AF814327

Recommended by **Teachers**
Trusted by **Toppers**

All in One®

GEOGRAPHY

Class 12

EVERYTHING YOU NEED TO SCORE

- Simplified Theory
- NCERT, Diksha & Other Imp. Ques.
- CBQs; MCQs, A-R, Source Based
- Board Questions Upto 2025
- Sample Question Papers

CBSE Exams 2026

Author
Shruti Sharma

arihant
SUCCESS AND NOTHING LESS

arihant
SUCCESS AND NOTHING LESS

ARIHANT PRAKASHAN
(School Division Series)

ADMINISTRATIVE & PRODUCTION OFFICES

Regd. Office

'Ramchhaya' 4577/15, Agarwal Road, Darya Ganj, New Delhi -110002
Tele: 011- 47630600, 43518550; Fax: 011- 23280316

Head Office

Kalindi, TP Nagar, Meerut (UP) - 250002, Tel: 0121-7156203, 7156204

SALES & SUPPORT OFFICES

Agra, Ahmedabad, Bengaluru, Bareilly, Chennai, Delhi, Guwahati, Hyderabad, Jaipur, Jhansi, Kolkata, Lucknow, Nagpur & Pune.

PO No : TXT-XX-XXXXXXX-X-XX

Published By Arihant Publications (India) Ltd.

For further information about the books published by Arihant, log on to www.arihantbooks.com or e-mail at info@arihantbooks.com

Follow us on

PRICE ₹ 475.00

PRODUCTION TEAM

Publishing Managers	Cover Designer	Inner Designer
Mahendra Singh Rawat & Keshav Mohan	Salman Shaikh	Ankit Prajapati
Project Head	*Page Layouting*	*Proof Reader*
Shivam Gupta	Sundar Bisht	Sundip Giri

Index *cum* Study Planner

		Studied	Revised	Exam ready

UNIT 2

UNIT 3

One Book- Endless Features

to Help you Succeed

Complete Theory in Each Chapter

Each chapter has Complete, Easy to Understand Simplified theory covering latest syllabus and NCERT Textbook. Theory is developed in such a way that it is suitable for all types of learners.

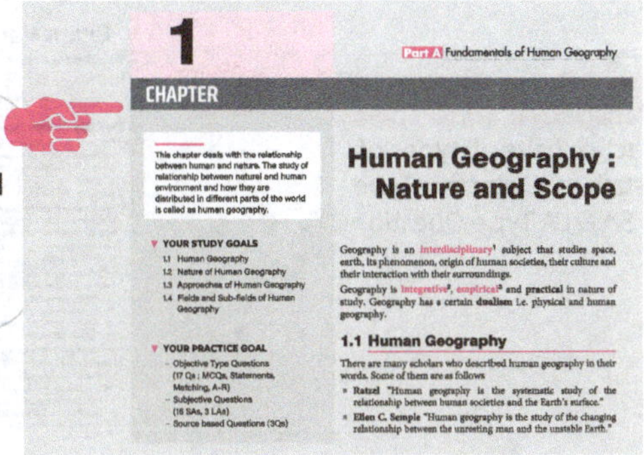

1 CHAPTER

Part A Fundamentals of Human Geography

This chapter deals with the relationship between human and nature. The study of relationship between natural and human environment and how they are distributed in different parts of the world is called as human geography.

YOUR STUDY GOALS
1.1 Human Geography
1.2 Nature of Human Geography
1.3 Approaches of Human Geography
1.4 Fields and Sub-fields of Human Geography

YOUR PRACTICE GOAL
- Objective Type Questions (17 Qs ; MCQs, Statements, Matching, A-R)
- Subjective Questions (16 SAs, 3 LAs)
- Source based Questions (3Qs)

Human Geography : Nature and Scope

Geography is an interdisciplinary[1] subject that studies space, earth, its phenomenon, origin of human societies, their culture and their interaction with their surroundings.

Geography is integrative[2], empirical[3] and practical in nature of study. Geography has a certain dualism i.e. physical and human geography.

1.1 Human Geography

There are many scholars who described human geography in their words. Some of them are as follows

- Ratzel "Human geography is the systematic study of the relationship between human societies and the Earth's surface."
- Ellen C. Semple "Human geography is the study of the changing relationship between the unresting man and the unstable Earth."

Mind Map

A quick revision visual tool for the complete chapter.

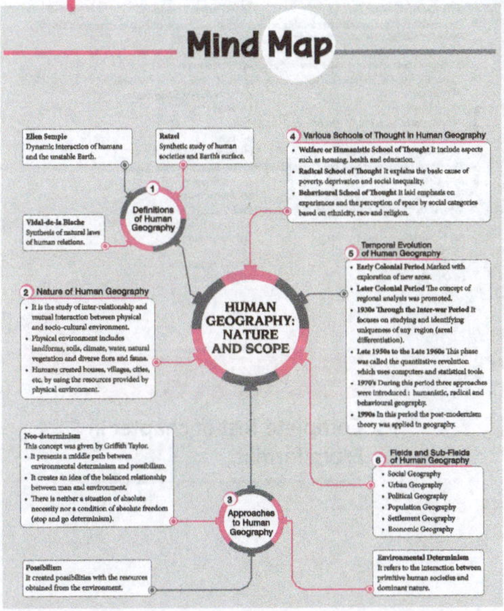

Mind Map

HUMAN GEOGRAPHY: NATURE AND SCOPE

1 Definitions of Human Geography
- Ellen Semple: Dynamic interaction of humans and the unstable Earth.
- Ratzel: Synthetic study of human societies and Earth's surface.
- Vidal-de-la Blache: Synthesis of natural laws of human relations.

2 Nature of Human Geography
- It is the study of inter-relationship and mutual interaction between physical and socio-cultural environment.
- Physical environment includes landforms, soils, climate, water, natural vegetation and diverse flora and fauna.
- Humans created houses, villages, cities, etc. by using the resources provided by physical environment.

3 Approaches to Human Geography
- Neo-determinism: This concept was given by Griffith Taylor. It presents a middle path between environmental determinism and possibilism. It creates an idea of the balanced relationship between man and environment. There is neither a situation of absolute necessity nor a condition of absolute freedom (stop and go determinism).
- Possibilism: It created possibilities with the resources obtained from the environment.
- Environmental Determinism: It refers to the interaction between primitive human societies and dominant nature.

4 Various Schools of Thought in Human Geography
- Welfare or Humanistic School of Thought It include aspects such as housing, health and education.
- Radical School of Thought It explains the basic cause of poverty, deprivation and social inequality.
- Behavioural School of Thought It laid emphasis on experiences and the perception of space by social categories based on ethnicity, race and religion.

5 Temporal Evolution of Human Geography
- Early Colonial Period Marked with exploration of new areas.
- Later Colonial Period The concept of regional analysis was promoted.
- 1930s Through the Inter-war Period It focuses on studying and identifying uniqueness of any region (areal differentiation).
- Late 1950s to the Late 1960s This phase was called the quantitative revolution which uses computers and statistical tools.
- 1970's During this period three approaches were introduced: humanistic, radical and behavioural geography.
- 1990s In this period the post-modernism theory was applied in geography.

6 Fields and Sub-Fields of Human Geography
- Social Geography
- Urban Geography
- Political Geography
- Population Geography
- Settlement Geography
- Economic Geography

Quick Test 1

1 Which geographer defined Human Geography as the study between the unresting man and the unstable Earth?
2 Identify the term that refers to the stage when humans adapted to nature due to low technology.
3 What do primitive societies depend on directly for sustenance?
4 What concept describes modifying nature within limits?
5 Give an example of environmental damage caused by unregulated human activity.

Quick Test

To make students understand the chapter in a smooth part-by-part manner, Quick Tests have been given in each chapter. These help students to assess the understanding of related concepts at regular interval.

NCERT Folder

Complete explanations of all the questions of NCERT Exercises.

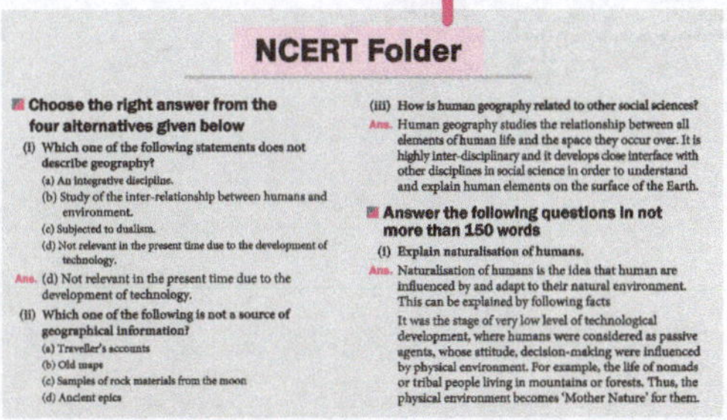

NCERT Folder

Choose the right answer from the four alternatives given below

(i) Which one of the following statements does not describe geography?
(a) An integrative discipline.
(b) Study of the inter-relationship between humans and environment.
(c) Subjected to dualism.
(d) Not relevant in the present time due to the development of technology.

Ans. (d) Not relevant in the present time due to the development of technology.

(ii) Which one of the following is not a source of geographical information?
(a) Traveller's accounts
(b) Old maps
(c) Samples of rock materials from the moon
(d) Ancient epics

(iii) How is human geography related to other social sciences?

Ans. Human geography studies the relationship between all elements of human life and the space they occur over. It is highly inter-disciplinary and it develops close interface with other disciplines in social science in order to understand and explain human elements on the surface of the Earth.

Answer the following questions in not more than 150 words

(i) Explain naturalisation of humans.

Ans. Naturalisation of humans is the idea that human are influenced by and adapt to their natural environment. This can be explained by following facts

It was the stage of very low level of technological development, where humans were considered as passive agents, whose attitude, decision-making were influenced by physical environment. For example, the life of nomads or tribal people living in mountains or forests. Thus, the physical environment becomes 'Mother Nature' for them.

One Book- Endless Features

to Help you Succeed

Exam Pattern Questions

Chapter Practice have all types of questions such as Objective Type Questions, SA & LA Type Questions.

Exam Pattern Questions

Objective Type Questions

Multiple Choice Questions (MCQs)

1. "Human Geography is the systematic study of relationship between human societies and Earth's surface." This definition was given by
   (a) Ratzel (b) Ellen .C Semple
   (c) Vidal de la Blache (d) None of these
2. Who among the following defined "Human geography is the study of the changing relationship between the unresting man and the unstable Earth"? CBSE Term I 2021
   (a) Ratzel (b) Griffith Taylor
   (c) Ellen C. Semple (d) Paul Vidal de la Blache
3. Which branch of geography deals with the relation between physical and socio-cultural environment?
   (a) Physical geography
   (b) Human geography
   (c) Environmental geography
   (d) None of the above
4. Which of the following statements reveals the core concept of Human geography? CBSE Diksha
   (a) It studies the elements of the physical environment.
   (b) It studies the laws of nature.
   (c) It studies the mutual interaction between the physical environment and human beings.
   (d) It studies the technical advancement of human beings.

(iii) Humans do not interact with environment.
Codes
(a) (i) and (ii) (b) (ii) and (iii)
(c) (i), (ii) and (iii) (d) (i) and (iii)

8. "Nature provides opportunities and human beings use these opportunities and slowly nature gets humanised." The statement above describes which of the following idea? Competency Based Que
   (a) Possibilism
   (b) Environmental determinism
   (c) Spatial analysis
   (d) Areal differentiation
9. Who among the following has introduced the concept of neo-determinism? CBSE Sample Paper Term II 2021
   (a) Ratzel (b) Griffith Taylor
   (c) Ellen C. Semple (d) Paul Vidal de la Blache
10. Which of the following is/are not a component of natural environment?
    (i) Farms (ii) Mountains
    (iii) Lakes (iv) Roads
    Codes
    (a) (i) and (ii) (b) (i) and (iii)
    (c) (i) and (iv) (d) (ii) and (iv)

Sample Question Papers

To make students practice of examination in real sense, there are 5 Sample Question Papers at the end. All these Sample Question Papers are exactly prepared on the latest syllabus & pattern of examinations.

SAMPLE QUESTION PAPER 1

A Highly Simulated Sample Question Paper for CBSE Class XII

(SOLVED)

GEOGRAPHY

- This question paper contains 30 questions. All questions are compulsory.
- This question paper is divided into five sections – Sections A, B, C, D and E.
- Section A – Questions no. 1 to 17 are Multiple Choice (MCQ) Type Questions carrying 1 mark each.
- Section B – Questions no. 18 and 19 are Source Based Questions carrying 3 marks each.
- Section C – Questions no. 20 to 23 are Short Answer (SA) Type Questions carrying 3 marks each. Answer to these questions shall be written in 80 to 100 words.
- Section D – Questions no. 24 to 28 are Long Answer (LA) Type Questions carrying 5 marks each. Answer to these questions shall be written in 120 to 150 words.
- Section E – Questions no. 29 and 30 are Map Based Questions.

Time : 3 hours **Max. Marks : 70**

SECTION A

1. Consider the following statements about primitive subsistence agriculture. (1)
   I. Shifting cultivation involves clearing a forest area, burning the vegetation and using the ash to fertilize the soil.
   II. After a few years of cultivation, the soil loses fertility and the farmers move to a new area.
   III. This method is widely practiced in densely populated regions of India.
   IV. Shifting cultivation is known by different names in different regions, such as Jhum in North-East India.
   Which of the above statements are correct?
   (a) II and IV (b) I, III and IV (c) I, II and IV (d) I, II and III
2. Arrange the following Indian ports from South to North in the Indian Ocean. (1)
   I. Tuticorin II. Chennai
   III. Vishakhapatnam IV. Haldia
   Codes
   (a) I, II, III, IV (b) II, I, IV, III (c) III, IV, II, I (d) IV, III, II, I

SELF ASSESSMENT TEST

Objective Type Questions

1. Who among the following emphasised on Human geography as a synthesis between human society and natural phenomena?
   (a) Ellen C. Semple (b) Ratzel
   (c) Griffith Taylor (d) Vidal de la Blache
2. Which approach of human geography focuses on identifying the uniqueness of any region and understanding how and why it was different from others?
   (a) Regional analysis (b) Areal differentiation
   (c) Spatial organisation (d) Quantitative revolution
3. Human geography is the inter-relationship between physical and socio-cultural environment. This fact can be established by which of the following?
   (a) Nature controls man (b) Man controls nature
   (c) Man modifies nature and is also impacted by nature (d) None of these
4. Interaction between primitive human society and forces of nature can be studied as
   (a) possibilism (b) environmental determinism
   (c) neo-liberalism (d) None of these
5. The concept of 'Stop and Go determinism' was given by
   (a) Griffith Taylor (b) Ratzel
   (c) Vidal de la Blache (d) Ellen C. Semple
6. The subject matter of geography of leisure has been taken from which discipline?
   (a) Social Science (b) Anthropology
   (c) Sociology (d) Political Science
7. What are some of the consequences of an uncontrolled "free run" of development.
   (i) Green house effect (ii) Ozone layer depletion
   (iii) Improved environmental balance (iv) Global warming
   Options
   (a) Only (i), (ii), (iv) (b) Only (i) and (iii)
   (c) Only (ii) and (iv) (d) All of these

Self Assessment Test

Complete Test of chapter in Exam format.

Latest Course Structure

Fundamentals of Human Geography

Chapter No.	Chapter Name	Weightage
	Unit - I	
1	Human Geography	3
	Unit - II	
2	The World Population Density Distribution and Growth	8
3	Human Development	
	Unit - III	
4	Primary Activities	19
5	Secondary Activities	
6	Tertiary and Quaternary Activities	
7	Transport, Communication and Trade	
8	International Trade	
Map Work (Based on identification of features on World Political Map)		**5**
	Total	**35**

India : People and Economy

Chapter No.	Chapter Name	Weightage
	Unit - I	
1	Population Distribution Density Growth and Composition	5
	Unit - II	
2	Human Settlements	3
	Unit - III	
3	Land Resources and Agriculture	10
4	Water Resources	
5	Mineral and Energy Resources	
6	Planning and Sustainable Development in Indian Context	
	Unit - IV	
7	Transport and Communication	7
8	International Trade	
	Unit - V	
9	Geographical Perspective on Selected Issues and Problems	5
Map Work (Based on Marking and Labelling on a Political Map of India)		5
Total		**35**

COURSE CONTENT

Book: Fundamentals of Human Geography

Unit 1:

Chapter 1 Human Geography: Nature and Scope

- Introduction to Human Geography
- Approaches to study Human Geography Regional and Systematic Geography, Dualism
- Nature of Human Geography
- Naturalisation of Humans and Humanisation of Nature
- Schools of thought in Human Geography
- Fields and subfields of Human Geography

Unit 2:

Chapter 2 The World Population Distribution, Density and Growth

- Population-distribution and density
- Factors influencing the distribution of population
- Population Growth
- Components of Population change
- Demographic Transition
- Population Control Measures

Chapter 3 Human Development

- Human development - concept; selected indicators
- Growth and Development
- The four pillars of Human Development
- Approaches to Human Development
- Measuring Human Development- HDI, HPI and GNH
- International comparisons

Unit 3:

Chapter 4 Primary Activities

Concept and types

- Hunting and Gathering, Pastoralism; Nomadic Herding, Commercial Livestock Rearing
- Types of agriculture:
  - Primitive Subsistence
  - Intensive Subsistence
- Commercial Agriculture
  - Plantation Agriculture
  - Extensive Commercial Grain Cultivation
  - Mixed Farming
  - Dairy farming
  - Mediterranean Agriculture
  - Market Gardening and Horticulture
  - Cooperative Farming
  - Collective Farming
- Mining, factors affecting mining
- Methods of Mining

Chapter 5 Secondary Activities

- Manufacturing: Characteristics of Modern large-Scale Manufacturing
- Factors influencing industrial Location
- Classification of manufacturing Industries: On the basis of Size, Inputs /raw material, Output /Products and Ownership
- Concept of High tech Industry

Chapter 6 Tertiary Activities

- Tertiary activities-concept and types
- Trade and commerce: Retail and Wholesale trading Transport, Factors Affecting Transport;
- Communication
- Services
- People engaged in tertiary activities
- Tourism, Major tourist regions
- Tourist attractions - some examples from selected countries
- Medical Services for Overseas Patients in India
- Quaternary and Quinary activities-concept
- The Digital Divide

Chapter 7 Transport and Communication

- Transport
- Modes of Transportation
- Land transport: Roadways, Highways, Road Density, Border Roads.
- Railways: Trans-continental Railways: Trans-Siberian, Trans Canadian, Australian Trans Continental,
- Water Transport: Important Sea Routes, Shipping Canals, Inland waterways
- Air transport: Inter-Continental air routes
- Pipelines
- Communications: Satellite Communications and Cyber Space- Internet

Chapter 8 International Trade

- History of International trade
- Why Does International Trade Exist?
- Basis of International Trade
- Balance of Trade
- Types of International Trade: Bilateral and Multi-lateral trade
- Case for Free Trade
- Concept of Dumping
- World Trade Organisation
- Regional Trade Blocs
- Concerns Related to International Trade
- Gateways of International trade: Ports
- Types of Port

Book: India: People and Economy

Unit 1:

Chapter 1 Population Distribution, Density, Growth and Composition

- Distribution of Population
- Density of Population
- Growth of population
- Four distinct phases of population growth
- Regional Variation in Population Growth
- Population Composition: Rural – Urban Composition, Linguistic Composition, Religious Composition
- Composition of Working Population
- Promoting Gender Sensitivity through 'Beti Bachao–Beti Padhao' Social Campaign.

Unit 2:

Chapter 2 Human Settlements

- Rural settlements - types and distribution
- Urban settlements - types, distribution
- Evolution of Towns in India
- Urbanisation in India
- Functional Classification of Towns
- Smart Cities Mission

Unit 3:

Chapter 3 Land Resources and Agriculture

- Land resources- general land use
- Land use categories
- Land-use Changes in India
- Common Property Resources
- Agricultural Land Use in India
- Cropping Seasons in India
- Types of Farming
- Geographical conditions and distribution of major crops (Wheat, Rice, Tea, Coffee, Cotton, Jute, Sugarcane and Rubber);
- Agricultural development in India
- Growth of Agricultural Output and Technology
- Problems of Indian Agriculture

Chapter 4 Water Resources

- Water resources- Surface water and Groundwater Resources
- Lagoons and Backwaters
- Water Demand and Utilisation - irrigation, domestic, industrial and other uses;
- Emerging Water Problems: Deterioration of Water Quality
- Water Conservation and Management; Prevention of Water Pollution; Rain water harvesting and Watershed management

Chapter 5 Mineral and Energy Resources

- Mineral Resources: Introduction and Types
- Major mineral belts of India
- Distribution of Ferrous Minerals (Iron ore and Manganese), Non-Ferrous Minerals (Bauxite and Copper); Non-metallic minerals (Mica)
- Energy Resources: Conventional sources (Coal, Petroleum and Natural gas) and non-conventional sources (Nuclear, Solar, Wind, Tidal and Wave and Geothermal and Bio energy)
- Conservation of Mineral Resources

Chapter 6 Planning and Sustainable Development in Indian Context

- Planning- Introduction
- Target Area Planning: Hill Area Development Programme, Drought Prone Area Programme.
- Concept of Sustainable Development

Case Studies

1. Integrated Tribal Development Project in Bharmaur* Region,
2. Indira Gandhi Canal (Nahar) Command Area

Unit 4:

Chapter 7 Transport and Communication

- Means of transport: Land (Road transport, Rail transport and Oil and Gas pipelines), Water transport (Inland waterways and Oceanic routes) and Air transport
- Communication Networks- Personal and Mass Communication Systems

Chapter 8 International Trade

- Changing Pattern of the Composition of India's Exports and Import
- Direction of Trade
- Sea Ports as Gateways of International Trade
- Major Seaports of India along with their hinterlands.
- Airports

Unit 5:

Chapter 9 Geographical Perspective on Selected Issues and Problems

- Environmental pollution- Introduction and types
- Urban-waste disposal

- Rural-Urban Migration: Case Study
- Problems of Slums
- Land degradation: Case study

Book- Geography Practical Part II

Chapter 1 Data – Its Source and Compilation

- What is Data, Sources of data: Primary, Secondary and Unpublished sources.
- Tabulation and Classification of Data
- Grouping of Data
- Frequency Polygon

Chapter 2 Data Processing

- Tabulating and processing of data
- Measures of Central Tendency: Mean, Median and Mode
- Comparison of Mean, Median and Mode

Chapter 3 Graphical Representation of Data

- Representation of data- General rules for drawing diagrams, graphs and maps, construction of line graphs, polygraphs, simple bar diagrams, line and bar diagram, Multiple bar, Compound bar, Pie diagram, Flowchart
- Thematic maps; Construction of Dot Map; Choropleth Map and Isopleth map

Chapter 4 Spatial Information Technology

- Introduction to GIS; Advantages of GIS, Components of GIS, Spatial data formats, Sequence of GIS activities; Spatial data input, Entering attribute data, Data Linkages and matching, Spatial analysis: Overlay Analysis Operation and Buffer Operation

Map items for identification only on outline political map of the world
Fundamentals of Human Geography

Chapter No	Chapter Name	No. of Periods
1	Human Geography	Nil
2	The World Population: Density, Distribution and Growth	Nil
3	Human Development	Nil
4	Primary Activites	• Areas of subsistence gathering (Fig 4.2) • Major areas of nomadic herding of the world (4.4) • Major areas of commercial livestock rearing (4.6) • Major areas of extensive commercial grain faming (4.12) • Major areas of mixed farming of the World (4.14)
5	Secondary Activities	Nil
6	Tertiary and Quaternary Activities	Nil
7	Transport and Communication	• Terminal Stations of Trans-continental Railways– Trans-Siberian, Trans Canadian, Trans-Australian Railways **Major Sea Ports** • **Europe**: North Cape, London, Hamburg • **North America**: Vancouver, San Francisco, New Orleans • **South America**: Rio De Janeiro, Colon, Valparaiso • **Africa**: Suez and Cape Town • **Asia**: Yokohama, Shanghai, Hong Kong, Aden, Karachi, Kolkata • **Australia**: Perth, Sydney, Melbourne

		Major Airports • **Asia**: Tokyo, Beijing, Mumbai, Jeddah, Aden • **Africa**: Johannesburg and Nairobi • **Europe**: Moscow, London, Paris, Berlin and Rome • **North America**: Chicago, New Orleans, Mexico City • **South America**: Buenos Aires, Santiago • **Australia**: Darwin and Wellington **Inland Waterways** Suez Canal, Panama Canal, Rhine Waterways and St Lawrence Seaways
8	International Trade	Nil

Map Items for Locating and Labelling on Political Outline Map of India
India : People and Economy

Chapter No	Chapter Name	No. of Periods
1	**Population :** Distribution, Density, Growth and Composition	State with highest population density and state with lowest population density (2011)
2	Human Settlements	Nil
3	Land Resources and Agriculture	Leading producing states of the following crops: (a) Rice (b) Wheat (c) Cotton (d) Jute (e) Sugarcane (f) Tea, and (g) Coffee
4	Water Resources	Nil
5	Mineral and Energy Resources	Mines: • **Iron-ore mines**: Mayurbhanj, Bailadila, Ratnagiri, Bellary • **Manganese mines**: Balaghat, Shimoga • **Copper mines**: Hazaribagh, Singhbhum, Khetari • **Bauxite mines**: Katni, Bilaspur and Koraput • **Coal mines**: Jharia, Bokaro, Raniganj, Neyveli • **Oil Refineries**: Mathura, Jamnager, Barauni
6	Planning and Sustainable Development in Indian Context	Nil
7	Transport and Communication	Nil
8	International Trade	Mark and label the major sea ports and airports on an outline map of India.of India. • **Major Sea Ports**: Kandla, Mumbai, Marmagao, Kochi, Mangalore, Tuticorin, Chennai, Visakhapatnam, Paradip, Haldia • **International Air ports**: Ahmedabad, Mumbai, Bengaluru, Chennai, Kolkata, Guwahati, Delhi, Amritsar, Thiruvananthapuram and Hyderabad.
9	Geographical Perspective on Selected Issues and Problems	Nil

UNIT 1

Part A Fundamentals of Human Geography

1 CHAPTER

Human Geography : Nature and Scope

This chapter deals with the relationship between human and nature. The study of relationship between natural and human environment and how they are distributed in different parts of the world is called as human geography.

YOUR STUDY GOALS

1.1 Human Geography
1.2 Nature of Human Geography
1.3 Approaches of Human Geography
1.4 Fields and sub-fields of Human Geography

YOUR PRACTICE GOAL

- Objective Type Questions (17 Qs ; MCQs, Statements, Matching, A-R)
- Subjective Questions (16 SAs, 3 LAs)
- Source Based Questions (3 Qs)

Geography is an **interdisciplinary**[1] subject that studies space, earth, its phenomenon, origin of human societies, their culture and their interaction with their surroundings.

Geography is **integrative**[2], **empirical**[3] and **practical** in nature of study. Geography has a certain **dualism** i.e. physical and human geography.

1.1 Human Geography

There are many scholars who described human geography in their words. Some of them are as follows

- **Ratzel** "Human geography is the systematic study of the relationship between human societies and the Earth's surface."
- **Ellen C. Semple** "Human geography is the study of the changing relationship between the unresting man and the unstable Earth."
- **Paul Vidal de la Blache** "Conception resulting from a more synthetic knowledge of the physical laws governing our Earth and of the relations between the living beings which inhabit it."

1 **Interdisciplinary** A subject that involves two or more areas of knowledge or study.
2 **Integrative** It means combining two or more things to form an effective unit or system.
3 **Empirical** Observations based on experiments and practical experience.

1.2 Nature of Human Geography

- Human geography is the study of **inter-relationship** and **mutual interaction** between **physical** and **socio-cultural** environment created by human beings.
- The elements of physical environment are landforms, soils, climate, water, natural vegetation and diverse flora and fauna.
- The humans have created various elements by using the resources provided by the physical environment. These include, houses, villages, cities, road-rail networks, industries and other elements of material culture.
- The physical environment has been modified by human beings which has impacted the human lives.

1.3 Approaches of Human Geography

The scholars introduced three major approaches to describe man- environment relationship and study human geography. These are

Environmental Determinism

- In early times, humans adapted to nature because of their low level of technology. Their social development was primitive, making them highly dependent on natural forces. The interaction between primitive human societies and dominant nature is termed as **environmental determinism**[4]. It shaped humans into naturalised beings who listened to, feared and worshipped the nature.
- The man- environment interaction at primitive stages was considered as the stage of **naturalisation of human** or **naturalised human**. At this stage the physical environment is worshipped as **'Mother Nature'**.

Possibilism

- People understood nature and their environment over time. Social and cultural development led to better technology.
- Humans created possibilities with the resources obtained from the environment. This state was termed as **possibilism**[5] by the early scholars.
- Humans moved from a condition of necessity to a situation of freedom, where they are not forced to follow the laws of nature.
- The presence of humans can be observed everywhere. For example, health resorts on highlands, huge urban expansion, fields, orchids in plains, oceanic routes on ocean surface and satellites in space.
- Nature provides opportunities and humans use them. Over time, nature becomes humanised, showing human efforts.

Humanisation of Nature

- With the development of technology nature slowly gets humanised.
- Technology developed by humans enabled them to overcome the limitations imposed by the natural environment. For example, the understanding of friction and heat helped the humans to discover fire and use it to make their lives easier.
- Another such example is understanding of DNA and genetics. It enabled humans to find cures for many diseases.

---

4. **Environmental determinism** It is a belief that physical geographic factors, such as climate and terrain, have a significant and direct impact on human activities and outcomes.
5. **Possibilism** This approach suggests that humans are not completely limited by the environment in their culture and actions.

Neo-determinism

- This concept was given by a geographer, **Griffith Taylor.**
- This concept presents a **middle path** between the two ideas of environmental determinism and possibilism.
- According to Taylor, there is neither a situation of **absolute necessity** (environmental determinism) nor a condition of **absolute freedom** (possibilism). That's why it is also known as **Stop and Go Determinism.**
- According to this approach, human beings without harming the natural environment, can modify nature according to their needs, when nature permits the modifications.
- Neo-determinism helps to create an idea of the balanced relationship between man and environment.

Quick Test 1

1 Which geographer defined Human Geography as the study between the unresting man and the unstable Earth?
2 Identify the term that refers to the stage when humans adapted to nature due to low technology.
3 What do primitive societies depend on directly for sustenance?
4 What concept describes modifying nature within limits?
5 Give an example of environmental damage caused by unregulated human activity.

Various Schools of Thought in Human Geography

- **Welfare or Humanistic School of Thought** It is concerned with the different aspects of social well-being of the people. These include aspects such as housing, health and education.
- **Radical School of Thought** It uses Marxian theory to explain the basic cause of poverty, deprivation and social inequality.
- **Behavioural School of Thought** It laid emphasis on experiences and the perception of space by social categories based on ethnicity, race and religion.

Temporal Evolution of Human Geography

Human geography has developed through the following stages

- **Early Colonial Period** This period is marked with exploration of new areas. A detail description of the areas was the major part of geographer's writing.
- **Later Colonial Period** In this period, the concept of regional analysis was promoted. Under this approach every aspect of region was studied.
- **1930s Through the Inter-war Period** In this period, the focus of study was on identifying uniqueness of any region. This approach is known as areal differentiation
- **Late 1950s to the Late 1960s** This period is marked by use of computers and statistical tools. This phase was called the **quantitative revolution.**
- **1970's** During this period, three new approaches in human geography named as humanistic, radical and behavioural geography were introduced. They made human geography more relevant to the socio-political reality.
- **1990s** In this period, the post-modernism theory was applied in geography. The importance of understanding each local context in its own right was emphasised.

1.4 Fields and sub-fields of Human Geography

- Human geography has close linkages with other sister disciplines in social sciences.
- The scope of human geography extends to the following fields and sub- fields

Fields of Human Geography	Sub-fields	Interface with Sister Disciplines of Social Sciences
Social Geography	—	Social Sciences-Sociology
	Behavioural Geography	Psychology
	Geography of Social Well-being	Welfare Economics
	Geography of Leisure	Sociology
	Cultural Geography	Anthropology
	Gender Geography	Sociology, Anthropology, Women's Studies
	Historical Geography	History
	Medical Geography	Epidemology
Urban Geography	—	Urban Studies and Planning
Political Geography		Political Science
	Electoral Geography	Psephology
	Military Geography	Military Science
Population Geography	—	Demography
Settlement Geography		Urban/Rural Planning
Economic Geography	—	Economics
	Geography of Resources	Resource Economics
	Geography of Agriculture	Agricultural Sciences
	Geography of Industries	Industrial Economics
	Geography of Marketing	Business Studies, Economics, Commerce
	Geography of Tourism	Tourism and Travel Management
	Geography of International Trade	International Trade

Quick Test 2

1 Which three schools of thought emerged in the 1970s?
2 Identify the field that focuses on identifying regional differences.
3 Name the revolution that occurred during the late 1950s to late 1960s in Geography.
4 What did post-modernism question in Human Geography?

Mind Map

HUMAN GEOGRAPHY: NATURE AND SCOPE

1 Definitions of Human Geography

Ellen Semple
Dynamic interaction of humans and the unstable Earth.

Ratzel
Synthetic study of human societies and Earth's surface.

Vidal-de-la Blache
Synthesis of natural laws of human relations.

2 Nature of Human Geography

- It is the study of inter-relationship and mutual interaction between physical and socio-cultural environment.
- Physical environment includes landforms, soils, climate, water, natural vegetation and diverse flora and fauna.
- Humans created houses, villages, cities, etc. by using the resources provided by physical environment.

3 Approaches to Human Geography

Neo-determinism
This concept was given by Griffith Taylor.
- It presents a middle path between environmental determinism and possibilism.
- It creates an idea of the balanced relationship between man and environment.
- There is neither a situation of absolute necessity nor a condition of absolute freedom (stop and go determinism).

Possibilism
It created possibilities with the resources obtained from the environment.

Environmental Determinism
It refers to the interaction between primitive human societies and dominant nature.

4 Various Schools of Thought in Human Geography

- **Welfare or Humanistic School of Thought** It include aspects such as housing, health and education.
- **Radical School of Thought** It explains the basic cause of poverty, deprivation and social inequality.
- **Behavioural School of Thought** It laid emphasis on experiences and the perception of space by social categories based on ethnicity, race and religion.

5 Temporal Evolution of Human Geography

- **Early Colonial Period** Marked with exploration of new areas.
- **Later Colonial Period** The concept of regional analysis was promoted.
- **1930s Through the Inter-war Period** It focuses on studying and identifying uniqueness of any region (areal differentiation).
- **Late 1950s to the Late 1960s** This phase was called the quantitative revolution which uses computers and statistical tools.
- **1970's** During this period three approaches were introduced : humanistic, radical and behavioural geography.
- **1990s** In this period the post-modernism theory was applied in geography.

6 Fields and Sub-Fields of Human Geography

- Social Geography
- Urban Geography
- Political Geography
- Population Geography
- Settlement Geography
- Economic Geography

NCERT Folder

Choose the right answer from the four alternatives given below

(i) **Which one of the following statements does not describe geography?**

(a) An integrative discipline.

(b) Study of the inter-relationship between humans and environment.

(c) Subjected to dualism.

(d) Not relevant in the present time due to the development of technology.

Ans. (d) Not relevant in the present time due to the development of technology.

(ii) **Which one of the following is not a source of geographical information?**

(a) Traveller's accounts

(b) Old maps

(c) Samples of rock materials from the moon

(d) Ancient epics

Ans. (c) Samples of rock materials from the moon

(iii) **Which one of the following is the most important factor in the interaction between people and environment?**

(a) Human intelligence (b) People's perception

(c) Technology (d) Human brotherhood

Ans. (c) Technology

(iv) **Which one of the following is not an approach in human geography?**

(a) Areal differentiation (b) Quantitative revolution

(c) Spatial organisation (d) Exploration and description

Ans. (b) Quantitative revolution

Answer the following questions in about 30 words

(i) **Define Human Geography.**

Ans. Human Geography is the study of the changing relationship between the physical/natural and the human worlds. It deals with the study of people, their communities, cultures, economies and interactions with the environment.

(ii) **Name some sub-fields of human geography.**

Ans. Behavioural geography, cultural geography, gender geography, military geography, geography of resources, geography of agriculture, geography of international trade, etc are some sub-fields of human geography.

(iii) **How is human geography related to other social sciences?**

Ans. Human geography studies the relationship between all elements of human life and the space they occur over. It is highly inter-disciplinary and it develops close interface with other disciplines in social science in order to understand and explain human elements on the surface of the Earth.

Answer the following questions in not more than 150 words

(i) **Explain naturalisation of humans.**

Ans. Naturalisation of humans is the idea that human are influenced by and adapt to their natural environment. This can be explained by following facts

It was the stage of very low level of technological development, where humans were considered as passive agents, whose attitude, decision-making were influenced by physical environment. For example, the life of nomads or tribal people living in mountains or forests. Thus, the physical environment becomes 'Mother Nature' for them.

Humans used to adjust themselves according to the possibilities provided by the nature. The environment greatly influenced the early human beings. They were afraid of natural forces, followed the nature and also worshipped and conserved it in order to be safe. This was considered as the stage of naturalised human.

According to naturalisation theory, human history, culture and life styles of development are influenced by the physical environment like, climate, soil, relief, etc.

(ii) **Write a note on the scope of Human Geography.**

Ans. Human Geography is the study of how humans interact with their environment and the spaces they live in. It focuses on understanding how people shape the world, how they use land, resources, and how culture, politics, and economics influence different places.

Human geography explores patterns like population distribution, migration, urban development, and how societies adapt to different environments.

The scope of human geography includes areas like settlement patterns, agriculture, industries, trade, transportation and communication. It also looks at the impact of humans on the environment, such as deforestation, pollution and climate change.

Through human geography, we learn about the diversity of human life across the globe, and how geography influences societies and their development. It helps in planning and managing resources, improving living conditions, and solving global challenges like urbanisation and environmental conservation.

Exam Pattern Questions

Objective Type Questions

Multiple Choice Questions (MCQs)

1. "Human Geography is the systematic study of relationship between human societies and Earth's surface." This definition was given by CBSE 2025

(a) Ratzel (b) Ellen .C Semple
(c) Vidal de la Blache (d) None of these

2. Who among the following defined "Human geography is the study of the changing relationship between the unresting man and the unstable Earth"? CBSE Term I 2021

(a) Ratzel (b) Griffith Taylor
(c) Ellen C. Semple (d) Paul Vidal de la Blache

3. Which branch of geography deals with the relation between physical and socio-cultural environment?

(a) Physical geography
(b) Human geography
(c) Environmental geography
(d) None of the above

4. Which of the following statements reveals the core concept of Human geography? CBSE Diksha

(a) It studies the elements of the physical environment.
(b) It studies the laws of nature.
(c) It studies the mutual interaction between the physical environment and human beings.
(d) It studies the technical advancement of human beings.

5. Which one of the following is not correctly matched?

Scholar		Approach
(a) Friedrich Ratzel	–	Environmental determinism
(b) Ellen C. Semple	–	Welfare geography
(c) Griffith Taylor	–	Stop and go determinism
(d) Vidal de la Blache	–	Possibilism

6. "Humans are restricted by the constraints of the natural environment." This idea can be described as Competency Based Que

(a) environmental determinism
(b) neo-liberalism
(c) possibilism
(d) spatial analysis

7. Consider the following statements about Environmental determinism and choose the correct option.

(i) Physical environment becomes Mother Nature for human beings.
(ii) Level of technological development is low.
(iii) Humans do not interact with environment.

Codes
(a) (i) and (ii) (b) (ii) and (iii)
(c) (i), (ii) and (iii) (d) (i) and (iii)

8. "Nature provides opportunities and human beings use these opportunities and slowly nature gets humanised." The statement above describes which of the following idea? Competency Based Que

(a) Possibilism
(b) Environmental determinism
(c) Spatial analysis
(d) Areal differentiation

9. The concept of 'Neodeterminism' was introduced by .... CBSE 2025

(a) Enrlich (b) C. Semple
(c) Griffith Taylor (d) Humboldt

10. Which of the following is/are not a component of natural environment?

(i) Farms (ii) Mountains
(iii) Lakes (iv) Roads

Codes
(a) (i) and (ii) (b) (i) and (iii)
(c) (i) and (iv) (d) (ii) and (iv)

11. 'The Radical School of Geography' was influenced by which of the following?

(a) Marxian Theory (b) Kant's Theory
(c) Gandhian Philosophy (d) None of the above

12. Behavioural School of Thought emphasised on which of the following aspects? CBSE Term I 2021

(a) Lived experience
(b) Causes of poverty and social inequality
(c) Different aspects of social well-being
(d) Housing, health and education

13. This age was marked by use of computers and sophisticated statistical tools. Laws of Physics were often applied to map and analyse.

Select the correct option. CBSE SQP Term I 2021

(a) Regional analysis
(b) Quantitative revolution
(c) Areal differentiation
(d) Spatial organisation

14. Consider the following situations and choose the correct option. **CBSE Diksha**

- The understanding of concepts of friction and heat helped us to discover fire.
- The understanding of the laws of aerodynamics helped us to develop faster planes.

Options

(a) Knowledge about machines only is important.
(b) Knowledge about nature is extremely important to develop technology.
(c) Technology and nature are not inter-related.
(d) Knowledge about nature is not necessary to develop technology.

Arrange the Following

15. Arrange the following approaches in ascending order on the basis of time. **CBSE SQP Term I 2021**

(i) Post-modernism in geography
(ii) Exploration and description
(iii) Areal differentiation
(iv) Regional analysis

Codes

(a) (i), (ii), (iii), (iv)
(b) (iv), (iii), (ii), (i)
(c) (iii), (i), (iv), (ii)
(d) (ii), (iv), (iii), (i)

Match the Following

16.

	List I (Sub-fields of Human Geography)	List II (Sister Disciplines)
A.	Behavioural Geography	1. Anthropology
B.	Geography of Leisure	2. Business Geography
C.	Geography of Marketing	3. Sociology
D.	Cultural Geography	4. Psychology

Codes **CBSE Term I 2021**

	A	B	C	D		A	B	C	D
(a)	4	3	2	1	(b)	1	2	3	4
(c)	3	4	2	1	(d)	3	2	1	4

Assertion-Reason

17. Assertion (A) Understanding of friction and heat helped the humans in discovering fire.

Reason (R) Technology enables the humans to overcome the limitations imposed by nature.

Codes

(a) Both A and R are true, but R is not the correct explanation of A.
(b) Both A and R are true and R is the correct explanation of A
(c) Both A and R are incorrect
(d) A is correct, but R is incorrect

Answers

1. (a) Ratzel
2. (c) Ellen C. Semple
3. (b) Human geography
4. (c) It studies the mutual interaction between the physical environment and human beings.
5. (b) Ellen C. Semple-Welfare geography
6. (a) environmental determinism
7. (a) (i) and (ii)
8. (a) Possibilism
9. (c) Griffith Taylor
10. (c) (i) and (iv)
11. (a) Marxian Theory
12. (a) Lived experience
13. (d) Spatial organisation
14. (b) Knowledge about nature is extremely important to develop technology.
15. (d) (ii), (iv), (iii), (i)
16. (a)
17. (b) Both A and R are true and R is the correct explanation of A

Subjective Questions

Short Answer Type Questions

1. Discuss the nature of human geography.

Ans. The nature of human geography is very complex. It deals with the inter-relationship between the natural physical environment and socio-cultural environment created by human beings through mutual interaction with each other.

All the phenomena such as houses, villages, cities, road-rail networks, industries, farms, parks, items of daily use and other elements of material culture have been created by human beings using the natural resources. By creating these phenomena, humans have modified the physical environment and have also been affected by it.

2. Differentiate between physical geography and human geography.

Or **On which basis geography can be classified as physical and human geography?**

Ans. Difference between physical and human geography are given below

Basis	Physical Geography	Human Geography
Area of study	Physical geography is concerned with the study of physical features found on the Earth.	Human geography is concerned with the study of man-made features found over the surface of the Earth.
Scope	Study of mountains, plains, valleys, atmosphere, oceans, etc are important examples with which physical geography deals.	The scope of human geography is very wide and involves the study of world population, activities of man and types of settlements in which he lives.
Sub-fields	The sub-fields of physical geography are hydrology, climatology, biogeography, geomorphology, pedalogy and meteorology.	The sub-fields of human geography are political geography, urban, behavioural, social, cultural, economic, agricultural and population geography.

3. "There is mutual interaction between the elements of physical geography and human geography." Support the statement with suitable examples.

Ans. Physical geography includes natural environment like landforms, climate, flora and fauna. Human geography includes the inter-relationship between the human beings and the physical environment.

Humans, through the use of technology create the socio-cultural environment or the cultural landscape. These creations are the action of mutual interaction between physical and human geography.

For instance, on highlands health resorts are created, oceanic routes are discovered on the surface of the oceans, houses in villages and cities are made so that physical environment can be used in a better way.

These examples show that there is mutual interaction between the elements of physical and human geography.

4. 'The dichotomy between physical and human is not a very valid one.' Explain the statement with an example. **CBSE 2024**

Ans. The dichotomy between physical and human geography is not valid because nature and humans are inseparably connected. Human activities, like building cities or farming, occur within the physical environment, shaping and modifying it. In turn, nature influences human life. For example, humans create roads and cities by altering natural landscapes, while climate and geography influence where humans settle. This interdependence shows that studying geography requires looking at both natural and human factors together, not separately.

5. "Nature and humans are inseparable elements". Justify the statement with suitable examples. **CBSE 2024**

Or **"The nature and human beings are so intricately intertwined that they cannot be separated." Explain.**

Ans. Nature and humans are inseparable elements. Man has created the socio-cultural environment within the physical environment by making roadways and railways to pass, go through and connect different landscapes. For example, the rivers are used as natural waterways.

Both physical and human phenomena are described in metaphors using symbols from the human anatomy such as the 'face' of Earth, 'eye' of storm, 'mouth' of the river, 'nose' of glacier, 'neck' of isthmus and 'profile' of the soil.

Man has described villages, towns, states and countries as organism and the network of roads and railways as arteries of circulation. Therefore, nature and human are intricately interwined.

6. "Human beings are directly dependent on nature for resources which sustain them." Examine the statement. Competency Based Que

Or "Humans are directly dependent on natural resources to sustain them." Explain the statement with examples. CBSE 2025

Ans. It is true that human beings are directly dependent on nature for resources which sustain them. In early periods, human was considered as a passive agent, who could easily be influenced by the environmental or physical factors i.e. climate, altitude, physiography, flora, fauna, etc which determined the decision-making and lifestyle of human beings. In early periods, human lived in primitive states where there was direct dependence of human beings on nature for resources which sustained them.

The physical environment for such societies became the 'Mother Nature', where these societies lived in complete harmony with their natural environment. As nature was considered a powerful force, people worshipped and conserved it. The period of environmental dominance is considered as 'environmental determinism'.

7. Explain the regional analysis approach of human geography. CBSE 2025

Ans. The regional analysis approach in human geography focuses on studying specific areas or regions by examining their unique characteristics, such as physical features, culture, economy, and population. It aims to understand how these factors interact and shape the development and identity of a region.

This approach helps in comparing different regions to identify patterns, trends, and spatial variations. It is crucial for effective regional planning, resource management, and understanding the relationship between human activities and the environment in different geographical contexts.

8. "The primitive communities were greatly influenced by their natural environment.' Justify the statement by giving any three points in the light of environmental determinism. CBSE Diksha

Or Explain the main aspects of environmental determinism. CBSE 2024

Ans. The primitive communities were greatly influenced by their natural environment in the following ways

(i) The level of technology was very low and the stage of human social development was also primitive.

(ii) This type of interaction between primitive human society and strong forces of nature was termed as environmental determinism.

(iii) At that stage of very low technological development we can imagine the presence of a naturalised human, who listened to nature, was afraid of its fury and worshipped it.

9. Explain the deterministic approach with suitable examples.

Or Explain the concept of 'determinism' with suitable examples.

Or Explain the concept of 'environmental determinism' with examples.

Ans. The approach of determinism states that humans are passive agents, influenced by the environmental factors i.e. physical factors like climate, flora, fauna, etc which determine the attitude, decision-making and lifestyle of human beings. They adapt to the limitations imposed by the nature and its various phenomenon.

For instance, the Eskimos of Tundra are adapted to the extremely cold climate. Their main food is whale, seals and walrus. They use animal oil for cooking, heating and lighting. They live in igloos whereas, Samang and Sakai of Malaysia and Pygmies of Congo basin lives in hot and humid condition. They feed on vegetable, hunting and fishing.

10. How is 'Naturalisation of Human' different from 'Humanisation of Nature'? CBSE SQP 2022

Ans. Naturalisation of Human is different from Humanisation of Nature in the following ways

	Naturalisation of Humans	Humanisation of Nature
Meaning	It refers to the process where human activities and behaviours are shaped by the natural environment.	This concept refers to the transformation of natural environments by human interferences.
Key Features	It reflects the concept of environmental determinism, where natural factors such as climate, terrain, and resources determine human life and activities.	It reflects the concept of possibilism, where humans are seen as active agents which is capable of modifying the environment according to their need.
Focus	Nature as the dominant force influence human actions.	Humans as the dominant force transform nature.

11. **"Physical environment has been greatly modified by human beings, it has also, in turn impacted human lives." Explain the statement.** Competency Based Que

Ans. Physical environment has been modified by human beings to a great extent. Through technology, we have interacted with our physical environment and obtained resources. With socio-cultural development, humans have developed better and more efficient technology. They have modified the natural landscape by creating their own cultural landscape in the form of health resorts, urban sprawls, fields, orchards and pastures, ports on the coast, oceanic routes, satellites in space, etc.

On the other hand, the nature has also impacted human lives. Humans have been influenced by the nature and have been able to develop technology after developing a better understanding of the natural laws. For example, the understanding of friction and heat has helped humans discover fire. In the early times, humans were greatly impacted by nature, they adapted to it, worshipped it and were afraid of its fury. Thus, physical environment has been greatly modified by human beings and humans have been impacted by nature too.

12. **Describe the concept of possibilism with suitable examples.**

Or **Explain the concept of 'possibilism' with three suitable examples.**

Ans. The concept of possibilism states that there are no necessities, but possibilities everywhere and man is referred to as a master of these possibilities. They are not influenced by the limitations imposed by natural environment. Man can adopt, adjust and modify the forces of his physical environment with his strength and innovation. His imprints could be seen everywhere. For instance

- Health resorts on highlands
- Huge urban sprawls
- Agricultural fields
- Orchards and pastures in plains and rolling hills
- Ports on the coasts
- Oceanic routes on the oceanic surface
- Satellites in the space

13. **Explain with example how nature gets humanised.**

Or **How humanisation of nature can be traced from human geography? Explain.**

Or **"The imprints of human activities are created everywhere." Evaluate the statement in context of humanisation of nature.** CBSE 2023

Or **Explain the concept of 'Humanisation of Nature' by giving examples.** CBSE 2024

Or **'Nature provides opportunities and human beings make use of these and slowly nature gets humanised and starts bearing the imprints of human endeavour.' Justify the given statement.** CBSE Diksha

Ans. 'Nature provides opportunities and human beings make use of these and slowly nature gets humanised and starts bearing the imprints of human endeavour'.

Humanisation of nature can be traced from human geography by understanding the following facts

- With social and cultural development, humans began to understand their environment and the forces of nature and they developed better and more efficient technology. With better technology they moved from a state of necessity to a state of freedom and created possibilities with the resources obtained from the environment.
- Humanisation of nature simply means that human have tendencies of grabbing opportunities which are given by the nature so that they are no longer constrained by the limitations imposed by nature.
- For instance, the imprints of human activities are created everywhere i.e. health resorts on highlands, huge urban sprawls, fields or orchards and pastures in plains and rolling hills, ports on the coasts, oceanic routes on the oceanic surface and satellites in the space.

14. **Explain the concept introduced by Griffith Taylor.**

Or **Explain the concept of 'neo-determinism' with suitable examples.**

Or **"Neo-determinism attempts to bring a balance between the two concepts of human-environment relationship." Examine the statement with examples.** CBSE 2024

Ans. The concept of 'neo-determinism' was introduced by Griffith Taylor which emphasises the middle path or *'Madhyam Marg'* between two ends of environmental determinism and possibilism.

It can be understood by the following facts

- The concept states that neither there is a situation of absolute necessity (i.e. environmental determinism) nor a condition of absolute freedom (i.e. possibilism).
- A human being can control nature by obeying it. Possibilities can be created within limits.
- If limits are not imposed, then it would lead to damage to the environment. For example, over exploitation of natural resources for the development of economy causes environmental problems like green house effect, ozone layer depletion, global warming, shrinking glaciers and degrading lands.

- The concept of neo-determinism conceptually balances the differences between environmental determinism and possibilism. It also eliminates the 'either' or dichotomy.

15. 'Those of you who live in cities, might have seen that traffic is regulated by lights on the cross- roads'. Discuss how the functioning of the traffic signals can be used to explain the concept of human of geography as introduced by Griffith Taylor. **CBSE Diksha**

Or **'The concept of neo-determinism is compared with traffic lights on the cross road'. Analyse the statement with examples.**

Ans. The concept of neo-determinism was introduced by Griffith Taylor. The concept shows that neither is there a situation of absolute necessity (environmental determinism) nor is there a condition of absolute freedom (possibilism). It means that human beings can conquer nature by obeying it. He used the concept of traffic lights to explain his approach in following ways

- Red light means to stop, amber light means to get set and green light means to go.
- In a similar way humans should take nature's hints as signals. They have to respond to the red signals and can proceed in their pursuits of development when nature permits the modifications.
- It means that possibilities can be created within the limits which do not damage the environment and there is no free run without accidents.

16. Explain the spatial organisation approach of human geography.

Ans. The spatial organisation approach in human geography focuses on understanding how human activities are distributed and arranged across space. It examines the patterns and processes that shape the location of people, settlements, industries, and resources.

This approach looks at factors like distance, accessibility, and transportation that influence spatial relationships. It also studies the impact of human actions on the environment, helping to explain the spatial structure of regions, cities, and networks of economic or social interactions across the globe.

Long Answer Type Questions

1. What do you mean by Human geography? Give some important definition of Human geography given by different scholars.

Ans. For answer refer to text page no. 1 under the heading 'Human Geography'.

2. Differentiate between determinism and possibilism.

Ans. The difference between determinism and possibilism are as follows

Determinism	Possibilism
This type of situation in which natural forces are more powerful than the human endeavour is termed as 'environmental determinism'.	This type of situation in which there are possibilities of human development has been termed as 'possibilism.'
It states that human activities are greatly influenced by natural environment.	It states that humans understand their environment and create possibilities by resources obtained from nature.
Human activities were dictated by forces of nature. Thus, the primitive man was almost completely controlled by the natural environment.	As the social and cultural development takes place, more efficient technology is developed. Humans shift from state of necessity to the state of freedom.
The scholars who supported this approach were Greek and Roman scholars.	Lucien Febvre and Vidal de la Blache advocated and developed systematically the school of possibilism.
For example, Eskimos living in Igloos, primitive tribes.	For example, Agricultural advancement, industrial revolution.

3. Describe various schools of thought that have developed in geography.

Ans. The various schools of thought that have developed in geography are discussed below

- **Welfare or Humanistic School of Thought** This school of thought seeks to put humans at the centre of geography. It is a part of human geography that is concerned with the different aspects of social well-being of the people like housing, health, education, etc. It deals with the concepts like human awareness, human agency, human consciousness and human creativity.
- **Radical School of Thought** This school has a strong Marxist base and holistic view of economics, society and polity. It explains the basic cause of poverty, deprivation and social inequality. According to this theory, capitalism creates the contemporary social problems in societies.

- **Behavioural School of Thought** This came in response to the dissatisfaction with the models and theories developed by the positivists. This school of thought lays great stress on lived experience and also perceives the notion of space by social categories based on ethnicity, race and religion.

Source Based Questions

1. Read the passage carefully and answer the questions that follow.

Benda lives in the wilds of the Abujh Maad area of central India. His village consists of three huts deep in the wilds. Not even birds or stray dogs that usually crowd villages can be seen in these areas. Wearing a small loin cloth and armed with his axe he slowly surveys the *Benda* (forest) where his tribe practices a primitive form of agriculture called shifting cultivation. Benda and his friends burn small patches of forest to clear them for cultivation. The ash is used for making the soil fertile. Benda is happy that the Mahua trees around him are in bloom. How lucky I am to be a part of this beautiful universe, he thinks as he looks up to see the Mahua, Palash and Sal trees that have sheltered him since childhood. Crossing the penda in a gliding motion, Benda makes his way to a stream.

As he bends down to scoop up a palmful of water, he remembers to thank Loi-Lugi, the spirit of the forest for allowing him to quench his thirst. Moving on with his friends, Benda chews on succulent leaves and roots. The boys have been trying to collect Gajjhara and Kuchla, from the forest. These are special plants that Benda and his people use. He hopes the spirits of the forest will be kind and lead him to these herbs. These are needed to barter in the madhai or tribal fair coming up the next full moon. He closes his eyes and tries hard to recall what the elders had taught him about these herbs and the places they are found in. He wishes he had listened more carefully. Suddenly there is a rustling of leaves. Benda and his friends know it is the outsiders who have come searching for them in the wilds. In a single fluid motion Benda and his friends disappear behind the thick canopy of trees and become one with the spirit of the forest.

(i) Benda and his family practises, which of the following type of agriculture?

(a) Horticulture (b) Plantation agriculture
(c) Slash and burn agriculture (d) Silviculture

Ans. (c) Slash and burn agriculture

(ii) The tribal people barter which of the following items in the tribal fair?

(a) Herbs (b) Wood
(c) River water (d) Clothes

Ans. (a) Herbs

(iii) The life of Benda in the forest shows which of the following approach?

(a) Neo-determinism
(b) Environmental determinism
(c) Possibilism
(d) Areal differentiation

Ans. (b) Environmental determinism

2. Read the passage carefully and answer the questions that follow.

In the primitive societies, there is direct dependence of human beings on nature for resources which sustain them. The physical environment for such societies becomes the 'Mother Nature'. The people begin to understand their environment and the forces of nature with the passage of time. With social and cultural development, humans develop better and more efficient technology. They move from a state of necessity to a state of freedom. They create possibilities with the resources obtained from the environment. The human activities create cultural landscape. The imprints of human activities are created everywhere; health resorts on highlands, huge urban sprawls, fields, orchards and pastures in plains and rolling hills, ports on the coasts, oceanic routes on the oceanic surface and satellites in the space. The earlier scholars termed this as possibilism. Nature provides opportunities and human being make use of these and slowly nature gets humanised and starts bearing the imprints of human endeavour.

(i) Which entity is considered sacred for primitive societies and why?

Ans. Nature is considered sacred for primitive societies because these are dependent on the Mother Nature.

(ii) How did human develop cultural landscape?

Ans. Human developed cultural landscape by creating possibilities with the resources obtained from the environment. With social and cultural development, humans developed better and more efficient technology, this helped humans to move from a state of necessity to a state of freedom.

(iii) State some examples of human activities which are associated with natural environment.

Ans. Some examples of human activities which are associated with his natural environment are

- Health resorts on highlands
- Huge urban sprawls, fields, orchards and pastures in plains and rolling hills
- Ports on the coasts
- Oceanic routes on the oceanic surface
- Satellites in the space

3. Read the passage carefully and answer the questions that follow.

Winters in the town of Trondheim mean fierce winds and heavy snow. The skies are dark for months. Kari drives to work in the dark at 8 am. She has special tyres for the winter and keeps the headlights of her powerful car switched on. Her office is artificially heated at a comfortable 23 degrees Celsius. The campus of the university she works in is built under a huge glass dome. This dome keeps the snow out in winter and lets in the sunshine in the summer.

The temperature is controlled carefully and there is adequate lighting. Even though fresh vegetables and plants don't grow in such harsh weather, Kari keeps an orchid on her desk and enjoys eating tropical fruits like banana and kiwi. These are flown in from warmer areas regularly. With a click of the mouse, Kari can network with colleagues in New Delhi. She frequently takes a morning flight to London and returns in the evening in time to watch her favourite television serial. Though Kari is fifty-eight years old, she is fitter and looks younger than many thirty year olds in other parts of the world.

(i) Which of the following helps Kari survive the harsh winters?

(a) Wood chimneys
(b) Artificial heaters
(c) Warm blankets
(d) Special clothes

Ans. (b) Artificial heaters

(ii) Which of the following describes the weather of Trondheim in winters correctly?

(a) Sunny weather
(b) Snowy and stormy weather
(c) Cool and windy weather
(d) Moderate weather

Ans. (b) Snowy and stormy weather

(iii) The life of Kari describes which of the following approaches of human geography?

(a) Environmental determinism
(b) Possibilism
(c) Neo-determinism
(d) Regional analysis

Ans. (b) Possibilism

SELF ASSESSMENT TEST

Objective Type Questions

1. Who among the following emphasised on Human geography as a synthesis between human society and natural phenomena?
   (a) Ellen C. Semple (b) Ratzel
   (c) Griffith Taylor (d) Vidal de la Blache
2. Which approach of human geography focuses on identifying the uniqueness of any region and understanding how and why it was different from others?
   (a) Regional analysis (b) Areal differentiation
   (c) Spatial organisation (d) Quantitative revolution
3. Human geography is the inter-relationship between physical and socio-cultural environment. This fact can be established by which of the following?
   (a) Nature controls man (b) Man controls nature
   (c) Man modifies nature and is also impacted by nature (d) None of these
4. Interaction between primitive human society and forces of nature can be studied as
   (a) possibilism (b) environmental determinism
   (c) neo-liberalism (d) None of these
5. The concept of 'Stop and Go determinism' was given by
   (a) Griffith Taylor (b) Ratzel
   (c) Vidal de la Blache (d) Ellen C. Semple
6. The subject matter of geography of leisure has been taken from which discipline?
   (a) Social Science (b) Anthropology
   (c) Sociology (d) Political Science
7. What are some of the consequences of an uncontrolled "free run" of development.
   (i) Green house effect (ii) Ozone layer depletion
   (iii) Improved environmental balance (iv) Global warming
   Options
   (a) Only (i), (ii), (iv) (b) Only (i) and (iii)
   (c) Only (ii) and (iv) (d) All of these

Short Answer Type Questions

8. State the main aspects of human environment which are included in the study of human geography.
9. Is it possible to separate human and nature? Give reason for your answer.
10. 'Determinism has a strong base since the early stages of human history'. Justify the statement.
11. "The neo-determinism nullifies the either or dichotomy". How?
12. Describe the three schools of thought in geography which started wide-ranging debates in the discipline of geography.

Long Answer Type Questions

13. "The scope of human geography is very vast." Substantiate the statement.
14. How does neo-determinism provide a solution to the environmental crises caused by unregulated development?

UNIT 2

2 CHAPTER

The population of the world is not spread equally in all places. Some areas have many people, while others have very few. The growth of the population depends on factors like births, deaths, and resources available in each region.

The World Population : Distribution, Density and Growth

▼ **YOUR STUDY GOALS**

2.1 Pattern of Population Distribution in the World
2.2 Population Growth

▼ **YOUR PRACTICE GOAL**

- Objective Type Questions (20 Qs ; MCQs, Statements, Matching, A-R)
- Subjective Questions (7 SAs, 9 LAs)
- Source/Graph Based Questions (4 Qs)

2.1 Pattern of Population Distribution in the World

- The growth and distribution of the population depends upon various factors such as physical, social, economic and cultural.
- The term **population distribution** refers to the way people are spread over the Earth's surface.
- 90 per cent of the world population lives in about 10 per cent of Earth's land area.

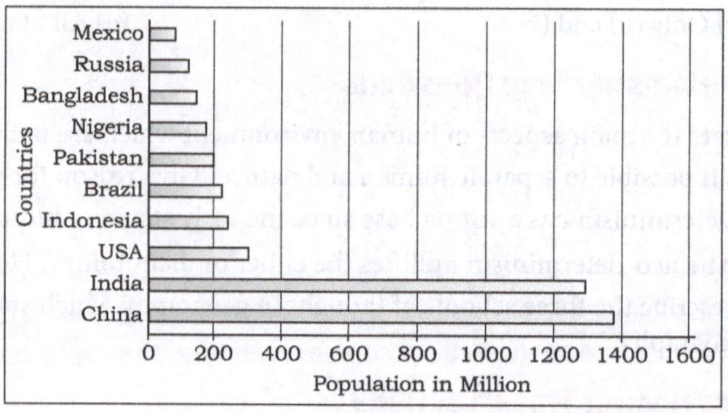

▲ *Most Populous Countries*

Density of Population

- **Population density** refers to the number of people living in per unit area.
  Density of population= Population/ Area

Factors Affecting Distribution of Population

Geographical Factors

- **Availability of water** People prefer to live in areas where fresh water is available. Hence, river valleys are densely populated.
- **Landforms** Plains and regions with gentle slopes are favourable for the agriculture and infrastructure development. So, the Ganga plains are among the most populated areas of the world.
- **Climate** Area with a comfortable climate, where there is not much seasonal variation, attracts more people. Regions with extreme climate like hot or cold deserts are uncomfortable for human settlements.
- **Soils** Regions with fertile loamy soils are densely populated. These soils supports intensive agriculture. Hence, these region preferred by human for settlement.

Economic Factors

- **Minerals** Regions with minerals attracts industries and job opportunities. So, semi- skilled and skilled workers moves in these regions and make them densely populated. The Katanga Zambia copper belt in Africa is a good example.
- **Urbanisation** Cities are highly populated because they provide employment opportunities, educational and medical facilites, better transportation and communication.
- **Industrialisation** Industrial belts provide job opportunities and attract large number of people. The Kobe-Osaka region in Japan has a large population because it has many industries.

Social and Cultural Factors

- Places with religious and cultural significance are highly populated.
- People tend to move away from the places of social and political unrest like civil disorders, strikes and riots.
- Many times government offers policies/incentives to move out from overcrowded places.

Quick Test 1

1. In which unit does density of population is measured?
2. The Katanga Zambia belt in Africa is famous for mining of which mineral?
3. Name two geographical factors affecting the distribution of population.
4. How social and cultural factors impact the population distribution?

2.2 Population Growth

- **Population growth** or population change refers to the change in number of people living in an area for a particular period of time. There can be positive or negative change in population.
- It is an indicator of economic development, **social upliftment** and historical and cultural background of the region.

Components of Population Change

- **Crude Birth Rate** (CBR) It refers to number of live births in a year per thousand of population.
  CBR= Number of live births during the year/ population of the area* 1000
- **Crude Death Rate** (CDR) It is measure to express number of deaths in a particular area.
  CDR= Number of deaths/ population of the area *1000

- **Mortality rate** It is impacted by the region's demographic structure, social advancement and levels of its economic development.
- **Migration** The movement of people from one place to another is called migration. The place from where people move is called **place of origin** and the place they move to is called the **place of destination.** Migration might be temporary or permanent. Human may migrate from rural to rural areas, rural to urban areas, urban to urban or urban to rural areas.
- When migrants move into a new place they are called *immigrants* and when migrants move out of a place, they are called *emigrants.*
- Factors affecting migrations are
  - **Push factors** These factors influence population to move out of the place. For example, political turmoil, unpleasant climate, natural disasters, etc.
  - **Pull factors** These factors influence population to move in the place. For example, better job opportunities, peace and security of life and property.

Demographic Transition

- Demographic transition theory can be used to describe and predict the population in future.

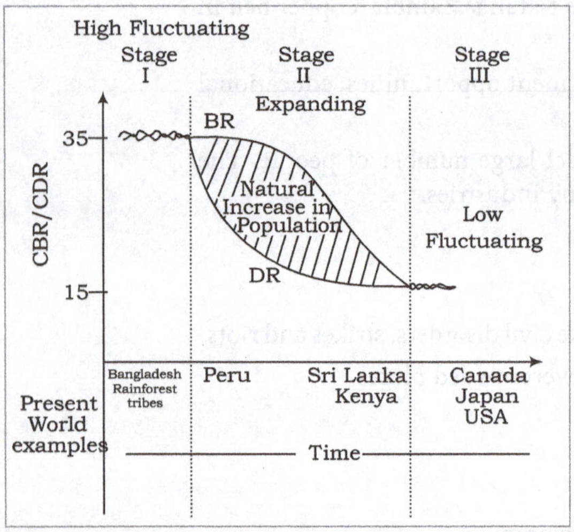

▲ *Demographic Transition Theory*

- The stages of demographic changes is called **demographic cycle.** These are discussed below
  - **Stage I** This stage is attributed with high birth rate and high death rate. The population growth is slow and large families were asset to the agricultural activities.
  - **Stage II** Initially birth rate is high in this stage but slowly declines. The mortality rate is reduced by the improved sanitation and health conditions.
  - **Stage III** Both fertility and mortality rate declines considerably in this stage. The population becomes urbanised, literate and has high technology.

Population Control Measures

- For sustainability of our resources, the world requires to control the rapid population increase.
- A proper family planning is an important factor in controlling population growth.
- **Propaganda**[2], free contraceptives availability and tax disincentives for large families are some of the measures which can help population control.

Quick Test 2

1. What are three important components of population change?
2. Give an example of pull factors of migration.
3. Which stage of demographic transition theory depicts population explosion?
4. What is the meaning of place of destination in migration?

2 **Propaganda** It is a communication that is primarily used to influence an audience.

Mind Map

THE WORLD POPULATION: DISTRIBUTION, DENSITY AND GROWTH

1 Pattern of Population Distribution in the World

- Shows the way people are spaced over Earth's surface.
- 10 most populous countries contributes 60% of the world's population.
- Asia is the most populous continent.

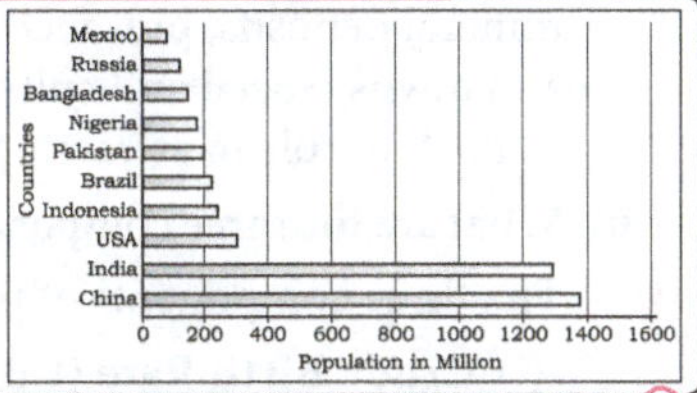

2 Density of population

Refers to the number of people living in per unit area.

$$\text{Density} = \frac{\text{Population}}{\text{Area}}$$

3 Factors Affecting Distribution of Population

Geographical Factors

- **Availability of Water** People prefer to live where fresh water is easily available.
- **Landforms** These areas are suitable for agriculture, manufacturing, etc.
- **Climate** People prefer to live in areas where there is not much seasonal variation (very hot or very cold).
- **Soil** Fertile soils offer optimal land for farming.

Social and Cultural Factors

People prefer to live in the areas that have religious and cultural significance and are socially and politically stable.

Economic Factors

- **Minerals Distribution** It attracts industries and job opportunities, e.g., Katanga Zambia copper belt in Africa.
- **Urbanisation** It provides employment opportunities, educational and medical facilities, better transportation and communication, e.g., cities.
- **Industrialisation** It provide job opportunities and attract large number of people, e.g., Kobe-Osaka region in Japan.

4 Population Growth

It is the change in number of inhabitants in a region.
It includes three components

(i) **Birth** It refers to number of live births in a year per thousand of population.
(ii) **Death** It refers to number of deaths in a particular area.
(iii) **Migration** It refers to movement of people from one place to another.

Migration is of two types

- **Immigration** When migrants move into a new place.
- **Emigration** When migrants move out of a place .

There are two factors that influence migration : **Push** and **Pull.**

5 Demographic Transition

Transition of population in a society.
It has three stages

(i) **High fluctuating** This stage is attributed with high birth rate and high death rate. Population growth is slow and large families were asset to the agricultural activities.
(ii) **Stagnant** Birth rate is high in this stage but slowly declines. Mortality rate is reduced by the improved sanitation and health conditions.
(iii) **Low fluctuating** Both fertility and mortality rate declines. Population becomes urbanised, literate and has high technological knowledge.

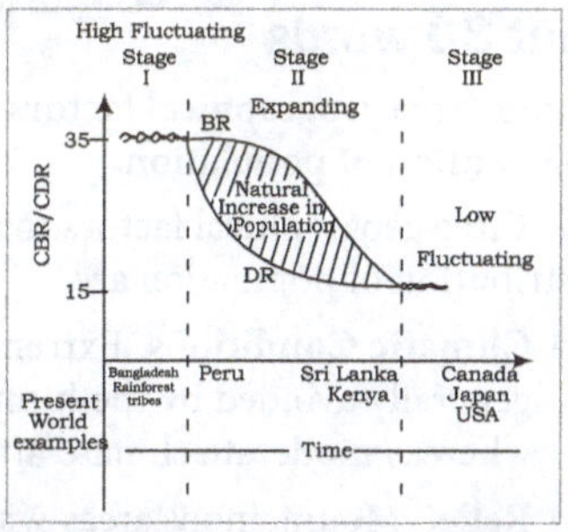

6 Population Control Measures

Include measures to control population, e.g., contraceptive, proper family planning, tax disincentives for large families, etc.

NCERT Folder

Choose the right answer from the four alternatives given below

(i) **Which one of the following continents has the highest growth of population?**

(a) Africa (b) South America
(c) Asia (d) North America

Ans. (a) Africa

(ii) **Which one of the following is not an area of sparse population?**

(a) The Atacama (b) South-East Asia
(c) Equatorial Region (d) Polar Regions

Ans. (b) South-East Asia

(iii) **Which one of the following is not a push factor?**

(a) Water shortage
(b) Medical/educational facilities
(c) Unemployment
(d) Epidemics

Ans. (b) Medical/educational facilities

(iv) **Which one of the following is not a fact?**

(a) Human population increased more than ten times during the past 500 years.
(b) Population growth is high in the first stage of demographic transition.

Ans. (b) Population growth is high in the first stage of demographic transition.

Answer the following questions in about 30 words

(i) **Name three geographical factors that influence the distribution of population.**

Ans. The three geographical factors that influence the distribution of population are

(i) **Climatic Conditions** Extreme type of climate are generally avoided by the human for settlement, whereas moderate climate attract population.

(ii) **Relief** Mountainous areas with steep slope, exposed and rugged terrain have low population density. While flat plains have high population density.

(iii) **Water Facilities and Availability** Areas with fresh water are most preferred for settling.

(ii) **There are a number of areas with high population density in the world. Why does this happen?**

Ans. Areas having high density of population are due to various factors. These include physical factors such as availability of fresh water, fertile soil areas having gentle slope and flat plains, moderate and comfortable climate etc. and economic factors such as areas having high mineral deposits, presence of industries and urban cities and towns. Social and cultural factors also play an important role in attracting population.

(iii) **What are the three components of population change?**

Ans. The three components of population change are

(i) **Crude Birth Rate** (CBR) It is referred to as number of live births in a year per thousand of population. It is calculated as

$$CBR = \frac{B}{P} \times 1000$$

(ii) **Crude Death Rate** (CDR) It is expressed in terms of number of deaths in a particular year per thousand of population in a particular region. It is calculated as

$$CDR = \frac{D}{P} \times 1000$$

(iii) **Migration** It is an important component of population change. It is a movement of people from one place to another.

Distinguish between

(i) **Birth rate and death rate**

Ans. Difference between birth rate and death rate are as follows

Birth Rate	Death Rate
It defines the number of live births in a year per thousand of population.	It defines the number of deaths in a particular year per thousand of population in a particular region.
It is calculated as $CBR = \frac{B}{P} \times 1000$ Here, CBR = Crude Birth Rate Bi = Live births during the year P = Mid year population of the area.	It is calculated as $CDR = \frac{D}{P} \times 1000$ Here, CDR = Crude Death Rate D= Number of deaths P= Estimated mid year population of that year.
If Crude Birth Rate exceeds the death rate between two points of time, it results in positive growth of population.	If Crude Death Rate exceeds birth rate between two points of time, it results in negative growth of population.

(ii) Push factors and pull factors of migration

Ans. Difference between push factors and pull factors of migration are as follows

Push Factors	Pull Factors
The unfavourable factors which make the place of origin less attractive are known as push factors.	The favourable factors which make a place of destination more attractive are known as pull factors.
Generally, these factors result in migration from rural to urban areas.	Generally, these factors result in migration from urban to urban and rural to urban areas.
The important factors are unemployment, poverty, poor facilities of education, health sanitation, recreation, etc.	The important factors are better employment opportunities, living conditions, peace, stability security of life, property and pleasant climate.

Answer the following questions in about 150 words

(i) Discuss the factors influencing the distribution and density of population.

Ans. There are three factors that influence the distribution and density of population. These are discussed below

(a) **Geographical Factors** These include the following sub-factors

Availability of Water People usually prefer to live in areas where fresh water is easily available.

Landforms/Relief Plains provide relief which is suitable for cultivation of crops, to build roadways, railways and to set up industries. Thus, plains are densely populated in the world.

Climate People prefer to live in normal climatic regions whereas heavy rainfall regions and very hot and very cold deserts are not favourable to live.

Soils People prefer to live in those areas which have fertile soils, where agricultural development can take place.

(b) **Economic Factors** These include the following sub-factors

Minerals Industries are generally set up near resource rich regions which generate employment opportunities for people.

Urbanisation Better employment opportunities, educational and medical facilities, etc attract people to live in the cities.

Industrialisation Industrial regions have a number of job creating sectors like transport operators, factory workers, teachers, doctors and other service providers.

(c) **Social and Cultural Factors** These include the following sub-factors

Cultural Significance Places with social as well as cultural values, customs, traditions attract people.

Social and Political Unrest Wars and conflicts often lead to out migration from place of origin to new place, this affects the distribution of population.

Government Aided Schemes Many a times government provide incentives to people to move from overcrowded places to less crowded places and sometimes to move people for developing sparsely populated areas.

(ii) Discuss the three stages of demographic transition.

Or **What is 'demographic cycle'? Describe three stages of Demographic Transition Theory.**

Or **Examine three stages of demographic transition theory.** **CBSE 2025**

Or **Explain the 'demographic transition theory' with reference to the world.**

Ans. Demographic cycle represent the changes in the population of a region as it moves from high births and high deaths to low births and low deaths. The three stages of Demographic Transition Theory are as follows

(a) **Stage I** This stage is characterised by high fertility and high mortality rates. There are more number of deaths due to epidemics and variable food supply and people reproduce more to compensate it. This leads to slow growth of population. People mostly live in rural areas and their main occupation is agriculture. The large size of families is considered as an asset. Life expectancy is low due to high deaths. This period is also a time of illiteracy and less technological advancement.

(b) **Stage II** This is the stage of population explosion where fertility remains constantly high in the beginning, but it declines with time. This period is characterised by reduced mortality rate. This is due to an expansion in medical and health facilities and also improvements in sanitation conditions, etc. Due to the widening gap between the birth and death rates, population grows at an exceptionally high rate. Thus, this period denotes a period of population explosion.

(c) **Stage III** This stage is characterised by a decline in fertility and mortality rates. Birth rate is nearly equal to death rate and there is little growth in population. In this period, population becomes more urbanised, literate and has high technical know how and deliberately controls the family size.

(To represent these three stages of Demographic Transition Theory, **refer to the diagram on pg. no. 18.**)

Exam Pattern Questions

Objective Type Questions

Multiple Choice Questions (MCQs)

1. The ratio between the number of people to the size of land is known as ....

(a) population distribution (b) population density
(c) population growth (d) crude birth rate

2. Which of the following is an example of a densely populated region?

(a) The Ganga plains
(b) The Sahara desert
(c) The Himalayan mountains
(d) The Amazon rainforest

3. Which among the following is an economic factor responsible for uneven distribution of population in the world ? CBSE 2023

(a) Urbanisation (b) Soils
(c) Climate (d) Political unrest

4. Which one of the following is a social factor affecting the distribution of population ? CBSE 2023

(a) Minerals (b) Urbanisation
(c) Industrialisation (d) Political Unrest

5. Which of the following formula correctly depicts natural growth of population?

(a) Births -Deaths
(b) Births-Deaths-In Migration + Out Migration
(c) Births-Deaths + In Migration
(d) Births -Deaths + In Migration -Out Migration

6. Which one of the following is a main component of population change? CBSE Term I 2021

(a) Density of population (b) Urbanisation
(c) Industrialisation (d) Migration

7. Which of the following is a push factor for migration?

(a) Job opportunities
(b) Peace and stability
(c) Socio-economic backwardness
(d) Pleasant climate

8. Which of the following feature(s) is/are related to the second stage of Demographic Transition Theory? CBSE SQP 2022

(a) Fertility and mortality decline considerable.
(b) Decline in mortality but fertility remains high.
(c) Fertility and mortality are high.
(d) Fertility declines and mortality high.

9. Which of the following country is in the first stage of Demographic transition?

(a) Bangladesh (b) India
(c) Peru (d) Canada

10. According to Malthus, which of these is a preventive check for population control?

(a) Famine (b) Disease
(c) War (d) Tax Disincentives

11. Read the following factors of migration carefully and choose the correct option related to 'push factor' CBSE 2024

(i) Peace and stability (ii) Protection of property
(iii) Epidemics (iv) Unpleasant climate

Options

(a) Only (i) and (ii) are correct
(b) Only (ii) and (iii) are correct
(c) Only (iii) and (iv) are correct
(d) Only (i) and (iv) are correct

12. Read the following factors of migration carefully and choose the correct option related to pull factors

(i) Peace and stability
(ii) Unfavourable climate
(iii) Protection of property
(iv) Economic backwardness CBSE 2024

Options

(a) Only (i) and (ii) are correct
(b) Only (i) and (iii) are correct
(c) Only (ii) and (iv) are correct
(d) Only (ii) and (iii) are correct

13. Consider the following and choose which of them can be reason/reasons for scarce population in an area.

(i) Presence of river valleys
(ii) Mountains and hills
(iii) Harsh climate
(iv) Rich mineral deposits

Codes

(a) (i) and (iv) (b) (i), (iii) and (iv)
(c) (ii) and (iii) (d) (ii), (iii) and (iv)

14. Which of the following are economic factors influencing population distribution?

(i) Climate (ii) Minerals
(iii) Industrialisation (iv) Soils

Codes
(a) (i), (ii) and (iii)
(b) (i), (ii) and (iv)
(c) (ii) and (iii)
(d) (i) and (iv)

Arrange the Following

15. **Arrange the following stages of demographic transition in a chronological order and choose the correct option.**
(i) High fertility, High mortality
(ii) Birth rate equal to death rate
(iii) Population explosion

Codes
(a) (i), (ii), (iii)
(b) (i), (iii), (ii)
(c) (iii), (ii), (i)
(d) (ii), (iii), (i)

16. **Arrange the following countries in order of their population from highest to lowest.**
(i) China
(ii) USA
(iii) India
(iv) Indonesia

Codes
(a) (ii), (i), (iv), (iii)
(b) (i), (iii), (ii), (iv)
(c) (iii), (iv), (i), (ii)
(d) (i), (iii), (iv), (ii)

Match the Following

17.

List I	List II
A. Population Density	1. $\frac{B}{P} \times 100$
B. Crude Birth Rate	2. $\frac{D}{P} \times 100$
C. Crude Death Rate	3. $\frac{Population}{Area}$

Codes

	A	B	C
(a)	3	1	2
(b)	1	2	3
(c)	2	1	3
(d)	1	3	2

Assertion-Reason

Directions (Q. Nos. 18-20) In the questions given below are two statements labelled as Assertion (A) and other is labelled as Reason (R). In the context of two statements, which one of the following is correct?

Codes
(a) Both A and R are true, but R is not the correct explanation of A
(b) Both A and R are true and R is the correct explanation of A
(c) Both A and R are incorrect
(d) A is correct, but R is incorrect

18. **Assertion** (A) Technology has helped in population growth.

Reason (R) Technology has led to improvement in medical facilities and sanitation.

19. Assertion (A) Mediterranean regions have been inhabited from early periods in history. **CBSE SQP 2022**

Reason (R) Plain areas are favourable for the production of crops and to build roads and industries.

20. **Assertion** (A) Areas with mineral deposits and industries are densely populated.
Reason (R) "Mining and industrial activities generate employment opportunities and thus attract large population." **CBSE 2024 C**

Answers

1. (b) population density
2. (a) The Ganga plains
3. (a) Urbanisation
4. (d) Unrest
5. (d) Births -Deaths + In Migration -Out Migration
6. (d) Migration
7. (c) Socio- economic backwardness
8. (b) Decline in mortality but fertility remains high
9. (a) Bangladesh
10. (d) Tax Disincentives
11. (c) Only (iii) and (iv) are correct
12. (b) Only (i) and (iii) are correct
13. (c) (ii) and (iii)
14. (c) (ii) and (iii)
15. (b) (i), (iii), (ii)
16. (b) (i), (iii), (ii), (iv)
17. (a)
18. (b) Both A and R are true and R is the correct explanation of A
19. (a) Both A and R are true and R is not the correct explanation of A
20. (b) Both A and R are true and R is the correct explanation of A

Subjective Questions

Short Answer Type Questions

1. Patterns of population distribution and density help us to understand the demographic characteristics of any area. Validate the statement.

Ans. Patterns of population distribution help us to understand the demographic characteristics of any area in the following ways

- Population distribution shows how people are distributed over the Earth's surface. 90 per cent of the world population lives on 10 per cent of the land. About 60 per cent of this population lives in only 10 countries.
- Places which are sparsely populated have low population density. On the other hand, places which are densely populated have large number of people living per km^2.
- Place such as Antarctica where there is harsh climate, population is low. On the other hand, place like Europe where climate is favorable, population is high.

2. What do you mean by density of population? Explain with examples the physical and economic factors which affect population distribution. **CBSE SQP 2022**

Ans The density of population is the ratio between the numbers of people living in a square kilometer of area. It is a measure of human and land relationship. It helps us in getting a better understanding of spatial distribution of population in relation to land.

Physical factors which affect population distribution include availability of water, terrain, fertile soil and climate. Most of the physical factors influence population distribution indirectly through climatic conditions. For instance, the North India plains, deltas and coastal plains have a higher proportion of population than other regions of the country.

Economic factors which affect population distribution include industrialisation, urbanisation and development of transport networks causes high concentration of population in urban regions of Delhi, Mumbai, Kolkata, Bangalore, Pune, etc.

3. Science and technology has contributed in population growth. Verify how.

Or **How does science and technology help in the increase of population in the world?** **CBSE 2024**

Ans. Population growth or population change refers to the change in number of inhabitants of a region during a specific period of time.

Science and technology helped in population growth in following ways

- The steam engine replaced human and animal energy and also provided mechanised energy of water and wind. This increased agricultural and industrial production leading to decline in deaths that were occurring due to variable food supply.
- Immunisation against epidemics and other communicable diseases led to decline in deaths due to epidemics.
- Improvement in medical facilities and sanitation lead to decline in mortality.

All these factors provided a strong base for population growth.

4. Analyse the impact of urbanisation and industrialisation on population growth. How do cities and industries attract large numbers of people?

Ans. Urbanisation and industrialisation significantly impact population growth by creating job opportunities, better living conditions, and improved infrastructure. Cities offer diverse employment options, educational and healthcare facilities, and enhanced transport networks, making them attractive to migrants from rural areas. Industries contribute by providing specialised jobs, increasing demand for workers, and fostering economic growth. This leads to a concentration of people in urban areas, resulting in population growth. Additionally, urban centers often offer better civic amenities and higher standards of living, drawing individuals seeking better opportunities, leading to the expansion of cities and further industrialisation.

5. Discuss the concept of 'Natural Growth' and 'Actual Growth' of population. How do migration and the difference between birth and death rates contribute to population changes?

Ans. 'Natural Growth' refers to population change due to the difference between births and deaths. A higher birth rate than death rate leads to natural growth. 'Actual Growth' includes both natural growth and migration-people moving into or out of a region. Migration impacts population size by adding people (immigration) or reducing it (emigration). Therefore, while natural growth depends on birth-death rates, actual growth considers both internal factors (births and deaths) and external factors (migration).

6. Describe any three characteristics of the first stage of 'Demographic Transition Theory'.

Ans. The Demographic Transition Theory is used to describe and predict the population and its growth in an area.

This stage is characterised by the following

(i) There is high fertility and high mortality rates. The number of deaths increase due to epidemics and variable food supply.

(ii) The life expectancy of the population is low due to the epidemics and variable food supply. Thus, people reproduce more and the growth of population is low.

(iii) The people mostly live in rural areas and there is low level of technological advancement. The main occupation of people is agriculture.

7. Describe any three characteristics of the last stage of Demographic Transition theory.

Ans. The last stage of Demographic transition has the following characteristics

(i) In this stage, there is decline in both the fertility and mortality rate due to improvement in the field of health and education.

(ii) The population in this stage either becomes stable or grows slowly. The population consists of a greater number of old people.

(iii) In this stage, there is increase in urbanisation and literate people and advancement in technology. These advancements lead to control in the family size.

Long Answer Type Questions

1. What is the meaning of density of population? Examine the four geographical factors that influence the distribution of population in the world with suitable examples.

Or **What do you mean by density of population? Explain with examples the four physical factors influencing the distribution of population in the world.**

Or **Landform as a factor influences the population density of a region. Elucidate the statement.**

Ans Landform as a factor influences how population is distributed over a space. This can be explained through following examples

- People prefer living on flat plains and gentle slopes. This is because such areas are favourable for the production of crops and they are also favourable for building roads and industries. Hence, these areas are densely populated.
- The mountainous and hilly areas act as an obstacle in the development of transport network and hence these areas are not good for agricultural and industrial development. So, these areas tend to be less populated.
- The Ganga plains are among the most densely populated areas of the world while the mountain zones in the Himalayas are scarcely populated.

2. Explain three economic and two social and cultural factors influencing the distribution of population in the world.

Or **Explain with examples the three economic factors influencing the population distribution in the world.**

Or **Explain the economic and cultural factors that influence the distribution of population in the world.**

Or **Explain with examples any three economic factors affecting population distribution in the world.** CBSE 2024

Or **Explain the factors affecting the population distribution in the world.** CBSE 2025

Ans The three economic factors influencing the distribution of population in the world are as follows

(i) **Minerals** Areas with mineral deposits attract industries, which generate huge employment and skilled and semi skilled workers that settle in these areas.

(ii) **Urbanisation** Urban centres offer better employment opportunities, education and medical facilities and better means of communication which attract population.

(iii) **Industrialisation** Industrial belts provide job opportunities. These attract not only factory workers, but also transport operators, shopkeepers, bank employees, doctors, teachers and other service providers.

Two social and cultural factors influencing the distribution of population in the world are as follows

(i) **Religious and Cultural Significance** Places having religious importance and cultural significance tend to attract number of people due to which they are densely populated.

(ii) **Social and Political Unrest** Places where there is political turmoil and social unrest are not fit for living. Thus, people tend to move away from those areas. This makes them sparsely populated.

3. Name the areas having high density of population in the world. Also mention the factors responsible for high population density in these areas.

Ans The regions having high density of population are as under

- **Eastern Asia** Countries like China, Japan, Korea and Philippines have high population density.

  The reason of high concentration of people is that these regions have fertile soils, level plains of river valley, sufficient water supply and transport facilities. They also have indented coastline, moderate climate, large fishing grounds, mechanisation and development.

- **South and South-East Asia** Countries include India, Pakistan, Sri Lanka, Nepal, Bhutan, Myanmar, Thailand, Vietnam, Malaysia and Indonesia.
These regions have attracted people because of fertile valleys of various rivers. These regions are also called 'Rice bowl' of the world. Besides these, transport facilities and development of agriculture and industries also attract people.
- **North-West Europe** It comprises of UK, France, Belgium, Netherland, Denmark and Germany. The reasons of high concentration are industrial development, scientific and technological changes, development of mechanised form of energy and rapid means of transport.
- **North-Eastern America** It includes central regions of USA and Canada. These regions have high concentration of population because European settlers brought high technology to exploit rich resources of America. People established industries and developed urban centres all along the coast.

4. "90 per cent of the world population lives in about 10 per cent of its total land area, whereas remaining 10 per cent population resides in the 90 per cent of its land area". Support the statement with suitable examples.

Ans It is true that 90 per cent of the world population lives in about 10 per cent of its total land area, whereas remaining 10 per cent population resides in the 90 per cent of its land area. Almost 60% of this population resides only in the 10 countries of world. The factors which affect the distribution of population in the world are

- **Cultural Factors** Traditions and culture of a place influence the distribution of population. People like to migrate in areas where common tradition and culture are found.
- **Physical Factors** Relief, climate, soil and mineral are the physical factors which determine the population of any place. Tibet is the region of very less population, whereas Indo-Gangetic plain is over populated.
- **Means of Transport** Regions with better facilities of means of transport lead to better economic condition. This leads to high density of population. Mumbai-Pune industrial region is the best example.
- **Economic Condition** Industrial and agriculture regions of the world are thickly populated due to presence of huge employment opportunities and favourable living conditions. For example Industrial regions of India, USA, Japan, UK.

5. Explain the term 'migration'. What are the different patterns of migration?

Ans 'Migration' is the movement of people from one place to another with the intention of settling at the new location. The movement is typically over long distances i.e. from one country to another, but internal migration is also possible. It may be permanent or semi-permanent change of a person's place of residence. The patterns of migration have been classified in various ways which may be rural to rural; rural to urban; urban to urban; urban to rural; inter-regional and international.

The above patterns of migration can be described as follows

- **International Migration** It refers to the displacement of people between countries and continents. People move to other regions in search of better opportunities and life.
- **Rural Urban Migration** It refers to the displacement of people from rural-urban areas of a country to other regions offering better opportunities. The movement of rural population to the growing urban centres is caused by push and pull factors.
- **Urban to Urban Migration** In countries, where three-quarters of total population is urbanised, the bulk of migrants tend to be inter-urban i.e. migrants frequently moving from one urban centre to another.
- **Rural to Rural Migration** Movement of people from rural to rural areas in search of better job opportunities such as in mining, plantation industries, etc.

6. Explain any three push and any two pull factors that influence the migration of population in the world.

Or **How is the mortality rate of a region affected? Explain any four push factors responsible for emigration.**

Ans The mortality rate of region is affected by a number of factors such as by the regions's demographic structure, social advancement and levels of its economic development.

Push factors The four push factors responsible for emigration are as follows

(i) **Unemployment** Whenever people find it difficult to live in circumstances of poverty, they want to escape from the place which have less or no opportunity of employment.

(ii) **Poor Living Conditions** Poor living conditions force people to move out of that particular area. Thus, people want to take a quick move to the places having good opportunities to sustain life.

(iii) **Internal Conflicts and War** When these situations arise in a particular place, people feel compelled to move to a new place which has no such situations.

(iv) **Unpleasant Climate** People usually prefer to live in favourable climate and avoid harsh climates. When they are hit by any natural disaster, they are compelled to leave their home town.

Pull Factors The two pull factors are as follows

(i) **Better Job Opportunities** People need work for their livelihood. Thus, when they find job opportunities they move to places for the sake of earning a better income.

(ii) **Better Living Conditions** Now, everyone wants a life full of leisure and comfort, that bring people from rural areas to urban areas as urban areas have more basic amenities than rural areas to give people a comfortable living.

7. Explain the measures of population control in the world. CBSE 2025

Ans Population control measures have been implemented globally to address issues like overpopulation, resource depletion, and environmental degradation. Some key measures include

Family Planning Programs Many countries have promoted family planning to reduce birth rates. These programs offer education on contraceptive use, health services, and counseling, aiming to empower individuals to make informed decisions about family size.

Government Policies Countries like China introduced the "One-Child Policy" (later relaxed) to directly control population growth. India also launched its "National Population Policy" to promote smaller families and improve reproductive health.

Improvement in Health Services Better healthcare, including maternal care, vaccination, and treatment for diseases, has led to a decline in infant mortality, allowing families to have fewer children while ensuring their survival.

Education Raising awareness, particularly among women, about the benefits of smaller families and reproductive health has played a significant role in reducing fertility rates globally.

8. What would be the consequences of the condition of positive population growth and negative population growth/decline? Explain.

Ans Increase or decrease in population may result in certain consequences, these are discussed below

Positive Population Growth Growth of population at high rate, beyond a certain level creates problem in the way of development.

Some consequences of positive population growth are given below

- The growth of population leads to pressure on land and its natural resources.
- The drinking water will not be available and it will become scarce. The water reserves are depleting in many regions of the world.
- Forests are being cleared for demand of more land and soil for agriculture which leads to soil erosion.
- The growth of population leads to adverse effects on the quality of workforce. Therefore, per capita income of work may go down.
- The important consequences are poverty, unemployment, disparity and malnutrition which also rise rapidly.

Negative Population Growth/Decline in Population
The decline in population is also a major problem. It can be understood from following points

- The population declines when the available resources are insufficient to support the population.
- The basic structure of the society itself becomes unstable. Due to it, there occurs a great chaos.
- Lesser number of people are available for working as most of population comprises of old and aged people.
- Thus, the growth and decline of population both leads to adverse impact on the economic and social framework of a country.

9. "Family planning helps limit population growth and improve women's health through measures like availability and tax disincentives. Justify this statement."

Ans. Family planning plays a crucial role in controlling population growth by allowing families to decide the number and timing of children. The availability of contraceptives empowers individuals to prevent unintended pregnancies, ensuring better health outcomes for women by reducing the risks associated with frequent childbearing. Tax disincentives for large families encourage people to have fewer children, promoting more sustainable population growth. These measures also improve women's health by reducing the physical and emotional stress of frequent pregnancies, while enabling women to pursue education and careers. By limiting family size, family planning contributes to better economic stability, reduced poverty, and improved quality of life. Thus, family planning is an effective tool for population control and overall societal development.

Source/Graph Based Questions

1. Study the graph given below and answer the questions that follow. **CBSE SQP 2024**

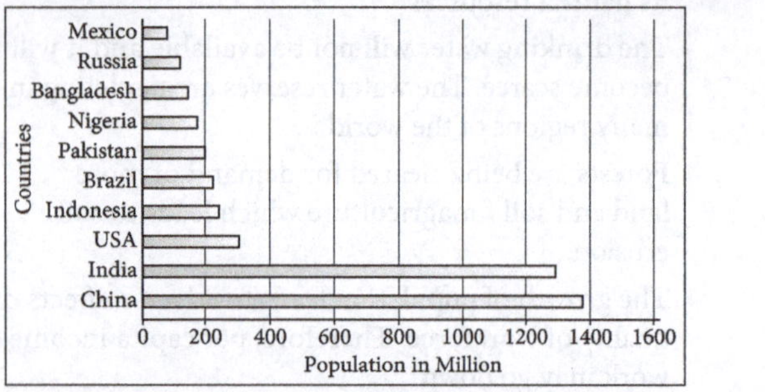

(i) Identify the highest populous country?
(a) Russia (b) India (c) Canada (d) China

Ans. (d) China

(ii) Identify the African country that has very high population.
(a) Mexico (b) Brazil (c) Pakistan (d) Nigeria

Ans. (d) Nigeria

(iii) Which continent has the highest number of the world's most populous countries?
(a) Africa (b) North America
(c) Asia (d) South America

Ans. (c) Asia

2. Study the given graph and answer the questions that follow

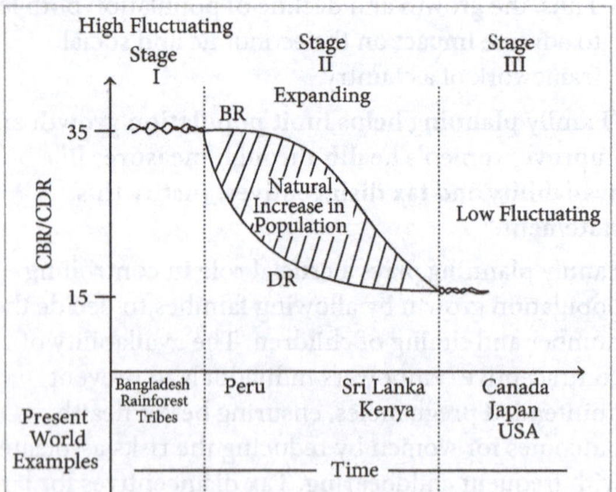

(i) Which one of the following statements regarding Stage I of demographic transition is true?
(a) Stage I has high fertility and high mortality.
(b) Population growth is high.
(c) Most of the people are engaged in industrial activities.
(d) Life expectancy is moderate.

Ans. (a) Stage I has high fertility and high mortality.

(ii) Which one of the following is applicable to Stage II of demographic transition? Choose the most appropriate option.
(a) Stage II is marked by the reduction in mortality rate.
(b) Health and sanitation conditions remained the same as in Stage I.
(c) In spite of high birth rate, high death rate lowers the population.
(d) By the end of the first half of Stage II, the gap between birth rate and death rate is low.

Ans. (a) Stage II is marked by the reduction in mortality rate.

(iii) Which one of the following is a characteristic of the last stage of demographic transition? Choose the most appropriate option.
(a) Both fertility and mortality decline considerably.
(b) Growth of population is moderately high.
(c) People are largely involved in agriculture.
(d) Technological application is moderately low.

Ans. (a) Both fertility and mortality decline considerably.

3. Stages of Demographic Transition Theory **CBSE 2024**

The first stage has high fertility and high mortality because people reproduce more to compensate for the deaths due to epidemics and variable food supply. The population growth is slow and most of the people are engaged in agriculture where large families are an asset. Life expectancy is low, people are mostly illiterate and have low levels of technology. Two hundred years ago all the countries of the world were in this stage.

Fertility remains high in the beginning of second stage but it declines with time. This is accompanied by reduced mortality rate. Improvements in sanitation and health conditions lead to decline in mortality. Because of this gap the net addition to population is high. In the last stage, both fertility and mortality decline considerably. The population is either stable or grows slowly. The population becomes urbanised, literate and has high technical know- how and deliberately controls the family size. This shows that human beings are extremely flexible and are able to adjust their fertility. In the present day, different countries are at different stages of demographic transition.

(i) 'The people at this stage are engaged in agricultural activities where large families are an asset. Life expectancy is also low.' Identify the stage.
(a) Only last stage
(b) Only first stage
(c) Both first and last stage
(d) Only second stage.

Ans. (b) Only first stage

(ii) **Choose the most appropriate option from the following regarding components of population change.**

(a) Births, deaths and migration

(b) Births, density and migration

(c) Density, literacy and age-structure

(d) Deaths, literacy and sex-ratio

Ans. (a) Births, deaths and migration

(iii) **Which of the following stage/ stages has/ have a slow growth of population?**

(a) Only the first stage

(b) Only the second stage

(c) Only second and last stage

(d) Only first and last stages

Ans. (d) Only first and last stages

4. Read the passage carefully and answer the questions that follow.

The population growth or population change refers to the change in number of inhabitants of a territory during a specific period of time. This change may be positive as well as negative. It can be expressed either in terms of absolute numbers or in terms of percentage. Population change in an area is an important indicator of economic development, social upliftment and historical and cultural background of the region.

There are three components of population change – births, deaths and migration. The Crude Birth Rate (CBR) is expressed as number of live births in a year per thousand of population. Death rate plays an active role in population change. Population growth occurs not only by increasing births rate but also due to decreasing death rate. Crude Death Rate (CDR) is a simple method of measuring mortality of any area. CDR is expressed in terms of number of deaths in a particular year per thousand of population in a particular region. Apart from birth and death there is another way by which the population size changes. When people move from one place to another, the place they move from is called the Place of Origin and the place they move to is called the Place of Destination. The place of origin shows a decrease in population while the population increases in the place of destination.

(i) **What does a population change in a region indicates?**

Ans. Population growth in a region indicates that there is change in the number of inhabitants of a territory during a specific period of time.

(ii) **Death is an important factor in determining the change in population. Comment.**

Ans. Decline in death rate because of improved health facility and good life style results in the rise in population leading to population change in a region.

(iii) **What is the other factor other than birth and death that changes population of a region?**

Ans. Migration is a determinant factor that changes the population of a region. Movement of people from one place to another affects the population of both the places.

SELF ASSESSMENT TEST

Objective Type Questions

1. Which of the following is an economic factor that favours population growth?
   (a) Soil (b) Minerals (c) Landforms (d) Water
2. .... region has the lowest population density.
   (a) Africa (b) Europe (c) Oceania (d) Asia
3. Migrants who move into a new place are called ....
   (a) emigrants (b) immigrants (c) refugees (d) None of these
4. Which of the following is a pull factor of migration?
   (a) Unpleasant climate (b) Security of life
   (c) Natural disasters (d) Unemployment
5. Which of the following correctly defines positive growth rate of population?
   (a) Birth rate is less than death rate (b) Death rate is less than birth rate
   (c) Death rate is equal to birth rate (d) Immigration is equal to outmigration
6. According to Malthus, which of the following statement is correct?
   (a) Population increases slower than food supply.
   (b) Population increases faster than food supply.
   (c) Physical checks are better than preventive checks.
   (d) Food supply increases faster than population.

Short Answer Type Questions

7. What is the effect of climate on population distribution?
8. Distinguish between immigration and emigration.
9. In spite of having an attractive life, cities are places where newly migrated people face a lot of difficulties. Explain the reasons.
10. Positive population growth leads to a number of problems. Explain.
11. Which situations push a person to leave his/her hometown to move to a new place? Elaborate the reasons.

Long Answer Type Questions

12. Discuss the factors which influence the distribution of population.
13. Explain the economic consequences of migration.
14. How demographic transition theory can be used to describe and predict the future population of any area? Elaborate with the help of an example.
15. Why do developing nations always face situation of population explosion?

3

CHAPTER

The terms growth and development are associated with change over a period of time. Growth is quantitative and can be measured. It can be positive or negative. On the other hand, development is a qualitative change. Development occurs when positive growth takes place.

▼ **YOUR STUDY GOALS**

3.1 Concept of Human Development
3.2 Measuring Human Development
3.3 International Comparisons of Human Development

▼ **YOUR PRACTICE GOAL**

- Objective Type Questions (23 Qs ; MCQs, Statements, Matching, A-R)
- Subjective Questions (11 SAs, 8 LAs)
- Source Based Questions (4 Qs)

Human Development

3.1 Concept of Human Development

- Dr. Mahbub-ul-Haq introduced the concept of human development. He described human development as enlarging people's choices and improving their lives. These choices vary from person to person.
- The basic goal of human development is to create a condition where people can live **meaningful lives**.
- In 1990, Dr. Haq created the **Human Development Index**. Since 1990 the Human Development Report has been published annually by the **United Nations Development Programme (UNDP)**.

Four Pillars of Development

The following concepts support the idea of human development

Equity

- It refers to making equal access to opportunities available to everybody.
- There should be no discrimination based on gender, race, income, caste and religion.

Sustainability

- It refers to the continuous availability of opportunities.

- To achieve sustainable human development, equal opportunities must be given to all generations without any misuse of natural resources and the environment.

Productivity

- It refers to the productivity of human labour or productivity in terms of human work.
- It is important to increase human knowledge or provide better health facilities for better work efficiency.

Empowerment

- It refers to having power that enables people to make choices.
- Good governance and people-oriented policies empower the people to make choices.

Approaches to Human Development

Some of the important approaches are

Income Approach

- According to this idea, the level of income decides the level of freedom an individual enjoys.
- It is assumed that if a nation has a higher level of income, it leads to a higher level of human development.

Welfare Approach

- Human beings are at the central position under this approach. People are only passive recipients and not participants in the process of development.
- This approach emphasises on the government expenditure on education, health and social amenities.

Basic /Minimum Needs Approach

- It was proposed by the **International Labour Organisation** (ILO).
- It focuses on six basic needs as important for human development. These are health, education, food, water supply, sanitation and housing.

Capability Approach

- This approach was proposed by **Prof. Amartya Sen.**
- According to this approach, capability should be increased in health, education and access to resources, to increase the level of human development.

Quick Test 1

1. Who introduced the concept of human development?
2. By whom the human development report is published?
3. Name any two approaches to human development.
4. Which approach to human development was proposed by Prof. Amartya Sen?

3.2 Measuring Human Development

The two important measures of calculating human development[1] are as follows

Human Development Index

- It ranks the countries based on their performance in sectors of **health**, **education** and **access to resources.** Each indicator has an equal value of one-third.

1 Human Development It is defined as the process of enlarging people's freedoms and opportunities and improving their well-being.

- Indicators used in the Human Development Index are as follows
  - **Health** To assess the health, life expectancy[2] at birth is measured. Higher life expectancy refers to a higher chance of living a long and healthier life.
  - **Education** The level of education is measured by the adult literacy rate[3] and gross enrolment ratio[4].
  - **Access to Resources** It is measured through purchasing power[5] (in U.S. dollars).
- The ranking is done between 0 to 1 where closer ranking 1 shows a higher level of human development.
- The Human Development Index measures attainments[6] in human development.

Human Poverty Index

- This index measures the shortfall[7] in human development. It is a non-income measure.
- It reveals the facts like those who do not have access to clean water, sanitation, education and health services.

Gross National Happiness (GNH)

- Gross National Happiness is a measure of a country's well-being that goes beyond economic indicators like GDP.
- It considers factors such as environmental protection, cultural preservation, good governance, and the overall satisfaction and quality of life of citizens.
- This concept is originated in Bhutan. It aims to balance material progress with spiritual and emotional fulfilment for a more broad view of national development.

3.3 International Comparisons of Human Development

- Human development is not directly dependent on the income of the country. Sometimes smaller countries with less income perform better than their rich neighbouring countries. For example, smaller economies like Sri Lanka, Trinidad and Tobago have a higher rank than India in the Human Development Index (HDI).
- Classification of countries on the basis of Human Development scores
  - **Very high** (above 0.800) As per 2021-22 reports of UNDP there are 66 countries under this category. Some of the examples are Switzerland, Norway, Iceland, Australia, Denmark, etc.
  - **High** (between 0.700 to 0.799) There are 49 countries in this category. In these countries, the government gives priority to education and healthcare. Most of the countries are early imperial powers.
  - **Medium** (between 0.550 to 0.699) There are 44 countries at this level of human development. Most of these countries emerged after World War II and others were former colonies.
  - **Low** (below 0.549) There are 32 countries in this category. Most of these small countries are going through political turmoil and social instability.

---

2 Life Expectancy It is the average number of years a newborn is expected to live.
3 Adult Literacy Rate The adult literacy rate is the percentage of people aged 15 and older who can read and write with comprehension.
4 Gross Enrolment Ratio It is a statistical tool that measures the percentage of a population that is enrolled in a specific level of education.
5 Purchasing Power It is the value of a currency expressed in terms of the amount of goods or services that one unit of money can buy.
6 Attainments It reflects what has been achieved in the key areas of human development.
7 Shortfall It is a measure to identify the lack of human development in the region.

Human Development: Categories, Criteria and Countries

Level of Human Development	Score in Development Index	Number of Countries
Very High	above 0.800	66
High	between 0.700 up to 0.799	49
Medium	between 0.550 up to 0.699	44
Low	below 0.549	32

Source Human Development Report, 2021-22

Quick Test 2

1. What is the weightage given to each dimension in the Human Development Index?
2. Name an indicator used to show a shortfall in education in the human poverty Index.
3. Name a country in South Asia that has a higher rank in human development than India.
4. Which is the first country to adopt a gross national happiness index?

Mind Map

HUMAN DEVELOPMENT

1 Concept of Human Development

- The concept was introduced by Dr. Mahbub-ul-Haq.
- According to him choices vary from person to person.
- Its basic goal is to create a condition where people can live meaningful lives.

2 The Four Pillars of Human Development

- **Equity** Equal access to opportunities available to everyone.
- **Sustainability** Continuous availability of opportunities.
- **Productivity** In terms of human work.
- **Empowerment** Having power to make choices

3 Approaches to Human Development

- **Income Approach**
  Level of income shows the development, example, if a nation has a higher level of income, it leads to a higher development.
- **Welfare Approach**
  Looks at human beings as beneficiaries. It emphasizes on the government expenditure on education, health, etc.
- **Basic-Needs Approach**
  Looks after the 6 basic needs- health, education , food, water supply, sanitation and housing. It was initially proposed by the International Labour Organisation (ILO)
- **Capability Approach**
  Building human capabilities in areas of health, education and resource access. It was proposed by Prof. Amartya Sen.

4 Measuring Human Development

- **Measured by Human Development Index (HDI)** It ranks the countries based on their performance in sectors of health, education and access to resources.
- Score range between 0-1
- Indicators are
  - **Life expectancy** The average number of years a new born is expected to live.
  - **Literacy** Level of education is measured by the adult literacy rate and gross enrolment ratio.
  - **Per capita income** The total amount earned per person in a nation or geographic region.
- UNDP publishes HDI since 1990.

5 International Comparisons of Human Development

- Countries are classified into four groups
  - (i) Very high HDI (>0.800)
  - (ii) High HDI (0.700-0.799)
  - (iii) Medium HDI (0.550-0.699)
  - (iv) Low HDI (<0.549)
- 66 countries scores high HDI
- 32 countries scores low HDI

NCERT Folder

Choose the right answer from the four alternatives given below

(i) Which one of the following best describes development?

(a) An increase in size.
(b) A constant in size.
(c) A positive change in the quality.
(d) A simple change in the quality.

Ans. (c) A positive change in the quality.

(ii) Which one of the following scholars introduced the concept of human development?

(a) Prof. Amartya Sen (b) Ellen C. Semple
(c) Dr Mahbub-ul-Haq (d) Ratzel

Ans. (c) Dr Mahbub-ul-Haq

Answer the following questions in about 30 words

(i) What are the three basic areas of human development?

Ans. The three basic areas of human development are

(i) **Health** A healthy population leads to positive human development.
(ii) **Education** It indicates high literacy level and gross enrolment ratio of a country.
(iii) **Access to Resources** It includes purchasing power of people in a country.

Building people's capabilities in areas of health, education and access to resources is important in enlarging people's choices.

(ii) Name the four main components of human development.

Ans. The four components of human development are

(i) **Equity** It means that equal access to opportunity should be given to all without any discrimination on the basis of gender, race, income, caste and religion.
(ii) **Sustainability** It refers to continuous flow of availability of opportunities.
(iii) **Productivity** It refers to productivity of human labour or productivity in terms of human work.
(iv) **Empowerment** It refers to the power that enables people to make choices.

(iii) How are countries classified on the basis of Human Development Index?

Ans. The Human Development Index (HDI) classifies countries on the basis of their performance in three dimensions of human development i.e. health, education and access to resources.

These rankings are based on scores between 0 to 1. A score, more near to 1 indicates higher human development.

For example, if a country has a score of 0.983, it would come in very high human development category. Whereas, if a country has a score of 0.268, it would be in very low human development category.

Answer the following questions in not more than 150 words

(i) What do you understand by the term human development?

Ans. Human development refers to the process of enhancing people's well-being by expanding their choices, opportunities and freedoms. It focuses on improving the quality of life rather than just economic growth. The concept, popularised by the United Nations Development Programme (UNDP), emphasises development that is people-centered.

Key dimensions of human development include

- **Health** Ensuring a long and healthy life through access to healthcare and nutrition.
- **Education** Providing knowledge and skills through quality education.
- **Standard of Living** Enhancing income levels and ensuring access to basic needs like housing and utilities.

It is measured using the Human Development Index (HDI), which combines indicators of health (life expectancy), education (mean and expected years of schooling) and income (GNI per capita). Unlike traditional economic measures, human development recognises that economic growth is a means, not an end, and seeks to reduce inequalities and empower individuals for sustainable progress.

(ii) What do equity and sustainability refer to within the concept of human development?

Ans. Human development has four concepts i.e. equity, sustainability, productivity and empowerment. These ensure the progress of human development in any country.

Equity It means availability of equal opportunities to an individual. The opportunity should be for all without any discrimination on the grounds of gender, race, income and caste. In India, persons from socially and economically backward groups are deprived of education. This indicates how choices of these groups are limited due to unequal opportunities.

Sustainability It refers to continuity in the availability of opportunities. Human development is possible when opportunities are available to the present and future generation of a country. It must be ensured that opportunities are available to the next generation without misusing the natural resources and harming environment. For example, unlimited use of fossil fuels leads to its exhaustibility from the Earth. If the use of fossil fuels continue at this rate, the future generation would not be able to use it.

Exam Pattern Questions

Objective Type Questions

Multiple Choice Questions (MCQs)

1. According to Dr Mahbub-ul-Haq, which of the following means human development?
(a) Development which increase people's incomes
(b) Development which enlarges people's choices
(c) Development which makes people strong
(d) Development which makes people smart

2. The idea of human development gives .... a central position in the process of development.
(a) income (b) health (c) people (d) education

3. Which of the following is not a pillar of human development?
(a) Equity (b) Equality
(c) Sustainability (d) Empowerment

4. Which among the following explains the 'equity concept of development'?
(a) Equal access to opportunities
(b) Capabilities building in people
(c) Power to make choice
(d) Opportunities for future generation

5. Which of the following is sustainability in context of human development?
(a) Giving equal opportunities to all generations
(b) Using natural resources widely
(c) Continuity in the availability of resources
(d) All of the above

6. In which one of the following approaches of human development are human beings the targets of all developmental activities? Choose the most appropriate option. **CBSE 2025**
(a) Income Approach (b) Welfare Approach
(c) Basic Needs Approach (d) Capability Approach

7. Which of the following was the only criterion used for many decades to measure a country's level of development? **CBSE Diksha**
(a) In terms of economic growth
(b) In terms of literacy rate
(c) In terms of basic amenities
(d) In terms of health facilities

8. The .... is chosen as an indicator to assess health in human development.
(a) purchasing power (b) knowledge
(c) vaccination level (d) life expectancy

9. International Labour Organisation initiated which one of the following approaches of human development? **CBSE 2024**
(a) Income (b) Welfare
(c) Capability (d) Basic Needs

10. Countries having lower human development can be characterised by which of the following?
(a) Political Turmoil
(b) More spending on defence
(c) Social unrest
(d) All of the above

11. Which one of the following is correct about growth and development? **CBSE 2025**
(a) Both growth and development are always positive.
(b) Growth may be positive or negative, but development is always positive.
(c) Development may be positive or negative, but growth is always positive.
(d) Both growth and development may be positive or negative.

12. Which of the following countries has the highest ranking in 'Human Development Index'?
(a) Belgium (b) Iceland
(c) Norway (d) Canada

13. The Human Poverty Index measures the shortfall in human development on the basis of which parameter/s? **CBSE SQP 2024**
(a) The adult literacy rate and the life expectancy at birth.
(b) Access to resources in terms of purchasing power.
(c) The number of small children who are underweight.
(d) The number of children enrolled in the school.

14. **There are four pillars of human development. Identify the one from the given description.**

A good example is about the importance of sending girls to school. If a community does not stress the importance of sending its girl children to school, many opportunities will be lost to these young women when they grow up. Their career choices will be severely curtailed and this would affect other aspects of their lives. So each generation must ensure the availability of choices and opportunities to its future generations.

Options

(a) Equity (b) Sustainability
(c) Productivity (d) Empowerment

15. **Consider the following statements and choose the correct option.**

(i) Human Development Index was created by Amartya Sen.
(ii) Human Poverty Index is related to human development.
(iii) A value closer to 1 shows lower human development on the HDI.

Codes

(a) (i) and (ii) (b) (i), (ii) and (iii)
(c) Only (ii) (d) Only (i)

16. **Which of the following are key aspects of human development?**

(i) Health (ii) Education
(iii) Police (iv) Access to Resources

Codes

(a) (i), (ii) and (iii) (b) (ii), (iii) and (iv)
(c) (i), (ii) and (iv) (d) (i), (ii), (iii) and (iv)

17. **Read the following statements and choose the correct option.**

Statement I An uneducated child cannot make the choice to be a doctor.

Statement II His/her choice has got limited by her lack of education.

Options

(a) Only I is correct
(b) Only II is correct
(c) Both I and II are incorrect
(d) Both statements are correct, statement II explains statement I

Arrange the Following

18. **Arrange the following countries in order of their Human Development Index ranks.**

(i) Norway (ii) Sweden
(iii) Switzerland (iv) Australia

Options

(a) (iii), (i), (iv), (ii) (b) (i), (iv), (iii), (ii)
(c) (iii), (ii), (i), (iv) (d) (i), (iii), (ii), (iv)

Match the Following

19.

List I	List II
A. Health	1. Purchasing power parity
B. Education	2. Life expectancy
C. Access to resources	3. Adult literacy rate

Codes

	A	B	C		A	B	C
(a)	2	3	1	(b)	3	2	1
(c)	1	2	3	(d)	2	1	3

20.

List I	List II
A. Income Approach	1. Emphasis was on the provision of the needs only.
B. Welfare Approach	2. The areas of health, education and access to resources are the key to human development.
C. Basic Needs Approach	3. The level of income reflects the level of freedom
D. Capability Approach	4. Human beings are beneficiaries of all development activities

Codes **CBSE Diksha**

	A	B	C	D		A	B	C	D
(a)	3	4	1	2	(b)	1	2	3	4
(c)	4	3	2	1	(d)	2	1	4	3

Assertion-Reason

Directions (Q. Nos. 21-23) In the questions given below are two statements labelled as Assertion (A) and other is labelled as Reason (R). In the context of two statements, which one of the following is correct?

Codes

(a) Both A and R are true, but R is not the correct explanation of A
(b) Both A and R are true and R is the correct explanation of A
(c) Both A and R are incorrect
(d) A is correct, but R is incorrect

21. **Assertion** (A) To have sustainable human development, each generation must have the same opportunities.

Reason (R) Indiscriminate use of resources will lead to fewer opportunities. **CBSE Diksha**

22. **Assertion** (A) Good governance and people-oriented policies are required to empower people.

Reason (R) Power comes from increasing freedom and capabilities.

23. Assertion (A) Often smaller countries have done better than larger ones and relatively poorer nations have been ranked higher than richer neighbours in terms of human development.

Reason (R) Size of the territory and per capita income are not directly related to human development. Countries with higher human development are those where a lot of investment in the social sector has taken place. **CBSEE SQP 2024**

Answers

1. (b) Development which enlarges people's choices
2. (c) people
3. (b) Equality
4. (a) Equal access to opportunities
5. (d) All of the above
6. (b) Welfare Approach
7. (a) In terms of economic growth
8. (d) life expectancy
9. (d) Basic Needs
10. (d) All of these
11. (b) Growth may be positive or negative, but development is always positive.
12. (c) Norway
13. (a) The adult literacy rate and the life expectancy at birth.
14. (b) Sustainability
15. (c) Only (ii)
16. (c) (i), (ii) and (iv)
17. (d) Both statements are correct, statement II explains statement I
18. (a) (iii), (i), (iv), (ii)
19. (a)
20. (a)
21. (b) Both A and R are true and R is the correct explanation of A
22. (b) Both A and R are true and R is the correct explanation of A
23. (b) Both A and R are true and R is the correct explanation of A

Subjective Questions

Short Answer Type Questions

1. "Development is a qualitative change, which is always value positive." Support this statement. **Competency Based Que**

Ans. Development means a qualitative change which is always value positive. This means that development cannot take place unless there is an increment or addition to the existing conditions. Development occurs when positive growth takes place. The given statement can be supported by the following two arguments

(i) Countries with better economic conditions are more developed, while poor nations are less developed. Quality of life of the people of a country, the opportunities they have, freedom of living, etc are important aspects of development.

(ii) Dr Mahbub-ul-Haq described human development as development that enlarges people's choice and improves their lives. He believed that people are central to all development and the main aim of development is to create a situation and environment where people are able to live meaningful lives.

2. "Misuse of any resources will lead to fewer opportunities for future generations." Explain the statement with examples in the context of sustainable development. **CBSE 2024**

Ans. Misuse of resources can harm future generations by depleting what they need to thrive. For example, overusing water for industries or wasting energy leads to shortages. Deforestation for farming or urban expansion destroys habitats and reduces biodiversity. Unsustainable practices like excessive mining or pollution damage the environment, making it harder for future generations to meet their needs. Sustainable development emphasises using resources wisely, conserving energy, and protecting nature to ensure opportunities for everyone. By acting responsibly today, we secure a better future for generations to come.

3. Differentiate between growth and development with an example.

Ans. Difference between growth and development are as follows:

Growth	Development
Growth is quantitative and it can be measured	Development is qualitative approach.
It can be positive or negative.	Development cannot take place unless there is an increment in existing conditions. Hence, it always value positive.
For example, if the population of a city grows from one lakh to two lakh over a period of time, we can say that the city has expanded.	For example, despite increase in population, if facilities like housing, provision of basic services and other characteristics remain the same, then this growth has not been accompanied by development.

4. "Equity refers to making equal access to opportunities available to everybody." Support the statement with suitable arguments. CBSE 2024

Ans. "Equity refers to making equal access to opportunities available to everybody." This statement highlights the importance of fairness in society. Equity ensures that everyone, regardless of their background, has the resources they need to succeed. For example, providing scholarships to underprivileged students or building ramps for people with disabilities allows them to access education and public spaces equally. By addressing inequalities, equity promotes social justice and ensures that no one is left behind. This creates a fair society where everyone has an equal chance to grow and contribute.

5. Explain the concept of 'equity' and 'sustainability' as the pillars of human development. CBSE Diksha

Ans. Refer to NCERT Folder Q. no. (ii) (under the 150 words category).

6. Explain any three features of welfare approach of human development.

Or **Explain any three characteristics of 'welfare approach' of human development in the world.**

Or **Explain the main aspects of 'welfare approach' of human development.** CBSE 2024 C

Ans. The three characteristics of welfare approach are as follows

- The welfare approach of human development is an approach which looks at human beings as beneficiaries or targets of all development activities.
- According to this approach, the government is responsible for increasing levels of human development by increasing expenditure on welfare such as on education, health, housing, sanitation, etc.
- In this approach, people are passive recipients of the benefits of human development, while the government is the provider of those benefits.

7. Explain the 'basic needs approach' to human development in the World.

Or **Explain the main aspects of the 'Basic Needs Approach of human development.** CBSE 2024 C

Ans. The basic needs approach to human development was initially proposed by International Labour Organisation (ILO). In this approach, the question of human choices is ignored, and the emphasis is laid on the provision of basic needs. These basic needs are the necessities that enables a person to survive and fulfil the essential requirements. There are six basic needs identified in this approach. These are as follows

(i) **Health** Proper health is required to maintain a healthy lifestyle.

(ii) **Education** Provision of schools and colleges ensures access to education.

(iii) **Food** Nutritious food is required to fulfil daily requirements.

(iv) **Water Supply** Provision of clean drinking water to everyone.

(v) **Sanitation** Proper sanitation facility to maintain hygiene.

(vi) **Housing** Proper dwelling place with basic facilities.

8. What is Human Poverty Index? Mention the four indicators used to measure this index.

Ans. The Human Poverty Index is used by UNDP to measure the limitations in human development. It is related to the Human Development Index. This index is an indication of the poverty in a community of a country. It is a non income measure.

The HPI concentrates on the deprivation of three essential elements in human lives-life expectancy, education and a decent standard of living.

To show the limitations in human development in any region, the following four indicators are used

- Probability of not surviving till age of 40.
- The adult literacy rate.
- Number of people who do not have access to clean water.
- Number of children who are underweight.

9. Discuss the importance of human development.

Ans. The importance of human development can be understood by the following points

- It improves the quality of life of individual.
- It provides an individual with various choices.
- It ensures the minimum investment to enhance economic productivity of human beings.
- It makes people aware about their abilities.
- It enhances the conditions of physical environment.
- It provides a stable political system to a country.
- It shows the limitations of existing system.
- It works for a long and reasonable healthy human life.

10. Analyse the importance of per capita income in human development.

Ans. The importance of per capita income in human development are as follows

- Per capita income refers to the mean income of population in a given area. There is a contradiction over per capita income in using it as an indicator of human development.
- If per capita income of a country is high, it may represent the high level of development in that region.
- It significant for high quality of life. But it often generates other problems such as inequality, poverty, environmental degradation, etc.
- Population below poverty line may be very high due to these reasons and access to resources could be limited to the rich persons only.

11. "Gross National Happiness (GNH) is the measure of the country's progress." Evaluate the statement. **Competency Based Que**

Or **'Bhutan is the only country in the world to officially proclaim the Gross National Happiness as the measure of the country's is progress. State the reasons behind adopting this approach.** **CBSE Diksha**

Ans. Bhutan is unique because it uses Gross National Happiness (GNH) to measure its progress, instead of just focusing on economic growth like most other countries. This means Bhutan values people's happiness, culture and environment more than just money or material success. Before adopting new technologies or pursuing big projects, Bhutan carefully considers whether they might harm the environment, culture, or the happiness of its people.

The idea is that development shouldn't only mean getting richer but also improving the quality of life in ways that make people genuinely happy and fulfilled.

Long Answer Type Questions

1. What is human development? Analyse the four pillars of human development.

Or **What do you mean by 'human development'? Explain the four pillars of human development.**

Ans. Human Development is defined as the process of enlarging people's freedoms and opportunities and improving their well-being. This concept was developed by the economist Mahbub-ul-Haq.

Human development have four concepts such as equity, sustainability, productivity and empowerment. These concepts are based on human development and are called as pillars of human development. These four pillars are

(i) **Equity** It refers to equal access to opportunity for all. There should not be any discrimination on the basis of gender, race, income, caste, creed etc. For example, it will be interesting to note that dropouts from the schools are of which community or what are the reasons they dropped out of schools.

(ii) **Sustainability** It refers to the continuity in availability of opportunities. To achieve sustainability, equal opportunities should be given to all the generations. There should not be any misuse of natural resources and environment. All resources must be used keeping in mind the future generations.

(iii) **Productivity** It means the productivity of human labour or productivity in terms of human work. Productivity has to be improved by building capabilities of people by increasing their knowledge and providing them better facilities.

(iv) **Empowerment** It means having power that enables people to make choices they want. Increasing freedom and capabilities gives such power. There should be good governance and policies so that all the people, including the socially and economically disadvantaged groups are empowered.

2. "The size of a territory and per capita income are not directly related to human development." Support the statement with examples. **Competency Based Que**

Ans. It is true that size of the territory and per capita income are not directly related to human development as

- According to United Nations Development Programme, human development is standing on four basic pillars like equity, sustainability, productivity and empowerment. Per capita income or size of the territory is not mentioned in it.
- These pillars consider all the aspects that affect human life like health, education, access to resources of a country and other social indicators alongwith economic indicators. No country can achieve a desired goal of

human development on the basis of per capita income alone. Human development is about all round development of people in all aspects of life.

- The economic structure of a country is the most important indicator of human development. The size of a territory does not play any role in it. The advanced countries have higher level of economic prosperity, while the less developed and backward countries are at lower level of economic growth.
- The developed country's per capita income is indirectly related to economic structure. The size of a territory and per capita income are not directly related to human development but it does play some role.

3. There are many ways of looking at the problem of human development. Analyse some of them. Competency Based Que

Or **Explain the concept of 'human development'. Examine four approaches to human development.** **CBSE 2025**

Ans. The concept of human development, introduced by Dr. Mahbub-ul-Haq, focuses on enlarging people's choices and improving their lives. It emphasises health, education and access to resources, enabling individuals to lead meaningful, purposeful lives.

(i) **Welfare Approach** This approach puts human beings at a central position where he/she is the beneficiary of all the developmental activities. Here people do not participate in the process of development but they are only passive recepients. The government is responsible for providing health, education and social services.

(ii) **Income Approach** In this approach, human development is linked to income. The level of income decides the level of freedom an individual enjoys. It is believed that if a nation has higher level of income, it leads to higher level of human development.

(iii) **Minimum Needs Approach** It was proposed by the International Labour Organisation. It considers six basic needs as most important for development of human beings-health, education, food, water supply, sanitation and housing.

(iv) **Capabilities approach** This approach emphasises upon building human capabilities in areas of health, education and access to resources for their human development.

4. "People usually blame the culture or religion for low human development of a country." Do you agree? What are the reasons for low and high human development in a country. Competency Based Que

Ans. When international comparisons are made on the levels of human development of countries, people blame a particular culture or religion for low levels of human development. For example, X country has lower human development because its people follow Y religion or belong to Z community.

I agree that it is wrong to associate a particular community or religion with low level of human development as it is entirely misleading. In reality, there are some factors responsible which keep a country in the lower HDI list constantly. These factors are

- Pattern of government expenditure on the social sector.
- Political environment of the country.
- Amount of freedom people have.
- Other possible reasons for their backwardness are their political and economic instability which compel these countries to spend more on defence rather than social sectors.

On the other hand, countries with high level of human development have the following characteristics which place these countries into the high HDI list

- More investment in the social sectors.
- Free from political turmoil and instability.
- Distribution of the resources is equitable.

5. How are countries classified under different categories under the HDI?

Ans. According to the Human Development Scores earned by countries, these are classified into four categories

(i) **Countries with very High HDI** These are the countries that have a score of more than 0.800 according to the Human Development Report, 2022. This group includes 66 countries.

(ii) **Countries with High HDI** These are the countries that have a score between 0.700 upto 0.799. These countries invest a lot in social sectors like education, healthcare, etc. They are characterised by good governance and welfare of the people. These include 49 countries according to HDR, 2022.

(iii) **Countries with Moderate HDI** These countries have a score between (0.550 upto 0.699). Many of these countries are trying improve their human development score by adopting more people oriented policies and reducing social discrimination. These countries have higher social diversity and have faced political instability and social uprising in recent part. They include 44 countries as per HDR 2022.

(iv) **Countries with Low HDI** These countries have scores below 0.549. These countries face political turmoil, social instability, civil war famines, wars and high incidence of diseases. These include 32 countries as per HDR 2022.

6. Which country has the highest rank in the World in 'Human Development Index' in 2020? Explain four approaches of human development. **CBSE 2024**

Ans. In 2020, Norway ranked first in the World on the **Human Development Index (HDI)**. The HDI measures the overall development of a country, considering factors like life expectancy, education, and per capita income.

The four approaches to human development are

- **The Human-Centered Approach** Focuses on enhancing individual well-being, emphasising people's health, education and income.
- **The Equity Approach** Ensures that all individuals have equal access to opportunities, reducing disparities.
- **The Participatory Approach** Encourages active involvement of people in decision-making and development processes.
- **The Sustainability Approach** Aims for long-term development by using resources responsibly to preserve them for future generations.

7. "The ways to measure human development are constantly being redefined". Evaluate this statement keeping in mind the attainments and shortfall in human development. **Competency Based Que**

Or **"The ways to measure human development are constantly being refined." Support the statement with suitable arguments.** **CBSE 2024**

Ans. The statement "The ways to measure human development are constantly being redefined" reflects the evolving understanding of what development truly means. Initially, development was measured mainly by economic growth, with the belief that a bigger economy meant better lives. However, this approach ignored essential aspects of human well-being. For example, economic growth does not always improve education, health, or living conditions for everyone.

Experts like Dr. Mahbub-ul-Haq and Prof. Amartya Sen introduced new ways to measure development by focusing on people's well-being. This led to the creation of the Human Development Index (HDI), which measures life expectancy, education, and income. While HDI is a major improvement, it still does not capture inequalities or shortfalls like poverty, lack of healthcare, or education access.

To address these gaps, the Human Poverty Index (HPI) was developed, highlighting areas where human development is lacking, such as high child mortality or lack of clean water. These newer ways to measure development reveal both achievements and areas needing improvement. As human development is complex, researchers are continuously finding better ways to measure progress, considering factors like political freedom and inequality .

8. How is the 'Human Development Index' measured? Explain key areas of human development. **CBSE 2024**

Or **What does the 'Human Poverty Index' measure? What are the various components used to measure it?** **CBSE Diksha**

Ans. There are three indicators that is used to measure Human Development Index (HDI). They are health, education and access to resources. These areas show how well people are living in a country.

The key areas of human development are as follows

- **Health** This is measured by life expectancy at birth. A higher life expectancy means people are living longer and healthier lives, which is a key sign of development.
- **Education** This is measured by the adult literacy rate and the gross enrolment ratio. The adult literacy rate shows the percentage of adults who can read and write, while the enrolment ratio reflects how many children are attending school. Both indicators show how much access people have to knowledge.
- **Access to resources** This is measured by income, using a country's Gross National Income (GNI) per person. It shows how much money people have to meet their basic needs, like food, shelter and healthcare.

Each of these three areas is given equal weight in the HDI. The index ranks countries based on their scores, which range from 0 to 1. A score closer to 1 means a higher level of human development. Together, these key areas reflect the quality of life in a country.

Source Based Questions

1. Read the passage carefully and answer the questions that follow.

Both growth and development refer to changes over a period of time. The difference is that growth is quantitative and value neutral. It may have a positive or a negative sign. This means that the change may be either positive (showing an increase) or negative (indicating a decrease). Development means a qualitative change which is always value positive. This means that development cannot take place unless there is an increment or addition to the existing conditions. Development occurs when positive growth takes place.

The idea that the quality of life people enjoy in a country, the opportunities they have and freedoms they enjoy, are important aspects of development, is not new. These ideas were clearly spelt out for the first time in the late eighties and early nineties. The works of two South Asian economists, Mahbub-ul-Haq and Amartya Sen are important in this regard. The concept of human development was introduced by Dr Mahbub-ul-Haq. Dr Haq has described human development as development that enlarges people's choices and improves their lives. People are central to all development under this concept. These choices are not fixed but keep on changing. The basic goal of development is to create conditions where people can live meaningful lives. A meaningful life is not just a long one. It must be a life with some purpose. This means that people must be healthy, be able to develop their talents, participate in society and be free to achieve their goals.

(i) What is the most important feature of human development?

(a) Enlarging people's choices
(b) Freedom to achieve one's goals
(c) Living healthy lives
(d) All of the above

Ans. (d) All of the above

(ii) Which of the following will reduce the human development of a region?

(a) Social discrimination
(b) Education
(c) Sustainable development
(d) High purchasing power

Ans. (a) Social discrimination

(iii) The concept of human development keeps which of the following at the centre of development?

(a) Nature (b) Resources
(c) Governments (d) People

Ans. (d) People

2. Read the passage carefully and answer the questions that follow.

The idea of human development is supported by the concepts of equity, sustainability, productivity and empowerment. Equity refers to making equal access to opportunities available to everybody. The opportunities available to people must be equal irrespective of their gender, race, income and in the Indian case, caste. Yet this is very often not the case and happens in almost every society. In India, a large number of women and persons belonging to socially and economically backward groups drop out of school.

Sustainability means continuity in the availability of opportunities. To have sustainable human development, each generation must have the same opportunities. All environmental, financial and human resources must be used keeping in mind the future. Misuse of any of these resources will lead to fewer opportunities for future generations.

Productivity means human labour productivity or productivity in terms of human work. Such productivity must be constantly enriched by building capabilities in people. Ultimately, it is people who are the real wealth of nations.

Empowerment means to have the power to make choices. Such power comes from increasing freedom and capability. Good governance and people-oriented policies are required to empower people. The empowerment of socially and economically disadvantaged groups is of special importance.

(i) What are the factors that can lead to empowerment of people?

Ans. Good governance and people oriented policies are required factors that can lead to empowerment of people.

(ii) 'Human development is supported by four pillars'. Comment.

Ans. Human development is supported by the concepts of equity, sustainability, productivity and empowerment. These acts as a pillar for the development.

(iii) Mention about the core concept of sustainable development.

Ans. Sustainable development focuses on sustainable human development, this means each generation must have the same opportunities.

3. Read the passage carefully and answer the questions that follow.

The Human Development Index (HDI) ranks the countries based on their performance in the key areas of health, education and access to resources. These rankings are based on a score between 0 to 1 that a country earns from its record in the key areas of human development. The more a score is closer to 1 the more is the human development.

The indicator chosen to assess health is the life expectancy at birth. A higher life expectancy means that people have a greater chance of living longer and healthier lives. The adult literacy rate and the gross enrolment ratio represent access to knowledge. Access to resources is measured in terms of purchasing power (in U S dollars). Each of these dimensions is given a weightage of one/third. The Human Development Index is a sum total of the weights assigned to all these dimensions.

The Human Development Index measures attainments in human development. It reflects what has been achieved in the key areas of human development. Yet it is not the most reliable measure. This is because it does not say anything about the distribution. The Human Poverty Index is related to the Human Development Index. This index measures the shortfall in human development. The ways to measure human development are constantly being refined and newer ways of capturing different elements of human development are being researched. Researchers have found links between the level of corruption or political freedom in a particular region.

(i) How one can measure the access to resource in Human Development Index?

Ans. In the Human Development Index, the access to resources is measured in terms of purchasing power.

(ii) Which new indicators can be used to measure the level of human development in a region?

Ans. New indicators to measure the level of human development in a region can be

- political freedom
- level of corruption

(iii) Mention the characteristics of countries with medium level of human development.

Ans. Countries with medium level of human development have following characteristics

- These countries have higher social diversity than countries with higher human development score.
- Most of these countries have faced political instability and social uprising in recent past.

4. Study the table given below and answer the questions that follow.

Level of Human Development	Score in Development Index	Number of Countries
Very High	above 0.800	66
High	between 0.700 up to 0.799	49
Medium	between 0.550 up to 0.699	44
Low	below 0.549	32

Source : Human Development Report, 2021-22

(i) Identify the human development score for the countries classified as having Medium Human Development?

Ans. Countries classified as having Medium Human Development have a Human Development Index (HDI) score between 0.550 and 0.699. This score reflects moderate achievements in education, health, and income levels.

(ii) What can you infer about the well-being of people living in countries with a high level of human development?

Ans. People in countries with a high level of human development generally experience better well-being. These countries prioritise education and healthcare, ensure equitable resource distribution, and have stable governance, leading to improved living standards and opportunities.

(iii) Give reasons for low level of human development in 32 countries.

Ans. The 32 countries with low levels of human development face challenges due to

- **Political Instability** Frequent political turmoil and civil wars disrupt progress.
- **Social Instability** High social discrimination and inequality prevail.
- **Health Crises** High incidence of diseases and famine affects well-being.
- **Misallocation of Resources** More spending on defense rather than education and healthcare.
- **Limited Freedom and Inequity** Unequal resource distribution and restricted freedoms hinder growth.

SELF ASSESSMENT TEST

Objective Type Questions

1. According to the eminent economist, Prof Amartya Sen, main objective of development is
   (a) increase freedom (b) decrease freedom
   (c) increase economic growth (d) Both (a) and (b)
2. International Labour Organisation is associated with which of the following approach to human developement?
   (a) Basic Needs Approach (b) Capability Approach
   (c) Welfare Approach (d) Income Approach
3. Which of the following statements describe 'growth'?
   (a) Provision of basic facilities.
   (b) More residential areas for the people
   (c) Population increasing from ten lakhs to fifteen lakhs.
   (d) Availability of training institutes
4. Which of the following factors determine human development of a country?
   (a) Government expenditure on social sector (b) Political environment of a country
   (c) Freedom available to people (d) All of these
5. Which of the following organisations proposed the basic need approach?
   (a) WHO (b) IMF
   (c) UNDP (d) ILO
6. Consider the following statements regarding 'four pillars of human development' and choose the correct option.
   (a) Among the four concepts, equity is the most important.
   (b) Among the four concepts, productivity is least important.
   (c) All the four concepts are of equal importance.
   (d) All the four concepts may not be present always.

Short Answer Type Questions

7. How people centric policies and good governance are deriving units of human development?
8. Explain the reasons of low Human Development Index.
9. Explain the different approaches of human development.
10. 'The opportunities available to people must be equal irrespective of any criteria'. Validate the statement with example.
11. How can we maximise our human development score? Suggest some ways.

Long Answer Type Questions

12. Explain the role of education and healthcare in shaping human development. How do these factors influence a country's HDI ranking?
13. How many groups can be classified on the basis of the human development scores earned? Explain.
14. Substantiate that the existing myths about human development are misleading.

UNIT 3

4

CHAPTER

Human activities that generate income are known as economic activities. These activities can be grouped as **primary**, **secondary**[1], **tertiary**[2] and **quaternary**[3].

▼ **YOUR STUDY GOALS**

4.1 Types of Primary Activities
4.2 Agriculture
4.3 Types of Farming
4.4 Mining

▼ **YOUR PRACTICE GOAL**

- Objective Type Questions (28 Qs ; MCQs, Statements, Matching, A-R)
- Subjective Questions (15 SAs, 12 LAs)
- Source Based Questions (6 Qs)
- Map Based Questions (2 Qs)

Primary Activities

- Primary activities are those, that are directly dependent on the environment. Some examples of primary activities are hunting, gathering, fishing, forestry, agriculture and mining[4], and quarrying[5]. People involved in primary activities are known as **red-collar workers**.

4.1 Types of Primary Activities

Hunting and Gathering

- These are some of the earliest economic activities when humans depended on the environment for their sustenance.
- People located in extreme conditions of cold and hot climates were dependent on **hunting**.
- **Gathering** is practised in regions with harsh climatic conditions. It includes a collection of both plants and animals for satisfying human needs like food, shelter and clothing.
- Gathering is practised in high-latitude zones like Northern Canada, Eurasia and Southern Chile. It is also practised in low-latitude zones like the Amazon Basin, Tropical Africa and the Northern fringe of Australia and interior parts of South-East Asia.

1 Secondary activity Secondary economic activities transform raw materials into finished products, for example, manufacturing
2 Tertiary activity Tertiary economic activities provide services to consumers and businesses, for example, transportation services, lawyers, etc.
3 Quaternary activity Quaternary economic activities focus on creating, processing, and sharing information and knowledge, for example, research and development
4. Mining It is the process of digging or excavation of the earth's surface in search of minerals
5. Quarrying It involves the extraction of stones, rocks, sand, mud, etc.

- These activities require a small amount of capital investment and operates at very low cost and little or no surplus is produced.
- In modern times, gathering is market-oriented and has become commercial. It has a low chance of becoming a global activity because synthetic products have replaced its products with better quality and lower priced goods.

Pastoralism

- Pastoralism is a form of animal husbandry where domesticated animals known as "livestock" are released onto large pastures for grazing.
- People living in different climatic conditions choose the animals found in their regions.
- Based on geographical factors and technological development, animal rearing is practised at subsistence or the commercial level.

Nomadic Herding

- It is also known as **pastoral nomadism**. It is a primitive subsistence activity.

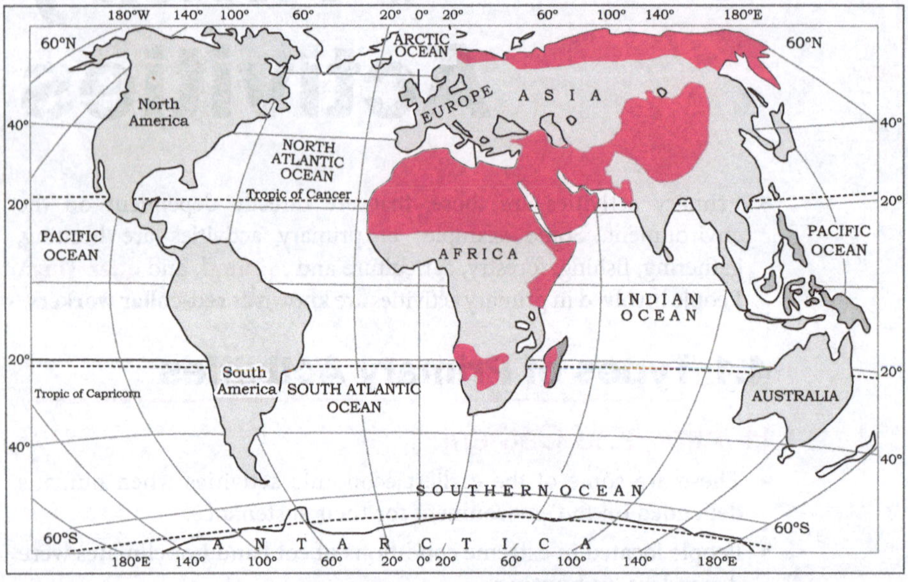

▲ *Areas of Nomadic Herding*

- In this type of activity, herders are dependent on animals for food, clothing, shelter, tools and transport.
- Herders move from one place to another along with their livestock in search of quality pastures and water. Movement in search of pastures is undertaken either horizontally or vertically.
- The process of migration from plain areas to pastures on mountains during summers and again from mountain pastures to plain areas during winters is known as **transhumance**. For example, in Himalayan regions tribes like **Gujjars, Bakarwals, Gaddis** and **Bhotiyas.**
- In tropical Africa, cattle are the most important livestock, while in Sahara and Asiatic deserts, sheep, goats and camel are reared. In the mountainous areas of Tibet and Andes, yak and llamas and in the Arctic and sub Arctic areas, reindeer are the most important animals.
- Each nomadic community occupies a well-defined territory.
- Pastoral nomadism is associated with three important regions
  - (i) The core region extends from the **Atlantic shores** of North Africa towards the **Arabian Peninsula, Mongolia** and **Central China.**
  - (ii) The second region extends over the tundra region of Eurasia.
  - (iii) The third region is around small areas in **South-West Africa** and on the island of Madagascar.
- The number of pastoral nomads is decreasing due to the following reasons
  - Due to the imposition of political boundaries.
  - Due to new settlement plans by different countries.

Commercial Livestock Rearing

- It is more organised and capital intensive. It is mainly associated with Western cultures and is practised on permanent **ranches**[6].
- Ranches cover large areas and are divided into several parcels, which are fenced to regulate grazing. When the grass of one parcel is grazed, animals are moved to another parcel.
- The main emphasis is on breeding, genetic improvement, disease control and health care of the animals.
- The number of animals in the pasture is kept according to the carrying capacity of the pastures.
- Only one type of animal is reared in commercial livestock rearing. Important animals include sheep, cattle, goats and horses.
- Products like meat, wool, hides and skin are processed and packed scientifically and exported to the global market.
- Major countries where commercial livestock rearing is practised are **New Zealand, Australia, Argentina, Uruguay** and the USA.

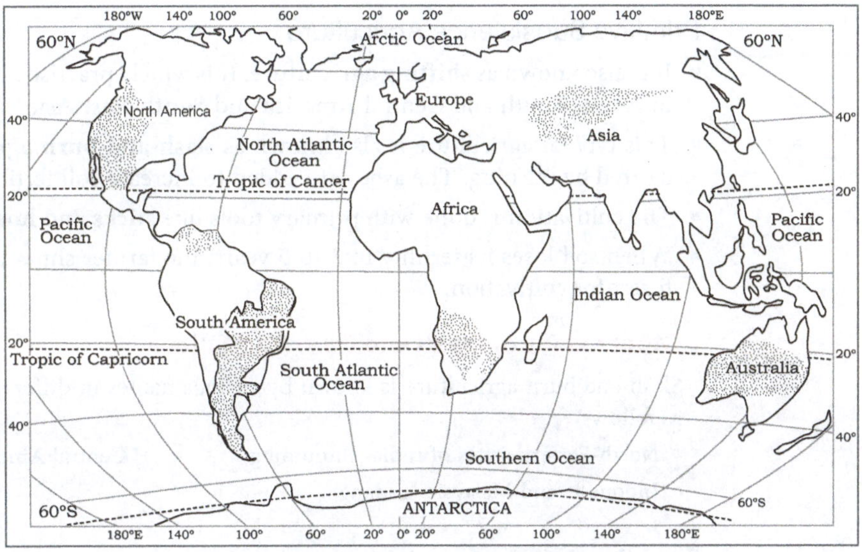

▲ *Commercial Livestock Rearing*

Quick Test 1

1. What term is used for the people working in primary activities?
2. Name an area in the world where the gathering is still practised.
3. In which areas nomadic herding is practised?
4. What type of primary activity is practised in permanent ranches?

4.2 Agriculture

- Agriculture is practised under multiple combinations of physical and socio-economic conditions.
- Types of agricultural systems based on methods of farming, different types of crops are grown and livestock raised are shown in the given chart.

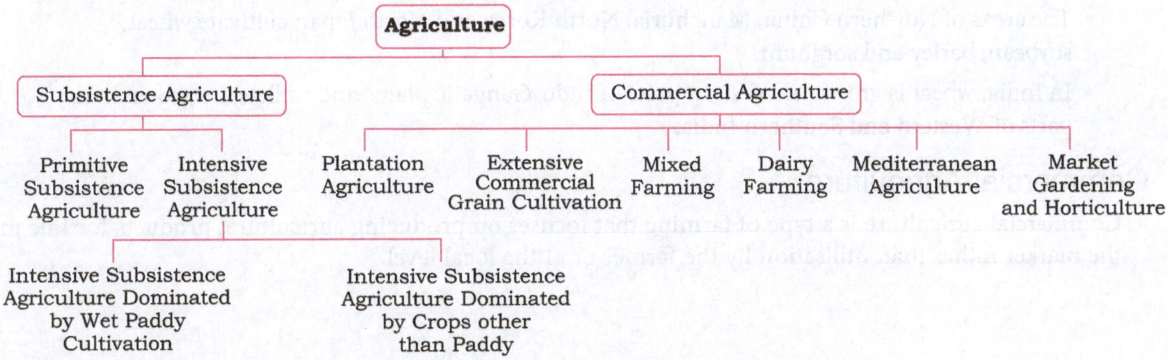

6 **Ranches** It is a farm for breeding and raising of cattle, sheep, or horses on rangeland.

Subsistence Agriculture

- In this type of farming, all or nearly all the production of the farm is consumed by the producers or the locality.
- It is divided into two sub-categories; Primitive subsistence agriculture and Intensive subsistence agriculture.

Primitive Subsistence Agriculture

- It is also known as **shifting agriculture**. It is widely practised by tribes living in **tropical regions**, mainly in Africa, South and Central America and **South-East** Asia.
- This type of agriculture is also known as **slash-and-burn agriculture** because a small patch of land is cleared by burning. The ashes are added to increase soil fertility.
- The cultivation is done with primary tools like **sticks** and **hoes**.
- When soil loses its fertility in 3 to 5 years, the farmer shifts to other parts and clears another patch of forest for cultivation.

Other names of Slash and Burn Agriculture

Slash and burn agriculture is known by various names in different regions. Some of the examples are as follows

- North-Eastern states of India- Jhumming
- Central America and Mexico- Milpa
- Indonesia and Malaysia- Ladang

Intensive Subsistence Agriculture

- This type of agriculture is mainly practised in **densely populated** regions. It can be sub-divided into two groups
  (i) Intensive subsistence agriculture dominated by wet paddy cultivation
  - It is characterised by the dominance of **rice crops**.
  - Due to the high density of the population, land holdings are very small.
  - Family works as labour and limited machinery is used.
  - The fertility of soil is maintained by using manure and chemical fertilisers. This leads to intensive use of land holdings.
  - The yield per unit area is high but per labour productivity is low.

  (ii) Intensive subsistence agriculture dominated by crops other than paddy
  - Many parts of **monsoon Asia** are not well suited to grow rice due to climatic, relief, soil and other geographical factors.
  - The areas of Northern China, Manchuria, North Korea and North Japan cultivate wheat, soybean, barley and sorghum.
  - In India, wheat is grown in Western parts of Indo-Gangetic plains and millets are grown in dry parts of Western and Southern India.

Commercial Agriculture

- Commercial agriculture is a type of farming that focuses on producing agricultural products for sale in the market rather than utilisation by the farmer or at the local level.

- Different types of commercial agriculture are as follows

Plantation Agriculture

- This type of agriculture was introduced by the Europeans in their colonies located in tropical regions.
- Tea, coffee, cocoa, rubber, cotton, oil palm, sugarcane, etc are some examples of plantation crops.

▲ *Tea Plantation*

- The cocoa and coffee plantations in West Africa were established by France.
- Tea gardens in India and Sri Lanka were established by the Britishers.
- Rubber plantations in Malaysia and sugarcane and banana plantations in the West Indies were established by the Britishers.
- Plantation agriculture requires large capital investment and a large estate of land holding.
- It requires single-crop specialisation and managerial and technical support.
- It also requires a good transportation system to link the estates to the factories and markets for the export of products.

Extensive Commercial Grain Cultivation

- It is practised in the interior parts of semi-arid lands of the mid-latitudes. The main crop is wheat and other major crops are corn, barley, oats and rye.
- The landholdings are very large and most of the operations are done using machines. There is a low yield per acre but a high yield per person.
- Eurasian steppes, the Canadian and American Prairies, the Pampas of Argentina, the Velds of South Africa, the Australian Downs and the Canterbury plains of New Zealand are the major regions in which commercial grain farming is practised.

Mixed Farming

- This type of agriculture is mainly practised in highly developed parts of the world. For example, North-Western Europe, Eastern North America, parts of Eurasia and the temperate latitudes of Southern continents.
- Mixed farming requires high capital expenditure on farm machinery and building. It requires extensive use of chemical fertilisers and green manures.
- The land holdings are moderate in size. There is equal importance given to crop cultivation and animal husbandry.
- The major crops grown in mixed farming are wheat, barley, oats, rye, maize, fodder and root crops. The animals like cattle, sheep, pigs and poultry are additional sources of income.

▲ *A Dairy Farm in Austria*

- The soil fertility is maintained through the practice of **crop rotation**[7] and **intercropping**[8].

Dairy Farming

- It is the most advanced and efficient type of rearing of milch animals. It is practised mainly near urban and industrial centres which provide neighbourhood markets for fresh milk and dairy products.
- It requires high capital investment in animal sheds, storage facilities, fodder, feeding and milking machines.

---

7 **Crop rotation** It is the practice of growing different types of crops in the same area across seasons to improve soil health, optimise nutrients and control pests and diseases.

8 **Intercropping** It is the practice of growing two or more crops together in the same field at the same time to maximise land use and increase overall productivity.

- It specifically focuses on cattle breeding, health care and veterinary services. It is highly labour-intensive as labour is required in feeding and milking of cattle.
- The development of transportation, refrigeration, pasteurisation and other preservation processes have increased the storage capacity of various dairy products.
- Commercial dairy farming is practised in three main regions. There are North-Western Europe (largest), Canada, and South-Eastern Australia, New Zealand and Tasmania belt.

Mediterranean Agriculture

- It is highly specialised commercial agriculture.
- It is practised in the countries on both sides of the Mediterranean Sea in Europe.
- It is also practised in North Africa from Tunisia to the Atlantic coast, Southern California, Central Chile, the South-Western part of South Africa and South-Western parts of Australia.
- Mediterranean agriculture benefits from growing valuable crops such as fruits and vegetables during winters, which are in great demand in European and North American markets. This region is an important supplier of citrus fruits.

Viticulture

- Viticulture or **grape cultivation** is a speciality of the Mediterranean region. This region also produces olives and figs.
- The best quality of wine with different flavours is made from high-quality grapes. The lower-quality of grapes are dried to make raisins and currants.

Market Gardening and Horticulture

- It specialises in the cultivation of high-value crops such as vegetables, fruits and flowers, for the urban markets.
- This type of cultivation is done on small farms, that are close to good transportation systems and urban centres.
- It is both labour and capital-intensive. It requires expenditure on HYV seeds, irrigation, fertilisers, insecticides, greenhouses and artificial heating in colder regions.
- Market gardening and horticulture are well developed in densely populated industrial districts of North-West Europe, the North-Eastern United States of America and the Mediterranean regions.
- The Netherlands specialises in growing flowers and horticultural crops, especially tulips.
- A modern development in the industrial regions of Western Europe and North America is called **factory farming.**
- In factory farming livestock, particularly poultry and cattle rearing is done in stalls and pens, fed on manufactured feedstuff and carefully supervised against diseases. This requires heavy capital investment in terms of building, machinery for various operations, veterinary services and heating and lighting.

Truck Farming

- Farming in the regions where farmers specialise in vegetables only is known as truck farming.
- The distance of truck farms from the market is controlled by the distance that a truck can cover overnight.

4.3 Types of Farming

- The farming organisation is affected by how farmers own their farms and various policies of the government that help to run these farms.
- The two types of farming based on farming organisations are as follows

Co-operative Farming

- Co-operative[9] societies help farmers to collect all important inputs of farming, sell the products at the most favourable terms and help in the processing of quality products at cheaper rates.
- A group of farmers form a cooperative society by pooling their resources for more efficient and profitable farming.
- The individual farmer's ownership remains with him and farming is cooperative among the group.
- The cooperative movement originated hundreds of years ago. It has been successful in many Western European Countries like Denmark, Netherlands, Belgium, Sweden, Italy, etc.

Collective Farming

- This type of farming is based on social ownership of the means of production and collective labour.
- Collective farming or the model of **Kolkhoz** was introduced in the erstwhile Soviet Union to boost agricultural production for self-sufficiency.

4.4 Mining

- The use of minerals can be observed throughout history in terms of the Copper Age, Bronze Age and Iron Age. The development of mining began with the industrial revolution.
- The developed countries are reducing mining activities due to high labour costs. On the other hand, several countries in Africa and a few of South America and Asia have over 50% of the earnings from the minerals alone.

Factors Affecting Mining Activity

(i) Physical factors which include the size, grade and mode of occurrence of the deposits.

(ii) Economic factors such as the demand for the mineral, technology available and used, capital to develop infrastructure and labour and transport costs.

Methods of Mining

- The methods of mining depend on the mode of occurrence of the mineral and the nature of the ore.
- The two types of mining are given below

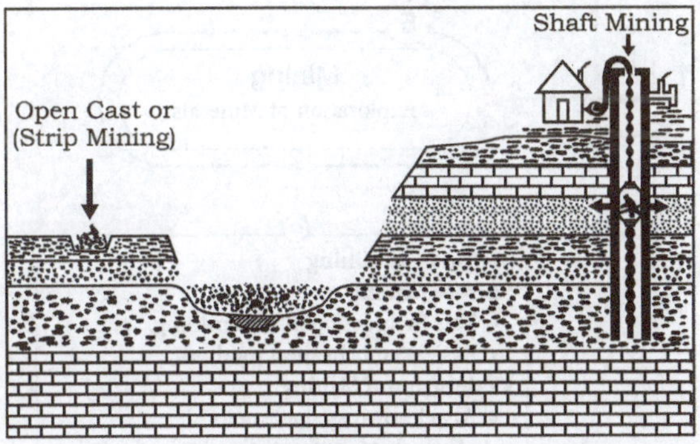

▲ *Methods of Mining*

- **Surface mining** (open-cast mining) It is the easiest and cheapest way of mining minerals that are found close to the surface. The cost of safety precautions and equipment is relatively low in this method.
- **Underground mining method** (shaft method) This method is used when ore lies deep below the surface. In this method, a vertical shaft is sent below the surface to reach the minerals. It requires specially designed lifts, drills, haulage vehicles, and ventilation systems for the safety and efficient movement of people and materials. This method is risky as there might be poisonous gases, fires, floods and caving, leading to fatal accidents.

Quick Test 2

1. Name two types of subsistence agriculture.
2. In which country tulips are grown?
3. On which model collective farming is based?
4. Name two physical factors determining the profitability of mining.

9 Co-operative A farm run by joint activity of two or more farmers.

Mind Map

PRIMARY ACTIVITIES

1 Hunting and Gathering
- Primitive societies sustained on these activities.
- Practised in regions with harsh climate
- Yield per person is very low.
- Practised in Canada, Southern Chile, Eurasia Amazon Basin.

2 Pastoralism
- Includes domestication of animals.
- Practised at domestic/subsistence and commercial level.

Nomadic Herding
- Includes primitive society which performed subsistence activities.
- Practised in shores of North Africa, Central China, Tundra regions.

Commercial Livestock Rearing
- Organised and capital intensive.
- Focus on breeding, genetic improvement, diseases control.
- Practised in-New Zealand, Australia and Argentina.

3 Agriculture
- Practised under multiple physical and socio-economic conditions.
- Different types of crops are grown and livestock raised based on methods of farming.

Subsistence Agriculture
- Practised by tribes
- Includes slash and burn, shifting cultivation

Grouped into two Categories

(I) Primitive subsistence agriculture

(ii) Intensive subsistence agriculture (practised in densely populated areas)

4 Types of Agricultural Systems

Plantation Agriculture
- It is characterised by large estates, large capital, investment, managerial and technical support, scientific methods of cultivation, single crop specialisation, cheap labour and a good system of transportation.
- Crops grown are (tea, coffee, cocoa, rubbers, oil palm)

Extensive Commercial Grain Farming
- Practised in interior parts of semi-arid lands of mid-latitudes.
- Crops grown are wheat, barley, oats, rye.

Mediterranean Agriculture
- Practised in Mediterranean countries
- Viticulture (grape cultivation)

Market Gardening and Horticulture
- Cultivation of high value crops like vegetables, fruits, flowers

Collective Farming
- Multiple farmers work together on their land as a joint enterprises.

Dairy Farming
- Advanced and highly capital intensive.
- Focus on cattle breeding, health care, vetereniary services.

Mixed Farming
- Found in highly developed parts of the world.
- Crops grown are maize, rye, wheat, fodder.

Co-operative Farming
- Farmers work together to reserve resources and share benefits of doing business together.
- Practised in Denmark, Netherland, Beligium

5 Mining
Exploration of Minerals

Factors affecting Mining
- **Physical Factors** Size, grade and mode of occurence of deposits.
- **Economic Factors** Demand of mineral, technology, capital, transport cost.

Methods of Mining

Surface Mining
- This includes open-cost mining.
- Easiest and cheapest method.

Underground Mining
- Also known as shaft method.
- Minerals are extracted and transported to the surface by sunking vertical shaft underground.

NCERT Folder

Choose the right answer from the four alternatives given below

(i) **Which one of the following is not a plantation crop?**

(a) Coffee (b) Sugarcane
(c) Wheat (d) Rubber

Ans. (c) Wheat

(ii) **In which one of the following countries, co-operative farming was the most successful experiment?**

(a) Russia (b) Denmark
(c) India (d) The Netherlands

Ans. (b) Denmark

(iii) **Growing of flowers is called**

(a) truck farming (b) factory farming
(c) mixed farming (d) floriculture

Ans. (d) floriculture

(iv) **Which one of the following types of cultivation was developed by European colonists?**

(a) Kolkhoz (b) Viticulture
(c) Mixed farming (d) Plantation

Ans. (d) Plantation

(v) **In which of the following regions is extensive commercial grain cultivation not practised?**

(a) American Canadian Prairies
(b) European Steppes
(c) Pampas of Argentina
(d) Amazon Basin

Ans. (d) Amazon Basin

(vi) **In which of the following types of agriculture is the farming of citrus fruit very important?**

(a) Market gardening (b) Plantation agriculture
(c) Mediterranean agriculture (d) Co-operative farming

Ans. (c) Mediterranean agriculture

(vii) **Which one type of agriculture amongst the following is also called 'slash and burn agriculture'?**

(a) Extensive subsistence agriculture
(b) Primitive subsistence agriculture
(c) Extensive commercial grain cultivation
(d) Mixed farming

Ans. (b) Primitive subsistence agriculture

(viii) **Which one of the following does not follow monoculture?**

(a) Dairy farming (b) Mixed farming
(c) Plantation agriculture (d) Commercial grain farming

Ans. (b) Mixed farming

Answer the following questions in about 30 words

(i) **Future of shifting cultivation is bleak. Discuss.**

Ans. The future of shifting cultivation is bleak because farmers have to leave their farming areas every three to five years when the soil loses its fertility. Farmers have to shift to other lands and clear forested areas which decrease the land under forest.

(ii) **Market gardening is practised near urban areas. Why?**

Ans. Market gardening is practised near urban areas because:

- Most of the urban centres have good transportation links with the farming areas.
- Urban areas have more demand and consumption of high value crops such as fruits, vegetables and flowers.
- High income group consumer are located in urban areas who are ready to pay good prices for these products.

(iii) **Large scale dairy farming is the result of the development of transportation and refrigeration.**

Ans. A number of goods and utilities are required in dairy farming in which transportation and refrigeration are most important. Dairy products are perishable goods so they need quick access to market. Thus, the duration of storage of various dairy products have increased because of the development of transportation, refrigeration, pasteurisation and other preservation processes.

Answer the following questions in not more than 150 words

(i) **Differentiate between nomadic herding and commercial livestock rearing.**

Ans. Difference between nomadic herding and commercial livestock rearing are as follows

Nomadic Herding	Commercial Livestock Rearing
Nomadic herding is practised mainly in primitive societies of Sahara, East Africa, South-West and Central Asia, Tundra in Eurasia, South-West Africa and Western part of Madagascar.	Commercial livestock rearing is practised in developed societies of North America, Central America, South Africa, Australia and New Zealand.
Nomadic herders have to move from one place to another in search of pastures, fodder for their animals.	Permanent pastures and grazing lands are available for animals.

Nomadic Herding	Commercial Livestock Rearing
Management of livestock is carried out in a natural way.	Management of livestock is done scientifically.
Animals are reared for the subsistence of herders.	Animals are reared for selling their products in the markets.
Animals are selected by considering climate and usefulness.	Animals are selected considering market demand.

(ii) **Discuss the important characteristics of plantation agriculture. Name a few important plantation crop from different countries.**

or **Describe any five characteristics of plantation agriculture in the world.**

or **Analyse the main features of plantation agriculture in the world.** CBSE 2024

Ans. Characteristics of Plantation Agriculture

- Plantation agriculture was introduced by the Europeans in their colonies situated in tropics.
- Cash crops are grown under plantation agriculture. It means that these crops are cultivated to sell in the market for profit. These include crops like coffee, sugarcane and rubber.
- Estates or plantations are large and the capital invested in them is also huge.
- Work in these plantations is done by specialised labour and there is application of machinery and fertilisers to get high yields and a large output.
- Nearly all the production in plantation agriculture is exported to the international market. Thus, it is characterised by packaging and processing facilities.
- Managerial and technical support is provided and cultivation is done by scientific methods.
- Generally, there is single crop specialisation i.e. only one crop is cultivated at a time.
- Cheap labour and good transportation system which links the estates to the factories and markets for the export of products are essential for such agriculture.

Important Plantation Crops

The Europeans introduced different crops in different countries

- **In West African Countries** Cocoa and coffee were introduced by the French.
- **In India and Sri Lanka** Tea was introduced by the British.
- **In Malaysia** Rubber was introduced by the British.
- **In West Indies** Sugarcane and banana were introduced by the British.
- **In Philippines and Indonesia** Coconut and sugarcane were introduced by Spanish and Americans, while in Indonesia, they were introduced by the Dutch.

Exam Pattern Questions

Objective Type Questions

Multiple Choice Questions (MCQs)

1. They move from one place to another along with their livestock, depending on the amount and quality of pastures and water.
The above-mentioned line is an important characteristic of which of the following activities? CBSE Diksha

(a) Subsistence agriculture (b) Nomadic herding
(c) Plantation agriculture (d) Collective farming

2. In the Arctic and Sub-Arctic areas, which of the following animal is reared by the Nomads?

(a) Yak (b) Reindeer
(c) Llamas (d) Horde

3. Which one of the following features is correct regarding nomadic herding ? CBSE 2023

(a) Nomadism is a modern commercial activity .
(b) It is practiced on permanent pastures.
(c) A wide variety of cattle are reared in different regions.
(d) Nomadism is associated with modern technology.

4. Seasonal migration of herders from plains to mountains and vice-versa is known as

(a) Nomadic herding
(b) Pastoral grazing
(c) Transhumance
(d) Livestock rearing

5. Which of the following is the chief characteristic of commercial livestock rearing? CBSE Diksha

(a) Organised and capital intensive
(b) Practised on permanent ranches
(c) Only one type of animal is reared
(d) All of the above

6. Intensive subsistence agriculture is characterised by which of the following factors? CBSE Diksha

(a) Landholdings are very small due to the high density of the population
(b) The yield per unit area is high but per labour productivity is low
(c) Single crop specialisation
(d) Only (a) and (b) are correct

7. Which of the following is not a feature of mixed agriculture?

(a) Mixed farms are big in size.
(b) Fodder crops are an important component of mixed farming.
(c) Equal emphasis is laid on crop cultivation and animal husbandry.
(d) Crop rotation and inter-cropping play an important role in maintaining soil fertility.

8. Which of the following colonial super power had monopoly over sugarcane plantation in Indonesia?

(a) British (b) French
(c) Dutch (d) Americans

9. Which of the following crops are mainly grown in 'Mediterranean agriculture'?

(a) Grape, figs, olives
(b) Wheat, barley, ragi
(c) Jowar, bajra, maize
(d) Rubber, cotton, sugarcane

10. In which of the following countries is Milpa known as primitive subsistence agriculture?

(a) Mexico (b) Malaysia
(c) India (d) Indonesia

11. Viticulture is speciality of which of the following type of agriculture?

(a) Dairy farming
(b) Mediterranean agriculture
(c) Extensive commercial grain agriculture
(d) Intensive subsistence agriculture

12. Highly specialised agriculture in the Mediterranean Region for cultivation of grapes is called ....

(a) Pisiculture
(b) Viticulture
(c) Factory farming
(d) Horticulture

13. Which one of the following is an important region for subsistence gathering ?

(a) South Africa (b) Amazon Basin
(c) Indonesia (d) Mexico

14. Which of the following is an economic factor determining the profitability of mining activities?

(a) Technology available for use of mineral
(b) Size of deposit
(c) Grade of deposit
(d) Occurrence of deposit

15. Why are the developed economies retreating from mining, processing and refining stages of production?

(a) Low labour cost
(b) High labour cost
(c) More opportunities of employment
(d) Lack of labour force

16. Which is not a characteristic of shaft method of mining?

(a) Cheapest way of mining
(b) Vertical shafts have to be sunk
(c) Specially designed lifts drills used
(d) Gases, fires and floods lend to fatal accidents

17. Identify the type of agriculture predominantly practiced in the Australian Downs. CBSE 2025

(a) Mixed farming
(b) Plantation agriculture
(c) Co-operative farming
(d) Extensive commercial grain cultivation

18. Consider the following characteristics of the type of agriculture and identify it from the options given below.

Best quality wines in the world with distinctive flavours are produced from high quality grapes in various countries of this region. The inferior grapes are dried into raisins and currants. This region also produces olives and figs.

Options

(a) Cooperative farming (b) Plantation farming
(c) Mediterranean farming (d) Extensive grain farming

19. Transhumance is practised by which of the following tribes?

(i) Gujjars (ii) Bakkerwals
(iii) Bhotiyas (iv) Pygmies

Codes

(a) (i) and (ii) (b) (ii), (iii) and (iv)
(c) (i), (ii) and (iii) (d) (i) and (iii)

20. Which of the following areas are famous for the practise of nomadic herding?

(i) Atlantic shores in North Africa
(ii) Central China
(iii) Mongolia

Codes

(a) (i) and (ii) (b) (ii) and (iii)
(c) (i), (ii) and (iii) (d) (i) and (iii)

21. Which of the following is true regarding mixed farming?

(i) Farms are huge in size.
(ii) Fodder crops are important crops.
(iii) Crop rotation and inter cropping maintain the fertility of soil.

Codes

(a) (i) and (ii) (b) (ii) and (iii)
(c) (i), (ii) and (iii) (d) (i) and (iii)

22. Consider and evaluate the following statements and choose the correct option from the given options for the same. **CBSE Diksha**

I. Products of gathering cannot compete in the world market.
II. Synthetic products are often of better quality and at lower prices.

Options

(a) Only statement II is correct
(b) Both statements I and II are correct and statement II is the true cause behind statement I
(c) Both statements are incorrect
(d) Only statement I is true

23. Consider the following statements and choose the correct option for the same.

I. Grape cultivation is the specialty of the Mediterranean agriculture.
II. Wines are produced from high quality grapes and the inferior grapes are dried into raisins and Currants.

Codes

(a) Only I is correct (b) Both I and II are correct
(c) Only II is correct (d) Both are incorrect

Match the Following

24.

List I (Shifting Cultivation)	List II (Countries)
A. Jhumming	1. North-East India
B. Milpas	2. Indonesia
C. Ladang	3. Central America

Codes

	A	B	C		A	B	C
(a)	1	2	3	(b)	3	2	1
(c)	2	1	3	(d)	1	3	2

25.

List-I (Areas of Nomadic Herding)	List-II (Animals)
A. Sahara Desert	1. Llamas
B. Andes mountain	2. Reindeer
C. Arctic	3. Camel
D. Tropical Africa	4. Cattle

Codes

	A	B	C	D		A	B	C	D
(a)	3	2	1	4	(b)	3	1	2	4
(c)	4	1	2	3	(d)	4	2	1	3

26.

List-I (Type of Activity)	List-II (Features)
A. Subsistence Agriculture	1. Introduced in colonies
B. Plantation Agriculture	2. Supplies citrus fruits
C. Dairy Farming	3. Rearing of Milch animals
D. Mediterranean Agriculture	4. Producers are consumers

Codes

	A	B	C	D		A	B	C	D
(a)	4	1	2	3	(b)	1	2	3	4
(c)	1	3	2	4	(d)	4	1	3	2

Assertion-Reason

Directions (Q. Nos. 27-28) In the questions given below are two statements labelled as Assertion (A) and other is labelled as Reason (R). In the context of two statements, which one of the following is correct?

Codes

(a) Both A and R are true, but R is not the correct explanation of A
(b) Both A and R are true and R is the correct explanation of A
(c) Both A and R are incorrect
(d) A is correct, but R is incorrect

27. **Assertion** (A) Nomadic herding is practised over vast horizontal as well as vertical distances.

Reason (R) Nomads migrate from plains to high altitude pastures during winter season and from high altitude pastures to plains during summer season.

28. **Assertion** (A) In truck farming, farmers only specialises in vegetable cultivation.

Reason (R) There is emphasis on social ownership of means of production in truck farming.

Answers

1. (b) Nomadic herding
2. (b) Reindeer
3. (c) A wide variety of cattle are reared in different regions.
4. (c) Transhumance
5. (d) All of the above
6. (d) Only (a) and (b) are correct
7. (a) Mixed farms are big in size.
8. (c) Dutch
9. (a) Grape, figs, olives
10. (a) Mexico
11. (b) Mediterranean agriculture
12. (b) Viticulture
13. (c) Indonesia
14. (a) Technology available for use of mineral
15. (b) High labour cost
16. (a) Cheapest way of mining
17. (d) Extensive commercial grain cultivation
18. (c) Mediterranean farming
19. (c) (i), (ii) and (iii)
20. (c) (i), (ii) and (iii)
21. (b) (ii) and (iii)
22. (b) Both statements I and II are correct and statement II is the true cause behind statement I.
23. (b) Both I and II are correct
24. (d)
25. (b)
26. (d)
27. (d) A is correct, but R is incorrect
28. (d) A is correct, but R is incorrect

Subjective Questions

Short Answer Type Questions

1. Why inhabitants of coastal and plain regions are engaged in fishing and agricultural activity respectively?

Ans. Fishing is practised by the inhabitants of coastal areas due to the following reasons

(i) **Nutritional Security** Fish is the main source of food for coastal inhabitants.

(ii) **Economic Security** Fish has huge demand in the market and it serves as a livelihood for these communities.

(iii) **Favourable Geographical Factors** Coastal areas have moderate climate and abundant water resources, which favours fishing.

The inhabitants of plains practise agriculture due to the following reasons

(i) **Favourable Geographical Factors** Plain areas have fertile soil and flat relief which favours agriculture.

(ii) **Irrigation Facilities** Plains have irrigation facilities which supports agriculture.

(iii) **Livelihood** Agriculture is a source of livelihood for the people living in plains.

2. Gathering has little chances of becoming important at global level. Why?

Ans. In modern times, though gathering is market oriented and it has become commercial but it has little chances of becoming important at the global level because of the following reasons

(i) This requires a small amount of capital investment and operates at a very low level of technology. Thus, the products of this activity cannot compete at global level.

(ii) The yield per person is very low and very little or no surplus is produced which cannot be sold in the market.

(iii) Synthetic products, often of better quality and a lower price have replaced many items supplied by gatherers in the tropical rainforests.

3. What is Pastoral Nomadism? Name three regions where it is practised. Why is it declining?

Ans. Pastoral nomadism or Nomadic herding is a primitive subsistence activity in which the herders rely on animals for food, clothing, shelter, tools and transport. They move from one place to another along with their livestock, depending on the amount of quality of pastures and water.

Pastoral nomadism is associated with three regions

- Region extending from Atlantic shores of North Africa Eastwards across the Arabian Peninsula into Mongolia and Central China.
- Tundra region in Eurasia.
- The region in Southern hemisphere in South West Africa and the Island of Madagascar.

4. "In modern times some gathering is market oriented and has become commercial". Explain. **Competency Based Que**

Ans. Gathering is a primary economic activity practised in the regions with harsh climatic conditions. It involves primitive societies, who extract both plants and animals to satisfy their needs for food, shelter and clothing.

But, in modern times gathering has become market oriented and commercial. It is evident from the following points

- The gatherers collect valuable plant parts such as leaves, bark of trees and medicinal plants. After simple processing, they sell the products in the market.
- The gatherers use different parts of plants to make products that are in demand in the market. These include quinine, cork and tannin from the bark, beverages, drugs, cosmetics, fibres and fabrics from leaves, food and oil from nuts and rubber, balata, gums and resins from trunk.

5. "There is low yield per acre but high yield per person in the interior parts of semi-arid lands of the mid latitudes in the world." Support the statement with suitable examples. **Competency Based Que**

Ans. The interior parts of semi-arid lands of the mid latitudes in the world are the areas where extensive commercial grain cultivation takes place. There is low yield per acre but high yield per person because the size of farms is very large and population is in small number. That is why entire operations of cultivation right from ploughing to harvesting is mechanised. Therefore, yield per person is high as the number of people working in farms is less and lot of machines are used.

However, the size of the farms are very large due to which per acre production or yield is low even though the total production is high. This type of agriculture is practised in Eurasian Steppes, Canadian and American Prairies, Pampas of Argentina, Velds of South Africa, Australian Downs and the Canterbury Plains of New Zealand. Wheat is the principal crop and other crops are corn, barley, oats and rye.

6. Explain any five characteristics of extensive commercial grain cultivation practised in the world.

***Or* Analyse the main features of extensive commercial grain cultivation in the world.** **CBSE 2024**

Ans. The main characteristics of extensive commercial grain cultivation are as follows

- The interior parts of semi-arid lands of the mid-latitudes are suitable for this cultivation.
- The main crop is wheat. It is accompanied by other crops like corn, barley oats and rye.
- Due to larger area of the farm, all the operations from ploughing to harvesting are mechanised.
- It is recorded that there is low yield per acre but high yield per person.
- Important areas of this cultivation are European Steppes, the Canadian and American Prairies, the Pampas of Argentina, the Velds of South Africa, the Australian Downs and Canterbury Plains of New Zealand.

7. "Dairy farming is the most advanced and efficient type of rearing of milch animals in the world." Analyse the statement with examples. **Competency Based Que**

Ans. It is true that dairy farming is the most advanced and efficient type of rearing of milch animals in the world. This is because it is highly capital as well as labour intensive.

For example, animal sheds, storage facilities for fodder, feeding and milching machines add to the cost of dairy farming. Special emphasis is laid on cattle breeding, healthcare and veterinary services.

It is labour intensive also due to the caring, feeding and milching processes involved. The developed means of transportation, refrigeration, pasteurisation and other preservation processes are used to increase the duration of storage of various dairy products. Thus, due to these specialised operations, dairy farming is very advanced and efficient form of rearing activity.

8. "Mediterranean agriculture is highly specialised.". Validate the statement.

Ans. Mediterranean agriculture is highly specialised agriculture because of high valued crops grown here.

Important crops cultivated in this type of agriculture are

- Citrus fruits, olives and figs.
- Grape cultivation or viticulture which is used to produce wines and raisins and currants.

The main advantage of Mediterranean agriculture is that more valuable crops such as fruits and vegetables are grown in Winters where there is great demand in European and North American markets.

9. Explain major features of co-operative farming.

Ans. The features of cooperative farming are as follows:

- **Pooling Resources** In cooperative farming, a group of farmers pool their resources voluntarily. Farming is a matter of cooperative initiative.
- **Efficient and Profit Oriented** It is more efficient and profit oriented than individual farming.
- **Support of Cooperative Societies** The cooperative societies help farmers to procure important inputs of farming, sell the products at more favourable terms and help in processing of quality products at cheaper rates.
- **Practised in Western Countries** This type of farming is mainly practised in the Western countries such as Denmark, Netherlands, Belgium, Sweden, Italy, etc. In Denmark, the movement has been so successful that practically every farmer is a member of a cooperative.

10. Explain the Kolkhoz model of farming.

Ans. The Kolkhoz model of farming is a collective model of farming that was introduced in the Soviet Union (Russia). The basic principle of this type of farming is that the means of production are socially owned and there is collective labour where each farmer compliments each other in the farming activity.

Method of Farming In this model of farming, the farmers used to pool their resources like land, livestock and labour. However, they were allowed to retain very small plots of land to grow crops to meet their daily requirements of food. The reasons for introducing this method of farming was

- To improve upon the efficiency of previous methods of agriculture.
- To boost agriculture production for self-sufficiency.

11. What is mining? Briefly describe the different types of mining.

Ans. Mining is the extraction of valuable minerals or other geological materials from the Earth from an ore, lode, vein or placer deposit. On the basis of mode of occurrence and the nature of ore, mining is of two types

(i) **Surface Mining** Surface mining is also known as open cast mining. It is used to extract minerals occurring closer to the surface. The advantages of this type of mining are
- It is easy and cheap.
- Cost of safety precautions and equipment is low in this method.
- Output is large and rapid.

(ii) **Underground Mining** It is also known as shaft method. It is the method of mining minerals when the ore lies deep below the surface.

This method of mining has following disadvantages
- It requires specially designed lifts, drills, haulage vehicles, ventilation system for moving people and materials.
- Poisonous gases, fires, floods and cavings can lead to deadly accidents.

12. Explain any three features of underground mining methods practiced in different countries of the world.

Ans. The three features of underground mining methods in different countries of the world are as follows

(i) It is done when the ore lies deep below the surface. In this method, vertical shafts have to be sunk, from where underground galleries radiate to reach the minerals.

(ii) For underground mining, lifts, drills, haulage vehicles, ventilation system for safety and efficient movement of people and materials are required.

(iii) The method used in underground mining is risky because poisonous gases, fires, floods and caving can lead to fatal accidents.

13. Study the given map, showing dairy farming regions carefully and answer the following questions.

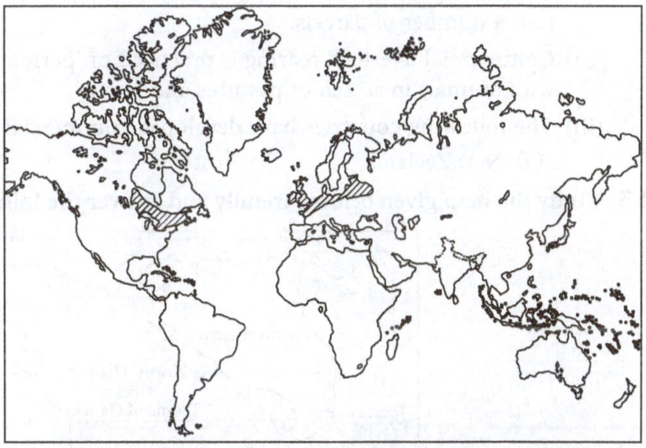

(i) What type of activities are done under dairy farming?

(ii) Explain any one characteristics of dairy farming.

(iii) How a country can develop the practice of dairy farming?

Ans. (i) Dairy farming include farming practice where milch animals are reared using scientific methods and techniques.

(ii) Dairy farming is highly capital intensive, as it requires animal sheds, storage facilities, fodder, milching machines, etc.

(iii) A country can improve its transportation facility and increase refrigerated storages to develop dairy farming.

14. **Study the map of commercial livestock rearing carefully and answer the following questions.**

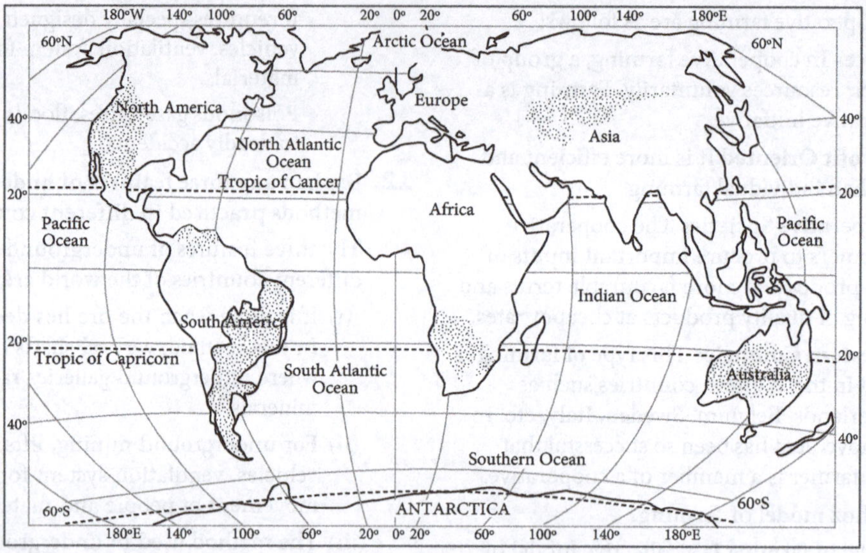

(i) Describe the characteristics of ranches used in commercial livestock rearing.
(ii) Write a major difference between commercial livestock rearing and nomadic herding.
(iii) Which countries have developed commercial livestock rearing practices?

Ans. (i) Ranches used in commercial livestock rearing are permanent and these ranches covers large areas and are divided into a number of parcels.

(ii) Commercial livestock rearing is practiced on permanent grazing fields, while in nomadic herding, the herders move with animals in search of pastures and water.

(iii) The following countries have developed commercial livestock rearing practices

(a) New Zealand (b) Australia (c) Argentina (d) Uruguay.

15. **Study the map given below carefully and answer the following questions.**

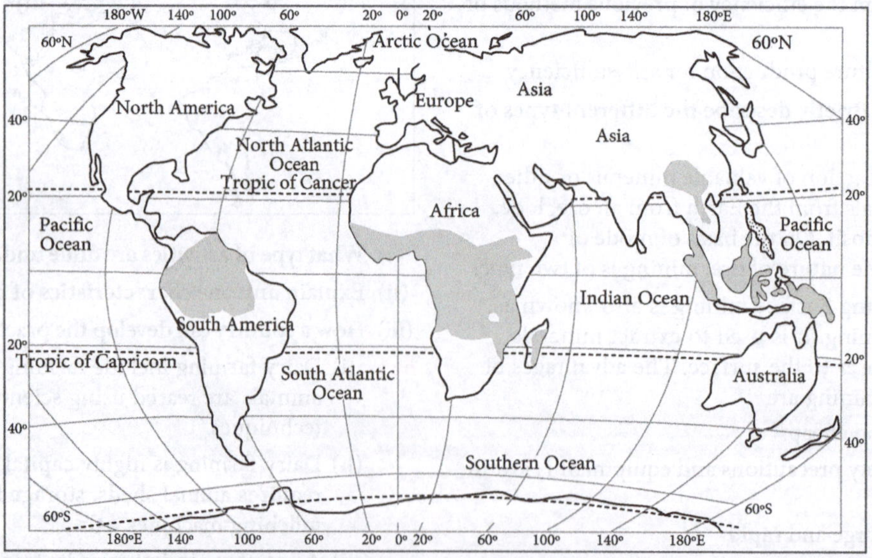

(i) What is meant by primitive subsistence agriculture?
(ii) In which area in India it is practised and locally known as jhumming cultivation?
(iii) Why do the farmer leave their farm land after 3 to 5 years?

Ans. (i) Primitive subsistence agriculture or shifting cultivation is a primitive type of agriculture in which a patch of forest is burnt and crops are grown in cleared field. Ash of trees is used as manure to make the soil fertile.

(ii) In North-Eastern part of India, shifting cultivation is practised and is locally known as 'jhuming'.

(iii) Farmers leave their farm land after (3-5) years because the soil looses its fertility. The farmer may return to the land after sometime.

Long Answer Type Questions

1. The earliest human beings depend on their immediate environment for sustenance. Validate the statement in light of hunting and gathering practices. Competency Based Que

Ans. The earliest human beings depend on their immediate environment for sustenance and they survived on hunting and gathering, this can be validated by following points

(i) Hunting and gathering are the well-known oldest economic activities.

(ii) Gathering is practised in region with harsh climate conditions. It often involves primitive societies, which extract both plants and animals for food, shelter and clothing.

(iii) People living in very cold and extremely hot climates, survive on hunting.

(iv) The early man used stone, tools, twigs or arrows, so animals were hunted in limited numbers. Now due to excessive and illegal hunting (poaching), many species have become extinct or endangered.

(v) Gatherers collect valuable plants, leaves, bark of trees. Gatherers also collect medicinal trees. After simple processing, they sell the products in the markets.

2. "Gathering and hunting are the primitive economic activities meant for the subsistence of tribal societies, but in modern times gathering is market oriented and has become commercial." Examine the statement.

Ans. Gathering and hunting are the primitive or ancient activity. People living in the ancient societies depend on this type of activities heavily. People used to survive in harsh climate by hunting animals. But now the concept of gathering and hunting has changed, it has now become market oriented and are now done/practised for commercial purposes.

In modern times, gathering is market-oriented because gatherers collect plants and other items on a large scale for selling in the market. Gatherers sell products made from valuable plants.

They use various parts of the plant, for example, the bark is used for quinine, tannin extract and cork-leaves supply materials for beverages, drugs, cosmetics, fibres and fabrics; nuts for food and oils and tree trunk give rubber, balata, gums and resins. Gathering has become a major way of earning income so it has become commercial.

3. Define the term 'nomadic herding'? Explain its any four characteristics.

Or **Explain any five characteristics of 'Pastoral Nomadism' in the World.**

Ans. Nomadic herding is also called pastoral nomadism. It is basically primitive subsistence activity, in which herders depend upon animals for food, clothing, shelter, tools and transport.

Characteristics of nomadic herding are as follows

(i) Nomadic herders move from one place to other place with their livestock in search of quality pastures and water. Each nomadic community occupies a well identified territory as a matter of tradition.

(ii) Different variety of animals are reared in different regions of the world e.g. in Tropical Africa, cattles are most important livestock; in the hilly areas of Tibet and Andes, Yak and Llamas and in Arctic and Sub-Arctic areas, Reindeer is the most important livestock.

(iii) Movement in search of pastures is undertaken either over vast grassland or mountainous regions. Movement from plains to mountains in summer season and vice-versa is called transhumance.

(iv) It is practised by tribes such as Gujjars, Bakkerwals and Gaddis in the mountain region of Himalayas where they move from plain to mountains in summers and from mountain to plains in winters.

(v) Now-a-days, number of pastoral nomads are declining and their areas are also reducing in size due to imposition of political boundaries and new settlement plans by different countries.

4. Define the term commercial livestock rearing. Explain any four characteristics.

Or **Describe any five characteristics of 'commercial livestock rearing' practised in the world.** CBSE Diksha

Or **Explain the main features of 'commercial livestock rearing' in the world.** CBSE 2024 C

Ans. Commercial livestock rearing is a specialised activity in which only one type of animal is reared for products such as meat, wool, hides, which are processed, packed and exported.

The five characteristics of commercial livestock rearing are as follows

(i) Commercial livestock rearing is more organised and capital intensive.

(ii) Commercial livestock rearing is practised on permanent ranches. These ranches are of large size and are divided into parcels which are fenced to regulate the grazing. When one parcel is grazed, then animals are moved to another parcel. All animals are kept according to the carrying capacity of pasture.

(iii) Only one type of animals are reared in commercial livestock rearing. Some important animals are sheep, goats, horses, etc. They produce meat, wool, hides and skin. These products are processed and packed scientifically and exported to different world markets.

(iv) Ranches are managed scientifically and they emphasise on breeding, genetic improvement, disease control and health care of the livestock.

(v) USA, Argentina, New Zealand, Australia and Uruguay are important countries where commercial livestock rearing is practised.

5. Explain the main features of 'primitive subsistence agriculture' in the world. **CBSE 2024 C**

Ans. Primitive subsistence agriculture is also known as shifting cultivation. It is widely practiced by many tribes in tropical regions, including Africa, South and Central America, and South-East Asia. This type of farming involves clearing vegetation by fire, and the ashes help fertilise the soil. Farmers use simple tools like sticks and hoes to cultivate small patches of land. After a few years, the soil loses fertility, and the farmer shifts to another part of the forest. The cycle of shifting land becomes shorter as the soil fertility decreases. This practice is known by different names in various regions, such as Jhumming in North-East India, Milpa in Central America, and Ladang in Indonesia and Malaysia. It is prevalent in tropical areas but can lead to environmental degradation if not managed properly.

6. Classify intensive subsistence agriculture into two categories practised in the world. How are they different from each other? Explain.

Or **Describe the main characteristics of intensive subsistence agriculture. In which parts of the world this type of agriculture is practiced?**

Or **State the areas where intensive subsistence agriculture practiced in the world. What are its two types? Describe any two characteristics of each type.**

Ans. The term 'intensive subsistence agriculture' is used to describe a type of agriculture characterised by high output per unit of land and relatively low output per worker. This form of agriculture is best developed in and practically confined to the monsoon lands of Asia. It is found in China, Japan, Korea, India, Pakistan, Sri Lanka, the greater part of South-East Asia.

There are two categories of intensive subsistence agriculture which are practised in the world

(i) Intensive subsistence agriculture dominated by wet paddy cultivation.

Characteristics of intensive subsistence dominated by wet paddy cultivation are

- It is characterised by dominance of rice crop. Land holding are very small due to the high density of population.
- Use of machinery is limited and most of the agricultural operations are done by manual labour.

(ii) Intensive subsistence agriculture dominated by crops other than paddy.

Characteristics of intensive subsistence dominated by crops other than paddy are

- Wheat, soybean, barley and sorghum are grown in Northern China, Manchuria, North Korea and North Japan. In India, wheat is grown in Western parts of the Indo-Gangetic plains and millets are grown in dry parts of Western and Southern India.
- Irrigation system are used frequently as this type of agriculture is practised in dry areas.

7. Describe any five features of extensive commercial grain farming in the world. **CBSE 2024**

Ans. Extensive commercial grain farming has several key features that distinguish it from other types of farming

- **Large Scale** This type of farming covers vast areas of land, often extending over thousands of acres. It is typically practiced in regions with vast plains, such as the Great Plains in North America, the steppes of Russia, and parts of Argentina.
- **Mechanisation** Extensive commercial grain farming relies heavily on machinery for ploughing, sowing, irrigation, and harvesting. Tractors, combine harvesters, and other advanced tools increase efficiency and productivity.
- **Use of Modern Technology** The farming process benefits from modern technologies like fertilisers, pesticides, and genetically modified crops, which boost yields and protect crops from pests and diseases.
- **Commercial Purpose** The primary goal is to produce grains for sale in national and international markets rather than for local consumption. The crops are often exported globally, contributing to the agricultural economy.

8. Define the term 'mixed farming'. Explain any four characteristics of mixed farming practised in the world.

Ans. Mixed farming refers to the primary activity in which animal husbandry is practised along with crop cultivation. Important animals are cattle, sheep, pigs and poultry animals.

The characteristics of mixed farming are

(i) This type of farming involves high capital investment on constructing farms, buildings and machines for animal husbandry and agriculture.

(ii) In this type of activity, chemical fertilisers and green manures are used on a large scale. Farmers require skills and expertise in this farming.

(iii) Fodder crops are important components of mixed farming as they are used to feed animals.

(iv) The farms in mixed farming are moderate in size.

(v) Inter-cropping and crop rotation are used here for growing crops such as wheat, barley, oats, rye, maize, etc.

(vi) Mixed farming practised in highly developed regions of the world. For example, North Western Europe, Eastern North America, Eurasia and Temperate latitudes of Southern Continents.

9. State the areas where dairy farming is practised in the world . Discuss any four characteristics of this type of farming.

Ans. Dairy farming is one of the most efficient and modernised type of rearing in which milching of animal is done. This farming is capital intensive and it is practised in different parts of the world. There are three main regions of commercial dairy farming. The largest is North Western Europe, the second is Canada and the third belt includes South Eastern Australia, New Zealand and Tasmania.

Characteristics of dairy farming

- **Specialised Farming** This farming focuses on milk production, with by-products like cheese and butter.
- **High Input** This farming requires quality feed, veterinary care and mechanisation.
- **Proximity to Markets** This type of farming is located near urban areas to ensure fresh delivery.
- **Labour-Intensive** This involves regular animal care and milking.

10. What is the meaning of market gardening and horticulture? Describe any four characteristics of this type of agriculture of the world.

Ans. Market gardening or horticulture specialises in the production of high value crops such as vegetables, fruits and flowers, mainly for the urban markets. These farms are located near urban areas.

Four characteristics of market gardening and horticulture are as follows

(i) Farms are small in size and located near urban centers where good transportation facilities are available.

(ii) It is both labour and capital intensive and lays emphasis on the use of irrigation, HYV seeds, fertilisers, insecticides, greenhouses and artificial heating systems in colder regions.

(iii) The regions where farmers specialise in cultivation of vegetables only is known as truck farming.

(iv) This type of agriculture is practised in well developed and densely populated regions of North-West Europe, North-Eastern USA and the Mediterranean regions. The Netherlands specialises in growing flower and horticultural crops, especially tulips.

11. Differentiate between co-operative farming and collective farming, stating five points of distinction.

Ans. Difference between co-operative farming and collective farming are as follows

Co-operative Farming	Collective Farming
Co-operative farming takes place when farmers pool their resources voluntarily for efficient and profitable farming.	Collective farming takes place when there is social ownership of means of production.
In co-operative farming, farmers have individual ownership of the resources.	In collective farming, farmers pool all their resources, though they are allowed to keep very small piece of land for their own use.
Co-operative societies help farmers in buying farm inputs on favourable terms.	In collective farming, all farm inputs are provided by the government.
Co-operative societies also help the farmers in selling the farm products profitably.	In collective farming, farm products are sold to the state at a fixed price.
Co-operative farming has been successful in many European countries and that is why, it is practised in many other countries of the world.	It was introduced in erstwhile Soviet Union in order to improve the inefficiency of previous method of agriculture.

12. The profitability of mining operations depends on physical as well as economic factors. Support the statement.

Ans. Mining activities are influenced by both physical factors as well as economic factors. These are:

(i) Formation, size, depth, grade and the mode of occurrence of deposits. The minerals that are near to the surface are extracted easily whereas the minerals deep inside the Earth are extracted by underground mining.

(ii) Mining activities require sophisticated tools for cutting tunnels, sinking of shaft and other works. Hence, the availability of technology is another important factor.

(iii) Desirable knowledge, cheaper technology, demand of mineral in market, supply of labour and finance to develop infrastructure is also required.

(iv) Sufficient transport availability to link mining sites with the markets and industries is also important.

(v) Processing machines and industries are also required to process the extracted minerals and convert them into useful products is also required.

Source Based Questions

1. Read the passage carefully and answer the questions that follow.

Gathering and hunting are the oldest economic activity known. These are carried out at different levels with different orientations. Gathering is practised in regions with harsh climatic conditions. It often involves primitive societies, who extract, both plants and animals to satisfy their needs for food, shelter and clothing. This type of activity requires a small amount of capital investment and operates at very low level of technology. The yield per person is very low and little or no surplus is produced. Gathering is practised in high latitude zones which include Northern Canada, Northern Eurasia and Southern Chile; Low latitude zones such as the Amazon Basin, tropical Africa, Northern fringe of Australia and the interior parts of South-East Asia. Gatherers collect valuable plants such as leaves, barks of trees and medicinal plants and after simple processing sell the products in the market. Synthetic products often of better quality and at lower prices, have replaced many items supplied by the gatherers in tropical forests. It is led to a decrease in gathering activity.

(i) What is the most important reason that has led to decline in gathering?

(a) Political boundaries (b) Environmental treaties
(c) Synthetic products (d) Decline of forests

Ans. (c) Synthetic products

(ii) Which of the following still practise gathering and hunting?

(a) Settled agriculturists (b) Commercial companies
(c) Tribal societies (d) All of these

Ans. (c) Tribal societies

(iii) Gathering is not practised in which of these regions?

(a) Amazon Basin (b) Southern Chile
(c) Northern Canada (d) New Zealand

Ans. (d) New Zealand

2. Read the passage carefully and answer the questions that follow.

Nomadic herding or pastoral nomadism is a primitive subsistence activity, in which the herders rely on animals for food, clothing, shelter, tools and transport. They move from one place to another along with their livestock, depending on the amount and quality of pastures and water. Each nomadic community occupies a well-identified territory as a matter of tradition. A wide variety of animals is kept in different regions. In tropical Africa, cattle are the most important livestock, while in Sahara and Asiatic deserts, sheep, goats and camel are reared. In the mountainous areas of Tibet and Andes, yak and llamas and in the Arctic and sub-Arctic areas, reindeer are the most important animals.

(i) Nomadic herding can be classified as what type of activity?

(a) Commercial Activity (b) Primitive Activity
(c) Subsistence Activity (d) Both (b) and (c)

Ans. (d) Both (b) and (c)

(ii) Cattle is an important animal kept by the Nomads in which of the following regions?

(a) Andes mountain (b) Arctic region
(c) Tropical regions (d) Sahara desert region

Ans. (c) Tropical regions

(iii) Which of the following means transhumance?

(a) Movement over vast areas
(b) Movement in desert regions
(c) Seasonal migration over mountains and plains
(d) Movement in forests

Ans. (c) Seasonal migration over mountains and plains

3. Read the passage carefully and answer the questions that follow.

Plantation agriculture was introduced by the Europeans in colonies situated in the tropics. Some of the important plantation crops are tea, coffee, cocoa, rubber, cotton, oil palm, sugarcane, bananas and pineapples. The characteristic features of this type of farming are large estates or plantations, large capital investment, managerial and technical support, scientific methods of cultivation, single crop specialisation, cheap labour, and a good system of transportation which links the estates to the factories and markets for the export of the products. The French established cocoa and coffee plantations in West Africa. The British set up large tea gardens in India and Sri Lanka, rubber plantations in Malaysia and sugarcane and banana plantations in West Indies. Spanish and Americans invested heavily in coconut and sugarcane plantations in the Philippines. The Dutch once had monopoly over sugarcane plantation in Indonesia. Some coffee fazendas (large plantations) in Brazil are still managed by Europeans. Today, ownership of the majority of plantations has passed into the hands of the government or the nationals of the countries concerned.

(i) Which colonial power established plantations in Malaysia?

(a) French (b) Portuguese (c) British (d) Dutch

Ans. (c) British

(ii) Which of the following is must for setting up plantation agriculture?

(a) Specialised labour

(b) Large capital investment

(c) Research and development

(d) Multiple cropping

Ans. (b) Large capital investment

(iii) Fazendas of Brazil are the plantations of which crop?

(a) Tea (b) Pineapple (c) Coffee (d) Banana

Ans. (c) Coffee

4. Read the passage carefully and answer the questions that follow.

Market gardening and horticulture specialise in the cultivation of high value crops such as vegetables, fruits and flowers, solely for the urban markets. Farms are small and are located where there are good transportation links with the urban centre where high income group of consumers is located. It is both labour and capital intensive and lays emphasis on the use of irrigation, HYV seeds, fertilisers, insecticides, greenhouses and artificial heating in colder regions. This type of agriculture is well developed in densely populated industrial districts of north-west Europe, north eastern United States of America and the Mediterranean regions. The Netherlands specialises in growing flowers and horticultural crops especially tulips, which are flown to all major cities of Europe. The regions where farmers specialise in vegetables only, the farming is known as truck farming. The distance of truck farms from the market is governed by the distance that a truck can cover overnight, hence the name truck farming. In addition to market gardening, a modern development in the industrial regions of Western Europe and North America is factory farming.

(i) Mention an important component of livestock factory farming.

Ans. Scientific breeding is one of the important component of livestock factory farming.

(ii) Why marked gardening is practised near urban areas?

Ans. Market gardening is practised in urban areas because it produces high valued crops. The urban population have purchasing capacity for such products.

(iii) Mention any two inputs required by the horticulture crops.

Ans. Horticulture crops require following inputs

(i) High yielding seeds (ii) Skilled labour

6. Study the given picture carefully and answer the questions that follow.

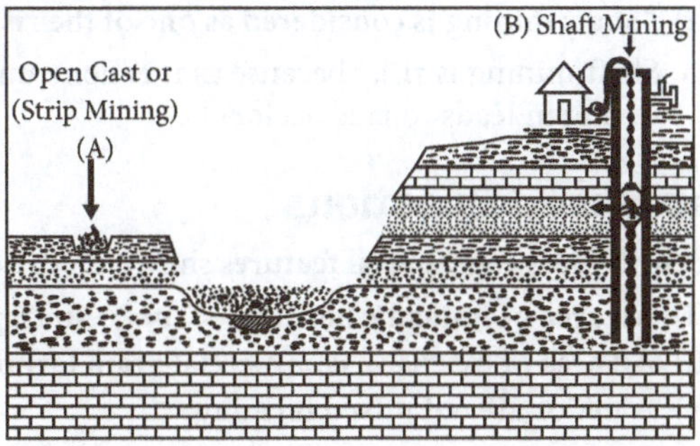

(i) In which type of mining, the output is large and rapid?

Ans. In open cast mining, the output is large and rapid.

(ii) What type of accidents can occur in the mining process indicated by symbol B?

Ans. The accidents that can occur in the mining process indicated by symbol (B) are as follows

(a) Underground fires

(b) Leakage of poisonous gases

(c) Flooding

(iii) Which countries are heavily dependent upon mining of minerals?

Ans. Some countries like Africa and few South American countries and Asia are dependent on mining of minerals.

6. Read the passage carefully and answer the questions that follow. **CBSE 2023**

Methods of Mining

Depending on the mode of occurrence and the nature of the ore, mining is of two types i.e. surface and underground mining. The surface mining also known as open-cast mining is the easiest and the cheapest way of mining minerals that occur close to the surface. Overhead costs such as safety precautions and equipment are relatively low in this method. The output is both large and rapid. When the ore lies deep below the surface, underground mining method (**shaft method**) has to be used. In this method, vertical shafts have to be sunk, from where underground galleries radiate to reach the minerals. Minerals are extracted and transported to the surface through these passages. It requires specially designed lifts, drills, haulage vehicles, ventilation system for safety and efficient movement of people and material. This method is risky. Poisonous gases, fires, floods and caving in lead to fatal accidents. Have you ever read about mine fires and flooding of coal mines in India ?

(i) **Explain the main difference between surface and underground mining.**

Ans. The main difference between surface and underground mining is that the surface mining is the easiest and the cheapest way of mining minerals that occur close to the surface. On the other hand, when the ore lies deep below the surface, underground mining method (shaft method) is used which needs more capital.

(ii) **Why is open-cast mining the easiest way of mining ?**

Ans. Open-cast mining is an easiest way of mining because excavation through rock is not necessary in this mining method.

(iii) **"Shaft mining is considered as one of the risky method of mining." Justify the statement.**

Ans. Shaft mining is risky because as it is done underground so there are chances of poisonous gases, fires, and floods and caving in leads to fatal accidents.

Map Based Questions

1. Identify the geographical features shown on the outline map of the world.

(i) **An area of nomadic herding.** *or* **An important area of nomadic herding.**

(ii) **An area of extensive commercial grain farming.** CBSE 2024

(iii) **An area of subsistence gathering.** CBSE 2024

(iv) **A major area of mixed farming.**

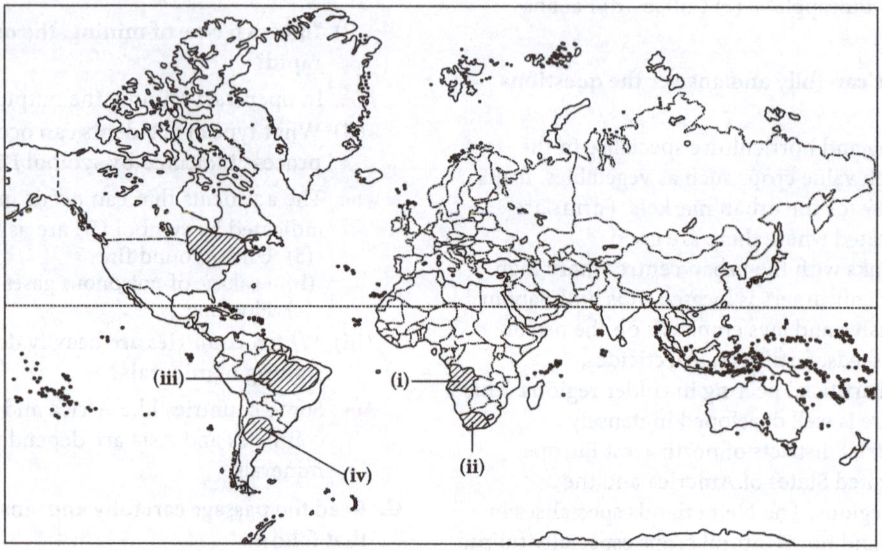

Ans.

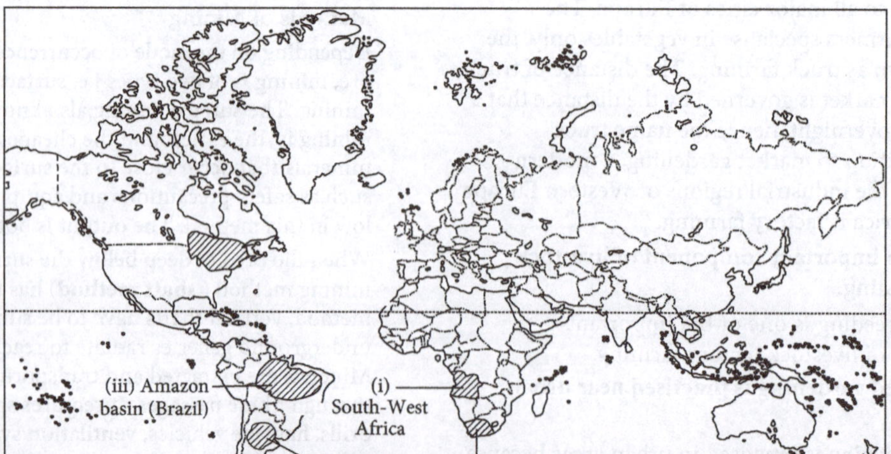

2. Identify the geographical features shown on the map.

(i) An area of extensive commercial grain farming.

(ii) An area of subsistence gathering.

(iii) A major area of commercial livestock rearing. **CBSE 2024**

(iv) A major area of mixed farming.

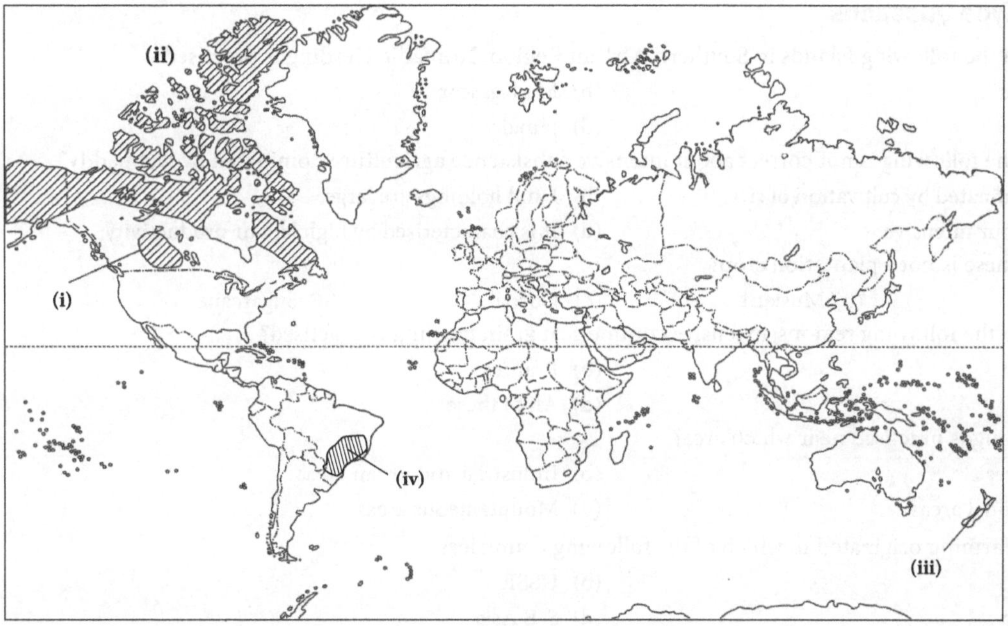

Ans.

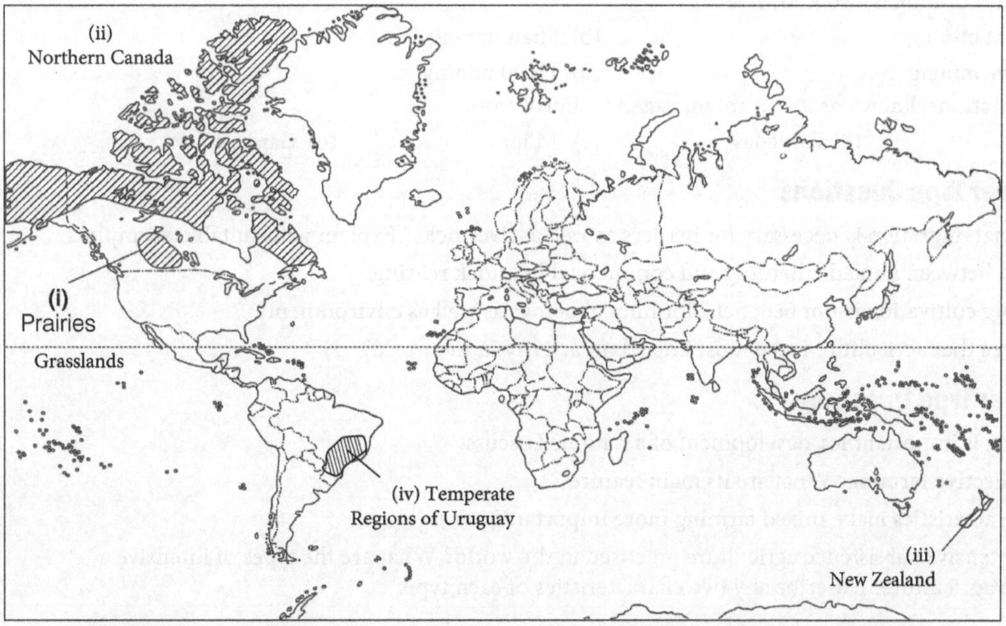

SELF ASSESSMENT TEST

Objective Type Questions

1. In which of the following Islands in Southern African Region, Nomadic Herding is practised?
   (a) Malaysia (b) Madagascar
   (c) Java (d) Jamaica
2. Which of the following is not correct about intensive subsistence agriculture dominated by wet paddy?
   (a) It is dominated by cultivation of rice. (b) Land holdings are large.
   (c) It is labour intensive. (d) It is characterised by high labour productivity.
3. Which of these is not a plantation crop?
   (a) Cotton (b) Mustard (c) Cocoa (d) Sugarcane
4. In which of the following regions, extensive commerical grain farming is practised?
   (a) Stepees (b) Prairies
   (c) Velds (d) All of these
5. Dairy farming is practised near which area?
   (a) Rural areas (b) Industrial and urban areas
   (c) Educational areas (d) Mountaineous areas
6. Collective farming originated in which of the following countries?
   (a) Europe (b) USSR
   (c) America (d) S-E Asia
7. Underground mining is also known as
   (a) Open cast mining (b) Shaft mining
   (c) Collective mining (d) Flood mining
8. Coffee plantations, known as .... are managed by Europeans.
   (a) Estates (b) Fazendas (c) Milpas (d) Gardens

Short Answer Type Questions

9. How seasonal migration is necessary for herders as well as livestocks? Explain with suitable examples.
10. Distinguish between nomadic herding and commercial livestock rearing.
11. Why shifting cultivation is not beneficial for human beings as well as environment?
12. Do you agree that agriculture is the most important activity in the world?

Long Answer Type Questions

13. Why mining is important for development of a nation? Discuss.
14. What is collective farming? What are its main features?
15. Which characteristics make mixed farming more important?
16. Where is intensive subsistence agriculture practised in the world? What are the types of intensive subsistence agriculture? Describe any two characteristics of each type.

5

CHAPTER

Secondary Activities

Secondary activities transform raw materials into valuable products and provide finished goods for consumer consumption. These are mainly concerned with manufacturing, processing and construction industries.

▼ YOUR STUDY GOALS

5.1 Manufacturing
5.2 Classification of Manufacturing Industries

▼ YOUR PRACTICE GOAL

- Objective Type Questions (19 Qs ; MCQs, Statements, Matching, A-R)
- Subjective Questions (17 SAs, 8 LAs)
- Source Based Questions (2 Qs)

5.1 Manufacturing

- **Manufacturing** is the process of turning raw materials or parts into finished goods with tools, human labour, machinery and chemical processing.
- Manufacturing includes production from handicrafts to moulding iron and steel, and to assembling delicate computer components or space vehicles.
- The common characteristics of any manufacturing are the use of power, mass production of identical products and specialised labour in a factory.

Characteristics of Modern Large-scale Manufacturing

Modern large-scale manufacturing has the following characteristics

- **Specialisation of Skills/Methods of Production** Industries differ in their output based on the skills employed and production methods they use. For example, the 'craft' method focuses on producing only a few custom items per order, as per specific requirements. In contrast, mass production involves creating large quantities of standardised items, where each worker performs specific, repetitive tasks to contribute to the final product.

- **Mechanisation** It is a systematic process designed to perform a specific function or achieve a particular outcome. Modern manufacturing heavily dependent on mechanical devices and automated equipment to enhance production efficiency. Mechanisation introduces various automated tools to handle different stages of the production process, making manufacturing faster and less labour-intensive.
- **Automation** It is an advanced stage of manufacturing. It allows manufacturing processes to operate with minimal to no human dependence. The highly automated factories reduce the need for manual labour while enhancing productivity.
- **Technological Innovation** Innovation in technology is essential for quality control, minimising waste, and reducing inefficiencies. Technological advancements also help industries address environmental concerns, making production more eco-friendly and sustainable.
- **Organisational Structure and Stratification** Modern manufacturing operations demand a structured organisational setup to handle complex machine technology, with a high level of specialisation and division of labour that allows for greater production output with less effort and lower costs. These industries require huge capital investments, a large organisational framework, and an efficient executive bureaucracy to support smooth operations.
- **Uneven Geographic Distribution** Global manufacturing is unevenly spread, with a significant concentration in less than 10% of the world's land area. These manufacturing centres become important regions because of their strong economic and political influence.

Difference between 'manufacturing' industry and 'manufacturing industry'

Manufacturing means making things, usually by hand or with machines. Today it means turning raw materials into finished products using machines, to sell them in nearby or far away markets.

An 'industry' is a place where this manufacturing happens, usually in a factory, with a proper system to keep track of everything. Sometimes, people use the word 'industry' to mean manufacturing, like when they talk about the 'steel industry' or the 'chemical industry.'

However, not all industries make things in factories. For example, the 'entertainment industry' and the 'tourism industry' don't create physical products, but they are still called industries. That's why the term 'manufacturing industry'is used when we want to clear that it's about making things in factories.

Factors Affecting the Location of Industries

1. Access to Market

- The existence of a market for manufactured goods is the most important factor in the location of industries.
- **'Market'** refers to the people who demand manufactured goods and have the ability to purchase them.
- The developed regions of Europe, North America, Japan and Australia provide large **global markets**[1] as the purchasing power of the people is very high.
- The densely populated regions of South and South-East Asia are also large markets.
- Remote areas inhabited by a few people offer small markets.
- Some industries like aircraft and arms manufacturing also have global markets.

2. Access to Raw Material

- Industries based on cheap, bulky, and **weight-losing materials**[2] are located close to the sources of raw materials. For example, steel, sugar and cement industries.

1 **Global Market** The global market refers to the interconnected marketplace where goods, services and capital are exchanged internationally across countries and regions.

2 **Weight-losing materials** A weight-losing material is a raw material that loses significant weight during the production process, making it more economical to locate industries near the source of the material.

- **Perishability**[3] is an important reason for industries to be located near the source of raw materials. Thus, agro-processing and dairy products are processed close to the sources of production or supply.

3. Access to Labour Supply

- Many manufacturing industries require skilled and semi-skilled labour. Hence industries are located around the places where labour is easily available.
- Increased mechanisation, automation and flexibility of industrial processes have reduced the dependence of industry upon the labourers.

4. Access to Sources of Energy

- Industries that use more power are located close to the source of the energy. For example, the aluminium industry.
- Earlier coal was the main source of energy, today hydroelectricity and petroleum are also important sources of energy for many industries.

5. Access to Transportation and Communication Facilities

- Efficient transportation facility to carry raw materials to the factory and manufactured goods to the market is required for the development of industries.
- Improved transportation led to integrated economic development and regional specialisation of manufacturing.
- Western Europe and Eastern-North America have highly developed transport systems which have always supported the concentration of industries in these areas.
- Communication among industries is important for the exchange and management of information.

6. Government Policy

- Government policies are framed to support industrial development at different locations. Governments frame 'regional policies' to promote 'balanced' economic development and set up industries in particular areas.

7. Access to Agglomeration Economies/ Links between Industries

- Industries get benefitted from nearness to a leader- industry and other industries. These benefits are termed as **agglomeration economies**.
- Savings are derived from the linkages that exist between different industries.

Footloose Industries

- These industries can be located in a wide variety of places. They are not dependent on any specific raw material.
- They produce in small quantities and also employ a small labour force.
- The important factor in their location is accessibility by road network.

Quick Test 1

1. Name any two characteristics of modern large-scale manufacturing firms.
2. What is an advanced stage of automation known as?
3. Name any three factors determining the location of industries.
4. Why are heavy industries located near the source of power?

3 **Perishability** It refers to the tendency of goods, especially food or biological products, to spoil, decay, or become unusable within a limited time.

5.2 Classification of Manufacturing Industries

Manufacturing industries are classified based on size, raw materials, output/products and ownership.

Classification of Industries

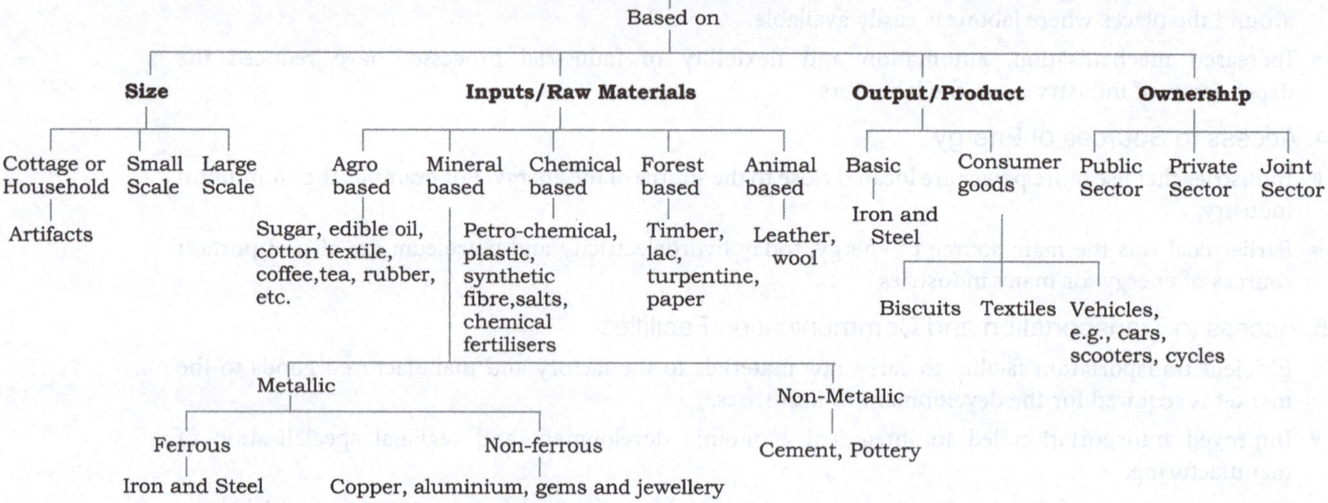

Industries Based on Size

The size of an industry is determined by the number of employees and volume of production. Under this category, industries can be classified as household or cottage, small-scale and large-scale.

Household Industries or Cottage Manufacturing

- It is the smallest manufacturing unit. The artisans manufacture goods in their homes using locally available raw materials. They often take help from their family members or part-time labourers.
- The produce might be used within the household or sold out in local markets for barter[4].
- This type of manufacturing has a low commercial significance and most of the tools are devised locally.
- These industries produce goods like foodstuffs, fabrics, mats, furniture, pottery, etc.

Small-scale Manufacturing

- Small-scale manufacturing is distinguished from household industries by its production techniques and place of manufacture (a workshop outside the home/cottage of the producer).
- This type of manufacturing uses local raw materials, simple power-driven machines and semi-skilled labour.
- It provides employment and raises local purchasing power.
- Countries like India, China, Indonesia, Brazil, etc have developed labour-intensive small-scale manufacturing industries.

▲ *Products of cottage industry on sale in Assam*

Large-Scale Manufacturing

- It involves a large market, various raw materials, energy, specialised workers, advanced technology, assembly-line mass production and large capital.
- This kind of manufacturing developed in the last 200 years, in the United Kingdom, the North-Eastern USA and Europe and now all over the world.

4 **Barter** It means the exchange of goods or services for other goods or services without using money.

- Based on the system of large-scale manufacturing, the world's major industrial regions can be grouped as
  - **Traditional large-scale industrial regions** These are thickly clustered in a few more developed countries.
  - **High-technology large-scale industrial regions** These are found in less developed countries.

Industries Based on Inputs/Raw Materials

- **Agro-based industries Agro-processing** involves processing raw materials from the field and the farm into finished products. For example food processing industries, sugar, pickles, fruit juices, spices, oils, etc. **Food processing** includes canning, producing cream, fruit processing and confectionery. Some preserving techniques, such as drying, fermenting[5] and pickling, have been known since ancient times, but these had limited applications.

Agri-business

- It is a form of commercial farming on an industrial scale. The capital and other investments are often financed by a business whose main interest is not in agriculture. For example, large corporations in the tea plantation business.
- Such farms are large, highly structured, reliant on chemicals and may be described as **agro-factories.**

- **Mineral-based industries** These industries use minerals as raw materials. Some industries use **ferrous metallic minerals** which contain ferrous (iron), such as iron and steel industries but some use non-ferrous metallic minerals, such as aluminium, copper and jewellery industries. Many industries use non-metallic minerals such as cement and pottery industries. For example, iron is used in the iron and steel industry, gold and silver are used in jewellery industries, and non-metallic minerals such as cement and soil are used in pottery industries.
- **Chemical-based industries** These industries use natural chemical minerals as their raw materials. For example, mineral oil (petroleum) is used in the petro-chemical industry. Chemical industries are also based on raw materials obtained from wood and coal. Synthetic fibre, plastic, etc are other examples of chemical-based industries.
- **Forest-based raw materials using industries** These industries use major and minor products of forests are used as raw materials. For example, timber for the furniture industry, wood, bamboo and grass for the paper industry, etc.
- **Animal-based industries** The raw material for such industries is obtained from animals. For example, leather for the leather industry and wool for woollen textiles are obtained from animals.

▲ *A pulp mill in the heart of the Ketchikan's timber area of Alaska*

Industries Based on Output/Product

- **Basic Industries** Industries that produce goods which are used by other industries to produce goods, are known as basic industries. For example, iron and steel industries products are used by other industries to manufacture machinery and other goods.
- **Consumer Goods Industries** These products are directly used by consumers. For example, these industries produce bread and biscuits, tea, soaps and toiletries, paper for writing, etc.

5 Fermenting A metabolic process that converts sugar to acids, gases and alcohol.

Industries Based on Ownership

- **Public Sector Industries** These are owned and managed by governments. India have a large number of Public Sector Undertakings (PSUs). Mixed economies have both Public and Private sector enterprises. On the other hand, socialist countries have many state-owned industries.
- **Private Sector Industries** These industries are owned and managed by individual or private organisations. In capitalist countries, the majority of industries are privately owned.
- **Joint Sector Industries** These industries are established and managed by joint stock companies or sometimes the private and public sectors.

High Technology Industry

- It is also known as the high-tech industry and it is the latest generation of manufacturing activities.
- Advanced scientific and engineering products are manufactured with intense research and development. Highly skilled professionals (white-collar workers) contribute at a large scale to the total workforce of the high-technology industry, as compared to actual production workers (blue-collar workers).
- Some examples of high-tech industries are robotics on the assembly line, Computer-Aided Design (CAD) and manufacturing.
- Characteristics of high technology industries are
    - They have neatly spaced areas.
    - They require low, modern, dispersed, office plant buildings rather than massive areas.
    - Planned business parks for high-tech start-ups have become part of regional and local development schemes.
- The high-tech industries that are regionally concentrated, self-sustained and highly specialised are called technopolis. For example, Silicon Valley near San Francisco and Silicon Forest near Seattle.

Quick Test 2

1. Name any two characteristics based on which industries can be classified.
2. Which type of industries provide more employment opportunities in developing countries like India?
3. Give three examples of industries that use chemical minerals as inputs.
4. What is the term used for industries whose products are used to make other goods by processing them?

Mind Map

SECONDARY ACTIVITIES

1 Meaning of Secondary Activities

- Adds value to natural resources.
- Involves process like manufacturing processing and construction.

2 Manufacturing

- It is the process of turning raw materials into finished goods.
- It involves application of power mass production, specialised labour in factory.

3 Characteristics of Modern Large-Scale Manufacturing

- **Specialisation of Skills/Methods of Production** It involves production of large quantities of standardised items where each worker performs specific, repetitive tasks to contribute to the final product.
- **Mechanisation** It is a systematic process designed to perform a specific function. It is heavily dependent on mechanical devices and automated equipment.
- **Automation** It is an advanced stage of manufacturing. It allows manufacturing processes to operate without human dependence.
- **Organisational Structure and Stratification** Require huge capital investments, a large organisational framework, and an efficient executive bureaucracy to support smooth operations.
- **Technological Innovation** Essential for quality control, minimising waste, and reducing inefficiencies. Help industries address environmental concerns.
- **Uneven Geographic Distribution** Manufacturing is spread in less than 10% of the world's land area.

4 Factors Affecting the Location of Industries

- Access to market
- Access to raw material
- Access to labour supply
- Access to sources of energy
- Access to transportation and communication facility
- Government policies
- Access to agglomeration economies/links between industries

5 Classification of Manufacturing Industries

Based on Size

- **Cottage or Household Industries** Artisans manufacture goods in their homes using locally available raw materials, e.g., mats, furniture, pottery, etc.
- **Small Scale Industries** Refers to the production of goods on a small scale by using limited resources, e.g., a workshop outside the home/cottage of the producer.
- **Large Scale Industries** Involves large market, various raw materials, energy, specialised workers, advanced technology.

Large Scale Industry (Motor Company)

High Technology Industry

- These industries involve advanced technology and innovation in fields like electronics, aerospace, etc.
- These industries mainly creates blue collar jobs.

Based on Ownership

- **Public Sector Industries** Owned and managed by governments.
- **Private Sector Industries** Owned and managed by individual or private organisations.
- **Joint Sector Industries** Established and managed by joint stock companies or sometimes the private and public sectors.

Based on Input/Raw Material

- Agro based industries (sugar, tea)
- Minerals based industries (copper, iron)
- Chemical based industries (petro-chemical)
- Forest based industries (timber, lac)
- Animal based industries (leather, wool)

Food Processing Industry (Tea Factory)

Based on Output/Product

- Basic industries (iron and steel)
- Consumer goods industries (biscuit, paper)

NCERT Folder

Choose the right answer from the four alternatives given below

(i) **Which one of the following statements is wrong?**

(a) Cheap water transport has facilitated the jute mill industry along the Hugli.

(b) Sugar, cotton textiles and vegetable oils are footloose industries.

(c) The development of hydro-electricity and petroleum reduced, to a great extent, the importance of coal energy as a locational factor for industry.

(d) Port towns in India have attracted industries.

Ans. (b) Sugar, cotton textiles and vegetable oils are footloose industries.

(ii) **In which one of the following types of economy are the factors of production owned individually?**

(a) Capitalist (b) Mixed

(c) Socialist (d) None of these

Ans. (a) Capitalist

(iii) **Which one of the following types of industries produces raw materials for other industries?**

(a) Cottage Industries

(b) Small-scale Industries

(c) Basic Industries

(d) Footloose Industries

Ans. (c) Basic Industries

(iv) **Which one of the following pairs is correctly matched?**

(a) Automobile Industry : Los Angeles

(b) Shipbuilding Industry : Lusaka

(c) Aircraft Industry : Florence

(d) Iron and Steel Industry : Pittsburgh

Ans. (b) Shipbuilding Industry : Lusaka

Write a short note on the following in about 30 words

(i) **High-Tech Industry**

Ans. It is simply known as high-tech industry and it is the latest generation of manufacturing activities. Advance scientific and engineering products are manufactured by intensive research and development.

Robotics on the assembly line, Computer-Aided Design (CAD) and manufacturing, electronic controls of smelting and refining processes, and the development of new chemical and pharmaceutical products are the most prominent examples of high-tech industry.

(ii) **Manufacturing**

Ans. Manufacturing refers to the conversion of raw materials into finished goods by the application of power. Manufacturing may be done with modern methods or may be primitive. Modern manufacturing is characterised by the application of power, mass production, specialised labour and production of standardised products.

(iii) **Footloose Industries**

Ans. Footloose industries can be located in a wide variety of places. They are not dependent on any specific raw material. These industries are dependent on component parts and generally are non polluting industries. The important factor in their location is nearby road network. These industries employ small amount of labour and production is also small.

Answer the following in not more than 150 words

(i) **Differentiate between primary and secondary activities.**

Ans. The differences between primary and secondary activities are as follows

Primary Activities	Secondary Activities
They are concerned with the extraction of raw material from the Earth's surface.	This activity incorporates the conversion of raw material into finished goods with higher value.
Hunting and gathering, pastoralism, fishing, forestry, mining and agriculture are the examples of primary activities.	Manufacturing clothes in textile industries, steel from iron-ore in iron and steel industries are examples of secondary activities.
It provides raw material for further processing or manufacturing.	It is involved in processing of raw material.
The types of workers in this sector include farmers, coal miners and hunters.	The types of workers in this sector include, factory workers or craftsmen.
Most of the developed countries are showing a declining trend in the proportion of the population that work in this sector.	The development in this sector is due to demand for more goods and food, which leads to industrialisation.

(ii) Discuss the major trends of modern industrial activities especially in the developed countries of the world.

Or **"Major concentrations of modern manufacturing have flourished in a few number of places in the world." Support the statement with examples.** Competency Based Que

Ans. The major trends of modern industrial activities especially in the developed countries of the world can be understood by the following points

- Modern industrial activities are carried out at a few number of places in developed countries.
- The structure and form of industries change with the progress of economy, scientific and technological advancements. For example, the textile industry in UK witnessed constant growth up to first half of 20th century.
- The industry declined with the shift of the textile industry to less developed countries like India where labour costs are low.
- High-tech industries have been diffusing to less developed countries from more developed countries. For example, in earlier days, Germany developed iron and steel industry by importing iron from Brazil. Now, Brazil might make steel and Germany would import steel and work with these to make engineering products such as cars, computers, etc.
- Other changes that have been observed are that large factories are giving way to smaller units dispersed over large areas and employing several thousands of people. These regions have become the centres of economic and political power.

(iii) Explain why high-tech industries in many countries are being attracted to the peripheral areas of major metropolitan centres.

Or **"High-tech industry is the latest generation of manufacturing in the world." Examine the statement.** CBSE 2023

Ans. High-tech industries are the latest generation of manufacturing industries in the world. It involves the application of intensive research and development for manufacturing scientifically advance and engineered products.

High-tech industries are being attracted to the peripheral areas of major metropolitan centres because

- Periphery of metropolitan areas have open spaces which are neat and clean as compared to core areas. It is suitable for setting up high-tech firms.
- Business parks are planned and developed by the governments at the periphery, which has free spaces as opposed to the congested core areas.
- In the peripheral areas, there is connectivity with the major roads and highways. Whereas the core is congested with heavy traffic.
- It requires modern set-ups which are neatly spaced having low and dispersed buildings. This can be planned in the peripheral areas as large land is available in peripheral areas of metropolitans.

(iv) Africa has immense natural resources and yet it is industrially the most backward continent. Comment. Competency Based Que

Ans. Africa is backward continent not only industrially, but also politically and socially. But the continent is blessed with immense natural resources.

Unfortunately, Africa lacks in the optimum utilisation of the natural resources due to the following reasons

- Lack of demand and absence of market for manufactured goods.
- Absence or lack of required energy or power sources.
- Poorly developed transportation and communication facilities are equally responsible for the underdeveloped industrial structure.
- Political instability and improper government and regional policies lead to unbalanced economy.
- The climate of most of the countries where mineral-based industries could be set-up is not favourable.
- The African countries do not have the advanced technology, therefore are backward in industrialisation.

Exam Pattern Questions

Objective Type Questions

Multiple Choice Questions (MCQs)

1. Identify the sector concerned with the work of converting raw materials into finished products. **CBSE 2025**

(a) Primary (b) Secondary
(c) Tertiary (d) Quaternary

2. The dependence of industries on labour has reduced because of ....

(a) quality control (b) hydroelectricity
(c) infrastructure (d) automation

3. When many industries are concentrated in a particular region to share factors of production, it is termed as ... .

(a) flexibility (b) joint sector
(c) professionalisation (d) agglomeration economies

4. What is the primary purpose of manufacturing?

(a) To produce goods for local consumption only
(b) To transform raw materials into higher-value finished goods
(c) To reduce raw material costs
(d) To increase factory sizes

5. Small-scale manufacturing is characterised by

(a) simple power-driven machines
(b) highly skilled labour
(c) use of imported raw materials
(d) All of the above

6. Which of the following is a high-tech industrial region?

(a) California valley (b) Iron valley
(c) Silicon valley (d) Computer valley

7. Which of the following is a basic industry?

(a) Soap industry (b) Iron industry
(c) Bamboo industry (d) All of these

8. Which of the following is/are characteristic(s) of technopolis?

(a) Regional concentration of high-tech industries.
(b) Presence of highly specialised industries.
(c) Presence of self-sustaining industries.
(d) All of the above

9. Synthetic fibre and plastic manufacturing is an example of which one of the following? **CBSE 2024**

(a) Mineral-based industry (b) Chemical-based industry
(c) Forest-based industry (d) Animal-based industry

10. A large factory producing steel tools and machinery is located near a source of iron ore. It uses advanced technology and has a significant workforce. Which of the following is the primary reason for the factory's location?

(a) Access to a large consumer market
(b) Proximity to raw materials
(c) Availability of skilled labour
(d) Government incentives

11. Which type of industry fits the following description?

It is produced in small quantities. It is not dependent on any specific raw material. It employs a small workforce and is generally not polluting.

Options

(a) Agro-based Industry (b) Cottage Industry
(c) Footloose Industry (d) Mineral-based Industry

12. Modern manufacturing is distinguished by

(i) Complex technology (ii) Division of labour
(iii) Specialisation
(iv) Small capital investment

Codes

(a) (i) and (ii) (b) (ii), (iii) and (iv)
(c) (i), (ii) and (iii) (d) (i), (iii) and (iv)

13. Consider the following statements and choose the correct option.

(i) Modern industries require specialisation in skills.
(ii) Research and development strategies have an important role in modern industries.

Codes

(a) Only (i) (b) Only (ii)
(c) Both (i) and (ii) (d) None of these

14. Read the following features of cottage manufacturing and choose the correct option . **CBSE 2023**

(i) Place of manufacturing outside the home.
(ii) It is the smallest unit of manufacturing.
(iii) Use local raw materials.
(iv) Simple tools are used.

Codes

(a) Only (i), (ii) and (iii) are correct
(b) Only (ii), (iii) and (iv) are correct
(c) Only (i), (ii), (iv) are correct
(d) Only (i), (iii) and (iv) are correct

Match the Following

15.

List I (Industry Type)	List II (Raw Material)
A. Agro-based Industries	1. Iron Ore
B. Mineral-based Industries	2. Cotton
C. Chemical-based Industries	3. Petroleum
D Forest-based Industries	4. Timber

Codes

	A	B	C	D		A	B	C	D
(a)	2	1	3	4	(b)	4	2	1	3
(c)	1	3	2	4	(d)	3	1	4	2

16.

List I (Industry)	List II (Example)
A. Agro-based	1. Soaps
B. Forest-based	2. Salts
C. Chemical-based	3. Lac
D Product-based	4. Vegetable oil

Codes

	A	B	C	D		A	B	C	D
(a)	3	4	2	1	(b)	3	4	1	2
(c)	4	3	2	1	(d)	4	3	1	2

Assertion-Reason

Directions (Q. Nos. 17-19) In the questions given below are two statements labelled as Assertion (A) and other is labelled as Reason (R). In the context of two statements, which one of the following is correct?

Codes

(a) Both A and R are true, but R is not the correct explanation of A

(b) Both A and R are true and R is the correct explanation of A

(c) Both A and R are incorrect

(d) A is correct, but R is incorrect

17. **Assertion** (A) Footloose industries can be located in a wide variety of places.

Reason (R) The important factor in the location of foot loose industries is accessibility by transport network. **CBSE 2024**

18. **Assertion (A) Many Industries benefit from nearness to a leader industry.**

Reason (R) Linkages between industries increases savings and profits for all the industries.

19. **Assertion (A) Mechanisation in manufacturing industries increases production efficiency.**

Reason (R) Mechanisation reduces the need for raw materials in production.

Answers

1. (b) Secondary
2. (d) automation
3. (d) agglomeration economies
4. (b) To transform raw materials into higher-value finished goods
5. (a) simple power-driven machines
6. (c) Silicon valley
7. (b) Iron industry
8. (d) All of the above
9. (b) Chemical-based industry
10. (b) Proximity to raw materials
11. (c) Footloose Industry
12. (c) (i), (ii) and (iii)
13. (c) Both (i) and (ii)
14. (b) Only (ii), (iii) and (iv) are correct
15. (a)
16. (d)
17. (b) Both A and R are true, but R is the correct explanation of A
18. (b) Both A and R are true and R is the correct explanation of A
19. (d) A is correct, but R is incorrect

Subjective Questions

Short Answer Type Questions

1. Secondary activities add value to natural resources. Justify with three examples. Competency Based Que, CBSE Diksha

Ans. Secondary activities add value to the natural resources by transforming raw materials into valuable products.

The three examples are as follows

(i) Cotton boll has limited use but after transforming into yarn, it becomes more valuable and can be used for making clothes.

(ii) Iron-ore cannot be used directly from the mines but after being converted into steel, it can be used for making many valuable machines, tools, etc.

(iii) Materials from the farms, forest products and resources of the sea can be put into greater use by secondary activities.

2. Explain the process of mechanisation in modern large scale manufacturing industry in three points.

Ans. The process of mechanisation in modern large scale manufacturing industries are as follows

(i) Mechanisation refers to using gadgets to accomplish tasks. For example, powerlooms in textile has led to higher production levels.

(ii) The advanced stage of mechanisation is automation that refers to completion of tasks without the aid of humans thinking during the manufacturing process.

(iii) There are automatic factories with feedback and closed loop computer control systems where machines are developed to think. These kinds of mechanised processing units have sprung up all over the world.

3. How manufacturing industries impacts the economic development of a country?

Ans. Manufacturing industries have played a major role in the economic development of countries. It is very important for the economic development of a region due to following reasons

- Manufacturing industries process the raw material into useful goods and products essential for consumption in a country.
- It adds value to a product and improves its quality that is essential for creating diversified products.
- Manufacturing sector creates jobs and provides employment to the people.
- Other industries such as service industry is also dependent upon the manufacturing sector.
- Urbanisation and social development of a region are also supported by the manufacturing sector.

4. Why are modern manufacturing industries concentrated in few places in the world?

Ans. Modern manufacturing industries are concentrated in a few places in the world because of the following reasons

(i) **Raw Material** Modern industries require large quantities of raw material. Industries are mainly located near mines, farms and seas. For example, jute mills in West Bengal, cotton textile in Maharashtra, etc.

(ii) **Power Resources** The main sources of power are coal, oil and hydro-power that are not evenly distributed. For instance, iron and steel industries get coal from Jharia and Raniganj coal-field.

(iii) **Means of Transport** The modern industries require cheap, developed and quick means of transport. For example, the world's great industrial region is situated at the end of North Atlantic Ocean route. Great lakes in USA provide cheap transport to the industrial centres.

5. Distance is the most important factor in determining the location of industries. Why? Competency Based Que

Ans. Distance is the most important factor in determining the location of industries because

- Access to market for the products of industry depends upon the distance between the location of industry and the nearby market.
- Distance between the site of raw material and industry influences the location of industry.
- Heavy industries depend upon power sources. Hence, they are located close to the sources of power.
- Efficient transportation system, which can travel large distances in short time is essential for the development of industries.

6. How does access to market affect the location of industries?

Ans. The existence of a market for manufactured goods is the most important factor in the location of industries in the following ways

- Remote areas inhabited by a few people offer small markets.
- The developed regions of Europe, North America, Japan and Australia provide large global markets as the purchasing power of the people is very high.

- The densely populated regions of South and South-East Asia also provide large markets.
- Some industries, like aircraft manufacturing and arms manufacturing also have global markets.

7. What are the basis on which industries are classified? Give examples.

Ans. Industries are classified on various basis. These are

- **On the Basis of Size** On this basis, industries are classified as cottage or household industries, small scale industries and large-scale industries. The size is determined by capital, number of workers and volume of production.
- **On the Basis of Inputs/Raw Materials** On this basis, industries are agro-based industries, chemicals-based industries, mineral-based industries, etc. The nature of input determines their operations.
- **Industries Based on Output/Product** On this basis, industries are classified as basic industries and consumer goods/non basic industries.
- **On the Basis of Ownership** On this basis, industries are classified into public sector, private sector and joint sector industries.

8. 'Aman weaving a bamboo basket by the roadside in Arunachal Pradesh. Which kind of industry is he running? Examine its features. Competency Based Que

Ans. Aman is running a household industry. Household industries are the smallest and simplest type of industries. In these industries, the artisans with local raw materials and simple tools produce everyday goods.

The characteristics of these industries are

- The work in these industries is done at home with the help of family members or with part-time labour. They manufacture daily use products.
- There is not much requirement of capital in these industries. There is not much requirement of a transportation system as products are created locally and it has low commercial significance.
- The finished products of this industry may be for local consumption in the same household or village or local markets.

9. 'Industries of the world are classified on the basis of ownership'. Discuss the types and features of each type.

Ans. On the basis of ownership, the industries of the world can be classified into three groups

(i) **Public Sector Industries** In this sector, government has the main authority to own and manage these industries. For example, India has many Public Sector Undertakings (PSUs). In socialist countries, these industries are directly owned and managed by the state.

(ii) **Private Sector Industries** Individual investors and private organisations have the authority to own and manage industries. In capitalist countries, industries are generally owned privately.

(iii) **Joint Sector Industries** These industries are managed by joint stock companies or sometimes the private and public sectors together establish and manage these industries.

10. Small-scale industries provides employment and raises local purchasing power. Comment. Competency Based Que

Ans. Small-scale industries are extended form of cottage industry. But the methods used in small-scale industry are different from those of cottage industry. It is characterised by the use of local raw materials, simple power-driven machines and semi-skilled labour.

Small-scale industries also contribute to the manufacturing and industrial output of a country. They contribute to the industrial exports and provide a base for the large-scale industries. They have flexibilities in operations and small market. There is more use of domestic resource in a productive manner.

This industry raises employment and increases the purchasing capacity of local people. Developing countries like India, China, Brazil, etc depend upon the small-scale industries to generate employment for their large population.

11. Technological innovations an important aspect of modern manufacturing industries. Explain any three aspects in this regard. Competency Based Que

Ans. Technological innovations through research and development strategies are an important aspect of modern manufacturing for quality control, eliminating waste and inefficiency and combating pollution.

Three aspects of modern manufacturing industries are

(i) Complex machine technology is needed so that high quality goods are produced at less time.

(ii) It requires vast capital so that machines with latest technology can be used in manufacturing.

(iii) Extreme specialisation and division of labour is required, that can work efficiently on the machines.

12. Give the meaning of high-tech industry. State any two characteristics of this industry.

Or **Explain the concept of 'High Technology Industry' with examples.**

Or **Explain the main features of 'High Tech' industries in the world.** CBSE 2025

Ans. High technology industry or high-tech industry is the latest generation of manufacturing activities. It involves the application of intensive Research and Development

(R and D) efforts leading to the manufacturing of products of an advanced scientific and engineering character.

Robotics on the assembly line, Computer-Aided Design (CAD) and manufacturing, electronic controls of smelting and refining processes, and the constant development of new chemical and pharmaceutical products are notable examples of a high-tech industry.

Characteristics of high-tech industry are as follows

(i) Professional (white collar) workers mak-up a large share of the total workforce and greatly outnumber the actual production (blue collar) workers.

(ii) These industries have neatly spaced, low, modern, dispersed, office-plant-lab buildings rather than massive assembly structures.

13. Distinguish between cottage industry and small-scale industry.

Ans. The differences between cottage industry and small-scale industry are

Cottage Industry	Small-Scale Industry
It is the smallest manufacturing unit where work is done at home by family members or part-time labour, e.g., artisans producing handicrafts.	It is generally bigger than cottage industries and employs semi-skilled labour. It is set up outside the cottage e.g., a small workshop.
It uses local raw materials and simple tools.	The raw material may be locally obtained, which are processed with simple power-driven machines.
Finished products may be for consumption in the household or to sell in the local village market.	Finished products are for local markets.
It has low commerical significance.	It provides employment to large number of people and raises local purchasing power.

14. Explain any five characteristics of 'large-scale manufacturing' in the world.

Or **Analyse the main characteristics of large scale manufacturing industries in the world.** **CBSE 2024 C**

Or **Explain the main features of large scale manufacturing industries in the world.** **CBSE 2025**

Ans. The characteristics of modern large-scale manufacturing industries are as follows

(i) Modern large scale industrial processes consist of multiple complex activities to run the industries.

(ii) The specialised and skilled labour is required in the modern manufacturing industries. Thus, skilled manpower is employed.

(iii) These industries widely use huge power to run the heavy machines in the production process.

(iv) For the quality control, special measures are taken in these type of industries.

(v) The main features in large-scale manufacturing is the specialisation in production.

(vi) Products of large-scale industries are sold in local as well as international markets.

15. What are the traditional large-scale industrial regions? Give any two characteristics of them.

Ans. Traditional large-scale industrial regions are associated with heavy industries like metal smelting, heavy engineering, chemical manufacturing and textile production. They are usually located near coalfields. These are also called smokestack industries because they are the most polluting industries.

The two characteristics of these industries are as follows

(i) The large labour force is engaged in production. It is also characterised by crowded and low-quality poor houses. The environment is unpleasant and full of pollution, waste disposal, etc.

(ii) Large unemployment and high out-migration are the present situation in these regions because of the closure of factories due to a worldwide fall in demand.

16. Examine any five characteristics of footloose industries in the world.

Ans. Footloose industries are those industries that can be located at a wide variety of places and are not dependent on any specific raw material. The characteristics of these type of industries are

(i) These industries require a smaller plant size as compared to heavy and small industries.

(ii) It needs skilled workers as the industrial process is advanced. The labour force is small and production is in small quantities.

(iii) These are environment-friendly industries and do not create any pollution.

(iv) These industries produce goods that are high in value but smaller in size, so, transport cost is negligible and products are transported by road networks.

(v) The do not require specialised raw materials. The raw material of these industries can be obtained at any place.

17. Differentiate between agro-based industries and mineral-based industries in the world.

Ans. The differences between agro-based industries and mineral-based industries are as follows

Agro-based Industries	Mineral-based Industries
Agro-based industries use plant and animal based products as their raw materials.	These industries use mineral ores as their raw materials.
These industries do not involve large investment.	These industries involve large investment and are capital intensive units.
These industries are a source of employment for rural people.	These industries are a source of employment for both rural as well as urban population.
The raw materials of these industries are fruits, vegetables, dairy products and so on.	The raw materials of these industries are different types of minerals such as iron-ore, aluminium, mica and so on.
Examples of these industries are dairy industry, cotton textile industry, jute textile industry, food processing industry and so on.	Examples of these industries are iron and steel industry, heavy machinery, ship building, machine tools, engineering industries and so on.

Long Answer Type Questions

1. Examine any five factors that influence the location of industries in the world. **CBSE Diksha**

Or **Explain five factors that influence the industrial location in the world.**

Or **Describe any five factors influencing industrial location in the world.**

Or **Analyse five main factors affecting location of industries in the world.** **CBSE 2023**

Ans. The five factors influencing the industrial location in the world are as follows

(i) **Access to Market** Market is a place where people, who have demand for goods and the ability to purchase, buy from the sellers, selling their goods at that place. Market affects the location of an industry. A manufacturing unit is established near the market area. Areas having more population are big markets for manufactured goods, as compared to areas having less population. Apart from it, areas having population with more purchasing power form big markets.

(ii) **Access to Raw Material** Industries that use heavy, bulky and weight-losing raw material are established near the source of raw material. For example, in sugar industries, sugarcane is a perishable and weight-losing raw material. To reduce the transport cost, industries are located near the source of raw material.

(iii) **Access to Sources of Energy** Industries using more power and energy are established near the source of energy. For example, aluminum industry.

(iv) **Access to Transportation and Communication** Industries are located in areas that have efficient transport network to get raw material from various regions and supply manufactured goods to market. Communication network is also needed to communicate ideas. Thus, transport and communication are important factors that affect the location of an industry.

(v) **Government Policies** Favourable government policies that promote industrialisation is also important in deciding the location of an industry.

2. Assess the factors that contributed to the development of large-scale industries all over the world. **CBSE SQP 2024**

Ans. Large-scale industries developed globally due to several key factors

- **Abundance of Raw Materials** The availability of natural resources, such as coal, iron, and cotton, played a crucial role. For example, Britain's coal reserves supported its industrial revolution.
- **Technological Advancements** Innovations like the steam engine and mechanised tools allowed industries to produce goods faster and more efficiently. This made large-scale production possible.
- **Improved Transportation** The construction of railways, ports, and canals made it easier to move raw materials to factories and finished goods to markets. This boosted trade and industrial growth.
- **Urbanisation** The growth of cities provided a steady labour force for industries, as many people migrated from rural areas in search of better job opportunities.
- **Capital Investment** Wealthy entrepreneurs and financial institutions provided the funds needed to build factories, purchase machinery, and expand production.
- **Growing Markets** Rising populations and expanding trade networks created high demand for industrial products like textiles, steel, and machinery.
- **Government Support** Policies like subsidies, protective tariffs, and infrastructure development encouraged industrialisation in many countries.

3. 'Access to transportation and communication facilities are essential for the development of industries.' Justify the statement with suitable example. CBSE SQP 2024

Ans. Access to transportation and communication facilities is essential for the development of industries as they ensure the smooth movement of raw materials, goods, and information.

Transportation systems play an essential role by reducing costs and saving time. Industries depend on efficient transport to carry raw materials to factories and move finished goods to markets. For instance, highly developed transportation networks in regions like Western Europe and Eastern North America have led to the concentration of industries in these areas. Improved transportation facilitates regional specialisation and integrated economic growth, making it a key factor in industrial location.

Communication is equally important for the exchange and management of information within industries. Effective communication systems enable industries to coordinate operations, manage supply chains, and make informed decisions. For example, modern industries rely on advanced technologies like computer-aided systems to enhance productivity.

Without reliable transportation, raw materials cannot reach factories efficiently, and finished goods cannot reach consumers. Similarly, without effective communication, industries face challenges in management and market connectivity. Therefore, transportation and communication facilities work together to support industrial growth and ensure the smooth functioning of industries.

4. Classify manufacturing industries on the basis of size into three categories and explain the important characteristics of each type.

Ans. On the basis of their size, industries are classified into the following three categories

(i) **Cottage Manufacturing Industries**
- It is the smallest manufacturing unit.
- The artisans use local raw materials.
- Part-time labour or artisan's family members produce everyday goods in their homes with the help of simple tools.
- Finished goods may be used for consumption in the same household or for sale in the local market.

(ii) **Small-scale Manufacturing**

For the characteristics of small-scale manufacturing industries, refer to Pg. 74 under the heading Small-Scale Manufacturing.

(iii) **Large-scale Manufacturing Industries**
- It needs enormous energy and various raw materials.
- It also requires specialised workers, advanced technology, assembly-line mass production and huge capital.
- It requires a large market.

5. Define the term manufacturing. Explain any four features of small-scale manufacturing.

Ans. Manufacturing refers to the conversion of raw materials into finished goods through the application of power. Manufacturing can be modern, which include modern forms of power and machinery or it can be primitive.

Four features of small-scale manufacturing are *(Any four)*

(i) Small-scale manufacturing units are characterised by production at a smaller scale such as in a workshop outside the home or cottage of the producer.

(ii) These industries use raw materials which are obtained from local sources. Production takes place with the help of simple power-driven machines and semi-skilled labour.

(iii) They do not require large capital investments to setup and operate. The level of technology used is very low and the production is meant for local or regional markets.

(iv) These industries are mainly located in the developing countries where they provide local employment and raises the purchasing power of people.

(v) Small-scale manufacturing also contribute to the manufacturing and industrial output of a country. These contribute to the industrial exports and provide a base for the large-scale industries. They have flexibilities in operations and small markets. There is more use of domestic resources in a productive manner.

6. Classify the industries on the basis of inputs/raw materials.

Ans. On the basis of inputs or raw materials, industries are classified as

- **Agro-based Industries** These industries involves the processing of raw materials of the products which are obtained from agricultural farms and fields. The finished products are sold in the rural and urban markets. These industries include food processing, sugar, pickles, fruit juices, spices, textiles, etc.

- **Minerals-based Industries** Minerals are used as raw materials in these industries. These include ferrous metallic minerals such as iron and steel industry, non-ferrous metallic minerals such as aluminium, copper, gold, etc and non-metallic minerals based industries like cement industry.
- **Chemical-based Industries** These industries use natural chemical minerals. These include petroleum, salt, sulphur, potash, plastic industries. They also use raw materials obtained from wood and coal.
- **Forest-based Industries** These industries use major and minor forest products such as wood, timber, etc. These raw materials are used for making furnitures, papers, lacs, etc.
- **Animal-based Industries** These industries are based on the products obtained from animals. These include leather industry, woollen, textile industry, etc.

7. Distinguish between cottage and large-scale industries.

or **How are large scale industries different from cottage industries? Explain.** **CBSE Term II 2022**

or **Explain the difference between cottage and large-scale industries in the world, with examples.** **CBSE 2024**

Ans. The differences between cottage and large-scale industries are as follows

Cottage Industries	Large-scale Industries
These are small-scale operations, often run from home or small workshops. An example of cottage industries includes **weaving, jewellery, pottery, etc.**	These are large manufacturing units. These industries cater to national and international markets. An example of large-scale industries includes **automobile manufacturing, Telecommunication, Information technology, iron and steel etc.**
They generally require minimal capital investment and use basic, manual tools. For example, **pottery making** or **carpentry.**	These industries require significant capital investment and use high-tech machinery. For example, industries like **steel manufacturing and Information Technology** require massive investment in machinery and infrastructure.
The labour force in cottage industries is small, often family-based or using part-time labour.	These industries employ a large number of workers, often skilled labourers and technicians.

8. Distinguish between large-scale industries and small-scale industries by stating five points of each.

Or **Differentiate between 'small-scale manufacturing' and 'large-scale manufacturing' in the world.**

Ans. The differences between large-scale manufacturing industry and small-scale manufacturing industry are as follows

Small-scale Manufacturing Industry	Large-scale Manufacturing Industry
This type of manufacturing has smaller operations such as a workshop.	In large-scale manufacturing, operations are on a large scale like large factories.
It is characterised by low capital investment and simple technology.	It requires very high capital investments and advanced technology.
It uses local raw materials, simple power-driven machines and semi-skilled labour.	Raw materials may be local or imported but there is large use of energy for assembly-line mass production and specialised workers.
The production is consumed in local or regional markets.	The production is for export purposes in the international markets.
They are located mainly in developing countries.	They are located in both developing and developed countries.
Examples include disposable crockery, handbags, spices industry, etc.	Examples include iron and steel, cement industry, automotive industry, etc.

Source Based Questions

1. Read the passage carefully and answer the questions that follow.

High technology, or simply high-tech, is the latest generation of manufacturing activities. It is best understood as the application of intensive Research and Development (R and D) efforts leading to the manufacture of products of an advanced scientific and engineering character. Professional (white collar) workers make up a large share of the total workforce. These highly skilled specialists greatly outnumber the actual production (blue collar) workers. Robotics on the assembly line, Computer -Aided Design (CAD) and manufacturing, electronic controls of smelting and refining processes, and the constant development of new chemical and pharmaceutical products are notable examples of a high-tech industry. Neatly spaced, low, modern, dispersed, office-plant-lab buildings rather than massive assembly structures, factories and storage areas mark the high-tech industrial landscape. Planned business parks for high-tech start-ups have become part of regional and local development schemes. High-tech industries which are regionally concentrated, self-sustained and highly specialised are called technopolies. The Silicon Valley near San Francisco and Silicon Forest near Seattle are examples of technopolies.

(i) Which of the following is a feature of high-tech industry?

(a) Research and Development (b) Skilled specialists
(c) Massive assembly lines (d) All of these

Ans. (d) All of these

(ii) Professional workers contributes maximum to the high-tech industry. By which other name these workers are known?

(a) Blue collar workers (b) White collar workers
(c) Grey collar workers (d) Red collar workers

Ans. (b) White collar workers

(iii) Highly specialised and localised high-tech industries are known as

(a) Metropolis (b) Technopolis
(c) Megalopolis (d) Necropolis

Ans. (b) Technopolis

2. Read the passage carefully and answer the question that follows.

The existence of a market for manufactured goods is the most important factor in the location of industries. 'Market' means people who have a demand for these goods and also have the purchasing power (ability to purchase) to be able to purchase from the sellers at a place. Remote areas inhabited by a few people offer small markets. The developed regions of Europe, North America, Japan and Australia provide large global markets as the purchasing power of the people is very high. The densely populated regions of South and South-East Asia also provide large markets. Some industries, such as aircraft manufacturing, have a global market. The arms industry also has global markets.

Labour supply is an important factor in the location of industries. Some types of manufacturing still require skilled labour. Increasing mechanisation, automation and flexibility of industrial processes have reduced the dependence of industry upon the labours. Speedy and efficient transport facilities to carry raw materials to the factory and to move finished goods to the market are essential for the development of industries. The cost of transport plays an important role in the location of industrial units. Western Europe and Eastern-North America have a highly developed transport system which has always induced the concentration of industries in these areas. Modern industry is inseparably tied to transportation systems. Improvements in transportation led to integrated economic development and regional specialisation of manufacturing.

(i) Why are markets important for industries?

Ans. Markets are important for industries because industries manufacture goods and commodities and search for people who have demand for these products. Markets provide such locations where people who have a demand for these goods and also have the purchasing power (ability to purchase), to be able to purchase from the sellers at a place.

(ii) Which industries have a global market?

Ans. Industries such as aircraft manufacturing, arms industry and basic industries (e.g., iron and steel) have a global market.

(iii) Which reasons are responsible that have reduced the dependence of industries upon the labours?

Ans. Following reasons are responsible that have reduced the dependence of industries upon the labours such as

- Increasing mechanisation
- Automation and flexibility of industrial processes

SELF ASSESSMENT TEST

Objective Type Questions

1. Which of the following is not a secondary economic activity?
   (a) Mining
   (b) Manufacturing
   (c) Timber processing
   (d) All of these
2. Which of the following factors promote large-scale manufacturing?
   (a) Large use of energy
   (b) Advance technology
   (c) Assembly lines
   (d) All of these
3. .... is a type of consumer goods industry.
   (a) Iron industry
   (b) Bread and biscuit industry
   (c) Cement industry
   (d) Cotton textile industry
4. Which of the following is not a characteristic of modern large-scale manufacturing?
   (a) Extreme specialisation
   (b) High dependence on labour
   (c) Vast capital investment
   (d) Use of advanced technology
5. Which of the following are the characteristics of the agri-business farm?
   (i) Farms are mechanised and large in size.
   (ii) It is commercial farming on an industrial scale often financed by a business whose main interest lies outside agriculture.
   (iii) Reliant on chemicals.

   Codes
   (a) (i) and (ii)
   (b) (ii) and (iii)
   (c) (i) and (iii)
   (d) All of these

Short Answer Type Questions

6. Explain the difference between metallic and non-metallic industries.
7. 'Basic goods industries and consumer goods industries differs from one another'. Comment.
8. Discuss any four features of small scale manufacturing industries.
9. 'Automation is the advanced stage of mechanisation'. Justify the statement.

Long Answer Type Questions

10. Aluminium industries are located near the source of energy. Explain why?
11. 'Household industries has low commercial significance'. Justify the statement.

CHAPTER 6

Tertiary activities provide services like healthcare and education, while quaternary activities focus on knowledge-based services like research and consulting.

YOUR STUDY GOALS

6.1 Tertiary Activities
6.2 Quaternary Activities

YOUR PRACTICE GOALS

- Objective Type Questions (25 Qs ; MCQs, Statements, Matching, A-R)
- Subjective Questions (13 SAs, 7 LAs)
- Source Based Questions (5 Qs)

Tertiary and Quaternary Activities

6.1 Tertiary Activities

- Tertiary activities include both **production** and **exchange**. These activities produce services. They do not include direct processing of raw material into physical goods.
- Production involves the 'provision' of **services** that are **'consumed'**.
- Exchange involves trade, transport and communication facilities that are used to overcome distance.
- In a developed economy, the majority of the population is employed under tertiary activities.

Types of Tertiary Activities

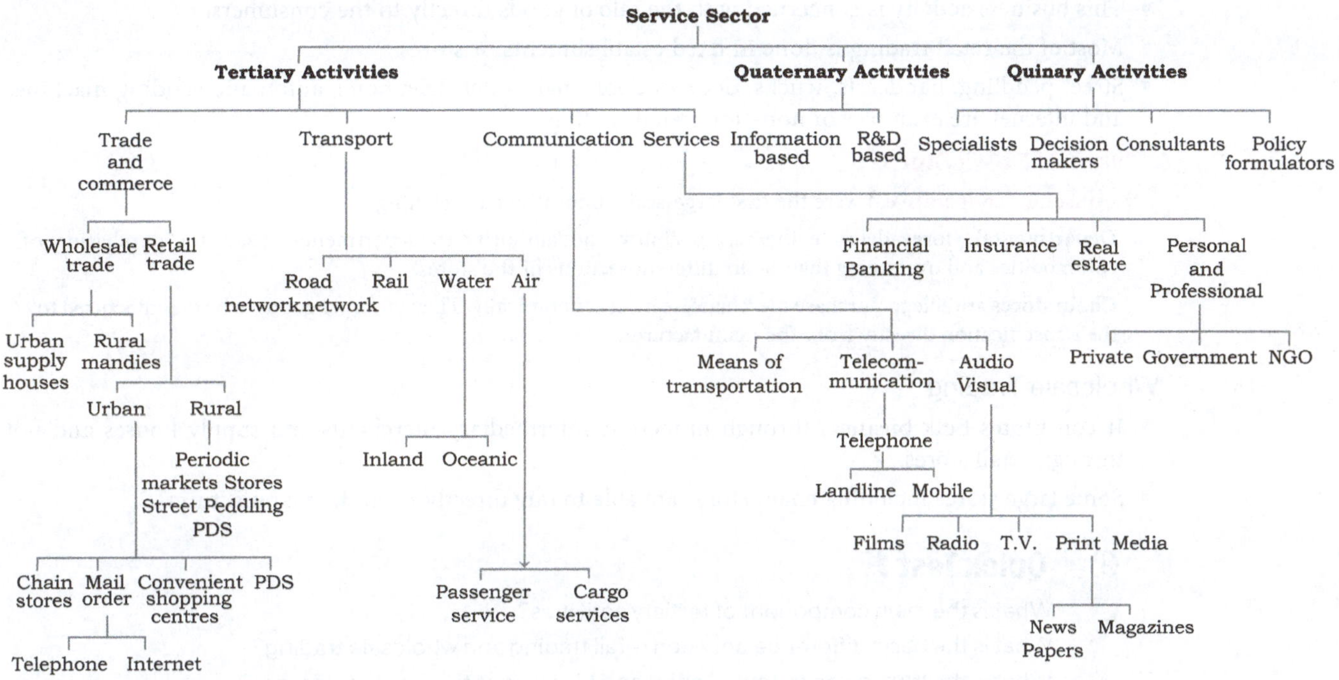

Trade and Commerce

- Trade refers to the **buying** and **selling** of items produced elsewhere. **Retail** and **wholesale** trading is specifically done to gain profit.
- The towns and cities where trade and commerce activities take place are known as **trading centres.**

Trading centres can be divided into the following types

Rural Marketing Centres

- These centres provide services to nearby settlements.
- These are quasi-urban and act as traditional trading centres. Personal and professional services are not well-developed here.
- These centres may include *mandis* (wholesale markets) and retailing areas.
- These centres provide the goods and services which are demanded by the rural population regularly.

Periodic Markets

- Such markets are found in rural areas where there is no regular markets.
- The periodic markets are organised at different temporal intervals. These may be weekly or bi-weekly to fulfil the demands of people.
- There is no permanent structure of shops hence, shopkeepers remain busy on all days while a large area is served by them.

Urban Marketing Centres

- They have more specialised urban services.
- They provide both common and specialised goods and services.
- They develop specialised markets for labour, housing and semi or finished goods.
- Services of teachers, lawyers, consultants, physicians, dentists and veterinary doctors are available.

Retail Trading

- This business activity is concerned with the sale of goods directly to the consumers.
- Most of the retail trading is done in fixed establishments or stores.
- Street peddling, handcarts, trucks, door-to-door, mail order, telephone, automatic vending machines and internet are examples of non-store retail trading.

Types of Retail Stores

- Consumer cooperatives[1] were the first large-scale innovations in retailing.
- **Departmental stores** delegate the responsibility and authority to departmental heads for purchasing of commodities and overseeing the sale in different sections of the stores.
- **Chain stores** are able to purchase merchandise most economically. They often get goods to be manufactured to their specification directly from the manufacturer.

Wholesale Trading

- It constitutes bulk business through numerous intermediary merchants and supply houses and not through retail stores.
- Some large stores including chain stores are able to buy directly from the manufacturers.

Quick Test 1

1. What is the main component of tertiary activities?
2. What is the basic difference between retail trading and wholesale trading?
3. What is the term given to towns, cities and big villages that carry out trades?
4. Name two types of non-store retail trading.

Transport

- Transport is a service or facility by which people, materials and manufactured goods are physically carried from one location to another.
- Modern society requires a speedy and efficient transport system to support the production, distribution and consumption of goods.
- Transport distance can be measured as actual distance by route length (**km distance**) or the time taken to travel (**time distance**) and expense of travelling (**cost distance**).
- Isochrone lines are drawn on a map to join places equal in terms of the time taken to reach them.

Factors Affecting Transport

- **Demand for Transport** It is influenced by the size of the population. A huge population will demand more transport services.
- **Transport Routes** It affects the connectivity among cities, towns, villages, industrial centers.

Network and Accessibility

- As transportation grows, different places connect to make a network. A network is like a web of paths linking places together.
- In a network, a **node** is where two or more paths meet, like a starting point, ending point, or a big town along the way.
- Every road that connects two nodes is called a **link**. When a network has lots of links, it means places are well-connected, making it easier to travel from one place to another.

---

1 Consumer co-operatives These are retail establishments that are organised and operated by the consumers themselves to obtain products of daily use at reasonably low prices.

Communication

- Communication services involve the transmission of **words** and **messages**, **facts** and **ideas**.
- All forms of transport can transfer messages, for example, boats, roads, rail and air. Therefore, these forms of transport are also referred to as **lines of communication**.
- Technologies like mobile telephony and satellites have made communications independent of transport.

Forms of Communication Services

Telecommunications

- It is linked to the development of modern technology. It revolutionised the communication system by reducing the time taken to send a message.
- It provides direct and instant connection anywhere in the world within seconds.
- The recent advancements like **mobile telephony** have made communications direct and instant, and provide communication at any time and from anywhere.
- **Radio, newspaper** and **television** spread news, pictures, and audio to vast audiences, hence termed mass media[2].
- Satellite communication relays information from the Earth and space.
- The **internet** is the most revolutionary development in global communication.

Services

- Services are provided to individual consumers who can afford to pay for them. For example, the gardener, the launderers and the barber do primarily physical labour. Teachers, lawyers, physicians, musicians and others perform mental labour.
- Services occur at many different levels. Some of the services are provided to industry, some to people and some to both industry and people. For example, the transport systems.
- **Low-order services**, such as grocery shops and laundries, are more widespread than **high-order services** or more specialised ones like accountants, consultants and physicians.
- State and union legislation have established corporations to supervise and control the marketing of transport, telecommunication, energy and water supply services.
- Services can be classified in two forms as follows
  (i) **Professional Services** The services such as primary health care, engineering, law and management are examples of professional services.
  (ii) **Personal Services** Such services are made available to the people to facilitate their work in daily life.

Unorganised Workers

- These workers migrate from rural to urban areas in search of employment.
- Most of these workers are unskilled. They are employed in domestic services as housekeepers, cooks and gardeners.

Tourism: An Example of a Tertiary Activity

- Tourism is travel undertaken for purposes of **recreation** rather than business. It has become the world's single largest tertiary activity in total registered jobs (250 million) and total revenue (40 per cent of the total GDP).
- Tourism employs many local people. They provide services like accommodation, meals, transport and entertainment.

---

2 Mass media It is a form of communication that reaches a large number of people, such as newspapers, radio, television, or the Internet.

- Tourism leads to the development of infrastructure industries, retail trading, and craft industries (souvenirs).
- In some regions, tourism is seasonal because the vacation period is dependent on favourable weather conditions, but many regions attract visitors all year round.

Tourist Attraction

- **Climate** People have specific climatic requirements, either higher temperatures than their homelands or snow cover suitable for skiing. Most people from colder regions choose warm, sunny weather for beach holidays. This is one of the main reasons for the importance of tourism in Southern Europe and the **Mediterranean lands.**
- **Landscape** People like to spend their holidays in an attractive environment. Hence, they choose mountains, lakes, spectacular sea coasts and landscapes.
- **History and Art** The history and art of an area have potential attractiveness. People visit ancient or picturesque towns and archaeological sites and enjoy exploring castles, palaces and churches.
- **Culture and Economy** These attract tourists who love to experience ethnic and local customs.
- **Cost of travel** If a region provides for the needs of tourists cheaply, it is likely to become very popular. Home-stay has emerged as a profitable business such as heritage homes in Goa, Madikeri and Coorg in Karnataka.

Medical Services for Overseas Patients in India

- About 55,000 patients from the U.S.A. visited India in 2005 for treatment. India has emerged as the leading country of medical tourism worldwide.
- World-class hospitals located in metropolitan cities cater to patients all over the world.
- Medical tourism brings abundant benefits to developing countries like India, Thailand, Singapore and Malaysia.
- Hospitals in India, Switzerland and Australia have been performing certain medical services from reading radiology images to interpreting Magnetic Resonance Images (MRIs) and ultrasound tests.

People Engaged in Tertiary Activities

- Today, services are provided in all societies. But in more developed countries, a higher percentage of workers is employed in providing services as compared to less developed countries.
- The trend in employment in this sector has been increasing while it has remained unchanged or decreasing in the primary and secondary activities.

Quick Test 2

1. What is Isochrone line?
2. Name a factor that influences the demand for transport.
3. What is line of communication?
4. Name the most revolutionary development in global communication.

6.2 Quaternary Activities

- Quaternary activities include research and development and an advanced form of services involving **specialised knowledge** and **technical skills.**
- Some examples of quaternary activities include the collection, production and dissemination of information or even the production of information.

- In developed economies, most of the workers are in the '**Knowledge Sector**'.
- Personnel working in office buildings, elementary schools and university classrooms, hospitals and doctors' offices, theatres, accounting and brokerage firms, all belong to quaternary activities.

Quinary Activities

- These services focus on the creation, re-arrangement and interpretation of new and existing ideas; data interpretation and the use and evaluation of new technologies.
- The highest level of decision makers or policy makers perform quinary activities.
- Workers involved in quinary activities are referred to as 'gold collar' professionals. They have the special and highly paid skills of senior business executives, government officials, research scientists, financial and legal consultants, etc.

Outsourcing

- Outsourcing or contracting out is giving work to an outside agency to improve efficiency and reduce costs.
- Outsourcing is emerging in those countries where cheap and skilled workers are available.
- **Knowledge Processing Outsourcing** (KPO) and '**home shoring**' are new trends in quinary activities.
- It has created new jobs in countries like India, China, Eastern Europe, Israel, the Philippines and Costa Rica. These are also outmigrating countries.
- The KPO industry is distinct from **Business Process Outsourcing** (BPO) as it involves highly skilled workers. It is information-driven knowledge outsourcing.
- KPO enables companies to create additional business opportunities. For example, KPOs include research and development (R and D) activities, e-learning, business research, intellectual property (IP) research, the legal profession and the banking sector.

The Digital Divide

- There are wide-ranging economic, political and social differences among countries. While developed countries in general have moved forward, developing countries are behind and this is known as the **digital divide**.
- Similarly, digital divides exist within countries. For example, in a large country like India or Russia, certain areas like metropolitan centres have better connectivity and access to the digital world as compared to rural areas.

Quick Test 3

1. In which terms distance can be measured in transportation activity?
2. Name two specialised services provided by countries to its medical tourists.
3. Give an example of quaternary activity.
4. What is the term used for uneven development of the IT industry in developed and developing countries?

Mind Map

Communication
Involves transmission of words messages, facts and ideas.

Personal Communication
- Telephone
- Telegraph
- Mobiles

Mass-Communication
- Mass media, newspaper, internet.
- Radio
- TV

Transport
Service by which people and goods are carried. Transport distance can be measured as
- Km distance (actual distance)
- Time distance (time taken to travel)
- Cost distance (expense of travelling)

Tertiary Activities
Includes both production and exchange.

1

Trade and Commerce
- It involves buying and selling of items.
- Towns and cities where trade and commerce takes place is known as trading centres such as
  - Rural marketing centres
  - Periodic markets
  - Urban marketing centres

Wholesale Trading
- Constitutes bulk business through numerous intermediary merchants and supply houses.

Retail Trading
- Sales of goods directly to the consumers, e.g., departmental stores.

Services
Occurs at many different levels

Types of Services
- **Law Order** It involves grocery, shops and laundries.
- **High Order** It involves accountant and physician.
- **Professional services** It involves Engineering, Law, Management.
- **Personal Services** Workers migrating from rural areas for employment.

TERTIARY AND QUATERNARY ACTIVITIES

2 Tourism: An Example of a Tertiary Activity
- Undertaken for purposes of recreation rather than business.
- It provides services like accommodation, meals, transport.

3 People Engaged in Tertiary Activities
Employment in this sector has been increasing while it has remained unchanged or decreasing in the primary and secondary activities.

4 Quaternary Activities
Involves collection, production and dissemination of information.

Outsourcing
It refers to giving work to an outside agency to improve efficiency and reduce costs.

Digital Divide
- When developed countries in general have moved forward, the developing countries are lagged behind.
- Example, countries like india and Russia have better connectivity and access to the digital world as compared to rural areas

5 Quinary Activities
Involves creation, re-arrangement and interpretation.
Involves following activities
- Advanced Medical Research
- Software Development
- Scientific Research (including R/D)

NCERT Folder

Choose the right answer from the four alternatives given below

(i) Which one of the following is a tertiary activity?

(a) Farming (b) Trading

(c) Weaving (d) Hunting

Ans. (b) Trading

(ii) Which one of the following activities is not a secondary sector activity?

(a) Iron smelting (b) Catching fish

(c) Making garments (d) Basket weaving

Ans. (b) Catching fish

(iii) Which one of the following sectors provides most of the employment in Delhi, Mumbai, Chennai and Kolkata?

(a) Primary (b) Quaternary

(c) Secondary (d) Service

Ans. (d) Service

(iv) Jobs that involve high degrees and level of innovations are known as

(a) Secondary activities (b) Quaternary activities

(c) Quinary activities (d) Primary activities

Ans. (b) Quaternary activities

(v) Which one of the following activities is related to quaternary sector?

(a) Manufacturing computers

(b) Paper and raw pulp production

(c) University teaching

(d) Printing books

Ans. (c) University teaching

(vi) Which one out of the following statements is not true?

(a) Outsourcing reduces costs and increases efficiency.

(b) At times engineering and manufacturing jobs can also be outsourced.

(c) BPOs have better business opportunities as compared to KPOs.

(d) There may be dissatisfaction among job seekers in the countries that outsource the job.

Ans. (c) BPOs have better business opportunities as compared to KPOs.

Answer the following questions in about 30 words

(i) Explain retail trading service.

Ans. Retail trading service links the producers with consumers. It is the business activity concerned with the sale of goods directly to consumers. Street peddling, handcarts, trucks, online ordering, etc are examples of non-store retail trading. Whereas, permanent shops are example of fixed retail trading.

(ii) Describe quaternary services.

Ans. Quaternary activities refer to the more intellectual occupations, whose task is to think, research and develop ideas. It is concerned with high-order of professional and administrative service, information generation, processing and transmission. Over half of all workers in developed economies are in the knowledge sector.

(iii) Name the fast emerging countries of medical tourism in the world.

Ans. The fast emerging countries of medical tourism in the world are India, Thailand, Singapore, Malaysia, Switzerland and Australia.

(iv) What is digital divide?

Or **Give the meaning of digital divide.**

Ans. Digital divide basically describes the uneven development of information and communication technology industry in the world. The main deciding factor of the differences in the development of Information and Communication Technology (ICT) services is that how actively countries can provide ICT access to its citizens.

Answer the following questions in not more than 150 words

(i) Discuss the significance and growth of the service sector in modern economic development.

Ans. Service sector is significant for modern economic development for the following reasons

- **Facilitates Flow of Money** Service sector facilitates the flow of money in an economy. For example, buying and selling of items. Trading helps in the exchange of money and commodities among different regions.
- **Contributes in GDP** In developed countries, a large proportion of GDP is contributed by service sector, as it is a major sector of economy in these countries.
- **Provides Employment** Apart from generating revenue, service sector also provides employment to people. About 45 to 75 per cent of population in developed countries is engaged in service sector.

- **Growth of Towns** Growth of services contributes in growth of existing centres and emergence of new centres. For example, new forms of trade which include money exchange at international level has produced many centres and institutions such as trading centres or collection and distribution points.
- **Supports Economic Development** In the initial stages of economic development, larger proportion of people work in the primary sector. As economy develops proportion of population in tertiary activity increases. Making and maintaining highways and bridges, maintaining fire fighting departments and supplying or supervising education and customer care are among the services most often supervised or performed by governments or companies.

(ii) Explain in detail the significance of transport and communication services.

Ans. The significance of transport services are as follows

- A developed system of transportation helps a country to develop fast.
- Transport helps in connecting raw material providing areas to industries and industries to markets. It supplies labour, machineries, fuels, emergency services at right time.
- It enlarges the service area of markets. It connects local markets to regional markets, regional markets to national markets and national markets to international markets.
- It facilitates the overall development of a nation. It facilitates the transportation of building and construction material to remote areas which is essential to develop infrastructures such as roads, highways, buildings, schools, colleges, etc.
- Development of roads, railways, etc in border areas and strategic areas helps in defence preparedness. These are used to transport military equipment and soldiers during war.

The significance of communication services are as follows

- A developed network of mass communication is essential to spread knowledge and ideas.
- It educates the masses.
- To bring the far-flung and remote areas closer to other areas developed means of communication are essential.
- Means of communication are also helpful in the national integration.
- Satellite communication is important for the weather forecast, monitoring of natural calamities, surveillance of border areas, telecommunication, etc.

Exam Pattern Questions

Objective Type Questions

Multiple Choice Questions (MCQs)

1. Which of the following is regarded as a Tertiary activity? CBSE 2024 C

(a) Cattle rearing (b) Farming
(c) Work of plumbers (d) Industrial work

2. Which one of the following is an example of 'Gold Collar' professional? CBSE 2025

(a) Policy (b) Bank Clerk
(c) Teacher (d) Insurance Provider

3. Which of the following is the feature of rural marketing centres?

(a) They provide very basic services.
(b) Professional services are not well developed.
(c) They provide facilities for local collection.
(d) All of the above

4. Which one of the following is able to purchase merchandise more economically, by contacting the manufacturers to produce the goods according to their specification? CBSE 2024

(a) Trading centres
(b) Consumer cooperation
(c) Departmental stores
(d) Chain stores

5. ……… lines are drawn on a map to join places equal in terms of the time taken to reach them.

(a) Isomers (b) Isochrone
(c) Isobar (d) Isotot

6. Which of the following is an example of mass media?

(a) Television (b) Newspaper
(c) Radio (d) All of these

7. Which one of the following will not choose the site within or near CBD (Central Business District) CBSE Diksha

(a) Golf course (b) Multiplexes
(c) Restaurants (d) Markets

8. Automatic vending machines and the internet are examples of which of the following types of trade? CBSE 2025

(a) Rural Marketing Centres
(b) Wholesale Trading
(c) Urban Marketing Centres
(d) Retail Trading

9. Which of the following is not included in Knowledge processing outsourcing (KPO)?

(a) Highly skilled labours
(b) E-learning
(c) Legal-profession
(d) Tele-marketing

10. Which of the following is incorrectly matched pair?

(a) Secondary – Oil and gas extraction
(b) Tertiary – Transport
(c) Quaternary – Research and development
(d) Quinary – Consultants

11. Production of information is related to which one of the following sectors? CBSE 2024

(a) Primary (b) Secondary
(c) Tertiary (d) Quaternary

12. Tourism sector is affected by many factors. Identify the factor by the given description.

Many people like to spend their holidays in an attractive environment, which often means mountains, lakes, spectacular sea coasts and landscapes not completely altered by man.

(a) Climate
(b) History and Art
(c) Landscape
(d) Culture and Economy

13. There is a decline in the trend of employment in primary sectors. Choose from the following the correct options regarding the reasons.

(i) Increasing level of education
(ii) Shifting to tertiary sectors
(iii) Low income
(iv) All of the above

Codes

(a) Only (i) and (ii) (b) Only (iv)
(c) Only (iii) and (i) (d) All of these

14. Which of the following is true about tertiary activities?

(i) Tertiary activities are related to service sector.
(ii) Manpower is the main component of tertiary activities.
(iii) Mining is a tertiary activity.

Codes

(a) (i) and (ii) (b) (i), (ii) and (iii)
(c) (ii) and (iii) (d) (i) and (iii)

15. Which of the following is a tertiary activity?

(i) Teaching (ii) Legal services
(iii) Publishing (iv) Transport
(v) Plumbing

Codes

(a) (i), (ii) and (iii)
(b) (ii), (iii) and (v)
(c) (i), (ii) and (v)
(d) All of these

16. Read the following characteristics of wholesale trading carefully and choose the correct option. CBSE 2024

(i) It is constituted by numerous intermediaries, merchants and supply houses.
(ii) Wholesalers often extend credit to retail stores.
(iii) Generally retailers operate very largely on the wholesaler's capital.
(iv) Mail order, automatic vending machines, street vendors are some of its examples.

Option

(a) Only (i), (ii) and (iii) are correct
(b) Only (ii), (iii) and (iv) are correct
(c) Only (i), (iii) and (iv) are correct
(d) Only (i), (ii) and (iv) are correct

17. Which of the following are the examples of quaternary activities? CBSE Diksha

(i) Accounting, mutual fund managers and software developers.
(ii) Software developers, gardeners and tax consultants
(iii) Tax consultants, brokerage firms and statisticians.
(iv) Whole sellers, theatre personnel and mutual fund managers.

Codes

(a) (i) and (iv) (b) (ii) and (iii)
(c) (i) and (iii) (d) (i) and (ii)

18. Which of the following are the features of rural marketing centres? CBSE Diksha

(i) Well-developed personal and professional services.
(ii) Most of the centres have wholesale and retail areas.
(iii) Serve as trading centres of the most rudimentary type.
(iv) Services of educational institutions and professionals are available.

Codes

(a) (i) and (ii) (b) (i) and (iv)
(c) (ii) and (iii) (d) (iii) and (iv)

19. **Statement I** Most of the quaternary activities can be outsourced. **CBSE 2024**

Statement II These services are not necessarily based on resources and market.

Options

(a) Statement I is correct, but Statement II is incorrect
(b) Statement I is incorrect, but Statement II is correct
(c) Statements I and II both are correct and Statement II is the correct explanation of Statement I
(d) Statements I and II both are correct, but Statement II is not the correct explanation of Statement I

Match the Following

20.

List-I (Tourist Regions)	List-II (Examples)
A. Warmer places	1. City of Varanasi
B. Winter sports region	2. Mediterranean coast
C. Historic towns	3. Himalayas

Codes

	A	B	C
(a)	1	2	3
(b)	2	3	1
(c)	2	1	3
(d)	3	2	1

Assertion-Reason

Directions (Q. Nos. 21-25) In the questions given below are two statements labelled as Assertion (A) and other is labelled as Reason (R). In the context of two statements, which one of the following is correct?

Codes

(a) Both A and R are true, but R is not the correct explanation of A
(b) Both A and R are true and R is the correct explanation of A
(c) Both A and R are incorrect
(d) A is correct, but R is incorrect

21. **Assertion** (A) Manpower is an important component of the service sector. **CBSE 2024**

Reason (R) Most of the tertiary activities are performed by skilled labour and professionally trained experts.

22. **Assertion** (A) Over 40% of the GDP of world is generated by tourism.

Reason (R) As a country develops, the number of people working in the primary sector declines whereas those in the tertiary sector increases.

23. **Assertion** (A) India has emerged as the leading country in medical tourism in the world.

Reason (R) There has been a positive growth in the medical facilities in India during the past 30 years.

24. **Assertion** (A) Most of the developed countries have a higher percentage of workers in service sectors.

Reason (R) A higher standard of education in the developed countries. **CBSE Diksha**

25. **Assertion** (A) The tourism industry has become the world's largest tertiary activity in total registered jobs and total revenue. **CBSE Diksha**

Reason (R) People migrate from one place to another.

Answers

1. (c) Work of plumbers
2. (a) Policy formulator
3. (d) All of the above
4. (d) Chain Stores
5. (b) Isochrone
6. (d) All of these
7. (a) Golf course
8. (c) Urban Marketing Centres
9. (d) Tele-marketing
10. (a) Secondary – Oil and gas extraction
11. (d) Quaternary
12. (c) Landscape
13. (d) All of these
14. (a) (i) and (ii)
15. (d) All of these
16. (a) Only (i), (ii) and (iii) are correct
17. (c) (i) and (iii)
18. (c) (ii) and (iii)
19. (d)
20. (b)
21. (c) Both A and R are incorrect
22. (a) Both A and R are true, but R is not the correct explanation of A
23. (a) Both A and R are true, but R is not the correct explanation of A
24. (a) Both A and R are true and R is the correct explanation of A
25. (a) Both A and R are true, but R is not the correct explanation of A

Subjective Questions

Short Answer Type Questions

1. Explain any three characteristics of periodical markets of rural areas in the world.

Ans. The three characteristics of periodical markets of rural areas in the world are as follows:

(i) Periodical markets in rural areas are found where there are no regular markets. Local periodical markets are organised at different intervals.

(ii) There may be weekly, bi-weekly markets and people from the surrounding areas come here to fulfil their accumulated demands.

(iii) These markets are held on specific days and move from one place to another. Thus, the shopkeepers remain busy on all the days, while a large area is served by them.

2. Describe the different types of retail stores.

Ans. Different types of retail stores are as follows

- **Consumer Co-operatives** These are retail establishments which are organised and operated by the consumers themselves to obtain products of daily use at reasonably low prices.
- **Departmental Stores** It is a large retail business unit which has number of stores engaged in purchasing and selling of different products.
- **Chain Stores** These may direct goods to be manufactured as per their customised specification. They employ highly skilled specialists in many executive tasks. They have the ability to experiment in one store and apply the results to many.

3. Differentiate between rural and urban marketing centres of the world in three points.

Ans. Differences between rural and urban marketing centres of the world are as follows

Rural Marketing Centres	Urban Marketing Centres
They provide services to nearby settlements.	They serve the need of large areas as compared to rural marketing centres.
They serve as trading centres of quasi-urban type. Personal and professional services are not well-developed here.	They provide ordinary goods and services as well as many of the specialised goods and services.
They are local collecting and distributing centres. Most of these have *mandis* (wholesale markets) and also retailing areas.	Urban centres offer manufactured goods as well as many specialised markets. For example, markets for labour, housing, semi or finished products, services of educational institutions and professionals such as teacher, lawyers, physicians, etc.

4. Telecommunication has revolutionised communication. Validate the statement. **Competency Based Que**

Ans. Telecommunication is the exchange of information over significant distances by electronic means.

Importance of telecommunication are

- Modern technology has changed the old pattern of communication. It has made communication independent of transport.
- The use of mobile phones and internet has brought a revolution in modern communication.
- It has reduced the speed with which messages are sent to destination. It has reduced the communication time from weeks to minutes.
- It has made the communication direct and instantaneous at any time and from anywhere irrespective of location.
- It is now easier to cater to a wide range of audience across the world through radio, television or internet.

5. Give the reasons for the rise in service sector.

Ans. Service sector is an important tertiary activity that is used by the households as well as the industry.

The service sector has grown enormously over past few decades. This is because of the following reasons.

- **Rapid Urbanisation** As more people start living in the cities, there is rising demand for various services in urban areas.
- **Increase in Population** The necessity for basic services has increased due to increase in the population. These services are hospitals, education, banking, etc.
- **Increase in Living Standard** The increasing living standard of the people has resulted in rising demand for services such as transport, tourism, sports, etc.

- **Rising Income** The rising incomes of people have led to increase in the services required by them. These services include retailing, tourism, education, etc.
- **Improvement in Technology** Improvements in technology have resulted in expansion of service sector in the international markets.

6. How do the different forms of service sector play significant roles in the modern economy? CBSE Diksha

Ans. Service sector is very important for the development of economy in the world. It involves to all kinds of services like-education, health, welfare, business services, etc. This sector also provides employment to a large number of people. The five major components of service sector are as follows

(i) Many services have been regulated by the government. It includes making and maintaining highways, bridges, supplying education and health services, transport, telecommunications, energy, etc.

(ii) Professional services include primary health care, engineering, law etc.

(iii) Personal services are for the people to facilitate their work in daily life.

(iv) Recreational and entertainment services are widely distributed.

(v) Whole sale and retail trading with the producers and consumers.

7. Tourism has become the world's single largest tertiary activity. Elucidate the statement. Competency Based Que

Ans. Tourism is the largest sector of tertiary activities in terms of providing employment. Tourism is a travel which is done for the purposes of recreation. It generates the largest revenue among tertiary activities in the world. Around 40 per cent of the world's total GDP is generated by tourism sector.

Tourism not only boosts the infrastructure, but also the local as well as global economy. It provides base for making a living for many people residing adjacent to tourist places. Local people are employed to provide variety of services like accommodation, food, transport, special shops and entertainment. It enhances the growth of retail trading, art and craft business or industries.

8. How does the climate of a region attract tourists? Explain with examples from different regions of the world.

Ans. The climatic conditions of any region decide the demand for tourism. The climate of a region attracts tourists in the following ways

- People from colder places seek to visit warm places. That's why the Mediterranean lands and Southern Europe, due to their considerable higher temperature, sunny days and less rainfall attract tourists from Europe.
- People from warmer regions like to visit colder places. That's why tourists from Northern plains of India prefer to go to tourist places located in the Himalayan region or other hill stations.
- Climatic conditions of a region also provide some adventurous activities to do and attract tourists. For example, ice skating and skiing in snowy regions, sea surfing on beaches, etc.

9. Medical tourism in India is a growing sector within the country's economy. Discuss about its importance in India. Competency Based Que

Ans. India has emerged as the leading country for medical tourism in the world. World class hospitals located in metropolitan cities cater to patients all over the world. Medical tourism brings abundant benefits to developing country like India. These benefits are

- Medical tourism creates employment opportunities in India.
- It contributes to the GDP of the country by generating income.
- It helps in increasing the foreign exchange reserves by increasing foreign exchange earnings.
- It helps in developing medical infrastructure in the country.
- It leads to innovation in healthcare services.
- It also raises India's image as a global leader in healthcare industry.
- India has nearly 18% of global medical tourism market in the world.

10. What are quaternary activities? Explain any three characteristics of quaternary activities.

Ans. Quarternary activity is a segment of service sector that is knowledge oriented. It has replaced most of the primary and secondary employment as the basis for economic growth. These include mutual fund managers, tax consultants, software developers and statisticians.

The three characteristics of quarternary activities include

- **Information Centric** These activities involve the collection, production and dissemination of information or even the production of information.
- **Research Oriented** Quarternary activities focus upon research, development and may be seen as an advanced form of service involving special knowledge and technical skills.
- **Outsourcing** These services are not tied to resources, affected by the environment or necessarily localised by the market. Thus, they can also be outsourced.

11. What kind of functions are performed by people involved in quinary activities?

Ans. Quinary activities includes the provision of highly specialised services. The people involved in quinary activities perform the following functions

- They are at the highest level of decision-making and policy-making.
- They focus upon creation, re-arrangement and interpretation of new and existing ideas, data interpretation and use and evaluation of new technologies.
- These people perform 'gold collar' professions, representing special and highly paid skills of senior business executives, government officials, research scientists, financial and legal consultants, etc.

12. Define the term outsourcing. What are the consequences of outsourcing?

Ans. Outsourcing or contracting out is giving work to an outside agency to improve efficiency and to reduce costs. Business activities that are outsourced includes IT, human resources, customer support and call centre services. At times it includes manufacturing and engineering.

The consequences of outsourcing are

- It is resulted in opening up of a large number of support call centres in India, China, Eastern Europe, Israel, Philippines and Costa Rica. Thus, it helps to create new jobs.
- It has helped in reducing migration in the out-migrating countries which have abundant cheap and skilled workers.
- It has led to resistence from the job seeking youths in the outsourcing countries.

13. "Outsourcing has resulted in opening up a large number of job opportunities in several countries." Analyse the statement with three suitable examples.

Competency Based Que

Ans. Outsourcing has resulted in the opening up of a large number of call centres in India, China, Eastern Europe, Israel, Philippines and Costa Rica. It has created new jobs in these countries. Outsourcing is coming to those countries where cheap and skilled workers are available. These are also out-migrating countries.

This can be explained through these examples

- The Knowledge Processing Outsourcing (KPO) industry involves highly skilled workers that are available in the developing countries at lower wages.
- In developing countries, skilled IT staff is available with good communication skills at lower wages as compared to developed countries.
- Data processing is another IT related service that employs large number of people in Asian countries.

Long Answer Type Questions

1. How can you say that different marketing centres try to provide services by targeting different markets?

Ans. There are three types of trading centres or marketing centres which provide different services to target their markets. These are

(i) **Rural Marketing Centres** These centres provide facilities to nearby settlements. These are quasi-urban centres. Here, personal and professional services are not well-developed. These are in the form of local collecting and distribution centres. Most of these have mandis (wholesale markets) and also retailing areas. They are significant centres for making available goods and services which are most frequently demanded by rural people.

(ii) **Periodic Markets** These markets are found where there are no regular markets and local periodic markets are organised at different temporal intervals. These may be weekly, bi-weekly markets from where people from the surrounding areas meet their temporally accumulated demand. These markets are held on specific days and move from one place to another. The shopkeepers thus, remain busy on all the days while a large area is served by them.

(iii) **Urban Marketing Centres** These have more widely specialised urban services. They provide ordinary goods and services as well as many of the specialised goods and services required by people. Urban centres, therefore, offer manufactured goods, as well as many specialised markets develop. For example, markets for labour, housing and semi or finished products. Different services are also available in these markets like services of educational institutions such as teachers, lawyers, consultants, physicians, dentists and veterinary doctors, etc.

2. What are services? Describe various types of services.

Ans. Services means to provide assistance to some one. Services are provided to individual customers who can pay for them. Services are of both physical and mental nature. It includes gardeners, barbers, teachers, lawyers, musicians, etc.

Types of services include

(i) **Government Aided Services** Government provides various services such as making and maintaining highways and bridges, maintaining fire fighting departments, supplying and supervising health, education, etc.

(ii) **Infrastructural Development Services** These type of services include transport, telecommunication, energy and water supply various corporations have been established by governments to control and supervise these services.

(iii) **Professional Services** These services include healthcare, engineering, law and management. These services are provided by both public and private companies.

(iv) **Personal and Domestic Services** Personal services are provided by domestic workers. The services help in making the lives of people easier. These services include gardeners, cooks, housekeepers, etc.

(v) **Services Based on Market** These services include recreational and entertainment services. Their location depends upon the market. It includes restaurants, multiplexes, etc.

3. "The modern economic development in the world is mainly the result of development of quaternary service". Explain with suitable examples. Competency Based Que

Or **The quaternary sector along with the tertiary sector has replaced most of the primary and secondary employment? Support the statement.** CBSE Term II 2022

Ans. The given statement can be supported by the following fact that the service sector is a knowledge oriented sector which involve research and development. This sector is different from primary and secondary sector as it provides specialised skill and technical knowledge.

Comparative to primary and secondary sector, quaternary sector involve 50 per cent of the working population and this provide a strong base to modern economic development in the world.

The quaternary and tertiary sector together have now replaced the primary and secondary sectors as the base of economic growth in many countries.

There has been very high growth in demand and consumption of information and knowledge based quarternary services. These include managers, consultants, software developers, etc.

The quarternary services are not bound with any type of resources that are affected by the environment or the market. Hence, these grow at a faster rate than the other sectors.

These services can be outsourced. This has resulted in its rapid growth beyond the national boundaries to international regions. It has made their operations profitable and it has resulted in the quarternary sector contributing to the economic development of the modern economies.

4. Justify the tremendous growth of the service sector in developed and developing countries than the manufacturing sector? Explain giving suitable examples. CBSE SQP 2022

Or **Assess the growth and significance of service sector in the development of the world economy.** CBSE 2025

Ans. Tertiary sector (service sector) is a skilled and knowledge oriented sector, which works on the components of skilled man power. This sector includes both production and exchange of services, trading, transportation, tourism, etc. It is providing a strong base to modern economic development in the world. In both developed and developing countries, the tertiary sector is contributing more than manufacturing and agriculture sector. Over 50% of all the workforce in developed countries is involved in the tertiary sector.

There has been very high growth in demand and consumption of transportation, trading, tourism and other services. These include both technical and non-technical services. Many services were also outsourced which resulted in growth of this sector beyond national boundaries to interaction regions.

One of the major example of expanding contribution of tertiary sector is tourism. It is the world's largest tertiary activity, with total registered jobs around 250 million and total revenue about 40 per cent of total GDP. Besides many local persons, are employed to provide services like transport, catering accommodation, entertainment, etc. Tourism fasters the growth of infrastructure industries, retail trading and craft industries.

5. How do quaternary services differ from tertiary services? Give three reasons why the service sector in developing and developed countries is growing faster than the manufacturing sector? CBSE Sample Paper Term II 2021

Ans. Tertiary and quaternary activities differ from one another in various ways, they are mentioned below

- **Nature** Tertiary activities are related to service sector while quaternary activities are related to intellectual and knowledge-based services.
- **Skill level** Tertiary activities require skilled people who provide services to the people against payment of fees while quaternary activities include high skilled workers such as researchers and developers.

Examples Tertiary activities include activities like doctors, lawyers, publishers while quaternary activities include activities like CEO of a MNC, medical transcription, etc.

The service sector in developing and developed countries is growing faster than the manufacturing sector due to following reasons

- The rising per capita income in both, developed and developing countries has generated proportionately larger increase in the many kinds of services such as trade, transport, real estate financial banking, etc.
- There is also demand for educational services at all levels with the increase in the demand for literacy and computer skills at the workplace.
- The increasing living standard of people has resulted in rising demand for services such as transport, tourism, sports, etc.

6. Assess the growth and significance of transport and communication services in the world economy. **CBSE 2025**

Ans. For answer, refer to NCERT Folder in 150 words category (ii) on Page 98.

7. What is medical tourism? Explain the scope of medical services for overseas patients in India.

Or **What is medical tourism? What is the reason for popularity of medical tourism in developing countries?** **CBSE DIksha**

Ans. When medical treatment is combined with international tourism activity, it is known as medical tourism.

The reason for popularity of medical tourism in developing countries like India are as follows

- The growing medical facilities in India during last few decades have made the country a favourable destination for medical tourists.
- The medical infrastructure also has developed to meet the world class demand of overseas patients.
- In India, many world class hospitals located in metropolitan cities have provisions for the patients all over the world.
- These hospitals provide a variety of medical treatment at lower cost. About 55,000 patients from USA, visited India in 2005 for medical treatment.
- Thus, looking at these scopes we may conclude that India has emerged as the leading country of medical tourism in the world.
- Despite these advancements India is still not as much advanced as USA, where each year millions of surgeries are performed.
- Medical tourism brings a lot of benefits to developing countries like India, Thailand, Singapore and Malaysia.

Source Based Questions

1. Read the passage carefully and answer the questions that follow.

Trade is essentially buying and selling of items produced elsewhere. All the services in retail and wholesale trading or commerce are specifically intended for profit. The towns and cities where all these works take place are known us trading centres. Rural marketing centres cater to nearby settlements. These are quasi-urban centres. They serve as trading centres of the most rudimentary type. Here personal and professional services are not well-developed. These form local collecting and distributing centres. Most of these have mandis (wholesale markets) and also retailing areas. Periodic markets in rural areas are found where there are no regular markets and local periodic markets are organised at different temporal intervals. These may be weekly, biweekly markets from where people from the surrounding areas meet their temporally accumulated demand. These markets are held on specified dates and move from one place to another. The shopkeepers thus, remain busy on all the days while a large area is served by them. Urban marketing centres have more widely specialised urban services. They provide ordinary goods and services as well as many of the specialised goods and services required by people. Urban centres, therefore, offer manufactured goods as well as many specialised markets develop, e.g. markets for labour, housing, semi or finished products.

(i) Retail and wholesale trading is carried out for which of the following purpose?

(a) Welfare (b) Distribution
(c) Profit (d) All of these

Ans. (c) Profit

(ii) Which of the following type of markets provide specialised services?

(a) Rural marketing centres
(b) Urban marketing centres
(c) Periodic markets
(d) Consumer Cooperatives

Ans. (b) Urban marketing centres

(iii) Which marketing centres are setup to temporally accumulated demands?

(a) Malls (b) Chain stores
(c) Weekly markets (d) Mandis

Ans. (c) Weekly markets

2. Read the passage carefully and answer the questions that follow.

Communication services involve the transmission of words and messages, facts and ideas. The invention of writing preserved messages and helped to make communication dependent on means of transport. These were actually carried by hand, animals, boat, road, rail and air.

That is why all forms of transport are also referred to as lines of communication. Where the transport network is efficient, communications are easily disseminated. Certain developments, such as mobile telephony and satellites, have made communications independent of transport. All forms are not fully disassociated because of the cheapness of the older systems. Thus, very large volumes of mail continue to be handled by post offices all over the world.

The use of telecommunications is linked to the development of modern technology. It has revolutionised communications because of the speed with which messages are sent. The time reduced is from weeks to minutes. Besides, the recent advancements like mobile telephony have made communications direct and instantaneous at any time and from anywhere. The telegraph, morse code and telex have almost become things of the past. Radio and television also help to relay news, pictures, and telephone calls to vast audiences around the world and hence they are termed as mass media. They are vital for advertising and entertainment. Newspapers are able to cover events in all corners of the world. Satellite communication relays information of the earth and from space. The internet has truly revolutionised the global communication system.

(i) Why all forms of transport were referred to as lines of communication?

Ans. All forms of transport were referred to as lines of communication as in old times, all communication was done using different modes of transports only.

(ii) After all the new developments in the communication technology, why large volumes of mail still continue to be handled by post offices all over the world?

Ans. All forms of communication are not fully disassociated with transport because of the cheapness of the older systems. Thus, very large volumes of mail continue to be handled by post offices all over the world.

(iii) Give some examples of old forms of communication.

Ans. Some examples of old forms of communication are

- The telegraph
- Morse code
- Telex

3. Read the passage carefully and answer the questions carefully. CBSE 2024

Services occur at many different levels. Some are geared to industry, some to people and some to both industry and people, e.g. the transport systems. Low-order services, such as grocery shops and laundries, are more common and widespread than high-order services or more specialised ones like those of accountants, consultants and physicians. Services are provided to individual consumers who can afford to pay for them. For example, the gardener, the launderers and the barber do primarily physical labour. Teacher, lawyers, physicians, musicians and others perform mental labour. Many services have now been regulated. Making and maintaining highways and bridges, maintaining fire fighting departments and supplying or supervising education and customer-care are among the important services most often supervised or performed by governments or companies. State and union legislation have established corporations to supervise and control the marketing of such services as transport, telecommunication, energy and water supply. Professional services are primarily health care, engineering, law and management. The location of recreational and entertainment services depends on the market.

(i) Mention any one example of common and widespread services.

Ans. Low-order services, such as grocery shop is an examples of common and widespread services.

(ii) Who supervises and controls the marketing of services?

Ans. The state and union legislation have established corporations to supervise and control the marketing of services.

(iii) "Services occur at many different levels". Support the statement.

Ans. Services occur at many different levels in the following ways

- Some services cater to the needs of people and some to the needs of industries.
- Some services are meant for both people and industries.

4. Read the passage carefully and answer the questions that follows. CBSE SQP 2024

Tourism

Tourism has become the world's single largest tertiary activity in total registered jobs (250 million) and total revenue (40 per cent of the total GDP). Besides, many local persons, are employed to provide services like accommodation, meals, transport, entertainment and special shops serving the tourists. Tourism fosters the growth of infrastructure industries, retail trading, and craft industries (souvenirs). In some regions, tourism is seasonal because the vacation period is dependent on favourable weather conditions, but many regions attract visitors all the year round. The warmer places around the Mediterranean Coast and the West Coast of India are some of the popular tourist destinations in the world. Others include winter sports regions, found mainly in mountainous areas, and various scenic landscapes and national parks, which are scattered. Historic towns also attract tourists, because of the monument, heritage sites and cultural activities.

(i) What constitutes tourism?

Ans. Tourism involves travel for recreation, including services like accommodation, meals, transport, entertainment and special shops for tourists.

(ii) List two renowned global tourist destinations.

Ans. Two renowned global tourist destinations are

(i) The West Coast of India.

(ii) Winter sports regions in mountainous areas.

(iii) "Tourism has become the largest tertiary activity in the world". Comment.

Ans. Tourism, the largest tertiary activity globally, generates significant employment and revenue. It promotes local industries, infrastructure, and services. Attractions like climate, landscapes, and culture, along with medical tourism, drive its growth.

5. Read the passage carefully and answer the questions that follow.

Outsourcing or contracting out is giving work to an outside agency to improve efficiency and to reduce costs. When outsourcing involves transferring work to overseas locations, it is described by the term off - shoring, although both off - shoring and outsourcing are used together. Business activities that are outsourced include Information Technology (IT), human resources, customer support and call centre services and at times also manufacturing and engineering. Data processing is an IT related service easily be carried out in Asian, East European and African countries. In these countries IT skilled staff with good English language skills are available at lower wages than those in the developed countries. Thus, a company in Hyderabad or Manila does work on a project based on GIS techniques for a country like U.S.A or Japan. Overhead costs are also much lower making it profitable to get job-work carried out overseas, whether it is in India, China or even a less populous country like Botswana in Africa.

Outsourcing has resulted in the opening up of a large number of call centres in India, China, Eastern Europe, Israel, Philippines and Costa Rica. It has created new jobs in these countries. Outsourcing is coming to those countries where cheap and skilled workers are available. These are also out-migrating countries. With the work available through outsourcing, the migration in these countries may come down.

(i) Which of these is the advantage of outsourcing?

(a) Low operating cost (b) Transfer of technology
(c) Tax saving (d) All of these

Ans. (a) Low operating cost

(ii) Which of the following activities are usually outsourced?

(a) Training of personnel
(b) Manufacturing
(c) Customer support
(d) Research

Ans. (c) Customer support

(iii) Why are most of the services outsourced to Asian countries?

(a) Availability of cheap IT staff
(b) Low taxes in Asia
(c) Large number of customers in Asia
(d) None of the above

Ans. (a) Availability of cheap IT staff

SELF ASSESSMENT TEST

Objective Type Questions

1. Tertiary activities involve commercial output of services rather than production of ……… goods.
   (a) Permanent (b) Commercial
   (c) Tangible (d) Intangible
2. Which of the following is not true about rural marketing centres?
   (a) They provide facility for local collection and distribution.
   (b) They include wholesale as well as retail areas.
   (c) They provide services to rural as well as urban centres.
   (d) They are very basic in nature.
3. Which factor is most associated with the popularity of Southern Europe and Mediterranean lands for tourism?
   (a) Cold weather
   (b) Consistent sunshine and warm weather
   (c) High cultural activities
   (d) Rich historical monuments
4. When outsourcing is involved in transferring of work to overseas locations, it is described by which of the following terms?
   (a) Outshoring (b) On shoring
   (c) Offshoring (d) Home shoring

Short Answer Type Questions

5. Justify how retail trading and wholesale trading differs from each other.
6. 'Where the transport network is efficient communications are easily disseminated'. Elucidate the statement.
7. Explain the difference between rural marketing and urban marketing centre.
8. Explain briefly about the telecommunication services and its growth.
9. 'Information and technology is important to revolutionise the society'. Explain why?
10. Climate acts as a major factor in tourism sector. Explain.

Long Answer Type Questions

11. Explain the relevance of medical tourism in India.
12. How 'digital divide' explains the development parameter of any region and country?
13. How quaternary activities are knowledge based? Explain.
14. Outsourcing is coming to those countries where cheap and skilled workers are available. Validate the statement.

7

CHAPTER

Transport and communication establish links between producing centres and consuming centres. Trade or the exchange of commodities relies on transportation and communication. High living standards and quality of life depend on efficient transportation, communications and trade.

Transport and Communication

YOUR STUDY GOALS

7.1 Transport
7.2 Land Transport
7.3 Water Transport
7.4 Air Transport
7.5 Pipelines
7.6 Communication

YOUR PRACTICE GOAL

- Objective Type Questions (31 Qs ; MCQs, A-R, Statements, Matching)
- Subjective Questions (26 SAs, 16 LAs)
- Source Based Questions (5 Qs) Map Based Questions (8 Qs)

7.1 Transport

- Transport is a service or facility to carry people and goods from one place to another, using humans, animals and different kinds of vehicles. Assured and speedy transportation, along with efficient communication, promotes cooperation and unity among peoples.
- Transportation is an organised service industry. It includes **transport arteries**[1], vehicles to carry people and goods, and the organisation to maintain arteries, to handle loading, unloading and delivery.
- Transport network joins several places together by a series of routes to form a pattern.
- Every nation has developed various kinds of transportation for defence purposes.
- Transportation can take place over land, water and air. Roads and railways form part of land transport, shipping waterways is a form of water transport and airways are an example of air transport.
- **Pipeline** is another form of transportation. It carries materials like petroleum, natural gas and ores in liquid form.

1 **Transport arteries** A transportation artery can refer to a highway, county road, township road, private road, or rail road.

Modes of Transportation

- The principal modes of world transportation are land, water, air and pipelines. These are used for **inter-regional** and **intra-regional** transport, and each one (except pipelines) carries both passengers and goods.
- The **international movement** of goods is generally handled by **waterways.**
- Road transport is cheaper and faster over short distances and for door-to-door services.
- Railways are most suited for large volumes of bulky materials over long distances within a country.
- Airways are suitable for the movement of high-value, light and perishable goods.

7.2 Land transport

- Most of the movement of goods and services takes place over land. In the early days, humans themselves were carriers. Later with the invention of the wheel, the use of carts and wagons became important.
- The old and elementary forms like the human porter, pack animal[2], cart or wagon are the most expensive means of transportation, while large freighters were the cheapest.
- The revolution in transport came after the invention of the **steam engine** in the **eighteenth century**. The first public railway line was opened in 1825 between **Stockton** and **Darlington** in Northern England and then onwards, railways became the most popular and fastest form of transport in the nineteenth century.
- Railways connected interior continents for commercial grain farming, mining and manufacturing in the USA.
- The invention of the **internal combustion engine** revolutionised road transport in terms of road quality and vehicles (motor cars and trucks).
- Pipelines, ropeways and cableways are new developments in roadways.
- Roadways are important in supplementing modern channels and carriers that moves through the interiors of large countries.

Roads

- Road transport is the most economical for short distances compared to railways. Freight transport by road offers door-to-door service.
- Roads on the basis of their form of construction are as follows
  - **Unmetalled roads** These roads are simple in construction. These roads are not effective and serviceable for all seasons. During the rainy season, heavy rains and floods, these roads become unusable.
  - **Metalled roads** These roads are made as all-season roads.
- Roads play a vital role in a nation's trade and commerce and in promoting tourism.
- The quality of the roads varies greatly between developed and developing countries because of the high expenditure included in road construction and maintenance.
- In developed countries, good quality roads are universal and provide long-distance links through motorways, autobahns (Germany), and inter-state highways for speedy movement.
- The world's total motorable road length is only about 15 million km, of which **North America** accounts for 33 per cent.
- The highest road density[3] and number of vehicles are registered in North America.

---

2 Pack Animal Animals that are used as carriers are known as pack animals. For example, horses, dogs, reindeers and mules.
3 Road Density It means the ratio of the total length of a country's roads to its land area. It can be defined as the length of road per square kilometre of area.

Traffic Flows

- Traffic flow is defined as the number of vehicles passing a point in a given time. It is expressed in vehicles per hour.
- **Peaks** (high points) and **troughs** (low points) of traffic flow can be seen on roads at particular times of the day, for example, peaks occurring during the rush hour before and after work.

Highways

- Highways are metalled roads connecting distant places. They are constructed in a manner for clear vehicular movement. Highways are 80 m wide, with separate traffic lanes, bridges, flyovers and dual carriageways to facilitate uninterrupted traffic flow.
- In developed countries, every city and port town is linked through highways. In North America, highway density is about 0.65 km per sq km. Every place is within 20 km of a highway.
- Cities located on the Pacific Coast (West) are well-connected with the cities on the Atlantic Coast (East). Likewise, the cities of Canada in the North are linked with those of Mexico in the South.

Highways in the World

- The **Trans-Canadian Highway** links **Vancouver** in British Columbia (West coast) to **St. John's City** in Newfoundland (East coast) and the Alaskan Highway links Edmonton (Canada) to Anchorage (Alaska).
- The **Pan-American Highway**, a large portion of which has been constructed, will connect the countries of South America, Central America and the USA Canada.
- The **Trans-Continental Stuart Highway** connects Darwin (North coast) and Melbourne *via* Tennant Creek and Alice Springs in Australia.
- **Europe** has a large number of vehicles and a well-developed highway network. But highways face a lot of competition from railways and waterways.
- In **Russia**, a dense highway network is developed in the industrialised region West of the Urals with Moscow as the hub. The important Moscow-Vladivostok Highway serves the region to the East. Due to the vast geographical area, highways in Russia are more important compared to railways.
- In **China**, highways criss-cross the country connecting all major cities such as Tsungtso (near the Vietnam boundary), Shanghai (Central China), Guangzhou (South) and Beijing (North). A new highway links Chengdu with Lhasa in **Tibet**.
- In **India**, there are many highways linking the major towns and cities. **The Golden Quadrilateral** (GQ) or **Super Expressway** is underway to connect the four metropolitan cities-New Delhi, Mumbai, Chennai and Kolkata.
- In **Africa**, a highway joins Algiers in the North to Conakry in Guinea. Similarly, Cairo is also connected to Cape Town.

▲ *Dharmavaram Tuni National Highway*

Border roads

- Roads laid along international boundaries are called border roads.
- They play an important role in integrating people in remote areas with major cities and providing defence.
- Almost all countries have border roads to transport goods to border villages and military camps.

Quick Test 1

1. Name two transport systems that carry both passenger and freight.
2. Which type of transport is most suited for large volumes of bulky materials over long distances within a country?
3. Which country accounts for most of the world's motorable road length?
4. Which cities are connected through super expressway?

Railways

- Railways are a mode of land transport for bulky goods and passengers over long distances. There are about 13 lakh km of railways open for traffic worldwide.
- Commuter trains are very popular in the UK, the USA, Japan and India.
- The railway gauges[4] vary in different countries. The gauges can be classified as
  - broad gauge (more than 1.5 m)
  - standard gauge (1.44 m) used in UK
  - metre gauge (1 m)
  - smaller gauge

▲ *Tube Train in Vienna*

Europe

- Europe has one of the most dense rail networks in the world.
- There are about 4,40,000 km of railways, most of these are double or multiple-tracked.
- **Belgium** has the **highest density** of 1 km of railway for every 6.5 sq km area.
- The important rail routes are London, Paris, Brussels, Milan, Berlin and Warsaw.
- Underground railways are important in London and Paris. **Channel Tunnel,** operated by **Euro Tunnel Group** through England, connects London with Paris.

Russia

- In Russia, railways account for about 90 per cent of the country's total transport with a very dense network West of the **Urals.**
- **Moscow** is the most important rail head with major lines radiating to different parts of the country's vast geographical area.
- Underground railways and commuter trains are also important in Moscow.

North America

- North America has one of the most extensive rail networks accounting for nearly 40 per cent of the world's total.
- In contrast to many European countries, the railways in North America are used more for long-distance bulky freight like ores, grains, timber and machinery than for passengers.
- The most dense rail network is found in the highly industrialised and urbanised region of East Central USA and adjoining Canada.
- In Canada, railways are in the public sector and distributed all over the sparsely populated areas. The trans-continental railways carry the bulk of wheat and coal tonnage.

Australia

- Australia has about 40,000 km of railways, of which 25 per cent exists in New South Wales.
- The West-East Australian National Railway line runs across the country from Perth to Sydney.
- New Zealand's railways are mainly in the North Island to serve the farming areas.

South America

- In South America, the rail network is the most dense in two regions, namely, the Pampas of Argentina and the coffee growing region of Brazil which together account for 40 per cent of South America's total route length.

---

4 **Rail Gauge** It defines the distance between the inner edges of the opposite rails.

- Chile is the only country in South America that has a good amount of roads connecting its coastal areas to the mining sites in the interiors of the country.
- Peru, Bolivia, Ecuador, Colombia and Venezuela have short single-track rail lines from ports to the interior with no inter-connecting links.
- There is only one trans-continental rail route linking Buenos Aires (Argentina) with Valparaiso (Chile) across the **Andes Mountains** through the **Uspallatta Pass**, located at a height of 3,900 m.

Asia

- In Asia, the rail network is the most dense in the thickly populated areas of Japan, China and India.
- West Asia is least developed in rail facilities because of vast deserts and sparsely populated regions.

Africa

- Africa, despite being the second largest continent, has only 40,000 km of railways.
- **South Africa** accounts for 18,000 km of railways. These railways links the mining areas of gold, diamond and copper.
- The important railway routes of the continent are
  - The **Benguela Railway** through Angola to the Katanga-Zambia Copper Belt
  - The **Tanzania Railway** from the Zambian Copper Belt to Dar-es-Salaam on the coast
  - The **railway through Botswana and Zimbabwe** linking the landlocked states to the South African network
  - the **Blue Train** from Cape Town to Pretoria in the Republic of South Africa.

Trans-Continental Railways

- Trans-continental railways run across the continent and link its two ends.
- They were constructed due to economic and political reasons.
- Major trans-continental rail routes are Trans-Siberian Railway, Trans-Canadian Railways, the Union and Pacific Railway, the Australian Trans-Continental Railway and the Orient Express.
- Trans-continental railway lines have now lost their importance to quicker and more flexible transport systems of airways and roadways.

Trans-Siberian Railways

- It is a major rail route in Russia. It runs from St. Petersburg in the West to Vladivostok on the Pacific Coast in the East passing through Moscow, Ufa, Novosibirsk, Irkutsk, Chita and Khabarovsk.
- It runs across the Ural Mountains, Ob and Yenisei rivers, Chita (agro-centre) and Irkutsk (fur centre).
- It is the **longest double-tracked (9,332 km)** and electrified transcontinental railway in the world.
- It has helped in connecting the Asian region to Western European markets.
- It has various connecting links to the South, namely, to Odessa (Ukraine), Baku on the Caspian Coast, Tashkent (Uzbekistan), Ulan Bator (Mongolia), and Shenyang (Mukden) and Beijing in China.

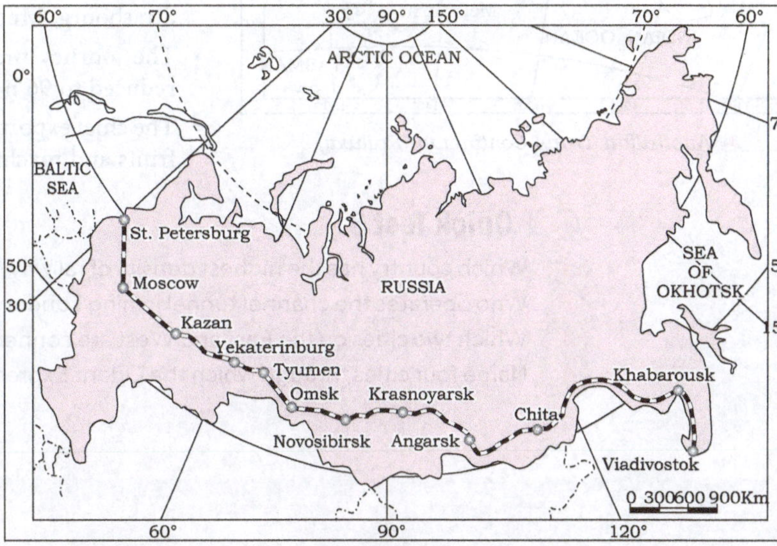

▲ *Trans-Siberian Railways*

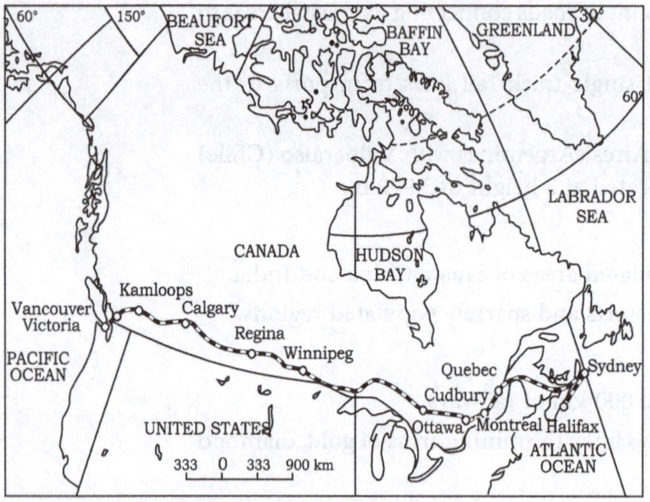

▲ *Trans-Canadian Railway*

Trans-Candian Railways

- This is a 7,050 km long rail-line in **Canada**. It runs from Halifax in the East to Vancouver on the Pacific coast. It passes through Montreal, Ottawa, Winnipeg and Calgary.
- It was constructed in 1886, initially as part of an agreement to make British Columbia on the West coast join the Federation of States.
- This rail-line gained economic significance because it connected the **Quebec-Montreal Industrial Region** with the wheat belt of the Prairie region and the Coniferous Forest region in the North.
- A loop line from Winnipeg to Thunder Bay (Lake Superior) connects this rail-line with one of the important waterways of the world.
- This line is the economic artery of Canada. Wheat and meat are the important exports on this route.

The Australian Trans-Continental Railways

- This rail-line runs West-East across the Southern part of the continent from Perth on the West coast, to Sydney on the East coast. It passes through Kalgoorlie, Broken Hill and Port Augusta.

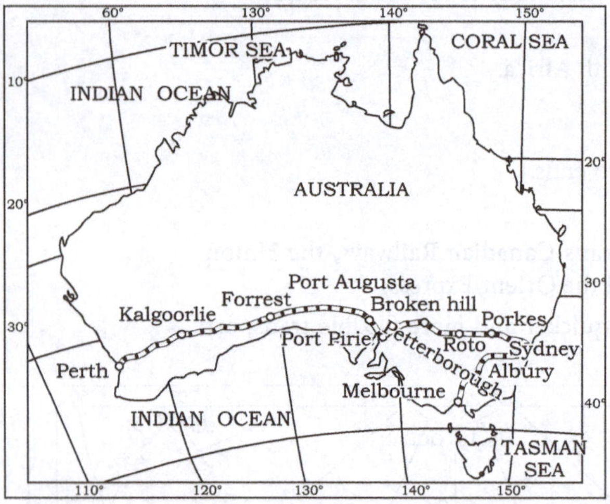

▲ *Australian Trans-Continental Railway*

The Union and Pacific Railways

- This rail-line connects New York on the Atlantic Coast to San Francisco on the Pacific Coast. It passes through Cleveland, Chicago, Omaha, Evans, Ogden and Sacramento.
- The most valuable exports on this route are ores, grain, paper, chemicals and machinery.

The Orient Express

- This line runs from Paris to Istanbul. It passes through Strasbourg, Munich, Vienna, Budapest and Belgrade.
- The journey time from London to Istanbul by this express is reduced to 96 hours as against 10 days by the sea route.
- The chief exports on this rail route are cheese, bacon, oats, wine, fruits and machinery.

Quick Test 3

1. Which country has the highest density of railway network?
2. Who operates the channel tunnel joining London and Paris?
3. Which two cities on the East and West are connected by the Trans- Siberian Railways?
4. Name four cities through which the Orient Express line passes.

7.3 Water Transport

- Water transport is the cheapest mode of transport. It is mainly used for international trade.
- Water transport is divided into sea routes and inland waterways. These are as follows

Sea Routes

- The oceans offer a smooth highway to travel in all directions with no maintenance costs.
- The transformation of oceans into a routeway by sea-going vessels is an important development in human adaptation to the physical environment.
- Compared to land and air transport, ocean transport is a cheaper means of haulage (carrying of load) of bulky material over long distances. For example, from one continent to another.
- Modern passenger and cargo ships have radar, wireless and other navigation aids.
- The development of refrigerated chambers for perishable goods, tankers and specialised ships has also improved cargo transport. The use of containers has made cargo handling at the world's major ports easier.

Important Sea Routes

The Northern Atlantic Sea Route

- This route links the North-Eastern USA and North-Western Europe. Both the coasts have highly advanced ports and harbour facilities.
- The foreign trade over this route is greater than the rest of the world combined.
- One-fourth of the world's foreign trade moves on this route. It is, therefore, the **busiest route** in the world. It is also called the **Big Trunk Route**.

The Mediterranean-Indian Ocean Sea Route

- This sea route passes through the centre of the Old World and serves more countries and people than any other route.

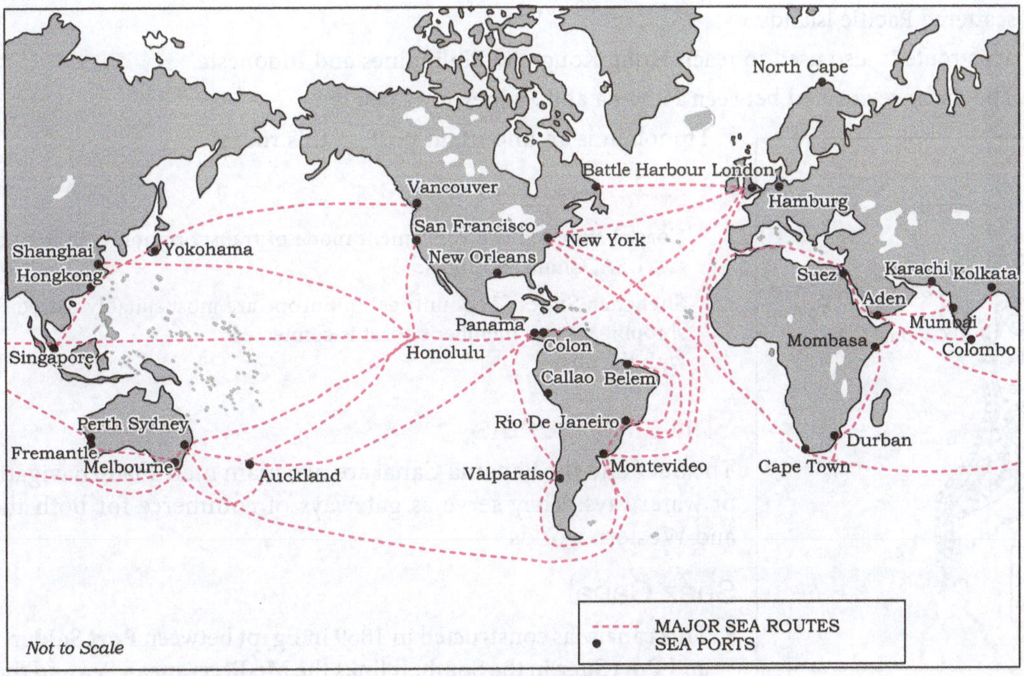

▲ *Important Sea Routes*

- Some of the important ports on this route are Port Said, Aden, Mumbai, Colombo and Singapore.
- The construction of the Suez Canal has greatly reduced the distance and time as compared to the earlier route through the Cape of Good Hope.

The Cape of Good Hope Sea Route

- This trade route connects the highly industrialised Western European region with West Africa, South Africa and South-East Asia.
- It also connects the commercial agriculture and livestock economies of Australia and New Zealand.
- The volume of trade and traffic between both East and West Africa is high due to the development of rich natural resources such as gold, diamond, copper, tin, groundnut, oil palm, coffee and fruits.

The South Atlantic Sea Route

- This sea route across the Atlantic Ocean connects **West European** and **West African countries** with Brazil, Argentina and Uruguay in **South America**.
- The traffic is less on this route because of the limited development and population in South America and Africa. Only South-Eastern Brazil and Plata estuary and parts of South Africa have large-scale industries.
- The traffic is less also because both South America and Africa have similar types of products and natural resources.

The North Pacific Sea Route

- This sea route links the ports on the West coast of **North America** with those of **Asia**.
- Trade across the vast North Pacific Ocean moves by several routes which converge at Honolulu.
- The direct route on the Great Circle links Vancouver and Yokohama and reduces the travelling distance (2,480 km) by half. These are Vancouver, Seattle, Portland, San Francisco and Los Angeles on the American side and Yokohama, Kobe, Shanghai, Hong Kong, Manila and Singapore on the Asian side.

The South Pacific Sea Route

- This sea route connects **Western Europe** and **North America** with **Australia**, New Zealand and the scattered Pacific islands.
- This route is also used to reach Hong Kong, the Philippines and Indonesia.
- The distance covered between Panama and Sydney is 12,000 km.
- Honolulu is an important port on this route.

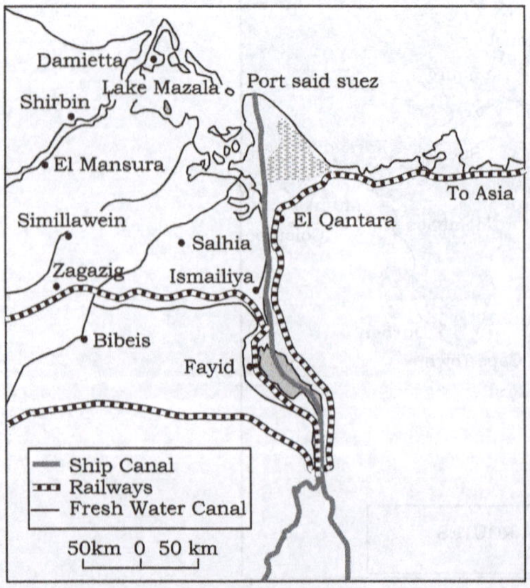

▲ *Suez Canal*

Coastal Shipping

- Coastal shipping is a convenient mode of transportation with long coastlines, e.g. USA, China and India.
- **Shenzhen States** (29 countries) in Europe are most suitably placed for coastal shipping, as one member's coast is connected with the other.

Shipping Canals

The Suez and the Panama Canal are two main man-made navigation canals or waterways. They serve as gateways of commerce for both the Eastern and Western worlds.

Suez Canal

- This canal was constructed in 1869 in Egypt between **Port Said** in the North and **Port Suez** in the South. It links the **Mediterranean Sea** and the **Red Sea**.

- It gives Europe a new gateway to the Indian Ocean and reduces the direct sea route distance between Liverpool and Colombo, as compared to the Cape of Good Hope route.
- It is a sea-level canal without locks. It is about 160 km long and 11 to 15 m deep. About 100 ships travel daily taking 10-12 hours to cross this canal.
- The tolls on this canal are so heavy that some find it cheaper to go by the longer Cape Route.
- A railway follows the canal to Suez, and from Ismailia, there is a branch line to Cairo. A navigable freshwater canal from the Nile also joins the Suez Canal in Ismailia to supply freshwater to Port Said and Suez.

Panama Canal

- This canal connects the **Atlantic Ocean** in the East to the **Pacific Ocean** in the West.
- It has been constructed across the **Panama Isthmus** between Panama City and **Colon** by the US government which purchased 8 km of area on either side and named it the **Canal Zone**.
- It shortens the distance between New York and San Francisco by 13,000 km by sea. Likewise, the distance between Western Europe and the West coast of the USA; the North-Eastern and Central USA and East and South-East Asia is shortened.
- Panama Canal is about 72 km long and depth of 12 km. It has a six-lock system and ships cross the different levels (26 m up and down) through these locks before entering the Gulf of Panama.
- The economic significance of this canal is relatively less than that of the Suez. However, it is vital to the economies of Latin America.

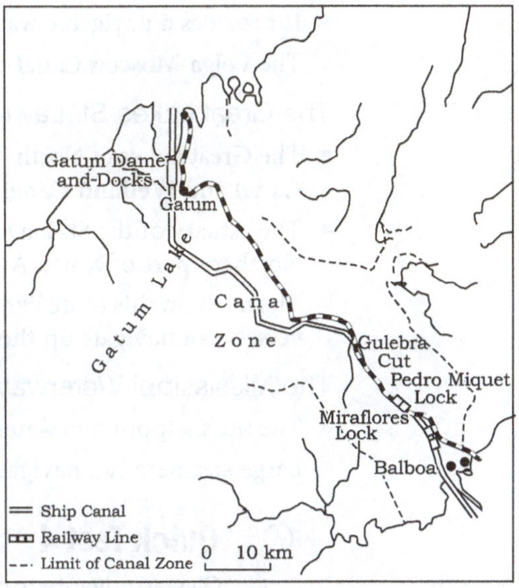

▲ *Panama Canal*

Inland Waterways

- The inland waterways are developed based on the navigability width and depth of the channel, continuity in the water flow and transport technology in use.
- Heavy cargo like coal, cement, timber and metallic ores can be transported through inland waterways.
- Due to the following reasons inland waterways lost their importance
    - It faced competition from railways.
    - Lack of water in rivers due to diversion for irrigation and poor maintenance.

Major Inland Waterways

The Rhine Waterways

- The Rhine river flows through **Germany** and the **Netherlands**. It is navigable for 700 km from Rotterdam, around its delta in the Netherlands to Basel in Switzerland.
- The ships going towards the Ocean can reach up to Cologne.
- The Ruhr river joins the Rhine from the East. It flows through a rich coalfield and the whole basin has become a prosperous manufacturing area. **Dusseldorf** is the Rhine port for this region.
- Huge cargo can move along the Southern parts of the route.
- This waterway is the world's most heavily used waterway. Each year more than 20,000 ocean-going ships and 2,00,000 inland vessels exchange their cargoes here.
- It connects the industrial areas of Switzerland, Germany, France, Belgium and the Netherlands with the North Atlantic Sea Route.

The Danube Waterway

- This is an important inland waterway in **Eastern Europe**.
- The Danube river originates in the **Black Forest** and flows Eastwards through many countries. It is navigable up to Taurna Severin.
- The chief export items through this route are wheat, maize, timber and machinery.

The Volga Waterway

- The Volga is one of the most important inland waterways in Russia.
- It provides a navigable waterway of 11,200 km and drains into the Caspian Sea.
- The **Volga-Moscow Canal** connects it with the Moscow region and the **Volga-Don Canal** with the Black Sea.

The Great Lakes-St. Lawrence Seaway

- The Great Lakes of North America, namely Superior, Huron Erie and Ontario are connected by the **Soo Canal** and **Welland Canal** to form an inland waterway.
- The estuary of the St. Lawrence river, along with the Great Lakes, forms a commercial waterway in the Northern part of North America.
- The ports on this route like Duluth and Buffalo have all the facilities as of ocean ports. Large ocean-going vessels can navigate up the river deep inside the continent to Montreal.

The Mississippi Waterways

- The Mississippi-Ohio waterway connects the interiors of the USA with the Gulf of Mexico in the South.
- Large steamers can navigate through this route up to Minneapolis.

Quick Test 4

1. Give an advantage of water transport over other modes of transport.
2. Which is the busiest sea route in the world in respect of foreign trade?
3. Name four important ports on the North Pacific sea route.
4. What is the total time taken by a ship to cross the Suez Canal?

7.4 Air Transport

- Air transport is the most costly and fastest means of transportation. It is preferred by passengers for long-distance travel.
- It helps in the rapid and worldwide movement of valuable cargo.
- Air transport is often the only means to reach inaccessible areas. Various goods can be transferred to Eskimos in Northern Canada by aeroplanes.
- In the Himalayan region, routes are often blocked by landslides, avalanches or heavy snowfall. At such times, air travel is the only alternative to reach a place.
- Airways also have great strategic importance. For example, the air strikes by US and British forces in Iraq.
- The manufacturing of aircrafts and their operations require a huge infrastructure. For example, hangars, landing, fuelling and maintenance facilities for the aircrafts. The construction of airports is also very expensive and has developed more in highly industrialised countries where there is a large volume of traffic.
- The UK initiated the use of **commercial jet transport**. The USA developed largely post-war international civil aviation. Today, more than 250 commercial airlines offer regular services to different parts of the world.
- **Supersonic aircraft**, cover the distance between London and New York within three and a half hours.

Inter-Continental Air Routes

- There is a distinct East-West belt of inter-continental air routes in the Northern hemisphere. A dense network exists in the Eastern USA, Western Europe and South-East Asia.
- USA alone accounts for 60 per cent of the airways of the world. New York, London, Paris, Amsterdam, Frankfurt Rome, Moscow, Karachi, New Delhi, Mumbai, Bangkok, Singapore, Tokyo, San Francisco, Los Angeles and Chicago are the nodal points where air routes converge or radiate to all continents.
- Africa, the Asian part of Russia and South America lack air services. Between 10-35 latitudes in the Southern hemisphere, there are limited air services due to a sparser population, limited landmass and economic development.

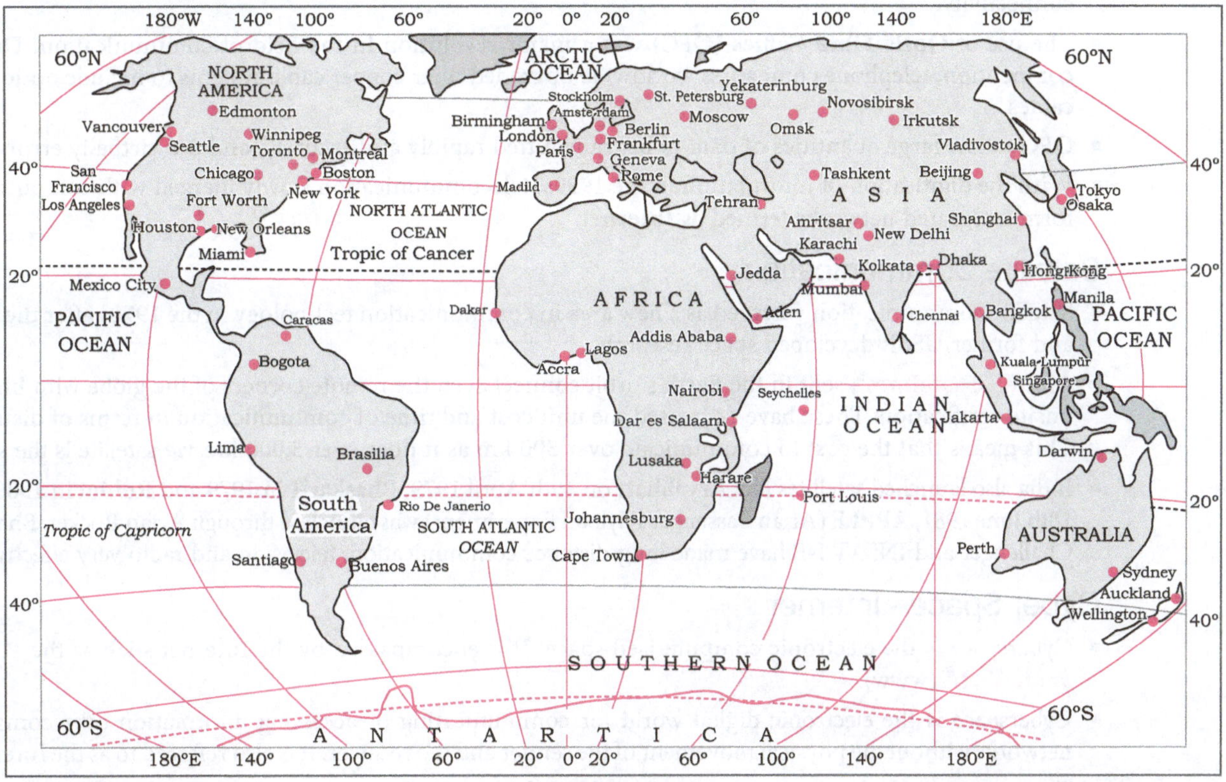

▲ *Major Airports*

7.5 Pipelines

- Pipelines are used extensively to transport liquids and gases such as water, petroleum and natural gas for an uninterrupted flow.
- Water supplied through pipelines is familiar to all. Cooking gas or LPG is supplied through pipelines in many parts of the world. Pipelines can also be used to transport liquified coal.
- In New Zealand, milk is being supplied to factories from farms through pipelines.
- In the USA there is a dense network of oil pipelines from the producing areas to the consuming areas. **Big Inch** pipeline carries petroleum from the oil wells of the **Gulf of Mexico** to the **North-Eastern States.**
- About 17 per cent of all freight per tonne-km. is carried through pipelines in the USA.
- In Europe, Russia, West Asia and India, pipelines are used to connect oil wells to refineries, and to ports or domestic markets. Turkmenistan in central Asia has extended pipelines to Iran and parts of China.
- The proposed Iran-India via Pakistan international oil and natural gas pipeline will be the longest in the world.

7.5 Communication

- Human beings had different methods to communicate over long distances. The **telegraph** and the **telephone** were important methods of communicating.
- The telegraph was used during the colonisation of the American West. During the early and mid-twentieth century, the **American Telegraph and Telephone Company** (AT&T) had a monopoly over the USA's telephone industry. Firms centralised their functioning at city headquarters and located their branch offices in smaller towns.
- In developing countries, the use of cell phones, made possible by satellites, is important for rural connectivity.
- The use of **Optic Fibre Cables** (OFC) was a major revolution in the field of communication. Due to competition, telephone companies worldwide upgraded their copper cable systems to include optic fibre cables.
- OFCs allow large quantities of data to be transmitted rapidly and securely, and are virtually error-free.
- With the digitisation of information in the 1990s, telecommunication slowly merged with computers to form integrated networks termed as **Internet**.

Satellite Communication

- Satellite communication emerged as a new area in communication technology in the 1970s after the USA and former USSR developed space research.
- **Artificial satellites**[5], sent in the Earth's orbit connect even the remote corners of the globe with limited onsite verification. These have decreased the unit cost and time of communication in terms of distance. This means that the cost to communicate over 500 km as it does over 5,000 km *via* satellite is the same.
- India also launched satellites like **Aryabhatt** on 19th April 1979, **Bhaskar-I** in 1979 and **Rohini** in 1980. On 18th June 1981, **APPLE** (Arian Passenger Payload Experiment) was launched through Arian Rocket. Bhaskar, Challenger and INSAT I-B have made long-distance communication, television and radio very effective.

Cyber Space - Internet

- Cyberspace is the electronic computerised space. It is encompassed by the Internet such as the **World Wide Web**[6] (www).
- Cyberspace is the electronic digital world for communicating or accessing information over computer networks without the physical movement of the sender and the receiver. It is also referred to as the Internet.
- The internet is the largest electronic network on the planet that connects about 1,000 million people in more than 100 countries.
- In the last few years, there has been a shift among global users from USA to the developing countries. The majority of the world's users are in the USA, UK, Germany, Japan, China and India.
- Cyberspace expands the contemporary economic and social space of humans through e-mail, e-commerce, e-learning and e-governance.

Quick Test 5

1. Give an advantage of air transport over other forms of transport.
2. Which country accounts for more than 50% of the airways of the world?
3. Name two regions where air transport has not developed well.
4. Which telephone company once enjoyed a monopoly over the USA's telephone industry?
5. Which rocket was used to launch the APPLE satellite?

---

5 **Artificial satellites** Artificial Satellites are human-built and sent by spaceships and carriers, these are objects orbiting the Earth and other planets in the Solar System.

6 **World Wide Web** It is a system of interconnected web pages that are accessible to the public through the internet

Mind Map

TRANSPORT AND COMMUNICATION

1 Land Transport

Movement of goods and services takes place over land.

Roads

Most economical for short distances

(i) Metalled Roads

(ii) Un-Metalled Roads

High ways

- 80 cm wide with separate traffic lanes.

Border Roads

- Runs along international boundaries.

Railways

- Used for bulky goods and passengers for long distances.
- **Trans-Continental Railways** Runs along continents and link two end of the continent.
- **Trans Siberian** Major rail route in Russia runs from St. Petersburg to Vladivostok.
- **Trans Canadian** It runs from Halifax to Vancouver.
- **The Union-Pacific** It connects New York to San-Francisco.
- **Australian-Trans-Continental** It runs from Perth to Sydney.
- **Orient-Express** It runs from Paris to Istanbul.

2 Water Transport

Exchange of goods and services takes place over water.

Sea-Routes

- **Northern-Atlantic** Connects North-Eastern USA with North-Western Europe.
- **The Mediterranean Indian Ocean** Passes through the centre of the Old World.
- **North-Pacific** Links the ports on the West coast of North America with Asia.
- **South Atlantic** Connects West European and West African countries with Brazil, Argentina and Uruguay in South America.
- **The Cape of Good Hope** Connects the highly industrialised Western European region with West Africa, South Africa and South-East Asia.
- **The South Pacific** Connects Western Europe and North America with Australia, New Zealand and the scattered Pacific islands.

Inland Waterways

- **The Rhine** Flows through Germany and the Netherlands. Navigable for 700 km.
- The Danube
- **The Volga** Navigable for 11,200 km
- **Great Lakes** St. Laurence Waterway
- The Mississippi

Shipping Canals

- **Suez canal** It was constructed in 1869. It links Mediterranean Sea and the Red sea.
- **Panama canal** It connects Atlantic Ocean to the Pacific Ocean. It is 72 km long and has depth of 12 km.

3 Air Transport

- Fastest and most expensive means of transportation.
- Dense network of air routes exists in the Eastern USA, Western Europe and South-East Asia.

4 Pipeline Transport

- Used to transport liquid and gases
- Big Inch is famous pipeline which carries petroleum from Gulf of Mexico to North-East states.

5 Communication

Cyber-space Internet

- It is the electronic computerised space.
- It is encompassed by the internet such as world wide web (www).
- It is the electronic digital world for communicating or accessing information over computer networks without physical movement of the sender or receiver.

Satellite Communication

- It emerged as a new area in communication technology in the 1970s after the USA and former USSR developed space research.
- Artificial satellites, sent in the Earth's orbit connect the remote corners of the globe with limited onsite verification.
- India has launched satellites like Aryabhatt in 1979, Bhaskar-I in 1979 and Rohini in 1980.
- It expands the contemporary economic and social space of humans through e-mail, e-commerce, e-learning and e-governance.

NCERT Folder

Choose the right answer from the four alternatives given below

(i) **The Trans-Continental Stuart Highway runs between**
(a) Darwin and Melbourne
(b) Edmonton and Anchorage
(c) Vancouver and St. John's City
(d) Chengdu and Lhasa

Ans. (a) Darwin and Melbourne

(ii) **Which country has the highest density of railway network?**
(a) Brazil (b) USA (c) Canada (d) Russia

Ans. (b) USA

(iii) **The Big Trunk Route runs through**
(a) the Mediterranean - Indian Ocean
(b) the North Atlantic Ocean
(c) the South Atlantic Ocean
(d) the North Pacific Ocean

Ans. (b) the North Atlantic Ocean

(iv) **The Big Inch pipeline transports**
(a) milk (b) Liquid Petroleum Gas (LPG)
(c) water (d) petroleum

Ans. (d) petroleum

(v) **Which one pair of the following places is linked by Channel Tunnel?**
(a) London - Berlin (b) Paris - London
(c) Berlin - Paris (d) Barcelona - Berlin

Ans. (b) Paris - London

Answer the following questions in about 30 words

(i) **What are the problems of road transport in mountainous, desert and flood prone regions?**

Ans. It is very difficult and expensive to construct and maintain roads in mountainous and desert areas.

In flood prone regions, roads are not sustainable. The unmetalled roads become unmotorable during rainy season and even the metalled roads are washed away during flood.

(ii) **What is a trans-continental railway?**

Ans. Trans-continental railways connect two ends of the continent while running across it. Trans-Siberian railway and Trans-Canadian railway are two important trans-continental railways.

(iii) **What are the advantages of water transport?**

Ans. The advantages of water transport are as follows
- The most important advantage of water transport is that the route construction is not required.
- It is also cheaper and energy efficient because of the less friction of water.

Answer the following questions in not more than 150 words

(i) **Elucidate the statement-"In a well managed transport system, various modes complement each other. "**

Ans. In developed countries producing centres and consuming centres are well connected through the various modes of transportation. Transport is the facility or service which provides movement of the goods and persons by using various modes.

Land, air, water and pipelines are important modes of transportation. These modes are used for transportation of man and materials within the country or between two countries and continents. Trans-continental railways are constructed to facilitate long distance travel in different directions. There are some factors like type of goods and services to be transported, costs of transport and the mode available, which determine the importance of a mode to be used.

Every mode of transport has its own significance, like road transport is cheaper for short distance travel as compared to railway. Railways are most suited for large volume of bulky materials. Airways are preferred for long distance travel and for the rapid movement of valuable goods on a worldwide scale. Pipelines are used to carry liquids and gaseous materials without any interruption.

Hence, these modes are complement each other in providing an efficient and well managed transport system.

(ii) **What are the major regions of the world having a dense network of airways?**

Ans. The major regions with dense airways networks are as follows
- **Eastern United States** Highly urbanised and industrialised regions of cities like New York and Chicago are included in this region.
- **Western Europe** This region includes UK, France and Germany. Major hubs of this region are London, Paris and Frankfurt.

- **South-East Asia** It includes countries like Singapore, Bangkok and Hong Kong. They have dense air network due to high tourism and trade.
- **Eastern Asia** It includes the countries like Japan and South Korea.
- **Middle East** This region includes the cities like Dubai and Doha.
- **Australia** It is an island nation. It is well connected through airways for domestic and international level. Major cities are Sydney and Melbourne.

(iii) **What are the modes by which cyberspace will expand the contemporary economic and social space of humans?**

Ans. Cyberspace or the internet is the electronic digital world for communicating or accessing data and information over computer networks without the physical movement of sender and receiver. Cyberspace will expand the contemporary economic and social space of humans through the following modes

- **E-commerce** Facilitates online buying and selling, making global trade easier and more convenient.
- **E-learning** Provides access to education worldwide through online courses, allowing learning regardless of location.
- **E-governance** Offers digital government services, increasing efficiency and making information accessible to citizens.
- **Global Communication** Connects people instantly across the world through e-mails and social media, enhancing social interactions.
- **Access to Information** Integrates tools like television, radio and fax, making information sharing quicker and easier.
- **Global Village Concept** Reduces the importance of physical distance, bringing people closer and creating a sense of global community.

These developments make the exchange of information, goods and services more efficient, contributing to a more interconnected world where geography matters less.

Exam Pattern Questions

Objective Type Questions

Multiple Choice Questions (MCQs)

1. Which of the following modes of transport can only carry freight?
(a) Airways (b) Railways
(c) Pipelines (d) Roads

2. Which type of transport is most suitable for large volume of bulky materials over long distances within a region?
(a) Airways (b) Roadways
(c) Railways (d) Seaways

3. The Trans-Canadian highway connects
(a) Edmonton to Anchorage
(b) Vancouver to St. John's City
(c) Edmonton to Vancouver
(d) Vancouver to Anchorage

4. Trans-Continental Stuart Highway passes through which of these continents?
(a) Australia
(b) Europe
(c) North Canada
(d) Asia

5. The West-East Australian National Railway line runs across the country from
(a) Melbourne to Sydney (b) Perth to Sydney
(c) Sydney to Alice (d) Alice to Perth

6. Which of the following is the highest railway line in the world?
(a) Peruvian Railways (b) Darjeeling Railways
(c) Nilgiri Rail line (d) Quinghai-Tibet Train

7. Which railway line runs through Katanga-Zambia Copper Belt?
(a) Tanzania Railways (b) Benguela Railways
(c) Peruvian Railways (d) Trans-Siberian Railways

8. The Trans-Canadian rail line connects which of these places
(a) London to Istanbul (b) Paris to Istanbul
(c) San Francisco to Ogden (d) Vancouver to Halifax

9. After the construction of which of these canals, the travelling time between Mediterranean Sea and Indian Ocean has been greatly reduced?
(a) Panama canal (b) Suez canal
(c) Kra canal (d) Java canal

10. **The South Pacific Sea Route connects**
(a) Western Europe with Australia
(b) West Asia with New Zealand
(c) Western Africa with North America
(d) South America with Oceania

11. **Which river supplies freshwater to the Suez canal?**
(a) Amazon (b) Nile
(c) Congo (d) Murray

12. **Which of the following sea routes connects Vancouver and Yokohama?** CBSE 2024
(a) South Atlantic Sea Route
(b) North Pacific Sea Route
(c) North Atlantic Sea Route
(d) Mediterranean- Indian Ocean Route

13. **Valuable cargo and perishable goods can be transferred through which of the following modes of transportation?**
(a) Seaways (b) Airways
(c) Roads (d) Railways

14. **Which one of the following is known as 'Big Inch' pipeline?** CBSE 2024
(a) Iran-India *via* Pakistan
(b) Iran-China *via* Afghanistan
(c) Hazira-Vijaipur to Jagdishpur
(d) Gulf of Mexico to North-Eastern USA

15. **What was the number of internet users in 1995 AD?**
(a) 20 million (b) 50 million
(c) 120 million (d) 2 billion

16. **Identify the incorrect statement regarding the importance of transport and communication for humans.** CBSE Diksha
(a) The high living standards and quality of life.
(b) Establish links between producing centres and consuming centres
(c) Exchange of commodities relies on transportation and communication.
(d) It does not links the producers and the consumers.

17. **Identify the rail route based on the characteristics given below.**
This line runs from Paris to Istanbul passing through Strasbourg, Munich, Vienna, Budapest and Belgrade. The journey time from London to Istanbul by this express is now reduced to 96 hours as against 10 days by the sea route. The chief exports on this rail route are cheese, bacon, oats, wine, fruits and machinery.
Options
(a) Trans-Asiatic Railway
(b) The Orient-Express
(c) The Union and Pacific Railway
(d) Trans-Siberian Railway

18. **Identify the waterway based on the characteristics given below.**
This trade route connects the highly industrialised Western European region with West Africa, South Africa, South-East Asia and the commercial agriculture and livestock economies of Australia and New Zealand. The volume of trade and traffic between both East and West Africa is on the increase due to the development of rich natural resources such as gold, diamond, copper, tin, groundnut, oil palm, coffee and fruits.
Options
(a) Cape of Good Hope Sea Route
(b) North Atlantic Sea Route
(c) South Pacific Sea Route
(d) The North Pacific Sea Route

19. **The Trans-Siberian railways does not pass through which of these cities?**
(i) Chicago (ii) Omaha
(iii) Irkutsk (iv) Vladivostok (v) Chita
Codes
(a) (i) and (ii) (b) (i), (ii) and (iii)
(c) (ii), (iii) and (iv) (d) (i), (ii) and (v)

20. **Which of the following is/are the advantages offered by water transport?**
(i) It does not require any construction and thus reduces costs.
(ii) The energy cost is low in water transport.
(iii) The oceans are linked and can be navigated in all directions.
Codes
(a) (i), (ii) and (iii) (b) (ii) and (iii)
(c) (i) and (iii) (d) (i) and (ii)

21. **Which of the following statements are true about the Suez canal?**
(i) It connects the Mediterranean Sea to the Red Sea.
(ii) It was constructed in 1969.
(iii) It shortens the route from Europe to Asia.
(iv) It is 160 km long and free of locks.
Codes
(a) (i) and (ii) only (b) (i), (iii), and (iv) only
(c) (ii) and (iii) only (d) (i), (ii), and (iv) only

22. **Which of the following are the advantages offered by Air transport?**
(i) Reduced travel time
(ii) Inaccessible areas becoming accessible
(iii) Strategic advantages
Codes
(a) (i) and (ii) (b) (ii) and (iii)
(c) (i), (ii) and (iii) (d) (i) and (iii)

Arrange the Following

23. **Arrange the following modes of transport from the most economical to the least for short distances:**

(i) Railways (ii) Roads
(iii) Air transport (iv) Water transport

Codes

(a) (iv), (ii), (i), (iii) (b) (ii), (iv), (i), (iii)
(c) (i), (iv), (ii), (iii) (d) (ii), (i), (iv), (iii)

Match the Following

24. **CBSE Diksha**

	List I (Modes of Transport)		List II (Significance)
A.	Road Transport	1.	Suited for large volumes of bulky materials over long distances within a country.
B.	Airways	2.	International movement of goods is handled by ocean freighters.
C.	Waterways	3.	Cheaper and faster over short distances and for door to door services.
D.	Railways	4.	High-value, light and perishable goods are best moved by this means of transport.

Codes

	A	B	C	D		A	B	C	D
(a)	2	4	3	1	(b)	4	3	1	2
(c)	3	4	2	1	(d)	3	1	2	4

25.

	List I (Railway Gauge)		List II (Length)
A.	Broad Gauge	1.	1 metre
B.	Standard Gauge	2.	1.5 metre or more
C.	Metre Gauge	3.	1.44 metre

Codes

	A	B	C		A	B	C
(a)	3	1	2	(b)	2	1	3
(c)	2	3	1	(d)	1	2	3

26.

	List I (Connects)		List II (Sea Route)
A.	West Europe and West Africa	1.	North Atlantic Sea Route
B.	North America and Asia	2.	North Pacific Sea Route
C.	North-Eastern USA and North-Western Europe	3.	Cape of Good Hope Sea Route

Codes

	A	B	C		A	B	C
(a)	1	3	2	(b)	3	2	1
(c)	2	1	3	(d)	2	3	1

27.

	List I (Routes)		List II (Connects)
A.	Trans-Siberian Railway	1.	Australia
B.	Trans-Canadian Railway	2.	North America
C.	Trans-Continental Stuart Highway	3.	Russia
D.	Big Trunk Route	4.	North Atlantic Ocean

Codes

	A	B	C	D		A	B	C	D
(a)	3	2	1	4	(b)	2	1	4	3
(c)	4	3	2	1	(d)	1	4	3	2

Assertion-Reason

Directions (Q. Nos. 28-31) In the questions given below are two statements labelled as Assertion (A) and other is labelled as Reason (R). In the context of two statements which one of the following is correct?

Codes

(a) Both A and R are true, but R is not the correct explanation of A
(b) Both A and R are true and R is the correct explanation of A
(c) Both A and R are incorrect
(d) A is correct, but R is incorrect

28. Assertion (A) Railways are most suited for large volume bulky materials over longer distances.

Reason (R) As compared to railways, road transport is economical for short distances.

29. Assertion (A) The length and quality of roads differs greatly between developed and developing countries.

Reason (R) Road construction and maintenance requires heavy expenditure.

30. Assertion (A) Water transport is the cheapest way to move bulky goods over long distances.

Reason (R) The friction of water is far less than that of land, making energy costs lower.

31. Assertion (A) In ancient times, riverways were the main highways of transportation. **CBSE Diksha**

Reason (R) Rivers lost their importance because of competition from railways, lack of water due to diversion for irrigation, and their poor maintenance.

Answers

1. (c) Pipelines
2. (c) Railways
3. (b) Vancouver to St. John's City
4. (a) Australia
5. (b) Perth to Sydney
6. (d) Quinghai-Tibet Train
7. (b) Benguela Railways
8. (d) Vancouver to Halifax
9. (b) Suez canal
10. (a) Western Europe with Australia
11. (b) Nile
12. (b) North Pacific Sea Route
13. (b) Airways
14. (d) Gulf of Mexico to North-Eastern USA
15. (b) 50 million
16. (d) It does not links the producers and the consumers.
17. (b) The Orient Express
18. (a) Cape of Good Hope Sea Route
19. (a) (i) and (ii)
20. (a) (i), (ii) and (iii)
21. (b) (i), (iii), and (iv) only
22. (c) (i), (ii) and (iii)
23. (d) (ii), (i), (iv), (iii)
24. (c)
25. (c)
26. (b)
27. (a)
28. (a) Both A and R are true, but R is not the correct explanation of A
29. (b) Both A and R are true and R is the correct explanation of A
30. (b) Both A and R are true and R is the correct explanation of A
31. (b) Both A and R are true and R is the correct explanation of A

Subjective Questions

Short Answer Type Questions

1. Classify Indian roads on the basis of construction and maintenance and explain them. **CBSE 2025**

Ans. Indian roads are classified into five categories based on construction and maintenance, as outlined by the Ministry of Road Transport and Highways (MoRTH).

- **National Highways (NH)** These are major roads that connect important cities, ports, and states across India. They are constructed and maintained by the central government. They play a crucial role in interstate trade and transport.
- **State Highways (SH)** These roads connect state capitals to districts and major towns. Constructed and maintained by the respective state governments, state highways facilitate intra-state connectivity.
- **District Roads** Managed by state governments, these roads link district headquarters to other towns and rural areas. They are essential for local transportation and access to administrative centers.
- **Rural Roads** Connecting villages to the main road network, these roads are crucial for rural development, agriculture, and connectivity. They are part of government schemes like the Pradhan Mantri Gram Sadak Yojana (PMGSY).
- **Border Roads** These roads are built near international borders, especially in remote and strategic areas. They are maintained by the Border Roads Organisation (BRO) for defense and connectivity purposes.

2. What are the important characteristics of border roads?

Ans. The important characteristics of border roads are as follows

- These roads are constructed on the international borders by specialised agency in a country.
- These roads are important for strategic as well as defence purposes as they help in providing access to strategically important areas along the borders.
- These roads are important for the economy of the people living along the border areas as these are used to supply goods and connect the border areas with major cities.
- It helps in providing security to the country as in case of any conflict at the borders, sufficient action can be taken early.

3. Describe any three major problems of road transport in the world.

Ans. Road transport plays an important role in the economy of a country. But it faces various problems, which include

(i) During rainy days, the roads which are unmetalled are damaged seriously. Even unmetalled roads are washed away by floods, which results in breaking up the road network.

(ii) The road transport system records heavy traffic. When roads cannot cope up with the demands of traffic on the road, roads are heavily congested.

(iii) Huge amount of money is required for construction and maintenance of roads which affects the quality of roads, mainly in developing countries. Road networks of the world are not fully developed.

4. Road transport plays a vital role in the promotion of trade and tourism in the world. Support this statement with three suitable arguments. **Competency Based Que**

Ans. Road transport plays a vital role in the promotion of trade and tourism in the world. It can be supported with the following examples

(i) Modern society requires speedy and efficient road transport system to assist in the production, distribution and consumption of goods.

(ii) The opening-up of tourist areas has been aided by improvement in transport facilities. Road transport provides link between the origin and destination of tourist places.

(iii) Road transport facilitates the movements of holiday makers, business travellers, people visiting relatives and those undertaking educational and health tourism.

5. What are the different roles played by pack animals in transportation in different parts of the world?

Ans. Pack animals are those animals which are used as a means of transportation. Some of the roles played by pack animals are as follows

- In Western countries horses are used as a draught animal.
- Dogs and reindeers are used to draw sledges over snow covered ground in North America, North Europe and Siberia.
- Camels are used in desert for caravan movement, the bullocks are used for pulling carts.
- Mules are used in mountain areas for carrying people as well as goods.

6. Mention the three major regions of the world which have a very dense network of railways.

Ans. The three regions of the world having a very dense network of railways are as follows

(i) **North America** It accounts for 40 per cent of the world's total railway network. The densest rail networks are present in the highly industrialised and urbanised region of East Central USA and adjoining Canada.

(ii) **Europe** There are about 4,40,000 km of railways in Europe. London, Paris, Brussels, Milan, Berlin and Warsaw are some of important rail headquarters.

(iii) **Asia** The rail network is dense in the thickly populated areas of Japan, China and India.

7. Write short note on the following ocean routes.
(i) North Atlantic Sea Route
(ii) The South Atlantic Sea Route

Ans. (i) The North Atlantic Sea Route connects the two industrially developed regions of the world which are North-Eastern USA and North-Western Europe. It accounts for one-fourth of world's foreign trade. It is the busiest route in the world. The other name of this route is Big Trunk Route. This route has highly advanced ports and harbour facilities.

(ii) The South Atlantic Sea Route route links West European and West African countries with Brazil, Argentina and Uruguay in South America. There is limited development and population in South America and Africa. Hence, there is little traffic on this route. The traffic is very low on the route between Rio de Janeiro and Cape Town.

8. Describe any six advantages of water transport in the world.

Or **Mention any six advantages of oceanic routes.**

Ans. Advantages of water transport or oceanic routes are as follows

(i) There is no need to construct routes over the oceans due to which the construction cost is saved.

(ii) Because of the less friction of water as compared to land, it is much cheaper mode of transport.

(iii) Compared to land and air, ocean transport is a cheaper means for carrying of bulky materials over long distances.

(iv) Water transport is energy efficient.

(v) It does not require maintenance.

(vi) Oceans are linked with each other and the ship of various sizes can be accommodated.

9. Name any two inland waterways of Europe. Explain any two factors that influence inland waterways.

Ans. The two important inland waterways of Europe are

(i) **The Rhine Waterway** The Rhine river flows through Germany and Netherlands. It is navigable for 700 km from Rotterdam in Netherlands to Basel in Switzerland.

It connects industrial areas of Switzerland, Germany, France, Belgium and Netherlands with the North Atlantic Sea Route.

(ii) **Danube Waterway** It rises near the Black forest mountains and flows Eastwards through many countries. It serves Eastern Europe. It is navigable up to Turnu Severin.

Factors that influence inland waterways are

(i) The navigability, width and depth of the channel. Rivers are modified so that they can be used as waterways.

(ii) The continuity in water flow and the level of technology also affect inland waterways.

10. Why is Rhine the world's most heavily used waterway? Explain any three reasons.

Or 'The Rhine waterways is the world's most heavily used inland waterway'. In the light of this statement, examine the significance of waterway.

Or Explain main features of the Rhine waterways. CBSE 2024

Ans. The Rhine flows through Germany and the Netherlands. The reasons for the Rhine to be the world's most heavily used waterway are as follows

(i) The river Rhine is navigable for 700 km from Rotterdam in Netherlands to Basel in Switzerland.

(ii) It flows through a rich coalfield which has made the whole region a prosperous manufacturing area.

(iii) The waterway links the industrial areas of Germany, France, Switzerland, Belgium, Netherlands with North Atlantic sea routes.

(iv) The Ruhr river joins the Rhine from its East. There is movement of huge volumes of freight to the South of Ruhr river. More than 20,000 ships and 20,00,000 inland vessels exchange their cargoes annually in this region.

11. Mention the famous oil pipeline of the USA. How are pipelines one of the most convenient modes of transport?

Ans. There is a dense network of oil pipelines in USA which run from the oil producing areas to consuming areas. One such famous pipeline is called Big lnch. It carries petroleum from the oil wells of the Gulf of Mexico to the North-Eastern states.

Pipelines are one of the most convenient modes of transport as they are used extensively to transport liquids and gases such as water, petroleum, oil and natural gas. They can carry liquid and gaseous materials for a long distance without any interruption or delays. The pipelines directly link the producing areas to the consuming areas.

12. There is increasing popularity of air transport in the recent time, inspite of its high cost. Why? Give reasons.

Ans. Air transport is the fastest mode of transport which has revolutionised the world connectivity. It is very costly, still it is becoming popular due to following reasons

- Valuable and perishable goods can be easily transported rapidly on a world wide scale from one country to another.
- The areas which were previously inaccessible have now become easily accessible due to air transport. For example, Himalayan region, Alaska region, etc.
- Travelling time has also reduced from months to days and hours.
- Air transport provides strategic and military advantage as tactical operations can be carried out easily. For example, US strikes in Iraq.

13. Write briefly about inter-continental air routes.

Ans. Different parts of the world are connected by air routes. A distinct East-West belt of inter-continental air routes is found in the Northern Hemisphere. Eastern USA, Western Europe and South-East Asia have a dense network of air routes. USA accounts for almost 60 per cent of the airways of the world.

These air routes are important for transporting goods and passengers between two continents. It has reduced the travel time and improved trade, commerce as well as relations between various countries in the world.

The important nodal points where air routes converge or radiate to all continents are New York, London, Paris, Amsterdam, Frankfurt, Rome, Moscow, Karachi, New Delhi, Mumbai, Bangkok, Singapore, Tokyo, San Francisco, Los Angeles and Chicago.

14. State any three advantages of satellite communication in India.

Ans. Three advantages of satellite communication in India are as follows *(Any three)*

(i) Satellites are an important mode of communication. The use of satellite in getting a continuous and synoptic view of larger area has made satellite communication very useful.

(ii) India has made great strides in satellite development. Bhaskar, Challenger and INSAT I-B have made long distance communication, television and radio very effective.

(iii) Today weather forecasting through television is a boon of satellite communication. Through it, monitoring of natural calamities is easy.

(iv) Satellites are also used to forecast monsoon rains in India. These forecast help farmers in planning their crops during monsoon.

15. What is cyberspace? Describe any two advantages of internet.

Ans. Cyberspace or internet refers to the electronic digital world that is used for communicating or accessing data information over computer networks without any physical movement of the sender and the receiver.

The cyberspace works within the World Wide Web (WWW) cyberspace can be accessed anywhere. For example in offices, at homes, in schools, etc. In the last few years, it has expanded rapidly. The user base has shifted from the developed countries like to USA to less developed countries such as China and India. There were about 2 billion internet users in the world in 2010 AD.

The two advantages of internet are

(i) It expands the social and economic space of people with the help of e-mail, e-commerce, e-learning, e-governance, etc.

(ii) Internet communication has connected more and more people across the world. It has made the concept of global village a reality.

16. Distinguish between National Highways and State Highways.

Ans. Differences between National Highways and State Highways are as follows

National Highways	State Highways
They connect state capitals and big cities across the nation.	They connect all the big cities within a particular state.
They are managed and maintained by the Public Works Department under Central Government.	They are managed and maintained by the Public Works Department under State Government.
These are important for the economy of the whole nation.	These are important for the economy of a particular state and surrounding regions.
In India, the total length of National Highways is 1,31,326 km.	In India total length of State Highways is about 1,79,535 km.

17. In modern times, communication has become specialised. Explain. **Competency Based Que**

Ans. Earlier people majorly used transport system not only for movement of goods and people but also to send their messages through men. Communication system was not much developed in that period. Gradually, communication developed and use of different means came into existence, like telegraphs, pagers, telephones, etc.

Communication has become specialised today. New forms of communication like mobile phones, satellite communication, internet, television, radio have been developed which have enhanced the connectivity and brought people more closer to each other. These specialised and modern communication systems have globalised the world.

18. 'Air transport has brought about a connectivity revolution in the world.' Explain this statement. **Competency Based Que**

Ans. Air transport has brought a connectivity revolution in the world. At present, no place in the world is more than 35 hours away due to developments in air transport. More than 250 commercial airlines offer transport services throughout the world.

The areas which were previously inaccessible due to difficult terrain and harsh climate can now be accessed easily by air transport services. For example, the airplanes supply various items of common use to the Eskimos living in regions where the ground is permanently frozen and roads and railways cannot reach there. The areas in mountain regions, which become inaccessible due to landslide and avalanches can be reached by air transport.

The travelling time has reduced from months to days and hours. Two places in the world are not much far away inspite of the distance between them with new developments such as supersonic aircrafts, the distance between two places will reduce greatly and air transport will become more convenient.

19. What are the five factors of development which have enhanced the efficiency of ocean transport?

Ans. Ocean transport is more economical as compared to land and air transport in case of haulage of bulky material over the continents.

The factors of development that have enhanced the capacity of ocean transport are as follows

(i) Use of radar, wireless and other navigation aids in modern passenger ships.

(ii) The introduction of refrigerated chambers for transporting perishable goods.

(iii) The development of tankers and other specialised ships and use of container.

(iv) The oceans provide smooth flow of traffic in all directions with no maintenance costs.

(v) The introduction of technology including advanced data capturing system has also enhanced the efficiency of ocean transportation.

20. Explain why all forms of transport are also referred to as lines of communication. **CBSE 2023**

Ans. All forms of transport also referred to as lines of communication. It is due to the fact that in ancient times means of transport and communication both were complimentary to each other. In older periods, when there was no invention of mobile telephony and internet services, the communication was dependent on means of transport alone as written messages were carried by hand, animals, boat, road, rail and air from one place to another place.

With the invention of new technologies in communication like internet, satellite communication, etc this dependence on means of transport is reducing. But all forms of communication are not fully disassociated with transport because of the cheapness of the older systems. Thus, very large volumes of mail continue to be handled by post offices all over the world.

21. Study the map given below carefully and answer the questions that follow.

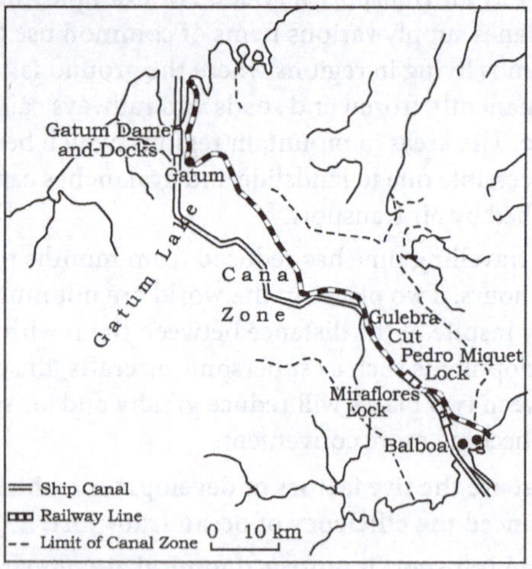

(i) Identify and name the canal shown in the map.

(ii) Write any two characteristics of this canal.

(iii) How economically significant is this canal for world?

Ans. (i) This map shows Panama canal.

(ii) Two characteristics of this canal are

(a) This connects the Atlantic Ocean with the Pacific Ocean.

(b) It is constructed by US Government across Panama Isthumus between Panama City and Colon.

(iii) The economic significance of this canal is relatively less than that of the Suez. However, it is vital to the economies of Latin America.

22. Study the following map of the Suez Canal carefully and answer the questions that follow. CBSE SQP 2024, 2024 C

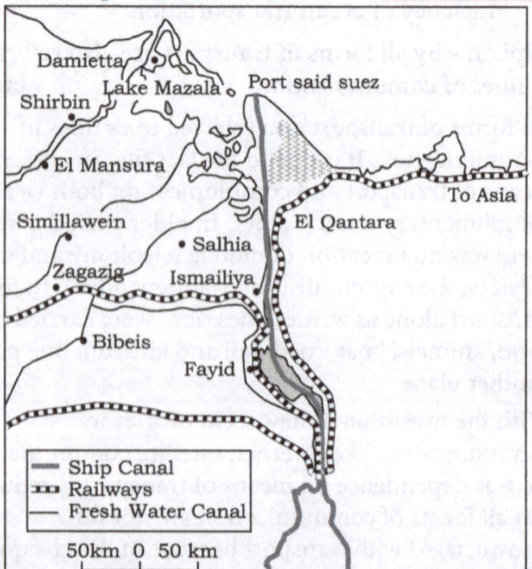

(i) Name the two seas connected by the Suez Canal.

(ii) Why do we consider this as Europe's gateway to the Indian Ocean?

(iii) Write one characteristic of the Suez Canal.

Ans. (i) The Suez Canal connects the Mediterranean Sea and the Red Sea.

(ii) The Suez Canal is considered Europe's gateway to the Indian Ocean because it provides a direct maritime route between Europe and Asia without requiring ships to navigate around the Southern tip of Africa (Cape of Good Hope).

(iii) The Suez Canal is a vital man-made waterway connecting the Mediterranean Sea to the Red Sea, significantly reducing travel time for ships by avoiding the long route around Africa's Cape of Good Hope.

23. Study the map given below carefully and answer the following questions.

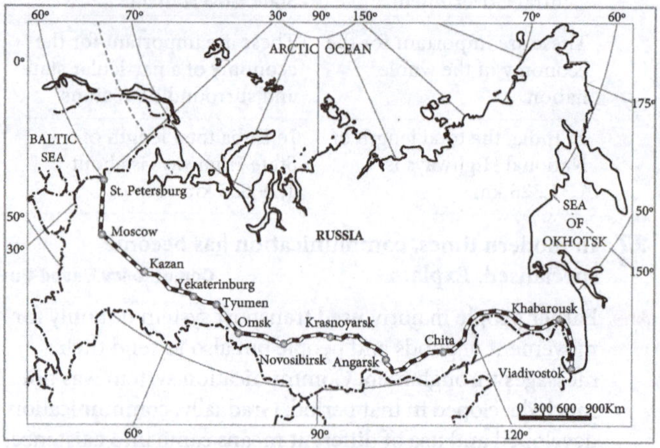

(i) Identify and name the railway line shown on the map.

(ii) Name the continents linked by this rail route.

(iii) Explain how this railway line is helpful for the promotion of trade in this region.

Ans. (i) Trans-Siberian railway line has been shown on the map.

(ii) It connects Asia and Europe.

(iii) This railway line runs across the Ural Mountains and connects agro-centres like Chita and Irkutsk. It also acts as a linkage between different manufacturing centres.

24. **Study the map given below carefully and answer the following questions.**

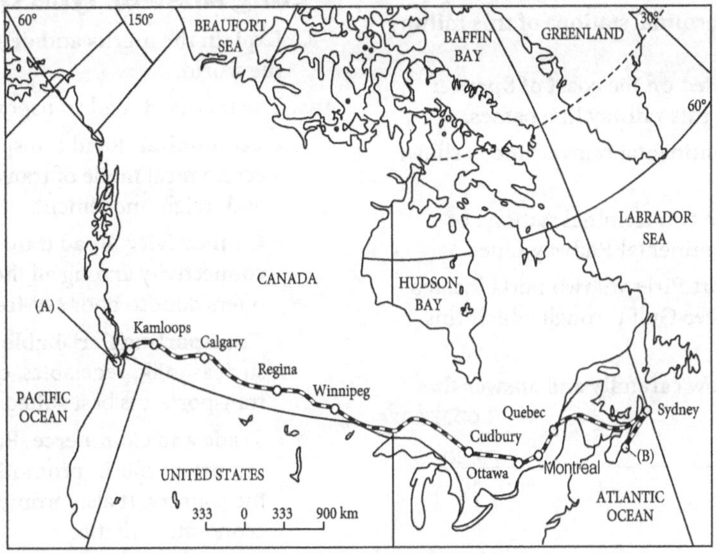

CBSE 2024

(i) **Name the railway line given in the map.**

(ii) **Name the places marked as '(A)' and '(B)' in the given map.**

(iii) **Explain the importance of the railway line given on the map.**

Ans. (i) The railway line given in the map is Trans-Canadian railway line.

(ii) (A) Vancouver (B) Halifax

(iii) The railway line connects the Atlantic and Pacific coasts of Canada, facilitating transportation of goods and passengers, promoting trade, and linking major cities, thus supporting economic growth and regional connectivity.

25. **Study the map given below carefully and answer the following questions.**

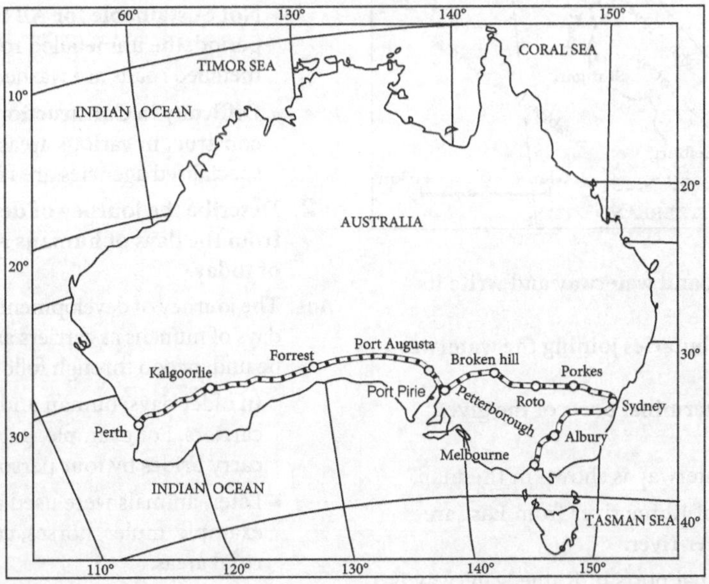

(i) Name the railway line shown in the given map.

(ii) Which are the two terminal stations of this railway line?

(iii) Name the ports located on the coast of Spencer Gulf through which this railway line passes.

Ans. (i) Australian Trans-Continental railway line is shown in the given map.

(ii) Perth and Sydney are two terminal stations of Australian Trans-Continental Railway Line.

(iii) Port Augusta and Port Pirie are two ports located on the coast of Spencer Gulf through which this railway line passes.

26. Study the map given below carefully and answer the following questions. **CBSE 2024**

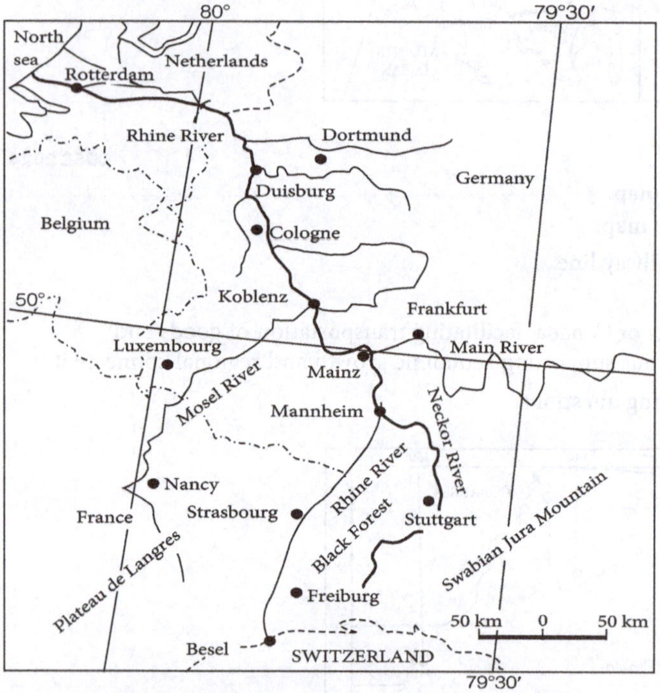

(i) Identify the given inland waterway and write its name.

(ii) Mention any two tributaries joining the waterway from East.

(iii) Write the names of terminal ports of the given waterways.

Ans. (i) The Rhine inland waterway is shown in the map.

(ii) The two tributaries of Rhine river from East are Main river and Necker river.

(iii) The important terminal ports of Rhine waterway is Dusseldorf.

Long Answer Type Questions

1. Explain the merits and demerits of road transport in the world.

Ans. The merits of road transport are

- **Economical** Road transport is cheap and most economical mode of transport for short distance travel and freight movement.
- **Connectivity** Road transport offers the best connectivity among all the means of transport as it offers door to door services.
- **Transporting Perishable Goods** Perishable goods such as milk, vegetables, etc are transported by road transport. It is best suited for transporting these items.
- **Trade and Commerce** Road transport plays an important role in promoting trade and commerce in the country. It also promotes tourism and other economic activities.
- **Flexible** Road transport is flexible in nature as multiple routes can be travelled to reach a particular place.

The demerits of road transport are

- **Heavy Expenditures** The construction and maintenance of roads require heavy expenditures. This affects road quality.
- **Traffic** Road transport is severely affected by traffic and congestion. When roads are not able to cope up with the demands of the traffic, then congestion occurs.
- **Not Sustainable for All Seasons** During the rainy period, the unmetalled roads are damaged. Even the metalled roads are washed away during floods.
- **Difficulty in Construction** Roads are difficult to construct in various areas such as mountains. Here, specialised agencies are required to construct roads.

2. Describe the journey of development of land transport from the days of humans as carriers and the cableways of today.

Ans. The journey of development of land transport from the days of humans as carriers and the cableways of today can be understood through following facts

- In older days, human and animals were important carriers. For example, palanquin (*palki/doli*) was used to carry brides by four persons (*Kahars* in North India).
- Later, animals were used as means of transport. For example, mules, horses, camels, oxen, etc were used in rural areas.
- With the invention of the wheel, the use of carts and wagons became important.

- The 18th century marks the revolution in transport which came about only after the invention of the steam engine.
- In the 19th century, railways became the most popular and fastest form of transport with the opening of the first public railway line in 1825 between Stockton and Darlington in Northern England.
- In USA, the development of railways also facilitated commercial grain farming, mining and manufacturing in the continental interiors of the country.
- On the other hand, the invention of the internal combustion engine revolutionised road transport in terms of road quality and vehicles (motor cars and trucks) flying over them.
- The newer forms of land transportation have emerged in recent times. It includes pipelines, ropeways and cableways. These are faster and more efficient as compared other means of transport.

3. Which continent has the highest road density? Why do traffic congestions occur on road? Explain any three measures to solve the problem of traffic congestion.

Ans. North America has the highest road density. About 33% of world's total motorable road length is present in North America. North America also accounts for the highest number of vehicles as compared to Europe.

Problem of Traffic Congestion There is a problem of chronic traffic congestion in most of the cities of the world. The congestion occurs because of the failure of the road networks in meeting the demands of traffic. In recent years, the traffic on roads has substantially increased. We can see peaks and troughs of traffic flow on roads at different times of the day.

The three measures to solve the problem of traffic congestion are as follows

Increasing Parking Fee The parking fee for private vehicles should be increased. It will discourage them in using their private vehicles. This will reduce the number of vehicles on the roads and reduce traffic congestion.

Public Transport Public transport facilities such as public bus service, metro rails, trains, etc should be improved. It will encourage people to use public transport facilities which will substantially reduce the road traffic. Public transport connectivity should be enhanced.

Expressways Highways and expressways should be constructed. These expressways and highways are wider and larger. They provide seamless connectivity to the people and also accommodate more number of vehicles. This also reduces congestion considerably.

4. What is the importance of railways as a mode of land transport? Explain any four main features of the railway network in Europe.

Or **Explain any five characteristics of rail transport in Europe.**

Or **Explain the importance of rail transport in India.**

CBSE 2024

Ans. Importance of railways as a mode of land transport are discussed below

- Railways provide the cheapest and most convenient mode of passenger transport both for long distance and sub-urban traffic.
- Railways have played a significant role in development and growth of industries. These help in supplying raw materials and other facilities to the factory sites and finished goods to the market.
- They also form the connecting link between the ocean vessels, barges, boats, motor trucks and pipelines.
- Railways are specially suited for transport of bulky materials like coal, petroleum and ores over long distances.

The characteristics of rail transport in Europe are

- The density of rail network is high in Europe. It is considered as one of the most dense rail networks in the world.
- The rail network is either double tracked or multiple-tracked. The total length of rail network is 4,40,000 km.
- Railways carries more passenger traffic as compared to freight in European countries.
- The rail network has underground railways in Europe. For example, underground railways in London, Paris, Moscow.
- There are various cities that form important nodes in the rail network. These are London, Paris, Milan, Berlin, Warsaw, etc.

5. Which is the longest trans-Continental Railway of North America? Describe its any four features.

Or **'Trans-Canadian railway line is considered as the economic artery of Canada.' Support the statement with suitable examples.**

Or **Explain the characteristics of Trans-Canadian Railways.**

CBSE 2025, 2024

Ans. The longest trans-continental railway line in North America is Trans-Canadian Railway line. It covers a distance of 7050 km, running from Halifax in the East to Vancouver on the Pacific Coast.

The Trans-Canadian railway line is considered the economic artery of Canada due to the following characteristics

(i) It connects the important industrial cities of Montreal, Ottawa, Winnipeg and Calgary. Goods and people can be easily transported to and from these economic centres with the railways.

(ii) It connects Quebec-Montreal industrial region with the wheat but of Prairie region. Thus, raw materials and finished products are transported with these railways.

(iii) The line also connects the Coniferous forest region in the North to the Quebec-Montreal and the Prairies. All these regions have become complementary to each other and they support economic activities.

(iv) A loop line from Winnipeg to Thunder Bay (Lake Superior) connects this rail line with one of the most important waterways in the world. This is used for exporting various products.

6. Name the longest trans-continental railway of the world. Describe its any four features.

Or **Explain the characteristics of Trans-Siberian Railways.** **CBSE 2025, 2024**

Ans. Trans-Siberian Railway is the longest trans- continental railway of the world. The Trans-Siberian railways runs from St. Petersburg in the West to Vladivostok on the Pacific coast in the East. It is Asia's most important route. Characteristics of the Trans-Siberian railways are as follows

- It connects various important commercial and industrial centres such as Moscow, Ufa, Irkustsk, Chita, etc. These centres are important for the economy of the region.
- In Asia, it is the longest as well as double-tracked and electrified railways. Due to this, it is possible to link Asian and European markets.
- This railway line has connecting links further Southwards. It connects Odessa in Ukraine, Baku on the Caspian Coast, Tashkent in Uzbekistan, etc.
- This railway line is important for trade and commerce between the continents of Asia and Europe. It provides integration of both continents in terms of their economy and society.

7. State any three characteristics of water transport. Why is traffic far less on the South Atlantic sea route?

Ans. Three characteristics of water transport are as follows

(i) Water transportation does not require route construction. The oceans are linked with each other and offer smooth routes that are accessible in all directions with less maintenance costs.

(ii) It is cheaper means of transportation because the friction of water is less than that of the land and energy cost is lower.

(iii) Very heavy cargo like coal, cement, timber and metallic ores can be transported through inland waterways.

The reasons for less traffic on South Atlantic Sea route are

- The population is very less in South America and Africa. There is less development in the countries of South America as well as Africa. Due to this, the demand in these regions is very less and trade is very low.
- Both South America and Africa have similar products and resources. Due to this the trade declines as trade of similar products is not economically feasible.
- There are very few industrial regions in both the continents. Only parts of South Africa and South-Eastern Brazil and Plata Estuary have industrial regions. This leads to lesser trade between these regions and tesser traffic on the South Atlantic Sea route.

8. "Pipelines are used extensively to transport liquids and gases in the world". Support the statement with appropriate arguments. **CBSE 2023, Competency Based Que**

Ans. Pipelines are extensively used worldwide to transport liquids and gases due to their efficiency, safety and cost-effectiveness. They provide an uninterrupted flow, making them ideal for petroleum, natural gas, water and even liquid coal.

The following factors make pipelines an important method of liquid transportation

- **Cost-Effectiveness** Pipelines require less energy for transportation than roads or rail. Once installed, they operate continuously with minimal labour costs, making them a cheaper option for long-term use.
- **Reliability** Pipelines offer a steady and uninterrupted supply of resources, reducing the chances of delays caused by weather or traffic.
- **Safety** Pipelines reduce the risk of accidents compared to transporting hazardous materials by road or rail. They are less prone to spills and leaks when properly maintained.
- **Environmental Benefits** Pipelines decrease carbon emissions by avoiding the need for trucks or trains. They also occupy less land than highways or railway tracks.
- **Wide Usage** Countries like the USA have dense networks of pipelines transporting petroleum and natural gas from production areas to consumption centres. The 'Big Inch' pipeline is a famous example in the USA, carrying petroleum efficiently. Similarly, in India, pipelines connect oil fields to refineries and markets.
- **Innovative Applications** In New Zealand, pipelines are even used to transport milk from farms to factories.

9. Explain the significance of each of the transport and communication services available in the world.

Ans. The significance of various transport services are as follows

Road Transport It is cheaper and faster mode of transport over short distance and for door-to-door services.

Railways It is best suited for bulky goods and passengers for long distances.

Water Transport It is the cheapest mode of transport because of less friction of water. Ocean routes are cheaper for carrying of bulky material from one continent to another.

Air Transport It is the fastest means of transportation. It is best suited for long distance travel and worldwide transportation of valuable cargo.

Pipelines It is used to carry liquids and gases from the producing areas to the consuming areas.

Significance of various communication services are as follows

Satellite Communication In contemporary, world, satellite communication has become very important with internet as the largest electronic network on the planet connecting about 1000 million people in more than 100 countries.

Cyber Space-Internet This electronic network has spread rapidly. The number of users have increased from 400 million in 2000 AD to over two billion in 2010. It has brought people from different parts of world closer to each other.

10. What is the significance of inland waterways? Explain the three factors responsible for the development of inland waterways in the world.

Or **Analyse the three factors that affect the development of inland waterways. Explain the significance of Rhine inland waterways.**

Ans. The significance of inland waterways are

- Inland waterways are suitable for transportation with the help of rivers, canals, creeks, etc.
- These are used for carrying both passengers and cargo.
- These are the only means of transport in the dense forests.
- They are suitable for carrying heavy cargo like coal, cement, timber, metallic ores, etc.

The three factors responsible for the development of inland waterways in the world are:

(i) **Navigability** The width and depth of the channel makes navigation possible.

(ii) **Water Flow** A continuous flow of water throughout the year helps ships, boats to easily move in the waterways.

(iii) **Transport Technology** Development of proper technology so that very heavy cargo like coal, timber, metallic ores can also be easily transported through inland waterways.

The Rhine waterways is significant in the following ways

- It is world's heavily used waterway with more than 20,000 ocean going ships and 200,000 inland vessels exchange their cargo on this route.
- Huge tonnage moves along this stretch of the waterway.
- The river Rhine is navigable for 700 km from Rotterdam in Netherlands to Basel in Switzerland.
- It flows through a rich coal field which has made the whole region prosperous manufacturing area.
- The waterway links the industrial areas of Germany, France, Switzerland, Belgium, Netherlands with North Atlantic sea routes.

11. Analyse the distribution of highways in the world.

Ans. For answer refer to text page. no. 111 under the heading 'Highways in the World'.

12. Analyse the distribution of railway network in the world.

Ans. For answer refer to page no. 112 under the heading 'Railways'.

13. 'The Suez and the Panama canals are two vital man-made navigation canals, which serve as the gateways of commerce for both the Eastern and Western worlds.' In the light of this statement, explain the economic significance of these two canals. **Competency Based Que**

Ans. The Suez and Panama canals are very important navigational canals that are significant for the Eastern as well as Western Worlds. The Panama Canal joins the Atlantic Ocean in the East to the Pacific Ocean in the West. Economically it is significant in the following ways

(i) It is important for the economies of North America as well as Latin America as it is used for carrying out trade between these regions.

(ii) The distance between Eastern and Western coasts of USA is significantly reduced due to the opening up of this canal. It has resulted in boosting the US economy and easing World Trade.

(iii) There has been a significant reduction in the distance between Western Europe and America. This results in improvements in their trade and commercial relations.

The Suez Canal connects Mediterranean Sea and Red Sea. It was constructed in 1869 in Egypt between Port Said in North and Port Suez in South.

Suez Canal is economically significant in the following ways

(i) After the opening of this canal, the sea distance between Europe and Asia has reduced. This has lead to rise in trade between both the continents.

(ii) It is important for the economies of Europe as well as African nations as ships carrying essential goods part through this canal.

(iii) Railway lines have also been constructed from the Suez Canal to supply goods and improve trade even in the interior parts of the region.

14. Name the canal connecting the Atlantic Ocean and the Pacific Ocean. Explain its main features. CBSE 2024

Ans. The Panama Canal joins the Atlantic and the Pacific Oceans. It was constructed by the US Government across the Panama Isthumus between Panama City and Colon.

The main features of Panama canal are

- Its total length is 72 km and involves a very deep cutting for a length of 12 km.
- It reduces the distance between New York and San Francisco by 13,000 km by the sea route, benefitting the economy of USA.
- It has six-lock system and ships cross different levels (26m up and down) through these locks before they enter the Gulf of Panama.
- It has also reduced the distance by sea route between Western Europe and West coast of USA, North-Eastern and Central USA and East and South-East Asia.
- It is vital for the economies of Latin America as most of the trade in these countries takes place through the Panama Canal.

15. Explain the importance of communication services in the world.

Ans. Communication is the exchanging of information, by speaking, writing or using some other means. For example, telephone, television, satellites, internet, etc.

Communication services are important because of the following reasons

- Communication connects the people in different parts of the world. They can exchange, information, ideas and make it easy to send or receive message.
- Communication through optic fibre networks allows large amount of datas to be transmitted rapidly, securely and error free.
- Development of communication networks has become a crucial factor in developing urbanisation in various countries, e.g. in America.
- In developing countries, use of cell phones has made it possible to connect the rural areas of the country.
- New technologies such as satellite communication has made it possible to communicate with anyone anywhere in the world. Thus, communication has become faster.
- The use of internet for communication has made the concept of global village a reality.

16. Explain with examples the importance of 'Satellite Communication' in the world. CBSE 2024

Ans. Satellite communication has revolutionised global connectivity, offering seamless communication across vast distances. Since its inception in the 1970s, satellite technology has enabled reliable communication, overcoming geographical barriers. This has been particularly crucial in connecting remote and rural areas, especially in developing countries. For example, satellite communication plays a vital role in rural India, enabling people to access mobile services and connect with others through cell phones.

Satellites have also made global broadcasting, including television and radio, more effective. Countries can now broadcast programs worldwide, making entertainment and educational content accessible to millions. In addition, satellites support weather forecasting, allowing accurate predictions that help in disaster management and agricultural planning.

The launch of artificial satellites such as India's Aryabhatt, Bhaskar-I, and INSAT-I has significantly contributed to the country's communication infrastructure. Satellites make long-distance communication efficient and cost-effective, as it is the same cost to communicate over 500 km or 5,000 km. Overall, satellite communication has made the world more interconnected and has transformed how we live, work, and interact.

Source Based Questions

1. Read the passage carefully and answer the questions that follow.

The revolution in transport came about only after the invention of the steam engine in the 18th century. Perhaps the first public railway line was opened in 1825 between Stockton and Darlington in Northern England and then onwards, railways became the most popular and fastest form of transport in the 19th century. It opened up continental interiors for commercial grain farming, mining and manufacturing in USA. The invention of the internal combustion engine revolutionised road transport in terms of road quality and vehicles (motor cars and trucks) plying over them. Among the newer developments in land transportation are pipelines, ropeways and cableways. Liquids like mineral oil, water, sludge and sewers are transported by pipelines. The great freight carriers are the railways, ocean vessels, barges, boats and motor trucks and pipelines. In general, the old and elementary forms like the human porter, pack animal, cart or wagon are the most expensive means of transportation and large freighters are the cheapest. They are important in supplementing modern channels and carriers which penetrate the interiors in large countries.

(i) Which of the following technology revolutionised road transport?

(a) Invention of Tyres
(b) Internal Combustion Engine
(c) Cart and Wagon
(d) Metalled Roads

Ans. (b) Internal Combustion Engine

(ii) Pipelines cannot be used to transport which of the following?

(a) Mineral oil (b) Water
(c) Sewage (d) Passengers

Ans. (d) Passengers

(iii) Which type of transport can be used to provide connectivity to interior of the countries?

(a) Airways (b) Roadways
(c) Waterways (d) All of these

Ans. (b) Roadways

2. Read the passage carefully and answer the questions that follow.

Rivers, canals, lakes and coastal areas have been important waterways since time immemorial. Boats and steamers are used as means of transport for cargo and passengers. The development of inland waterways is dependent on the navigability width and depth of the channel, continuity in the water flow, and transport technology in use. Rivers are the only means of transport in dense forests. Very heavy cargo like coal, cement, timber and metallic ores can be transported through inland waterways. In ancient times, riverways were the main highways of transportation as in the case of India. But they lost importance because of competition from railways, lack of water due to diversion for irrigation, and their poor maintenance.

The significance of rivers as inland waterways for domestic and international transport and trade has been recognised throughout the developed world. Despite inherent limitations, many rivers have been modified to enhance their navigability by dredging, stabilising river banks, and building dams and barrages for regulating the flow of water.

(i) Which of the following has led to decline in waterway transport?

(a) Competition from railways
(b) Diversion of rivers
(c) Poor maintenance of waterways
(d) All of the above

Ans. (d) All of the above

(ii) Which of the following transport is used in navigating the dense forests?

(a) Railways (b) Road transport
(c) Riverways (d) Airways

Ans. (c) Riverways

(iii) Which of these can be transported by inland waterways?

(a) Metallic ores (b) Timber
(c) Cement (d) All of these

Ans. (d) All of the above

3. Study the map and answer the questions that follows.

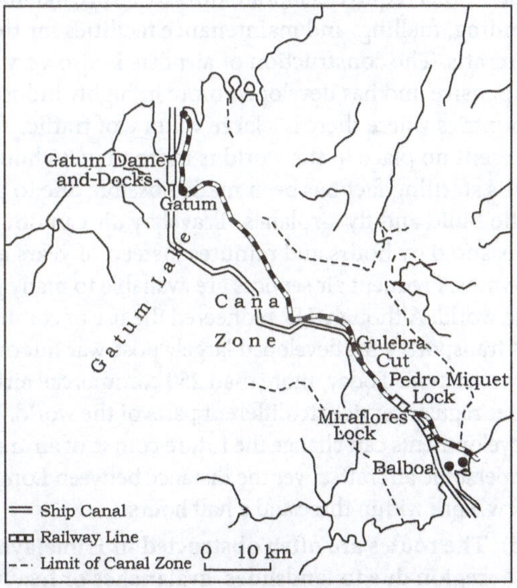

(i) Which two oceans does the Panama Canal connect?

(a) Atlantic Ocean and Indian Ocean
(b) Pacific Ocean and Indian Ocean
(c) Atlantic Ocean and Pacific Ocean
(d) Southern Ocean and Arctic Ocean

Ans. (c) Atlantic Ocean and Pacific Ocean

(ii) Observe the image and analyse the primary purpose of the locks in the canal.

(a) To connect different rivers.

(b) To adjust the water level for ships to cross different elevations.

(c) To prevent flooding in the region.

(d) To provide a water source to nearby cities.

Ans. (b) To adjust the water level for ships to cross different elevations.

(iii) Identify the economic importance of the Panama Canal.

(a) Facilitates faster shipping between the Eastern and Western hemispheres.

(b) Provides drinking water to surrounding regions.

(c) Acts as a tourist destination.

(d) Generates hydroelectric power.

Ans. (a) Facilitates faster shipping between the Eastern and Western hemispheres.

4. Read the passage carefully and answer the questions.

In the Himalayan region, the routes are often obstructed due to landslides, avalanches or heavy snowfall.

At such times, air travel is the only alternative to reach a place. The manufacturing of aircrafts and their operations require elaborate infrastructure like hangars, landing, fuelling, and maintenance facilities for the aircrafts. The construction of airports is also very expensive and has developed more in highly industrialised countries where there is a large volume of traffic. At present no place in the world is more than 35 hours away. This startling fact has been made possible due to people who build and fly airplanes. Travel by air can now be measured by hours and minutes instead of years and months. Frequent air services are available to many parts of the world. Although, UK pioneered the use of commercial jet transport, USA developed largely post-war international civil aviation. Today, more than 250 commercial airlines offer regular services to different parts of the world. Recent developments can change the future course of air transport. Supersonic aircraft, cover the distance between London and New York within three and a half hours.

(i) The routes are often obstructed in Himalayan region due to landslides, avalanches or heavy snowfall. How necessary goods can be transported to the people?

Ans. The necessary goods are provided to the people through the airways, when routes in Himalayan region are obstructed due to landslides, avalanches or heavy snowfall.

(ii) What is the main infrastructure requirement for the manufacturing and operation of aircraft?

Ans. The main infrastructure required for the manufacturing and operation of aircraft are hangars, landing, fuelling, and maintenance facilities for the aircraft.

(iii) Which country pioneered the use of commercial jet transport?

Ans. The UK pioneered the use of commercial jet transport.

5. Read the passage carefully and answer the questions.

Cyberspace is the world of electronic computerised space. It is encompassed by the internet such as the World Wide Web (WWW). In simple words, it is the electronic digital world for communicating or accessing information over computer networks without the physical movement of the sender and the receiver... It is also referred to as the internet. Cyberspace exists everywhere. It may be in an office, sailing boat, flying plane and virtually anywhere.

The speed at which this electronic network has spread is unprecedented in human history. There were less than 50 million internet users in 1995, about 400 million in 2000 AD and over two billion in 2010. In the last few years, there has been a shift among global users from USA to the developing countries. The percentage share of the USA has dropped from 66 in 1995 to only 25 in 2005. Now the majority of the world's users are in the USA, UK, Germany, Japan, China and India.

(i) What is the significance of the rapid spread of cyberspace globally?

Ans. The rapid spread of cyberspace has led to a significant increase in global internet users, with a notable shift from the USA to developing countries.

(ii) What trend is observed in the global distribution of internet users from 1995 to 2005?

Ans. There has been a shift in global internet users from the USA to developing countries, with the USA's percentage share decreasing from 66% in 1995 to 25% in 2005.

(iii) Which countries currently have the majority of the world's internet users?

Ans. The majority of the world's internet users are currently in the USA, UK, Germany, Japan, China, and India.

Map Based Questions

1. Identify the following on the political map of the world.

(i) An International airport **CBSE SQP 2024**
(ii) Two important airports in South America
(iii) An important shipping canal **CBSE 2024 C**
(iv) A major air port
(v) The terminal station of Trans-continental Railway

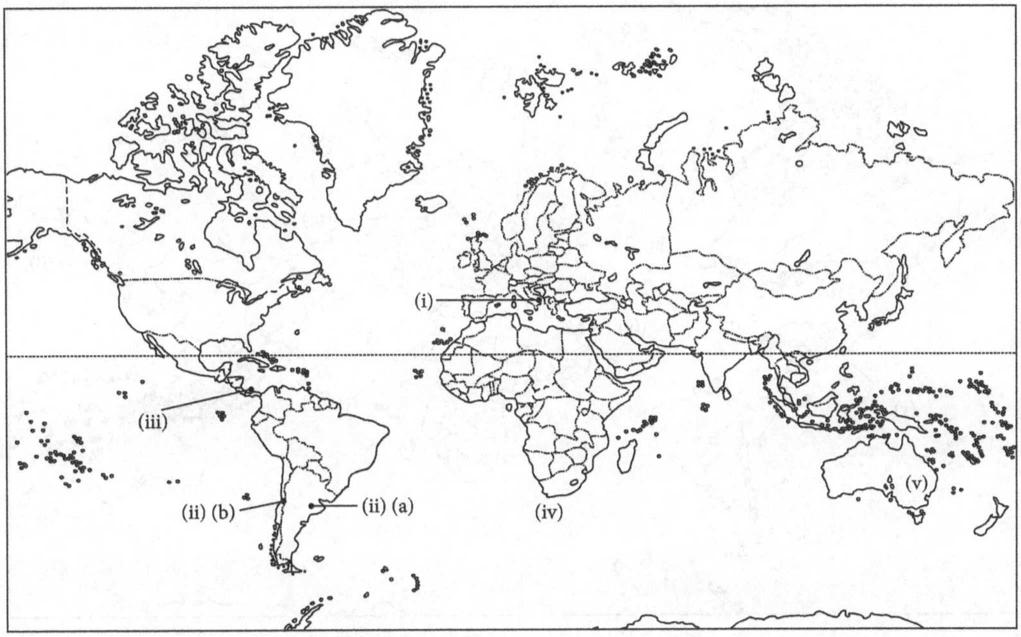

Ans.

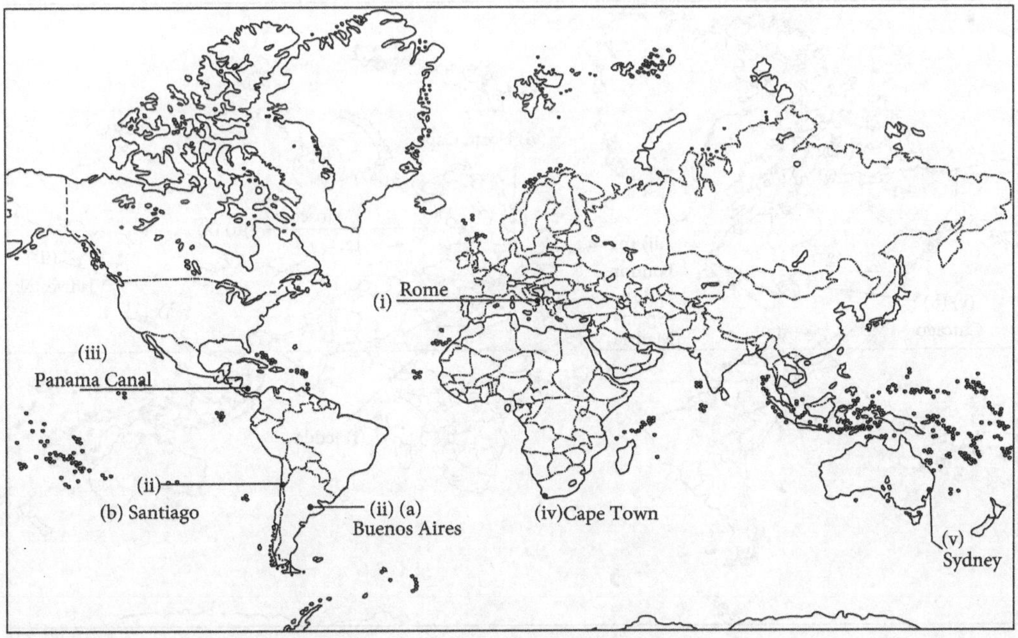

2. Identify the following on a political map of the world.

(i) A major airport

(ii) Eastern terminal station of Trans-Siberian railway

(iii) Two major airports of Europe.

(iv) An international airport

(v) Two major airports of North America.

(vi) A major sea port in Europe

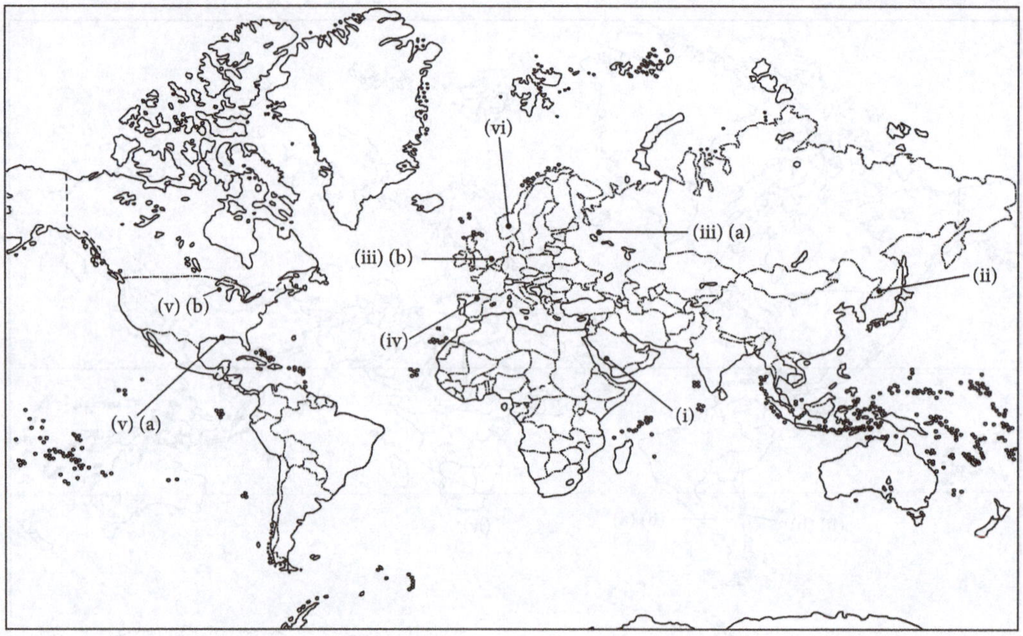

Ans.

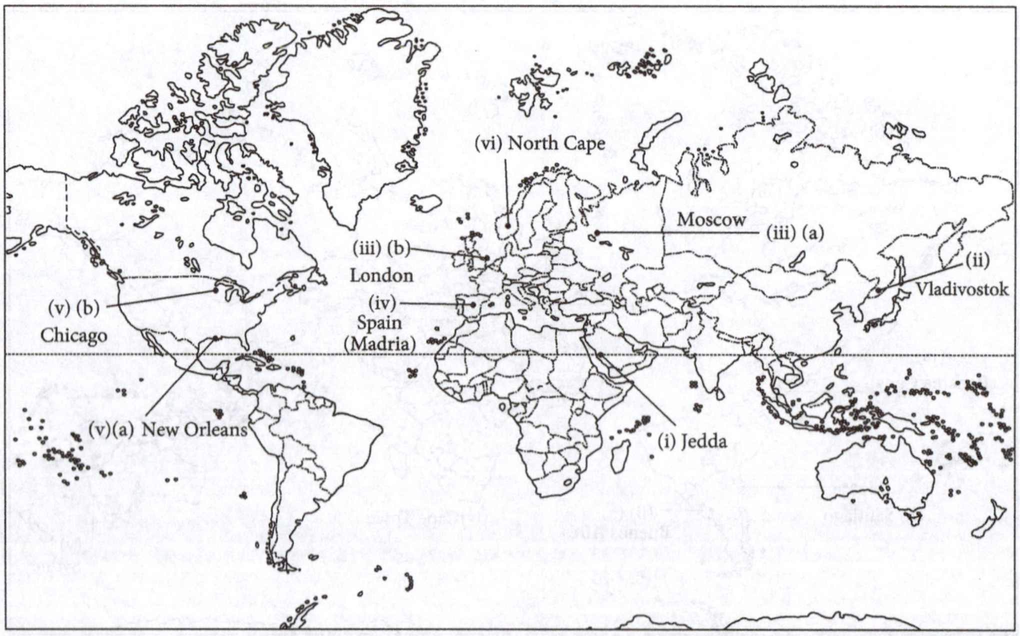

3. Identify the following on a political map of the world.

(i) A major sea port in Australia **CBSE 2024**

(ii) A major seaport

(iii) A major sea port

(iv) A major sea port in North America

(v) A major sea port

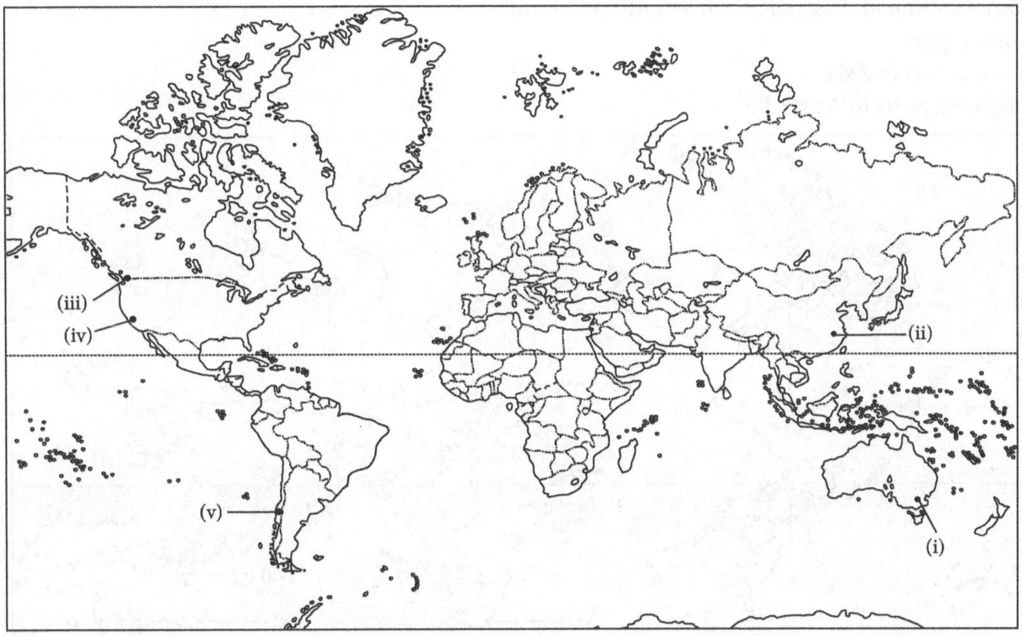

Ans.

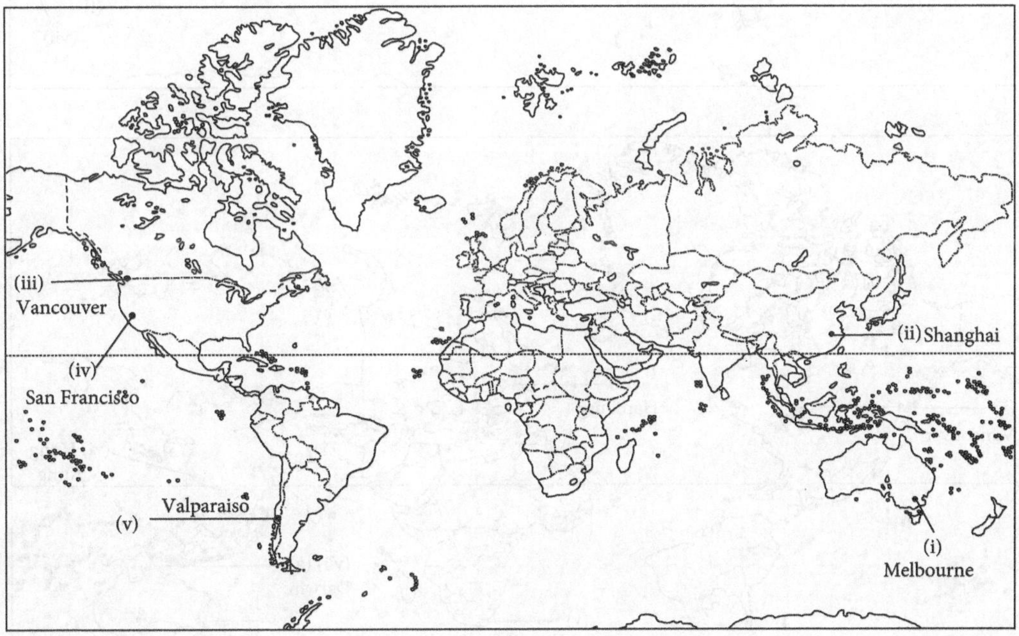

4. Identify the following on a political map of the world.

(i) Railway terminal station
(ii) A terminal station of Trans-Canadian railway line
(iii) An important seaport
(iv) A terminal station of Australian trans-continental railway
(v) A major sea port
(vi) A major sea port in Asia
(vii) Two major airports in Australia

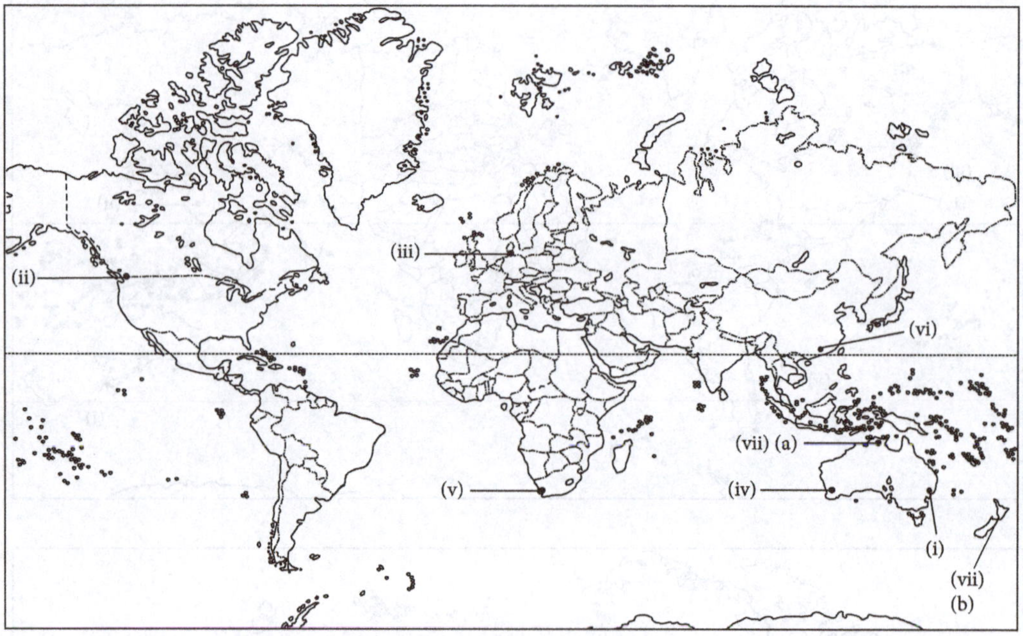

Ans.

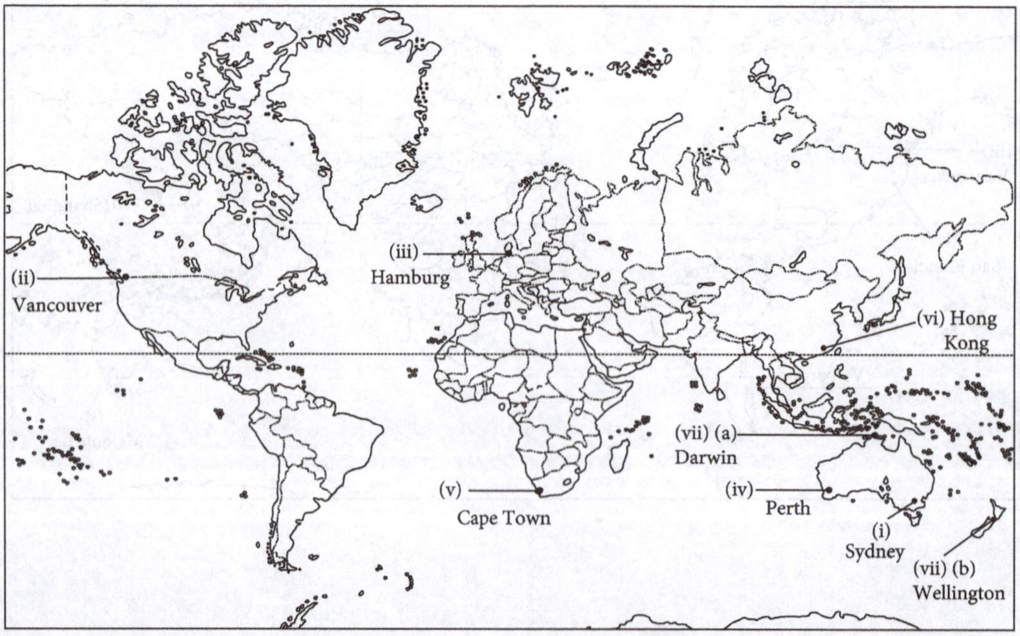

5. **Identify major airports marked on the following political map of the world.**

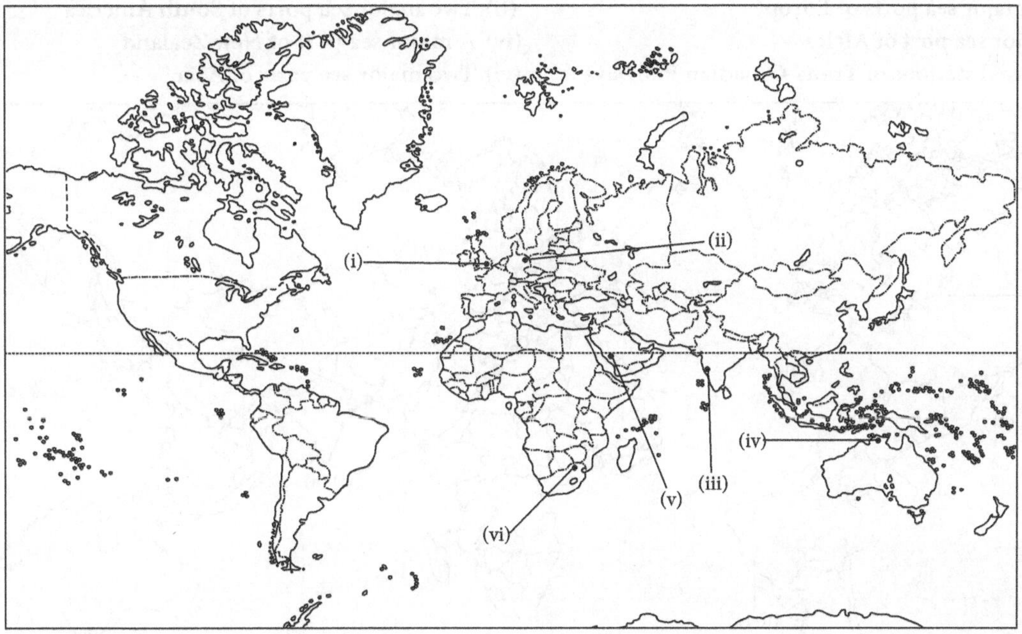

Ans.

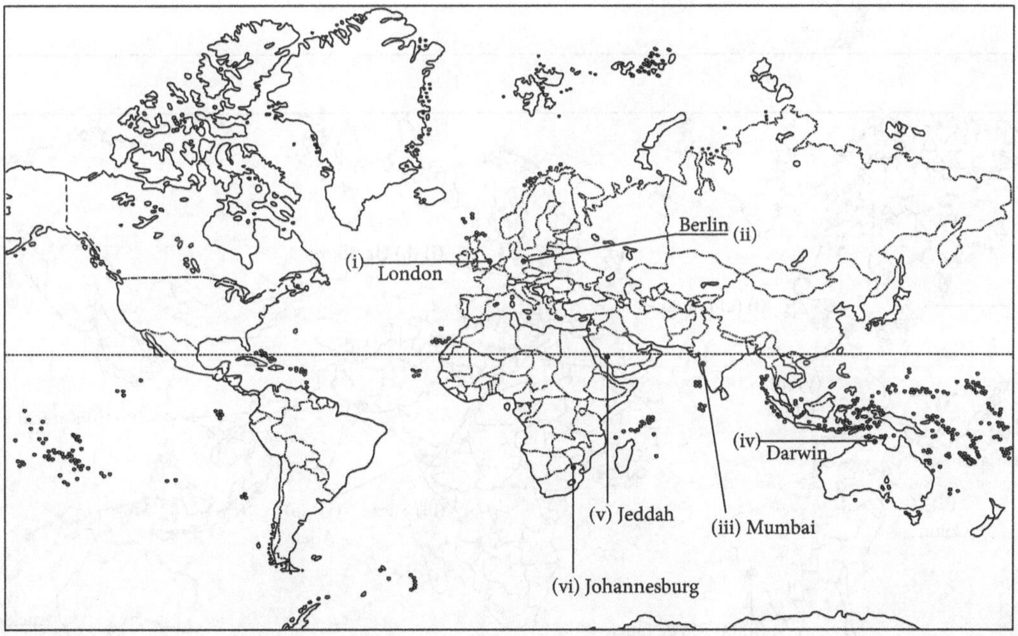

6. On the map of the world, identify the following.

(i) Two major sea ports of Europe
(ii) Two major sea ports of South America
(iii) A major sea port of Africa
(iv) A major sea port of New Zealand
(v) Terminal stations of Trans-Canadian Railways
(vi) Two major sea parts of Asia

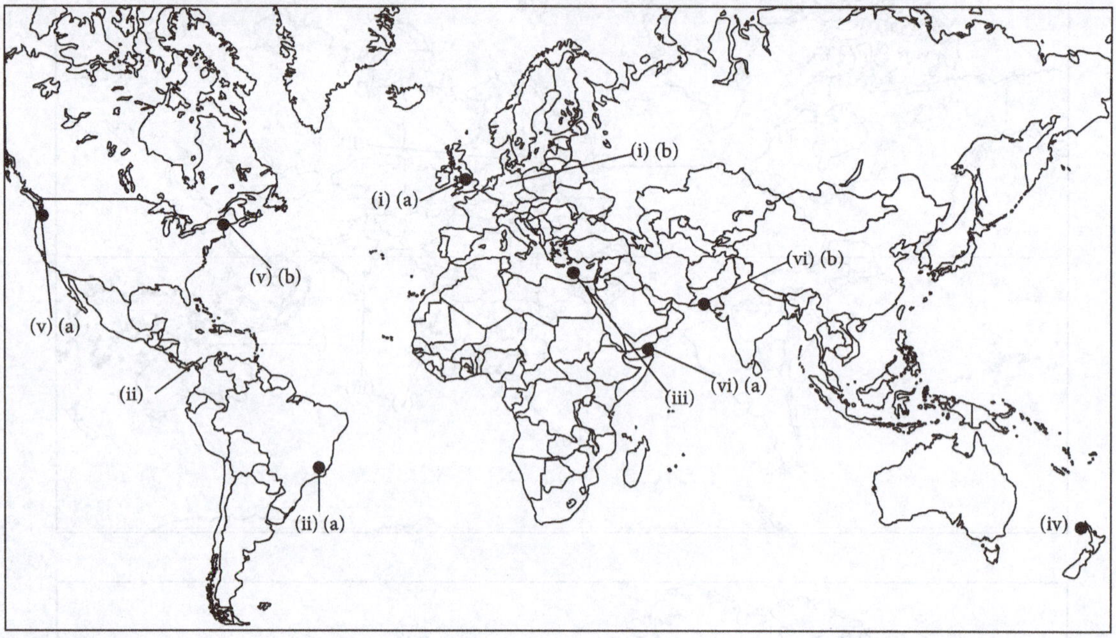

Ans.

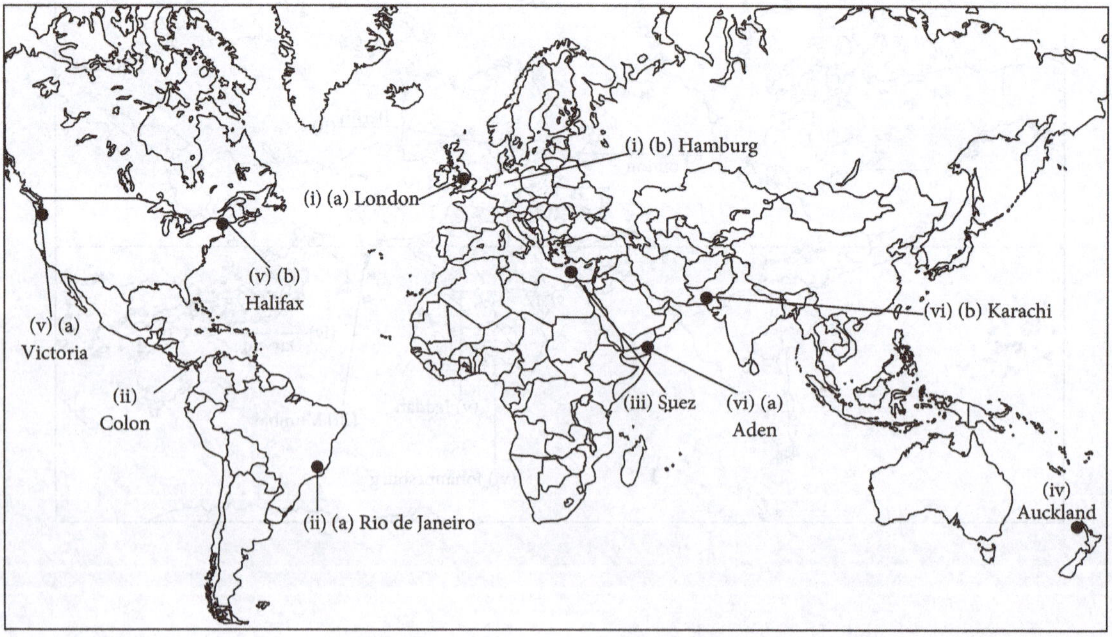

7. On the map of the world, identify the following

(i) An inland waterway
(ii) Two major airports of Asia
(iii) Terminal station of Trans-Siberian Railway
(iv) A major sea port of Asia
(v) Two major airports of North America
(vi) A major airport of Africa

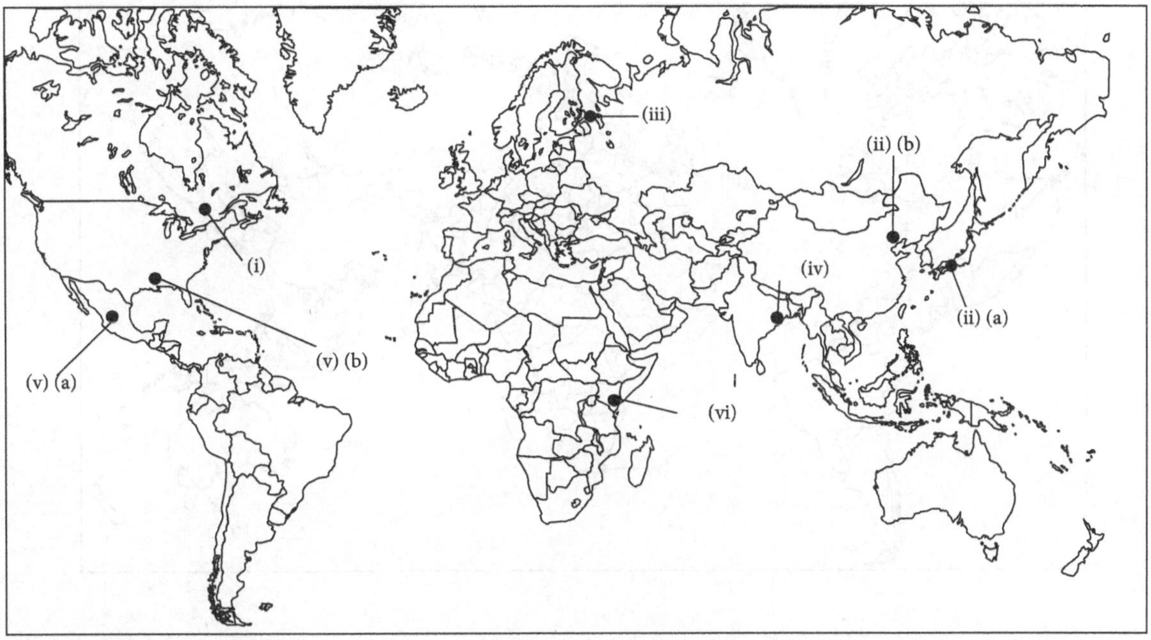

Ans.

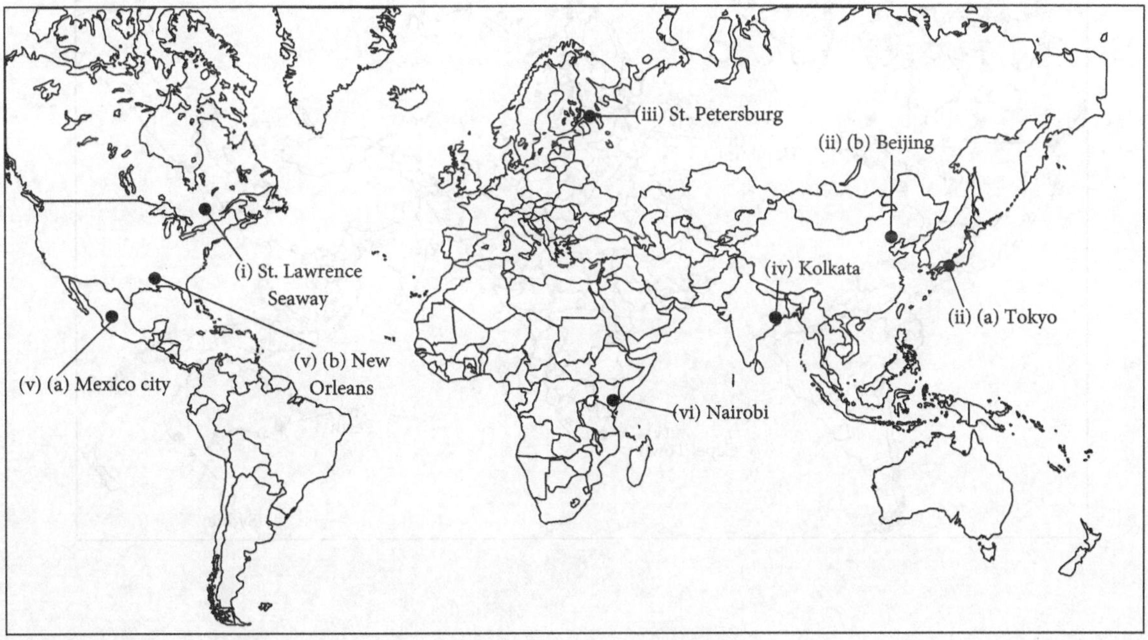

8. Identify the following in the political map of the world.

(i) Railway terminal station
(ii) A terminal station of Trans-Canadian Railway line
(iii) An important seaport
(iv) A terminal station of Australian Trans-continental railway
(v) A major sea port

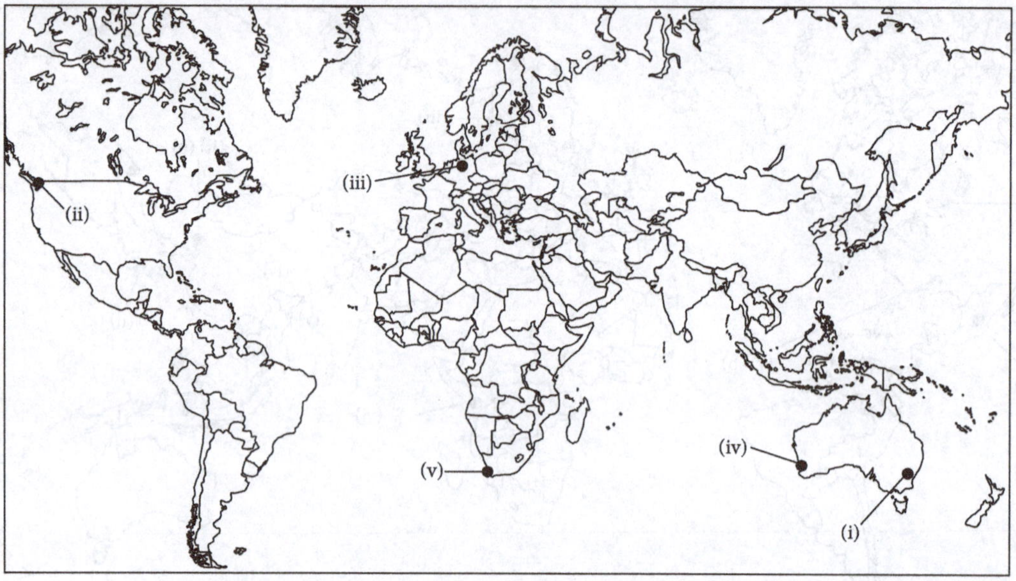

Ans.

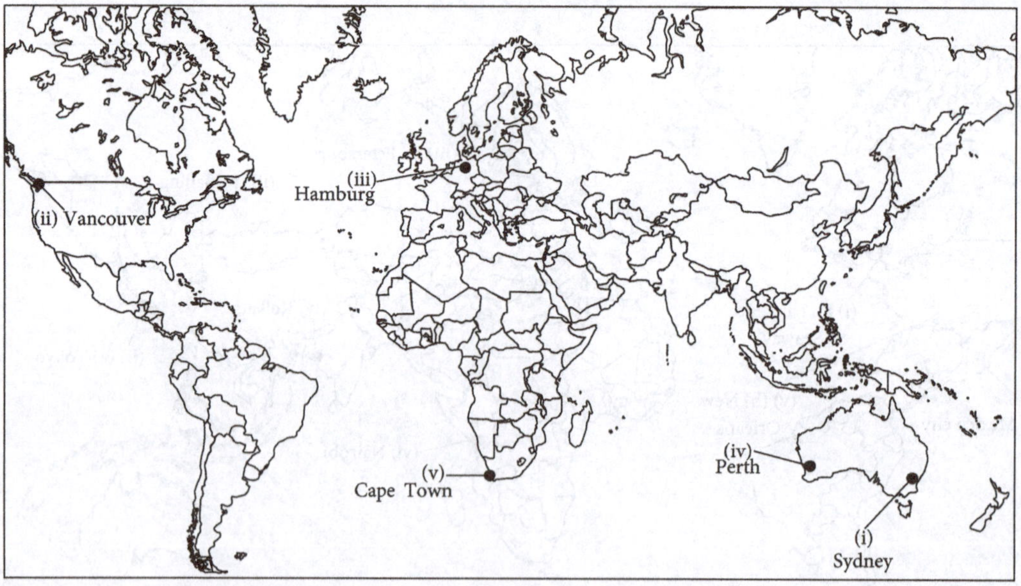

SELF ASSESSMENT TEST

Objective Type Questions

1. What is the primary function of trans-continental railways?
   (a) To connect mining centers within a single country
   (b) To link the two ends of a continent for economic and political reasons
   (c) To facilitate urban transport within a city
   (d) To replace road networks in hilly areas
2. The Peruvian Railways are located in which of these mountains?
   (a) Andes (b) Rockies
   (c) Himalayas (d) Atlas
3. The length of Australian rail network is about ....
   (a) 6000 km (b) 50,000 km
   (c) 40,000 km (d) 120,000 km
4. The Union and Pacific Railways connects which of these two cities?
   (a) New York to Los Angeles (b) New York to San Francisco
   (c) New York to Chicago (d) Chicago to San Francisco
5. Which of these sea routes is also known as the Big Trunk Route?
   (a) North Atlantic sea route (b) North Pacific sea route
   (c) South Pacific sea route (d) South Atlantic sea route

Short Answer Type Questions

6. How do transport and communication unite scattered people?
7. How is the Trans-Siberian railway economically significant?
8. Give an account of the rail network of Asia.
9. What are the changes which have occurred in last few years in the use of internet?
10. Compare the significance of Danube and the Volga waterways.
11. How has the increasing use of cyberspace contributed to the idea of a 'global village'?
12. What is the reason for the high energy efficiency of waterways?

Long Answer Type Questions

13. Give the two phases of the communication development in the world.
14. Analyse the importance of the highways of the world.
15. Explain the technological innovations used in the Panama Canal and their role in overcoming natural barriers.
16. Why do countries likes Russia and the USA rely more on railways for long-distance freight transport?

8

CHAPTER

Trade means the voluntary exchange of **goods** and **services**. Two parties must trade where one person sells and the other purchases. For both parties, trade is mutually beneficial.

International Trade

YOUR STUDY GOALS

8.1 History of International Trade
8.2 Basis of International Trade
8.3 Gateways of International Trade

YOUR PRACTICE GOAL

- Objective Type Questions (21 Qs ; MCQs, Statements, Matching, A-R)
- Subjective Questions (17 SAs, 9 LAs)
- Source Based Questions (2 Qs)

- The initial form of trade in primitive societies was the **barter system**, where direct exchange of goods took place. In other words, goods were exchanged for goods. The introduction of money overcame the difficulties of the barter system.
- Earlier, rare objects with very high intrinsic value were used as money. For example, flintstones, obsidian, cowrie shells, tiger's paws, whale's teeth, dog's teeth, skins, furs, cattle, rice, peppercorns, salt, small tools, copper, silver and gold.
- Trade may be conducted at two levels: **international** and **national**.

8.1 History of International Trade

- In ancient times, transporting goods over long distances was risky, hence trade was restricted to local markets.
- The **Silk Route** is an early example of long distance trade connecting Rome to China through the 6,000 km route. The traders exchanged Chinese silk, Roman wool, precious metals and many other high value commodities from intermediate points in India, Persia and Central Asia.
- After the disintegration of the Roman Empire, European commerce developed around the twelfth and thirteenth centuries with the development of ocean. There was increase in warships trade between Europe and Asia and the discovery of the Americas.

- Fifteenth century onwards, European countries began to colonise the countries along with the trade of exotic commodities.
- During this period, a new form of trade emerged which was called the **slave trade**. The **Portuguese, Dutch, Spaniards** and **British** captured African natives and forcefully shifted them to the newly discovered Americas for their labour in the plantations.
- The slave trade was a huge business for more than two hundred years till it was abolished in **Denmark** in 1792, **Great Britain** in 1807 and the **United States** in 1808.
- After the **Industrial Revolution**, the demand for raw materials like grains, meat and wool also increased, but their monetary value declined in comparison to the manufactured goods.
- The industrialised nations used to import raw materials from non-industrialised nations and exported the value added finished products back to the non-industrialised nations.
- In the late nineteenth century, regions producing primary goods were no longer important, and industrial nations became each other's major customers.
- During World Wars I and II, countries imposed trade taxes and quantitative restrictions for the first time on trading activities.
- The **General Agreement for Tariffs** and Trade was formed after the end of World War II. It helped in reducing tariffs.

International Trade

- **International trade** is the exchange of goods and services among countries across national boundaries. Countries trade to obtain commodities, which they cannot produce themselves or they can purchase elsewhere at a lower price.
- International trade happens because different countries are good at making different things. When countries focus on what they do best, they can trade with others and everyone benefits. This is called **specialisation.**
- Countries trade is based on three main ideas
  (i) **Comparative advantage** It means making what they are best at;
  (ii) **Complementarity** It is trading things that fit well with what another country needs;
  (iii) **Transferability** It is how easily goods and services can be moved from one country to another.
  These principles make trade beneficial for both sides.
- In today's world, trade is very important for the global economy, and it's linked to the relationships between countries. With the help of modern transportation and communication, no country wants to miss out on the benefits of trading with others. It helps everyone get what they need and boosts the economy.

Types of International Trade

- **Bilateral Trade** Bilateral trade is done by two countries with each other. They agree to trade specified commodities among themselves. For example, country A may agree to trade some raw material with an agreement to purchase some other specified item to country B or vice versa.
- **Multi-lateral Trade** Multi-lateral trade is conducted between many trading countries. The same country can trade with several other countries. The country may also grant the status of the **Most Favoured Nation** (MFN) to some of its trading partners.

Quick Test 1

1. Name a place where barter trade still exists in India.
2. The native of which continent were captured and treated as slaves?
3. In which year, slave trade started to decline in Great Britain?
4. Name a principle based on international trade.

8.2 Basis of International Trade

- **Difference in National Resources** The world's national resources are unevenly distributed because of differences in their physical structure as follows
  - (i) **Geological Structure** It determines the mineral resource base. Due to topographical differences, the diversity of crops and animals raised can be observed. Lowlands have greater agricultural potential. Mountains attract tourists and promote tourism.
  - (ii) **Mineral Resources** They are unevenly distributed worldwide. The availability of mineral resources provides the basis for industrial development.
  - (iii) **Climate** It influences the type of flora and fauna that can survive in a particular region. It also maintains diversity in the range of various products. For example, wool production can take place in cold regions, and bananas, rubber and cocoa can grow in tropical regions.
- **Population Factors** The size, distribution and diversity of people between countries affect the type and volume of goods traded.

  These factors are discussed below
  - (i) **Size of Population** Densely populated countries have a large volume of internal trade but little external trade because most of the agricultural and industrial production is consumed in the local markets. The living standard of the population determines the demand for better quality imported products because with a low standard of living only a few people can afford to buy costly imported goods.
  - (ii) **Cultural Factors** Different forms of art and craft develop in certain cultures that are valued worldwide. For example, China produces the finest porcelains and brocades. Carpets of Iran are famous while North African leather work and Indonesian batik cloth are prized handicrafts.
- **Stage of Economic Development** At different stages of economic development of countries, the nature of items traded changes. In agriculturally important countries, agro products are exchanged for manufactured goods whereas industrialised nations export machinery and finished products, and import food grains and other raw materials.
- **Extent of Foreign Investment** Foreign investment can boost trade in developing countries that lack in capital required for the development of mining, oil drilling, heavy engineering, lumbering and plantation agriculture. By developing such capital intensive industries in developing countries, the industrial nations ensure the import of food stuff and minerals and create markets for their finished products. This entire cycle increases the volume of trade between nations.
- **Transport** In olden times, lack of adequate and efficient means of transport restricted trade to local areas. Only high-value items, like gems, silk and spices were traded over long distances. With the development of rail, ocean and air transport, as better means of refrigeration and preservation, trade has experienced spatial expansion.

Balance of Trade

- Balance of trade is the record of the volume of goods and services imported as well as exported by a country to other countries.
- Based on the value of trade, there can be two types of balance of trade among countries : negative or positive.
- If the value of imports is more than the value of a country's exports, the country has a **negative** or unfavourable balance of trade. If the value of exports is more than the value of imports, then the country has a **positive** or favourable balance of trade.

- Balance of trade and **balance of payments**[1] have a great influence on a country's economy. A negative balance refers that the country spends more on buying goods than it can earn by selling its goods. This would lead to the over-utilisation of financial reserves.

Free Trade

- When economies open up for trading at the international level it is known as free trade or trade **liberalisation**. This is done by bringing down **trade barriers**[2] like tariffs.
- Trade liberalisation allows goods and services from everywhere to compete with domestic products and services.
- Globalisation and free trade can affect the economies of developing countries negatively by not giving equal trading capacities by imposing unfavourable conditions.
- The development of transport and communication systems makes goods and services travel faster and farther than before.
- Free trade should not only let rich countries enter the markets but also allow developed countries to keep their markets protected from foreign products. Countries also need to be cautious about **dumped goods**.

World Trade Organisation

- To liberate the world from high customs tariffs and various other types of restrictions, the **General Agreement for Tariffs and Trade** (GATT) was formed in 1948 by some countries. The GATT was transformed into the **World Trade Organisation** on 1st January, 1995.
- WTO Headquarters are located in Geneva, Switzerland. India has been one of the founding members of the WTO.
- WTO is the only international organisation that deals with global rules of trade between nations. It sets the rules for the global trading system and resolves disputes between its member nations.
- WTO also covers trade in services, such as telecommunication and banking, and other issues such as **intellectual rights**[3].
- The WTO has however been criticised. WTO is opposed by the countries that are worried about the effects of free trade and economic globalisation. The free trade does not make ordinary people's lives more prosperous. It is increasing the difference between rich and poor by making rich countries more rich. This is because the influential nations in the WTO focus on their commercial interests.
- Moreover, many developed countries have not fully opened their markets to products from developing countries. It is also argued that issues of health, worker's rights, child labour and environment are ignored.

Regional Trade Blocs

- Regional trade blocs encourage trade between countries that are closely located.
- Regional trade blocs have similarities and complementarities in trading items and they reduce restrictions on trade in the developing world.
- Currently, 120 regional trade blocs generate 52 per cent of the world trade. These trading blocs are developed as a response to the failure of global organisations to speed up intra-regional trade.

---

1 **Balance of Payments** It is the record of all international financial transactions made by the residents of a country.

2 **Trade barriers** These restrictions are introduced by the government on international trade. These barriers may be tariffs or non-tariffs.

3 **Intellectual rights** It is a term sometimes used to refer to the legal protection afforded to owners of intellectual capital. This idea is more commonly referred to as intellectual property.

Concerns Related to International Trade

- International trade can be harmful to nations if it leads to dependence on other countries and uneven levels of development.
- International trade often leads to exploitation and commercial rivalry that leads to wars.
- Global trade affects many aspects of life; it can impact everything from the environment to the health and well-being of people around the world.
- When countries compete to trade more, then production and the use of natural resources increase. This leads to overutilisation of resources. This further results in marine life depletion, deforestation and river basins being sold off to private drinking water companies.
- Multinational corporations trading in oil, gas mining, pharmaceuticals and agri-business keep expanding their operations at all costs. Their mode of work is in such a way that they do not follow the norms of sustainable development and create more pollution.
- If organisations are aimed only towards profit making, and environmental and health concerns are not addressed, then it could lead to serious implications in the future.

Quick Test 2

1. Name two factors that determine international trade.
2. In the current period, which sector is showing an increase in international trade?
3. Give any one limitation of international trade.

8.3 Gateways of International Trade

Ports

- The chief gateways of the world's international trade are the harbours and ports. Cargoes and travellers pass from one part of the world to another through the ports.
- The ports provide facilities for docking, loading, unloading and storage facilities for cargo. To provide these facilities, the port authorities make arrangements for maintaining navigable channels, arranging tugs and barges, and providing labour and managerial services.
- The importance of a port is judged by the size of the cargo and the number of ships handled. The quantity of cargo handled by a port is an indicator of the level of development of its surroundings.

Types of Port

Types of port according to cargo handled

- **Industrial Ports** These ports specialise in bulk cargo, like grain, sugar, ore, oil, chemicals and similar materials.
- **Commercial Ports** These ports handle general cargo-packaged products and manufactured goods. These ports also handle passenger traffic.
- **Comprehensive Ports** These ports handle bulk and general cargo in large volumes. Most of the world's great ports are classified as comprehensive ports.

Types of port based on location

- **Inland Ports** These ports are located away from the sea coast. They are linked to the sea through a river or a canal. Such ports are accessible to flat bottom ships or barges. For example, Manchester is linked with a canal; Memphis is located on the river Mississippi; Rhine has several ports like Mannheim and Duisburg; and Kolkata is located on the river Hoogli, a branch of the river Ganga.

- **Out Ports** These are deep water ports built away from the actual ports. These serves the parent ports by receiving those ships that are unable to approach them due to their large size. Example of this kind of port is Athens and its out port in Greece.

Types of port based on specialised functions

- **Oil Ports** These ports deal in the processing and shipping of oil. Some of these are tanker ports and some are refinery ports. Maracaibo in Venezuela, Esskhira in Tunisia and Tripoli in Lebanon are tanker ports. Abadan on the Gulf of Persia is a refinery port.
- **Ports of Call** These are the ports that originally developed as calling points on main sea routes where ships used to anchor for refuelling, watering and taking food items. Later on, they developed into commercial ports. Aden, Honolulu and Singapore are examples of commercial ports
- **Packet Station** These are also known as **ferry ports**. These packet stations are exclusively concerned with the transportation of passengers and mail across water bodies covering short distances. These stations occur in pair, and they are located in such a way that they face each other across the water body, e.g. Dover in England and Calais in France across the English Channel.
- **Entrepot Ports** These are collection centres where the goods are brought from different countries for export. Singapore is an entrepot for Asia, Rotterdam for Europe and Copenhagen for the Baltic region.
- **Naval Ports** These are ports which have only strategic importance. These ports serve as warships and have repair workshops for them. Kochi and Karwar are examples of such ports in India.

Quick Test 3

1. The WTO was established in which year?
2. Memphis port is located on which river?
3. Give an example of a tanker port.

Mind Map

INTERNATIONAL TRADE

1 History of International Trade

- Barter system was a popular method of trade in the primitive societies.
- Silk route is an early example of international trade.
- During World War I and World War II, countries imposed trade taxes and quantitative restrictions.
- General Agreement for Tariffs (GATT) was formed after war period in 1948.

2 Types of International Trade

- **Bilateral Trade** Done by two countries with each other.
- **Multilateral Trade** Conducted by many trading countries.

3 Basis of International Trade

- **Differences in National Resources** Geological structure, Mineral Resources, climate are distributed unevenly.
- **Population Factors** Size distribution and diversity of people between countries affects trade.
- **Stage of Economic Development** Nature of trade changes with different level of economic development.
- **Extent of Foreign Investment** Foreign investment boosts trade.
- **Transport** Adequate and efficient transport affects trade.

4 Balance of Trade

- Records the volume of goods and services imported and exported between countries.
- **Positive** When export is more than import.
- **Negative** When import is more than export.

5 Free Trade

- Trading without barriers like tariffs.
- Trade liberalisation is promoted.

6 Trading Blocs

- **World Trade Organisation** International organisation that deals with global rules of taxes.
- **Regional Trade Blocs** Encourage trade between countries that are densely connected.

7 Concerns Related to International Trade

- Regional imbalance
- Commercial rivalry
- Environment depletion
- Depletion of marine life
- Exploitation of resources

8 Types of Ports

Based on Location

- **Inland Port** Located away from sea coast, e.g., Memphis.
- **Out Ports** Deep water ports built away from actual ports, e.g., Piraceus.

Based on Cargo Handled

- **Industrial Ports** Specialised in bulk cargo like grain, sugar, ore, etc.
- **Commercial Ports** Handle general cargo packaged products.
- **Comprehensive Ports** Handles bulk and general cargo in large volumes.

Based on Specialised Functions

- **Oil Ports** Deals in the processing and shipping of oil.
- **Ports of Call** Calling points on main sea routes where ships used to anchor for refuelling, watering and taking food items.
- **Packet Stations** It is also known as ferry ports.
- **Entrepot Ports** Collection centres where the goods are brought from different countries for exports.
- **Naval Ports** Serve as warships

NCERT Folder

Choose the right answer from the four alternatives given below

(i) **Most of the world's great ports are classified as**

(a) Naval ports (b) Comprehensive ports
(c) Oil ports (d) Industrial ports

Ans. (b) Comprehensive ports

(ii) **Which one of the following continents has the maximum flow of global trade?**

(a) Asia (b) Europe (c) North America (d) Africa

Ans. (b) Europe

Answer the following questions in about 30 words

(i) **What is the basic function of the World Trade Organisation?**

Ans. The World Trade Organisation (WTO) sets the rules for the global trading system and resolves disputes between its member nations. WTO also covers trade in services, such as telecommunication and banking, and other issues including intellectual rights.

(ii) **Why is it detrimental for a nation to have negative balance of payments?**

Ans. A negative balance of payment has serious implications over the financial resources of a country. Negative balance would mean that the country spends more on buying goods than it can earn by selling goods. This would ultimately lead to exhaustion of its financial resources. Therefore, it is detrimental (disadvantageous) for a nation to have negative balance of payments.

(iii) **What benefits do nations get by forming trading blocs?**

Ans. Regional trade blocs are set up to encourage trade between countries with geographical closeness, similarity and complementarities in trading items. These are also to keep restrictions on trade of the developing world under control.

Answer the following questions in not more than 150 words

(i) **How are ports helpful for trade? Give a classification of ports on the basis of their location.**

Ans. The usefulness of ports for trade can be justified by the following points

- Ports are important for global trade because trains and waterways are not available everywhere.
- Harbours and ports acts as the best gateways of the world of international trade.
- These ports facilitates the passage of goods/cargos and travellers.
- Ports provide other facilities like docking, loading and unloading and storage facilities for cargos.

Classification of Ports on the Basis of their Location

- **Inland Ports** These are located away from the sea port and are connected to sea through a river or a canal. Examples of such ports are Manchester which is connected with a canal, Memphis located on the river Mississippi, Mannheim and Duisburg on the river Rhine, and Kolkata located on the river Hoogli, a branch of the river Ganga.
- **Out Ports** These are deep water ports built away from the actual ports. These ports serve as the parent ports by receiving those ships which are unable to approach them due to their large size. For example, Athens and its out port Piraeus in Greece.

(ii) **How do nations gain from international trade?**

Ans. Nations gain from international trade in the following ways

- International trade provides opportunity to sell goods and services in international markets to earn foreign exchange.
- Nations obtain technological and managerial support from different countries of the world.
- By importing raw materials, they can support their industries.
- Some essential commodities can be imported to fulfil the needs of the people of the country.
- Trade creates employment opportunities and hence, improves the living standard of the citizens.
- Trade between different nations improve their relationship which provides opportunities for other bilateral agreements.
- Trade opens the way for the exchange of ideas and knowledge which are helpful in social and economic transformation.
- International trade also leads to the better development of ports as their development is necessary to facilitate the international trade.

Exam Pattern Questions

Objective Type Questions

Multiple Choice Questions (MCQs)

1. Slave trade was a lucrative business for more than two hundred years. It was abolished in

(a) Denmark in 1792 and Great Britain in 1807
(b) Great Britain in 1807 and United States in 1808
(c) Denmark in 1792 and United States in 1808
(d) All of the above

2. The silk route had a length of .... connecting Rome to China.

(a) 2,000 km (b) 6,000 km
(c) 60,000 km (d) 1,200 km

3. Which statement is incorrect related to cultural factors in the context of International trade? **CBSE Diksha**

(a) China produces the finest porcelains and brocades.
(b) Iran produces metal works.
(c) North African produces leather work.
(d) Indonesian produce batik cloths.

4. European commerce grew after the disintegration of .... Empire with the development of ocean going warships in 12th century AD.

(a) Byzantine (b) Roman
(c) British (d) Mughal

5. Which of the following factors determines international trade between countries?

(a) Population (b) Mineral resources
(c) Foreign investment (d) All of these

6. Choose the correct option to fill the blank. .... were originally developed for refuelling, watering and collecting food items. **CBSE 2025**

(a) Entre ports (b) Ports of Call
(c) Packet stations (d) Comprehensive ports

7. Which one of the following is the headquarter of the World Trade Organisation? **CBSE 2024**

(a) New York (b) Delhi
(c) Geneva (d) London

8. Which of the following organisations sets the rules for the global trading among its member nations? Choose the most appropriate option. **CBSE 2024**

(a) United Nations
(b) World Trade Organisation
(c) North American Free Trade Association
(d) South Asian Free Trade Agreement

9. Choose the correct option to fill the blank. The act of opening up economies for trading is known as ....

(a) Balance trade (b) Unilateral trade
(c) Free trade (d) Bilateral trade

10. Which of the following pairs is matched correctly? **CBSE SQP 2022**

	Name of the country		Oil port
(a)	Tunisia	–	Tripoli
(b)	Lebanon	–	Esskhira
(c)	Venezuela	–	Maracaibo
(d)	Oman	–	Aden

11. Which of the following is an example of 'entrepot port'? **CBSE 2024**

(a) Abadan (b) Maracaibo
(c) Singapore (d) Tripoli

12. Which of the following ports are used as collection centres?

(a) Pocket station (b) Entrepot ports
(c) Naval ports (d) Call ports

13. Consider the following statements and choose the correct option.

(i) In primitive societies, barter trade was most prominent form of trade.
(ii) Barter system made trade very complex.
(iii) Difficulties of barter system reduced with introduction of money.

Codes
(a) (i), (ii) and (iii) (b) (i) and (ii)
(c) (i) and (iii) (d) (ii) and (iii)

14. Which of these objects served as a form of money initially before the introduction of paper currency?

(i) Obsidian (ii) Iron (iii) Cloth
(iv) Copper (v) Silver

Codes
(a) (i), (ii), (iii) and (iv) (b) (ii), (iii) and (iv)
(c) (i), (iv) and (v) (d) (ii), (iii) and (v)

15. Consider the following statements and choose the correct option from the given options.

I. The WTO has been criticised and opposed by those who are worried about the effects of free trade and economic globalisation.

II. Free trade does not make ordinary people's lives more prosperous. **CBSE SQP 2022**

Codes
(a) Only statement I is correct
(b) Both the statements are true and statement II correctly present the reason for statement I
(c) Only statement II is correct
(d) Both the statements I and II are incorrect

Arrange the Following

16. Arrange the following events in the history of international trade in a sequential order.
(i) Trade on silk route
(ii) Trade growth after industrial revolution
(iii) Slave trade
(iv) Growth of trade between Europe and Asia

Codes
(a) (i), (iii), (ii), (iv)
(b) (i), (iv), (iii), (ii)
(c) (ii), (i), (iii), (iv)
(d) (i), (ii), (iii), (iv)

Match the Following

17.

List I (Types of Port)	List II (Port)
A. Ports of Call	1. Memphis
B. Inland Port	2. Aden
C. Tanker Port	3. Tripoli

Codes

	A	B	C		A	B	C
(a)	1	3	2	(b)	2	1	3
(c)	2	3	1	(d)	1	2	3

Assertion and Reason

Directions (Q. Nos. 18-21) In the questions given below are two statements labelled as Assertion (A) and other labelled as Reason (R). In the context of two statements which one of the following is correct?

Codes
(a) Both A and R are true, but R is not the correct explanation of A
(b) Both A and R are true and R is the correct explanation of A
(c) Both A and R are incorrect
(d) A is correct, but R is incorrect

18. Assertion (A) Barter system did not promote trade and was very complex.
Reason (R) In primitive societies, it was almost impossible to find people who were in need of the same commodities as one needed to exchange.

19. Assertion (A) World Trade Organisation (WTO) is widening the gulf between rich and poor by making rich countries richer.
Reason (R) The influential nations in the WTO focus on their own commercial interests.

20. Assertion (A) Countries need to be cautious about dumped goods under free trade.
Reason (R) Dumping of goods can harm the domestic producers.

21. Assertion (A) 'Free international trade can prove to be detrimental to the under-developed countries.'
Reason (R) Under-developed countries are not at par to compete with developed countries. **CBSE 2024**

Answers

1. (d) All of the above
2. (b) 6,000 km
3. (b) Iran produces metal works
4. (b) Roman
5. (d) All of these
6. (b) Ports of Call
7. (c) Geneva
8. (b) World Trade Organisation
9. (c) Free Trade
10. (c) Venezuela – Maracaibo
11. (c) Singapore
12. (b) Entrepot ports
13. (a) (i), (ii) and (iii)
14. (c) (i), (iv) and (v)
15. (b) Both the statements are true and statement II correctly present the reason for statement I.
16. (b) (i), (iv), (iii), (ii)
17. (b)
18. (b) Both A and R are true and R is the correct explanation of A
19. (d) A is correct, but R is incorrect
20. (b) Both A and R are true and R is the correct explanation of A
21. (d) A is correct, but R is incorrect

Subjective Questions

Short Answer Type Questions

1. 'Trade plays an important role in boosting the economy of a country'. Justify the statement. Competency Based Que

Ans. Trade is the result of specialisation which not only benefits the mother country's economy but also world economy.

It plays an important role in boosting the economy of a country by following ways

- Trade provides opportunity to sell goods and services in international markets to earn foreign exchange and gain profit.
- The import of certain goods is required to develop infrastructure and industries in the country.
- Trade creates employment opportunities and hence, improves the living standard of citizens of the country.

2. Barter trade and monetary trade differs from one another. Explain how. Competency Based Que

Ans. Differences between barter trade and monetary trade are as follows

Barter Trade	Monetary Trade
It is earlier system of trade where exchange took place without the use of money.	It is modern system of trade where money is used as means of exchange.
It was limited to certain commodities.	All types of goods and services can be traded.
It was very complex and difficult.	It is simple and practical.
It is subjected to various government rules and regulations.	There are no government regulations.

3. How do differences in national resources become the basis of international trade? Explain with examples. CBSE 2024

Ans. Differences in national resources form the basis of international trade because countries have unique geological, climatic, and biological characteristics that influence resource availability. For example, nations with rich mineral deposits, like Saudi Arabia's oil, trade it globally as they have an abundance of this resource. On the other hand, Japan, which lacks mineral resources, relies on imports for raw materials while exporting technological goods. Climatic differences also play a role; tropical regions, like Brazil, produce coffee, while cooler climates, such as Canada, specialise in wheat. These variations encourage countries to trade for what they lack and export their surplus.

4. Explain with example how stage of economic development' and 'foreign investment become the basis of international trade.

Ans. The stage of economic development and foreign investment have become the basis of international trade due to following reasons

- **Stage of Economic Development** The nature of trade changes with the change in stage of economic development of countries. In developed economies, manufactured goods, machinery are traded for raw materials but in less developed economies, agro products are traded for industrial goods.
- **Foreign Investment** Developing countries lack in capital which is required for the development of mining, oil drilling, heavy engineering, lumbering and plantation agriculture. Foreign investment can boost trade in these countries. Like, in India, foreign investment in service sectors has made India one of the leading service providers in the world.

5. 'The pattern of world trade has changed since the past few decades'. Substantiate the statement. Competency Based Que

Ans. The pattern of world trade has changed since the past few decades. There has been huge changes in the volume of trade, composition as well as the direction of trade.

The volume of trade has increased over the past few decades. In the beginning of the 20th century, the trade of primary products was dominant. It has changed to manufactured goods and later to the service sector including travel, transportation and other commercial services. But manufactured goods still dominate the world trade.

In early times, valuable goods and artefacts were exported by developing countries to the European countries. During the second half of 20th century developing countries such as China, India and South-East Asian countries have started competing with the developed countries. There has also been change in the nature of the goods exported and imported. Thus, there has been a huge change in the pattern of the world trade.

6. Explain the criticisms faced by the World Trade Organisation. CBSE 2024

Ans. The World Trade Organisation (WTO) has faced criticism for widening the gap between rich and poor countries. Critics argue that free trade under the WTO benefits wealthy nations, making them richer, while developing countries struggle. Many developed countries do not fully open their markets to goods from poorer nations.

Additionally, issues like health, workers' rights, child labour, and the environment are often neglected. The WTO is also accused of focusing too much on commercial interests rather than addressing the needs of ordinary people.

7. Discuss about direction of foreign trade.

Ans. Direction of foreign trade means the countries where import of goods is done and the countries where export of goods is done. Direction of foreign trade shows the direction of destination of exports and sources of imports.

Earlier valuable goods and artefacts, etc were exported to European countries by the developing countries, but during the 19th century, there was export of manufactured goods by the European countries for exchange of food stuffs and raw materials from their colonies. Europe and USA became major trade partners in the world and emerged as leaders in the trade of manufactured goods.

During the second half of the 20th century, this pattern of world trade has undergone changes as Europe lost its colonies and developing countries like India, China started competing with the developed countries.

8. What is Balance of Trade? Explain the characteristics of 'Balance of Trade'. **CBSE 2024**

Ans. The Balance of Trade records the difference between a country's exports and imports. If a country exports more than it imports, it has a favourable balance (trade surplus). If imports exceed exports, the country faces a negative balance (trade deficit).

Characteristics of Balance of Trade are as follows

- It only considers the trade of goods, not services.
- A positive balance (surplus) is beneficial for the economy.
- A negative balance (deficit) may lead to financial strain.
- It influences a country's economic health and currency value.

9. What are the difference between imports and exports?

Ans. Differences between imports and exports are as follows

Imports	Exports
Under this goods and services are brought into the domestic country from other country or countries.	Under this goods and services are sold to other countries from the domestic country.
The main aim is to fulfill the demands of goods and services not available in the domestic country.	The main aim is to create more income and to increase the presence of domestic goods and services
Increase in import may have adverse effect on balance of payment.	Exports are promoted to reduce current account deficit.
Excessive import reduces foreign exchange of the importing country.	Excessive export increases foreign exchange of the exporting country.

10. How bilateral trade and multilateral trade differs from one another? Explain.

Ans. Differences between bilateral and multilateral trade are given below

Bilateral Trade	Multilateral Trade
It is the trade between two countries.	It is the trade among different trading partners.
Here, only two countries benefit from the trade and the trade between two countries increases.	Here, many countries benefit, which leads to increasing international trade.
In this type of trade, commodities of two countries are complementary.	The trade is not complementary but supplementary.
This type of trade is limited to certain commodities.	This type of trade includes exchange of various types of goods and services.

11. What is free trade? Give two advantages of free trade.

Ans. Free trade or trade liberalisation means opening a country's economy by making trade easier by reducing trade barriers such as tarrifs.

Advantages of free trade are as follows *(Any two)*

- It makes country's economy more open and increase its exports.
- Due to trade liberalisation, a country is able to produce specialised products and increase its output.
- Trade liberalisation or free trade creates the environment of competition between the goods produced globally and the domestic goods.
- It is the only type of truly fair trade beacuse it offers consumers with more choices and the best opportunities to improve their standard of living.
- Free trade promotes innovation because, along with goods and services, the flow of trade circulates new ideas.
- Free trade leads to growth in a country's economy, which also increases the level of employment.

12. Write a short note on WTO.

Ans. World Trade Organisation (WTO) is an international organisation associated with the free and liberal trade in the world. General Agreement for Tariffs and Trade (GATT) was formed in 1948 to make the world free from tariffs as well as non-tariff barriers.

On 1st January, 1995, the GATT was transformed into World Trade Organisation to set up an institution for the promotion of free and fair trade amongst different countries of the world.

The main functions of WTO are

- Setting up global rules of trade between nations.
- Resolve disputes between its member states.
- Overseeing the trade in services such as telecommunication and banking.
- Resolving issues related to the intellectual property rights.

13. Which shortcomings are responsible for the criticism of WTO?

Ans. The WTO has many shortcomings due to which it has been criticised and opposed by those countries who are worried about the negative effects of free trade and economic globalisation. For example,

- It is seen that the WTO does not minimise the negative effects of free trade and thus, widening the gap between rich and poor by making rich countries more rich.
- This situation developed because the influential nations in the WTO focus more on their own commercial interest.
- Besides these, many developed countries have not fully opened their markets to products from developing countries.
- It is also seen that some important issues like health, worker's rights, child labour and environment are also ignored in WTO.

14. Classify ports of the world into two types on the basis of their location. Explain any two features of each type of ports.

Or **Explain the differences between the inland and outports with examples.** **CBSE 2024**

Ans. Ports are classified into two types on the basis of their location

(i) Inland ports (ii) Out ports

Two features of each of these ports are as follows

Inland Ports

(a) These ports are connected to sea through a river or a canal and are located away from the sea coast.

(b) Flat bottom ships and barges are used to reach these ports.

(c) Examples of such ports are Manchester, Memphis, Mannheim, Duisburg and Kolkata ports.

Out Ports

(a) These ports serve as the parent ports by receiving their large ships as those ships can not reach to the main port because of their size.

(b) These are built away from the actual main ports in deep water.

For example, Athens and its out port Piraeus in Greece.

15. Discuss the major types of ports on the basis of cargo and location.

Ans. For answer refer to text on page no. 152 under the heading 'Types of ports according to cargo handled and location'.

16. Study the table given below carefully and answer the following questions.

World Imports and Exports (in US $)

	1955	1965	1975	1985	1995	2005
Exports Total Merchandise	95,000	190,000	877,000	1,954,000	5,162,000	10,393,000
Imports Total Merchandise	99,000	199,000	912,000	2,015,000	5,292,000	10,753,000

(i) Which decade shows the highest increase of total value of imports and exports of goods and services?

(ii) How much is the increase in total value of exports during 1955 to 2005?

(iii) How much is the increase in total value of imports during 1985 to 2005?

Ans. (i) 1965-1975 shows the highest increase of total value of imports and exports of goods and services.

(ii) The total value of exports increased by 10.2 million US $ during 1955 to 2005.

(iii) The total value of imports increased by 8.7 million US $ during 1985 to 2005.

17. Study the following table and answer the questions that follow.

World: Imports and Exports
(in millions of U.S. $)

Year	Exports Total Merchandise	Imports Total Merchandise
1955	95,000	99,000
1965	1,90,000	1,99,000
1975	8,77,000	9,12,000
1985	19,54,000	20,15,000
1995	51,62,000	52,92,000
2005	1,03,93,000	1,07,53,000
2015	1,55,83,232	1,56,28,204

(i) Which aspect of trade has shown rapid growth?
(ii) Has the total volume of trade increased or decreased?
(iii) Why does import take place? Write any two reasons.

Ans. (i) The imports of total merchandise has shown a rapid growth from 1955 to 2015.

(ii) The given table shows that the total volume of world trade has been steadily rising over the past decades.

(iii) Import takes place due to the following reasons

- When there is lack of some resources or services in a country then import takes place.
- When there is a demand of good quality foreign products then import takes place.

Long Answer Type Questions

1. "In modern times international trade is the basis of the world economy." Support the statement with example. Competency Based Que

Ans. The exchange of surplus goods and services between different countries is known as international trade.

It is the basis of world economy in modern times because of the following

- **Reduces Economic Differences** Different countries of the world have differences in their resource base. This leads to uneven economic development. International trade helps in reducing uneconomic development.
- **Provides Foreign Exchange** With international trade, developing and the underdeveloped countries earn foreign exchange. With the help of foreign exchange, these countries can invest in their economic development.
- **Provides Boost to Industries** As the international trade flourishes, the domestic industry gets a boost as it produces more to fulfil the demands of international markets.
- **Technology Transfer** Along with the international trade, new technologies and new ideas are also transferred between countries. With the help of this, countries innovate and make better products and provides better services.
- **Employment** Increase in international trade results in increasing employment generation as new industries are setup to fulfil the demands of exports.
- **Improve Standard of Living** Along with the economy, international trade also results in improved standard of living because of the increasing levels of economic and social developments in the country.

2. 'International Trade is mutually beneficial to Nations". Analyse.

Or **"International trade can prove to be detrimental to nations. It leads to dependence on the other countries". Justify the statement.** CBSE 2024 C

Ans. International trade is mutually beneficial to nations. It can be ascertained with the following points

- **More Variety of Products** International trade brings different varieties of products from different countries. It gives a wide number of choices, which will improve their quality of life.
- **Efficient Allocation of Resources** Efficient allocation of resources and their better utilisation prevents wasteful duplication of resources and gives the countries a comparative advantage.
- **Promotes Efficiency in Production** Trade promotes efficiency in production as countries try to adapt to better methods of production to keep their costs minimum to remain productive.
- **Employment Generation** International trade results in generation of more employment by establishment of newer industries to fulfil the demands of various countries.
- **Earning Foreign Exchange** International trade helps in earning foreign exchange, which increases the income of the country and reduces its dependence.
- **Cheaper Imports** International trade results in cheaper imports of products which are costly in the domestic market. It reduces the burdens on the citizen.

3. "The difference in national resources is the basis of international trade". Analyse the statement. Competency Based Que

Ans. The difference in national resources is considered as a basis of international trade because resources are not evenly distributed over the surface of Earth. Some countries are rich in a particular type of resource whereas other countries are rich in some other resources.

The factors that affect the uneven distribution of resource are the differences in physical settings like geology, relief, soil and climate of the countries.

(i) **Geological Structure** Differences in geological structure and topographical differences results in the diversity of crops and animals raised countries that have more plain areas can grow more crops whereas countries that have more highland or mountain areas are richer in forest resources.

(ii) **Mineral Resources** Different regions of the world have different proportions of mineral resources. These minerals provide the basis of different type of industries in different regions of the world. Some countries are rich in coal and petroleum while others are rich in minerals such as Uranium and Thorium. Some countries have more proportion of forest resources while other countries may be rich in metallic or non-metallic resources.

(iii) **Climate** The climate of a country influences its flora and fauna. It ensures that there is diversity in the range of products of a country. Regions which have colder climate have more production of wool. Regions that lie in tropical regions grow cocoa, coffee, rubber, etc.

Thus, these differences that there is complementarity between the countries and international trade can flourish.

4. Describe any five basis of international trade. **CBSE 2024**

Or **Examine the five basis of international trade which are responsible for promoting international trade.**

Ans. For answer refer to text page no 150 under the heading 'Basis of International Trade'.

5. Explain the two types of international trade. Examine any three possible negative impacts of globalisation alongwith free trade in the world.

Ans. International trade is the exchange of capital, goods and services across international borders or territories.

There are two types of international trade

(i) **Bilateral Trade** It refers to the trade between two countries. The two countries are specialised in certain commodities and hence, they enter into an agreement to trade specified commodities between them.

(ii) **Multi-lateral Trade** It is conducted with many trading countries. The same country can trade with a large number of other countries. The status of the Most Favoured Nation (MFN) can be granted by such country on some of the trading partners.

Three possible negative impacts of globalisation alongwith free trade in the world are as follows

(i) It does not provide level playing field by imposing unfavourable conditions hence, retard the growth of trade for developing countries.

(ii) Cheaper goods from foreign countries may harm the domestic producers.

(iii) The phenomena of dumping may be visible in the markets of developing countries.

When large amount of a product is dumped that is very cheap as compared to the domestic products. It affects the domestic producers.

6. Explain any two functions of WTO. Why has this organisation been criticised? Give three arguments in this regard.

Or **What is the role of 'World Trade Organisation' as an international organisation? Why has the World Trade Organisation been criticised by some countries?**

Ans. For answer refer to text page no. 151 under the heading 'World Trade Organisation'.

7. Discuss briefly the concerns related to international trade of the world.

Ans. The concerns related to international trade of the world are given below

- When international trade promotes regional specialisation, higher level of production, better standard of living, worldwide availability of goods and services, equalisation of prices and wages and diffusion of knowledge and culture, then it is mutually beneficial to nations.
- But it may prove to be detrimental when it leads to dependence on other nations, inequitable development, exploitation and commercial rivalry.
- Globalisation of trade affects every aspects of life from the environment to health and well- being of people around the world.
- As countries compete to trade more, production and the use of natural resources go up, resources get used up faster than they can be replenished.
- As a result, marine life is also depleting fast, forests are being cut down and river basins are sold to private drinking water companies.
- Multinational corporations trading in oil, natural gas mining, pharmaceuticals and agri-business keep expanding their operations at all costs creating more pollution. They do not follow the norms of sustainable development.

If organisations only work towards profit making and ignore environment and health concerns, then it could lead to serious implications in future.

8. Why are ports known as 'gateways of international trade'? Explain any three characteristics of inland ports.

Ans. Ports are called the 'gateways of international trade' because of the following reasons

- These ports facilitate the passage of cargoes and travellers from one country to another.
- These ports provide facilities of docking, loading, unloading and storage facilities for cargo, which are meant to export or import.

- In order to provide these facilities, the port authorities make arrangements for maintaining navigable channels, arranging tugs and barges, and providing labour and managerial services.
- Large ports offer particularly attractive locations for leading industries and distribution exporting enterprises.

Important characteristics of the inland ports are as follows

(i) Inland ports are located away from the sea coast.

(ii) They are linked to the sea through a river or a canal. For example, Manchester is linked with a canal.

(iii) Such ports are accessible by flat bottom ships or barges.

9. Describe any five types of ports in the world, on the basis of specialised functions. **CBSE 2024**

Ans. Ports are classified based on their specialised functions, handling specific types of cargo or services. Here are five types of ports based on their specialised functions

(i) **Oil Ports** These ports are specifically designed for the processing and shipping of oil. Some oil ports focus on receiving tankers, while others have refineries to process the oil. Examples include Maracaibo in Venezuela and Abadan in Iran.

(ii) **Ports of Call** These ports originally developed as stopping points for ships to refuel, resupply, and take on passengers. Over time, many evolved into commercial ports. Examples include Aden and Honolulu.

(iii) **Packet Stations** These are also known as ferry ports. These handle the transportation of passengers and mail over short distances. They are located in pairs, facing each other across bodies of water. A good example is the Dover-Calais route between England and France.

(iv) **Entrepot Ports** These ports serve as collection centers where goods from different countries are gathered for export. Singapore is an entrepot for Asia, and Rotterdam for Europe, are famous examples.

(iv) **Naval Ports** These ports have strategic military importance. They serve warships and often have repair facilities. Kochi and Karwar in India are examples of naval ports.

Source Based Questions

1. Read the passage carefully and answer the questions that follow.

In ancient times, transporting goods over long distances was risky, hence trade was restricted to local markets. People then spent most of their resources on basic necessities – food and clothes. Only the rich people bought jewellery, costly dresses and this resulted in trade of luxury items. The silk route is an early example of long distance trade connecting Rome to China – along the 6,000 km route. The traders transported Chinese silk, Roman wool and precious metals, and many other high value commodities from intermediate points in India, Persia and Central Asia. After the disintegration of the Roman Empire, European commerce grew during twelfth and thirteenth century with the development of ocean going warships trade between Europe and Asia grew and the Americas were discovered.

Fifteenth century onwards, the European colonialism began and along with trade of exotic commodities, a new form of trade emerged which was called slave trade. The Portuguese, Dutch, Spaniards, and British captured African natives and forcefully transported them to the newly discovered Americas for their labour in the plantations. Slave trade was a lucrative business for more than two hundred years till it was abolished in Denmark in 1792, Great Britain in 1807 and United States in 1808.

(i) **Which countries were connected through the silk route?**

Ans. Rome and China were connected with the silk route. The silk route is an early example of long distance trade in the world. It was 6,000 km long route.

(ii) **Which commodities were transported through silk route?**

Ans. Chinese silk, Roman wool and precious metals, and many other high value commodities were transported by the traders from intermediate points in India, Persia and Central Asia.

(iii) **Why during 15th century European colonies were engaged in slave trade?**

Ans. During fifteenth century, Portuguese, Dutch, Spaniards and British were engaged in slave trade. They captured African natives and forcefully transported them to the newly discovered Americas for their labour in the plantations.

2. Read the passage carefully and answer the questions that follow.

Globalisation along with free trade can adversely affect the economies of developing countries by not giving equal playing field by imposing conditions which are unfavourable. With the development of transport and communication systems goods and services can travel faster and farther than ever before. But free trade should not only let rich countries enter the markets, but allow the developed countries to keep their own markets protected from foreign products.

Undertaking international trade is mutually beneficial to nations if it leads to regional specialisation, higher level of production, better standard of living, worldwide availability of goods and services, equalisation of prices and wages and diffusion of knowledge and culture.

International trade can prove to be detrimental to nations if it leads to dependence on other countries, uneven levels of development, exploitation, and commercial rivalry leading to wars. Global trade affects many aspects of life; it can impact everything from the environment to health and well-being of the people around the world.

(i) Discuss about the benefits of international trade.

Ans. Benefits of international trade involves diffusion of knowledge, regional specialisation and increasing reach of goods and services.

(ii) How international trade can be detrimental to other developing countries?

Ans. International trade can be detrimental to other developing countries if there is uneven level of development, exploitation and commercial rivalry leading to wars.

(iii) Mention one advantage of developing transport and communication system.

Ans. With the development of transport and communication systems, goods and services can travel faster and farther than ever before.

3. Read the passage carefully and answer the questions that follow.

In 1948, to liberalise the world from high customs, tariffs and various other types of restrictions, General Agreement for Tariffs and Trade (GATT) was formed by some countries. In 1994, it was decided by the member countries to set up a permanent institution for looking after the promotion of free and fair trade amongst nation and the GATT was transformed into the World Trade Organisation from 1st January, 1995. WTO is the only international organisation dealing with the global rules of trade between nations. It sets the rules for the global trading system and resolves disputes between its member nations. WTO also covers trade in services, such as telecommunication and banking, and others issues such as intellectual rights. The WTO has however been criticised and opposed by those who are worried about the effects of free trade and economic globalisation. It is argued that free trade does not make ordinary people's lives more prosperous. It is actually widening the gulf between rich and poor by making rich countries more rich. This is because the influential nations in the WTO focus on their own commercial interests. Moreover, many developed countries have not fully opened their markets to products from developing countries. It is also argued that issues of health, worker's rights, child labour and environment are ignored.

(i) Which of the following was the predecessor organisation of WTO?

(a) World Bank (b) GATT
(c) IMF (d) United Nations

Ans. (b) GATT

(ii) Which of the following is not true about WTO?

(a) It was setup in 1995.
(b) It covers trade in goods only.
(c) Both developed and developing countries are its members.
(d) WTO is a permanent body.

Ans. (b) It covers trade in goods only

(iii) WTO is criticised on the basis of which of the following issues?

(a) International trade ignores worker's rights
(b) With international trade rich countries are becoming more rich
(c) Developed countries influence WTO for their interests
(d) All of the above

Ans. (d) All of the above

SELF ASSESSMENT TEST

Objective Type Questions

1. In primitive societies, the trade took place through which of these systems?
   (a) Currency (b) Money
   (c) Barter (d) Exchange
2. Positive balance of trade occurs when the value of .... is more than value of ....
   (a) imports; Exports
   (b) exports; Imports
   (c) commodities; Services
   (d) services; Commodities
3. Which of the following is an entrepot port for Asia?
   (a) Rotterdam (b) Singapore
   (c) Kolkata (d) Kochi
4. International trade is based on which of the following principles?
   (i) Comparative Advantage (ii) Complementarity
   (iii) Transferability
   Codes
   (a) (i) and (ii) (b) (i), (ii) and (iii)
   (c) (i) and (iii) (d) (ii) and (iii)
5. Which of the following factors would promote international trade?
   (i) Industrialised economy (ii) Well developed transport
   (iii) Better standard of living
   Codes
   (a) (i) and (ii) (b) (i), (ii) and (iii)
   (c) (ii) and (iii) (d) (i) and (iii)

Short Answer Type Questions

6. Negative balance of trade has serious implications over the country's financial reserves. Explain.
7. Discuss about the concept of sustainable development.
8. Explain how climate become the basis of international trade?
9. 'There was growth of European commerce after the disintegeration of Roman Empire'. Explain why?
10. Discuss about the existence of slave trade during Colonial period.

Long Answer Type Questions

11. The members of GATT formed World Trade Organisation for development of international trade. Give a critical comment on the role of WTO in development of international trade.
12. 'Ports are classified on the basis of specialised functions'. Discuss about the five types of ports.

UNIT 1

Part B India-People and Economy

1

CHAPTER

Population : Distribution, Density, Growth and Composition

India is the second most populous country after China with a total population of 1,210 million (2011). India's population is larger than the total population of North America, South America and Australia.

YOUR STUDY GOALS

- 1.1 Distribution of Population
- 1.2 Density of Population
- 1.3 Growth of Population
- 1.4 Population Composition

YOUR PRACTICE GOAL

- Objective Type Questions (29 Qs ; MCQs, Statements, Matching, A-R)
- Subjective Questions (18 SAs, 11 LAs)
- Source Based Questions (6 Qs)
- Map Based Question (1 Qs)

- Population data are collected through Census operations held every 10 years in India. The first population **Census** in India was conducted in 1872 but its first complete Census was conducted only in 1881.
- It is often argued that, India's large population puts pressure on a country's resources and is also responsible for many socio-economic problems in the country.

1.1 Distribution of Population

- India has a highly uneven pattern of population distribution. **Uttar Pradesh** has the highest population followed by Maharashtra, Bihar and West Bengal.
- Uttar Pradesh, Maharashtra, Bihar, West Bengal, Andhra Pradesh along with Tamil Nadu, Madhya Pradesh, Rajasthan, Karnataka and Gujarat, together account for about 76 per cent of the total population of the country. On the other hand, states like Jammu & Kashmir (1.04%), Arunachal Pradesh (0.11%) and Uttarakhand (0.84%) have small populations.
- This uneven spatial distribution of population in India suggests a close relationship between population and physical, socioeconomic and historical factors.

- The physical factors affecting population distribution are climate, terrain and availability of water. Therefore, the North Indian Plains, deltas and Coastal Plains have a higher population than the interior districts of the Southern and Central Indian states, the Himalayas and some of the North-Eastern and Western states.
- The development of irrigation (Rajasthan), availability of mineral and energy resources (Jharkhand) and development of transport network (Peninsular States) have resulted in moderate to high population in areas that were previously very thinly populated.
- The socio-economic and historical factors of the population distribution, include the evolution of settled agriculture and agricultural development; pattern of human settlement; development of transport network, industrialisation and urbanisation.
- It is observed that the regions falling in the river plains and coastal areas of India have remained the regions of larger population concentration even after depletion of resources like land and water. This is because of the history of human settlement and the development of transport networks.
- The urban regions of Delhi, Mumbai, Kolkata, Bengaluru, Pune, Ahmedabad, Chennai and Jaipur have high concentrations of population due to industrial development and urbanisation drawing large numbers of rural-urban migrants.

1.2 Density of Population

- The density of the population is expressed as several persons per unit area. It helps in the understanding of the spatial distribution of population in relation to land.
- There has been a steady increase in the density of the population in India. The density of the population increased from 117 persons/ sq km in 1951 to 382 persons/sq km in 2011.
- There is spatial variation in the density of the population. It ranges from as low as 17 persons per sq km in Arunachal Pradesh to 11,297 persons in the National Capital Territory of Delhi.
- The spatial distribution of states based on their density is as follows
    - **High density states** Bihar (1102), West Bengal (1029) and Uttar Pradesh (828) have higher densities, while Kerala (859) and Tamil Nadu (555), all Union Territories except Andaman and Nicobar islands.
    - **Moderate density states** Assam, Gujarat, Andhra Pradesh, Haryana, Jharkhand and Odisha.
    - **Low-density states** The hill states of the Himalayan region and North-Eastern states of India (excluding Assam).

Types of Population Density

In an agricultural country like India, the physiological and agricultural densities are calculated. The formulas to calculate them are as follows

- **Physiological density** = Total population / net cultivated area
- **Agricultural density** = Total agricultural population / net cultivable area
- The agricultural population includes cultivators, agricultural labourers and their family members.

Quick Test 1

1. What is the total population of India according to Census 2011?
2. Which state in India has the highest population?
3. Name two states that have moderate population density in India.
4. What is the formula to calculate physiological density?

1.3 Growth of Population

- It is the change in the number of people living in a particular area between two points of time. Its rate is expressed in percentage.
- **Population Doubling Time** is the time taken by any population to double itself at its current annual growth rate.
- Population growth has two components as follows
  - **Natural growth** This is analysed by assessing the crude birth and death rates.
  - **Induced growth** This is assessed by the volume of inward and outward movement of people in any given area.
- The decadal and annual growth rates of the population in India are both very high and steadily increasing over time. The annual growth rate of India's population is 1.64 per cent (2011).
- The growth rate of population in India over the last century has been caused by annual birth rate, death rate and rate of migration, and thereby shows different trends.

Decadal Growth Rates in India, 1901-2011

Census Years	Total Population	Growth Rate*	
		Absolute Number	% of Growth
1901	238396327	....	....
1911	252093390	(+) 13697063	(+) 5.75
1921	251321213	(–) 772117	(–) 0.31
1931	278977238	(+) 27656025	(+) 11.60
1941	318660580	(+) 39683342	(+) 14.22
1951	361088090	(+) 42420485	(+) 13.31
1961	439234771	(+) 77682873	(+) 21.51
1971	548159652	(+) 108924881	(+) 24.80
1981	683329097	(+) 135169445	(+) 24.66
1991	846302688	(+) 162973591	(+) 23.85
2001	1028610328	(+) 182307640	(+) 21.54
2011**	1210193422	(+) 181583094	(+) 17.64

* Decadal growth rate: $g = \frac{P_2 - P_1}{P_1} \times 100$, where P_1 = Population of the base year and P_2 = Population of the present year

** ***Source**: Census of India, 2011 (Provisional)*

Phases of Population Growth

The phases are analyse based on average growth rate of the country, but there is wide variation in growth rate from one area to another.

Phase I

- The period from 1901-1921 had a **stagnant** or **stationary** phase of growth of India's population.
- In this period, growth rate was very low, even recording a negative growth rate during 1911-1921.

- Both the birth and death rates were high hence overall rate of growth was low.
- During this phase the reason for high birth and death rates were poor health and medical services, illiteracy of people at large and inefficient distribution system of food and other necessities.

Phase II

- The decades 1921-1951 **had steady population growth**. An overall improvement in health and sanitation throughout the country reduced the mortality rate.
- The crude birth rate remained high in this period leading to a higher growth rate than the previous phase.
- This phase also experienced the **Great Economic Depression**, of the 1920s and World War II.

Phase III

- The decades 1951-1981 were the period of **population explosion**[1] in India. It was caused by a rapid fall in the mortality rate but a high fertility rate in the country. The average annual growth rate was as high as 2.2 per cent.
- During this period, developmental activities were introduced through a **centralised planning process** and the economy started to develop ensuring a better standard of living at large scale. Consequently, there was a high natural increase and higher growth rate. Migration was another factor of population growth at that time.
- An increased international migration bringing in Tibetans, Bangladeshis, Nepalies and even people from Pakistan contributed to the high growth rate.

Phase IV

- Post 1981 till the present, the growth rate of the country's population though remained high, has started slowing down gradually. A downward trend in the crude birth rate is held responsible for such a population growth.
- The low birth rate is the result of the increase in the age of marriage and improved quality of life, particularly the education of females in the country.
- The growth rate of population is still high. As per World Development Report, population of India will touch 1.350 million in 2025.

Regional Variation in Population Growth

- The growth rate of population during 1991- 2001 in Indian States and Union Territories shows a particular pattern.
- States like Kerala, Karnataka, Tamil Nadu, Andhra Pradesh, Odisha, Puducherry and Goa show a low rate of growth not exceeding 20 per cent over the decade. Kerala registered the lowest growth rate (9.4 per cent) in the country.
- A continuous belt of states from West to East in the North-West, North and North-Central parts of the country has a relatively high growth rate than the Southern states.
- The population growth rate on average remained high with 20-25 per cent in the states like Gujarat, Maharashtra, Rajasthan, Punjab, Haryana, Uttar Pradesh, Uttarakhand, Madhya Pradesh, Sikkim, Assam, West Bengal, Bihar, Chhattisgarh and Jharkhand.

1 **Population Explosion** A sudden, large increase in the size of the population.

- During 2001-2011, the growth rates of almost all States and Union Territories registered a lower growth rate compared to the previous decade (1991-2001). The decline is the lowest for Andhra Pradesh (3.5% percentage points) and highest for Maharashtra (6.7 percentage points).
- Tamil Nadu (3.9 percentage points) and Puducherry (7.1 percentage points) have registered some increase during 2001-2011 over the previous decade.

Adolescent Population

- The share of **adolescents**[2] is about 20.9 per cent (2011), among which male adolescents constitute 52.7 per cent and female adolescents constitute 47.3 per cent.
- The adolescent population is the youthful population having high potential, but at the same time, they are quite vulnerable if not guided properly.
- There are many challenges for society as far as these adolescents are concerned. Some of these are as follows
  - Lower age at marriage
  - Illiteracy-particularly female illiteracy, school dropouts
  - Low intake of nutrients
  - High rate of maternal mortality among adolescent mothers
  - High rate of HIV and AIDS infections
  - Physical and mental disability or retardedness, drug abuse and alcoholism, juvenile delinquency and commitment of crimes, etc.
- To overcome these issues, the Government of India has undertaken certain policies to provide proper education to the adolescent groups so that their talents are better channelised and properly utilised. Some of these are as follows
  - **National Youth Policy** It has been designed to look into the overall development of the large youth and adolescent population of India.
  - The National Youth Policy was launched in February 2014 and proposes a 'vision' for the youth of India, which is "To empower the youth of the country to achieve their full potential and through them enable India to find its rightful place in the community of nations".
  - The NYP-2014 has defined 'youth' as persons in the age group of 15-29 years.
- **National Policy for Skill Development and Entrepreneurship** The Government of India also formulated this policy in 2015. This policy provides a single framework for all skilling activities within the country and provides them the jobs according to their skills.

Quick Test 2

1 What is the annual growth rate of India's population during the period of 2001-2011?
2 During which decades, India had a steady population growth?
3 During which phase, India has shown a downward trend in the growth rate of population?
4 How much is the male adolescent population among total adolescent population?

1.4 Population Composition

- Population composition is a field of population geography.
- This field of study covers the analysis of age and sex, place of residence, ethnic characteristics, tribes, language, religion, marital status, literacy and education, occupational characteristics, etc.

2 **Adolescent** A young person usually between the ages of 10 to 19 years who is growing into an adult.

The population composition of the Indian population can be studied in the following ways

Rural-Urban Composition

- The population composition based on places of residence is an important indicator of social and economic characteristics.

Rural Population

- In India, about 68.8 per cent of its total population lives in villages (2011).
- India has 640,867 villages according to the Census 2011 out of which 597,608 (93.2 per cent) are inhabited villages. However, the distribution of the rural population is not uniform throughout the country.
- The states like Himachal Pradesh and Bihar have a very high percentage of rural population while the states of Goa and Mizoram have only a little over half of their total population residing in villages. On the other hand, the Union Territories have a smaller proportion of the rural population, except Dadra and Nagar Haveli (53.38 per cent).
- The size of villages also varies in places. There may be less than 200 persons in the hill states of North-Eastern India, Western Rajasthan and Rann of Kuchchh and as high as 17 thousand persons in the states of Kerala and parts of Maharashtra.
- As per studies of population distribution patterns, the relative degree of urbanisation and rural-urban migration regulates the concentration of the rural population.

Urban Population

- The proportion of the urban population (31.16 per cent) in India is quite low but it has a much faster rate of growth over the decades. The growth rate of the urban population has accelerated due to enhanced economic development and improvement in health and hygienic conditions.
- Almost all the States and Union Territories, have seen a considerable increase in urban population. This indicates both the development of urban areas in terms of socio-economic conditions and an increased rate of rural-urban migration.

Rural-Urban Migration

- The **rural-urban migration** is seen in particular regions on the following basis
  - Urban areas along the main road links and railroads in the North Indian Plains.
  - The industrial areas around Kolkata, Mumbai, Bengaluru-Mysuru, Madurai-Coimbatore, Ahmedabad-Surat, Delhi-Kanpur and Ludhiana-Jalandhar.
  - The agriculturally stagnant parts of the middle and lower Ganga Plains, Telangana, non-irrigated Western Rajasthan, remote hilly, tribal areas of the North-East, along the flood-prone areas of Peninsular India and the Eastern part of Madhya Pradesh, the degree of urbanisation remained low.

Linguistic Composition

- India is a land of linguistic diversity. According to **Grierson** (Linguistic Survey of India, 1903-1928), there were 179 languages and as many as 544 dialects in the country.
- In modern India, there are about 22 scheduled languages and several non-scheduled languages.
- Among the scheduled languages, the speakers of Hindi have the highest percentage. The smallest language groups are Sanskrit, Bodo and Manipuri speakers (2011).
- The linguistic regions in the country do not have a sharp and distinct boundary, rather they gradually merge and overlap in their respective frontier zones.

Linguistic Classification

The speakers of major Indian languages belong to four language families, which have their sub-families and branches or groups. These are as follows

Classification of Modern Indian Languages

Family	Sub-Family	Branch/Group	Speech Areas
Austric (*Nishada*) 1.38%	Austro-Asiatic	Mon-Khmer	Meghalaya, Nicobar Islands
		Munda	West Bengal, Bihar, Odisha, Assam, Madhya Pradesh, Maharashtra
	Austro-Nesian		Outside India
Dravidian (*Dravida*) 20%		South- Dravidian	Tamil Nadu, Karnataka, Kerala
		Central Dravidian	Andhra Pradesh, Madhya Pradesh, Odisha, Maharashtra
		North- Dravidian	Bihar, Odisha, West Bengal, Madhya Pradesh
Sino- Tibetan (*Kirata*) 0.85%	Tibeto- Myanmari	Tibeto-Himalayan	Jammu and Kashmir, Himachal Pradesh, Sikkim
		North Assam	Arunachal Pradesh
	Siamese- Chinese	Assam- Myanmari	Assam, Nagaland, Manipur, Mizoram, Tripura, Meghalaya
Indo- European (Aryan) 73%	Indo-Aryan	Iranian	Outside India
		Dardic	Jammu and Kashmir
		Indo-Aryan	Jammu and Kashmir, Punjab, Himachal Pradesh, Uttar Pradesh, Rajasthan, Haryana, Madhya Pradesh, Bihar, Odisha, West Bengal, Assam, Gujarat, Maharashtra, Goa

Religious Composition

- Religion is one of the most dominant forces affecting the cultural and political life of the majority of Indians.
- The spatial distribution of religious communities in the country shows that certain states and districts have a large numerical strength of one religion, while some states and districts have less distribution.
- **Hindus** are a major group distributed in many states with 70-90 per cent and above. While some states have a very little number of Hindus such as – Indo-Bangladesh border, Indo-Pak border, Jammu and Kashmir, Hill States of North-East and in scattered areas of Deccan Plateau and Ganga Plain.
- **Muslims** are the largest religious minority. They are concentrated in Jammu and Kashmir, certain districts of West Bengal and Kerala, many districts of Uttar Pradesh, in and around Delhi and in Lakshadweep. They form a majority in Kashmir Valley and Lakshadweep.
- The **Christian** population is distributed mostly in rural areas of the country. They are mainly concentrated along the Western coast around Goa, Kerala and also in the hill states of Meghalaya, Mizoram, Nagaland, Chotanagpur area and hills of Manipur.

- **Sikhs** are mostly concentrated in relatively small areas of the country, particularly in the states of Punjab, Haryana and Delhi.
- **Jains** and **Buddhists**, the smallest religious groups in India have their concentration only in selected areas of the country. Jains have a major concentration in the urban areas of Rajasthan, Gujarat and Maharashtra, while the Buddhists are concentrated mostly in Maharashtra. The other areas of the Buddhist majority are Sikkim, Arunachal Pradesh, Ladakh in Jammu and Kashmir, Tripura and Lahul and Spiti in Himachal Pradesh.
- The other religions of India include Zoroastrians, tribal and other **indigenous faiths** and **beliefs**. These groups are concentrated in small groups which are distributed throughout the country.

Religious Communities of India, 2011

Religious Group	2011	
	Population (in million)	% of Total
Hindus	966.3	79.8
Muslims	172.2	14.2
Christians	27.8	2.3
Sikhs	20.8	1.7
Buddhists	8.4	0.7
Jains	4.5	0.4
Other Religions and Persuasions (ORP)	7.9	0.7
Religion not stated	2.9	0.2

Source: *Census of India, 2011*

Religion and Buildings

- Religions show their presence in different places by building sacred buildings, using cemeteries and creating special areas with certain plants, animals or trees.
- Different religions have their special buildings, like temples, mosques, gurudwaras, monasteries and churches. These buildings can be big or small and have unique designs and shapes.

Composition of Working Population

- The population of India according to their economic status is divided into three groups: **main workers, marginal workers** and **non-workers.**
- In India, the proportion of workers (both main and marginal) is only 39.8 per cent (2011) and the proportion of non-workers about 60 per cent. This indicates an economic status in which there is a larger proportion of the dependent population, further indicating the possible existence of a large number of unemployed or under-employed people.
- The proportion of the working population, of the States and Union Territories shows a variation from about 29.1 per cent in Lakshadweep to about 51.9 per cent in Himachal Pradesh.
- The states with larger percentages of workers are Himachal Pradesh, Sikkim, Chhattisgarh, Andhra Pradesh, Karnataka, Arunachal Pradesh, Nagaland, Manipur and Meghalaya. Among the Union Territories, Dadra and Nagar Haveli and Daman and Diu have higher work participation rates.
- In a country like India, the work participation rate is meant to be higher in the areas of lower levels of economic development since several manual workers perform subsistence or near-subsistence economic activities.
- The **occupational composition** of India's population shows a large proportion of primary sector workers as compared to secondary and tertiary sectors.
- About 54.6 per cent of the total working population are **cultivators** and **agricultural labourers**, whereas only 3.8 per cent of workers are engaged in **household industries**. 41.6 per cent are **other workers**, including non-household industries, trade, commerce, construction and repair, and other services.
- Among the working composition of male and female population, it is observed that male workers are more than female workers in all three sectors.

Promoting Gender Sensitivity through 'Beti Bachao-Beti Padhao' Social Campaign

- Treating everyone fairly, irrespective of their gender is important for a healthy and developed society.
- Discrimination, especially against women and girls, is seen as a serious problem. It means not allowing fair chances for education, jobs, fair pay, or political roles.
- The Government of India has a program called 'Beti Bachao-Beti Padhao' to support girls' education and well-being.
- In the past, most women in India worked in farming, but recently more women are getting jobs in factories, offices and other services. Farming jobs are less common now, with more people moving to non-farming jobs, showing a shift in the economy.
- Some states like Himachal Pradesh and Nagaland have more farmers. Others, like Bihar and Odisha, have many agricultural labourers. Big cities like Delhi have fewer farmers because there's less land for farming and more jobs in cities.

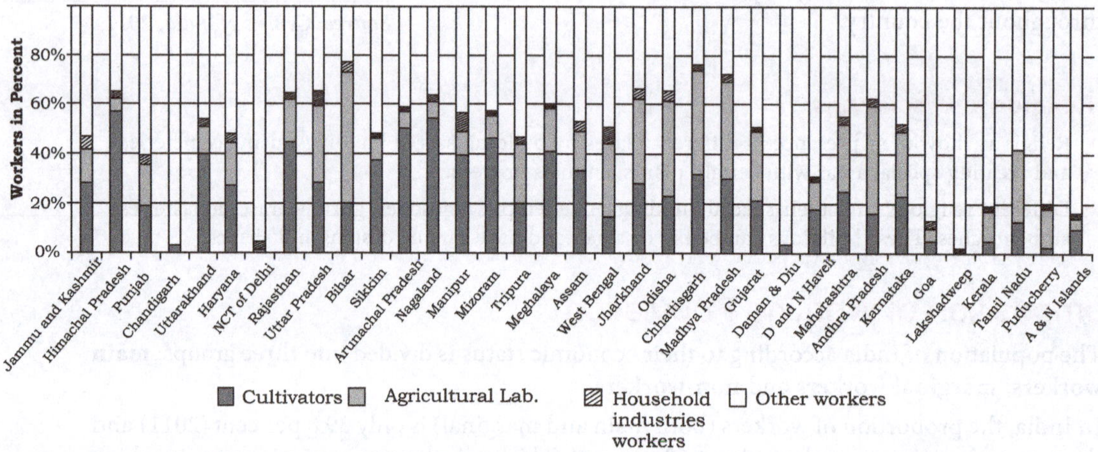

India-Occupational Structure, 2011

Sectoral Composition of Workforce in India, 2011

Categories	Population			
	Persons	% to Total Workers	Male	Female
Primary	26,30,22,473	54.6	16,54,47,075	9,75,75,398
Secondary	1,83,36,307	3.8	97,75,635	85,60,672
Tertiary	20,03,84,531	41.6	15,66,43,220	4,37,41,311

Quick Test 3

1. What percentage of India's population lives in villages?
2. Name a state where more than 80 per cent of the population lives in rural areas.
3. Name a state where the Austric family language is spoken.
4. What is the percentage of main and marginal workers in India?

Mind Map

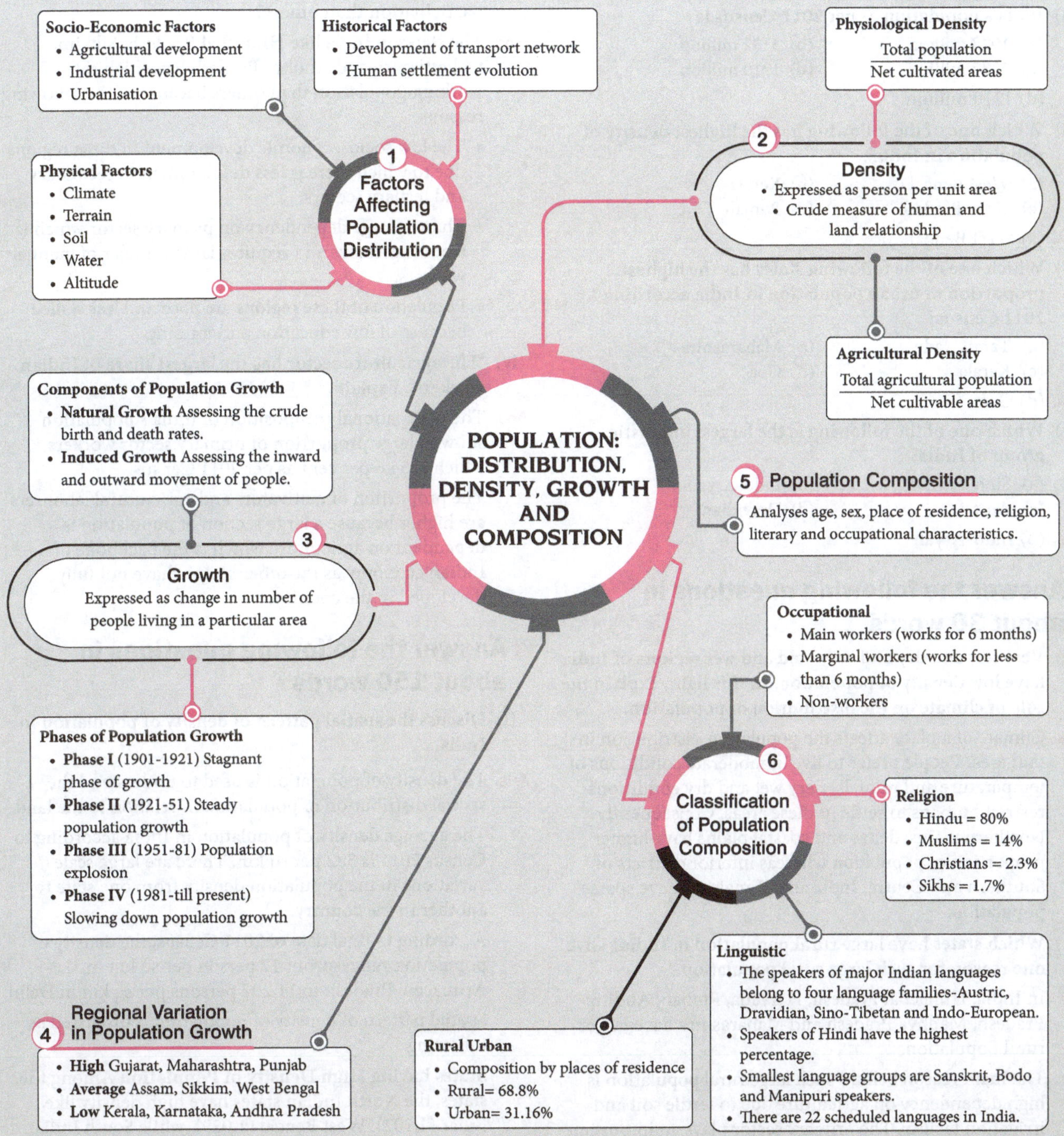
POPULATION: DISTRIBUTION, DENSITY, GROWTH AND COMPOSITION
1 Factors Affecting Population Distribution
Socio-Economic Factors
• Agricultural development
• Industrial development
• Urbanisation
Historical Factors
• Development of transport network
• Human settlement evolution
Physical Factors
• Climate
• Terrain
• Soil
• Water
• Altitude
2 Density
• Expressed as person per unit area
• Crude measure of human and land relationship
Physiological Density
Total population / Net cultivated areas
Agricultural Density
Total agricultural population / Net cultivable areas
3 Growth
Expressed as change in number of people living in a particular area
Components of Population Growth
• Natural Growth Assessing the crude birth and death rates.
• Induced Growth Assessing the inward and outward movement of people.
Phases of Population Growth
• Phase I (1901-1921) Stagnant phase of growth
• Phase II (1921-51) Steady population growth
• Phase III (1951-81) Population explosion
• Phase IV (1981-till present) Slowing down population growth
4 Regional Variation in Population Growth
• High Gujarat, Maharashtra, Punjab
• Average Assam, Sikkim, West Bengal
• Low Kerala, Karnataka, Andhra Pradesh
5 Population Composition
Analyses age, sex, place of residence, religion, literary and occupational characteristics.
6 Classification of Population Composition
Occupational
• Main workers (works for 6 months)
• Marginal workers (works for less than 6 months)
• Non-workers
Religion
• Hindu = 80%
• Muslims = 14%
• Christians = 2.3%
• Sikhs = 1.7%
Linguistic
• The speakers of major Indian languages belong to four language families-Austric, Dravidian, Sino-Tibetan and Indo-European.
• Speakers of Hindi have the highest percentage.
• Smallest language groups are Sanskrit, Bodo and Manipuri speakers.
• There are 22 scheduled languages in India.
Rural Urban
• Composition by places of residence
• Rural= 68.8%
• Urban= 31.16%

NCERT Folder

Multiple Choice Questions

(i) **India's population as per 2011 Census is**

(a) 1028 million (b) 3182 million
(c) 3287 million (d) 1210 million

Ans. (d) 1210 million

(ii) **Which one of the following has the highest density of population in India?**

(a) West Bengal (b) Kerala
(c) Uttar Pradesh (d) Punjab

Ans. (a) West Bengal

(iii) **Which one of the following states has the highest proportion of urban population in India according to 2011 Census?**

(a) Tamil Nadu (b) Maharashtra
(c) Kerala (d) Goa

Ans. (d) Goa

(iv) **Which one of the following is the largest linguistic group of India?**

(a) Sino-Tibetan (b) Indo-Aryan
(c) Austric (d) Dravidian

Ans. (b) Indo-Aryan

Answer the following questions in about 30 words

(i) **Very hot and dry and very cold and wet regions of India have low density of population. In this light, explain the role of climate on the distribution of population.**

Ans. Climate of a place affects the population distribution in that area. People prefer to live in moderate conditions of temperature and rainfall. Very wet and dry conditions restrict humans to settle in these areas. Consequently Northern plains, deltas and coastal plains have higher proportion of population whereas interior districts of Southern and Central India and Himalayas have sparse population.

(ii) **Which states have large rural population in India? Give one reason for such large rural population.**

Ans. In India, Himachal Pradesh, Haryana, Punjab, Andhra Pradesh, Madhya Pradesh and Maharashtra have large rural population.

The main reason behind such large rural population is high dependency on agriculture due to fertile soil and irrigation facility. The primary sector plays an important role in the economy of these states.

(iii) **Why do some states of India have higher rates of work participation than others?**

Ans. The states in India like Himachal Pradesh, Sikkim, Chhattisgarh and Andhra Pradesh have high rate of working population than others because of the following reasons

- The low socio-economic development in these regions due to which there is less development in secondary and tertiary sectors.
- There is large dependency on primary sector which is labour intensive and requires large number of manual workers.
- Population of these regions are poor and less skilled because of low education and training.

(iv) **'The agriculture sector has the largest share of Indian workers'. Explain.**

Ans. The occupational composition of India's population shows a large proportion of primary sector workers which is 54.6 per cent as per 2011 Census.

The proportion of cultivators and agricultural labourers are higher because a large section of population is dependent on agriculture which is the backbone of Indian economy as the other sectors have not fully developed in the country.

Answer the following questions in about 150 words

(i) **Discuss the spatial pattern of density of population in India.**

Ans. The density of population is used to understand the spatial distribution of population in relation to the land.

The average density of population in India according to Census 2011 is 382 per sq km. There are large scale variations in the population density from one state to another in the country.

According to final data of 2011 Census, the density of population ranges from 17 person per sq km in Arunachal Pradesh to 11,297 persons per sq km in Delhi. Spatial pattern of density of population is discussed as following

States having High Density of Population Among the states, the North Indian states have high density like Bihar (1,102), West Bengal (1,029) while South Indian states like Kerala (859) and Tamil Nadu (555) have higher densities among the Peninsular Indian states.

States having Moderate Density of Population States like Assam, Gujarat, Andhra Pradesh, Haryana, Jharkhand and Odisha.

States having Low Density of Population The hilly states of North India and North-East India have low density of population due to tough geographical and environmental conditions.

Population Density in Union Territories The population density in Union Territories is relatively high except Andaman and Nicobar.

In some way, the spatial distribution of population also varies from coastal regions to mid-peninsular regions and from Western to Eastern parts of India.

(ii) Give an account of the occupational structure of India's population.

Or **Explain with example the occupational structure of India's population.**

Ans. Occupational structure of India's population means the engagement of an individual in farming, manufacturing, trade, services, or any kind of professional activities. Occupations are generally classified as primary, secondary and tertiary.

The main feature of occupational structure in India is the engagement of maximum population in agriculture sector. The sectorwise distribution of occupations are

- The total working population as cultivator and agricultural labourer was 54.6% in 2011.
- The workers engaged in household industries was very low and just 3.8% of workers.
- The workers in non-households industries i.e. trade, commerce, construction and other services were 41.6%.

It is significant to note that proportion of agricultural workers declined from 69.49% in 1991 to 54.6% in 2011. The share of jobs generated in household industries reduced over the year. Although, the shift towards non-farm activities is a good indicator for Indian economy, but low growth in secondary sectors is still a big issue for the creation of jobs.

Exam Pattern Questions

Objective Type Questions

Multiple Choice Questions (MCQs)

1. The first population Census in India was conducted in

(a) 1901 (b) 1872
(c) 1857 (d) 1906

2. Which of these State/UT has the lowest population density in India?

(a) Assam
(b) Himachal Pradesh
(c) Arunachal Pradesh
(d) Jammu and Kashmir

3. Which one of the following states has the lowest population density? **CBSE Term I 2021**

(a) Mizoram (b) Nagaland
(c) Assam (d) Himachal Pradesh

4. Which one of the following Union Territories has the highest density of population? **CBSE Sample Paper Term I 2021**

(a) NCT Delhi
(b) Andaman and Nicobar Islands
(c) Chandigarh
(d) Puducherry

5. In which of these phases of population growth, both birth and death rates were high?

(a) Phase IV (b) Phase I (c) Phase II (d) Phase III

6. Which one of the following pairs is correctly matched? **CBSE Diksha**

(a) Phase I (1901-1921) : Period of high population growth
(b) Phase II (1921-1951) : Period of stagnant population growth
(c) Phase III (1951-1981): Period of population explosion
(d) Phase IV (1981-now): Period of declining population growth

7. Which one of the following is responsible for slowing down of growth rate after 1981? **CBSE Diksha**

(a) Decrease in death rates (b) Increase in death rates
(c) Female illiteracy
(d) Increase in mean age at marriage

8. Choose from the following states that has registered the highest fall in decadal growth rates during 2001-2011 compared to 1901-2001?

(a) Andhra Pradesh (b) Maharashtra
(c) Arunachal Pradesh (d) Bihar

9. Which one of the following policies is designed to look into the overall development of our large youth and adolescent population? CBSE Diksha

(a) National Policy for Digital India
(b) National Population Policy
(c) National Youth Policy
(d) National Policy for Skill Development and Entrepreneurship

10. The National Youth Policy 2014 has defined 'youth' in the age group of

(a) 16-24 years (b) 15-29 years
(c) 10-19 years (d) 12-14 years

11. Which one of the followings is the false reason of high growth rate of urban population in India? CBSE 2024

(a) Higher economic development in cities
(b) Improvement in health condition in cities
(c) Rapid expansion of urban areas
(d) Availability of employment opportunities in cities

12. Which one of the following language groups is the smallest in India? CBSE 2024

(a) Sanskrit, Bodo and Manipuri
(b) Kannada, Tamil and Telugu
(c) Dogri, Punjabi and Konkani
(d) Maithili, Gujarati and Bangla

13. Which one of the following is the smallest language group in India? CBSE Diksha

(a) Punjabi (b) Manipuri
(c) Tamil (d) Marathi

14. Which of the following is the smallest linguistic group in India ? CBSE 2023

(a) Austric (b) Dravidian
(c) Indo- European (d) Sino-Tibetan

15. Choose the correct pair. CBSE Term I 2021

(a) State having the highest density of population – West Bengal
(b) State having the highest literacy rate – Kerala
(c) State having the highest percentage of urban population – Punjab
(d) State having the highest percentage of rural population – Goa

16. There are four distinct phases of population growth identified in India over the last one century. Identify the phase from the given description. CBSE SQP 2024

This period is referred to as the period of population explosion in India, which was caused by a rapid fall in the mortality rate but a high fertility rate of population in the country. The average annual growth rate was as high as 2.2 per cent. It is in this period that developmental activities were introduced through a centralised planning process and economy started showing up ensuring the improvement of living condition of people at large. Consequently, there was a high natural increase and higher growth rate.

(a) Phase I 1901-1921
(b) Phase II 1921-1951
(c) Phase III 1951-1981
(d) Phase IV post 1981 till present

17. Consider the following statements "India has a highly uneven pattern of population distribution." CBSE Diksha

I. Uttar Pradesh has the highest population followed by Maharashtra.
II. Top 10 states together account for about 90 per cent of the total population of the country.
III. The regions falling in the river plains and coastal areas have dense population concentrations.
IV. ·The interior districts of Southern and Central Indian States, some of the North-Eastern have high population concentration.

Of these statements

(a) I, II, III and IV are correct (b) I, II and III are correct
(c) I and III are correct (d) II and IV are correct

18. Read the following objectives regarding the National Policy for Skill Development and Entrepreneurship (2015) carefully and choose the most appropriate option. CBSE 2024

I. To improve the literacy rate of different age groups in India.
II. To provide an umbrella framework for all skilling activities.
III. To align all skilling activities to common standards.
IV. To link skilling activities with demand centres.

Options

(a) Only I, II and III are correct.
(b) Only II, III and IV are correct.
(c) Only I, III and IV are correct.
(d) Only I, II and IV are correct.

19. Which of the following are branches of Dravidian language in India? CBSE 2025

I. Central Dravidian II. East Dravidian
III. South Dravidian IV. North Dravidian

Options

(a) Only I, II and III (b) Only II, III and IV
(c) Only I, III and IV (d) Only I, II and IV

20. Which of these factors has led to increasing density of population in Jharkhand which was earlier sparsely populated?

I. Availability of mineral resources
II. Better transport facility

III. Irrigation system

Codes

(a) I and II (b) Only I (c) Only II (d) I and III

Arrange the Following

21. **Which of the following States/UTs are arranged in decreasing order of their percentage of urban population correctly?**

(i) Delhi (ii) Kerala
(iii) Maharashtra (iv) Assam

Codes

(a) (ii), (i), (iii), (iv) (b) (i), (ii), (iii), (iv)
(c) (i), (iv), (ii), (iii) (d) (iii), (iv), (i), (ii)

22. **Arrange the following states in the decreasing order in terms of their population density.**

(i) Uttar Pradesh (ii) West Bengal
(iii) Bihar

Codes

(a) (i), (ii), (iii) (b) (ii), (i), (iii)
(c) (iii), (i), (ii) (d) (iii), (ii), (i)

23. **Consider the density of the population in the following states.** **CBSE Diksha**

(i) West Bengal (ii) Bihar
(iii) Kerala (iv) Uttar Pradesh

Select the correct sequence in order of decreasing importance in the density of the population.

(a) (i), (ii), (iii) and (iv) (b) (i), (iii), (iv) and (ii)
(c) (ii), (iv), (iii) and (i) (d) (ii), (i), (iv) and (iii)

24. **Arrange the following states in order of their population from highest to lowest.** **CBSE SQP 2024-2025**

(i) Bihar (ii) Maharashtra
(iii) Uttar Pradesh (iv) West Bengal

Codes

(a) (i), (iii), (ii), (iv) (b) (iv), (iii), (ii), (i)
(c) (iii), (ii), (i), (iv) (d) (ii), (i), (iv), (iii)

Match the Following

25.

List I (Phase of Population Growth)	List II (Characteristics)
A. Phase I	1. Steady population growth
B. Phase II	2. Population explosion
C. Phase III	3. Negative growth rate

Codes

	A	B	C		A	B	C
(a)	3	2	1	(b)	3	1	2
(c)	1	2	3	(d)	1	3	2

26.

List I (Religious Group)		List (% of Total Population)
A. Hindus	1.	2.3%
B. Muslims	2.	79.8%
C. Christians	3.	14.2%
D. Sikhs	4.	1.7%

Codes

	A	B	C	D
(a)	2	3	1	4
(b)	3	1	2	4
(c)	4	1	2	3
(d)	4	2	1	3

Assertion-Reason

Directions (Q. Nos. 27-29) In the questions given below are two statements labelled as Assertion (A) and other labelled as Reason (R). In the context of two statements which one of the following is correct?

Codes

(a) Both A and R are true, but R is not the correct explanation of A
(b) Both A and R are true and R is the correct explanation of A
(c) Both A and R are incorrect
(d) A is correct, but R is incorrect

27. **Assertion (A) Socio-economic factors affect the distribution of population in India.**

Reason (R) Climate is one of the important socio-economic factor.

28. **Assertion (A) India has highly uneven pattern of population distribution.** **CBSE 2025**

Reason (R) Population distribution is highly associated with physical, socio-economic and historical factors.

29. **Assertion (A) The states with larger percentages of workers are Himachal Pradesh, Sikkim, Chhattisgarh, etc.**

Reason (R) The work participation rate tends to be higher in the areas of lower levels of economic development.

Answers

1. (b) 1872
2. (c) Arunachal Pradesh
3. (a) Mizoram
4. (a) NCT Delhi
5. (b) Phase I
6. (c) Phase III (1951-1981): Period of population explosion
7. (d) Increase in mean age at marriage
8. (b) Maharashtra
9. (c) National Youth Policy
10. (b) 15-29 years
11. (c) Rapid expansion of urban areas
12. (a) Sanskrit, Bodo and Manipuri
13. (b) Manipuri
14. (d) Sino-Tibetan
15. (b) State having the highest literacy rate-Kerala
16. (c) Phase III 1951-1981
17. (c) I and III are correct.
18. (b) Only II, III and IV are correct.
19. (c) Only I, III and IV
20. (b) Only I
21. (b) (i), (ii), (iii), (iv)
22. (d) (iii), (ii), (i)
23. (d) (ii), (i), (iv) and (iii)
24. (c) (iii), (ii), (i), (iv)
25. (b)
26. (a)
27. (c) Both A and R are incorrect
28. (b) Both A and R are true and R is the correct explanation of A
29. (a) Both A and R are true, but R is not the correct explanation of A

Subjective Questions

Short Answer Type Questions

1. State the physical factors which determine the pattern of population distribution.

Ans. In India, there is uneven distribution of population due to various factors.

Important physical factors which determine the pattern of population distribution are given below

- There is a close relationship between climate and population distribution. The climate, terrain and availability of water largely determine the pattern of the population distribution.
- Since, there is availability of sufficient water and fertile plain land in Northern plains, the population density in Northern part of India is high in comparison to Southern states. Whereas, there is rough terrain in Himalayas, therefore population density is also low in Himalayan states like Himachal Pradesh, Sikkim and Arunachal Pradesh.
- However, due to availability of transport, communication, resources and other developmental facilities, the concentration of population has become moderate to high in areas which were earlier sparsely populated e.g. Rajasthan, Jharkhand.

2. What are the two main components of population growth in India? Describe the main features of each component.

Ans. The two main components of population growth in India are

(i) **Natural Growth** It refers to the growth in population which is caused by birth rate and death rate. It is estimated by the difference between birth rate and death rate.

Features of natural growth in India are as follows

- In India, it is more influential in population growth.
- This high growth rate shows the medical, technological and social advancement of Indian society.

(ii) **Induced Growth** It refers to the growth in population caused by the migration. It is measured by the difference between in-migrants and out-migrants.

Features of induced growth rate are as follows

- In India, it was more influential in population growth during the partition in 1947 and Bangladesh war of 1971.
- This type of growth is caused by the economic advancement of a society that attracts migrants from other areas.

3. Explain any five causes for the stagnant growth of India's population from 1901 to 1921.

Or **"The period from 1901 to 1921 is referred to as a stagnant phase of India's population growth." Substantiate the statement.** Competency Based Que

Or **Analyse the growth of population in India since 1921.** CBSE2025

Ans. The period from 1901-1921 is referred to as a period of stagnant or stationary phase of growth of India's population. Following causes are responsible for stagnant growth

- High birth rate and high death rate resulted into stationary growth.
- Due to lack of medical, health and sanitation facilities, death rate was high.
- The improper public distribution system resulted into hunger and famine.

- Low level of economic development and occurance of First World War was also responsible for decrease in population growth.
- Illiteracy, lack of family planning and lack of social awareness etc, were the factors for stagnant growth rate in India.

4. Why did the growth rate of population in Phase IV slow down in India? Give three reasons.

Ans. The decades after 1981 marked the slow growth rate of population due to low birth rate and low death rate.

The reasons which are responsible for the slow growth rate of population in phase-IV are as follows

- The fall in crude birth rate due to family planning is responsible for such slow population growth.
- The progressive social development and increase in mean age of marriage lower down the birth rate in the country.
- The improved quality of life particularly education of females and increasing economic progress helped to reduce the growth rate of population.

5. How far the trend of birth and death rate in India has determined the growth of population?

Ans. The growth of population is determined by two components i.e. natural growth and induced growth. The birth rate and death rate are the basic parameters of natural growth, whereas induced growth includes the volume of inward and outward movement of people in any given area.

From the decade of 1901 to 1941, the growth rate in India was slow due to high death rate in comparison to birth rate. After 1941, the birth rate continued to be high but the death rate increased which caused high growth rate in India. After 1941, due to partition of India, there was large scale migration from the Pakistan to India which increased the population. In same way, in decade of 1961-1971, there was a large scale migration from the border of Bangladesh to India which was also a reason for population explosion in India.

Therefore, both natural i.e. birth rate and death rate as well as induced population growth are responsible for growth of population in India.

6. "The decades of 1951-81 are referred to as the period of population explosion in India." Explain the statement by giving three reasons.

Or Explain any five causes of the rapid growth of population in India from 1951 to 1981.

Ans. The decades of 1951 to 1981 marked a drastic increase in population as compared to prior decades.

These decades are referred to as the period of population explosion in India because of rapid fall in death rate and high birth rate, which has the following reasons

- High mortality rate was uncontrolled by improvement in medical and sanitation facilities.
- Birth rate was high because of developmental activities which were started with a centralised planning process.
- Due to illiteracy, the efforts for family planning were not successful.
- Better transportation has resulted into the improved distribution system which is responsible for high birth rate also.
- Due to better health and food security, the life expectancy was also increased i.e. from 23 years to 55 years.

7. What is the meaning of population growth? Describe two main features of the first phase of Indian demographic history. **CBSE Diksha**

Ans. Growth of population is the change in the number of people living in a particular area between two points of time. Its rate is expressed in percentage. Population growth has two components namely; natural and induced.

The two main features of phase I of Indian demographic history are as follows

(i) The period from 1901-1921 is referred to as a period of stagnant or stationary phase of growth of India's population.

(ii) In this period, growth rate was very low, even recording a negative growth rate during 1911-1921 due to the high birth rate and death rate.

8. Discuss the status of adolescent population in India. Also state its challenges.

Or With respect to adolescent population, analyse the challenges of Indian society. **CBSE 2025**

Ans. In India, the share of adolescents i.e. people in the age group of 10-19 years is about 20.9 per cent as per 2011 Census. Among these, male adolescents constitute 52.7 per cent and female adolescents contribute 47.3 per cent. This youthful population has high potential which can be utilised in socio-economic and political development of the country. But this population is highly vulnerable to various challenges like drug addicts, alcoholism, radicalism, etc.

There are many traditional challenges for the adolescents in the society such as

- Lower age of marriage.
- Illiterary among youth, particularly in females.
- Increasing school dropouts.
- Low intake of nutrients.
- High rate of maternal mortality of adolescent mothers.
- High rate of HIV/AIDS infection.

9. Enumerate the challenges confronting society regarding the adolescent population. Enlist a few measures to overcome these problems. CBSE SQP 2024

Ans. The adolescent population faces challenges like lack of education, unemployment, health issues, early marriages and poor awareness about reproductive health. Many adolescents also struggle with mental stress, peer pressure and lack of proper guidance, leading to risky behaviour.

Following are the measures to overcome these problems

- Provide better education and skill development programs.
- Improve access to healthcare and counselling services.
- Spread awareness about reproductive health and nutrition.
- Encourage community programs to support adolescents.
- Create job opportunities to ensure a secure future for them.

10. Explain the main aspects of 'National Youth Policy' of government of India launched in 2014.

or What is the main thrust of the National Youth Policy of Government of India 2014?

Ans. The National Youth Policy has been launched by government in 2014 in the view of challenges against adolescents population.

Major aspects of this policy are as follows

- To impart education to adolescent group so that their talent and potential are better analysed and properly utilised.
- Imparting skill quality and training to youths.
- All round development of the youth is to be undertaken.
- Empowering women and girl child to bring equality in the male and female status.
- Providing youth, health facilities that make them creative, aware and innovative in the field of science and technology.

11. "The distribution of rural population is not uniform throughout India". Support this statement with three suitable examples. Competency Based Que

Ans. The Census of 2011 revealed the facts that the distribution of rural population in India is uneven. There are 6.4 lacs villages in India out of which 5.9 lacs are inhabited. Some of the findings show the uneven distribution of population. These are

- There is variation in rural population among states e.g: Himachal Pradesh has 90 per cent rural population, whereas Goa has only 38 per cent of rural population.
- There is a huge variation between states and UTs. Almost all Union Territories have rural population less than 50 per cent. The UTs like Delhi and Chandigarh have rural population of 2.5 per cent and 2.7 per cent.
- There is also a variation in size of rural population. For example, it is less than 200 persons in the hill states of North-Eastern India, Western Rajasthan and Rann of Kachchh and as high as 17 thousand persons in the states of Kerala and in parts of Maharashtra.

12. Explain any three characteristics each of rural and urban composition in India.

Ans. There are three characteristics each of rural and urban composition in India which are discussed below

Rural Composition

- As per Census 2011, 68.8 per cent of India's population lives in rural areas.
- India has 640,867 villages according to Census 2011.
- States like Himachal Pradesh, Sikkim and Bihar have very high percentage of rural population.

Urban Composition

- The proportion of urban population is 31.16 per cent in India.
- There is wide variation in distribution of urban population across the country.
- Economic development has played critical role in growth of urban population.

13. "India is a land of linguistic diversity." Support the statement.

Ans. India is a land of linguistic diversity, this statement can be supported by following

- As per linguistic survey of India (1903-1928) by Grierson, there were 179 languages and 544 dialects in the country.
- As present, there are 22 scheduled languages and a number of non-scheduled languages.
- Different families of languages are spoken in country such as, Austric Dravidian, Sino-Tibetan and Indo-European.
- There is no sharp and clear boundry between zones of different languages.

14. How is the main worker different from the marginal worker? State the four occupational categories as per the Census of India. CBSE Diksha

Ans. The main worker is different from the marginal worker in terms of number of days they work, as a main worker works for at least 183 days while a marginal worker works for less than 183 days.

The 2011 Census has divided the working population of India into four major categories.

These categories are as follows

1. Cultivators
2. Agricultural Labourers
3. Household Industrial Workers
4. Non-household Industrial Workers

15. Which are the three groups of Indian population according to their economic status? Explain the main characteristics of each group.

Ans. On the basis of economic status, India's population is divided into the following three categories

(i) **Main Worker** A person who works for atleast 183 days in a year.

Characteristics of main workers are as follows

- They are the main contributors in a nation's GDP.
- They constitute large proportion of workers in India.

(ii) **Marginal Workers** A person who works for less than 183 days in a year.

Characteristics of marginal workers are as follows

- They are mostly engaged in agricultural sector.
- They constitute a short proportion of workers in India.

(iii) **Non-Workers** A person who does not work for his/her livelihood.

Characteristics of non-workers are as follows

- They are dependent on working population for their needs.
- They represent a larger proportion of Indian population.

16. "The female work participation rate is low in comparison to male in India". Give reason for this statement.

Ans. In the occupational composition, the male workers out number female workers in all three sectors.

Following are the reasons behind this

- The patriarchal system of society does not allow females to work outside the house.
- Low level of literacy among females.
- The joint family system put greater family responsibility over females.
- Early child marriage, low level of nutrition, insecure atmosphere are the problems which results in low female participation in workforce.
- Wage disparity discourages women to participate in workforce.
- Harassment by fellow male workers.

17. Why was 'Beti Bachao Bati Padhao' social campaign launched by the Government of India ? Examine. **CBSE 2023**

Ans. The social campaign 'Beti-Bachao-Beti Padhao' was launched by the government of India in 2015 for the following purposes

- The Indian government introduced the Beti Bachao-Beti Padhao (BBBP) scheme to address concerns of gender discrimination and women empowerment in the country.
- The name Beti Bachao-Beti Padhao translates to 'Save the Girl Child, Educate the Girl Child'. The scheme aims to educate citizens against gender bias and improve efficacy of welfare services for girls.
- It also aims to prevent gender-biased, sex selective elimination.
- It encourages education and participation of the girl child.
- It aims to improve the child sex ratio.
- It ensures gender equality and women empowerment.

18. Discuss in brief the responsible factors for the declination of worker in agricultural sector.

Ans. In the last few decades, agricultural sector has shown a declining trend in the proportion of workers which has various reasons such as

- Decreasing availability of agricultural land due to increase in urbanisation.
- Due to use of technology in agriculture, there is no need of employment in farm sector.
- There is a shift of workers from agriculture or rural area to urban areas due to industrialisation.
- Less productivity and low income opportunities do not attract many people to work in farms.
- The tertiary and secondary sectors are more attractive due to permanent jobs and higher income as compared to agriculture.

Long Answer Type Questions

1. What is the source of population data in India? Explain the distribution of population in India.

Ans. In India, population data is collected through Census which is held every 10 years in our country. The recent Census was conducted in 2011.

In India, spatial pattern of population distribution is very uneven. As some areas are sparsely populated, whereas others are dense. These states can be categorised into three categories

(i) **States with High Population** Uttar Pradesh (highest population), Maharashtra, Bihar, West Bengal, Andhra Pradesh, Tamil Nadu together account for 76 per cent of population.

(ii) **States with Moderate Population** Assam, Haryana, Jharkhand, Chhattisgarh, Kerala, Punjab and Goa have moderate population.

(iii) **States with Low Population** Hilly and tribal areas like Jammu and Kashmir (now UT), Uttarakhand, all North-Eastern states (except Assam) and Union Territories excluding Delhi and Chandigarh have low population.

Population is mainly affected by climate, terrain and availability of water. For example, the North Indian Plains, deltas and coastal plains are densely populated, whereas the mountainous areas and interior areas of Central and Southern India have relatively low population. Besides these, evolution of settled agriculture and urbanisation are the socio-economic and historical factors of distribution of population.

2. "An uneven distribution of population suggests a close relationship between population and physical and socio-economic factors". Support the statement with suitable examples.

Or What is density of population? Explain with examples the physical and economic factors which affect the population distribution in India.

Or How are physical and economic factors responsible for uneven distribution of population in India? Explain with examples.

Or Explain any five factors affecting the uneven distribution of population in India. **CBSE 2024**

Ans. Population density is a measure of persons living in per unit area of land. The distribution of population over space is not uniform. It varies from place to place. There are some factors that affects the distribution of population of a place.

These are as follows

- Physical factors like climate, terrain and availability of water affects the distribution of population. People prefer to live in areas with favourable climate and terrains. The development of irrigation, availability of mineral resource and energy resource have impacted the distribution of population.
- Socio economic factors like evolution of settled agriculture and agricultural development, patterns of human settlements, transport network and industrialisation and urbanisation are included in this factor. History of human settlement and development of transport network plays an important role in the distribution of population over the space.

3. "The decadal and annual growth rates of population in India are both very high and steadily increasing over time." Substantiate the statement.

Ans. The growth of population is the change in the number of people living in a particular area between two point of time. The decadal and annual growth rates of population in India are both very high and steadily increasing this can be substantiated by following points

- In the decades of 1951–81, mortality rate declined rapidly but the fertility and rate of population was high in the country. This resulted in high decadal and growth in the population.
- The developmental activities and improvement in socio-economic condition further increased the growth rate. But after the year 1981 the decadal and annual growth rate started declining.
- At present, the annual growth rate of India's population is 1.64 per cent according to Census 2011. Still the growth rate of population is high in India as compared to other countries.

4. What is population doubling time? Explain the characteristics of the growth of population in India in Phase-I and Phase-II.

Or Explain any three characteristics of phase II of growth of population in India. **CBSE 2024**

Ans. Population doubling time is the time taken by any population to double itself at its current annual growth rate. At present, the annual growth of India's population is 1.64 per cent (2011). At this current rate of increase, it is estimated that country's population will double itself in 30 to 35 years.

For the characteristics of the growth of population in India in Phase I and Phase II, refer to text page. no. (04) under the heading 'Phase I' and 'Phase II'.

5. Explain the main characteristics of the Phase III (1951-81) of population growth in India. **CBSE 2024**

Ans. The Phase III of population growth in India (1951-1981) is known as the **period of population explosion**. This phase witnessed a rapid rise in population due to significant improvements in health conditions and a decline in the death rate, while the birth rate remained high. Key characteristics of this phase include

- **Decline in Death Rate** Post-independence, improvements in medical facilities, sanitation, and public health measures significantly reduced mortality rates, leading to population growth.

- **High Birth Rate** Although efforts were made to control population growth, birth rates remained high due to socio-cultural factors, lack of awareness and limited adoption of family planning.
- **Economic Development and Urbanisation** Economic activities expanded, and industrialisation began to grow, leading to rural-to-urban migration. However, population growth outpaced economic progress.
- **Challenges** Rapid population growth strained resources, employment opportunities, healthcare, and education systems, leading to poverty and urban overcrowding.

6. Discuss in brief about urban composition of population of India.

Ans. For answer refer to text page. no. 171 under the heading 'Urban Population'.

7. State the important steps which have been taken by the Government of India to solve the problems of adolescence.

Ans. The government of India has undertaken several steps to solve the problems of adolescence, one among them is NYP (National Youth Policy).

Following are the points of National Youth Policy.

- The National Youth Policy is one example which has been designed to look into the overall development of our large youth and adolescent population.
- The National Youth Policy (NYP–2014) was launched in February 2014.
- This policy proposes a holistic 'vision' for the youth of India, with the aim "To empower the youth of the country to achieve their full potential, and through them enable India to find its rightful place in the community of nations".
- The Government of India also formulated the National Policy for Skill Development and Entrepreneurship in 2015 to provide a single framework to all skilling activities being carried out within the country.

8. Analyse the major problems of the youth population in India. Suggest two measures to overcome the problems. CBSE 2024 C

Ans. India's youth, forming a significant part of the population, face pressing challenges impacting their development and well-being.

The major problems of youth population in India are as follows

- High unemployment rates, particularly among educated youth, stem from limited job opportunities, resulting in economic instability and mental health issues.
- Inadequate access to quality education and skills training leads to a skills mismatch, where young people are often unprepared for the labour market.
- Societal pressures, including early marriage and inadequate healthcare, restrict youth potential, especially in rural and underdeveloped regions.

Two key measures to overcome these problem are

(i) **Enhanced Education and Skill Development** Implementing comprehensive skill development programs, such as the National Skill Development Mission, can equip youth with practical skills aligned with industry needs. Promoting vocational training and internship opportunities can bridge the education-employment gap.

(ii) **Youth-Centric Policies for Employment** Policies should focus on creating jobs, especially in sectors like technology and renewable energy, which have high growth potential. Encouraging entrepreneurship through financial support and mentorship programs can enable youth to create self-sustaining careers, promoting overall economic growth.

9. Discuss the religious composition in population of India which shows the secular fabric of Indian society.

Ans. The spatial distribution of religious communities in the country shows that there are certain states and districts having large numerical strength of one religion. India is the land of multiple religions. It is a place of origin of various religions like Hinduism, Buddhism and Jainism but there are large numbers of Christians, Muslims and Zoroastrians.

The distribution of religious communities shows the statistical facts which proves the above argument

Hindus They range from 70-90 per cent and are found in majority in various states except Jammu and Kashmir and in some North-East states.

Muslims They are the largest minority religious groups and covers 14.23 per cent of total population. They are concentrated in Jammu and Kashmir, West Bengal, Kerala, Uttar Pradesh, Delhi and Lakshadweep and are in majority in Jammu and Kashmir and Lakshadweep.

Christians They are 2.30 per cent of total population and are concentrated along the Western coast of Goa, Kerala, Meghalaya, Mizoram, Nagaland, Chota Nagpur plateau and hills of Manipur.

Sikhs Population of Sikh community is 1.72 per cent but they are the most prosperous religious community. They are concentrated in small area of country particularly in Punjab, Haryana and Delhi.

Jains and Buddhists They are the smallest religious groups. Jains are concentrated in Western part of India in the states of Rajasthan, Gujarat and Maharashtra. Buddhists are concentrated in Maharashtra, Sikkim, Arunachal Pradesh and Ladakh.

Zoroastrians These are the natives of Iran and are concentrated in Mumbai, Goa and Gujarat. This community is very progressive in business and trade.

10. How is discrimination on the basis of gender a crime against humanity? Suggest two measures to overcome the problem. CBSE 2024 C

Ans. Gender discrimination is a profound violation of human rights, depriving individuals of equality, dignity and opportunities based on gender biases. It is a crime against humanity as it perpetuates cycles of inequality, limiting women's and girls' access to education, healthcare and fair employment, thereby impeding societal progress. Gender discrimination not only leads to economic disparity but also reinforces stereotypes, contributing to social injustice and restricting personal growth.

Two measures to overcome these problems are as follows

1. **Education and Awareness** Integrating gender sensitivity into education can change mindsets from a young age, promoting values of equality and respect. Campaigns like "Beti Bachao Beti Padhao" play a crucial role in shifting societal perceptions and encouraging female participation across various fields.
2. **Enforcing Gender-Equal Laws** Stronger legal frameworks, like equal pay laws and anti-discrimination legislation, can protect against workplace and societal bias. Implementing these laws with stringent penalties and ensuring workplace equality can significantly reduce gender discrimination and contribute to a fair and inclusive society.

11. How does the highly uneven spatial distribution of the population in India suggest its close relationship with physical, social, economic and historical factors? Analyse with examples. CBSE 2024

Ans. The highly uneven spatial distribution of the population in India reflects its close relationship with physical, social, economic, and historical factors. These are as follows

- **Physical Factors** Population density is higher in fertile plains like the Ganga Plain because of agriculture, while regions like the Himalayas, deserts of Rajasthan, and dense forests of central India remain sparsely populated due to harsh conditions.
- **Social Factors** Areas with better living conditions and social infrastructure, like education and healthcare, attract more people. For example, Kerala and Tamil Nadu have high literacy rates, leading to higher population concentrations.
- **Economic Factors** Industrial and urbanised regions, such as Maharashtra, Delhi, and Gujarat, have higher populations due to job opportunities in industries, services, and trade. In contrast, less developed states like Jharkhand and Chhattisgarh see lower densities.
- **Historical Factors** Historical development of cities like Kolkata, Mumbai, and Chennai as colonial trade centers led to dense populations. Similarly, regions like the Indo-Gangetic plains have been inhabited for centuries due to agricultural prosperity.

Thus, population distribution in India is shaped by the interplay of natural resources, opportunities, and historical developments.

Source Based Questions

1 Read the passage carefully and answer the questions that follow.

The division of the society into male, female and transgender is believed to be natural and biological. But, in reality, there are social constructs and roles assigned to individuals which are reinforced by social institutions. Consequently, these biological differences become the basis of social differentiations, discriminations and exclusions. The exclusion of over half of the population becomes a serious handicap to any developing and civilised society. It is a global challenge, which has been acknowledged by the UNDP when it mentioned that, "If development is not engendered it is endangered" (HDR UNDP 1995). Discrimination, in general, and gender discrimination, in particular, is a crime against humanity. All efforts need to be made to address the denial of opportunities of education, employment, political representation, low wages for similar types of work, disregard to their entitlement to live a dignified life, etc. The number of female workers is relatively higher in primary sector where there are very less wages and insecurity of employment.

(i) **Which among the following creates discriminations and exclusions in the society?**

(a) Biological differences
(b) Social institutions
(c) Schools
(d) Government

Ans. (b) Social institutions

(ii) **The Beti Bachao Beti Padhao scheme has been started by the government for which of the following purposes?**

(a) Remove discrimination against teachers
(b) Remove gender discrimination
(c) Improve school enrolment of girls
(d) Give cash to women

Ans. (b) Remove gender discrimination

(iii) **Gender discrimination manifests itself as which of the following?**

(a) Low wages for women
(b) Low political representation
(c) Denial of education
(d) All of the above

Ans. (d) All of the above

2 Read the passage carefully and answer the questions that follow.

The hill states of the Himalayan region and North Eastern states of India (excluding Assam) have relatively low densities while the Union Territories (excluding Andaman and Nicobar Islands) have very high densities of population. The density of population is a crude measure of human and land relationship. To get a better insight into the human-land ratio in terms of pressure of population on total cultivable land, the physiological and the agricultural densities should be found out which are significant for a country like India having a large agricultural population.

(i) **Choose the incorrect statement from the following regarding population density.**

(a) Density of population shows how the population is distributed over the space.
(b) Over the last 50 years there is steady increase of population.
(c) Arunachal Pradesh shows the lowest population density.
(d) The density of population shows the nature human relationship.

Ans. (b) Over the last 50 years there is steady increase of population.

(ii) **Which of these is a crude measure to determine human land relation is called ....**

(a) Agricultural density (b) Physiological density
(c) Population density (d) None of these

Ans. (c) Population density

(iii) **Which of the following North-Eastern state has high population density?**

(a) Sikkim (b) Arunachal Pradesh
(c) Assam (d) Mizoram

Ans. (c) Assam

3. Study the following table and answer the questions that follow. **CBSE Sample Paper Term I 2021**

Decadal Growth Rates in India, 1901-2011

Census Years	Total Population	Growth Rate*	
		Absolute Number	% of Growth
1901	238396327	—	—
1911	252093390	(+) 13697063	(+) 5.75
1921	251321213	(–) 772117	(–) 0.31
1931	298977238	(+) 27656025	(+) 11.60
1941	318660580	(+) 39683342	(+) 14.22
1951	361088090	(+) 42420485	(+) 13.31
1961	439234771	(+) 77682873	(+) 21.51
1971	548159652	(+) 108924881	(+) 24.80
1981	683329097	(+) 135169445	(+) 24.66
1991	846302688	(+) 162973591	(+) 23.85
2001	1028610328	(+) 182307640	(+) 21.54
2011**	1210193422	(+) 181583094	(+) 17.64

***Decadal growth rate:* $g = \frac{P_2 - P_1}{P_1} \times 100$

where P_1 = Population of the base year
P_2 = Population of the present year
***Source : Census of India, 2011 (Provisional)*

(i) **Which year has seen a negative population growth rate in India?**

(a) 1931 (b) 1921
(c) 1911 (d) 1941

Ans. (b) 1921

(ii) **What was the highest recorded growth rate of population in India?**

(a) 24.66 (b) 24.80
(c) 23.85 (d) 21.54

Ans. (b) 24.80

(iii) **How much population increase has been registered between the census years 1911 to census year 2011?**

(a) 900789600 (b) 182307640
(c) 181583094 (d) 971797095

Ans. (d) 971797095

4. Read the passage carefully and answer the questions that follow.

An important aspect of population growth in India is the growth of its adolescents. At present the share of adolescents i.e., up to the age group of 10-19 years is about 20.9 per cent (2011), among which male adolescents constitute 52.7 per cent and female adolescents constitute 47.3 per cent. The adolescent population, though, regarded as the youthful population having high potentials, but at the same time they are quite vulnerable if not guided and channelised properly.

There are many challenges for the society as far as these adolescents are concerned, some of which are lower age at marriage, illiteracy – particularly female illiteracy, school dropouts, low intake of nutrients, high rate of maternal mortality of adolescent mothers, high rate of HIV and AIDS infections, physical and mental disability or retardedness, drug abuse and alcoholism, juvenile delinquency and commitence of crimes, etc. In view of these, the Government of India has undertaken certain policies to impart proper education to the adolescent groups so that their talents are better channelised and properly utilised. The National Youth Policy is one example which has been designed to look into the overall development of our large youth and adolescent population. The National Youth Policy (NYP–2014) launched in February 2014 proposes a holistic 'vision' for the youth of India, which is "To empower the youth of the country to achieve their full potential, and through them enable India to find its rightful place in the community of nations".

(i) **Mention one of the aim of National Youth Policy of 2014.**

Ans. This policy aims at overall development of the large youth and adolescent and motivate them to empower their full potential.

(ii) **What per cent of India's population constitutes the adolescents?**

Ans. 20.9 per cent of India's population constitutes the adolescents.

(iii) **Adolescent population is vulnerable to which bad things?**

Ans. Adolescent population is vulnerable to delinquency, drug abuse, alcoholism, etc.

5. Read the passage carefully and answer the questions that follow.

Regional Variation in Population Growth

The growth rate of population during 1991-2001 in Indian States and Union Territories shows very obvious pattern. The States like Kerala, Karnataka, Tamil Nadu, Andhra Pradesh, Odisha, Puducherry and Goa show a low rate of growth not exceeding 20 per cent over the decade. Kerala registered the lowest growth rate (9-4) not only in this group of states, but also in the country as a whole. A continuous belt of states from West to East in the North-West, North and North Central parts of the country has relatively high growth rate than the Southern states. It is in this belt comprising Gujarat, Maharashtra, Rajasthan, Punjab, Haryana, Uttar Pradesh, Uttarakhand, Madhya Pradesh, Sikkim, Assam, West Bengal, Bihar, Chhattisgarh and Jharkhand, the growth rate on the average remained 20-25 per cent.

During 2001-2011, the growth rates of almost all States and Union Territories have registered a lower figure compared to the previous decade, namely, 1991-2001. The percentage decadal growth rates of the six most populous States, namely, Uttar Pradesh, Maharashtra, Bihar, West Bengal, Andhra Pradesh and Madhya Pradesh have all fallen during 2001-2011 compared to 1991-2001, the fall being the lowest for Andhra Pradesh (3.5 percentage points) and highest for Maharashtra (6.7 percentage points). Tamil Nadu (3.9 percentage points) and Puducherry (7.1 percentage points) have registered some increase during 2001-2011 over the previous decade. **CBSE Term I 2021**

(i) **What is the trend of growth rate of population from West to East of the country mostly in the Northern states?**

Ans. When we go from West to East of India mostly in the Northern States we see high growth rate of population than the Southern states.

(ii) **Mention the states that has seen highest decrease in the population growth rate during 2001 – 2011.**

Ans. States that has seen highest decrease in the population growth rate during 2001-2011 are Uttar Pradesh, Maharashtra, West Bengal, Andhra Pradesh and Bihar and Madhya Pradesh.

(iii) **Discuss about some of the states who witnessed average growth rate of 20-25 per cent.**

Ans. States like Rajasthan, Punjab, Madhya Pradesh, Sikkim, Assam, Chhattisgarh, Gujarat, Uttarakhand witnessed average growth rate of 20-25 per cent.

6. Study the following graph and answer the questions that follow.

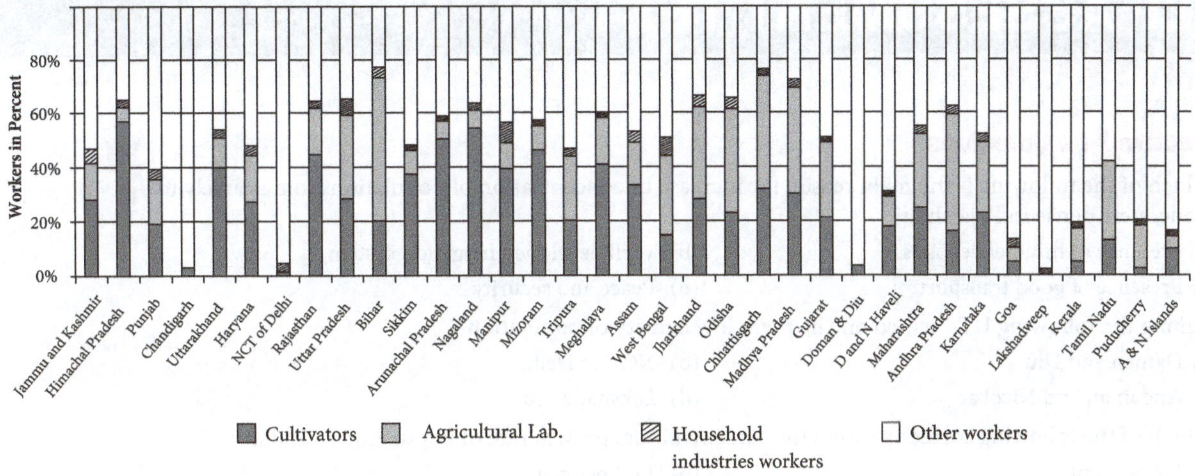

India-Occupational Structure, 2011

(i) **Mention states which are having higher proportion of cultivators as compared to others.**

Ans. States that record higher number of cultivators as compared to others are Rajasthan, Himachal Pradesh, Uttarakhand, Mizoram, Nagaland, Meghalaya, Arunachal Pradesh, Jammu and Kashmir, Haryana, Sikkim.

(ii) **Write one characteristics of marginal worker.**

Ans. Marginal workers are those workers who work for less than 183 days or 6 months in a year.

(iii) **According to the graph, what major activity is done in India?**

Ans. The graph shows that majority of workers in India are engaged in primary activities like agriculture.

Map Based Question

1. On an outline map of India, locate the following.

(i) **State with highest population density.** (ii) **State with lowest population density**

Ans.

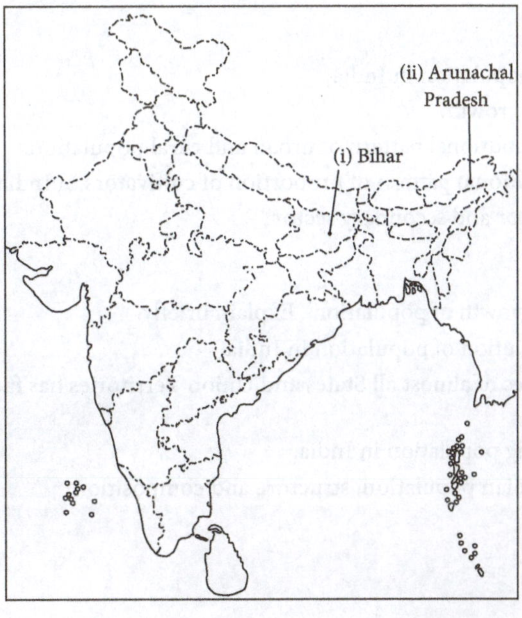

SELF ASSESSMENT TEST

Objective Type Questions

1. Which of the following is the main reason for increase in concentration of population from sparsely to moderately dense in Rajasthan?
   (a) Presence of mineral deposits
   (b) Well developed irrigation system
   (c) Presence of good transport
   (d) Peace and security
2. Among the following UTs, which one has very low density of population?
   (a) Daman and Diu
   (b) NCT of Delhi
   (c) Andaman and Nicobar
   (d) Lakshadweep
3. Which of the following correctly shows the current annual growth rate of population in India?
   (a) 1.2 per cent
   (b) 1.64 per cent
   (c) 2.3 per cent
   (d) 1.01 per cent
4. Which of the following are correctly arranged in increasing order of their numbers in India?
   (a) Hindus, Jains, Sikhs, Muslims
   (b) Sikhs, Jains, Hindus, Muslims
   (c) Hindus, Jains, Muslims, Sikhs
   (d) Jains, Sikhs, Muslims, Hindus
5. Which of these correctly describes a marginal worker?
   (a) A person who works for atleast 183 days in a year
   (b) A person who works for atleast 266 days in a year
   (c) A person who works for less than 183 days in a year
   (d) A person who works for less than 92 days in a year
6. More than 50% of working population of India is engaged as
   (a) household workers
   (b) agricultural labourers and cultivators
   (c) industrial workers
   (d) unskilled labourers

Short Answer Type Questions

7. Discuss about the distribution of population in India.
8. Explain the concept of population growth.
9. Give reasons for the different distributional pattern of urban and rural population.
10. 'There is differences in the distributional pattern of proportion of cultivators in India'. Explain.
11. Differentiate between primary sector and secondary sector.

Long Answer Type Questions

12. 'There are four distinct phases of growth of population'. Explain briefly.
13. Give reasons for the uneven distribution of population in India.
14. 'During 2001-2011, the growth rates of almost all States and Union Territories has faced lower growth rates'. Elucidate with example.
15. Explain the composition of working population in India.
16. Elucidate the salient features of Indian population, structure and composition.

UNIT 2

2 CHAPTER

Human settlement means a group of houses of different types or sizes where humans live. To develop a settlement, humans build houses and other infrastructures to support their economic base and control a particular land.

Human Settlements

YOUR STUDY GOALS

2.1 Rural Settlements
2.2 Urban Settlements
2.3 Evolution of Towns in India

YOUR PRACTICE GOAL

- Objective Type Questions (23 Qs ; MCQs, Statements, Matching, A-R)
- Subjective Type Questions (15 SAs, 3 LAs)
- Source Based Questions (4 Qs)

- Human settlements vary in size. They can be small and spacious or large and densely populated.
- The sparsely located small settlements are called villages or **rural settlements.** Villages are specialised in agriculture or other primary activities.
- On the other hand, larger settlements are called **urban settlements** which are specialised in secondary and tertiary activities.

2.1 Rural Settlements

- In India, the compact or clustered village of a few hundred houses is a common feature, particularly in the Northern plains. However, several areas have other forms of rural settlements.
- The various factors and conditions responsible for having different types of rural settlements in India are as follows
  - (a) **Physical Factors** These include the nature of terrain, altitude, climate and availability of water.
  - (b) **Cultural and Ethnic Factors** These include social structure, caste and religion.
  - (c) **Security Factors** These include defence against thefts and robberies.

- Rural settlements in India can broadly be divided into four types: clustered settlements, semi-clustered settlements, hamleted settlements and dispersed settlements.

Clustered Settlements

- The clustered rural settlement is a compact or densely built area of houses. In this type of settlement, the general living area is different from the surrounding farms, barns and pastures.

▲ *Clustered Settlements in the North-Eastern States*

- The closely built-up area and its interconnected streets create patterns or geometric shapes, such as rectangular, radial, linear, etc. Such settlements are generally found in fertile alluvial plains and the North-Eastern states.
- Sometimes, people live in compact villages for security or defence reasons. For example, in the Bundelkhand region of central India and Nagaland.
- Due to the scarcity of water in Rajasthan, people live in compact settlements, for maximum utilisation of water resources.

Semi-Clustered Settlements

- Semi-clustered or **fragmented settlements** are generally found in areas with limited land resources for settlement.

▲ *Semi-Clustered Settlements*

- Such a pattern results from segregation or fragmentation of a large compact village. In village society one or more sections choose or are forced to live a little away from the main cluster or village.
- Generally, the land-owning and dominant community occupies the central part of the main village, whereas people of lower status in society and menial workers settle on the borders of the village.
- Such settlements are widespread in the Gujarat plain and some parts of Rajasthan.

Hamleted Settlements

- Hamleted settlements are parts of a larger village that have split into smaller groups of houses. Even though these groups are separated from each other, they all share the same village name.
- These units are locally called *panna*, *para*, *palli*, *nagla*, *dhani*, etc in various parts of the country. This grouping of a large village is often based on social and ethnic factors.
- Such villages are generally found in the middle and lower Ganga plain, Chhattisgarh and lower valleys of the Himalayas.

Dispersed Settlements

▲ *Dispersed Settlements*

- In India, dispersed and **isolated**[1] settlements are small groups of huts or single houses that are spread far apart. These can be found in remote jungles or on small hills, with farms or pastures on the nearby slopes.
- Extreme dispersion of settlement is often caused by the fragmented nature of the landforms and land resources.
- Areas of Meghalaya, Uttarakhand, Himachal Pradesh and Kerala have this type of settlement.

1 **Isolated** A place that is separated from others.

2.2 Urban Settlements

- The Census of India, 1991 defines urban settlements as "All places which have municipality, corporation, cantonment board or notified town area committee and have a minimum population of 5000 persons with at least 75 per cent of male workers are engaged in non-agricultural activities and a density of population of at least 400 persons per square km are urban."
- Urban settlements are generally compact and larger. People living in urban areas are engaged in various non-agricultural, economic and administrative functions.
- Cities are functionally linked to rural areas around them. Cities are connected directly as well as indirectly with the villages and also with each other. Thus, there is a continuous direct or indirect exchange of goods and services through market towns and cities.

Basic Differences between Rural and Urban Settlements

- The rural settlements are involved in land-based primary economic activities, whereas urban settlements depend on the processing of raw materials and manufacturing of finished goods, and a variety of services.
- Cities provide goods and services not only to people living in urban areas but also to the people of the rural areas in their surroundings. This functional relationship between urban and rural settlements takes place through transport and communication networks.
- Rural and urban settlements differ in terms of social relationship, attitude and outlook. Rural people have strong social relations among the people. On the other hand in urban areas, the way of life is complex and fast, and social relations are formal.

Quick Test 1

1. Name two physical factors influencing the location of rural settlements.
2. In which regions of India hamleted settlements are found?
3. Give examples of clustered settlements in India.
4. How are urban settlements identified in India?

2.3 Evolution of Towns in India

- Towns have been developed and flourished since prehistoric times in India. During the Indus Valley Civilisation, towns like Harappa and Mohanjodaro were found in India.
- The evolution of towns continued with periodic ups and downs until the arrival of Europeans in India in the eighteenth century.
- Based on their evolution in different periods, Indian towns may be classified into the following types

Ancient Towns

- Several towns in India have historical backgrounds. Their history spans over 2000 years.
- Most of the ancient towns are developed as religious and cultural centres. For example, Varanasi, Prayagraj (Allahabad), Pataliputra (Patna) and Madurai.

Medieval Towns

- During medieval period, 100 of Indian towns were developed. Most of them were developed as headquarters of principalities and kingdoms.
- These towns were built on the ruins of ancient towns. For example, Delhi, Hyderabad, Jaipur, Lucknow, Agra and Nagpur.

Modern Towns

- The British and other Europeans have developed several towns in India. They first developed some trading ports such as Surat, Daman, Goa, Pondicherry, etc. The British later controlled three principal locations i.e. Mumbai (Bombay), Chennai (Madras) and Kolkata (Calcutta). These cities were built in the British style.
- The British established their administrative centres by extending their domination either directly or through control over the princely states.
- They also built hill towns as summer resorts and added new civil, administrative and military areas for them.
- Towns based on modern industries also evolved after 1850. For example, **Jamshedpur**.
- After independence, a large number of towns have been developed as administrative headquarters, e.g., Chandigarh, Bhubaneswar, Gandhinagar, Dispur, etc., and industrial centres, such as Durgapur, Bhilai, Sindri, Barauni.
- Some old towns are developed as **satellite towns** around metropolitan cities. For example, Ghaziabad, Rohtak and Gurugram around Delhi.
- With increasing investment in rural areas, many medium and small towns have developed all over the country.

Functional Classification of Towns

- **Administrative Towns and Cities** Towns that support administrative headquarters are called administrative towns. For example, Chandigarh, New Delhi, Bhopal, Shillong, Guwahati, Imphal, Srinagar, Gandhinagar, Jaipur, Chennai, etc.
- **Industrial Towns** Industrial towns are surrounded by industries. For example, Mumbai, Salem, Coimbatore, Modinagar, Jamshedpur, Hugli, Bhilai, etc.
- **Transport Cities** They may be ports that are primarily engaged in export and import activities. For example, Kandla, Kochchi, Kozhikode, Visakhapatnam, etc., or hubs of inland transport, such as Agra, Dhulia, Mughalsarai, Itarsi, Katni, etc.
- **Commercial Towns** Towns and cities specialising in trade and commerce are called commercial towns. For example, Kolkata, Saharanpur, Satna, etc.
- **Mining Towns** These towns are developed in mineral rich areas and major activity in these towns is mining. For example, Raniganj, Jharia, Digboi, Ankaleshwar, Singrauli, etc.
- **Garrison Cantonment Towns** These towns emerged as garrison towns or basement towns for defence staff. For example, Ambala, Jalandhar, Mhow, Babina, Udhampur, etc.
- **Educational Towns** These towns are major education hubs. Some of the towns have grown into major campus towns. For example, Roorkee, Varanasi, Aligarh, Pilani, Allahabad, etc.

- **Religious and Cultural Towns** These towns are developed due to their **religious/cultural significance**. For example, Varanasi, Mathura, Amritsar, Madurai, Puri, Ajmer, Pushkar, Tirupati, Kurukshetra, Haridwar and Ujjain
- **Tourist Towns** These towns are developed as tourist destinations. Nainital, Mussoorie, Shimla, Pachmarhi, Jodhpur, Jaisalmer, Udagamandalam (Ooty) and Mount Abu are some of the tourist towns.

Urbanisation in India

- The level of urbanisation in India in 2011 was 31.16 per cent, which is quite low in comparison to developed countries.
- The level of urbanisation is measured in terms of percentage of urban population to total population. The total urban population has increased eleven-times during the twentieth century.
- The enlargement of urban centres and the emergence of new towns have played a significant role in the growth of urban population and urbanisation in the country. However, the growth rate of urbanisation has slowed down during the last two decades.

Smart Cities Mission

- The objective of the Smart Cities Mission is to promote cities that provide core infrastructure, a clean and sustainable environment, and give a decent quality of life to its citizens.
- One of the features of smart cities is to apply smart solutions to infrastructure and services to make them better. For example, making areas less vulnerable to disasters, using fewer resources and providing cheaper services.
- The focus of smart cities mission is on sustainable and inclusive development.

Quick Test 2

1. Name two mining towns in India.
2. How are tourist towns identified?
3. Which type of trend is visible in the urbanisation of India?
4. In which year the smart cities mission was launched?

Mind Map

HUMAN SETTLEMENTS

1 Meaning

Cluster of dwellings of any type or size where human beings live.

Factors and Conditions required for the Rural Settlement

- **Physical Factors** Terrain, climate, altitude
- **Cultural and Ethnic Factors** Social structure, caste, religion
- **Security Factors** Defence against thefts, robberies

2 Rural Settlements

People living in rural settlement derive their life support from land based primary economic activity.

Types of Rural Settlements

- **Clustered Settlements** Compact or closely built up areas, found in fertile alluvial plain.
- **Semi-Clustered Settlements** Results from fragmentation of large compact villages found in Gujarat plains.
- **Hamleted Settlements** Fragmented into several units, locally called- Para, Palli, Nagla.
- **Dispersed Settlement** Isolated huts found in Uttarakhand, Meghalaya.

Dispersed Settlement

3 Urban Settlements

- Compact and large in size.
- People living in urban settlements perform non-agricultural activities.

Towns Based on Function

- **Administrative Town** e.g., New Delhi, Chennai
- **Industrial Towns** e.g., Mumbai, Bhilai
- **Transport Cities** e.g., Agra, Mughalsarai
- **Commercial Towns** e.g., Satna, Saharanpur
- **Mining Towns** e.g., Digboi, Jharia
- **Garrison (defence)** Cantonment Towns e.g., Ambala, Mhow
- **Educational Towns** e.g., Aligarh, Pilani
- **Religious and Cultural Towns** e.g., Varanasi, Tirupati.
- **Tourist Towns** e.g., Mussoorie, Nainital, Jodhpur.

Evolution of Towns

- Towns flourished since prehistoric times.
- Early examples includes Indus Valley Civilisation, Harappa.

Towns Based on Period of Evolution

- **Ancient Towns** Older than 2000 years, e.g., Varanasi, Allahabad, Madurai.
- **Medieval Towns** Built on the ruins of ancient towns. It includes Jaipur, Lucknow, Agra.
- **Modern Towns** Developed by Britishers and Europeans. It includes Goa, Pondicherry, Mumbai.

Ancient Town (Varanasi)

NCERT Folder

Choose the right answers of the following from the given options

(i) **Which one of the following towns is not located on a river bank?**

(a) Agra (b) Bhopal
(c) Patna (d) Kolkata

Ans. (b) Bhopal

(ii) **Which one of the following is not the part of the definition of a town as per the census of India?**

(a) Population density of 400 persons per sq km.
(b) Presence of municipality, corporation, etc.
(c) More than 75% of the population engaged in primary sector.
(d) Population size of more than 5,000 persons.

Ans. (c) More than 75% of the population engaged in primary sector.

(iii) **In which one of the following environments does one expect the presence of dispersed rural settlements?**

(a) Alluvial plains of Ganga
(b) Arid and semi-arid regions of Rajasthan
(c) Lower valleys of Himalayas
(d) Forests and hills in North-East

Ans. (d) Forests and hills in North-East

Answer the following questions in about 30 words

(i) **What are garrison towns? What is their function?**

Ans. Garrison towns are towns which are meant for the army and defence purpose, e.g. towns like Ambala, Jalandhar, Mhow, Babina, Udhampur, etc.

Functions of garrison towns are as follows

- These are the places where army troops are posted.
- These provide places for important activities like training centres, offices and residence complexes.

(ii) **What are the main factors for the location of villages in desert regions?**

Ans. The main factors for the location of villages in desert regions are as follows

- Due to lack of water resources compact villages are found in desert regions, for maximum utilisation of water.
- Due to limited availability of fertile land, villages are either compact or semi-compact in desert regions.

Answer the following questions in about 150 words

(i) **Discuss the features of different types of rural settlements. What are the factors responsible for the settlement pattern in different physical environments?**

Ans. The features of different types of rural settlements are as follows

- **Clustered Settlements** The clustered rural settlement is a compact or closely built up area of houses. In this type of village, the general living area is distinct and separated from the surrounding farms, barns and pastures.
- **Semi-Clustered Settlements** Semi-clustered or fragmented settlements may result from tendency of clustering in a restricted area of dispersed settlement.
- **Hamleted Settlements** Hamlet is formed when the settlement is fragmented into several units, physically separated from each other bearing a common name. These units are locally called panna, para, palli, nagla, dhani, etc. in various parts of the country.
- **Dispersed Settlements** These settlements appear in the form of isolated huts or hamlets of few huts in remote jungles, or on small hills with farms or pasture on the slopes.

Following are the factors responsible for settlements in different physical environment

- **Availability of Water** Generally rural settlements are located near water bodies specially in desert region where there is scarcity of water.
- **Nature of Land** People prefer to settle in plain areas where opportunities for livelihood are more in comparison to other regions.
- **Resources** These are very important factors of determining settlements. Early villages were built in forest where woods and fruits were in plenty. Resources attract people from longer distance.

(ii) **Can one imagine the presence of only one-function town? Why do the cities become multi-functional?**

Ans. It is difficult to imagine about the presence of only one functional town at present time. The demands and aspiration of people for services changes with time and this results in the change/increase in the town size and population. Hence, towns are modified according to the desired services and becomes multi-functional.

Each town performs multiple functions. Even the specialised cities with time become multi-functional, wherein industries, transport, marketing and other functions become important. These functions become so intertconnected that it is difficult to classify a city on the basis of a specialised function.

A town is engaged in various activities for fulfilling the needs of its population. To support the main activity of the town various supporting services are also developed. For example, Mumbai was developed as a port town but it emerged as a hub of international trade, which made it a trading centre. It also transformed into the commercial capital of the country due to large scale commerical activities.

This shows that presence of a single specialised function attracts various other activities to the towns which creates favourable conditions for the development of other functions, making the towns multifunctional in nature. The functions performed by towns are dynamic in nature.

Exam Pattern Questions

Objective Type Questions

Multiple Choice Questions (MCQs)

1. Local names like Panna, Para, Palli, Nagla, Dhani, etc. are examples of which of the following types of rural settlements in India? CBSE 2025

(a) Clustered Settlement (b) Semi-clustered Settlement
(c) Hamleted Settlement (d) Dispersed Settlement

2. Which one of the following is a reason for the emergence of clustered settlements in Rajasthan? CBSE 2024

(a) For the maximum utilisation of land resources
(b) For external security and defence
(c) For maximum utilisation of available water resources
(d) For internal security and defence

3. Which of the following are the features of urban settlements in India? CBSE SQP 2022

(a) Complex way of life, manufacturing of finished goods, nodes of economic growth.
(b) Intimate social relations, mainly primary economic activities, people are less mobile.
(c) Economy mainly based on primary activities, providing food and raw materials and social relations are formal.
(d) Provide a variety of services, poor transport networks, social relations are intimate.

4. Identify the classification of towns on the basis of their evolution in different periods in India. CBSE Term I 2021

(a) First, Second and Third Category
(b) Ancient, Medieval and Modern
(c) Transport, Commercial and Industrial
(d) Cantonment, Religious and Educational

5. Identify the town developed in medieval period.

(a) Delhi (b) Madurai
(c) Mumbai (d) Kolkata

6. Which of the following is a good example of fort town? CBSE Sample Paper Term I 2021

(a) Jaipur (b) Banaras
(c) Mathura (d) Rameswaram

7. Ghaziabad, Rohtak, Gurugram are the examples of ....

(a) Port towns (b) Garrison towns
(c) Satellite towns (d) Transport towns

8. Which of the following is an example of a Modern City? CBSE 2024

(a) Surat (b) Nagpur
(c) Madurai (d) Hyderabad

9. Which one of the following towns has developed as an administrative headquarter after independence?

(a) Delhi (b) Chandigarh
(c) Prayagraj (d) Madurai

10. Which of the following types of town is 'Babina'?

(a) Garrison (b) Commercial
(c) Transport (d) Industrial

11. Choose the correct option regarding mining towns of India. CBSE 2024

(a) Kandla, Kochchi and Kozhikode
(b) Ankaleshwar, Singrauli and Digboi
(c) Mumbai, Salem and Modinagar
(d) Varanasi, Roorkee and Aligarh

12. **Which of the following pairs is correctly matched?**
(a) Satellite Town – Pachmarhi
(b) Tourist Town – Ujjain
(c) Industrial Town – Hugli
(d) Cultural Town – Ghaziabad

13. **Choose the correct option related to garrison towns in India.** CBSE 2024
(a) Raniganj, Digboi and Jharia
(b) Mhow, Babina and Udhampur
(c) Itarsi, Katni and Kandla
(d) Modinagar, Jamshedpur and Bhilai

14. **Which of the following pairs is not matched correctly?** CBSE Sample Paper Term I 2021

	Cities		Basis of Development
(a)	Prayagraj (Allahabad)	–	On religious and cultural basis
(b)	Lucknow	–	Based on the remnants of ancient cities
(c)	Kolkata	–	On cultural basis
(d)	Mumbai	–	In the form of commercial port

15. **Read the following characteristics of settlements carefully and identify it's type** CBSE 2024
- It is seen in the form of isolated huts in the forest.
- It is visible on the slopes of small hills.
- This kind of settlements are found in different parts of Meghalaya, Uttarakhand and Himachal Pradesh.

Settlement types
(a) Nucleated (b) Fragmented
(c) Hamleted (d) Dispersed

16. **Study the following statements carefully and choose the correct option.** CBSE 2024
Statement I In India, after independence, some old towns around metropolitan cities developed as satellite towns.
Statement II Delhi is a good example of such metropolitan cities.
Options
(a) Only statement I is correct.
(b) Only statement II is correct.
(c) Both statements I and II are correct and statement II is the correct example of statement I.
(d) Both statements I and II are correct, but statement II is not the correct example of statement I.

17. **Which of these is true about rural settlements?**
(i) They are sparsely populated.
(ii) Population of rural settlements is engaged in secondary activities.
(iii) Rural settlements provide raw materials to occupations in the urban settlements.

Codes
(a) (i) and (ii) (b) (i) and (iii)
(c) (i), (ii) and (iii) (d) (ii) and (iii)

18. **The formation of various types of rural settlements depend upon**
(i) Climate (ii) Ethnic factors
(iii) Security (iv) Terrain

Codes
(a) (i), (ii) and (iii) (b) (ii), (iii) and (iv)
(c) (ii) and (iii) (d) All of these

19. **Which of these are the characteristics of semi-clustered settlements?**
(i) They are formed by fragmentation of a large compact village.
(ii) The land-owning and dominant community occupies the central portion of the main village.
(iii) They are found in lower portions of mountain slopes.

Codes
(a) (i) and (ii) (b) (i), (ii) and (iii)
(c) (ii) and (iii) (d) (i) and (iii)

20. **Study the following facts regarding urbanisation in India and choose the correct option.** CBSE Term I 2021
(i) The level of urbanisation in India in 2011 was 31.15 per cent.
(ii) It is quite low in comparison to developed countries.
(iii) The growth rate of urbanisation has increased during the last two decades.

Codes
(a) Only (i) and (ii) are correct
(b) Only (ii) and (iii) are correct
(c) Only (i) and (iii) are correct
(d) (i), (ii) and (iii) are correct

Match the Following

21. CBSE Term I 2021

	List I		List II
A.	Educational town	1.	Jodhpur
B.	Tourist town	2.	Aligarh
C.	Commercial town	3.	Kurukshetra
D.	Religious and Cultural town	4.	Sharanpur

Codes

	A	B	C	D		A	B	C	D
(a)	2	1	4	3	(b)	1	2	3	4
(c)	3	4	2	1	(d)	4	3	2	1

22.

	List I		List II
A.	Transport city	1.	Jaipur
B.	Mining city	2.	Ambala
C.	Garrison town	3.	Itarsi
D.	Administrative town	4.	Singrauli

Codes **CBSE SQP 2023**

	A	B	C	D
(a)	4	3	2	1
(b)	1	2	3	4
(c)	3	4	2	1
(d)	2	1	4	3

Assertion-Reason

Direction (Q. No. 23) In the question given below are two statements labelled as Assertion (A) and other labelled as Reason (R). In the context of two statements which one of the following is correct.

(a) Both A and R are true, but R is not the correct explanation ofA

(b) Both A and R are true and R is the correct explanation of A

(c) Both A and R are incorrect

(d) A is correct, but R is incorrect

23. **Assertion (A) In rural settlements social relation among people are strong in comparison to urban settlements.**

Reason (R) In rural settlements pople are less mobile.

Answers

1. (c) Hamleted settlements
2. (c) For maximum utilisation of available water resources
3. (a) Complex way of life, manufacturing of finished goods, nodes of economic growth.
4. (b) Ancient, Medieval and Modern
5. (a) Delhi
6. (a) Jaipur
7. (c) Satellite towns
8. (c) Madurai
9. (b) Chandigarh
10. (a) Garrison
11. (b) Ankaleshwar, Singrauli and Digboi
12. (c) Industrial Town - Hugli
13. (b) Mhow, Babina and Udhampur
14. (c) Kolkata-On cultural basis
15. (d) Dispersed
16. (c) Both statements I and II are correct and statement II is the correct example of statement I.
17. (b) (i) and (iii)
18. (d) All of these
19. (a) (i) and (ii)
20. (a) Only (i) and (ii) are correct
21. (a)
22. (c)
23. (b) Both A and R are true and R is the correct explanation of A

Subjective Questions

Short Answer Type Questions

1. **Explain any three physical factors responsible for different types of rural settlements in India.**

Ans. Physical factors which are responsible for different types of rural settlements in India are

- **Water Supply** People need water to survive. That is why settlements are concentrated near the source of water. For example, in Rajasthan, scarcity of water has forced people to live in compact villages for maximum utilisation of available water resources.
- **Climate** People usually prefer areas which have favourable climatic conditions. Harsh climate like very hot and cold regions have less or no settlements there. For example, coastal plains have favourable climate thus, are densely populated regions.
- **Nature of Terrain** It plays an important role in determining the shape and size of rural settlements. For example, plain areas have compact and larger settlements with dense population, whereas mountainous areas have scattered and hamleted rural settlements, e.g. Meghalaya, Uttarakhand and Himachal Pradesh have scattered types of rural settlement.

2. Explain any three basic differences between rural and urban settlements in India. **CBSE 2024**

Ans. The differences between rural and urban settlements are as follows

Rural Settlements	Urban Settlements
The major economic activities in rural areas are agriculture and other primary activities.	Urban settlements are specialised in industries and services.
They are dependent on natural resources, mainly land for their income.	They provide various types of services like transport and communication, etc.
Agricultural and other productions in rural areas support industries of urban area. Rural areas provide raw material to the industries.	Cities provide manufactured goods to rural areas and also to the people of cities.
Social bonds in rural areas are stronger and life is simple.	Social bonds in urban areas are formal and life is complex, fast and surrounded with various problems.

3. Explain any three characteristics of clustered rural settlement of India.

Or **What type of rural settlements are generally found in the fertile alluvial plains of India? Mention any two features of such type of settlements.**

Or **Explain the main features of clustered settlements in India.** **CBSE 2024 C**

Ans. Clustered or compact settlements are generally found in the fertile alluvial plains.

The important features of these settlements are as follows

(i) In this type of rural settlements, space between the houses are less or they have no space. The houses in this type of settlement are closely built up, often they share walls with other houses.

(ii) People live in a distinct area of settlement. This living place is surrounded by farms, barns or pastures. In compact settlements, many settlement patterns form such as rectangular, linear, triangular, radial, etc.

(iii) This type of settlements generally develop in riverine fertile plains and North-Eastern states.

4. Explain any three features of semi-clustered rural settlements of India.

Or **Mention any three characteristics of semi-clustered rural settlements of India.**

Ans. The characteristics of semi-clustered rural settlements in India are as follows

(i) These are developed by the concentration of houses in a restricted area of a dispersed settlement. These settlements are also developed due to fragmentation of a large compact village.

(ii) In the case of fragmentation, a particular group is forced to live far from the centre or main village. In this condition, the dominant community or land-owning community captures the most important part in the main village and may force people of lower strata (level) to live away.

(iii) In India, these types of settlements are mostly found in the plains of Gujarat and Rajasthan.

5. Give the meaning of 'dispersed settlement'. Explain any two reasons for the development of such settlements in India.

Ans. Dispersed settlements in India appear in the form of isolated huts or hamlets of few huts in remote jungles, or on small hills with farms or pastures on the slopes.

There are multiple reasons/factors responsible for the formation of this type of settlement. The two main reasons are as follows

(i) The most dominating factors for the formation of dispersed settlement is rugged and difficult terrain. Because of this reason, dispersed settlements are mainly found in Himachal Pradesh, Meghalaya, etc.

(ii) Such settlements are also found in dense forested areas and in other areas which have very few resource base. Uttarakhand also depicts such settlement type.

6. "Compact or clustered village is a universal feature in the Northern plains". Elucidate the statement. **Competency Based Que**

Ans. 'Compact or clustered village is a universal feature in the Northern Plains'. This statement can be elucidated by the following fact that in Northern part of India, the land is mostly plain which provides fertile productive agriculture, base for the livelihood of the people. Suitable climatic condition and flat topography are another attractive factors for settlement.

Therefore, in Northern plains, clustered or compact village is a universal feature. In such settlements, the general living area is distinct and separated from the surrounding forms and pastures. In some parts, people live in compact village. Due to favourable physiographic, socio-cultural and economic factors in the Northern plain, compact or clustered villages are universal features.

7. Differentiate between hamleted and dispersed rural settlement of India.

Ans. The differences between hamleted settlements and dispersed settlements are as follows

Hamleted Settlements	Dispersed Settlements
It is fragmented into several units physically separated from each other.	It is isolated form of huts or hamlets situated in remote areas or jungles.
The segmentation of large villages is due to social and ethnic factors.	It is formed due to rugged terrain and few resources.
Found in the middle and lower Ganga plain, Chhattisgarh and lower valleys of the Himalayas.	Found in the areas of Meghalaya, Uttarakhand, Himachal Pradesh and Kerala.

8. Explain any three characteristics each of hamleted and dispersed rural settlement in India?

Or **Describe any three characteristics of hamleted settlements in India.** **CBSE 2024**

Ans. Charateristics of hamleted settlements are as follows

- Some settlements are fragmented into several units and physically separated from each other are known as hamleted settlements.
- The segmentation of large villages is due to social and ethnic factors.
- Mostly primary activities like hunting and gathering are done in such settlements.
- These settlements are found in the middle and lower Ganges plain, Chhattisgarh and lower valleys of the Himalayas.

Characteristics of dispersed rural settlement are as follows

- Some settlements which appear in the form of isolated huts or hamlets are known as dispersed settlements.
- It is formed due to rugged terain and few resources.
- These settlements are also found in dense forested areas.

9. Distinguish between clustered and dispersed rural settlements of India by stating three points of distinction of each.

Ans. Differences between clustered and dispersed rural settlements of India are as follows

Clustered Rural Settlements	Dispersed Rural Settlements
Space between the houses are less. They are closely built up.	Space between the houses are more. They are scattered in areas.
These settlements are usually seen in the Northern Plains of India.	These settlements can be seen in remote hilly and mountainous areas or within the forests.
In clustered settlements, different types of settlement patterns emerge like rectangular, linear, radial and circular.	In dispersed settlements, no pattern emerges because of scattering of houses. Houses are scattered over large area

10. Discuss the salient features of urban settlements in India.

Or **Describe any three features of urban settlement in India.**

Ans. Urban centres or towns are dense and large settlements which are different from rural settlements. Following are some salient features of urban settlements

- In urban centre, most of the population are engaged in non-agricultural activities, mainly secondary, tertiary sector activities.
- These settlements are set up on the basis of different functions like industrial towns, administrative towns, tourist towns, etc.
- Urban settlements have very close relationship with technology and man-made things.
- In urban settlements, social relations are formal, way of life is fast moving and complex.

11. Explain the evolution of towns in India in three points.

Or **Classify Indian towns on the basis of their evolution in three different periods. Name one town of each period.**

Or **"Towns flourished since prehistoric times in India." Examine.**

Ans. In India, towns flourished since prehistoric times. The towns can be classified into the following groups on the basis of their evolution in different periods

(i) **Ancient Towns** These towns of India have historical background of over 2000 years. Varanasi, Prayagraj, Pataliputra (Patna), Madurai, etc were developed by the ancient kings.

(ii) **Medieval Towns** These towns were developed during the medieval period of India by kings and sultans of India as their headquarters for making their administration strong, e.g. Delhi, Hyderabad, Jaipur, Lucknow, Agra, etc.

(iii) **Modern Towns** These towns were developed by the Britishers and other Europeans in India like Surat, Daman and Goa, Kolkata, Mumbai, etc. Later, after independence some towns like Bhilai, Durgapur, Chandigarh, Gandhinagar were established.

12. Many of the modern towns of India were developed during the period of British. Comment. Competency Based Que

***Or* How have the modern towns developed in India? Explain.**

Ans. The British and other Europeans have developed a number of towns in India. Starting with their foothold on coastal locations, they first developed some trading ports such as Surat, Daman, Goa, Pondicherry (Puducherry), etc.

The British later consolidated their hold around three principal nodes i.e. Mumbai, Chennai and Kolkata. Towns based on modern industries also evolved after 1850.

After their domination over the princely states, they established their administrative centres, hill towns as summer resorts and added administrative and military areas to them.

13. What are ancient towns? Give four examples of ancient towns of India.

Ans. Ancient towns of India have historical background of over 2000 years. These towns emerged during the ancient period and were developed by the ancient kings. In comparison to medieval and modern cities, ancient cities were quite small in size. These cities were developed in unplanned manner.

Most of these were temple towns. Later, they had became the hub of religion and cultural activities. Varanasi, Prayagraj, Pataliputra (Patna), Madurai, etc are some of the ancient towns.

Among these cities Varanasi is considered as the oldest one. These cities, even today exhibit dot of ancient features in the form of temples.

14. Describe the development of medieval towns in India during the Mughal period.

Ans. Medieval towns were developed as headquarters of principalities and kingdoms during the Mughal period. The growth of towns happened at a faster pace in 16th, 17th century which continued upto the middle of 18th century. These were developed as fort towns and came up on the remains of the ancient fort towns.

The basic feature of a town was the presence of a market. The *qasba* is defined as the village with a market. There was a hierarchy of towns from the *qasba* to the district headquarter, to the provincial towns like Agra, Delhi, etc. Example of these towns are Hyderabad, Jaipur, Lucknow, Nagpur and so on.

15. Examine the level of urbanisation in India after independence.

Ans. Urbanisation is the transition of rural population into urban population. It is measured by the percentage of urban population to total population. At the time of independence, only 17% of the total population lived in the urban areas. It expanded to 28% in 2001 and 31% in 2011.

Total urban population increased eleven times during the 20th century.

Enlargement of urban centres and emergence of new towns have played a significant role in urbanisation since independence. But still the level of urbanisation in India is low as compared to the developed countries.

Long Answer Type Questions

1. Describe any three factors that determine the types of rural settlements in India. CBSE 2024

Ans. Types of rural settlements in India are determined by the following factors

Physical Factors Refer to SA Q. no. 1.

Cultural and Ethnic Factors Among these factors, social structure, caste and religion are important in India.

For examples, more often semi-clustered settlement pattern develops due to segregation or fragmentation of a large compact village. In this case, one or more sections of village society choose or is forced to live a little away from the main cluster or village. In such cases higher caste and rich people live in central part whereas people of lower strata (level) of society and menial workers forced to live on the outer flanks of the village. Such type of settlements are widespread in the Gujarat plain and some parts of Rajasthan.

Sometimes settlement is fragmented into several units physically separated from each other and bearing a common name. This segmentation is motivated by social and ethnic factors. For example, in middle and lower Ganga plain, Chhattisgarh and lower valleys of the Himalayas.

Security Factors It involves protection from thefts and attack. For example in the past, the border areas of North-Western plains were attacked frequently by outsiders. Therefore, security concerns favoured the evolution of nucleated type of settlements and people chose to construct houses closer to each other.

2. Name any three factors that determine the clustered or compact rural settlement in India.

Ans. The three factors that determine the clustered or compact rural settlement in India are as follows

Fertile Alluvial Plain It provides a plain surface where houses can be easily build. Fertile plains provide more agricultural land which attracts people to engage in agriculture. More concentration of population results in a compact or clustered rural settlement pattern.

Water Availability It is another reason that can cause people to live in compact conditions. Scarcity of water forces the people to live together for maximum utilisation of the available water, e.g. compact settlements of Rajasthan.

Security and Nature of Terrain Security is another reason that cause people to live in compact settlements, e.g. people of Bundelkhand region and Nagaland live in compact settlements for security reasons.

Nature of terrain plays an important role in determining the shape and size of rural settlements. For example, plain areas have compact and larger settlements with dense population, whereas mountainous areas have scattered and hamleted rural settlements. e.g. Meghalaya, Uttarakhand and Himachal Pradesh have scattered types of rural settlement.

3. Explain in brief the functional classification of towns in India.

Or **Classify Indian cities and towns on the basis of dominant and specialised fucntions?** CBSE Diksha

Ans. For answer refer to text page no. 194 under the heading 'Functional Classification of Town'.

Source/Graph Based Questions

1. Read the passage carefully and answer the questions that follow.

The clustered rural settlement is a compact or closely built up area of houses. In this type of village the general living area is distinct and separated from the surrounding farms, barns and pastures. The closely built-up area and its intervening streets present some recognisable pattern or geometric shape, such as rectangular, radial, linear, etc. Such settlements are generally found in fertile alluvial plains and in the North-Eastern states. Sometimes, people live in compact village for security or defence reasons, such as in the Bundelkhand region of Central India and in Nagaland. In Rajasthan, scarcity of water has necessitated compact settlement for maximum utilisation of available water resources.

Semi-clustered or fragmented settlements may result from tendency of clustering in a restricted area of dispersed settlement. More often such a pattern may also result from segregation or fragmentation of a large compact village. In this case, one or more sections of the village society choose or is forced to live a little away from the main cluster or village. In such cases, generally, the land-owning and dominant community occupies the central part of the main village, whereas people of lower strata of society and menial workers settle on the outer flanks of the village. Such settlements are widespread in the Gujarat plain and some parts of Rajasthan. Sometimes settlement is fragmented into several units physically separated from each other bearing a common name. These are hamleted settlements. This segmentation of a large village is often motivated by social and ethnic factors.

(i) What is the purpose to built compact or clustered settlements?

Ans. There are many purposes to built compact or clustered settlements such as

- For security purpose
- For scarcity of water
- For fertile soil

(ii) There are certain regions in India where compact or clustered settlements are found. Comment.

Ans. Compact or clustered settlements are generally found in fertile alluvial plains and in the North-Eastern States of India.

(iii) Sometimes settlement is fragmented into several units physically separated from each other bearing a common name. Discuss.

Ans. This fragmentation of large villages is often done on the basis of social and ethnic factors. Generally land owing community lives in the centre and community with lower states in society lives on borders of the village.

2. Read the passage carefully and answer the questions that follow.

Human settlement means cluster of dwellings of any type or size where human beings live. For this purpose, people may erect houses and other structures and command some area or territory as their economic support-base. Thus, the process of settlement inherently involves grouping of people and dividing territory as their resource base. Settlements vary in size and type. They range from a hamlet to metropolitan cities. With size, the economic character and social structure of settlements changes and so do its ecology and technology. Settlements could be small and sparsely spaced; they may also be large and closely spaced. The sparsely located small settlements are called villages, specialising in agriculture or other primary activities.

On the other hand, there are fewer but larger settlements which are termed as urban settlements specialising in secondary and tertiary activities.

The rural settlements derive their life support or basic economic needs from land based primary economic activities, whereas, urban settlements, depend on processing of raw materials and manufacturing of finished goods on the one hand and a variety of services on the other. Cities act as nodes of economic growth, provide goods and services not only to urban dwellers but also to the people of the rural settlements in their hinterlands in return for food and raw materials.

(i) **Large urban settlements are mainly engaged in which of these activities?**
(a) Primary activities (b) Secondary activities
(c) Tertiary activities (d) Both (b) and (c)

Ans. (d) Both (b) and (c)

(ii) **Urban and rural areas are functionally connected with each other by which of the following systems?**
(a) Satellites (b) Transport networks
(c) Internet (d) Mobile networks

Ans. (b) Transport networks

(iii) **Cities provide which of the following to the rural areas?**
(a) Manufactured goods (b) Water
(c) Raw materials (d) Food

Ans. (a) Manufactured goods

3. Read the given passage and answer the questions that follow.

Many towns and cities perform specialised services. Some towns and cities specialise in certain functions and they are known for some specific activities, products or services. However, each town performs a number of functions.

Towns supporting administrative headquarters of higher order are administrative towns, such as Chandigarh, New Delhi, Bhopal, Shillong, Guwahati, Imphal, Srinagar, Gandhinagar, Jaipur, Chennai, etc. Industries constitute prime motive force of industrial towns, such as Mumbai, Salem, Coimbatore, Modinagar, Jamshedpur, Hugli, Bhilai, etc. Transport cities may be ports primarily engaged in export and import activities such as Kandla, Kochchi, Kozhikode, Visakhapatnam, etc., or hubs of inland transport, such as Agra, Dhulia, Mughalsarai, Itarsi, Katni, etc.

Towns and cities specialising in trade and commerce are commercial towns. Kolkata, Saharanpur, Satna, etc., are some examples. Mining towns have developed in mineral rich areas such as Raniganj, Jharia, Digboi, Ankaleshwar, Singrauli, etc. Starting as centres of education, some of the towns have grown into major educational towns, such as Roorkee, Varanasi, Aligarh, Pilani, Prayagraj, etc. Varanasi, Mathura, Amritsar, Madurai, Puri, Ajmer, Pushkar, Tirupati, Kurukshetra, Haridwar, Ujjain came to prominence due to their religious/cultural significance.

(i) **Which of the following town mainly performs administrative functions?**
(a) Katni (b) Modinagar
(c) Srinagar (d) Jharia

Ans. (c) Srinagar

(ii) **Which of the following town has developed due to dominance of transport networks?**
(a) Kolkata (b) Kandla
(c) Delhi (d) Raniganj

Ans. (b) Kandla

(iii) **Towns can be classified functionally on which of the following basis?**
(a) Transport towns
(b) Mining towns
(c) Commercial towns
(d) All of the above

Ans. (d) All of the above

4. Study the given table carefully and answer the questions that follow **CBSE 2023**

India-Trends of Urbanisation 1901-2011

Year	Number of Towns/ UAs	Urban Population (In Thousands)	% of Total Population	Decennial Growth (%)
1901	1,827	25,851.9	10.84	–
1911	1,815	25,941.6	10.29	0.35
1921	1,949	28,086.2	11.18	8.27
1931	2,072	33,456.0	11.99	19.12
1941	2,250	44,153.3	13.86	31.97
1951	2,843	62,443.7	17.29	41.42
1961	2,365	78,936.6	17.97	26.41
1971	2,590	1,09,114	19.91	38.23
1981	3,378	1,59,463	23.34	46.14
1991	4,689	2,17,611	25.71	36.47
2001	5,161	2,85,355	23.78	31.13
2011	6,171	3,77,000	31.16	31.08

(i) **In which year was the decennial growth of urban population the highest in India?**

Ans. In the year 1981, the decennial growth of urban population was the highest in India.

(ii) **How much was the total urban population in the year 2001 ?**

Ans. 285355 was the total urban population in the year 2001.

(iii) **How much was the total growth of number of towns between the year 1901 to 2011 in India?**

Ans. 37110 was the total growth of number of towns between the years 1901 to 2011 in India.

SELF ASSESSMENT TEST

Objective Type Questions

1. Varanasi, Mathura, Amritsar, Tirupati are prominent as which of these type of towns?
   (a) Transport Towns (b) Educational Towns
   (c) Cultural Towns (d) Administrative Towns
2. Which of these is a satellite town of Delhi?
   (a) Ghaziabad (b) Greater Noida
   (c) Bhilai (d) Jaipur
3. Functional relationship between urban and rural settlements takes place through ....
   (a) transport and communication networks (b) power and energy systems
   (c) raw materials and finished goods (d) All of these
4.

	List I		List II
A.	Administrative Town	1.	Agra
B.	Industrial Town	2.	Dispur
C.	Satellite Town	3.	Rohtak
D	Medieval Town	4.	Barauni

Codes

	A	B	C	D		A	B	C	D
(a)	4	2	1	3	(b)	2	4	3	1
(c)	3	2	4	1	(d)	4	1	2	3

Short Answer Type Questions

5. Discuss about the different types of rural settlements in India.
6. 'Towns flourished since pre-historic times in India'. Explain.
7. Explain the main features of the dispersed settlements in India.
8. 'Clustered settlements are found only in certain parts/areas of India'. Explain why?
9. Towns are dynamic in their functions and gradually becomes multi-functional. Comment on the statement.

Lone Answer Type Questions

10. Discuss the evolution of urban settlement in India.
11. Explain the main objectives of 'Smart Cities Mission' in India.
12. Give an overview of the towns developed after Independence of India.
13. 'The rural settlements decline their life support from land based primary economic activities'. Discuss.

3

CHAPTER

The land around us can be used for different purposes. For example, some land is occupied by rivers, trees, roads and buildings. Human beings use land as a resource for production, residence and recreation.

Land Resources and Agriculture

▼ **YOUR STUDY GOALS**

3.1 Land-use Categories
3.2 Land-use Changes in India
3.3 Common Property Resources
3.4 Agricultural Land-use in India
3.5 Cropping Seasons in India
3.6 Foodgrains Grown in India
3.7 Agricultural Development in India
3.8 Problems of Indian Agriculture

▼ **YOUR PRACTICE GOAL**

- Objective Type Questions (34 Qs ; MCQs, Statements, Matching, A-R)
- Subjective Questions (13 SAs, 12 LAs)
- Source/Graph Based Questions (5Qs)
- Map Based Questions (2 Qs)

Different types of land are suited for various uses. Thus, the building of schools, roads, parks in which you play, fields in which crops are grown and the pastures where animals graze, represent different uses for land.

3.1 Land-use Categories

- The **Land Revenue Department** maintains the records of land use.
- The land-use categories are different from the geographical area.
- The **Survey of India** is responsible for measuring the geographical area of **administrative units** in India.
- The difference between the land-use records and administrative units is that land use records depends on the estimates of the land revenue records, while the administrative unit does not change and stays fixed as per survey of India measurements.
- The land-use categories as maintained by the Land Revenue Records in India are as follows
  - **Forests** The area under actual forest cover is different from the area classified as forest. This is the area that the government has identified and demarcated for forest growth. The land revenue records are fixed as per the definition given by the government. Thus, there may be an increase in this category without any increase in the actual forest cover.

- **Barren and Wastelands** The land which may be classified as a wasteland, cannot be brought under cultivation with the available technology. For example, barren hilly terrains, desert lands, ravines, etc.
- **Land put to Non-agricultural Uses** Land under settlements (rural and urban), infrastructure (roads, canals, etc.), industries, shops, etc., are included in this category. An expansion in the secondary and tertiary activities leads to an increase in this category of land use.
- **Area under Permanent Pastures and Grazing Lands** Most of this type of land is owned by the village 'Panchayat' or the Government. Only a small proportion of this land is privately owned. The land owned by the village panchayat comes under **Common Property Resources.**
- **Area under Miscellaneous Tree Crops and Groves** (Not included in Net Sown Area) The land under orchards and fruit trees is included in this category. Much of this land is privately owned.
- **Culturable Wasteland** Any land that is left fallow (uncultivated) for more than five years is included in this category. It can be brought under cultivation after improving it through reclamation[1] practices.
- **Current Fallow** This is the land which is left without cultivation for one or less than one agricultural year. Fallowing is a cultural practice adopted for giving rest to the land. The land regains the lost fertility through natural processes.
- **Fallow other than Current Fallow** This is also a cultivable land which is left uncultivated for more than a year but less than five years. If the land is left uncultivated for more than five years, it would be categorised as a culturable wasteland.
- **Net Area Sown** The physical extent of land on which crops are sown and harvested is known as Net Sown Area.

3.2 Land-use Changes in India

- Land-use in any region is influenced by the nature of economic activities carried out in that region.
- The economic activities of an area change with time but, like many other natural resources, land is fixed in terms of its area.
- Following are the three types of changes that an economy undergoes, which affect land-use
  (i) The **size of the economy** (measured in terms of value for all the goods and services produced in the economy) grows over time due to increasing population, changes in income levels, available technology and other associated factors. As a result, the pressure on land will increase with time and **marginal lands** will come under use.
  (ii) The **composition of the economy** changes over time. The secondary and tertiary sectors usually grow much faster than the primary sector, specifically the agricultural sector. This type of change is common in developing countries, like India. This process results in a shift of land from agricultural uses to non-agricultural uses. These changes are visible around large urban areas where agricultural land is used for building purposes.
  (iii) As the contribution of agricultural activities reduces over time, the **pressure on land** for agriculture does not decline. The reasons for continued pressure on agricultural land are
    - In developing countries, more population is dependent on agriculture while the share of agriculture in the GDP of the economy declines at a faster rate.
    - The number of people that the agricultural sector has to feed is increasing day by day.
- The Indian economy has undergone major changes over the past four or five decades. These changes influenced the land-use changes in the country.

1 Reclamation The process involved in making land suitable for construction or farming again.

- The percentages of land-use have been derived for the reporting area. The reporting area has remained constant over the years. The decline in one category usually leads to an increase in some other category.

Changes in Land-use Categories

- Share of area under forest, area under non-agricultural uses, current fallow lands and net area sown are increased.
- The rate of increase is the highest in the case of areas under non-agricultural use. This is due to the changing structure of the Indian economy. The Indian economy is the contribution of the industrial and services sectors and the expansion of related infrastructural facilities. Also, an expansion of area under both urban and rural settlements has added to the increase. Thus, the area under non-agricultural uses is increasing at the expense of wastelands and agricultural land.
- The increase in the share under forest may be due to changes in the criteria of accounting for any region as a forest.
- The increase in the current fallow cannot be explained from information about only two accounting years. The trend of current fallow fluctuates over the years, depending on the variability of rainfall and cropping cycles.
- The increase in net area sown is a recent phenomenon due to the use of culturable wasteland for agricultural purposes. Earlier it was registering a slow decrease.

Decrease in Land-use Categories

- The four categories that have registered a decline are barren and wasteland, culturable wasteland, areas under tree crops and **groves** and fallow lands.
- As the pressure on land increased, from both agricultural and non-agricultural sectors, the wastelands and culturable wastelands have witnessed a decline over time.
- The decline in land under tree crops and groves can be explained by pressure from agricultural land.

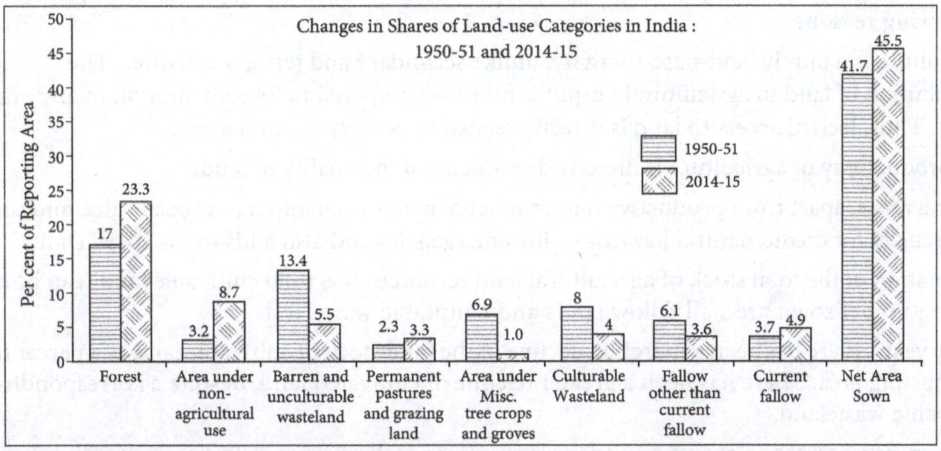

Important Facts

- For calculating actual increase, the difference of the land-use categories should be worked out over the two periods.
- For deriving the rate of increase, simple growth rate should be used. It is the difference of values between the two time points i.e. value of terminal year minus base year/base year (1960-61) value.

$$\frac{\text{Net Sown Area in 2014-15} - \text{Net Sown Area in 1950-51}}{\text{Net Sown Area in 1950-51}} \times 100$$

3.3 Common Property Resources

- According to its ownership, land can be broadly classified as-**private** land and **Common Property Resources** (CPRs). The private land is owned by an individual or a group of individuals, and CPRs are owned by the state and meant for the use of the community.
- CPRs can be defined as a community's natural resource, where every member has the right of access and usage with specified restrictions, and without anybody having property rights over them. Examples of CPRs are community forests, pasture lands, village water bodies and other public spaces where a group larger than a household or family unit have rights of use and carries responsibility for the management of land.
- CPRs provide fodder for the livestock and fuel for the households. They also provide other minor forest products like fruits, nuts, fibre, medicinal plants, etc. In rural areas, CPRs is important for the livelihood of the landless and marginal farmers and other weaker sections.
- CPRs are important for women also, for the collection of fodder and fuel. They have to devote long hours to collecting fuel and fodder from a degraded area of CPR.

Quick Test 1

1. How are geographical areas measured in India?
2. Who owns most of the land under permanent pastures and grazing?
3. Name two factors that affect the land-use in a country.
4. Name two categories of land-use that have registered a decline in their area.

3.4 Agricultural Land-use in India

- Land as a resource is more important for the people whose livelihood is dependent on agriculture, due to the following reasons
  - Agriculture is a purely land-based activity, unlike secondary and tertiary activities. The contribution of land to agricultural output is more as compared to its contribution in any other sector. Thus, lack of access to land is directly related to poverty in rural areas.
  - The productivity of agriculture is directly dependent on the quality of land.
  - In rural areas, apart from productive nature of land, land ownership has a social value and serves as a security for credit, natural hazards or life emergencies and also adds to the social status.
- An estimation of the total stock of agricultural land resources (i.e. total cultivable land) can be calculated by adding up net sown area, all fallow lands and culturable wasteland.
- Over the years, there has been a marginal decline in the total stock of cultivable land as a percentage of the total reporting area. There has been a greater decline of cultivated land, despite a corresponding decline of cultivable wasteland.
- There is an urgent need to evolve and adapt land-saving technologies in India. Such technologies can be classified as
  - those that raise the yield of any particular crop per unit area of land
  - those that increase the total output per unit area of land from all crops grown over one agricultural year by increasing **land-use intensity**.
- For countries like India, where labour force is abundant and land is less, there is need for high cropping intensity not only for maximum utilisation of land resource but also for reducing unemployment in the rural economy.

- The Cropping Intensity (CI) is calculated as Cropping Intensity in percentage = GCA/NSA × 100

Composition of Total Cultivable Land

Agricultural Land-use Categories	As a Percentage of Reporting Area		As a Percentage of Total Cultivated Land	
	1950-51	2014-15	1950-51	2014-15
Culturable Waste land	8.0	4.0	13.4	6.8
Fallow other than Current Fallow	6.1	3.6	10.2	6.2
Current Fallow	3.7	4.9	6.2	8.4
Net Area Sown	41.7	45.5	70.0	78.4
Total Cultivable Land	59.5	58.0	100.00	100.00

3.5 Cropping Seasons in India

- In the Northern and interior parts of India, there are three distinct cropping seasons: ***kharif***, ***rabi*** and ***zaid***.
  - **Kharif Season** occurs at the same time as the South-West monsoon. In this season, tropical crops are cultivated. For example, rice, cotton, jute, jowar, bajra and tur are possible.
  - **Rabi Season** begins with the onset of winter in October-November and ends in March-April. The low temperatures during this season facilitate the cultivation of temperate and subtropical crops such as wheat, gram and mustard.
  - **Zaid** is a short-duration summer cropping season that begin after the harvesting of rabi crops. The cultivation of watermelons, cucumbers, vegetables and fodder crops during this season is done on irrigated lands.
- These three cropping seasons only exist in Northern part of the country. Southern India has the high temperature to grow tropical crops during any period of the year, the only condition is that there should be availability of soil moisture. Therefore, the same crops can be grown thrice in an agricultural year.

Cropping Seasons in India

Cropping Season	Major Crops Cultivated	
	Northern States	Southern States
Kharif (June - September)	Rice, cotton, *bajra*, maize, *jowar*, *tur*	Rice, maize, ragi, *jowar*, groundnut
Rabi (October - March)	Wheat, gram, rapeseeds and mustard, barley	Rice, maize, ragi, groundnut, *jowar*
Zaid (April - June)	Vegetables, fruits, fodder	Rice, vegetables, fodder

Types of Farming

- Farming can be classified as **irrigated** and **rainfed** (barani) based on the main source of moisture for crops.
- Irrigated farming can be classified based on the objective of irrigation, i.e., **protective** or **productive**.
  - **Protective irrigation** protects the crops from the adverse effects of soil moisture deficiency. Here, irrigation acts as a supplementary source of water over and above the rainfall. This kind of irrigation provides soil moisture to the maximum possible area.
  - **Productive irrigation** provides sufficient soil moisture in the cropping season to achieve high productivity. In such irrigation, the water input per unit area of cultivated land is higher than protective irrigation.

- *Rainfed farming* is further classified based on the adequacy of soil moisture during the cropping season into **dryland** and **wetland farming**.
- In India, dryland farming is largely confined to the regions having annual rainfall of less than 75 cm. These regions grow hardy and drought-resistant crops such as *ragi, bajra, moong, gram* and *guar* (fodder crops) and practise various measures of soil moisture conservation and rainwater harvesting.
- Wetland farming requires more rainfall than the soil moisture requirement of plants during the rainy season. Such regions may face flood and soil erosion hazards. These areas grow various water-intensive crops such as rice, jute and sugarcane, and practise aquaculture in the freshwater bodies.

3.6 Foodgrains Grown in India

- In the Indian agricultural economy, foodgrains play a major role as these crops occupy about two-thirds of the total cropped area in the country.
- Foodgrains are dominant crops in all parts of the country whether they have subsistence or commercial agricultural economy.
- Based on the structure of the grain, the foodgrains are classified as **cereals** and **pulses**.

Cereals

- The cereals occupy about 54 per cent of the total cropped area in India.
- India produces about 11 per cent of cereals in the world and ranks third in production after China and the USA.
- India produces a variety of cereals. These are classified as **fine grains** (rice, wheat) and **coarse grains** (jowar, bajra, maize, ragi), etc.

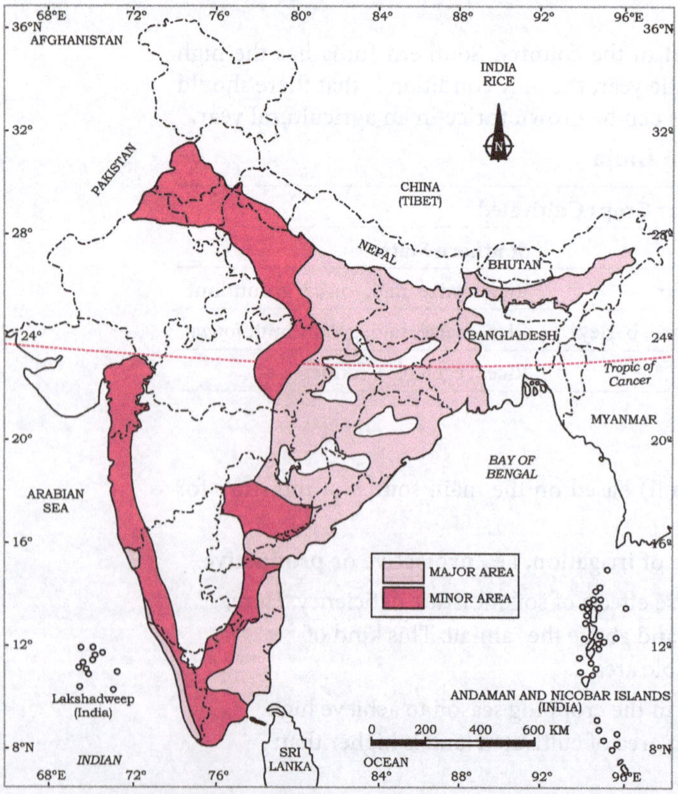

▲ *Rice transplantation in Southern parts of India*

Rice

- Rice is a staple food for the majority of the population in India.
- Rice is considered to be a crop of tropical humid areas. However, it has many varieties that are grown in different agro-climatic regions.
- Rice is successfully grown about 2,000 m above sea level.
- India contributes 22.07 per cent of the rice production of the world and ranks second after China in 2018. About one-fourth of the total cropped area in the country is under rice cultivation. West Bengal, Uttar Pradesh and Punjab are the leading rice-producing states in the country.
- The yield level of rice is high in Punjab, Tamil Nadu, Haryana, Andhra Pradesh, Telangana, West Bengal and Kerala. In Punjab, Tamil Nadu, Haryana and Andhra Pradesh, almost all land under rice cultivation is irrigated.
- There is a higher yield of rice in Punjab and Haryana due to the usage of genetically improved varieties of seed, relatively high usage of fertilisers and pesticides and lesser chance of pests due to dry climatic conditions.

- Punjab and Haryana are not traditional rice-growing areas. After the Green Revolution in the 1970s rice cultivation was introduced in the irrigated areas of Punjab and Haryana.
- In Southern states and West Bengal, the climatic conditions allow the cultivation of two or three crops of rice in an agricultural year. In West Bengal, farmers grow three crops of rice called ***aus***, ***aman*** and ***boro***.
- The yield of rice crops is very low in rainfed areas of Madhya Pradesh, Chhattisgarh and Odisha.
- In the Himalayas and North-Western parts of the country, rice is grown as a *kharif* crop during the South-West monsoon season.

Wheat

- Wheat is the second most important cereal crop in India after rice.
- India produces about 12.8 per cent of the total wheat production of the world (2017).
- It is primarily a crop of the **temperate zone**. It is cultivated in India during winter (*rabi* season).
- About 85 per cent of the total area under wheat crop is concentrated in the North and central regions of the country from the Indo-Gangetic Plain, Malwa Plateau and the Himalayas up to 2,700 m altitude.
- It is mostly grown under irrigated conditions. But it is a rainfed crop in Himalayan highlands and parts of Malwa Plateau in Madhya Pradesh.
- About 14 percent of the total cropped area in the country is under wheat cultivation. Uttar Pradesh, Madhya Pradesh, Punjab, Haryana and Rajasthan are leading wheat producing states.
- The yield level of wheat is very high (above 4,000 kg per ha) in Punjab and Haryana whereas Uttar Pradesh, Rajasthan and Bihar have moderate yields.
- The states like Madhya Pradesh, Himachal Pradesh, Jammu and Kashmir growing wheat under rainfed conditions have low yields.

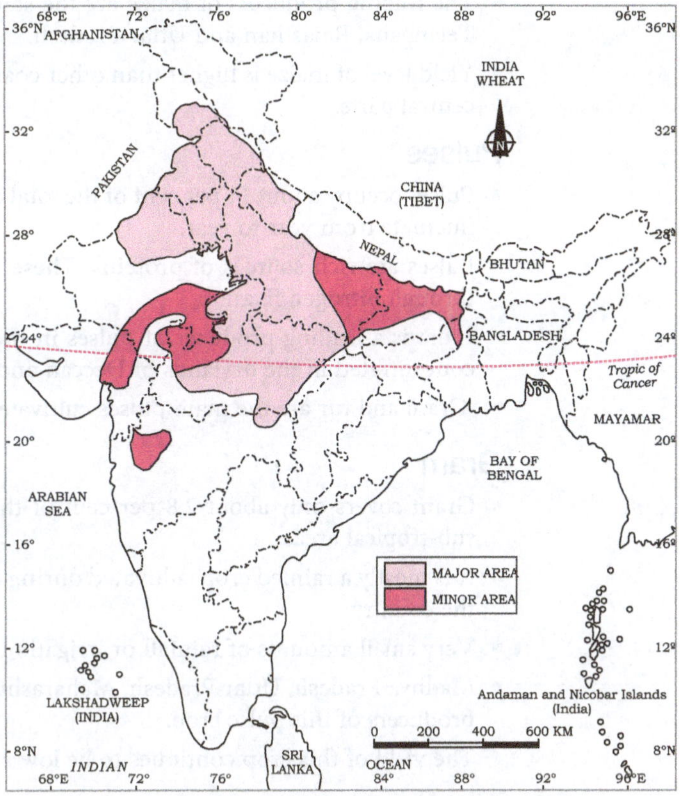

▲ *India – Distribution of Wheat*

Jowar

- The coarse cereals together occupy about 16.50 per cent of the total cropped area in the country. Among the coarse cereals, jowar or sorghum accounts for about 5.3 per cent of the total cropped area.
- It is sown in both *kharif* and *rabi* seasons in Southern states. It is a *kharif* crop in Northern India and is grown as a fodder crop.
- Jowar is the main food crop in semi-arid areas of central and Southern India. Maharashtra alone produces more than half of the total jowar production of the country. Other leading producer states of Jowar are Karnataka, Madhya Pradesh, Andhra Pradesh and Telangana.
- It is a rainfed crop in the South of Vindhyachal and its yield level is very low in this region.

Bajra

- Bajra occupies about 5.2 per cent of the total cropped area in the country. It is sown in hot and dry climatic conditions in the North-Western and Western parts of the country.
- It is a hardy crop that resists frequent drought in this region. It is cultivated alone as well as part of mixed cropping.

- The leading producers of bajra are Rajasthan, Maharashtra, Gujarat, Uttar Pradesh and Haryana.
- During recent years, the yield of bajra has increased in Rajasthan, Haryana and Gujarat, as drought-resistant varieties and irrigation facilities are developed.

Maize

- Maize occupies only about 3.6 per cent of total cropped area. Maize cultivation is not concentrated in any specific region. It is sown all over India except Punjab and Eastern and North-Eastern regions.
- Maize is a food as well as fodder crop. It grows under semi-arid climatic conditions and over inferior soils.
- The leading producers of maize are the states of Karnataka, Madhya Pradesh, Bihar, Andhra Pradesh, Telangana, Rajasthan and Uttar Pradesh.
- Yield level of maize is higher than other coarse cereals. It is high in Southern states and declines towards central parts.

Pulses

- Pulses occupy about 11 per cent of the total cropped area in the country. The yields of pulses are low and fluctuate from year to year.
- Pulses are rich sources of proteins. These are legume crops that increase the natural fertility of soils through nitrogen fixation.
- India is a leading producer of pulses in the world. The cultivation of pulses in the country is largely concentrated in the drylands of Deccan and Central Plateaus and North-Western parts of the country.
- Gram and tur are the main pulses cultivated in India.

Gram

- Gram covers only about 2.8 per cent of the total cropped area in the country. Gram is cultivated in sub-tropical areas.
- It is mostly a rainfed crop cultivated during *rabi* season in Central, Western and North-Western parts of the country.
- Very small amounts of rainfall or irrigation are required to grow this crop successfully.
- Madhya Pradesh, Uttar Pradesh, Maharashtra, Andhra Pradesh, Telangana and Rajasthan are the main producers of this pulse crop.
- The yield of this crop continues to be low and fluctuates from year to year even in irrigated areas.

Tur (Arhar)

- Tur crop occupies only about 2 per cent of the total cropped area of India. It is also known as **red gram** or **pigeon pea.**
- It is cultivated over marginal lands and under rainfed conditions in the dry areas of the Central and Southern states of the country. Maharashtra alone contributes about one-third of the total production of tur.
- Other leading producer states of tur are Uttar Pradesh, Karnataka, Gujarat and Madhya Pradesh.

Oilseeds

- Oilseeds occupy about 14 per cent of the total cropped area in the country. The oilseeds are produced for extracting edible oils.
- Groundnut, rapeseed, mustard, soyabean and sunflower are the main oilseed crops grown in India.
- Oilseeds growing regions of India are drylands of the Malwa Plateau, Marathwada, Gujarat, Rajasthan, Telangana, Rayalaseema region of Andhra Pradesh and Karnataka Plateau.

Groundnut

- India produces about 18.8 per cent of the total groundnut production in the world (2018). It covers about 3.6 per cent of the total cropped area in the country.
- It is largely a rainfed *kharif* crop of drylands. In Southern India, it is cultivated during *rabi* season as well.
- The leading producer states are Gujarat, Rajasthan, Tamil Nadu, Telangana, Andhra Pradesh, Karnataka and Maharashtra.
- The yield of groundnut is comparatively high in Tamil Nadu where it is partly irrigated. But its yield is low in Telangana, Andhra Pradesh and Karnataka.

Rapeseed and Mustard

- These oilseeds together occupy only about 2.5 per cent of the total cropped area in the country.
- Rapeseed and mustard comprise several oilseeds such as *rai*, *sarson*, *toria* and *taramira*. These are sub-tropical crops cultivated during the *rabi* season in the North-Western and Central parts of India.
- These crops are frost sensitive and their yields fluctuate from year to year. The expansion of irrigation and improvement in seed technology has improved and stabilised the yield of these crops.
- About two-third of the cultivated area under these crops is irrigated. Rajasthan contributes about one-third of the production of the whole country.
- Other leading producers of rapeseed and mustard are Haryana, Madhya Pradesh and Rajasthan.

Other Oilseeds

- **Soyabean** and **sunflower** are other important oilseeds grown in India.
- Soyabean is mostly grown in Madhya Pradesh and Maharashtra. These two states together produce about 90 per cent of the total output of soyabean in the country.
- Sunflower cultivation is done in Karnataka, Andhra Pradesh, Telangana and adjoining areas of Maharashtra. It is a minor crop in the Northern parts of the country where its yield is high due to irrigation.

Quick Test 2

1. How access to land and poverty are related in rural areas?
2. What is the formula for calculating crop Intensity?
3. What are the three cropping seasons in India?
4. In which type of region dryland farming is done?

Fibre Crops

These crops provide fibre for making cloth, bags, sacks, etc. Two main fibre crops grown in India are **cotton** and **jute**.

Cotton

- Cotton occupies about 4.7 per cent of the total cropped area in the country. Cotton is a tropical crop grown in *kharif* season in semi-arid areas of the country. Cotton requires a clear sky during the flowering stage.
- During the partition between India and Pakistan, India lost a large proportion of cotton growing area to Pakistan. However, its yield has increased considerably during the last 50 years.
- India grows both **short staple** (Indian) cotton as well as **long staple** (American) cotton called **narma** in North-Western parts of the country.

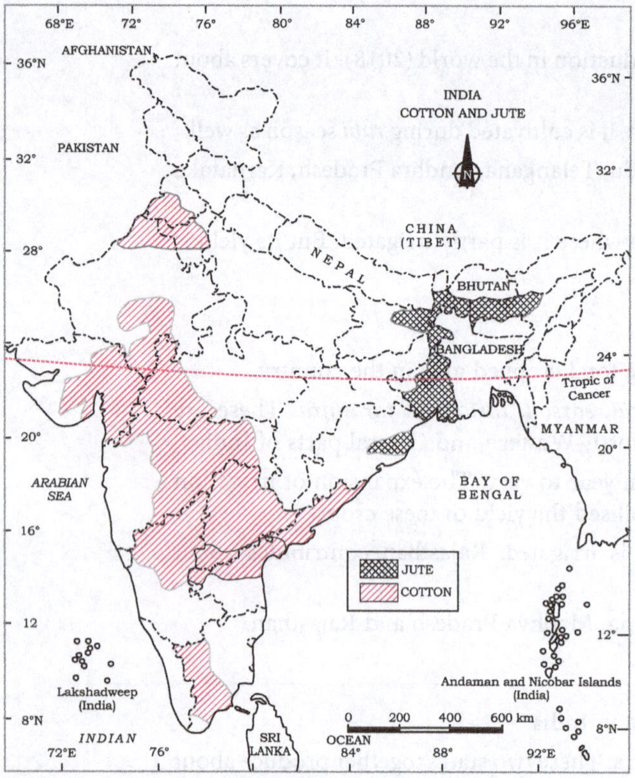

▲ *India – Distribution of Cotton and Jute*

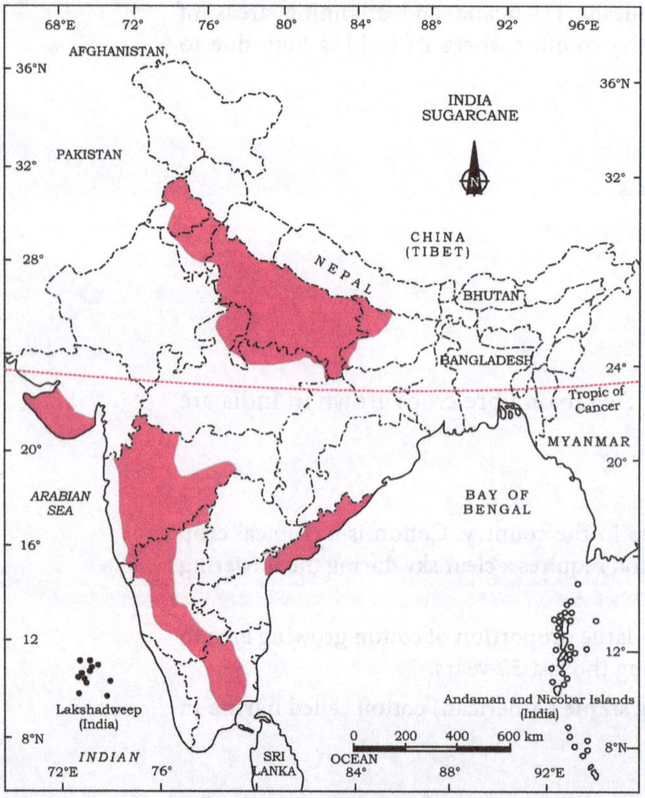

▲ *India – Distribution of Sugarcane*

- India ranks second in the world in the production of cotton after China. Leading producers of cotton are Gujarat, Maharashtra and Telangana.
- Per hectare output of cotton is high under irrigated conditions in North-Western region of the country. Its yield is very low in Maharashtra where it is grown under rainfed conditions.

Jute

- Jute accounts for only about 0.5 per cent of total cropped area in the country. Jute is used for making coarse cloth, bags, sacks and decorative items.
- It is a cash crop in West Bengal and adjoining Eastern parts of the country.
- India lost large jute growing areas to East Pakistan (Bangladesh) during partition. At present, India produces about three-fifth of jute production.
- West Bengal accounts for about three-fourth of the production in the country. Bihar and Assam are other jute growing areas.

Other Crops

Sugarcane, tea and coffee are other important crops grown in India.

Sugarcane

- Sugarcane occupies only 2.4 per cent of the total cropped area in the country. It is a crop of tropical areas. It can be cultivated in sub-humid and humid climates with irrigation facilities.
- India was the second largest producer of sugarcane after Brazil in 2018. It accounts for about 19.7 per cent of the world's production of sugarcane.
- Uttar Pradesh produces about two-fifth of the sugarcane of the country. Its yield is low in Northern India.
- Maharashtra, Karnataka, Tamil Nadu and Andhra Pradesh are other leading producers of sugarcane where the yield level of sugarcane is high.

Tea

- It is an indigenous crop of hills in Northern China.
- India is a leading producer of tea and accounted for about 21.22 per cent of total production in the world in 2018. India ranks second among tea-exporting countries in the world after China (2018).
- Tea is grown over hilly areas and well-drained soils in humid and sub-humid tropics and sub-tropics.

- In India, tea plantations started in the 1840s in the **Brahmaputra valley of Assam** which still is a major tea-growing area in the country. Later, it was introduced in the sub-Himalayan region of West Bengal (Darjeeling, Jalpaiguri and Cooch Behar districts).
- Tea is also cultivated on the lower slopes of Nilgiri and Cardamom hills in Western Ghats. West Bengal and Tamil Nadu are the other leading producers of tea.
- 'Tea leaves have rich content of caffeine and tannin.'
- Assam accounts for 53.2 per cent of the total cropped area and contributes more than half of total production of tea in the country.

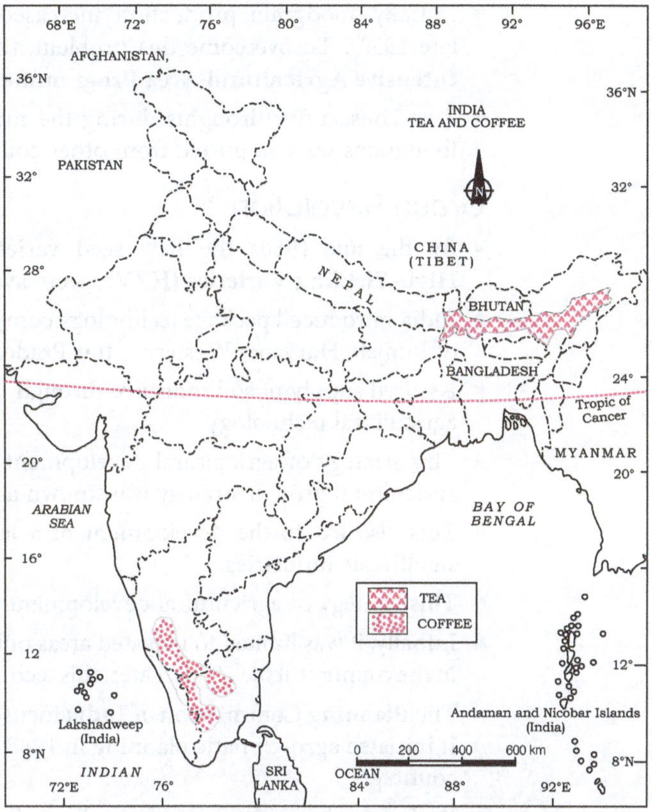

▲ *India – Distribution of Tea and Coffee*

Coffee

- Coffee is also a tropical plantation crop. Its seeds are roasted, ground, and are used for preparing a beverage.
- There are three varieties of coffee i.e. ***arabica***, ***robusta*** and ***liberica***. India mostly grows superior quality coffee, ***arabica***.
- India produces only about 3.17 per cent coffee of in the world and ranks **eighth** after Brazil, Vietnam, Indonesia, Colombia, Honduras, Ethiopia and Peru in 2018.
- Coffee is cultivated in the highlands of Western Ghats in Karnataka, Kerala and Tamil Nadu. Karnataka alone accounts for more than two-third of the total production of coffee in the country.

Quick Test 3

1. Name two crops that are grown during *rabi* season.
2. Give two examples of coarse grains.
3. What are the geographical requirements for wheat cultivation?
4. How much per cent of the total cropped area is under cultivation of pulses?
5. Name two plantation crops that are used as beverages.

3.7 Agricultural Development in India

- Indian agricultural economy was subsistence in nature before independence. It had a low performance in the first half of the twentieth century.
- During partition, about one-third of the irrigated land in undivided India went to Pakistan. This reduced the proportion of irrigated areas in independent India.
- After independence, the government aimed to increase foodgrain production. They took the following steps
  - Switching from cash crops to food crops
  - Practising intensified cropping over already cultivated land
  - Increasing cultivated area by bringing cultivable and fallow land under cultivation

- Initially, foodgrain production increased but agricultural production became stagnated during the late-1950s. To overcome this problem, the **Intensive Agricultural District Programme** (IADP) and **Intensive Agricultural Area Programme** (IAAP) were launched
- Two consecutive droughts during the mid-1960s resulted in a food crisis in the country. Therefore, foodgrains were imported from other countries.

Green Revolution

- By the mid-1960s the new seed varieties of wheat (Mexico) and rice (Philippines) known as **High-Yielding Varieties** (HYVs) were available for cultivation.
- India introduced package technology comprising HYVs, along with chemical fertilisers in irrigated areas of Punjab, Haryana, Western Uttar Pradesh, Andhra Pradesh and Gujarat.
- Assured supply of soil moisture through irrigation was a basic requirement for the success of this new agricultural technology.
- This strategy of agricultural development increased the foodgrains production at a very fast rate. This agricultural growth strategy was known as the Green Revolution.
- This also led to the development of a large number of agro-inputs, agro-processing industries and small-scale industries.
- This strategy of agricultural development made the country self-reliant in foodgrain production.
- Initially, it was limited to irrigated areas only, which led to regional inequality in agricultural development in the country till the 1970s. Later, this technology spread to the Eastern and Central parts of the country.
- The **Planning Commission of India** focused on the problems of agriculture in rainfed areas in the 1980s. It initiated agro-climatic planning in 1988 to induce regionally balanced agricultural development in the country.
- It also emphasised the need for diversification of agriculture and the development of dairy farming, poultry, horticulture, livestock rearing and aquaculture.
- The policy of liberalisation and free market economy in the 1990s influenced the development of Indian agriculture.

Growth of Agricultural Output and Technology

- The expansion of irrigation has played a crucial role in enhancing agricultural output in the country. It provided the basis for the introduction of modern agricultural technology, such as High-Yielding Varieties of seeds, chemical fertilisers, pesticides and farm machinery.
- Production and yield of many crops such as rice and wheat has increased at an impressive rate. Among the other crops, the production of sugarcane, oilseeds and cotton has also increased.
- The net irrigated area in the country has also increased.
- Modern agricultural technology has spread very fast in various areas of the country.
- The consumption of chemical fertilisers has increased by 15 times since the mid-sixties. Since the High-Yielding Varieties are highly vulnerable to pests and diseases, hence the use of pesticides has increased significantly since the 1960s.

National Mission for Sustainable Agriculture (NMSA)

- The National Mission for Sustainable Agriculture aims to make agriculture more productive, sustainable, remunerative and climate resilient.
- It promotes location specific integrated/composite farming systems and conserves natural resources through appropriate soil and moisture conservation measures.
- The government has been promoting organic farming in the country through schemes such as **Paramparagat Krishi Vikas Yojana** (PKVY) and **Rashtriya Vikas Yojana** (RKVY).

3.8 Problems of Indian Agriculture

Dependence on Erratic Monsoon

- The majority of cultivated land is dependent on the uneven rainfall pattern. Irrigation covers only about 33 per cent of the cultivated area in India. The crop production in the rest of the cultivated land directly depends on rain.
- The South-West monsoon also affects the supply of canal water for irrigation. On the other hand, the rainfall in Rajasthan and other drought-prone areas are highly unreliable.
- The areas receiving high annual rainfall experience considerable fluctuations too. This makes them vulnerable to both droughts and floods.
- Drought is a common phenomenon in the low rainfall areas, which may also experience occasional floods. The **flash floods** in the drylands of Maharashtra, Gujarat and Rajasthan in 2006 and 2017 are examples of this phenomenon.

Low Productivity

- The yield of the crops in the country is lower than at the international level.
- Per hectare output of most of the crops such as rice, wheat, cotton and oilseeds in India is much lower than that of the USA, Russia and Japan.
- Due to the high pressure on land resources, the labour productivity in Indian agriculture is also very low.
- The vast rainfed areas of the country, particularly drylands which mostly grow coarse cereals, pulses and oilseeds, have low yields.

Constraints of Financial Resources and Indebtedness

- The inputs of modern agriculture are very expensive. Marginal and small farmers have very little or no savings to invest in agriculture.
- Most farmers take credit from various institutions and moneylenders to purchase inputs of modern agriculture. Crop failures and low returns from agriculture create the trap of indebtedness.

Lack of Land Reforms

- Indian farmers had been exploited for a long time as there had been unequal distribution of land. There were three revenue systems operational during the British period, i.e., **Mahalwari**, **Ryotwari** and **Zamindari**. Zamindari was most exploitative for the peasants.
- After Independence, land reforms were not implemented effectively due to a lack of strong political will. The lack of implementation of land reforms has resulted in the continuation of unequal distribution of cultivable land which does not support agricultural development.

Small Farm Size and Fragmentation of Landholdings

- There are a large number of marginal and small farmers in the country. The average size of land holdings is decreasing under increasing population pressure.
- The small fragments of land is uneconomical, as the landholdings gets divided into parts for the next generation of a family and has no productivity.

Lack of Commercialisation

- A large number of farmers produce crops for self-consumption. These farmers do not have enough land resources to produce more than their requirement.
- Most of the small and marginal farmers grow foodgrains, which are meant for their family consumption.

Vast Underemployment

- There is a massive underemployment in the agricultural sector in India, particularly in the unirrigated land.
- In the agricultural sector, there is seasonal unemployment ranging from 4 to 8 months. Hence, the people engaged in agriculture don't have work around the year.

Degradation of Cultivable Land

- The degradation of land resources lead to the depletion of soil fertility.
- The situation is particularly increasing in irrigated areas. A large tract of agricultural land loses its fertility due to **alkalisation**[2] and **salinisation**[3] of soils and **waterlogging**[4].
- Excessive use of chemicals such as insecticides and pesticides led to the concentration of chemicals in toxic amounts in the soil profile.
- Leguminous crops have been displaced from the cropping pattern in the irrigated areas and duration of fallow has been reduced owing to multiple cropping. This has disturbed the process of natural fertilisation such as **nitrogen fixation**[5].
- Rainfed areas in humid and semi-arid tropics also experience degradation of several types. For example, soil erosion by water and wind erosion which are often induced by human activities.

Farmer's Portal of India

- The Farmer's Portal is a platform for farmers to seek any information related to agriculture.
- It provides detailed information on farmers' insurance, agriculture storage, crops, extension activities, seeds, pesticides, farm machineries, etc.
- It also provides details of fertilisers, market prices, package and practices, programmes and welfare schemes.
- Block level details related to soil fertility, storage, insurance, training, etc are available in an interactive map.
- Users can also download a farm-friendly handbook, scheme guidelines, etc.

Quick Test 4

1 From which countries the new HYV variety of seeds were brought to India?
2 When did the major growth come in Indian agriculture?
3 Name two states where consumption of chemical fertilisers is very high.
4 Mention two problems affecting Indian agriculture.

---

2 **Alkalisation** It is the process of making something alkaline by lowering the amount of acid in a solution.
3 **Salinisation** It is the process of an increase in the concentration of salt in soil or water.
4 **Waterlogging** It is a kind of condition in which an area becomes flooded with water, often due to heavy rainfall or poor drainage.
5 **Nitrogen Fixation** It is the process by which nitrogen in the atmosphere is converted into ammonia by certain bacteria.

Mind Map

LAND RESOURCES AND AGRICULTURE

1 Land Resources

Land classified on the basis of ownership
- **Private Land** Example, a piece of land, a house
- **Common Property Resources** Example, community forests, village water bodies

Land-Use Changes
Change in economy affects the land use of a region.
Changes which Affect Land-use
- **Size of the Economy** It is measured in terms of value for all the goods and services produced in the economy.
- **Composition of the Economy** It changes over time which are visible around large urban areas where agricultural land is used for building purposes.
- Pressure on land

Changes in Shares of Land-Use Categories (1950-51) and (2014-15)
Increase in Share of Land Use
- Forests
- Area under non-agricultural use
- Current fallow
- Permanent pasture and grazing land
- Net sown area

Decrease in Share of Land Use
- Barren and unculturable wasteland
- Area under tree crops and groves
- Fallow land

Land-Use Categories Shows the distribution of land for different purposes.
- Forests
- Barren and wasteland
- Land put to non-agricultural uses
- Area under permanent pastures and grazing lands
- Area under miscellaneous tree crops and groves
- Culturable wasteland
- Current fallow
- Fallow other than current fallow
- Net area sown

2 Agriculture

Agriculture Development
Before Independence
- Subsistence in nature

After Independence
- Switched to cash crops
- Intensification of cropping
- Increase in cultivated area
- Green Revolution
- Growth of agriculture output and technology

Problem of Indian Agriculture
- Dependence on monsoon
- Lack of financial resources and indebtness
- Lack of land reforms
- Low productivity
- Small farm size and fragmentation of landholding
- Lack of commercialisation
- Vast underemployment
- Land degradation

Types of Farming
Irrigated Farming
- **Protective Irrigation** Protect soil from moisture deficiency.
- **Productive Irrigation** Provide moisture for high productivity.

Rainfed Farming
- **Dryland Farming** Confined in area with rainfall less than 75 cm.
- **Wetland Farming** Excess of rainfall in rainy seasons.

Agriculture Land Use Show the distribution of land for agriculture purpose
- Culturable wasteland
- Fallow other than current fallow
- Current fallow
- Net area sown

Cropping Seasons
- **Kharif** June-September
  Crops: Rice Cotton, Maize
- **Rabi** October - March
  Crops: Wheat, Gram, Ragi
- **Zaid** April - June
  Crops: Vegetables, Fodder

Foodgrains
- Cereals
- Wheat
- Bajra
- Pulses
- Rice
- Jowar
- Maize

Oilseeds
- Groundnut
- Other oilseeds
- Rapeseed and mustard

Fibre Crops
- Cotton
- Jute

Other Crops
- Sugarcane
- Coffee
- Tea

NCERT Folder

Choose the right answers of the following from the given options

(i) Which one of the following is not a land-use category?

(a) Fallow land (b) Marginal land
(c) Net Area Sown (d) Cultivable land

Ans. (b) Marginal land

(ii) Which one of the following is the main reason due to which share of forest has shown an increase in the last forty years?

(a) Extensive and efficient efforts of afforestation
(b) Increase in community forest land
(c) Increase in notified area allocated for forest growth
(d) Better people's participation in managing forest area

Ans. (c) Increase in notified area allocated for forest growth

(iii) Which one of the following is the main form of degradation in irrigated areas?

(a) Gully erosion (b) Wind erosion
(c) Salinisation of soils (d) Siltation of land

Ans. (c) Salinisation of soils

(iv) Which one of the following crops is not cultivated under dryland farming?

(a) Ragi (b) *Jowar*
(c) Groundnut (d) Sugarcane

Ans. (d) Sugarcane

(v) In which of the following group of countries of the world, HYVs of wheat and rice were developed?

(a) Japan and Australia (b) USA and Japan
(c) Mexico and Philippines (d) Mexico and Singapore

Ans. (c) Mexico and Philippines

Answer the following questions in about 30 words

(i) Differentiate between barren and wasteland and culturable wasteland.

Ans. The difference between barren and wasteland and culturable wasteland are as follows

Barren and Wasteland	Culturable Wasteland
According to the land revenue records, the barren and wastelands cover all the uncultivable land that cannot be brought under cultivation with the use of current technology.	Cultivable wasteland is the land which is left fallow (uncultivated) for more than 5 years. It can be brought under cultivation after improving it through reforming practices.
It includes land such as barren hilly terrains, desert lands, etc.	Uncultivable land is the best example of culturable wasteland.

(ii) How would you distinguish between net sown area and gross cropped area?

Ans. **Net Sown Area** This represents the total area sown with crops and orchards. Area which is sown more than one time in the same year is counted only for one time.

Gross Cropped Area This represents the total area sown once and/or more than once in a particular year, i.e. the area is counted as many times as there is sowing in a year on the same piece of land.

(iii) Why is the strategy of increasing cropping intensity important in a country like India?

Ans. In a country like India, it is difficult to increase cultivable land due to increasing pressure of population and expansion of secondary and tertiary sectors.

Therefore, to fulfil the demand of the population, it is necessary to increase the output which can be achieved by increasing the yield of agricultural land. Intensity or crop intensity, which means growing more number of crops on the same piece of land in a particular time.

(iv) How do you measure total cultivable land?

Ans. Total cultivable land denotes how much area of land is among the productive category from the total reported area. It is the combination of total net sown and total fallow lands.

Total cultivable land of an area/region can be calculated by adding up of net sown area, all fallow lands and culturable wasteland.

(v) What is the difference between dryland and wetland farming?

Ans. Dryland farming is confined to the region having annual rainfall less than 75 cm. In this region, drought resistant crops are grown. This region grows crops such as ragi, *bajra*, moong, etc.

On the other hand, farming in areas which receive more than 75 cm of rainfall is called wetland agriculture. Crops grown include rice, jute, sugarcane, etc.

Answer the following questions in about 150 words

(i) **What are the different types of environmental problems of land resources in India?**

Ans. In India, land is a very crucial resource but it is facing multiple crisis in the form of environmental, physical and economic problems.

Following are the environmental problems of land resources in India

- Uneven rainfall is the major problem in India. At times there is excessive rainfall and floods which cause heavy damage to land fertility as running water causes large scale soil erosion.
- At some other occasion, rainfall may be deficit and drought conditions may prevail which also leads to soil erosion.
- In arid regions, badland topography develops due to a natural agents of soil erosion, i.e. wind. It leads to land degradation and reduces fertility of soil.
- In modern farming practices, excess use of fertiliser and chemical causes salinisation of land and problem of water logging. It also leads to alkalination.
- Deforestation is also related with land problem, as it not only causes loss of habitat but also promote soil erosion and land degradation.
- Excess canal irrigation also causes salinisation of land.
- Excessive use of chemical fertilisers and insecticides leads to toxicity in the soil.

(ii) **What are the important strategies for agricultural development followed in the post-independence period in India?**

Ans. After the independenc of India, focus was shifted to produce more food grains, and many strategies were adopted by the government for the same.

Following are some of the strategies adopted

- Green Revolution technologies were introduced by Indian government for agricultural development where High Yield Varieties of Seeds (HYVs) and various modern techniques were used to intensify agriculture.
- The emphasis shifted from cash crops to food crops especially after Green Revolution.
- Expansion of cultivated area by growing food crops on fallow and cultivable land.
- Intensive Agricultural District Programme (IADP) and Intensive Agricultural Area Programme (IAAP) were launched to increase production.
- In order to solve the problems related to agriculture and allied activities, the Planning Commission of India introduced agro-climatic planning in 1988.
- Policy of liberalisation and free market economy was introduced to influence the course of development of Indian agriculture in 1990s.

Exam Pattern Questions

Objective Type Questions

Multiple Choice Questions (MCQs)

1. Which of these correctly defines barren and wastelands?

(a) Land which is left uncultivated for more than 5 years.
(b) Land which cannot be brought under cultivation with the use of current technology.
(c) Physical extent of a land on which crops are sown.
(d) Land under orchards and fruit trees.

2. Which type of land-use is owned by the village panchayat or the government?

(a) Land put to non-agricultural uses
(b) Forests
(c) Area under permanent pastures and grazing lands
(d) Culturable wasteland

3. Any land which is left fallow (uncultivated) for more than five years is included in which category of land-use? **CBSE Diksha**

(a) Current fallow
(b) Culturable wasteland
(c) Net sown area
(d) Fallow other than current fallow

4. The physical extent of land on which crops are sown and harvested is known as

(a) Current fallow
(b) Net sown area
(c) Culturable wasteland
(d) Fallow other than current fallow

5. Which among the following land-use category has increased due to use of culturable wasteland?
(a) Net sown area (b) Current follow
(c) Forests (d) Barren and wasteland

6. Which of the following is an example of barren and unculturable wasteland?
(a) Permanent pasture (b) Desert and ravines
(c) Land used for infrastructure (d) Land used in settlements

7. Which of the following departments maintains the record of land use in India?
(a) Revenue (b) Income Tax
(c) Sales Tax (d) Estate

8. Which of the following is not used in the estimation of the total stock of agricultural land resources? **CBSE Diksha**
(a) All fallow land (b) Net sown area
(c) Pasture land (d) Culturable wastelands

9. Fallowing is a cultural practise adopted for giving rest to land so that ....
(a) land could be cultivated again
(b) land could regain its fertility
(c) land could be used for animal rearing
(d) land could be used to grow another crop

10. Choose the most appropriate statement defining the CPRs. **CBSE Diksha**
(a) Every member has the right to access and use with specific obligations
(b) It provides fodder for livestock
(c) It provides fuel for households
(d) All of the above

11. Which of the following categories of marginalised sections does not enjoy the benefits of CPRs in rural areas? **CBSE Diksha**
(a) The landless farmers (b) The marginal farmers
(c) The women (d) The slums

12. The land-saving technique of increasing the cropping intensity does not include **CBSE Diksha**
(a) increasing output from limited land
(b) fuller utilisation of land
(c) increasing fodder for livestock
(d) reducing unemployment in rural areas

13. The cropping intensity can be calculated by
(a) $\frac{GCA \times NSA}{100}$ (b) $\frac{GCA}{100 \times NSA}$
(c) $\frac{GCA}{NSA} \times 100$ (d) $\frac{NSA}{GCA} \times 100$

14. What is the other name of rainfed type of farming ? **CBSE 2024**
(a) Productive farming (b) Protective farming
(c) Barani (d) Zaid

15. More than 54% of total cropped area in India is occupied by
(a) cereals (b) pulses
(c) oilseeds (d) fibre crops

16. 'Aus', 'Aman' and 'Boro'are varieties of which crop?
(a) Wheat (b) Rice (c) Pulses (d) Oilseeds

17. Which of these crops is grown in rainfed areas?
(a) Rice (b) Sugarcane
(c) Gram (d) All of these

18. Which of the following fact, about jute cultivation in India, is true? **CBSE 2024**
(a) West Bengal is the leading producer of jute.
(b) Jute is cash crop for Punjab and Haryana.
(c) Madhya Pradesh and Maharashtra are other leading jute producing states.
(d) India produces about 30% of the jute production of the world

19. Choose the measure that was not adopted by the government immediately after the independence to increase foodgrain production. **CBSE Diksha**
(a) Increasing crop intensity
(b) Introducing liberalisation
(c) Switching from cash to food crops
(d) Increasing the cropped area

20. The Indian agriculture has been facing which of these problems?
(a) Low productivity
(b) Over dependence on monsoon
(c) Very small landholdings
(d) All of the above

21. Read the following information carefully and identify the correct option for the crop. **CBSE 2024**
- Grown in *kharif* season.
- Mainly grown in semi-arid area in India.
- Gujarat and Maharashtra are the leading producer states.

Options
(a) Cotton (b) Tea
(c) Jute (d) Sugarcane

22. The characteristics of an agricultural crop in India are given below. Read them carefully and identify the crop. **CBSE 2024**
- It is a crop of tropical humid area.
- West Bengal farmers grow it three crops in a year.
- It is grown as a *kharif* crop in North-Western parts.
- West Bengal, Uttar Pradesh and Punjab and major producing states.

Crops
(a) Wheat (b) Gram (c) Bajra (d) Rice

23. Wheat is mainly grown in India in which of these regions?

(i) Punjab (ii) Uttar Pradesh
(iii) Himachal Pradesh (iv) Gujarat

Codes

(a) (ii), (iii) and (iv) (b) (i), (ii) and (iii)
(c) (i), (iii) and (iv) (d) (i) and (iv)

24. Which of these categories of land-use has registered an increase from 1950-51 to 2014-2015?

(i) Land under forest (ii) Net sown area
(iii) Land under pastures

Codes

(a) (i), (ii) and (iii) (b) (i) and (ii)
(c) (ii) and (iii) (d) (i) and (iii)

25. Which of these is a *rabi* crop in the Northern India?

(i) Rice (ii) Cotton
(iii) Wheat (iv) Gram
(v) Mustard

Codes

(a) (i) and (ii) (b) (i), (ii), (iii), (iv) and (v)
(c) (ii), (iii) and (iv) (d) (iii), (iv) and (v)

26. Tea is mainly grown in which of these regions in India?

(i) Slopes of Nilgiris
(ii) Slopes of Cardamom hills
(iii) Slopes of Darjeeling hills

Codes

(a) (i), (ii) and (iii) (b) (ii) and (iii)
(c) (i) and (iii) (d) (i) and (ii)

27. Read the given resources and choose the correct option related to 'community's resources'. **CBSE 2023**

(i) Village water bodies
(ii) Village agriculture land
(iii) Village residential land
(iv) Pasture land

Codes

(a) Only (i) and (ii) are correct
(b) Only (ii) and (iii) are correct
(c) Only (iii) and (iv) are correct
(d) Only (i) and (iv) are correct

28. Which of these is true regarding the growth and development in Indian agriculture?

(i) The yields of crops like rice and wheat have increased since independence.
(ii) Net irrigated area in the country has declined in India in past 50 years.
(iii) There is decrease in the use of pesticides after 1960.

Codes

(a) (i) and (ii) (b) Only (i)
(c) Only (ii) (d) (i), (ii) and (iii)

Arrange the Following

29. Arrange the following states in sequence as per their position in the production of wheat.

(i) Uttar Pradesh (ii) Madhya Pradesh
(iii) Punjab (iv) Haryana

Codes

(a) (i), (ii), (iii), (iv) (b) (iii), (ii), (iv), (i)
(c) (iv), (iii), (ii), (i) (d) (ii), (iv), (iii), (i)

Match the Following

30.

List I (Land-use category)	List II (Definition)
A. Current Fallow	1. This is the area that government has identified.
B. Forests	2. Land left without cultivation for one or less than one year
C. Wasteland	3. Land which cannot be brought under cultivation

Codes

	A	B	C		A	B	C
(a)	1	3	2	(b)	1	2	3
(c)	2	1	3	(d)	2	3	1

31.

List I (Crop)	List II (Cultivating Region/State)
A. Rice	1. Maharashtra
B. Wheat	2. Malwa Plateau
C. *Tur* (Arhar)	3. West Bengal

Codes

	A	B	C		A	B	C
(a)	1	3	2	(b)	3	2	1
(c)	1	2	3	(d)	3	1	2

Assertion-Reason

Directions (Q. Nos. 32-34) In the questions given below are two statements labelled as Assertion (A) and other labelled as Reason (R). In the context of two statements which one of the following is correct?

Codes

(a) Both A and R are true, but R is not the correct explanation of A
(b) Both A and R are true and R is the correct explanation of A
(c) Both A and R are incorrect
(d) A is correct, but R is incorrect

32. Assertion (A) The contribution of agriculture has declined over time but the pressure on land for agriculture has not declined.
Reason (R) The number of people in India is increasing day by day.

33. Assertion (A) As per the land use data of 1950-51 to 2014-15, there has been an increase in area under forest.
Reason (R) There is an increase in demarcated areas under forest rather than an actual increase in forest cover.

34. Assertion (A) Degradation of land is particularly alarming in the irrigated areas.
Reason (R) A large tract of agricultural land has lost its fertility due to alkalisation and salinisation.

Answers

1. (b) Land which cannot be brought under cultivation with the use of current technology.
2. (c) Area under permanent pastures and grazing lands
3. (b) Culturable wasteland
4. (b) Net sown area
5. (a) Net sown area
6. (b) Desert and ravines
7. (a) Revenue
8. (c) Pasture land
9. (b) land could regain its fertility
10. (d) All of the above
11. (d) The slums
12. (c) increasing fodder for livestock
13. (c) $\frac{GCA}{NSA} \times 100$
14. (c) Barani
15. (a) cereals
17. (c) Gram
16. (b) Rice
18. (a) West Bengal is the leading producer of jute.
19. (b) Introducing liberalisation
20. (d) All of the above
21. (a) Cotton
22. (d) Rice
23. (b) (i), (ii) and (iii)
24. (b) (i) and (ii)
25. (d) (iii), (iv) and (v)
26. (a) (i), (ii) and (iii)
27. (d) Only (i) and (iv) are correct
28. (b) Only (i)
29. (a) (i), (ii), (iii), (iv)
30. (c)
31. (b)
32. (b) Both A and R are true and R is the correct explanation of A
33. (b) Both A and R are true and R is the correct explanation of A
34. (b) Both A and R are true and R is the correct explanation of A

Subjective Questions

Short Answer Type Questions

1. How would you differentiate among culturable wasteland, current fallow and fallow other than current fallow land?

Ans. Culturable wasteland, current fallow and fallow other than current fallow land differs in the following ways

Culturable Wasteland It is the land which is left fallow for more than five years. It can be brought under cultivation after improving it through reclamation (recovery) practices.

Current Fallow This is the land which is left without cultivation for one or less than one agricultural year to recover its lost fertility through natural processes.

Fallow other than Current Fallow It is a cultivable land which is left uncultivated for more than a year but less than five years. If the land is left uncultivated for more than five years, it would be categorised as culturable wasteland.

2. Describe the trend regarding increase in area under forest, area under non-agricultural uses and current fallow.

Ans. There is change in the trend regarding increase in area under forest, area under non-agricultural uses and current fallow. This can be stated by the following observations

- The rate of increase is the highest in case of area under non-agricultural uses. This is due to the changing structure of Indian economy. The Indian economy is increasingly depending on the contribution from industrial and services sectors and expansion of related infrastructural facilities.
- An expansion of area under both urban and rural settlements has added to the increase. Thus, the area under non-agricultural uses is increasing at the expense of wastelands and agricultural land.

- There is an increase in the share under forest due to increase in the demarcated area under forest.
- The trend of current fallow changes over years, depending on the variability of rainfall and cropping cycles.

3. Give three reasons for the decline of barren and wasteland, culturable wasteland, area under pastures and tree crops and fallow lands.

Ans. As per the land use categories of 1950-51 to 2014-15, following reasons are responsible for the decline of barren and wastelands, culturable wasteland, area under pastures and tree crops and fallow lands

- Due to increase in pressure on land from agricultural and non-agricultural sectors, wastelands and culturable wastelands have witnessed decline over time.
- Illegal encroachment due to expansion of cultivation on common pasture lands is largely responsible for this decline.
- Decline in land under pastures and grazing lands due to pressure from agriculture land.

4. Discuss the significance of land resources in India.

Ans. Land resource is important for the livelihood of the people depending on agriculture as

- Agriculture is purely land based activity unlike secondary and tertiary sectors. Its unavailability may lead to poverty.
- The role of quality of land is important in agriculture. The more the land is fertile, the more it gives output/production.
- Ownership of land resource is considered as a social status in rural areas. It is also seen as security for credit, natural hazards or life contingencies.
- As in rural areas a large number of population is engaged in agricultural activities. Thus, more land under cultivation may increase the employment opportunities to rural poors.

5. "Land resources are more crucial to the livelihood of the people depending on agriculture." Support this statement with any three suitable arguments.

Competency Based Que

Or **How is land resource more crucial to the livelihood of the people depending on agriculture in India? Explain.**

Ans. Most of the Indians are dependent on agriculture directly or indirectly for their subsistence. Thus, land resource becomes more important.

Importance of land resource in agriculture can be understood by following points

- Dependence of agriculture sector on land resources is high as compared to secondary or tertiary sector.
- Agriculture is directly affected by the quality of land but other sectors such as industry or service sector are not affected by the quality of land.
- Besides agricultural production, ownership of land resources also indicates a social status in rural areas.

6. State any two characteristics each of the three distinct cropping seasons of India.

Ans. The three distinct cropping seasons of India are

(i) ***Kharif*** The characteristics of *kharif* season are as follows

(a) *Kharif* season starts with the onset of South-West monsoon (June-September).

(b) The major crops which are cultivated in this season are rice, jute, cotton, *jowar*, *bajra*, *tur* and other tropical crops.

(ii) ***Rabi*** The characteristics of rabi season are as follows

(a) *Rabi* season in India starts from October-November with onset of winter and ends in March-April.

(b) The crops which are cultivated in this season are wheat, gram, mustard and other temperate and sub-tropical crops because of the low temperature condition.

(iii) ***Zaid*** The characteristics of *zaid* season are as follows

(a) *Zaid* is a short season between *rabi* and *kharif* in India (April-June).

(b) The crops which are cultivated in this season are watermelons, cucumbers, vegetables and fodder crops. Crops are cultivated mainly on irrigated lands.

7. Explain the importance of irrigation for agriculture in India.

Or **Why is demand of water to irrigation increasing day by day in India? Explain any three reasons.**

Or **Why is irrigation necessary in India? Explain any three reasons.**

Ans. Irrigation is necessary in India for the following reasons:

- **To Decrease the Dependency on Monsoon Rainfall** After decades of independence, India is still dependent on monsoon rainfall for agriculture production. Only 33% of agricultural land is irrigated and rest is dependent on rainfall for soil moisture. To decrease the dependency on monsoon rainfall, irrigation is necessary.
- **To Increase Production** Agricultural production and yield under rainfed areas are low. To increase the agricultural production in India, irrigation is necessary.
- **To Introduce Newer Farming Method** Irrigation is important to introduce newer farming methods like use of HYV seeds which need more irrigation. These newer methods replace old farming practices.

8. "Green Revolution was not equally successful in all parts of India". Explain why. Competency Based Que

Ans. Green Revolution in India was not much successful in all the parts of India. It created inequalities alongwith increasing productivity and production. Following are the reasons of limited success of Green Revolution

- Unavailability of irrigation facilities in all parts of India.
- Green Revolution did not take proper measures to create awareness among farmers about how to use chemical fertilisers and new varieties of seeds during agricultural practices.
- HYVs seeds were not easily available to all people due to faulty distribution and their high cost.
- Small size of land holdings also created obstacles in the path of success of Green Revolution.

9. "Land degradation caused by human made process are more harmful than natural processes in India". Analyse the statement with three suitable examples. Competency Based Que

Ans. Human activities are majorly responsible for degradation of land than natural resources. This degradation has started after Green Revolution where new methods and techniques were used intensively, e.g. chemical fertilisers, irrigation, etc.

Three examples for this are as follows

(i) Unregulated and over-irrigation have created problems of alkanisation, salinisation and waterlogging in irrigated areas of India.

(ii) It is estimated that about 15 million hectare land has lost its fertility due to faulty methods of agriculture.

(iii) Besides these, shifting cultivation, deforestation, mining activities, etc are human processes causing land degradation, that have caused harm to the soil fertility and agriculture in India.

10. Discuss the growth of agricultural output and improvement in technology in India.

Ans. Indian agriculture has witnessed a tremendous improvement in agricultural production and associated technology during the last sixty years. Following are some observations related to agricultural growth

- Production and yield of several crops such as rice, wheat, sugarcane, oilseeds, cotton, etc have increased considerably.
- India is the leading producer of pulses, tea, jute, milk, etc.
- Irrigation facilities have expanded to a great extent. This has helped to use modern agricultural technology like HYV seeds, chemical fertilisers, pesticides and farm machinery.
- Consumption of chemical fertilisers has increased by 15 times since 1960s.
- Since the HYVs are highly susceptible to pests and diseases, the use of pesticides has increased significantly since 1960s.

11. Differentiate between protective and productive irrigation.

Ans. Differences between protective irrigation and productive irrigation are as follows

Protective Irrigation	Productive Irrigation
Protective irrigation aims to protect the crops from adverse effects of soil moisture.	Productive irrigation aims to provide adequate moisture to soil to increase the productivity.
Due to fluctuating situation of rainfall, this irrigation system provides alternative source of water.	The water input per unit area of cultivated land is greater in the irrigation as compared to protective irrigation.
In this system of irrigation, the productivity remains low.	In this irrigation, the productivity remains high.

12. Modern agricultural technology has brought a significant increase in agricultural output in India. Elucidate the statement. Competency Based Que

Ans. The modern agricultural technology has brought a significant increase in agricultural output in India in the following ways

- Production and yield of several crops such as rice, wheat, sugarcane, oilseeds, cotton etc have increased considerably.
- India is the leading producer of pulses, tea, jute, milk, etc.
- Irrigation facilities have expanded to a great extent. This has helped to use modern agricultural technology like HYV seeds, chemical fertilisers, pesticides and farm machinery.
- Consumption of chemical fertilisers increased from a mere 292 thousand tonnes in 1960-61 to 18398 thousand tonnes in 2004-05.
- Since, the HYVs are highly susceptible to pests and diseases, the use of pesticides has increased significantly since 1960s.

13. "Indian farmers gamble with the monsoon". Illustrate this statement. Competency Based Que

Ans. Agriculture of India is based on monsoon and hence, it is said that good output production is based on good monsoon and therefore, Indian farmers gamble with the monsoon.

It is due to the following reasons

- Indian monsoon is highly uncertain. Sometimes we receive early monsoon, late monsoon or weak monsoonal rainfall.

- The distribution of rainfall is also unequal in the country. Some parts receive very high rainfall (even flood like situation) whereas other face drought like condition. This hit the agricultural production in India.
- Not all farmers have proper irrigation facilities. Small farmers are the most deprived ones.
- Under-developed technological base of agriculture.

Long Answer Type Questions

1. "Land-use in a region to a large extent is influenced by the nature of economic activities carried out in that region". Support the statement by giving three examples from India.

Or **Why is the area under pastures decreasing in India? How do the changes in the economy affect changes in land-use? Explain.**

Ans. Increasing population pressure on land is one of the major reasons which is responsible for the decline in land under pasture and grazing area.

There are three types of economic changes that affected the land-use in India which are as follows (*Any three*)

(i) As population increases, the size of economy also increases. High population pressurises land resources and force people to utilise every piece of land. Thus, marginal lands and barren wastelands would be used to support population.

(ii) When composition of an economy changes, it also changes the land uses because different sectors use land for different purposes, e.g. when agricultural area decreases, the area under other categories like area under non-agriculture use increases.

(iii) With the compositional change in economy and change in land-use, area under agriculture declines, but it does not reduce the population pressure on agriculture land.

(iv) As land is fixed in its size or area and due to intensive cultivation, the soil fertility is declined. Thus, it is very difficult to produce more from the same piece of land. So, more land is needed for agricultural practices and higher production for the growing population. Thus, pasture land is decreasing in India.

2. Mention any six land-use categories in India.

Ans. Under the land revenue records, land-use categories are as follows

(i) **Forests** Area under actual forest cover is different from area classified as forest. It is the area demarcated by government for forest growth. There may be an increase in area of forest without any increase in the actual forest cover.

(ii) **Land put to Non-agricultural Uses** Land under rural and urban settlements, infrastructure (road, canals, power project) industries, shops, etc are included in this category. Expansion in the secondary and tertiary activities would lead to an increase in this category of land-use.

(iii) **Barren and Wastelands** The land which normally cannot be brought under cultivation with the available technology is barren or wasteland. For example, barren hilly terrains, desert lands, ravines, etc.

(iv) **Area under Permanent Pastures and Grazing Lands** It includes all grazing land whether it is permanent pasture or not. Only a small proportion of this land is privately owned as most of the part is owned by 'Village Panchayat' or government which comes under 'Common Property Resources'.

(v) **Area under Miscellaneous Tree Crops and Groves** It includes land under orchards and fruit trees which is mainly privately owned.

(vi) **Culturable Wasteland** It is the land which is left fallow for more than five years. It can be brought under cultivation after improving it through reclamation (recovery) practices.

3. Explain the term cropping intensity. Describe the three cropping seasons in India.

Ans. Cropping intensity refers to producing more number of crops from the same field during one agriculture year. In this process, cropping area is counted twice or thrice depending upon the number of crops produced in the year.

For three cropping seasons, refer to page no. 211 under the heading 'Cropping Seasons in India.'

4. Explain the importance of foodgrains in the Indian agricultural economy. Describe any three characteristics of rice cultivation.

Ans. Foodgrains acquired special position in agriculture economy of India. Within agriculture, foodgrains production is by far the major activity, covering about two-third of the total cropped area in the country.

It dominates both subsistence and commercial farming all over India. Foodgrains provide almost all the calories and proteins consumed by the poor and provide the rural poor with the bulk of their employment and income. Rice, wheat, bajra, maize, pulses (gram, *tur*), etc are the examples of foodgrains.

Characteristics of rice cultivation are as follows

(i) For most of the Indians, rice is a staple food.

(ii) About 3000 varieties of rice are grown in various agro-climatic regions of India. India ranked second with the production of 21.2% of rice in the world.

(iii) Because of suitable climatic conditions, rice can be cultivated twice and even thrice in an agricultural year in Southern India and West Bengal.

It is cultivated in all parts of India from sea level to about 2000 m altitude and from humid area in the Eastern India to dry but irrigated areas of Punjab, Haryana, Western Uttar Pradesh and Northern Rajasthan.

5. Classify Indian farming into two groups on the basis of main source of moisture for crops. Write two features of each.

***Or* Classify Indian farming practices on the basis of source of moisture and describe them.** **CBSE 2025**

Ans. In India, farming is classified into following two groups on the basis of moisture available for crops

Irrigated Farming The main source of moisture for this farming is irrigation by various methods i.e. wells, tubewells, etc. It has two types i.e. protective and productive irrigation

(i) In protective farming/irrigation, the objective is to protect the crops from adverse effects of soil moisture deficiency which often means that irrigation acts as a supplementary source of water over and above the rainfall.

(ii) Productive irrigation is meant to provide sufficient soil moisture in the cropping season to achieve high productivity. In such irrigation, the water input per unit area of cultivated land is higher than protective irrigation.

Rainfed Farming (*Barani*) The main source of moisture for this farming is rainfall. Two types are dryland farming and wetland farming:

(i) Dryland farming is confined to the region having annual rainfall less than 75 cm. In this region, drought-resistant crops are grown such as *ragi, bajra, moong, gram* and *guar* (fodder crops). Measures of soil moisture conservation and rainwater harvesting are also done in this region.

(ii) In wetland farming, farming is done in areas which receive more than 75 cm of rainfall. Water intensive crops are grown in this farming such as rice, jute and sugarcane.

6. Discuss the plantation crops in India. What are conditions required for these crops to grow?

Ans. Among the major plantation crops, tea, coffee, sugarcane are prominent plantation crops in India.

The important plantation crops and their required conditions of growth are as follows

Sugarcane

It is an important cash crop of India. India is claimed to be the homeland of sugarcane.

Conditions Required to Grow

- Sugarcane is a long-duration crop, maturing in 10-12 months.
- It requires hot and humid climate with temperature ranging from 20°C to 30°C and rainfall ranging from 100 to 150 cm.
- Dry weather is necessary at the harvesting season.
- Frost is injurious to sugarcane, frequent irrigation is required in low rainfall areas.

Tea

It is the most important beverage crop in India. It contains caffeine and tannin. In India, tea plantation was introduced in 1840s in Brahmaputra valley of Assam which is still the largest producer of tea in the country.

Conditions Required to Grow

- Tea requires about 25°C to 30°C temperature and a well distributed rainfall of 200 to 250 cm.
- It grows well in loamy soil rich in organic matter.

Coffee

It is second most prominent beverage crop of India after tea. There are three varieties of coffee i.e. *arabica, robusta* and *liberica*. In India, it is grown in the region of Karnataka.

Conditions Required to Grow

- It requires hot and humid climate with 15° to 30°C temperature and rainfall 150-200 cm.
- It grows in frost free slopy area with height 800-1600 m from sea level.

7. Analyse any five major problems of Indian agriculture. **CBSE 2024**

***Or* Describe any five major problems of Indian agriculture.**

***Or* Describe any five major problems related to Indian agriculture.**

Ans. For answer refer to text page no. 219 and 220 under the heading 'Problems of Indian Agriculture'.

8. How the small size of landholdings and degradation of cultivable land are the two major problems of Indian agriculture? Explain both these problems with examples.

Ans. Problems of small size of landholdings in India are as follows

- Most of the Indian farmers are small and marginal. About 60% landholdings are smaller than one hectare and about 40% landholdings are smaller than 0.5 hectare.
- The average size of a farm in India is much smaller than developed countries. This average size of farm is becoming smaller every year because of increasing population pressure.
- Due to small landholdings, small farmers are able to only grow food for their self consumption.

- Small and fragmented lands are less productive and uneconomical.

For problems of degradation of cultivable land, refer to page no. 220 under heading 'Degradation of Cultivable Land'.

9. 'Erratic monsoon' and 'indebtedness' are the major problems of Indian agriculture. Suggest and explain the measures to overcome these problems.

Ans. **Erratic Monsoon** Nature of monsoon is very erratic in India. It is true that means of irrigation were developed after independence, but the cultivated area under irrigation is only 33%. So, there should be more stress on developing various means of irrigation especially in unirrigated areas of India.

Some of the measures are

- Water disputes between states should be ended in order to provide equitable water resources to each cultivable land in India.
- There should be stress on rainwater harvesting technique to improve and recharge groundwater table so that farmers can easily harvest their land with the use of these sources.
- Drought resistant crops should be used more in the areas where shortage of water occurs.

Indebtedness Indebtedness is the state of being in debt, or owing money to someone else. When a person is in debt, it means that he has borrowed money or received goods or services with a promise to pay the sum back.

To overcome the problem of indebtedness following measures could be taken

- Encouraging co-operative credits in rural areas so that farmers could get loans at cheaper rates. Private lending should be eliminated.
- Agriculture should be conducted on scientific basis so that the income of the farmers would increase and they could meet their expenses without borrowing money.
- Encourage minimum support price policy for all farmers. Rural banks and co-operative banks should provide storage facilities at cheap interest rates.

10. "Low productivity and fragmentation of landholding are the major problems of Indian agriculture". Suggest and explain measures to overcome these problems.

Ans. Measures to overcome the problems of low productivity are as follows

- To make aware all the farmers about new technologies like use of improved implements, seeds, chemicals, manures, etc.
- Double cropping, better rotation of crops, fighting plant diseases and pests, etc should be given due emphasis. Different sources of irrigation should be provided to all farmers.
- Timely soil testing should be done in rural areas by establishing soil testing labs.
- Institutional credit or loan facilities should be provided to all farmers at low interest rates, e.g. Kisan credit card scheme.

Measures to overcome the problems of fragmentation of landholdings are as follows

- Big areas of land which are lying waste can be reclaimed and made fit for cultivation.
- Co-operative farming can be helpful to check the sub-division and fragmentation of holding. This farming would result in the adoption of modern technology on big farms. In this way, agriculture will become profitable occupation.
- New agricultural policy should be framed to improve this situation.
- The stress of population on land should be reduced.

11. 'Fragmentation of land-holdings' and 'degradation of cultivable land' are the serious problems of Indian agriculture. Suggest and explain measures to overcome these problems.

Ans. Fragmentation of land-holdings and degradation of cultivable lands are the serious problems of Indian agriculture.

Following are the measures to overcome or reduce the problems of fragmentations

- Big areas of land that are of no use could be reformed and could be used.
- Cooperative farming can he helpful to check the sub-division and fragmentation of holding. This farms results in the adoption of new technology and make profit from agriculture.
- There should be new agricultural policy, that would help in the improvement of existing problems of agriculture.

Following are some measures for controlling land degradation

- Strip farming should be encouraged in which cultivated crops are sown in alternative strips to prevent water movement.
- Crop rotation should be in practice.
- In the hilly regions, contour farming should be done. As it is useful in collecting and diverting the run off water to avoid erosion.
- To minimise water logging and salinisation, modern techniques of irrigation in the fields should be adopted.

12. **"Lack of land reforms' and 'degradation of cultivable land' are the major problems of Indian agriculture". Substantiate the statement.**

Or **"Degradation of cultivable land is serious problem in India." Explain with examples.**

Ans. 'Lack of land reforms' and 'degradation of cultivable land' are the major problems of Indian agriculture.

Lack of Land Reforms (Problems of small size of land holdings) **in India** are

- Most of the Indian farmers are small and marginal. About 60% landholdings are smaller than one hectare and about 40% landholdings are smaller than 0.5 hectare.
- The average size of a farm in India is much smaller than developed countries.
- This average size of farm is becoming smaller every year because of increasing population pressure.
- Most of these farmers are only able to grow food and consume it within their families. Small and fragmented lands are less productive and uneconomical.

Degradation of Cultivable Land

The degradation of cultivable land is one of the serious problems in India as

- Intensive use of chemical fertilisers and irrigation have resulted into the degradation of cultivable land. It has reduced the fertility of soil in India.
- Unregulated and over irrigation has created problems of alkalisation and salinisation and waterlogging in irrigated cultivated areas of India.
- The natural fertilisation processes of soil like nitrogen fixation by cultivation of leguminous crops are not adopted because these crops are displaced with the commercial crops such as sugarcane.

Source/Graph Based Questions

1. **Read the passage carefully and answer the questions that follow.**

CPRs provide fodder for the livestock and fuel for the households along with other minor forest products like fruits, nuts, fibre, medicinal plants, etc. In rural areas, such land is of particular relevance for the livelihood of the landless and marginal farmers and other weaker sections since many of them depend on income from their livestock due to the fact that they have limited access to land. CPRs also are important for women as most of the fodder and fuel collection is done by them in rural areas. They have to devote long hours in collecting fuel and fodder from a degraded area of CPR. CPRs can be defined as community's natural resource, where every member has the right of access and usage with specified obligations, without anybody having property rights over them. Community forests, pasture lands, village water bodies and other public spaces where a group larger than a household or family unit exercises rights of use and carries responsibility of management are examples of CPRs.

(i) What is the most important feature of Common Property Resources?

(a) It is owned by women
(b) Every member has access to these resources
(c) It is controlled by the government
(d) None of the above

Ans. (b) Every member has access to these resources

(ii) The marginalised sections can obtain which of the following products from CPRs?

(a) Medicines (b) Fruits
(c) Fodder (d) All of these

Ans. (d) All of these

(iii) Common Property Resources are mainly found in which of the following areas?

(a) Rural areas (b) Urban areas
(c) Semi urban areas (d) Metropolitan areas

Ans. (a) Rural areas

2. **Read the passage carefully and answer the questions that follow.**

New seed varieties of wheat (Mexico) and rice (Philippines) known as High Yielding Varieties (HYVs) were available for cultivation by mid-1960s. India took advantage of this and introduced package technology comprising HYVs, along with chemical fertilisers in irrigated areas of Punjab, Haryana, Western Uttar Pradesh, Andhra Pradesh and Gujarat. Assured supply of soil moisture through irrigation was a basic pre-requisite for the success of this new agricultural technology.

This strategy of agricultural development paid dividends instantly and increased the foodgrains production at very fast rate. This spurt of agricultural growth came to be known as 'Green Revolution'. This also gave fillip to the development of a large number of agro-inputs, agro-processing industries and small-scale industries. This strategy of agricultural development made the country self-reliant in foodgrain production.

But Green Revolution was initially confined to irrigated areas only. This led to regional disparities in agricultural development in the country till 1970s, after which the technology spread to the Eastern and Central parts of the country. The Planning Commission of India focused its attention on the problems of agriculture in rainfed areas in 1980s. It initiated agro-climatic planning in 1988 to induce regionally balanced agricultural development in the country.

(i) **Foodgrains were imported in the country in the mid-1960s for which of the following reasons?**
(a) Floods (b) Cyclones
(c) Drought (d) Green Revolution

Ans. (c) Drought

(ii) **Which of the following measures were taken by the Planning Commission to induce regionally balanced agricultural development?**
(a) Green Revolution
(b) Horticulture Development
(c) Agro Climatic Planning
(d) Liberalisation

Ans. (c) Agro Climatic Planning

(iii) **Which of the following is/are component(s) of Green Revolution?**
(a) Irrigation supply (b) High yielding seed
(c) Fertilisers (d) All of these

Ans. (d) All of these

3. Read the passage carefully and answer the questions that follow.

Rice is a staple food for the overwhelming majority of population in India. Though, it is considered to be a crop of tropical humid areas, it has about 3,000 varieties which are grown in different agro-climatic regions. These are successfully grown from sea level to about 2,000 m altitude and from humid areas in Eastern India to dry but irrigated areas of Punjab, Haryana, Western Uttar Pradesh and Northern Rajasthan. In Southern states and West Bengal the climatic conditions allow the cultivation of two or three crops of rice in an agricultural year. In West Bengal farmers grow three crops of rice called 'aus', 'aman' and 'boro'. But in Himalayas and North-Western parts of the country, it is grown as a kharif crop during South-West monsoon season. India contributes 21.6 per cent of rice production in the world and ranked second after China in 2018. About one-fourth of the total cropped area in the country is under rice cultivation. West Bengal, Uttar Pradesh and Punjab are the leading rice producing states in the country.

(i) **What is the rank of India in terms of rice production in the world?**

Ans. The rank of India is second in terms of rice production in the world.

(ii) **In the Himalayan region and North-Western parts of the country, rice is grown during which season?**

Ans. In the Himalayan region and North-Western parts of the country, rice is grown during monsoon season.

(iii) **Mention the factors which significantly increase the production of rice in India.**

Ans. The inputs like HYV seeds, fertilisers and irrigation can increase the production of rice in India.

4. Read the passage carefully and answer the questions that follow.

The nature of problems faced by Indian agriculture varies according to agro-ecological and historical experiences of its different regions. Hence, most of the agricultural problems in the country are region specific. Yet, there are some problems which are common and range from physical constraints to institutional hindrances. Irrigation covers only about 33 per cent of the cultivated area in India. The crop production in rest of the cultivated land directly depends on rain. Poor performance of South-West monsoon also adversely affects the supply of canal water for irrigation. On the other hand, the rainfall in Rajasthan and other drought-prone areas is too restricted and highly unreliable. Even the areas receiving high annual rainfall experience considerable fluctuations. This makes them vulnerable to both droughts and floods. Drought is a common phenomenon in the low rainfall areas, which may also experience occasional floods.

(i) **Discuss about the variation in the problems faced by Indian agriculture.**

Ans. The nature of problems faced by Indian agriculture varies according to the agro-ecological and historical experiences in different regions.

(ii) **Discuss about the dependency of agriculture of India, apart from irrigational facilities.**

Ans. Apart from irrigation, Indian crops depends on another source of water, that is rain, mainly monsoonal rain.

(iii) **Mention the region of India, that is vulnerable to both flood and droughts.**

Ans. In India, regions lying in Rajasthan are vulnerable to both flood and droughts.

5. Study the graph carefully and answer the questions that follow. **CBSE 2024**

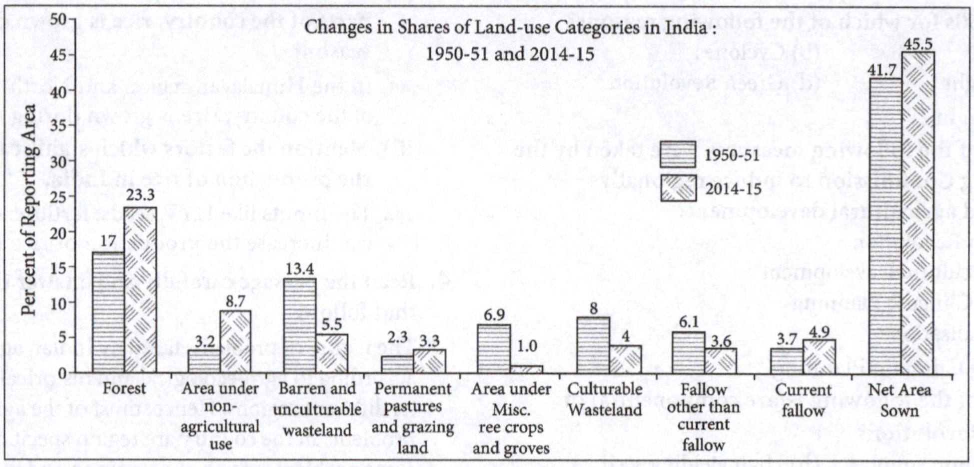

(i) In 2014-15, which category of land-use has undergone the highest net increase in comparison to 1950-51?

Ans. In 2014-15, the forest category of land-use has undergone the highest net increase in comparison to 1950-51.

(ii) In 2014-15, which category of land use has undergone the highest net decline in comparison to 1950-51?

Ans. In 2014-15, the area under miscellaneous tree crops and groves underwent the highest net decline in comparison to 1950-51.

(iii) Mention any two reasons for the decline in land under culturable wasteland.

Ans. The two reasons for the decline in land under culturable wastelands are as follows

(a) By using fertilisers the land is again put to use under cultivation.

(b) Due to the increasing population, this category of land is also put under non-agricultural use.

Map Based Questions

1. On the given political outline map of India, locate and label the following with appropriate symbols.

(i) The leading tea producing state

(ii) The leading jute producing state

(iii) Leading producer state of cotton

(iv) Leading producer of coffee

Ans.

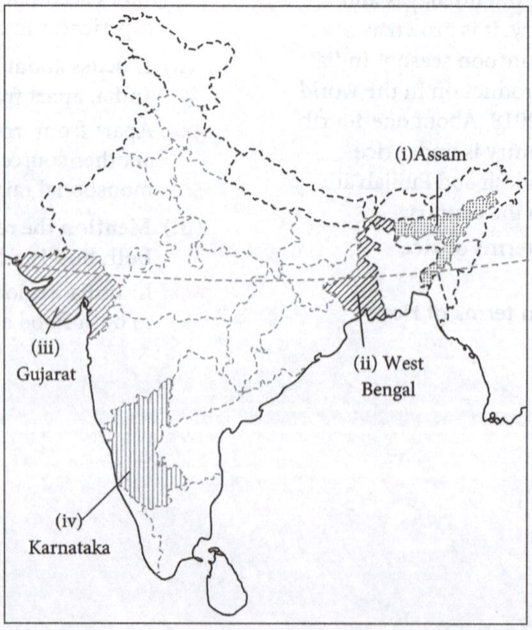

2. On a political map of India, locate the following

(i) Rice producing state of India **(ii) Wheat producing state of India**

(iii) Sugarcane producing state of India

Ans.

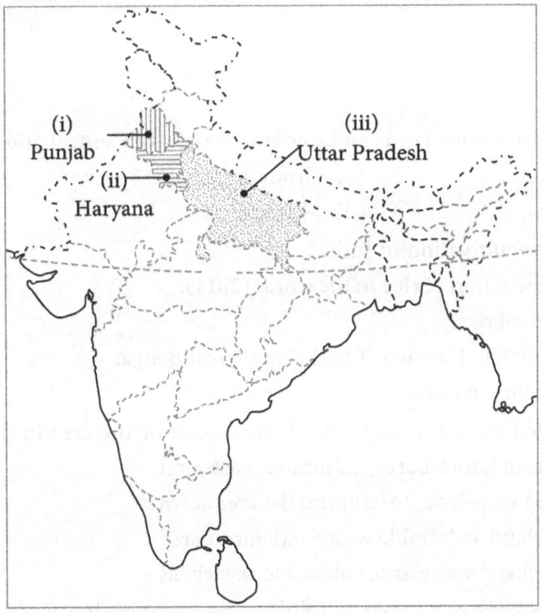

SELF ASSESSMENT TEST

Objective Type Questions

1. Which of the crop is cultivated by marginal lands and under dry areas of Central and Southern states?
   (a) Tur (b) Groundnut
   (c) Rapeseed (d) Mustard
2. Which of this is not true about rice cultivation in India?
   (a) India is ranked second in the production of rice in the world (2011).
   (b) *Aus*, *Aman* and *Boro* are varieties of rice.
   (c) The yield level of rice is low in Punjab, Haryana, Tamil Nadu, West Bengal.
   (d) Rice is grown in about 3000 varieties in India.
3. Which of these is correctly arranged according to their per cent of reporting area in the declining order?
   (a) Net area sown, barren and wasteland, forest area, culturable wasteland
   (b) Culturable wasteland, barren and wasteland, forest area, net area sown
   (c) Net area sown, barren and wasteland, culturable wasteland, forest area
   (d) Net area sown, forest area, barren and wasteland, culturable wasteland
4. Which of these land-use categories have registered a decline in area reported?
   (i) Wasteland (ii) Land pastures
   (iii) Forest area
   Codes
   (a) (i), (ii) and (iii) (b) (i) and (ii)
   (c) (ii) and (iii) (d) (i) and (iii)
5. Which of these crops are grown under dryland farming?
   (i) Ragi (ii) Bajra
   (iii) Rice (iv) Gram
   Codes
   (a) (i), (ii), (iii) and (iv) (b) (i), (ii) and (iv)
   (c) (i), (ii) and (iii) (d) (ii), (iii) and (iv)

Short Answer Type Questions

6. There are certain advantages of common property resources in India. Discuss.
7. Discuss some of the characteristics of wheat as a crop.
8. Explain the conditions for the growth of wheat.
9. Give reasons for the importance of pulses in our diet.

Long Answer Type Questions

10. 'Land use categories are maintained by the land revenue records'. Discuss.
11. Discuss the role of technology in agriculture.
12. Analyse the development of agriculture in India. Give two measures to boost development of agriculture.

4

CHAPTER

Water is a **cyclic resource**[1] which is present in abundance on the globe. Approximately 71% of the Earth's surface is covered with water in which freshwater is only 3% of the total water. A very small proportion of freshwater is effectively available for human use.

Water Resources

YOUR STUDY GOALS

4.1 Water Resources of India
4.2 Deterioration of Water Quality

YOUR PRACTICE GOAL

- Objective Type Questions (36 Qs ; MCQs, Statements, Matching, A-R)
- Subjective Type Questions (10 SAs, 9 LAs)
- Source Based Questions (3 Qs)

4.1 Water Resources of India

- India accounts for about 2.45% of the world's surface area. It has 4% of the world's water resources and more than 17% of the world's population.
- The total water available from annual precipitation is 4,000 cubic km.
- The water available from surface water and replenishable groundwater is 1,869 km. However, only 60% (1,122 cubic km) can be utilised from these resources.

Surface Water Resources

- Rivers, lakes, ponds and tanks are the four major sources of water in India.
- There are about 10,360 rivers and their tributaries are longer than 1.6 km each.
- The mean annual flow in all the river basins is estimated to be 1,869 cubic km. However, only about 690 cubic km (32%) of the available surface water can be utilised due to topographical, hydrological and other constraints.

1 **Cyclic resosource** Resource which can be formed again and again after being used.

- Water flow in a river depends on size of its **catchment area**[2] or **river basin**[3] and rainfall within its catchment area.
- The Ganga, the Brahmaputra and the Barak rivers have huge catchment areas and receive high rainfall. These rivers have 60% of the total surface water resources.
- Much of the annual water flow in South Indian rivers like the Godavari, the Krishna and the Kaveri has been utilised, but it is yet to be done in the Brahmaputra and the Ganga basins.

Groundwater Resources

- The total replenishable groundwater resources in the country are about 432 cubic km.
- The level of groundwater utilisation is relatively high in the river basins of North-Western region and parts of South India.

Groundwater Utilisation	States
Very high utilisation	Punjab, Haryana, Rajasthan, Tamil Nadu
Moderate utilisation	Gujarat, Uttar Pradesh, Bihar, Tripura, Maharashtra
Low utilisation	Chhattisgarh, Odisha, Kerala

Lagoons and Backwaters

- The coast is very rough in some states of India. Due to this, a number of **lagoons**[4] and lakes have formed.
- Kerala, Odisha and West Bengal have vast surface water resources in lagoons and lakes. Although, water is generally brackish in these water bodies, it is used for fishing and irrigating certain varieties of paddy crops, coconut, etc.

Water Demand and Utilisation

- India has traditionally been an agrarian economy with two-third of its population dependent on agriculture.
- Multipurpose river valleys projects, like the Bhakra-Nangal, Hirakud, Damodar Valley, Nagarjuna Sagar, Indira Gandhi Canal Project, etc., have been taken up in the Five Year Plans to increase agricultural production.
- 89% of the surface water and 92% of the groundwater is utilised by agriculture sector.
- Industrial sector uses 2% of the surface water utilisation and 5% of the groundwater. The share of domestic sector is higher (9%) in surface water utilisation as compared to groundwater.

Demand of Water for Irrigation

- In India, irrigation is needed due to spatio-temporal variability in rainfall. The large parts of the country are deficient in rainfall and are drought prone. For example, North-Western India and the Deccan Plateau.
- Winter and summer seasons are more or less dry in most part of the country. Hence, it is difficult to practise agriculture without assured irrigation during dry seasons.
- Some crops, such as rice, sugarcane, jute, etc., need extensive water, which makes irrigation necessary.

---

2 **Catchment Area** The area from which a river gets water from rainfall or other sources.
3 **River Basin** Total area drained by a river and its tributaries is called river basin.
4 **Lagoons** It is a shallow body of water separated from a larger body of water by barrier lands.

- Irrigation helps in multiple cropping and increases agricultural productivity. The High Yielding Varieties of crops need regular moisture supply, which is made possible only by a developed irrigation system.
- **Green Revolution** became successful in Punjab, Haryana and Western Uttar Pradesh due to better irrigation facilities.
- In Punjab, Haryana and Western Uttar Pradesh, more than 85% of their net sown area is under irrigation. Wheat and rice are grown mainly with the help of irrigation in these states.
- Of the total net irrigated area, 76.1% in Punjab and 51.3% in Haryana are irrigated through wells and tubewells. This has led to the depletion of groundwater.
- Over-withdrawals of groundwater in Rajasthan and Maharashtra have increased fluoride concentration in groundwater. This practice has led to an increase in the concentration of arsenic in parts of West Bengal and Bihar.

Pradhan Mantri Krishi Sinchayee Yojana (PMKSY)

The Central Government launched Pradhan Mantri Krishi Sinchayee Yojana during 2015-16 to ensure access to some means of protective irrigation for all agricultural farms. Some of its objectives are

- Increasing water access on the farm and expanding cultivable area under assured irrigation.
- Integrating water source, distribution and its efficient use.
- Improving water use efficiency to reduce wastage and increase availability.
- Introducing sustainable water conservation practices.
- Ensure the integrated development of rainfed areas using the waters held approach towards soil and water conservation, regeneration of ground water, providing livelihood options, etc.

Quick Test 1

1. How much water is available in India from annual precipitation?
2. Name the states where the Green Revolution became successful.
3. Name any two states with low groundwater utilisation.
4. Why is the per capita availability of water decreasing day-by-day?

4.2 Deterioration of Water Quality

- Water quality refers to purity of water, or water without unwanted foreign substances such as micro-organisms, chemicals, industrial and other wastes.
- When toxic substances enter lakes, streams, rivers, oceans and other water bodies, they get dissolved or lie suspended in water. This results in water pollution. Sometimes, these pollutants also seep down and pollute groundwater.

Water Conservation and Management

- Due to decline in availability of freshwater and increased demand, water conservation is necessary.
- Besides conservation of water, attempts should also be made to prevent pollution.
- Watershed development, rainwater harvesting, water recycling, resuse and combined use of water (surface + ground) should be encouraged for sustaining water supply in the long run.

Prevention of Water Pollution

- River water in plains is of low quality as compared to hilly areas. In plains, river water is used intensively for irrigation, drinking, domestic and industrial purposes.
- Water quality of national aquatic resources at 507 stations have been monitored by the **Central Pollution Control Board** (CPCB) in collaboration with **State Pollution Control Boards**. The data obtained from these stations show that organic and bacterial contamination continues to be the main source of pollution in rivers.
- The **Yamuna river** is the **most polluted river in India** between Delhi and Etawah. Other severely polluted rivers are the Sabarmati at Ahmedabad, the Gomti at Lucknow, the Kali, the Adyar, the Cooum (entire stretches), the Vaigai at Madurai, the Musi of Hyderabad and the Ganga at Kanpur and Varanasi.
- The legislative provisions such as the **Water (Prevention and Control of Pollution) Act 1974**, and **Environment Protection Act 1986** have not been implemented effectively. The project **Water Cess Act, 1977**, works on reducing the pollution.

Recycle and Reuse of Water

- Availability of freshwater can be improved by recycle and reuse of water.
- Industries can use water of lesser quality such as reclaimed wastewater for cooling and fire fighting to prevent their water cost.
- Water collected after bathing, washing utensils and vehicles can be used for gardening.
- At present, recycling of water is practised on a limited scale, but recycling has an enormous scope to replenish water.

Watershed Management

- Watershed management basically refers to efficient management and conservation of surface and groundwater resources. It aims at bringing about balance between natural resources on the one hand and society on the other.
- **Haryali** is a watershed development project sponsored by the Central Government, being executed by Gram Panchayats with people's participation. It aims to enable the rural population to conserve water for drinking, irrigation, fisheries and afforestation.
- **Neeru-Meeru** (Water and You) programme (in Andhra Pradesh) and Arvary Pani Sansad (in Alwar, Rajasthan) have initiated constructions of various water-harvesting structures such as percolation tanks, dug out ponds (Johad), check dams, etc., through people's participation.
- Tamil Nadu has made water harvesting structures in the houses compulsory.

Atal Bhujal Yojana

- Atal Bhujal Yojana (Atal Jal) is being implemented in 8220 water stressed Gram Panchayats of 229 administrative blocks/ talukas in 80 districts of seven states,viz. Gujarat, Haryana, Karnataka, Madhya Pradesh, Maharashtra, Rajasthan and Uttar Pradesh.
- These states account for about 37 per cent of the total number of water-stressed (over-exploited, critical and semi-critical) blocks in India.
- One of the key aspects of ATAL JAL is to bring in behavioural changes in the community, changing their mindset from consumption to conservation and smart water management.

Watershed Development in Ralegan Siddhi: A Case Study

- Ralegan Siddhi is a small village in the district of Ahmadnagar, Maharashtra. In 1975, this village was caught in a web of poverty and illegal liquor trade. A retired army personnel settled down in the village and took up the task of watershed development. He convinced villagers about the importance of family planning and voluntary labour; preventing open grazing, felling trees and liquor prohibition.

Initiatives Taken by the Villagers

- Voluntary labour was promoted to ensure minimum dependence on the government for financial aids.
- The percolation tank that got damaged was voluntarily repaired by the people.
- A youth group called **Tarun Mandal** was formed to work on issues like dowry system, caste discrimination and untouchability.
- Liquor distilling units were removed and prohibition imposed.
- The village imposed the ban on the cultivation of water-intensive crops like sugarcane. Crops such as pulses, oilseeds and certain cash crops with low water requirements were encouraged.
- All elections to local bodies began to be held on the basis of consensus. A system of Nyay Panchayats (informal courts) were also set up.
- A school costing ₹ 22 lakh was constructed using only the resources of the village.

Rainwater Harvesting

- Rainwater harvesting is a method to capture and store rainwater for various uses.
- It is a low cost and eco-friendly technique for preserving every drop of water by guiding the rain water to borewell, pits and wells.
- Traditional rainwater harvesting in rural areas is done by using surface storage bodies, like lakes, ponds, irrigation tanks, etc.
- In Rajasthan, rainwater harvesting structures locally known as **Kund** or **Tanka** (a covered underground tank) are constructed near or in the house or village to store harvested rainwater.

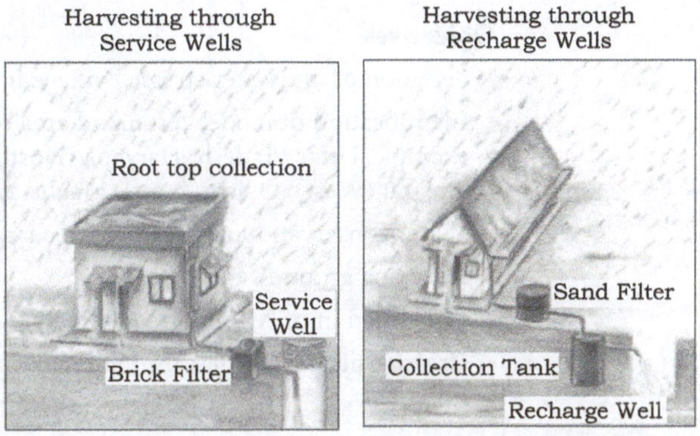

▲ *Various Methods of Rainwater Harvesting*

Benefits of Rainwater Harvesting

- It increases water availability.
- It checks the declining groundwater table.
- It improves the quality of groundwater through dilution of contaminants like florides and nitrates.
- It prevents soil erosion and flooding.
- It arrests salt water intrusion in coastal areas if used to recharge aquifers.
- It increases the dependence on groundwater for domestic use.
- It saves energy to pump groundwater as recharge leads to rise in groundwater table.

Other Methods to Solve Water Scarcity

- Water particularly in coastal areas and brackish water in arid and semi-arid areas can be used after **desalination**[5].
- Water can be transferred from water surplus areas to water deficit areas through inter-linking of rivers.

---

5 **Desalination** It is a process that removes salts from sea water or saline water.

India's National Water Policy, 2012

The objective of the National Water Policy, 2012 is to assess the existing situation and to propose a framework for a plan of action with a unified national perspective. Some of the salient features of this policy are

- Emphasis on the need for a national water framework law, comprehensive legislation for optimum development of inter-state rivers and river valleys.
- Water should be treated as an economic good after meeting essential needs to promote its conservation and efficient use.
- The policy highlights the need for adaptations strategies to address the impacts of climate change on water resource.
- Development of a system for benchmarks for water uses and water auditing.
- Removal of large disparity in stipulations for water supply in urban areas and in rural areas.
- Management of water resources and services with community participation.

Jal Kranti Abhiyan (2015-16)

The Government of India launched the Jal Kranti Abhiyan in 2015-16 with an aim to ensure water security through per capita availability of water in the country.

Objectives

- Selection of one water stressed village in each 672 districts of the country to create a 'Jal Gram'.
- Identification of model command area of about 1000 hectares in different parts of the country, for example, Uttar Pradesh, Haryana (North), Karnataka, Telangana, Tamil Nadu (South), Rajasthan, Gujarat (West), Odisha (East), Meghalaya (North-East).
- Water conservation and artificial recharge.
- Reducing groundwater pollution.
- Construction of Arsenic-free wells in selected areas of the country.
- Creating mass awareness through social media, radio, TV, print media, poster and essay writing competitions in schools.

Quick Test 2

1. What do you understand by the water quality?
2. Write the aim of Haryali project.
3. How is traditional rainwater harvesting practised in rural areas?
4. What is the aim of Jal Kranti Abhiyan?

Mind Map

WATER RESOURCES

1 Classification of Water Resources

Surface Water Resource
- It includes rivers, lakes, ponds.
- There are about 10,360 rivers.
- Water flow in a river depends on size of its catchment area or river basin(Ganga,Brahmaputra and Barak).

Lagoons and Backwaters
- These are a shallow body of water separated from a larger body of water by barrier lands.
- Due to very rough coast in some regions a number of lagoons and lakes have formed.

Groundwater Resources
- It includes wells and springs
- Total replenishable groundwater resources in the country is about 432 cubic km.

Groundwater Utilisation
- **Very High Utilisation** Punjab, Haryana, Rajasthan, Tamil Nadu
- **Moderate Utilisation** Gujarat, Uttar Pradesh, Bihar, Tripura, Maharashtra
- **Low Utilisation** Chhattisgarh, Odisha, Kerala

2 Water Demand and Utilisation

Domestic Sector
9% surface water

Industrial Sector
- 2% surface water
- 5% groundwater

Agriculture Sector
- 89% surface water utilisation
- 92% groundwater utilisation

Uses in Irrigation
North-Western part and Deccan plateau region uses irrigation as they do not receive rainfall.

3 Emerging Water Problems

Deterioration in Water Quality
Water gets polluted by unwanted toxic substance, such as chemical, industrial waste, micro-organisms.

4 Water Conservation and Management

Recycle and Reuse of Water
- Availability of freshwater can be improved by recycle and reuse of water.
- Reuse of poor quality water for industries, gardening and other domestic works.

Watershed Management
- Efficient management and conservation of surface and groundwater.
- **Haryali** It aims to enable the rural population to conserve water for drinking, irrigation, fisheries and afforestation.
- **Neeru-Meeru Arvary Pani Sansad** Constructed various water-harvesting structures such as percolation tanks, dug out ponds (Johad), check dams, etc.

Rainwater Harvesting
- It is a method to capture and store rainwater, also used for recharging ground water.
- Low cost and eco-friendly technique for preserving water by collecting rain water to borewell, pits and wells, e.g., kund, tanka.

Prevention of Water Pollution
- Includes monitoring of water bodies by State and Central Board
- Water Cess Act, 1977 works on reducing the pollution.

NCERT Folder

Choose the right answers of the following from the given options

(i) **Which one of the following types describe water as a resource?**

(a) Abiotic resource (b) Non-renewable resource
(c) Biotic resource (d) Non-cyclic resource

Ans. (a) Abiotic resource

(ii) **Which one of the following South Indian states has the highest groundwater utilisation (in per cent) of its total groundwater potential?**

(a) Tamil Nadu (b) Karnataka
(c) Andhra Pradesh (d) Kerala

Ans. (a) Tamil Nadu

(iii) **The highest proportion of the total water used in the country is in which one of the following sectors?**

(a) Irrigation (b) Industries
(c) Domestic use (d) None of these

Ans. (a) Irrigation

Answer the following questions in about 30 words

(i) **It is said that the water resources in India have been depleting very fast. Discuss the factors responsible for depletion of water resources.**

Ans. Following are the factors responsible for depletion of water resources

- Pollution by micro-organisms, chemicals and industrial wastes.
- When toxic substances enters lakes and streams, they pollute the waters of these water bodies.
- Over exploitation by human beings.

(ii) **What factors are responsible for the highest groundwater development in the states of Punjab, Haryana and Tamil Nadu?**

Ans. Factors that are responsible for the highest groundwater development in the states of Punjab, Haryana and Tamil Nadu

- In these states the main source of irrigation is groundwater. Due to success of Green Revolution, groundwater has been used at a high pace.
- Water intensive crops such as wheat, rice, are mainly grown in these states, which require assured irrigation.

(iii) **Why the share of agricultural sector in total water used in the country is expected to decline?**

Ans. Following are the reasons behind decrease in share of water use in agricultural sector

- The land-use is increasing for non-agricultural use and hence, farming land is shrinking day by day.
- Industrial and domestic sectors in country are likely to expand which increase use of water in these sectors in comparison to agriculture.

(iv) **What can be possible impacts of consumption of contaminated/uncleaned water on the people?**

Ans. The use of uncleaned water results in bad effects on the people. These include

- Diseases such as cholera, diarrhoea, tuberculosis, jaundice, etc.
- Increasing concentration of arsenic and flouride results in deadly diseases such as cancer.

Answer the following questions in about 150 words

(i) **Discuss the availability of water resources in the country and factors that determine its spatial distribution.**

Ans. India accounts 4% of world's water resources. The total water availability from precipitation in the country in a year is about 4,000 cubic km.

In India, water resources can be classified into

- **Surface Water** River, lakes, ponds and tanks are the major source of surface water. In the country, there are about 10,360 rivers and mean annual flow in all river basins in India is 1,869 cubic km.
- **Groundwater Resources** The total replenishable groundwater resources in the country are about 432 cubic km. The Ganga and the Yamuna basins have about 46% of the total replenishable water in India.
- **Lagoons and Backwater** The states like Kerala, Odisha, West Bengal have vast surface water in lagoons and backwaters.

  Factors that determine spatial distribution of water resources are

- **Natural Factors** The presence of rivers, lakes, ponds in the region. The percolation capacity of surface rocks determines the presence of groundwater table beneath the surface of the Earth.

- **Climatic Factors** The amount of rainfall determines total availability of water resources in a region, especially in Southern part of India.
- **Technological Factors** Watershed management and rainwater harvesting rich areas have better water resources than the areas which are not utilising their resources properly.

(ii) The depleting water resources may lead to social conflicts and disputes. Elaborate it with suitable examples.

Ans. The depleting water resources may lead to social conflicts and disputes due to the following reasons

- As the population is increasing, the demand for water resources is increasing. But due to depletion and pollution of water, the supply of resources in limited. It is bound to create conflicts.
- Due to careless management of water, excessive utilisation and increasing concentration of contaiminants, there is artificial scarcity of water. This results in some regions not getting adequate water supply than others which leads to disputes.
- Some regions of the country have surplus water resources while others have deficit resources. The water surplus regions share their water resources with water deficit regions that creates controversies among states.
- Contaimination of groundwater resources in regions of Rajasthan and West Bengal has further reduced the availability of water resources in these regions. It creates intra-state water disputes in these regions.
- Depletion of water in rivers, ponds, lakes also affects the fishing community for whom these water bodies are a source of livelihood. This will also increase conflict.

Some of the water disputes between states are

- Cauvery water dispute between Tamil Nadu, Karnataka, and Kerala.
- Sutlej-Yamuna link dispute between Punjab, Haryana and Rajasthan.

(iii) What is watershed management? Do you think it can play an important role in sustainable development?

Ans. Watershed management refers to efficient management
and conservation of surface and groundwater resources. It includes prevention of surface runoff and storage and recharge of groundwater by different methods such as percolation tanks, recharge wells, etc. It is a comprehensive strategy that involves following

- The conservation, regeneration and judicious use of all natural resources (land, water, plants and animals) and human resources.
- Creating a balance among natural elements as well as in society. Community participation is a key to success of a watershed development programme.

Yes, watershed management can play significant role in sustainable development in the following ways

- It will improve the quality of both the surface water resources as well as groundwater resources.
- It will conserve water, regulate water flow and help in reducing risks arising due to drought conditions.
- It helps in recharging groundwater levels and reduces the concentration of contaiminants.
- It improves agriculture in the region and helps in maintaining regular income for farmers.

Therefore, by increasing awareness regarding benefits of watershed development, management among people in the country and through integrated water resource management approach, water availability can be ensured on sustainable basis.

Exam Pattern Questions

Objective Type Questions

Multiple Choice Questions (MCQs)

1. Choose from the following the total amount of rainfall occuring in India. (In cubic kilometre)

(a) 2,000 (b) 3,000 (c) 4,000 (d) 5,000

2. What percentage of world's water resources are present in India?

(a) 2% (b) 3% (c) 4% (d) 5%

3. The water flow in a river does not depend upon which of the given factors? CBSE Diksha

(a) Size of catchment area
(b) Rainfall in catchment area
(c) Length of the river
(d) Gradient of the land

4. Ganga, Brahmaputra and Barak rivers account for ...... of total surface water resources of India.

(a) 68% (b) 75%
(c) 12% (d) 60%

5. Choose the correct option to fill in the blank. The groundwater utilisation is very high in .... If the present trend of groundwater utilisation continues, it would be very difficult to meet the water needs. CBSE 2024

(a) Punjab (b) Odisha
(c) Kerala (d) Chhattisgarh

6. In which of the following states lagoons and backwater sources of water are not found?

(a) Uttar Pradesh (b) Kerala
(c) Odisha (d) West Bengal

7. Which one of the following sectors utilises the highest surface and groundwater in India? CBSE 2024 C

(a) Industrial (b) Power
(c) Agricultural (d) Domestic

8. Irrigation in certain parts of the country is neccessary due to which of the following reasons?

(a) Rainfall deficiency
(b) Dry winters and summers
(c) Breaks in monsoon
(d) All of the above

9. The watershed management programme in Jhabua district of Madhya Pradesh is funded by which one of the following ministries? CBSE 2025

(a) Rural Development (b) Environment
(c) Transport (d) Irrigation

10. Which of the following is the correct abbreviation for stating the meaning of CPCB?

(a) Community Pollution Control Board
(b) Central Population Control Board
(c) Council of Pollution and Conservation Board
(d) Central Pollution Control Board

11. Neeru-Meeru watershed management programme is associated with which of the following states? CBSE 2024

(a) Rajasthan (b) Tamil Nadu
(c) Andhra Pradesh (d) Haryana

12. 'Haryali' – a watershed development project in India is sponsored by which one of the following? CBSE 2024 C

(a) Central Government (b) State Governments
(c) District Administration
(d) Non-Governmental Organisation

13. Which one of the following is not the objective of 'Haryali watershed development project'? CBSE Term I 2021

(a) Drinking water (b) Irrigation
(c) Fishing (d) Industries

14. Which of the following programmes sponsored by Central Government aims at enabling the rural population to conserve water for drinking, irrigation, fisheries and afforestation? CBSE Sample Paper Term I 2021

(a) Arvary Pani Sansad (b) Haryali
(c) Neeru-Meeru (d) Narmada Bachao

15. The success of watershed development in an area largely depends upon which of the following?

(a) Relief structure of the area
(b) Climatic conditions of the area
(c) Community participation
(d) Nature of river in the area

16. Which of these options correctly defines watershed management?

(a) A method to capture and store rainwater.
(b) Recycling and reuse of water.
(c) Efficient management and conservation of water resources.
(d) Awareness generation programmes.

17. Which of the following is not a characteristic of rainwater harvesting? CBSE Diksha

(a) It recharges ground water aquifers.
(b) It is high costing and not eco-friendly.
(c) It improves the quality of water.
(d) It checks the declining water table.

18. ***Kund*** **or** ***tanka*****, a covered underground tank is constructed for rainwater harvesting mainly in which of these states?**

(a) Haryana (b) Punjab
(c) Rajasthan (d) Uttar Pradesh

19. Which of the following is the main objective of 'Jal Kranti Abhiyan'? **CBSE 2024**

(a) Per capita water availability assurance
(b) Rainwater harvesting
(c) Conservation of water resources
(d) Providing sufficient water for agriculture

20. Which of the following city is majorly contributing towards polluting the river Ganga by disposing the industrial waste into it? **CBSE Diksha**

(a) Kanpur (b) Rishikesh (c) Varanasi (d) Agra

21. Identify the statement that is not true with regard to watershed management? **CBSE SQP-2024**

I. It refers to efficient management and conservation of surface and groundwater resources.
II. Watershed management includes judicious use of all resources – both natural and human with in a watershed.
III. Watershed management aims at bringing about balance between natural resources on the one hand and society on the other.
IV. The success of watershed development solely depends upon the state government.

Options

(a) Statement I and IV (b) Only II
(c) Only III (d) Statement IV

22. Which of the following statements is correct about water resources in India?

(i) India accounts for about 8% of the world's water resources.
(ii) The total water available from annual precipitation in India is about 4000 cubic km.
(iii) The total utilisable water resource in the country is only 1,869 cubic km.
(iv) Much of the annual water flow in South Indian rivers like the Godavari, the Krishna and the Kaveri has been harnessed.

Codes

(a) (i), (ii) and (iii) (b) (ii), (iii) and (iv)
(c) (i), (iii) and (iv) (d) (i), (ii) and (iv)

23. Which of the following statements is/are true?

(i) Agriculture accounts for 92% of groundwater utilisation in India.
(ii) Over-use of groundwater resources has led to depletion of groundwater in certain states.

Codes

(a) Only (i) (b) Both (i) and (ii)
(c) Only (ii) (d) None of these

24. Which of the following states have very low groundwater utilisation in India?

(i) Chhattisgarh (ii) Punjab
(iii) Kerala (iv) Tamil Nadu

Codes

(a) (ii), (iii) and (iv)
(b) (i), (ii), (iii) and (iv)
(c) (i) and (iii)
(d) (ii) and (iv)

25. Which of the following statements is/are true?

(i) Water quality is relatively better in upper hilly terrains.
(ii) The concentration of pollutants in the rivers remain high during the summer season.
(iii) Organic and bacterial contaminants are the main source of pollution in the rivers.

Codes

(a) (i) and (ii) (b) (ii) and (iii)
(c) (i), (ii) and (iii) (d) (i) and (iii)

26. Which of the following are the main objectives of the Jal Kranti Abhiyan?

(i) Water conservation and artificial recharge
(ii) Creating mass awareness
(iii) Reducing groundwater pollution

Codes

(a) (i) and (ii) (b) (i), (ii) and (iii)
(c) (ii) and (iii) (d) (i) and (iii)

27. Study the following facts and choose the correct option.

(i) These days 'rainwater harvesting' is being taken up on massive scale in many states.
(ii) Urban areas have benefited from rainwater harvesting.
(iii) Water demand has been increasing in most of the cities and towns.
(iv) There is no benefit of rainwater harvesting for rural areas. **CBSE Term I 2021**

Codes

(a) Only (i), (ii) and (iii) are correct.
(b) Only (ii), (iii) and (iv) are correct
(c) Only (i), (iii) and (iv) are correct.
(d) (i), (ii), (iii) and (iv) are correct.

Arrange the Following

28. Which of these states are correctly arranged in terms of groundwater utilisation (high to low)?

(i) Kerala (ii) Punjab
(iii) Uttar Pradesh

Codes

(a) (i), (ii), (iii) (b) (ii), (iii), (i)
(c) (iii), (ii), (i) (d) (i), (iii), (ii)

Match the Following

29.

List I (Sector)	List II (Water Utilisation)
A. Domestic	1. 89%
B. Agriculture	2. 2%
C. Industrial	3. 9%

Codes

	A	B	C		A	B	C
(a)	3	1	2	(b)	2	1	3
(c)	1	2	3	(d)	3	2	1

30.

List I (Act/Policy)	List II (Year)
A. Water (Prevention and Control Pollution) Act	1. 1986
B. Environment Protection Act	2. 1974
C. The Water Cess Act	3. 2012
D. National Water Policy	4. 1977

Codes

	A	B	C	D		A	B	C	D
(a)	3	4	1	2	(b)	2	1	4	3
(c)	1	4	2	3	(d)	3	1	4	2

31.

List I	List II
A. Yamuna	1. Lukhnow
B. Gomti	2. Delhi
C. Vaigai	3. Varanasi
D. Ganga	4. Madurai

Codes

	A	B	C	D		A	B	C	D
(a)	3	1	2	4	(b)	2	1	4	3
(c)	2	3	4	1	(d)	1	4	2	3

32.

List I	List II
A. Pradhan Mantri Krishi Sinchayee Yojana	1. Behavioural changes in water consumption
B. Atal Bhujal Yojana	2. Watershed management
C. Neeru-Meeru	3. Protective irrigation
D. Jal Kranti Abhiyan	4. Water security through per capita availability of water

Codes

	A	B	C	D		A	B	C	D
(a)	3	1	2	4	(b)	2	4	1	3
(c)	3	1	4	2	(d)	1	3	2	4

Assertion-Reason

Directions (Q. Nos. 33-36) In the questions given below are two statements labelled as Assertion (A) and other labelled as Reason (R). In the context of two statements which one of the following is correct?

Codes

(a) Both A and R are true, but R is not the correct explanation of A
(b) Both A and R are true and R is the correct explanation of A
(c) Both A and R are incorrect
(d) A is correct, but R is incorrect

33. Assertion (A) Irrigation is needed in India because of spatio-temporal variability of rainfall in the country.

Reason (R) Agriculture accounts for 92% of groundwater utilisation in India.

34. Assertion (A) India has to take quick steps and make policies and laws for conservation of water resources.

Reason (R) The per capita availability of water is declining due to increasing population and existing resources are getting polluted.

35. Assertion (A) The major rivers of the country generally retain better water quality in less densely populated upper stretches in hilly areas.

Reason (R) In plains, river water is used intensively for irrigation, drinking, domestic and industrial purposes.

36. Assertion (A) Laws are necessary but cannot deal effectively with the problem of water pollution.

Reason (R) Without public awareness laws to protect water will have a very limited impact.

Answers

1. (c) 4,000
2. (c) 4%
3. (c) Length of the river
4. (d) 60%
5. (a) Punjab
6. (a) Uttar Pradesh
7. (c) Agricultural
8. (d) All of the above
9. (a) Rural Development
10. (d) Central Pollution Control Board
11. (c) Andhra Pradesh
12. (a) Central Government
13. (d) Industries
14. (b) Haryali
15. (c) Community participation
16. (c) Efficient management and conservation of water resources.
17. (b) It is high costing and not eco-friendly.
18. (c) Rajasthan
19. (a) Per capita water availability assurance
20. (a) Kanpur
21. (d) Statement IV
22. (b) (ii), (iii), (iv)
23. (b) Both (i) and (ii)
24. (c) (i) and (iii)
25. (c) (i), (ii) and (iii)
26. (b) (i), (ii) and (iii)
27. (a) Only (i), (ii) and (iii) are correct.
28. (b) (ii), (iii), (i)
29. (a)
30. (b)
31. (b)
32. (a)
33. (a) Both A and R are true, but R is not the correct explanation of A
34. (b) Both A and R are true and R is the correct explanation of A
35. (b) Both A and R are true and R is the correct explanation of A.
36. (b) Both A and R are true and R is the correct explanation of A.

Subjective Questions

Short Answer Type Questions

1. Define water quality. Explain the reasons of deteriorating surface water quality in India.

Ans. Water quality refers to the physical, chemical and biological characteristics of water that determine its suitability for various uses. Water quality is deteriorating in India due to factors like industrial pollution, untreated sewage discharge, agricultural runoff containing pesticides and fertilisers and over-extraction of water. These activities lead to the contamination of rivers, lakes and groundwater. Additionally, rapid urbanisation and improper waste disposal further contribute to the worsening of water quality, making it unsafe for consumption.

2. Describe any three major problems related to water in India.

Or **Explain any three major problems related to water in India.**

Ans. The three major problems related to water in India are as follows

(i) **Insufficient Amount of Freshwater** In India, there is insufficient amount of freshwater available to meet the growing demand. Increasing population is also shrinking the per capita availability of water.

(ii) **Water Pollution** It has increased rapidly after industrialisation and urbanisation. They have contributed the most in water pollution in India.

(iii) **Uneven Distribution of Water Resources** Water resources in India are very unevenly distributed. Some regions are facing scarcity of water whereas other areas are facing floods.

3. Why should we reuse and recycle water? Suggest some ways by which water can be reused or recycled.

Ans. Water is a precious resource and we need it to fulfil our daily needs. The demand of freshwater is high but supply is less due to increased population. So, it is necessary to reuse and recycle water to conserve better quality water for drinking.

Ways to reuse and recycle water

- Industries can use water of lesser quality such as reclaimed wastewater for cooling and fire fighting to prevent their water cost.
- Water collected after bathing, washing utensils and vehicles can be used for gardening.

4. "The assessment, efficient use and conservation of water are necessary to ensure development." Explain in the light of values regarding conservation of water resources.

Or **Why is conservation of water resources necessary? Explain any three reasons.**

Ans. To ensure development, it is necessary to do assessment, efficient use and conservation of water. Without proper availability of water there will be no meaning of development.

There is need to conserve the water resources due to the following reasons

(i) **Low Availability of Freshwater** In India freshwater is not available to meet the demand of a large population. Increasing population is also shrinking the per capita availability of water.

To guarantee the adequate supply of freshwater, we need to create awareness among people for conservation of water resources.

(ii) **To Irrigate Crops** India is an agrarian economy. Most of its population is dependent on agriculture. Water is required to irrigate crops and ensure the employment of agrarian workers and development of economy.

(iii) **For Sustainable Development** Water is a life giving precious resource. If we do not save and conserve it, development cannot be possible. So, to ensure sustainable development, we need to be responsible citizen and sensitise people to positively cooperate for water conservation.

5. "Indiscriminate use of water by increasing population and industrial expansion has led to degradation of the quality of water considerably." Evaluate the statement. Competency Based Que

Ans. The quality of water is degraded by indiscriminate use of water by increasing population and industrial expansion. It can be explained through the following points

- Sewage, garbage and liquid waste of households and industries are discharged into lakes and rivers. These wastes contain harmful chemicals and toxins which make the water polluted.
- The use of various types of chemical fertilisers like inorganic fertilisers, pesticides and herbicides, etc also pollute groundwater, as they infiltrate the soil to reach the groundwater.
- Due to discharge of untreated waste into the rivers, the rivers get polluted which makes the water in the rivers unfit for human use.

6. Explain watershed management. What is its aim?

Ans. Watershed management refers to the technique of efficient management of surface and groundwater resources.

Major aims of watershed management are as follows

- Prevention of surface runoff.
- Storage and recharge of groundwater by different methods such as percolation tanks, recharge well, etc.
- The conservation, regeneration and judicious use of all natural resources (land, water, plants and animals) and human resources.
- To create balanced development and environment conservation.
- To involve community to take part for the success of watershed development programme.

7. Analyse the economic and social values of rainwater harvesting. Competency Based Que

Ans. The economic values associated with rainwater harvesting are

- It creates employment opportunities for the people as it leads to improvements in agriculture and allied activities.
- It leads to cost saving because people do not have to obtain water from wells, tubewells or municipal water supply.
- It also generate local employment as rainwater harvesting structures have to be created.

Social values of rainwater harvesting are

- The rainwater harvesting is environmental friendly and reduces social conflict among the people of the society.
- It reduces the harmful effects of droughts and floods that affect the vulnerable communities every year.
- It also leads to social cooperation betwen various communities in making the rainwater harvesting programmes successful.

8. State any three benefits of water harvesting. Also give another method to solve the problem of water scarcity in water deficit areas.

Ans. Three benefits of water harvesting are as follows

(i) With the help of water harvesting technique, we can use water all the year round for various purposes.

(ii) With the help of this technique the quality of groundwater can also be improved by dilution of pollution like fluoride and nitrates.

(iii) The areas which are prone to continuous soil erosion and flooding can also be benefitted by this technique.

Some other methods to solve water scarcity are

- To solve the problem of water scarcity, we can use brackish (salty) water of arid, semi-arid and coastal areas after desalinisation processes.
- By interlinking of rivers, water can be transferred from the water surplus areas to water deficit areas.

9. Write the objective of India's National Water Policy, 2012. Give any three salient features of this policy.

Or **Analyse any three key feaures of 'Indian National Water Policy'.** **CBSE 2024**

Ans. The objective of the National Water Policy, 2012 is to assess the existing situation and to propose a framework for a plan of action with a unified national perspective.

Salient features of National Water Policy 2012 are

(i) It emphasis on the need for a national water framework law, comprehensive legislation for optimum development of inter-state rivers and river valleys.

(ii) The policy highlights the need for adaptations strategies to address the impacts of climate change on water resource.

(iii) It is a system to evolve benchmarks for water uses for different purposes, i.e., water footprints, and water auditing be developed to ensure efficient use of water.

10. Analyse the three objectives of 'Jal Kranti Abhiyan' in India. **CBSE 2024**

Ans. The Jal Kranti Abhiyan was launched by the Government of India in 2015-16 with an aim to ensure water security through per capita availability of water in the country. The following activities have been proposed under the Jal Kranti Abhiyan

(i) Selection of one water stressed village in each 672 districts of the country to create a 'Jal Gram'.

(ii) Identification of model command area of about 1000 hectares in different parts of the country, for example, Uttar Pradesh, Haryana (North), Karnataka, Telangana, Tamil Nadu (South), Rajasthan, Gujarat (West), Odisha (East), Meghalaya (North-East).

(iii) Decreasing pollution is another objective which include

- Water conservation and artificial recharge.
- Reducing groundwater pollution.
- Construction of Arsenic-free wells in selected areas of the country.

Long Answer Type Questions

1. Write an account on the usability of surface water resources in India.

Ans. Surface water as a natural resource has a lot of usability to humans in many forms like drinking water, irrigation and in industries as well. This usability is not uniform in every sector as one sector requires more use of this resource while others uses a very less percentage of water as a resource.

Following are the major distribution of usage of water resource in India

- Agriculture accounts for most of the surface and groundwater utilisation, it accounts for 89 per cent of the surface water and 92 per cent of the groundwater utilisation.
- While the share of industrial sector is limited to 2 per cent of the surface water utilisation and 5 per cent of the ground-water,
- The share of domestic sector is higher nearly 9 per cent in surface water utilisation as compared to groundwater.
- The share of agricultural sector in total water utilisation is much higher than other sectors.

2. Describe any two sources of water pollution in India. Suggest any three measures to overcome the water pollution. **CBSE 2024**

Ans. The two major sources of water pollution in India are

(i) **Industrial effluents** Industries release harmful chemicals and other industrial waste into water bodies, which cause water pollution.

(ii) **Agricultural effluents** Drains carrying agricultural effluents such as fertilisers and insecticides join rivers and pollute them.

Ways to overcome water pollution

(i) Public awareness is necessary to overcome water pollution. The public should be made aware of the importance of water and the impacts of water pollution. Public awareness and action can be very effective in reducing the pollutants from agricultural activities and domestic and industrial discharges.

(ii) Industries should be located away from rivers. If they are located near rivers, they should adopt proper waste water treatment to reduce water pollution.

(iii) Farmers should be encouraged to use natural fertilisers over chemical fertilisers. The government should provide the necessary help and support to farmers so they can use natural fertilisers.

3. What are the major problems in the development of water resources in the country? Discuss in brief.

Ans. The major problems in the development of water resources in the country are as follows

- **Insufficient Availability of Water** Total available water resource in India has been estimated to be around 1,869 cubic km. Out of this, only 1,122 cubic km water potential is available for utilisation. Availability of water in ratio of population is low and per capita availability is decreasing day by day.

- **Uneven Distribution of Water** Distribution of water resource in India is very uneven. Some areas are facing scarcity while some have surplus. Hence, it creates difficulty improperly managing the resources.
- **Over Utilisation of Water** Due to over utilisation of this valuable resource, it is difficult to provide water to all regions. Over supply of water in urban areas results in lack of water supply in other areas.
- **Deteriorating Quality of Water** Despite having access to water supply, there is a major issue of quality of water. Poor quality water and polluted water resources causes various water borne diseases such as diarrhoea.

4. Write the aim and objectives of Pradhan Mantri Krishi Sinchayee Yojana.

Ans. Pradhan Mantri Krishi Sinchayee Yojana was launched by the Central Government during 2015-16 with an objective to ensure access to some means of protective irrigation for all agricultural farms in the country, thus bringing much desired rural prosperity.

Some of the broad objectives of this programmes are to

- Enhance the physical access of water on the farm and expand cultivable area under assured irrigation (*Har khet ko pani*)
- Promote integration of water source, distribution and its efficient use, to make best use of water through appropriate technologies and practices.
- Improve on-farm water use efficiency to reduce wastage and increase availability both in duration and exent; irrigation and other water saving technologies (Per drop more crop).
- Introduce sustainable water conservation practices.
- Ensure the integrated development of rainfed areas using the waters held approach towards soil and water conservation, regeneration of groundwater, providing livelihood options, etc.

5. "Irrigation is needed because of spatio-temporal variability in rainfall in the country". Elucidate.

Competency Based Que

Or **Why demand of water for irrigation increasing in India? Explain with example.**

Ans. In India, water is mainly used for irrigation in agriculture. Since, the agriculture of India is based on monsoon with spatial and temporal variation, need of irrigation is high.

Following are the reasons which show necessity of irrigation in India

- **Seasonal Rainfall** Rainfall in India is highly seasonal. Most of the rainfall occurs during four months from June to September. The remaining part of the year remains dry.
- **Uncertain Rainfall** Monsoonal rainfall is uncertain in time and space. Normal rainfall has variations from year to year which results in famines. Hence, irrigation is necessary for agriculture in areas of inadequate rainfall.
- **Unequal Distribution of Rainfall** The annual rainfall is unevenly distributed. About 30% of total land area receive less than 75 cm rainfall. In such areas, irrigation supplements rainfall.
- **Demand for Crops** Some particular crops like *rabi* crops and cash crops like cotton, sugarcane and jute require intensive irrigation.
- **To Increase Productivity** Expansion of irrigation facilities results in increase in productivity and enhances the production of food crops. This helps to meet the demand of foodgrains in India.

6. How do human beings pollute the water through industrial and agricultural activities? Explain.

Ans. Industrial and agricultural activities are the main causes of water pollution.

They are discussed below

Industrial Activities

- The waste generated in the industrial units are directly disposed in the lakes, streams, rivers, ocean and other water bodies.
- These waste contain toxic material/elements which are harmful for the aquatic life.
- The pollution in Ganga and Yamuna rivers is mainly caused due to disposing of industrial waste, especially in Delhi, Kanpur, Agra, etc.
- Industrial activities are also responsible for underground water pollution.

Agricultural Activities

- Agricultural activities are mainly responsible for the surface and groundwater pollution in India. The surface runoff from the agricultural field bring fertilisers into the lakes, streams, rivers, oceans and other water bodies.
- Fertiliser and other toxic material also seep down along with water in the aquifers. Hence, groundwater resources gets polluted due to agricultural activities.

7. What is included in watershed management in broad sense? Discuss some programmes and efforts by the government for watershed development and management.

Ans. Watershed development is a very important method to conserve water resources, increase agricultural production and stop ecological degradation and hence, it improves the living conditions of the people.

The Central and State Governments have initiated many watershed development and management programmes in the country. Some of these are

- Haryali is a watershed development project sponsored by the Central Government which aims at enabling the rural population to conserve water for drinking, irrigation, fisheries and afforestation. The project is being executed by Gram Panchayats with people's participation.
- Neeru-Meeru (Water and You) programme (in Andhra Pradesh) and Arvary Pani Sansad (in Alwar, Rajasthan) have taken up constructions of various water-harvesting structures such as percolation tanks, dug out ponds (Johad), check dams, etc., through people's participation.
- Tamil Nadu has made water harvesting structures in the houses compulsory. No building can be constructed without making structures for water harvesting.

8. Explain how 'watershed management' and 'rainwater harvesting' are the methods of efficient management and conservation of surface water resources in India.

Ans. **Watershed Management**

Watershed management ensures efficient management and conservation of surface water through following methods

- It prevents surface runoff through various methods like percolation tanks, recharge wells, etc. By using above method groundwater is recharged.
- It promote judicious use of surface water.
- Under watershed management, awareness campaign are launched for the conservation and efficient utilisation of the surface water.
- Afforestation initiatives have been under taken under this programme, which helped in seeping of surface water into the ground.
- Different initiative such as Haryali, Neeru- Meeru and Arvary Pani Sansad have been launched to built percolation tanks, dug out (Johad), check dams, etc.

Rainwater Harvesting

- It is a method to capture and store rainwater for various uses.
- It is a low cost and eco-friendly technique for preserving every drop of water by guiding the rainwater to borewell, pits and wells.
- There are numerous methods to harvest rainwater in India. In traditional rainwater harvesting techniques in rural areas water is usually collected in any surface water body i.e. lakes, ponds, irrigation tanks, etc.
- *Kund or Tanka* is a covered storage underground tank widely used in Rajasthan.

Thus, we can conclude that watershed management and rainwater harvesting are the methods of efficient management and conservation of surface water resources in India for sustainable development of the country.

9. Rainwater harvesting is an ancient art of water conservation and recently has gained lot of popularity. Support your answer giving reasons. **CBSE Diksha**

Ans. Rainwater harvesting is a method to capture and store rainwater for various uses. It is an ancient art of water conservation, as the community was rural and did not have permanent structures to save and store water. Traditional rainwater harvesting in rural areas is done by using surface storage bodies, like lakes, ponds, irrigation tanks, etc.

In Rajasthan, rainwater harvesting structures locally known as *kund* or *tanka* (a covered underground tank) are constructed near or in the house or village to store harvested rainwater.

It has gained popularity as a simple and economical method of conserving water, even in urban settlements. Harvesting rainwater decreases the community dependence on groundwater for domestic use. Besides bridging the demand supply gap, it can also save energy to pump groundwater as recharge leads to a rise in the groundwater table. These days, rainwater harvesting is being taken up on a massive scale in many states in the country. Urban areas can specially benefit from rainwater harvesting, as water demand has already outstripped supply in most of the cities and towns.

Source Based Questions

1. Read the passage carefully and answer the questions that follow.

India has traditionally been an agrarian economy, and about two-third of its population have been dependent on agriculture. Hence, development of irrigation to increase agricultural production has been assigned a very high priority in the Five Year Plans, and multipurpose river valleys projects, like the Bhakra-Nangal, Hirakud, Damodar Valley, Nagarjuna Sagar, Indira Gandhi Canal Project, etc., have been taken up. In fact, India's water demand at present is dominated by irrigational needs.

Agriculture accounts for most of the surface and groundwater utilisation, it accounts for 89 per cent of the surface water and 92 per cent of the groundwater utilisation. While the share of industrial sector is limited to 2 per cent of the surface water utilisation and 5 per cent of the groundwater, the share of domestic sector is higher (9 per cent) in surface water utilisation as compared to groundwater. The share of agricultural sector in total water utilisation is much higher than other sectors. However, in future, with development, the shares of industrial and domestic sectors in the country are likely to increase.

(i) Which of the following is an advantage of irrigation?

(a) Multiple cropping
(b) Increase in groundwater table
(c) Mixed farming
(d) Fixed agricultural production every year

Ans. (a) Multiple cropping

(ii) Which of the following states is not associated with the Green Revolution?

(a) Punjab
(b) Haryana
(c) Uttar Pradesh
(d) Himachal Pradesh

Ans. (d) Himachal Pradesh

(iii) Which of these crops would be suitable to grow in a region where groundwater table is low? **Competency Based Que**

(a) Barley (b) Wheat
(c) Rice (d) Sugarcane

Ans. (a) Barley

2. Read the passage carefully and answer the questions that follow. **CBSE SQP 2022**

Ralegan Siddhi is a small village in the district of Ahmednagar, Maharashtra. It has become an example for watershed development throughout the country. In 1975, this village was caught in a web of poverty and illicit liquor trade. The transformation took place when a retired army personnel settled down in the village and took up the task of watershed development. He convinced villagers about the importance of family planning and voluntary labour; preventing open grazing, felling trees and liquor prohibition. Voluntary labour was necessary to ensure minimum dependence on the government for financial aid. Even, those who were working outside the village contributed to the development by committing a month's salary every year. Work began with the percolation tank constructed in the village. In 1975, the tank could not hold water. The embankment wall leaked. People voluntarily repaired the embankment. The seven wells below it swelled with water in summer for the first time in the living memory of the people. The people reposed their faith in him and his visions. A youth group called Tarun Mandal was formed. The group worked to ban the dowry system, caste discrimination and untouchability. Liquor distilling units were removed and prohibition imposed. Open grazing was completely banned with a new emphasis on stall feeding. The cultivation of water intensive crops like sugarcane was banned. Crops such as pulses, oilseeds and certain cash crops with low water requirements were encouraged.

All elections to local bodies began to be held on the basis of consensus. "It made the community leaders complete representatives of the people." A system of Nyaya Panchayats (informal courts) were also set up. Since then, no case has been referred to the police.

A ₹ 22 lakh school building was constructed using only the resources of the village. No donations were taken. Money, if needed, was borrowed and paid back. The villagers took pride in this self-reliance. A new system of sharing labour grew out of this infusion of pride and voluntary spirit. People volunteered to help each other in agricultural operations. Landless labourers also gained employment.

(i) Which of the following methods of water conservation brought prosperity in Ralegan Siddhi?

(a) Rainwater harvesting
(b) Watershed development
(c) Groundwater recharge
(d) Construction of dams

Ans. (b) Watershed development

(ii) Which of the following measures were taken to increase democratic participation in the village?

(a) Construction of school
(b) Local body elections
(c) Liquor prohibition
(d) All of the above

Ans. (b) Local body elections

(iii) Which of the following made Ralegan Siddhi independent of government's financial aid?

(a) Prohibition of liquor
(b) Voluntary labour
(c) Local body election
(d) Agriculture

Ans. (b) Voluntary labour

3. Read the passage carefully and answer the questions that follow.

Neeru-Meeru (Water and You) Programme (in Andhra Pradesh) and Arvary Pani Sansad (in Alwar, Rajasthan) have taken up constructions of various water-harvesting structures such as percolation tanks, dug out ponds (Johad), check dams, etc., through people's participation. Tamil Nadu has made water harvesting structures in the houses compulsory. No building can be constructed without making structures for water harvesting.

Watershed development projects in some areas have been successful in rejuvenating environment and economy. However, there are only a few success stories. In majority of cases, the programme is still in its early stage. There is a need to generate awareness regarding benefits of watershed development and management among people in the country, and through this integrated water resource management approach water availability can be ensured on sustainable basis.

(i) What do you understand by the watershed management?

Ans. Watershed management basically refers to efficient management and conservation of surface and groundwater resources.

(ii) Why is haryali project initiated by the government of India?

Ans. Haryali is a watershed development project sponsored by the central government. It aims at enabling the rural population to conserve water for drinking, irrigation, fisheries and afforestation.

(iii) Name an Indian village which is an example of watershed development throughout the country.

Ans. Ralegan Siddhi in Ahmadnagar, Maharashtra is an example of watershed development throughout India.

SELF ASSESSMENT TEST

Objective Type Questions

1. The mean annual flow in the rivers of India is estimated about ....

   (a) 4,000 cubic km (b) 1,869 cubic km

   (c) 1,269 cubic km (d) 3,000 cubic km

2. Which of these programmes is associated with protective irrigation?

   (a) Atal Bhujal Yojana (b) Jal Kranti Abhiyan

   (c) Pradhan Mantri Krishi Sinchayee Yojana (d) Haryali project

3. In Punjab, Haryana and Western Uttar Pradesh, more than …….. of their net sown area is under irrigation.

   (a) 60% (b) 85% (c) 92% (d) 16%

4. Which of these rivers is severely polluted at Madurai?

   (a) Krishna (b) Kaveri (c) Godavari (d) Vaigai

Short Answer Type Questions

5. 'The major rivers of the country generally retain better water quality in less densely populated upper stretches in hilly areas'. Analyse this statement.
6. Give reasons for the degrading water resources in India.
7. 'Rain water harvesting is a solution to many problems in urban areas.' Explain how.
8. Give an overview of Pradhan Mantri Krishi Sinchayee Yojna and highlight source of its objectives.

Long Answer Type Questions

9. 'Provision of irrigation makes multiple cropping possible.' Justify the statement.
10. 'The per capita availability of water is decreasing day-by-day due to increasing population. Substantiate the statement.
11. Give reasons for the neccessity of public awareness-regarding water conservation and discuss some measures to help with the conservation of water.

5

CHAPTER

This chapter deals with the mineral and energy resource distribution throughout India. India is rich in variety of mineral and energy resources due to its varied geological structure.

Mineral and Energy Resources

▼ **YOUR STUDY GOALS**

5.1 Types of Mineral Resources
5.2 Distribution of Minerals in India
5.3 Ferrous Minerals
5.4 Non-Ferrous Minerals
5.5 Non-Metallic Minerals
5.6 Energy Resources
5.7 Conservation of Mineral Resources

▼ **YOUR PRACTICE GOAL**

- Objective Type Questions (27 Qs ; MCQs, Statements, Matching, A-R)
- Subjective Questions (11 SAs, 9 LAs)
- Source Based Questions (2 Qs)
- Map Based Questions (4 Qs)

- A mineral is a natural substance of organic or inorganic origin with definite chemical and physical properties.
- The bulk of valuable minerals are formed during the **pre-palaeozoic age**. These are generally found in metamorphic and igneous rocks of the peninsular India. The mineral resources provide the country with the necessary base for industrial development.

5.1 Types of Mineral Resources

- Based on chemical and physical properties, minerals may be grouped under two main categories : **metallics** and **non-metallics** which may further be classified as follows

Minerals

- **Metallic mineral**
  - Ferrous e.g. iron, manganese, etc.
  - Non-ferrous e.g. copper, bauxite, etc.
- **Non-metallic mineral**
  - Fuel mineral e.g. coal, petroleum, natural gas,etc.
  - Other non-metallics e.g. mica, limestone, graphite, etc.

▲ *Classification of Minerals*

- **Metallic Minerals** Metallic minerals are the sources of metals. For example, iron ore, copper and gold produce metal. Metallic minerals are further divided into **ferrous** and **non-ferrous** metallic minerals. Ferrous, refers to iron. Hence, all those minerals that have iron content are ferrous, e.g., iron ore. The minerals that do not have iron content are non-ferrous, e.g., copper, bauxite, etc.
- **Non-metallic Minerals** Non-metallic minerals are organic in origin such as fossil fuels (mineral fuels) which are derived from the buried animal and plant life such as coal and petroleum. The non-metallic minerals whose origin are inorganic are mica, limestone graphite, etc.

5.2 Distribution of Minerals in India

- Minerals are unevenly distributed over space. There is an inverse relationship between quality and quantity of minerals i.e. good quality minerals are less in quantity and low quality minerals are larger in quantity.
- All minerals are exhaustible over time. They take a long to develop geologically and cannot be regenerated immediately. Thus, they have to be conserved and not misused.
- Most of the metallic minerals in India occur in the **peninsular plateau** region in the old crystalline rocks. The vast alluvial plains of North India lack minerals of economic use.
- Approximately 97% of coal is found in the valleys of Damodar, Sone, Mahanadi and Godavari. Petroleum is found in Assam, Gujarat, Mumbai High, and Krishna-Godavari and Kaveri basins.
- Most of the major mineral resources occur to the East of a line linking Mangaluru and Kanpur.
- Minerals are generally concentrated in three broad belts in India. These belts are

The North-Eastern Plateau Region

- This belt covers Chhotanagpur (Jharkhand), Odisha Plateau, West Bengal and parts of Chhattisgarh.
- It has a variety of minerals *viz* iron ore, coal, manganese, bauxite and mica.
- The major iron and steel industries are located in this region.

The South-Western Plateau Region

- This belt extends over Karnataka, Goa and neighbouring Tamil Nadu uplands and Kerala. This belt is rich in ferrous metals and bauxite. It also contains high-grade iron ore, manganese and limestone.
- Kerala has deposits of monazite, thorium and bauxite clay. Goa has iron ore deposits.
- This belt lacks coal deposits except for **Neyveli lignite**.
- This belt does not have diversified mineral deposits like the North-Eastern belt.

The North-Western Region

- This belt extends along Aravali in Rajasthan and part of Gujarat. The minerals in this belt are associated with the Dharwar system of rocks. For example, copper and zinc. Dolomite and limestone provide raw materials for the cement industry.
- Rajasthan is rich in building stones, i.e. sandstone, granite and marble. Gypsum and Fuller's Earth deposits are also found in Rajasthan.
- Gujarat is known for its petroleum deposits. Gujarat and Rajasthan have rich sources of salt.

Himalayan and Assam Valley Belt

- The Himalayan belt is another mineral belt where copper, lead, zinc, cobalt and tungsten are found.
- They occur in both the Eastern and Western parts of the Himalayas.
- Assam Valley has mineral oil deposits. Oil resources are also found in off-shore areas near the Mumbai Coast (Mumbai High).

Quick Test 1

1 What is the term used for minerals having iron content?
2 Where are most of the metallic minerals found in India?
3 Name two minerals that are mainly concentrated in the South-Western plateau region.
4 Name two non-metallic minerals found in India.

5.3 Ferrous Minerals

- Ferrous minerals provide a strong base for the development of **metallurgical industries**[1].
- India is rich in ferrous minerals both in reserves and production.

Iron Ore

- India has the largest reserve of iron ore in Asia.
- The two main types of iron ore found in India are **haematite** and **magnetite**. It has great demand in the international market due to its superior quality.
- The iron ore mines occur near the coal fields in the North-Eastern plateau region.
- About 95 per cent of total reserves of iron ore are located in the states of Odisha, Jharkhand, Chhattisgarh, Karnataka, Goa, Telangana, Andhra Pradesh and Tamil Nadu.
- In **Odisha**, iron ore occurs in a series of hill ranges in Sundergarh, Mayurbhanj and Jhar. The important mines in Odisha are Gurumahisani, Sulaipet, Badampahar (Mayurbhaj), Kiruburu (Kendujhar) and Bonai (Sundergarh).
- **Jharkhand** has some of the oldest iron ore mines. The important mines of Jharkhand are Noamundi and Gua located in Poorbi and Pashchimi Singhbhum districts. This belt further extends to Durg, Dantewara and Bailadila. Dalli and Rajhara in Durg are the important mines of iron ore in India.
- In **Karnataka**, iron ore deposits occur in the Sandur-Hospet area of Ballari district, Baba Budan hills and Kudremukh in Chikkamagaluru district and parts of Shivamogga, Chitradurg and Tumakuru districts.

▲ *Metallic Minerals (Ferrous)*

- The districts of Chandrapur, Bhandara and Ratnagiri in **Maharashtra**, Karimnagar and Warangal districts of **Telangana**, Kurnool, Cuddapah and Anantapur districts of **Andhra Pradesh**, Salem and Nilgiris districts of **Tamil Nadu** are other iron mining regions. **Goa** has also emerged as an important producer of iron ore.

Manganese

- Manganese is an important raw material for smelting iron ore and is also used for manufacturing ferro-alloys.
- Manganese deposits are found in most rock structures but it is mainly associated with the Dharwar system.
- Madhya Pradesh and Odisha are the leading producers of manganese.

1 **Metallurgical Industries** These industries produces metals and alloys by extracting, refining and processing raw materials.

- In Odisha, major mines are located in the Central part of the iron ore belt of India, particularly in Bonai, Kendujhar, Sundergarh, Gangpur, Koraput, Kalahandi and Bolangir.
- The manganese belt of Madhya Pradesh extends to Balaghat-Chhindwara-Nimar-Mandla and Jhabua districts.
- The major mines of **Karnataka** are located in Dharwar, Ballari, Belagavi, North Canara, Chikkmagaluru, Shivamogga, Chitradurg and Tumakuru.
- In Maharashtra, manganese is mined in Nagpur, Bhandara and Ratnagiri districts. The disadvantage to these mines is that they are located far from steel plants.
- **Telangana, Goa** and **Jharkhand** are other minor producers of manganese.

5.4 Non-Ferrous Minerals

Bauxite

- India is poor in terms of non-ferrous metallic minerals except bauxite.
- Bauxite is used in the manufacturing of aluminium.
- Bauxite is found mainly in tertiary deposits[2]. It is generally found in laterite rocks either on the plateau or hill ranges of peninsular India and also in the coastal regions of India.
- **Odisha** is the largest producer of bauxite. Kalahandi and Sambalpur are the leading producers. The other two producers are Bolangir and Koraput.

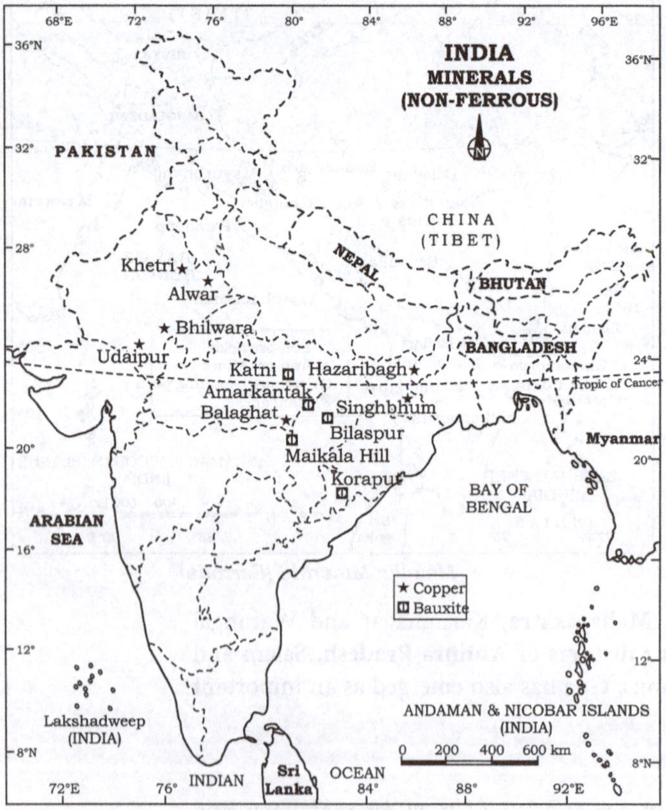

▲ *Minerals (Non-Ferrous)*

- The patlands of Lohardaga in **Jharkhand** have rich deposits of bauxite.
- In Gujarat, Bhavanagar and Jamnagar have the major deposits of bauxite.
- **Chhattisgarh** has bauxite deposits in the Amarkantak plateau.
- In Madhya Pradesh, Katni-Jabalpur area and Balaghat have important deposits of bauxite.
- Kolaba, Thane, Ratnagiri, Satara, Pune and Kolhapur in **Maharashtra** are important producers of bauxite.
- Tamil Nadu, Karnataka and Goa are minor producers of bauxite.

Copper

- Copper is an important metal in the electrical industry for making wires, electric motors, transformers and generators.
- It is alloyable[3], malleable[4] and ductile[5]. It is mixed with gold to provide strength to jewellery.
- The copper deposits mainly occur in Singhbhum district in **Jharkhand,** Balaghat district in **Madhya Pradesh** and Jhunjhunu and Alwar districts in **Rajasthan.**
- Minor producers of copper are Agnigundala in Guntur district (Andhra Pradesh), Chitradurg and Hasan districts (Karnataka) and South Arcot district (Tamil Nadu).

2 **Tertiary deposits** Tertiary deposits are sedimentary and volcanic deposits that are around 55 million years old.
3 **Alloyable** Something that can be mixed with some other substance and forms an alloy.
4 **Malleable** It is the property of a metal of being reshaped by beating with hammer or by the pressure of a roller.
5 **Ductile** It is the property of a metal of being transformed into a thin wire if pressure is applied on it.

5.5 Non-metallic Minerals

- Mica, limestone, dolomite and phosphate are some of the non-metallic minerals found in India.
- Mica is mainly used in the electrical and electronic industries. It can be split into thin sheets which are tough and flexible.
- Mica in India is produced in Jharkhand, Andhra Pradesh, Telangana and Rajasthan followed by Tamil Nadu, West Bengal and Madhya Pradesh.
- In **Jharkhand**, high quality mica is obtained in a belt extending over an area of about 150 km, in length and about 22 km in width in the lower Hazaribagh plateau.
- In **Andhra Pradesh**, Nellore district produces the best quality mica. In **Rajasthan**, the mica belt extends for about 320 km from Jaipur to Bhilwara and around Udaipur.
- Mica deposits also occur in Mysuru and Hasan districts of Karnataka, Coimbatore, Tiruchirapalli, Madurai and Kanyakumari in Tamil Nadu, Alleppey in Kerala, Ratnagiri in Maharashtra, Purulia and Bankura in West Bengal.

Quick Test 2

1. Where are Gurrmahisani, Sulaipet and Bonai iron ore mines located?
2. Which state is the leading producer of mica?
3. Name three regions in India where copper is produced.
4. Mention two uses of mica.

5.6 Energy Resources

Conventional Energy Resources

- Mineral fuels are essential for power generation which is required by agriculture, industry, transport and other sectors of the economy.
- Mineral fuels like coal, petroleum, natural gas (known as fossil fuels), and nuclear energy minerals, are the conventional sources of energy. These conventional sources are exhaustible resources.

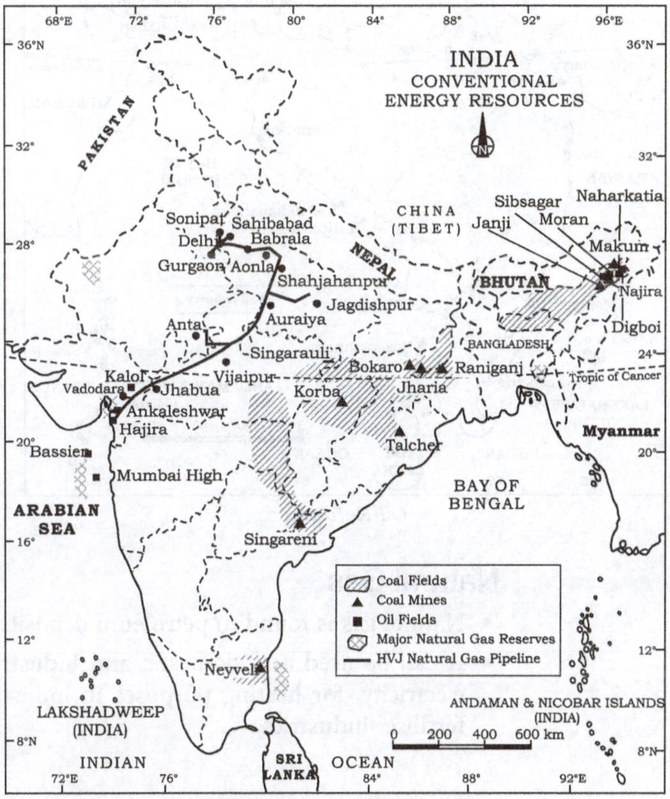

▲ *Conventional Energy Resources*

Coal

- Coal is an important mineral that is mainly used in the generation of thermal power and smelting of iron ore.
- Coal occurs in rock sequences mainly of two geological ages; **Gondwana** and **tertiary deposits**.
- About 80 per cent of the coal deposits in India are of **bituminous** type and are of **non-coking** grade.
- The most important Gondwana coal fields in India are located in **Damodar Valley**. It lies in the **Jharkhand-Bengal coal belt** and the important coal fields in this region are Raniganj, Jharia, Bokaro, Giridih and Karanpura. **Jharia is the largest coal field** followed by Raniganj.
- The other river valleys associated with coal are Godavari, Mahanadi and Sone.

- The most important coal mining centres are Singrauli in Madhya Pradesh (part of Singrauli coal field lies in Uttar Pradesh), Korba in Chhattisgarh, Talcher and Rampur in Odisha, Chanda-Wardha, Kamptee and Bander in Maharashtra and Singareni in Telangana and Pandur in Andhra Pradesh.
- **Tertiary coals** are found in Assam, Arunachal Pradesh, Meghalaya and Nagaland. It is extracted from Darangiri, Cherrapunji, Mewlong and Langrin (Meghalaya); Makum, Jaipur and Nazira in upper Assam, Namchik-Namphuk (Arunachal Pradesh) and Kalakot (Jammu and Kashmir).
- The **brown coal or lignite** occurs in the coastal areas of Tamil Nadu, Puducherry, Gujarat, and Jammu and Kashmir.

Petroleum

- Crude petroleum consists of hydrocarbons of liquid and gaseous states varying in chemical composition, colour and specific gravity.
- Petroleum is referred to **as liquid gold** because of its scarcity and diversified uses.
- It is an essential source of energy for all internal combustion engines in automobiles, railways and aircraft.

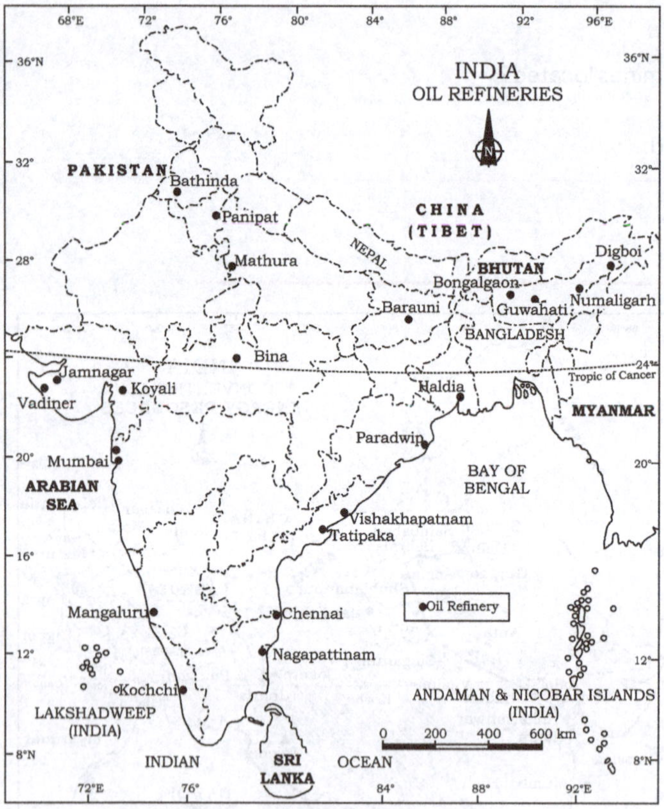

▲ *Oil Refineries*

- It has a number of by-products processed in petro-chemical industries, such as fertiliser, synthetic rubber, synthetic fibre, medicines, vaseline, lubricants, wax, soap and cosmetics.
- Oil extracted from the wells is crude oil and contains many impurities. It cannot be used directly. It needs to be refined. There are two types of refineries in India: **field-based** (Digboi) and **market-based** (Barauni).
- Crude petroleum occurs in sedimentary rocks of the tertiary period.
- In India, oil exploration and production were systematically taken up after the Oil and Natural Gas Commission was set up in 1956. Till then, Digboi in Assam was the only oil-producing region.
- New oil deposits have been found recently in the extreme Western and Eastern parts of the country.
- In **Assam**, Digboi, Naharkatiya and Moran are important oil-producing areas.
- The major oilfields of **Gujarat** are Ankaleshwar, Kalol, Mehsana, Nawagam, Kosamba and Lunej.
- **Mumbai High** which lies 160 km off Mumbai was discovered in 1973 and production commenced in 1976.
- Oil and natural gas have been found in exploratory wells[6] in the Krishna-Godavari and Kaveri basins on the East coast.

Natural Gas

- Natural gas is found in petroleum deposits and is released when crude oil is extracted to the surface.
- It can be used as a domestic and industrial fuel. It is used as fuel in the power sector to generate electricity, for heating purposes in industries, and as raw material in chemical, petro-chemical and fertiliser industries.

6 Exploratory Wells It is a deep hole drilled to find oil or gas in an area that was previously considered unproductive.

- With the help of the expansion of gas infrastructure and local city gas distribution (COD) networks, natural gas is also emerging as a preferred transport fuel (CNG) and cooking fuel (PNG) at homes.
- India's major gas reserves are found in the Mumbai High and nearby petroleum fields along the West coast. These are supplemented by the Cambay basin.
- Along the East Coast, new reserves of natural gas have been discovered in the Krishna-Godavari basin.

Non-Conventional Energy Sources

- These sources are renewable source of energy that are environment friendly and they are widely distributed. For example, Solar, wind, hydro geothermal and biomass.
- The non-conventional energy sources will provide more sustained, eco-friendly cheaper energy.

Nuclear Energy Resources

- Important minerals used for the generation of nuclear energy are **uranium** and **thorium.**
- Uranium deposits occur in the Dharwar rocks. Uranium ores occur in several locations along the Singbhum Copper belt. It is also found in the Udaipur, Alwar and Jhunjhunu districts of Rajasthan, the Durg district of Chhattisgarh, the Bhandara district of Maharashtra and the Kullu district of Himachal Pradesh.
- Thorium is mainly obtained from monazite and ilmenite in the beach sands along the coast of Kerala and Tamil Nadu. The **world's richest monazite deposits** occur in **Palakkad** and **Kollam** districts of Kerala, near **Visakhapatnam** in Andhra Pradesh and **Mahanadi** river delta in Odisha.
- The **Atomic Energy Commission** was established in 1948, but progress in thermal power generation could be made only after the establishment of the Atomic Energy Institute at Trombay in 1954, now known as the **Bhabha Atomic Research Centre** (1967).
- The important nuclear power projects are Tarapur (Maharashtra), Rawatbhata near Kota (Rajaṣthan), Kalpakkam (Tamil Nadu), Narora (Uttar Pradesh), Kaiga (Karnataka) and Kakarapara (Gujarat).

Solar Energy

- Sun rays are trapped in photovoltaic cells[7] to convert into energy, which is known as solar energy. The two processes in tapping solar energy are **photovoltaics** and **solar thermal technology**.
- Solar thermal technology is cost-competitive, environment friendly and easy to construct.
- Solar energy is 7 per cent more effective than coal or oil-based plants and 10 per cent more effective than nuclear plants. It is generally used more in appliances like heaters, crop dryers, cookers, etc.
- The Western part of India has greater potential for the development of solar energy in Gujarat and Rajasthan.

Wind Energy

- Wind energy is a pollution-free, inexhaustible source of energy.
- The kinetic energy of wind is converted into electrical energy through turbines. Permanent wind systems such the trade winds, westerlies and seasonal winds like monsoons have been used as sources of energy.
- The local winds, land and sea breezes can also be used to produce electricity.
- India, already has started generating wind energy. In Rajasthan, Gujarat, Maharashtra and Karnataka, favourable conditions for wind energy are present.

---

7 Photovoltaic Cells They generate power using devices that absorb energy from sunlight and convert it into electrical energy through semiconducting materials.

Tidal and Wave Energy

- Ocean currents are the store-house of infinite energy. Since the beginning of the seventeenth and eighteenth centuries, efforts have been made to create a more efficient energy system from tidal waves and ocean currents.
- Large tidal waves are known to occur along the West coast of India. Hence, India has great potential for the development of tidal energy along the West coast, but so far these have not yet been utilised.

Geothermal Energy

- When the magma from the Earth's interior comes out on the surface, it releases a huge amount of heat. This heat energy can successfully be tapped and converted to electrical energy.
- The hot water that flows out through the geyser wells is also used in the generation of thermal energy. It is popularly known as geothermal energy.
- The first successful (1890) attempt to tap the underground heat was made in the city of Boise, Idaho (U.S.A.), where a hot water pipe network was built to give heat to the surrounding buildings. This plant is still working.
- In India, a geothermal energy plant has been commissioned at Manikaran in Himachal Pradesh.

Bio-energy

- It refers to energy derived from biological products such as agricultural residues, municipal, industrial and other wastes.
- Bio-energy can be converted into electrical energy, heat energy or gas for cooking. It will also process the waste and garbage and produce energy.
- Bio-energy can be used to improve the economic life of rural areas in developing countries, reduce environmental pollution, enhance self-dependence and reduce pressure on fuel wood. A project converting municipal waste into energy is Okhla in Delhi.

5.7 Conservation of Mineral Resources

- Traditional methods of resource utilisation generate huge quantities of waste and create other environmental problems. Hence, **sustainable development**[8] requires the protection of resources for future generations.
- Sustainable development requires the integration of economic development with environmental conservation.
- Alternative energy sources like solar power, wind, wave and geothermal energy are inexhaustible resources. These should be developed to replace the exhaustible resources.
- In the case of metallic minerals, the use of scrap metals will enable the recycling of metals. The use of scrap is especially significant in metals like copper, lead and zinc in which India's reserves are less.
- The use of substitutes for scarce metals may also reduce their consumption.
- The export of strategic and scarce minerals must be reduced for longer utilisation of existing reserves.

Quick Test 3

1. Name two important coal mines where Gondwana coal is found.
2. Name two crude oil-producing regions of India.
3. Thorium deposits are found in which states of India?
4. Which states of India have high potential for the production of wind energy?

8 **Sustainable Development** Sustainable development is development that meets the needs of the present without compromising the ability of future generations to meet their own needs.

Mind Map

MINERAL AND ENERGY RESOURCES

1 Types of Minerals

Metallic Minerals These are the sources of metals.

(i) **Ferrous** Contains iron

Iron Ore
- Largest reserve are found in Asia.
- Two main types of iron ore found in India are haematite and magnetite.

Manganese
- Used for ferro alloys.
- Manganese deposits are found in rock structures but mainly associated with the Dharwar system.
- Madhya Pradesh and Odisha are the leading producers of manganese.

(ii) **Non-ferrous** No-iron content

Bauxite
- Used for manufacturing of aluminium.
- It is found mainly in tertiary deposits.
- Odisha is the largest producer of bauxite.

Copper
- Used in electrical industry.
- It is alloyable, malleable and ductile
- The copper deposits mainly occur in Singhbhum district in Jharkhand, Madhya Pradesh and Rajasthan.

Non-Metallic Minerals
These are organic in origin such as fossil fuels.

Mica
- Used in the electrical and electronic industries.

2 Distribution of Minerals

- **The North-Eastern Plateau** This covers Jharkhand, Odisha, West Bengal. Iron-ore, Manganese, Bauxite are found in these regions.
- **The South-Western Plateau Region** This covers Karnataka, Goa, Tamil Nadu. Monazite, iron-ore, bauxite, clay are found in these regions.
- **The North-Western Region** This covers Aravali, Gujarat. Copper, zinc, gypsum are found in these regions.
- **The Himalayan Belt** Copper, lead, zinc, cobalt are found in these regions.

3 Conservation of Mineral Resources

- Replacement of exhaustible energy resource
- Use of scrap metals
- Use of substitute for scarce metals
- Reducing strategic and scarce minerals

4 Conventional Energy Resources

Coal
- Used for generation of thermal power.
- Coal occurs in rock sequences mainly of two geological ages; Gondwana and tertiary deposits.
- 80 per cent of the coal deposits in India are of bituminous type.

Petroleum
- Used for combustion in automobiles.
- By-products processed in petro-chemical industries are fertiliser, synthetic rubber, synthetic fibre,medicines,soap, etc.

Natural Gas
- Used for generating electricity, heating.
- It is found in petroleum deposits.
- India's major gas reserves are found in the Mumbai High.

5 Non-Conventional Energy Resources

- **Nuclear Energy** Uses uranium and thorium.
- **Solar Energy** Sun rays gets converted into energy.
- **Wind Energy** Blowing wind gets converted into energy.
- **Tidal and Wave Energy** Ocean currents gets converted into energy.
- **Geothermal Energy** Earth's heat energy gets converted into electrical energy.
- **Bio-Energy** Energy derived from biological products.

NCERT Folder

Choose the right answer of the following from the given options

(i) In which one of the following states are the major oil fields located?

(a) Assam (b) Bihar
(c) Rajasthan (d) Tamil Nadu

Ans. (a) Assam

(ii) At which one of the following places was the first atomic power station started?

(a) Kalpakkam (b) Narora
(c) Rana Pratap Sagar (d) Tarapur

Ans. (d) Tarapur

(iii) Which of the following is non-renewable source of energy?

(a) Hydel (b) Solar
(c) Thermal (d) Wind power

Ans. (c) Thermal

Answer the following questions in about 30 words

(i) Give an account of the distribution of mica in India.

Ans. In India, mica is mainly found in Jharkhand, Andhra Pradesh, Rajasthan, Karnataka. Important regions producing mica are

- In Jharkhand, Hazaribagh plateau produces high quality of mica.
- In Andhra Pradesh, Nellore district is famous for mica production.
- A 320 km long belt from Jaipur to Bhilwara and around Udaipur produces mica in Rajasthan.
- Mysore and Hasan are important mica producers in Karnataka.

(ii) What is nuclear power? Mention the important nuclear power stations in India.

Ans. Nuclear power is generated using minerals such as uranium, plutonium, thorium, etc. The first nuclear power station in India was set up at Tarapur near Mumbai.

The important nuclear power plants are Rawatbhata (Rajasthan), Kalpakkam (Tamil Nadu), Narora (Uttar Pradesh), Kaiga (Karnataka), Kakarapara (Gujarat).

(iii) Name non-ferrous metals. Discuss their spatial distribution.

Ans. Bauxite, copper, silver are some of the important non-ferrous metals.

Spatial Pattern of Non-Ferrous Metals

Odisha is the largest producer of bauxite. Jharkhand, Gujarat, Chhattisgarh, Madhya Pradesh, Maharashtra are other producer states of bauxite.

The main copper producing areas are Singhbhum district of Jharkhand, Balaghat district of Madhya Pradesh, Jhunjhunu and Alwar districts of Rajasthan.

(iv) What are non-conventional sources of energy?

Ans. Non-conventional sources of energy are renewable in nature. These include solar, wind, geothermal and biomass energy.

These are environment friendly and cheaper energy resources. These are more equitably distributed and will provide sustained and cheaper energy. These are newly discovered and can be used as an alternative to the conventional sources of energy.

Answer the following questions in about 150 words

(i) Write a detailed note on the petroleum resources of India.

Or **Explain the significance and distribution of petroleum in India.** **CBSE Diksha**

Ans. All petroleum products are obtained from crude oil. Crude oil is found in sedimentary rocks of tertiary age. In India, Digboi was the only crude oil producing region before Independence.

In 1956, after foundation of Oil and Natural Gas Commission, excavation of oil resources started at a faster pace. In recent years, new oil deposits have been found at the extreme Western and Eastern parts of the country.

Distribution of Oil Fields in India

Following are the oil producing regions of India

- **North-Eastern Region** It is the oldest producing region of India. It extends over vast area in upper Assam Valley and Arunachal Pradesh. Important oil fields are Digboi, Naharkatiya, Moran, Rudrasagar, etc.

- **Gujarat Region** The major oil fields of this region are Ankleshwar, Kalol, Nawagam, etc.
- **Mumbai High** It is an oil bearing region about 160 km North-West off the Mumbai coast in the Arabian sea.
- **East-Coastal Region** This region extends over the Krishna, Godavari and Kaveri basin.
- **Western Region** Ankleshwar, Kalol, Mehsana, Nawagam, Kosamba and Lunej are important oil producing regions in Gujarat.

(ii) Write an essay on hydel power in India.

Ans. Hydel power is one of the important renewable sources of energy. Here electricity is generated by using potential energy of water. It is more sustained, eco-friendly cheaper energy.

India has one of the world's largest potential for hydroelectric power. Its potential is around 84,000 MW.

The Brahmaputra basin has the largest possible capacity of hydro power in India followed by Indus and Ganges basin.

At present, India is the 7th largest producer of hydroelectric power in the world with installed capacity of 44, 594 MW. India produces 13.5% hydroelectricity of its total utility power generation capacity.

First hydroelectric power plants were set up in Darjeeling (West Bengal) and Shivasamudram (Karnataka) in 1897 and 1902, respectively. States like Karnataka, Himachal Pradesh, Punjab, Uttarakhand, Tamil Nadu, Uttar Pradesh, Odisha, etc are the major producers of hydropower generation in India.

The National Hydroelectric Power Corporation (NHPC) is responsible for planning and promoting efficient development of hydroelectric power in the country.

Exam Pattern Questions

Objective Type Questions

Multiple Choice Questions (MCQs)

1. Which of the following is a metallic mineral?

(a) Coal (b) Bauxite (c) Mica (d) Graphite

2. Noamundi and Gua iron ore mines are located in which state?

(a) Haryana (b) Jharkhand (c) Odisha (d) Karnataka

3. Sandur-Hospet ,Baba Budan Hills ,Kudremukh are regions of iron ore concentration found in which of the following state of India? CBSE Diksha

(a) Madhya Pradesh (b) Karnataka
(c) Andhra Pradesh (d) Chhattisgarh

4. Balaghat-Chhindwara-Nimar-Mandla-Jhabua belt is famous for the mining of

(a) iron ore (b) copper
(c) manganese (d) mica

5. Which one of the following states in India is the leading producer of manganese? CBSE 2024

(a) Jharkhand (b) Madhya Pradesh
(c) Telangana (d) Bihar

6. High quality mica is produced in lower .... plateau in Jharkhand.

(a) Malwa (b) Hazaribagh
(c) Chhotanagpur (d) Bastar

7. The largest coal field containing Gondwana coal in India is ....

(a) Raniganj (b) Singrauli
(c) Bokaro (d) Jharia

8. Gondwana coal fields are located mainly in the .... valley.

(a) Ganga (b) Damodar
(c) Chambal (d) Narmada

9. Which one of the following is the largest coalfields in India? CBSE 2024

(a) Jharia (b) Raniganj
(c) Neyveli (d) Bokaro

10. Which of these is a market-based oil refinery?

(a) Digboi (b) Koyali (c) Barauni (d) Tatipaka

11. Which of the following oil refineries are correctly arranged from North to South?

(a) Visakhapatnam, Chennai, Nagapattinam, Haldia
(b) Haldia, Chennai, Nagapattinam, Visakhapatnam
(c) Haldia, Visakhapatnam, Chennai, Nagapattinam
(d) Visakhapatnam, Haldia, Chennai, Nagapattinam

12. The Oil and Natural Gas Commission was set up in .... .

(a) 1981 (b) 1947
(c) 1956 (d) 1921

13. **Uranium deposits are found in which rock system in India?**

(a) Cuddapah (b) Gondwana
(c) Dharwar (d) All of these

14. **Which of these states have high potential for development of solar energy?**

(a) Gujarat (b) Assam
(c) Arunachal Pradesh (d) Bihar

15. **Which of the following statements is not correct in the context of the conservation of minerals?** **CBSE Diksha**

(a) Use of scrap metals will enable recycling of metals.
(b) Export of strategic and scarce mineral should be reduced.
(c) Traditional methods of resource use results in reducing mineral waste.
(d) Use of substitutes will also help in conservation of precious minerals.

16. **Which of the following agencies is not involved in the exploration of minerals?** **CBSE Diksha**

(a) Geological Surivey of India (GSI).
(b) National Organic Chemical Industries Limited (NOCIL)
(c) Mineral Exploration and Consultancy Limited (MECL)
(d) OPI and Natural Gas Corporation (ONGC)

17. **Which one of the following is not a method of mining?** **CBSE Sample Paper Term I 2021**

(a) Shaft mining (b) Open-cast mining
(c) Underground mining (d) Refining

18. **Which of the following pairs is incorrectly matched?**

(a) Singrauli Coalmine	–	Madhya Pradesh
(b) Talcher Coalmine	–	Chhattisgarh
(c) Raniganj Coalmine	–	West Bengal
(d) Jharia Coalmine	–	Jharkhand

19. **Which of the following pairs is incorrectly matched?** **CBSE SQP 2022**

Name of the state		Coal Mining Centre
(a) Telangana	—	Singareni
(b) Maharashtra	—	Korba
(c) Odisha	—	Talcher
(d) West Bengal	—	Raniganj

20. **Choose the correct option to fill in the blank in the flow chart.** **CBSE 2024**

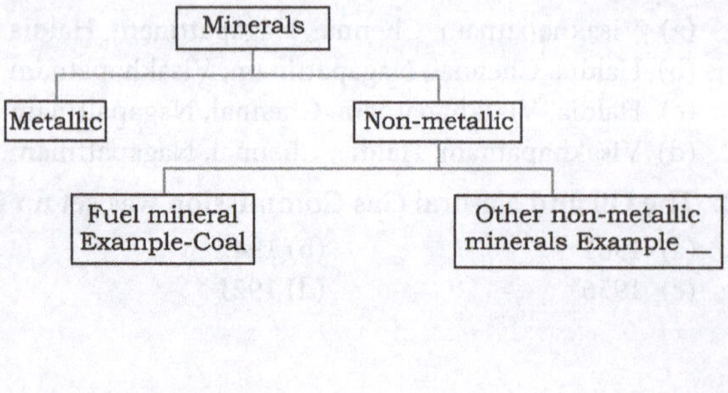

Options

(a) Gold (b) Bauxite
(c) Graphite (d) Manganese

21. **Consider the following characteristic and identify the mineral.**

It is an important raw material for smelting of iron ore and also used for manufacturing ferro alloys. It's deposits are found in almost all geological formations, however, it is mainly associated with Dharwar system. Madhya Pradesh and Odisha are its leading producers.

Options

(a) Iron (b) Bauxite
(c) Copper (d) Manganese

22. **The North-Eastern plateau region consists of mainly which of the following minerals?**

(i) Iron-ore (ii) Coal
(iii) Zinc (iv) Granite

Codes

(a) (i) and (ii) (b) (ii) and (iii)
(c) (iii) and (iv) (d) (i) and (iii)

23. **Manganese is mainly used in which of these activities?**

(i) Smelting of iron ore
(ii) Producing ferro-alloys
(iii) Manufacturing aluminium

Codes

(a) (i), (ii) and (iii) (b) (ii) and (iii)
(c) (i) and (ii) (d) (1) and (iii)

Arrange the Following

24. **Arrange the following in correct sequence. Following is the sequence of generating geothermal** **CBSE SQP 2022**

(i) It is so hot that when it rises to the Earth's surface, it turns into steam.
(ii) Groundwater in such areas (where the geothermal gradient is high) absorbs heat from the rocks and becomes hot.
(iii) This steam is used to drive turbines and generate electricity.
(iv) Geothermal energy exists, because the Earth grows progressively hotter with increasing depth.

Codes

(a) (iv), (ii), (i), (iii)
(b) (ii), (i), (iv), (iii)
(c) (i), (iv), (iii), (ii)
(d) (iii), (ii), (iv), (i)

Match the Following

25.

List I (State)	List II (Copper Producing Region)
A. Jharkhand	1. Agnigundala
B. Madhya Pradesh	2. Singhbhum
C. Rajasthan	3. Jhunjhunu
D. Andhra Pradesh	4. Balaghat

Codes

	A	B	C	D
(a)	1	2	4	3
(b)	1	2	3	4
(c)	2	4	3	1
(d)	4	1	2	3

Assertion-Reason

Directions (Q. Nos. 26-27) In the questions given below are two statements labelled as Assertion (A) and other labelled as Reason (R). In the context of two statements which one of the following is correct?

Codes

(a) Both A and R are true, but R is not the correct explanation of A
(b) Both A and R are true and R is the correct explanation of A
(c) Both A and R are incorrect
(d) A is correct, but R is incorrect

26. Assertion (A) There is an urgent need to conserve mineral resources in India.

Reason (R) For sustainable development economic growth must be integrated with environmental concerns.

27. Assertion (A) Ferrous minerals are rich in iron content.

Reason (R) Distribution of minerals is ubiquitous (even) in nature.

Answers

1. (b) Bauxite
2. (b) Jharkhand
3. (b) Karnataka
4. (c) manganese
5. (b) Madhya Pradesh
6. (b) Hazaribagh
7. (d) Jharia
8. (b) Damodar
9. (a) Jharia
10. (c) Barauni
11. (c) Haldia, Visakhapatnam, Chennai, Nagapattinam
12. (c) 1956
13. (c) Dharwar
14. (a) Gujarat
15. (c) Traditional methods of resource use results in reducing mineral waste.
16. (b) National Organic Chemical Industries Limited (NOCIL)
17. (d) Refining
18. (b) Talcher Coalmine – Chhattisgarh
19. (b) Maharashtra-Korba
20. (c) Graphite
21. (d) Manganese
22. (a) (i) and (ii)
23. (c) (i) and (ii)
24. (a) (iv), (ii), (i), (iii)
25. (c)
26. (b) Both A and R are true and R is the correct explanation of A
27. (d) A is correct, but R is incorrect

Subjective Questions

Short Answer Type Questions

1. Explain any three main characteristics of mineral resources.

Ans. The major characteristics of mineral resources are as follows

(i) Their distribution over the Earth's surface is uneven i.e. some regions have rich minerals, whereas others lack behind in availability of minerals.

(ii) Minerals of good quality are less in amount and minerals of low quality are more in amount on Earth. Thus, quality and quantity of minerals have an inverse relationship.

(iii) Minerals are exhaustible, i.e. once used they can't be used again. Minerals take long time to develop geologically and once they get exhausted, they cannot be replenished immediately at the time of need.

2. Describe the uneven distribution of mineral and energy resources in India by giving suitable examples.

Ans. India is a rich country in terms of minerals. However, there is uneven distribution of mineral and energy resources in country. It is explained through following examples

- Most of the metallic minerals occur in the Peninsular Plateau region in the old crystalline rocks.
- River valleys of Damodar, Sone, Mahanadi and Godavari have over 97% of coal reserves in India.
- Sedimentary basins of Assam and offshore region in the Arabian Sea (Gujarat and Mumbai High) are famous for their crude petroleum reserves.
- The area to the East of a line joining Mangaluru and Kanpur has most of the major mineral resources of India.
- Mineral are mainly concentrated in three broad belts, namely
  (i) The North-Eastern Plateau region
  (ii) The South-Western Plateau region
  (iii) The North-Western Plateau region

3. Discuss the distribution of iron ore in India.

Ans. India has largest iron ore reserves in Asia. Two of its superior quality types i.e. haematite and magnetite have a great demand in international market. Iron ore mines of India are found near the coalfields of North-Eastern plateau region which is an advantage for iron and steel industries of India. Only a few Indian states have about 95% of total iron ore reserves in India. These states are Odisha, Jharkhand, Karnataka, Maharashtra and Andhra Pradesh, Chattisgarh, Goa and Telangana.

Important iron ore producing regions are Sundergarh, Mayurbhanj, Jhar in Odisha, Noamundi and Gua in Poorbi and Paschimi Singbhum in Jharkhand, Sandur-Hospet region in Karnataka and Kurnool, Anantapur districts in Andhra Pradesh.

4. Discuss the production of bauxite in India.

Ans. Bauxite ore is found in laterite rocks mostly in the plateau or hilly regions of peninsular India and also in the coastal areas. Odisha is the largest producer of bauxite and important producing areas are Kalahandi, Sambhalpur, Bolangir and Koraput. The patlands of Lohardaga in Jharkhand have rich deposits. Chhattisgarh, Madhya Pradesh, Tamil Nadu and Karnataka are the other important producers of bauxite.

Bhavnagar and Jamnagar in Gujarat have the major deposits. Chhattisgarh has bauxite deposits in Amarkantak plateau while Katni-Jabalpur area and Balaghat in Madhya Pradesh have important deposits of bauxite. Tamil Nadu, Karnataka and Goa are minor producers of bauxite.

5. Give two advantages of 'copper'. Mention four copper mining areas of India.

Ans. Copper is a non-ferrous mineral found in India. It has various advantages such as

(i) Copper due to its alloyable, malleable and ductile properties is mostly used in electrical industry for making wires, electric motors, transformers and generators.

(ii) To give strength to jewelleries, copper is also mixed with gold.

Four copper producing regions of India are

(i) Copper deposits are mainly found in Singhbhum district in Jharkhand.

(ii) It is found in Balaghat district of Madhya Pradesh.

(iii) Alwar, Jhunjhunu, Bhilwara and Udaipur districts of Rajasthan are producers of copper.

(iv) Agnigundala in Guntur district of Andhra Pradesh. Chitradurg and Hasan districts of Karnataka and South Arcot district of Tamil Nadu are other producers of copper ore.

6. Give an account of production and use of coal in India.

Or **Coal occurs in rock sequences mainly in two geological ages, mention the names of geological ages and explain the distribution of each in brief.** **CBSE Diksha**

Ans. About 80% of coal found in India is bituminous coal of non-coking grade. In India, coal is found in two rock sequences

(i) **Gondwana** It is mainly found in river valleys of Damodar, Godavari, Mahanadi, Sone, etc. The important coal mines are Jharia, Raniganj, Bokaro, Korba, Singareni, etc.

(ii) **Tertiary Coal** It is found in Western and Eastern region of Himalayas. Meghalaya, Assam, Jammu and Kashmir, and Arunachal Pradesh are important states where tertiary coal is produced.

Uses of coal are as follows

- It is mainly used for generation of thermal power.
- It is also used in smelting of iron ore.

7. "The promotion of the use of non-conventional sources of energy in India is the need of the hour." Support the statement. **Competency Based Que**

Ans. It is true that promotion of the use of non-conventional sources of energy in India is the need of the hour due to the following reasons

- Unlike conventional sources of energy, most of the non-conventional energy sources are cheaper and renewable. The limitation and scarcity of fossil fuels have given rise to the urgent need for using the alternative energy sources such as renewable non-conventional energy resources.

- Power from non-conventional and renewable sources is must in order to reduce carbon dioxide (CO_2) emissions from the coal-based power plants. Non-conventional resources are environment friendly.
- Locally available non-conventional and renewable power resources like wind and solar can meet local rural energy needs with minimum costs.
- Thus, non-conventional energy resources will ensure sustainable development by meeting the needs of the present generation without harming the need of future generation.

8. Give two advantages of 'Wind energy.' Mention four states of India having favourable conditions for the development of wind energy.

Ans. Wind energy is a non-conventional source of energy. The two advantages of wind energy are as follows

(i) Wind energy is a clean fuel source. It does not pollute the air as compared to conventional sources like coal.

(ii) Wind energy is one of the low-cost renewable energy technologies available today. Even without government subsidies, wind energy is a low-cost fuel in many areas of the country.

In India, there are some states that are favourable for the generation of wind energy. These states include Rajasthan, Gujarat, Maharashtra and Karnataka.

9. Why is it necessary to develop bio-energy in India?

or Explain the significance of bio-energy to humankind in India.

Ans. Bio-energy refers to energy derived from biological product which includes agricultural residues, municipal, industrial and other wastes.

It is necessary to develop bio-energy in India because

- It is a potential source of energy conversion and can be converted into electrical energy, heat energy or gas for cooking food.
- It can solve the problem of garbage and waste in urban areas as energy can be derived from wastes.
- It can contribute to improving economic life of rural people in developing countries.
- It will enhance self-reliance and can reduce pressure on fuel wood and reduce oil imports.

10. "Conservation of minerals is more important than other resources". Explain by giving three arguments. **Competency Based Que**

Ans. Conservation of minerals is more important than other resources due to the following reasons

- Minerals are important as large number industries are dependent for raw materials completely on minerals.
- We are rapidly consuming mineral resources which require millions of years to form.
- Minerals are in insufficient quantities and are exhaustible.
- Mineral conservation is necessary because once they get exhausted, it will be difficult to find other resources to take their place.
- Economic and industrial development of a country depends on minerals.

11. Explain any three methods of conservation of minerals resources in India.

Ans. There are some methods through which we can conserve mineral resources. These are

(i) Adoption of renewable resources in place of exhaustible resources, like solar power, wind, wave, geothermal energy can save our non-renewable resources.

(ii) Use of recycled scrap metals should be encouraged. It can save the mining of newer metals. In India, scope of recycling scarce metallic minerals like zinc, copper, lead is more because India lacks behind in the availability of these minerals.

(iii) Substitutes for some precious and scarce metals should be encouraged. It can reduce their consumption.

Long Answer Type Questions

1 Classify minerals into two groups on the basis of chemical and physical properties and give one example of minerals of each group. Mention any two features of the three mineral belts of India.

***Or* Elaborate on distribution of minerals in India by focusing on the three major mineral belts of the country.** **CBSE Diksha**

Ans. Minerals are classified on the basis of their physical and chemical properties such as

Metallic Minerals Metallic minerals are those that are rich in metals. They are used to obtain a variety of metals like copper, gold, iron, etc. Bauxite, iron ore are some examples of metallic minerals. There are two types of metallic minerals i.e. ferrous and non-ferrous. Ferrous minerals include iron, manganese etc. Non-ferrous minerals include copper, bauxite, etc.

Non-metallic Minerals Non-metallic minerals are those that do not have metal components. Non-metallic minerals are mica, limestone, graphite, etc.

Features of the three mineral belts are

(i) **North-Eastern Plateau Region**

- It covers Chhotanagpur in Jharkhand, Odisha Plateau, West Bengal and parts of Chhattisgarh.

- It contains minerals such as iron-ore, coal, manganese, bauxite and mica.

(ii) **South-Western Plateau Region**

- It extends over Karnataka, Goa, Tamil Nadu uplands and Kerala.
- It is rich in ferrous minerals and iron-ore, manganese and limestone. It also contains Neyveli lignite coal.

(iii) **North-Western Region**

- It extends along Aravalli in Rajasthan and parts of Gujarat.
- Minerals are associated with Dharwar system of rocks. Minerals found here include copper, zinc, sandstone, granite and marble.

2. What is the use of manganese? Describe the statewise distribution of manganese in India.

Ans. The uses of manganese are as follows

- It is used as a raw material in iron and steel industry for smelting of iron-ore.
- It is used in the manufacturing of ferro alloys.
- It is also used in dry cell batteries.
- It is also used to make fungicide.
- It is used as a catalyst in different chemical reactions.

Statewise distribution of Manganese

The manganese deposits are mainly found in the rock of Dharwar system. It's statewise distribution are as follows

Odisha

- It is one of the leading producers of Manganese in India.
- Most of the manganese mines are located in central part of the iron-ore belt in the state.
- The mines are located in the districts of Bonai, Kendujhar, Sundergarh, Gangpur, Koraput, Kalahandi and Bolangir.

Karnataka

Dharwar, Bellari, Belgaum (Belagavi), North Canara, Chikkmagaluru, Shivamogga, Chitradurg and Tumakuru are districts having major manganese mines.

Madhya Pradesh

Most of the manganese mines in Madhya Pradesh are located in the belt of Balaghat-Chhindwara-Nimar-Mandla and Jhabua districts.

Maharashtra

In Maharashtra, manganese mines are situated away from iron and steel plants. The main mines are located in the districts of Bhandara, Nagpur and Ratnagiri.

Other producing states of manganese are Telangana, Goa and Jharkhand.

3. Explain in brief the production, distribution and use of petroleum in India.

Ans. Production, distribution and use of petroleum in India can be stated as following

Production Petroleum as a resource is formed from the sediments that are the main composition in sedimentary rocks.

Distribution Digboi in Assam was the only oil producing region but after 1956 new oil deposits have been found at the extreme Western and Eastern parts of the country. Some important petroleum sites in India includes Digboi, Naharkatiya and Moran. The major oilfields of Gujarat are Ankaleshwar, Kalol, Mehsana, Nawagam, Kosamba and Lunej. Mumbai high, Krishna-Godavari and Kaveri basin on the East coast.

Usage It is an essential source of energy for all internal combustion engines in automobiles, railways and aircraft. Its numerous by-products are processed in petrochemical industries, such as fertiliser, synthetic rubber, synthetic fibre, medicines, vaseline, lubricants, wax, soap and cosmetics.

4. "The non-conventional sources of energy in India will provide more sustained and environment friendly energy." Examine the statement. Competency Based Que

Ans. Non-conventional energy resources involve higher costs in setting up of large plants and equipments such as large wind mills, solar panels, nuclear plants, generators and storage equipments. If this cost is taken care of by providing subsidies, discounts and monetary support, the non-conventional energy resources will provide more sustained and environment friendly energy. It is because of following reasons

- Unlike conventional sources of energy, most of the non-conventional energy sources are cheaper and renewable. The overall limitation and scarcity of fossil fuels has given rise to the urgent need for exploiting alternative energy sources.
- Power from non-conventional and renewable sources is must in order to reduce carbon dioxide (CO_2) emissions of the coal-based power plants. Non-conventional sources are in exhaustible in nature and environment friendly.
- Locally available non-conventional and renewable power resources can meet localised rural energy with minimum transportational cost.
- The non-conventional energy sources are solar energy, wind energy, geothermal energy, biomass energy, etc. These are easily available in the country and can be harnessed with the help of modern technology.

- These sources are capable of regeneration. These can be renewed along with exploitation and hence, always available for us.

5. Explain any three features of the solar energy, tidal energy and geothermal energy resources.

Ans. Solar energy, tidal energy and geothermal energy are renewable energy sources. Their use ensure sustainable development as these are environment friendly and cheaper in nature. Important features of these resources are as follows

(i) **Features of Solar Energy**

- It is the most readily available source of energy. It can be trapped by two methods i.e. photovoltaic cells and solar thermal technology.
- It is environment friendly and easy to construct.
- It is generally used in appliances like heaters, crop dryers, cookers, etc.

(ii) **Features of Tidal Energy**

- Tidal energy refers to energy generated by tapping infinite energy present in ocean currents.
- Tides are more predictable than the wind and the solar energy. Thus, energy from this can be harnessed more than the other renewable energy sources.
- India has a long coastline thus has a great potential for the development of tidal energy.

(iii) **Features of Geothermal Energy**

- It refers to energy generated by the magma, hot springs, hot geysers, etc that comes over the Earth's surface. The heat energy from these sources can be converted into electrical energy by tapping it.
- Geothermal energy is gaining importance and can be used as an alternative to conventional energy sources.
- In Manikaran (Himachal Pradesh), a geothermal energy plant has been commissioned by India.

6. Nuclear energy is replacing the conventional sources in India. Do you think it as a viable source of energy in future keeping in view the availability of nuclear minerals in India. **Competency Based Que**

Or **"Nuclear energy has emerged as a viable source in recent times." Analyse the statement in context of India. CBSE 2025**

Ans. Nuclear energy is replacing the conventional sources of energy in India. Now, nuclear power plants are being constructed to replace thermal power plant in a phase wise manner. Nuclear energy has multiple benefit over other conventional sources. Country like India, which are deficient in energy resources are promoting nuclear energy to fulfil its demand.

Yes, nuclear energy is a viable source of energy for future keeping in view the availability of nuclear minerals in India. This is due to following reasons

- In nuclear power plant, uranium and thorium are used to generate energy.
- In India, uranium deposits found in the Dharwar rock system. Its main reserves are in Singhbum (Jharkhand), Udaipur, Alwar and Jhunjhunu (Rajasthan), etc.
- India has very rich deposits of the thorium in the world, which is the biggest reason for the viability of nuclear energy in India.
- Thorium is mainly obtained from monazite and ilmenite in the beach sands of India.
- The states which have rich monazite deposits are Kerala, Andhra Pradesh and Odisha.

Institutions such as Atomic Energy Commission and Bhabha Atomic Research Centre are working consistently to extract thorium from monazite in efficient manner, so that, India's dependence on convectional sources can be reduced.

7. "Conservation of mineral resources is essential for the development of India." Examine the statement. **Competency Based Que**

Or **"The challenge of sustainable development requires integration of quest for economic development with environmental concerns." Evaluate the statement in the context of conservation of mineral resources. CBSE 2023**

Ans. Conservation of minerals resources is essential for development of India because of multiple reasons. In the last few decades, mismanagement and over exploitations of resources has put India's development at risk.

Their conservation is essential because of following reasons

- In India, mineral resources are unevenly distributed throughout the country, if these resources get extinct, then it will a huge challenge to fulfil domestic requirement.
- Its conservation is important as large number of industries are dependent completely on mineral resources.
- If mineral resources are not conserved, then we have to import them from other countries which will put huge economical pressure.
- The formation of minerals takes number of years. Moreover, they finite and non-renewable. Once finished, they take millions of years for their replenishment.
- Every country has a moral responsibility to conserve resources for the future generation, so that, they can also use them for their development.

Hence, efficient and judicious of minerals is demand of time, if we want ensure development of India.

8. Analyse the relationship between the conservation of mineral resources and sustainable development in India. CBSE 2024

Ans. The conservation of mineral resources is essential for sustainable development in India, as these resources are limited and crucial for industrial growth. Sustainable development focuses on balancing economic growth with environmental preservation, ensuring resources for future generations. In India, minerals like coal, iron ore, and bauxite are heavily used but are non-renewable, and their extraction often causes environmental degradation, including deforestation and soil erosion.

To address these issues, India focuses on practices like recycling metals and promoting alternatives such as renewable energy sources. Using scrap metal, particularly for scarce metals like copper and zinc, reduces dependence on fresh mining and helps conserve limited reserves. Additionally, India is investing in renewable energy—solar, wind and bioenergy—which can reduce the pressure on mineral-based energy sources. Reducing the export of strategic minerals can also prolong resource availability. By prioritising these conservation strategies, India can support sustainable development while reducing environmental impacts.

9. Analyse the advantages of non-conventional energy sources by giving the example of solar energy in India. CBSE 2024

Ans. Non-conventional energy sources, like solar energy, provide important advantages for sustainable development in India.

Solar energy, in particular, is abundant, renewable, and environmentally friendly, which helps reduce dependence on exhaustible fossil fuels. Solar technology, such as photovoltaic cells, converts sunlight directly into electricity and can be used in areas with high solar potential, like Western India, including Gujarat and Rajasthan, which have significant solar energy resources. Solar energy has several benefits. It is cost-competitive with conventional energy sources, especially after the initial setup costs are covered. Solar technology is also more environmentally friendly, producing no emissions during operation, thus supporting India's efforts to reduce pollution and meet climate goals.

Solar energy systems can be used in various applications, such as heaters, cookers and crop dryers, contributing to energy access in remote and rural areas where conventional energy infrastructure may be limited.

Investing in solar energy not only supports cleaner energy production but also encourages local employment and reduces pressure on limited conventional resources, aligning well with India's long-term sustainability objectives.

Source Based Questions

1 Read the passage carefully and answer the questions that follow.

Metallic minerals are the sources of metals. Iron ore, copper, gold produce metal and are included in this category. Metallic minerals are further divided into ferrous and non-ferrous metallic minerals. Ferrous, as you know, refers to iron. All those minerals which have iron content are ferrous such as iron ore itself and those which do not have iron content are non-ferrous such as copper, bauxite, etc. Non-metallic minerals are either organic in origin such as fossil fuels also known as mineral fuels which are derived from the buried animal and plant life such as coal and petroleum. Other type of non-metallic minerals are inorganic in origin such as mica, limestone, graphite, etc. Minerals have certain characteristics. These are unevenly distributed over space. There is inverse relationship in quality and quantity of minerals i.e. good quality minerals are less in quantity as compared to low quality minerals. The third main characteristic is that all minerals are exhaustible over time. These take long to develop geologically and they cannot be replenished immediately at the time of need. Thus, they have to be conserved and not misused as they do not have the second crop.

(i) There lies a relationship between quality and quantity of minerals. Choose the correct statement from the following about this relationship.

(a) Quantity increases then quality decreases
(b) Quality decreases then quantity decreases
(c) Quantity increases then quality increases
(d) None of the above

Ans. (a) Quantity increases then quality decreases

(ii) Minerals like copper and bauxite falls into which type of categories?

(a) Non-ferrous (b) Ferrous
(c) Organic origin (d None of these

Ans. (a) Non-ferrous

(iii) Choose from the following the incorrect statement regarding minerals.

(a) Minerals are non-exhaustible in nature.
(b) They take long time to develop geologically.
(c) They cannot be replenished quickly.
(d) They are unevenly distributed.

Ans. (a) Minerals are non-exhaustible in nature.

3. Read the passage carefully carefully and answer the questions that follow.

India is endowed with fairly abundant resources of iron ore. It has the largest reserve of iron ore in Asia. The two main types of ore found in our country are haematite and magnetite. It has great demand in international market due to its superior quality. The iron ore mines occur in close proximity to the coal fields in the North-Eastern plateau region of the country which adds to their advantage. About 95 per cent of total reserves of iron ore is located in the states of Odisha, Jharkhand, Chhattisgarh, Karnataka, Goa, Telangana, Andhra Pradesh and Tamil Nadu. In Odisha, iron ore occurs in a series of hill ranges in Sundergarh, Mayurbhanj and Jhar. The important mines are Gurumahisani, Sulaipet, Badampahar (Mayurbhaj), Kiruburu (Kendujhar) and Bonai (Sundergarh). Similar hill ranges, Jharkhand has some of the oldest iron ore mines and most of the iron and steel plants are located around them. Most of the important mines such as Noamundi and Gua are located in Poorbi and Pashchimi Singhbhum districts. This belt further extends to Durg, Dantewara and Bailadila. Dalli and Rajhara in Durg are the important mines of iron ore in the country. In Karnataka, iron ore deposits occur in Sandur-Hospet area of Ballari district, Baba Budan hills and Kudremukh in Chikkamagaluru district and parts of Shivamogga, Chitradurg and Tumakuru districts. The districts of Chandrapur, Bhandara and Ratnagiri in Maharashtra, Karimnagar and Warangal district of Telangana, Kurnool, Cuddapah and Anantapur districts of Andhra Pradesh, Salem and Nilgiris districts of Tamil Nadu are other iron mining regions. Goa has also emerged as an important producer of iron ore.

(i) Which states are most important in terms of total reserves of iron ore in India?

Ans. States like Odisha, Jharkhand, Chhattisgarh, Karnataka, Goa, Telangana, Andhra Pradesh and Tamil Nadu are most important in terms of total reserves of iron ore are in India.

(ii) Analyse the significance of iron ore found in India.

Ans. India is the largest reserve of iron ore in Asia. Haematite and magnetite iron ore are found in India which are of great significance in international trade due to its superior quality.

(iii) Which districts of Karnataka are famous for iron ore deposits in the country?

Ans. Ballari district, Chikkamagaluru district and parts of Shivamogga, Chitradurg and Tumakuru districts of Karnataka are famous for iron ore deposits in the country.

2. Read the passage carefully and answer the questions that follow.

Nuclear energy has emerged as a viable source in recent times. Important minerals used for the generation of nuclear energy are uranium and thorium. Uranium deposits occur in the Dharwar rocks. Geographically, uranium ores are known to occur in several locations along the Singhbhum Copper belt. It is also found in Udaipur, Alwar and Jhunjhunu districts of Rajasthan, Durg district of Chhattisgarh, Bhandara district of Maharashtra and Kullu district of Himachal Pradesh. Thorium is mainly obtained from monazite and ilmenite in the beach sands along the coast of Kerala and Tamil Nadu. World's richest monazite deposits occur in Palakkad and Kollam districts of Kerala, near Visakhapatnam in Andhra Pradesh and Mahanadi river delta in Odisha. Atomic Energy Commission was established in 1948, progress could be made only after the establishment of the Atomic Energy Institute at Trombay in 1954 which was renamed as the Bhabha Atomic Research Centre in 1967. The important nuclear power projects are Tarapur (Maharashtra), Rawatbhata near Kota (Rajasthan), Kalpakkam (Tamil Nadu), Narora (Uttar Pradesh), Kaiga (Karnataka) and Kakarapara (Gujarat).

(i) Choose from the following incorrect statement regarding nuclear energy.

(a) Uranium and thorium are the important minerals used for the generation of this energy
(b) Thorium is the byproduct of monazite.
(c) Atomic Energy Commission was established in 1950.
(d) World's richest monazite deposit is found in Palakkad and Kollam.

Ans. (c) Atomic Energy Commission was established in 1950.

(ii) Copper deposits are found in which of the following regions of India?

(a) Manikaran (b) Kullu
(c) Singhbhum (d) Kollam

Ans. (c) Singhbhum

(iii) Production of power through nuclear power plants require which of the following minerals?

(a) Copper (b) Uranium
(c) Magma (d) Coal

Ans. (b) Uranium

Map Based Questions

1 Locate and label the following on the political outline map of India with appropriate symbols.

(i) Mayurbhanj an iron ore mining area
(ii) A copper mining area of Southern Jharkhand
(iii) An iron ore mine of Maharashtra
(iv) Name the place where an oil refinery is located in Gujarat
(v) A manganese mine in Karnataka

Ans.

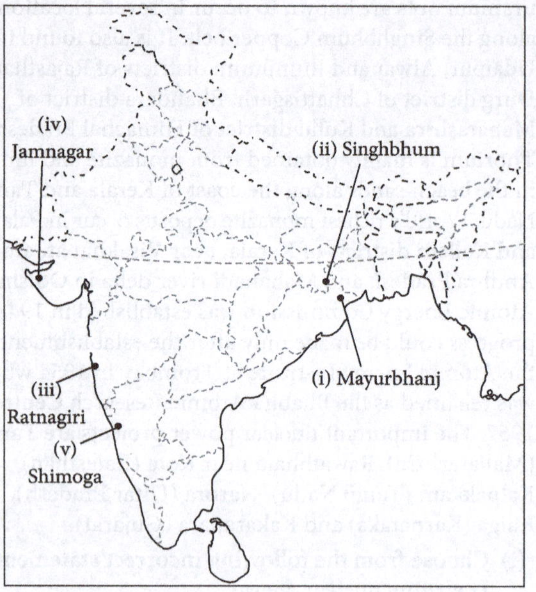

2 **In the given political outline map of India, locate and label the following with appropriate symbols.**

(i) An iron ore mine in Karnataka
(ii) The oil refinery located in Bihar
(iii) Raniganj coal mines.
(iv) Khetri copper mines
(v) Bokaro coal mines

Ans.

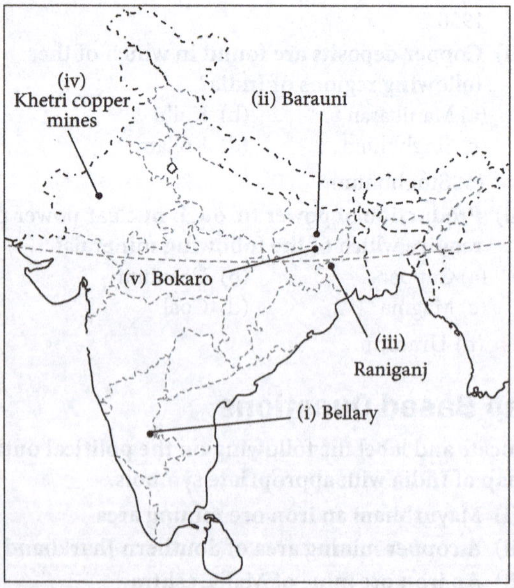

3 **On the map of India, locate the following**

(i) Bailadila iron-ore mine in Chhattisgarh
(ii) Bauxite mine in Chhattisgarh
(iii) Manganese mine in Madhya Pradesh
(iv) Famous bauxite mine in Odisha
(v) Coal mine in Jharkhand

Ans.

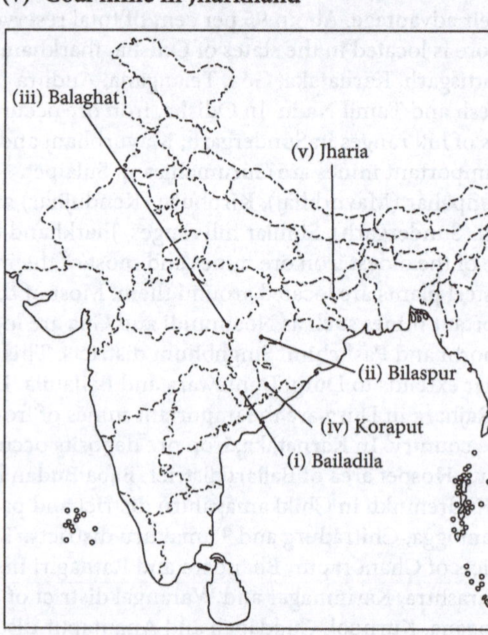

4 **On the map of India, locate the following**

(i) Hazaribagh copper mine of Jharkhand
(ii) Bauxite mine in Madhya Pradesh
(iii) Neyveli lignite coal field
(iv) Oil refinery in Uttar Pradesh

Ans.

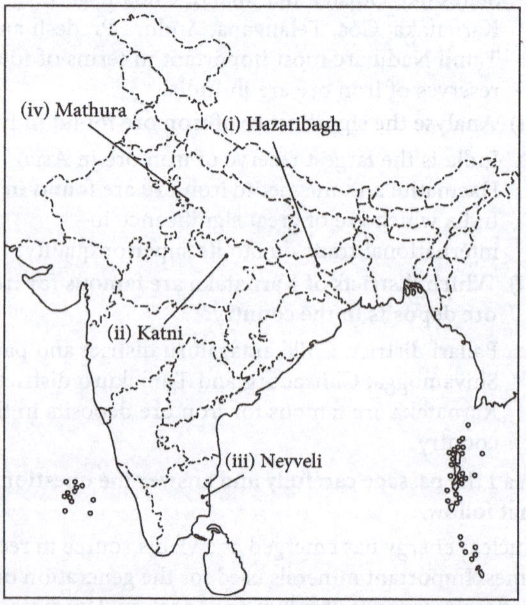

SELF ASSESSMENT TEST

Objective Type Questions

1. The South-Western plateau region is rich in which of the following minerals?
   (a) Iron ore, manganese, bauxite
   (b) Coal, petroleum, natural gas
   (c) Sandstone, granite, marble
   (d) Copper, mica, thorium
2. Which of these is a ferrous mineral?
   (a) Manganese
   (b) Copper
   (c) Bauxite
   (d) Mica
3. Good quality mica is produced in Rajasthan in a 320 km long belt from .... to .... and Udaipur.
   (a) Jaipur; Jhunjhunu
   (b) Jaipur; Bhilwara
   (c) Alwar; Jaipur
   (d) Bhilwara; Jhunjhunu
4. Singareni coal fields are located in ....
   (a) Odisha
   (b) Telangana
   (c) Tamil Nadu
   (d) Jharkhand
5. Why petroleum is also referred to as liquid gold?
   (a) Because of its golden black texture.
   (b) Because it is a hydrocarbon.
   (c) Because of its scarcity and multiple uses.
   (d) Because of its chemical composition and specific gravity.
6. Which of these oil refineries are correctly arranged from South to North?
   (a) Kochchi, Mumbai, Jamnagar, Mangaluru
   (b) Jamnagar, Mumbai, Mangaluru, Kochchi
   (c) Kochchi, Mangaluru, Mumbai, Jamnagar
   (d) Jamnagar, Kochchi, Mangaluru, Mumbai

Short Answer Type Questions

7. Minerals have distinct properties. Discuss about any three of them.
8. Give three point of distinction between ferrous and non-ferrous minerals.
9. Give reason for why petroleum as a resource is called as a liquid gold.
10. The non-conventional energy sources will provide more sustained, eco-friendly cheaper energy. Elucidate the statement.
11. Natural gas can be used as a domestic and industrial fuel. Discuss about its different usage.
12. Explain importance of solar energy in India context.

Long Answer Type Questions

13. India is endowed with fairly abundant resources of iron ore. Substantiate the statement.
14. Nuclear energy are the conventional sources of energy and these conventional sources are exhaustible resources. Explain.
15. Now a day's mineral resources need proper utilisation and conservation. Justify the statement.

6
CHAPTER

The word 'planning' involves the process of thinking, formulation of a scheme or programme and implementation of a set of actions to achieve some goal.

Planning and Sustainable Development in Indian Context

YOUR STUDY GOALS

6.1 Approaches to Planning
6.2 Integrated Tribal Development Project in Bharmaur Region- A Case Study
6.3 Sustainable Development

YOUR PRACTICE GOAL

- Objective Type Questions (19 Qs ; MCQs, Statements, Matching, A-R)
- Subjective Questions (11 SAs, 5 LAs)
- Source Based Questions (5 Qs)

- India adopted centralised planning after independence and later moved to decentralised **multi-level planning**[1]. The responsibility of making plans was given to the Planning Commission at the central, state and district levels.
- On 1st January 2015, the Planning Commission was replaced by the NITI Aayog. NITI Aayog has been set up to involve the states in economic policy-making for India to provide strategic and technical advice to the central and state governments.

6.1 Approaches to Planning

- There are two approaches to planning; **sectoral planning** and **regional planning**.
- Sectoral planning refers to the formulation and implementation of schemes or programmes aimed at developing various economic sectors, such as agriculture, irrigation, manufacturing, power, construction, transport, communication, social infrastructure and services.

1 **Multi-level Planning** Multi-level planning is a decentralised approach to planning and decision-making that involves multiple levels of government and local institutions.

- Regional planning refers to the implementation of plans in a particular region. There is uneven economic development over space in every country. The planners use regional ideas and draw plans to reduce regional imbalance in development.

Target Area Planning

- The planning process aims to address economically backward areas. While economic development depends on resources, it also requires technology and investment. Even resource-rich regions can remain underdeveloped.
- After 15 years of planning, it was observed that regional imbalances were increasing. To tackle this, the Planning Commission introduced 'target area' and 'target group' approaches.
- Target area programmes include the Command Area Development Programme, Drought Prone Area Development Programme, Desert Development Programme, and Hill Area Development Programme.
- Target group programmes include the Small Farmers Development Agency (SFDA) and Marginal Farmers Development Agency (MFDA).
- In the 8th Five Year Plan, special programmes were introduced to develop infrastructure in hill areas, North Eastern states, tribal regions, and other backward areas.

Drought-Prone Area Programme

- This programme was initiated during the Fourth Five-Year Plan. The objective of the plan was to employ the people in drought-prone areas and create productive assets.
- Initially, this programme focused on the construction of labour-intensive civil works. But later on, it focused on irrigation projects, land development programmes, afforestation, grassland development and the creation of basic rural infrastructure, such as electricity, roads, markets, credit and services.
- The **National Committee on Development of Backward Areas** reviewed the performance of this programme.
- This programme is largely related to development of agriculture and allied sectors with a major focus on the restoration of ecological balance between water, soil, plants, and human and animal populations.
- The Planning Commission of India (1967) identified 67 districts (entire or partly) of the country prone to drought.
- The drought-prone areas in India spread over semi-arid and arid areas of Rajasthan, Gujarat, Western Madhya Pradesh, Marathwada region of Maharashtra, Rayalaseema and Telangana plateaus of Andhra Pradesh, Karnataka plateau and highlands and interior parts of Tamil Nadu.
- Due to growing population pressure, the marginal lands are being used for agriculture. This leads to ecological degradation. This emphasised the need to create alternative employment opportunities in the drought-prone areas.
- The other strategies for the development of drought-prone areas include the development of **integrated watershed development** approaches at the micro-level.
- The **Irrigation Commission (1972)** introduced the criterion of 30 per cent irrigated land to demarcate the drought-prone areas.
- The drought-prone areas of Punjab, Haryana and North Rajasthan are largely protected due to the presence of irrigation facilities in these regions.

Hill Area Development Programme

- Hill Area Development Programmes were started during the Fifth Five-Year Plan. It covers 15 districts comprising all the hilly districts of Uttarakhand, Mikir hill and North Cachar hills of Assam, Darjeeling district of West Bengal and Nilgiri district of Tamil Nadu.

- The **National Committee on the Development of Backward Areas** in 1981 recommended that all the hill areas in the country above 600 m of height and not covered under tribal sub-plan be treated as backward hill areas.
- The detailed plans for the development of hill areas were made on the basis of landform, ecosystem, social and economic conditions.
- These programmes aimed at utilising the indigenous resources of the hill areas through the development of horticulture, plantation, agriculture, animal husbandry, poultry, forestry and small-scale and village industries.

Quick Test 1

1 When was Planning Commission replaced by the NITI Aayog?
2 Mention one objective of NITI Aayog.
3 What is the main focus of sectoral planning?
4 How many districts have been identified by Planning Commission under drought-prone areas?

6.2 Integrated Tribal Development Project in Bharmaur Region- A Case Study

Geographical Features of Bharmaur Region

- This region lies between 32° 11′ N and 32°41′ N latitudes and 76° 22′ E and 76° 53′ E longitudes.

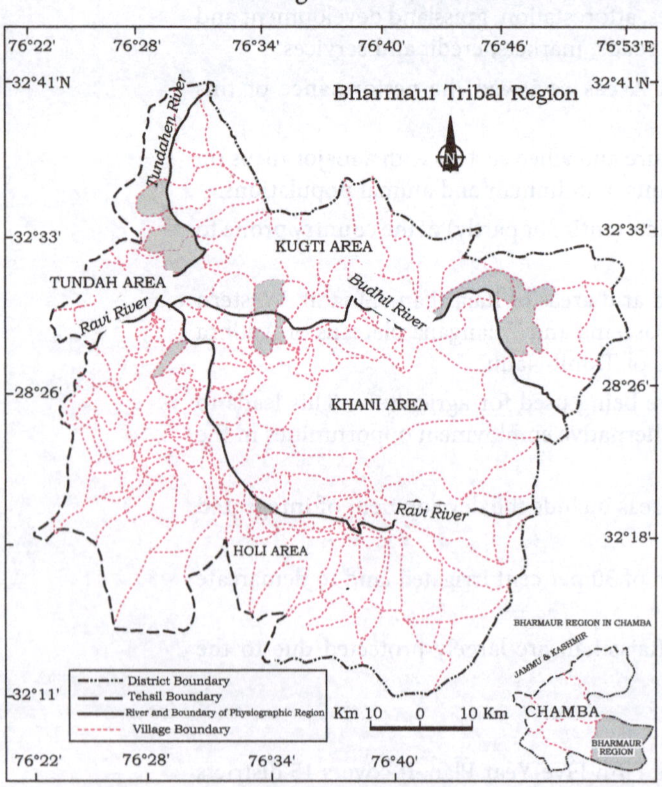

- It is spread over an area of about 1,818 sq km. The region mostly lies between 1,500 m to 3,700 m above the mean sea level.
- This region is surrounded by huge mountains on all sides. It has Pir Panjal in the North and Dhaula Dhar in the South. In the East, the extension of Dhaula Dhar merges with Pir Panjal near Rohtang Pass.
- The river Ravi and its tributaries-the Budhil and the Tundahen, flow in this region and create deep gorges. These rivers divide the region into four physiographic divisions; *Holi, Khani, Kugti* and *Tundah* areas.
- Bharmaur experiences cold weather conditions and snowfall in winter. Its mean monthly temperature in January remains 4°C and in July 26°C.
- According to the 2011 census, the total population of the Bharmaur sub-division was 39,113 with a density of 21 persons per sq km.

Tribal Area of Bharmaur

- Bharmaur tribal area includes Bharmaur and Holi tehsils of Chamba district of Himachal Pradesh. It was notified as the tribal area on 21st November, 1975. Bharmaur tribal region has harsh climate conditions, less resources and a fragile environment.
- '*Gaddi*', a tribal community that practises **transhumance**[2] and has unique *Gaddiali* dialects lives in the Bharmaur region.

2 **Transhumance** It is a type of pastoralism or nomadism, a seasonal movement of livestock between fixed summer and winters.

- It is one of the most economically and socially backward areas of Himachal Pradesh.
- Historically, the *Gaddis* have experienced geographical and political separation and socio-economic deprivation. The economy of this region is largely dependent on agriculture and allied activities such as sheep and goat rearing.
- The process of development of the tribal area of Bharmaur started in the 1970s when *Gaddis* were included among 'Scheduled Tribes'.

Integrated Tribal Development Project (ITDP) in Bharmaur

- Under the Fifth Five-Year Plan, the tribal sub-plan was introduced in 1974 and Bharmaur was designated as one of the five **Integrated Tribal Development Projects** (ITDP) in Himachal Pradesh.
- This plan was aimed at improving the quality of life of the *Gaddis* and reducing the disparities in the level of development between Bharmaur and other areas of Himachal Pradesh.

Achievements of ITDP

- The most significant contribution of the tribal sub-plan in the Bharmaur region is the development of infrastructure such as schools, healthcare facilities, potable water, roads, communications, electricity, agriculture and allied activities, and social and community services.
- The villages located along the river Ravi in Holi and Khani areas are the main beneficiaries of infrastructural development.
- The social benefits of ITDP include an increase in literacy rate, an improvement in the sex ratio and a decline in child marriage. The female literacy rate in the region increased from 1.88 per cent in 1971 to 65 per cent in 2011. The difference between males and females in literacy level i.e. gender inequality, has also declined.
- Traditionally, the *Gaddis* do subsistence agricultural and pastoral activities. However, in the last three decades of the twentieth century, the cultivation of pulses and other cash crops has increased in the Bharmaur region.
- At present only about one-tenth of the total population of *Gaddis* practise transhumance.

Limitations of ITDP

- The crop cultivation is still done with traditional technology.
- The remote villages in Tundah and Kugti areas still do not have sufficient infrastructure.
- Still, the *Gaddis* do seasonal migration and a small section of them move to Kangra and surrounding areas during winter to earn their livings from wage labour.

Quick Test 2

1. Which mountain surrounds Bharmaur region in the North?
2. Name the tribal community that lives in Bharmaur region.
3. Mention one limitation of Integrated Tribal Development Programme (ITDP).
4. The ITDP was started in Bharmaur during which Five-Year Plan?

6.3 Sustainable Development

- Development refers to the state of societies and the changes they experience over time.
- Throughout history, the state of societies has been shaped by interactions between humans and their environment. These interactions depend on the level of technology and institutions within a society.
- Technology and institutions have increased the pace of these interactions, which, in turn, have further driven technological and institutional progress.
- Development is a multi-dimensional concept involving positive, irreversible changes in the economy, society, and environment. It is dynamic and has evolved significantly since the mid-20th century.

- In the post-World War II era, the concept of development referred to economic growth which is measured in terms of temporal increase in **Gross National Product** (GNP) and per capita income/per capita consumption. But, even the countries having high economic growth, experienced a rise in poverty because of the unequal distribution of resources.
- During the 1970s, phrases such as redistribution and equity were added to the definition of development. It was realised that apart from economic development, the concept of development also includes issues such as improving the well-being and living standard of people, health, education and equality of opportunity and ensuring political and civil rights.
- By the 1980s, the meaning of development changed and it included widespread improvement in the social as well as material well-being of all in a society.
- The idea of **sustainable development** emerged as a general awareness of environmental issues in the late 1960s in the Western World. It showcased the concern of people about the unwanted effects of industrial development on the environment.
- The publication of **The Population Bomb** by **Ehrlich** in 1968 and **The Limits to Growth** by **Meadows** and others in 1972 further explained the thinking of environmentalists and people.
- The **United Nations** established a **World Commission on Environment and Development** (WCED) headed by the Norwegian Prime Minister Gro Harlem Brundtland.
- The Commission gave its report known as the **Brundtland Report** with the title **Our Common Future** in 1987. The report defines sustainable development as a 'development that meets the needs of the present without compromising the ability of future generations to meet their own needs.'
- Sustainable development focuses on ecological, social and economic aspects of development during the present times and conserves resources for future generations. It takes into account the development of the whole of humankind which have a common future.

Indira Gandhi Canal (Nahar) Command Area-A Case Study

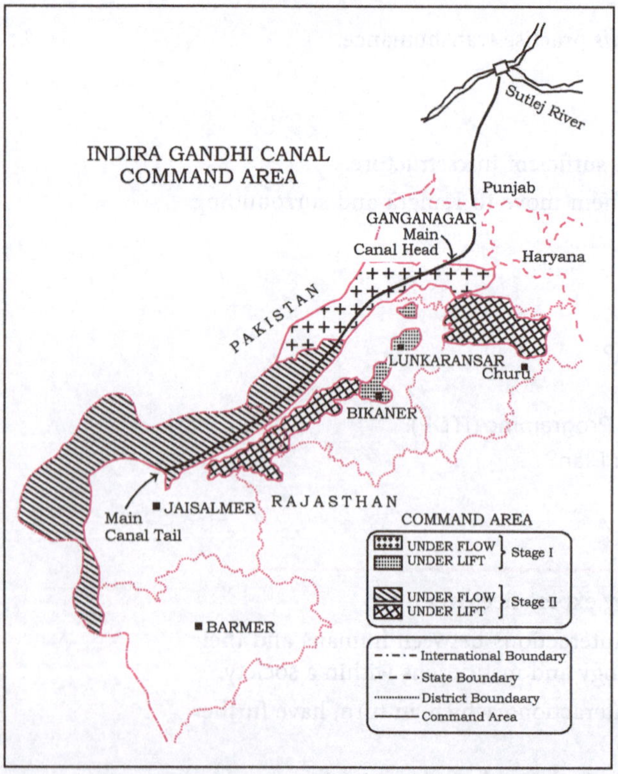

- Indira Gandhi Canal (Rajasthan Canal) is one of the largest canal systems in India. **Kanwar Sain** proposed the idea in 1948. The project was later launched on 31st March, 1958.
- The canal originates at Harike Barrage in Punjab and runs parallel to the Pakistan border at an average distance of 40 km in the Thar Desert (Marusthali) of Rajasthan.
- The total planned length of the system is 9,060 km. This canal provides the irrigation needs of a total culturable command area of 19.63 lakh hectares.
- Out of the total command area, about 70 per cent was supposed to be irrigated by a flow system and the rest by a lift system.
- The construction work of the canal system has been carried out through **two stages**
  (i) **Stage I** The command area of Stage-I lies in Ganganagar, Hanumangarh and Northern part of Bikaner districts. It has a gently uneven topography and its culturable command area is 5.53 lakh hectares.
  (ii) **Stage II** The command area of Stage-II is spread over Bikaner, Jaisalmer, Barmer, Jodhpur, Nagaur and Churu districts covering a total area of 14.10 lakh hectares. It comprises desert land comprising of shifting **sand dunes**[3] and temperatures reaching to 50°C in summer.

3 **Sand Dunes** It is any accumulation of sand grains shaped into a mound or ridge by the wind under the influence of gravity.

- In the lift canal, the water is lifted up to make it flow against the slope of the land. All the lift canals of the Indira Gandhi Canal system originate at the left bank of the main canal while all the canals on the right bank of the main canal are flow channels.
- Irrigation in Stage-I command area of the canal was introduced in the early 1960s, while the command area of Stage-II began receiving irrigation in the mid-1980s.
- The introduction of canal irrigation in this dry land has changed its ecology, economy and society. It has influenced the environmental conditions of the region both positively as well as negatively.
- The availability of soil moisture and various afforestation and pasture development programmes under Command Area Development (CAD) has resulted in increasing the green cover on this land. This has also helped in reducing wind erosion and **siltation**[4] of canal systems.
- The intensive irrigation and excessive use of water have led to the problems of waterlogging and soil salinity.
- The introduction of canal irrigation has transformed the agricultural economy of the region. The spread of canal irrigation has led to an increase in cultivated area and intensity of cropping.
- The traditional crops sown in the area i.e., gram, bajra and jowar have been replaced by wheat, cotton, groundnut and rice.

Measures for the Promotion of Sustainable Development

- The ecological sustainability of the Indira Gandhi Canal Project has been questioned due to environmental degradation over the last four decades.
- Achieving sustainable development in the command area requires a strong focus on ecological balance. Five out of seven proposed measures aim to restore this balance
  - (i) **Water Management Policy** Strict implementation of protective irrigation in Stage-I and extensive irrigation for crops and pasture development in Stage-II.
  - (ii) **Cropped Pattern Adjustments** Avoid water intensive crops and encourage plantation crops, such as citrus fruits, to conserve water.
  - (iii) **Canal Area Development (CAD) Programmes** Implement programmes like lining water courses, land levelling and the **warabandi system**[5] to reduce water loss through efficient distribution.
  - (iv) **Reclamation of Affected Areas** Reclaim areas impacted by waterlogging and soil salinity to restore agricultural productivity.
  - (v) **Eco-development Initiatives** Focus on afforestation, shelterbelt plantation, and pasture development to maintain ecological balance, particularly in Stage II's fragile environment.
  - (vi) **Social Support for Farmers** Provide financial and institutional support to economically disadvantaged land allottees for sustainable cultivation.
  - (vii) **Economic Diversification** Develop agriculture and allied activities along with other sectors of economy. This shall lead to diversification of economic base and establishment of functional links between villages, agro-service centers and markets.

Quick Test 3

1. Who published 'The Population Bomb' in 1968?
2. By which commission the report 'Our Common Future' was published?
3. Which district has benefitted with the command area of stage I of the Indira-Gandhi Canal?
4. Name three crops that are now being grown in the Indira Gandhi Command area.

4 **Siltation** Siltation is the process by which water becomes polluted with fine particles of soil or minerals, such as silt and clay.
5 **Warabandi system** Equal distribution of canal water in the command area of outlet.

Mind Map

PLANNING AND SUSTAINABLE DEVELOPMENT IN INDIAN CONTEXT

1 Planning

Involves the process of thinking, formulation and implementation of programmes.

2 Sectoral Planning

Focus on specific economic sector (e.g., agriculture manufacturing, transport, etc).

3 Regional Planning

- It refers to the implementation of plans in a particular region.
- Reduces regional development imbalance.

4 Target Area Planning

Focuses on special area that are economically backward.

Integerated Tribal Development Programme

- Improvement in the healthcare, education and infrastructure.
- This programme has benefitted Bharmaur Tribe.

Command Area Development

- Improving the use of irrigation potential and increasing agriculture productivity.
- Example, Indira Gandhi Canal

Hill Area Development Programme

- It was started during the Fifth Five-Year Plan.
- Focuses on the development of hill areas.

Drought Prone Area Programme

- It was initiated during the Fourth Five-Year Plan.
- Focused on irrigation projects, land development programmes, afforestation, etc.
- Provides employment to the people in drought prone areas.

5 Sustainable Development

Focusing on present development without compromising the future generation.

Measures for Sustainability

- Better water management practices
- Switch to non-water intensive crops
- Encouraging afforestation and ecological recovery
- Diversification in economic activities.
- Social support for farmers

Components of Sustainable Development

- Ecological balance
- Economic development
- Social inclusion

NCERT Folder

Choose the right answer of the following from the given options

(i) Regional planning relates to

(a) development of various sectors of economy.
(b) area specific approach of development.
(c) area differences in transportation network.
(d) development of rural areas.

Ans. (b) area specific approach of development.

(ii) ITDP refers to which one on the following?

(a) Integrated Tourism Development Programme
(b) Integrated Travel Development Programme
(c) Integrated Tribal Development Programme
(d) Integrated Transport Development Programme

Ans. (c) Integrated Tribal Development Programme

(iii) Which one of the following is the most crucial factor for sustainable development in Indira Gandhi Canal Command Area?

(a) Agricultural development
(b) Eco-development
(c) Transport development
(d) Colonisation of land

Ans. (b) Eco-development

Answer the following questions in about 30 words

(i) What are the social benefits of ITDP in the Bharmaur tribal region?

Ans. The social benefits of ITDP are

- Tremendous increase in literacy rate.
- Increase in female literacy rate from 1.88% in 1971 to 65% in 2011.
- Improvement in sex ratio and fall in child marriage.
- The difference between male and female literacy has also declined. This means decline in gender inequality.

(ii) Define the concept of sustainable development.

Ans. The term sustainable development was coined by Brundtland Commission with the publication of report 'Our Common Future' in 1987. It defined sustainable development as a development that meets the needs of the present generations without compromising the ability of future generations to meet their own needs.

(iii) What are the positive impacts of irrigation on Indira Gandhi Canal Command Area?

Ans. The positive impacts of irrigation on Indira Gandhi Canal Command Area are as follows

- The availability of soil moisture for a longer period of time resulted in greening of land.
- Spread of canal irrigation has led to increase in cultivated area and intensity of cropping.
- Significant increase in agricultural and livestock productivity.

Answer the following questions in about 150 words

(i) Write short notes on Drought Prone-Area Programme. How does this programme help in the development of dryland agriculture in India?

Ans. In Fourth Five-Year Plan, Drought-Prone Area Programme was initiated to provide employment to the rural poor in drought-prone areas and to create productive assets.

The main emphasis of this programme was on integrated development of the area through irrigation projects, land development programmes, afforestation, grassland development, rural electrification and programmes of infrastructural development such as electricity, roads, market, credit and services.

The Drought-Prone Area Development Programme has helped in developing the dryland agriculture in India by the creation of basic infrastructure such as roads, electricity, markets, etc.

It also helped in many other things which are described below

- Increasing the availability of soil moisture by providing irrigation. This has improved the productivity of agriculture and livestock.
- Longer availability of soil moisture and afforestation programmes have resulted in greening of land.

- Traditional crops have been replaced by cash crops and crops which have high value in the markets. This has improved farmer's incomes.

(ii) Suggest the measures of promotion of sustainability in Indira Gandhi Canal Command Area.

Or

Explain any five measures necessary for the promotion of sustainable development in 'Indira Gandhi Canal Command Area'.

Ans. The following measures are recommended to promote sustainability in the Indira Gandhi Canal Command Area

- **Water Management Policy** Strict implementation of protective irrigation in Stage-I and extensive irrigation for crops and pasture development in Stage-II.
- **Cropped Pattern Adjustments** Avoid water intensive crops and encourage plantation crops, such as citrus fruits, to conserve water.
- **Canal Area Development (CAD) Programmes** Implement programmes like lining water courses, land levelling and the warabandi system to reduce water loss through efficient distribution.
- **Reclamation of Affected Areas** Reclaim areas impacted by waterlogging and soil salinity to restore agricultural productivity.
- **Eco-development Initiatives** Focus on afforestation, shelterbelt plantation, and pasture development to maintain ecological balance, particularly in Stage II's fragile environment.
- **Social Support for Farmers** Provide financial and institutional support to economically disadvantaged land allottees for sustainable cultivation.
- **Economic Sustainability** Requires the development of agriculture, animal husbandry, and other sectors together. This will diversify the economic base and create links between villages, agro-service centers and market centers.

Exam Pattern Questions

Objective Type Questions

Multiple Choice Questions (MCQs)

1. The planning approach that aims to reduce regional imbalances in development is known as

(a) sectoral planning (b) target area planning
(c) regional planning (d) target group planning

2. Which of the following best describes 'development'? CBSE Sample Paper Term I 2021

(a) An increase in size
(b) A constant in size
(c) A positive change in quality
(d) A simple change in quality

3. The Hill Area Development Programme was started during which of the following Five-Year Plans?

(a) Sixth Five-Year Plan (b) Fifth Five-Year Plan
(c) Fourth Five-Year Plan (d) Eight Five-Year Plan

4. What does Warabandi system signify in the canal command area of the Rajasthan canal? CBSE Diksha

(a) Lining of water courses
(b) Levelling of land
(c) Equal distribution of canal water in the command area
(d) Shifting sand dunes in the command area

5. Which of the following areas of our country are deficient in rainfall and are drought-prone? CBSE Sample Paper Term I 2021

(a) North- Eastern states (b) Deccan Plateau
(c) Gangetic Plain (d) Brahmaputra valley

6. The Integrated Tribal Development Programme led to which of the following improvements in the Bharmaur Tribal Region?

(a) Increased cultivation of cash crops
(b) Decline in child marriages
(c) Improvement in female literacy
(d) All of the above

7. The Bharmaur region is surrounded by .... range in the North and .... range in the South.

(a) Pir Panjal, Zanskar (b) Ladakh, Dhaula Dhar
(c) Pir Panjal, Dhaula Dhar (d) Dhaula Dhar, Pir Panjal

8. Identify the area where lift irrigation is available in the 'Indira Gandhi Canal Command Area'? CBSE 2025

(a) Entire area to the right side of main canal.
(b) Entire area to the left side of main cannal.
(c) Entire area South of Bikaner district.
(d) Entire area North of Jaisalmer district.

9. Intensive irrigation in the canal command area in Rajasthan has brought twin problems which are associated with CBSE Diksha
(a) sedimentation and silting
(b) sheet and gully erosion
(c) water logging and soil salinity
(d) wind and soil erosion

10. Which one of the following is the positive impact of irrigation in the 'Indira Gandhi Canal Command Area'? CBSE 2024
(a) Waterlogging
(b) Increase in agricultural productivity
(c) Increase in soil salinity
(d) Increase in evaporation from canal water

11. Which one of the following pairs is matched correctly? CBSE 2024

	Target Area Planning	Area
(a)	Hill Area Development Programme	Semi-arid and Arid tracts of India
(b)	Drought-Prone Area Programme	15 Hilly Districts
(c)	Indira Gandhi Canal Command Area	Ganganagar, Hanumangarh
(d)	Integrated Tribal Development Project	Rajasthan and Gujarat

12. Identify the project based on the characteristics given below
It has influenced the environmental conditions of the region both positively as well as negatively.
The availability of soil moisture for a longer period and various afforestation and pasture development programmes under CAD have resulted in greening the land. This has also helped in reducing wind erosion and siltation of canal systems. However, intensive irrigation and excessive use of water have led to the emergence of twin environmental problems of waterlogging and soil salinity.
Options
(a) Integrated Tribal Development Programme
(b) Indira Gandhi Canal Command Area
(c) Hill Area Development Programme
(d) Drought-Prone Area Development Programme

13. Which of these are examples of Target Area Planning?
(i) Hill Area Development Programme
(ii) Desert Area Development Programme
(iii) Small Farmer's Development Agency
Codes
(a) (i), (ii) and (iii) (b) (i) and (ii)
(c) (ii) and (iii) (d) (i) and (iii)

14. The Hill Area Development Programme includes which of these components?
(i) Development of horticulture
(ii) Development of animal husbandry
(iii) Development of forestry
(iv) Development of poultry
Codes
(a) (i), (ii) and (iii) (b) (ii), (iii) and (iv)
(c) (i), (ii), (iii) and (iv) (d) (i), (iii) and (iv)

15. Which of these states/region constitute the drought-prone areas in India?
(i) Gujarat (ii) Rayalseema
(iii) Meghalaya (iv) Karnataka Plateau
Codes
(a) (i) and (ii) (b) (i), (ii) and (iv)
(c) (i), (iii) and (iv) (d) (ii), (iii) and (iv)

16. The Command Area of Stage-II Indira Gandhi Canal is spread over which of these districts?
(i) Bikaner (ii) Ganganagar
(iii) Jaisalmer (iv) Barmer
Codes
(a) (i), (iii) and (iv) (b) (i), (ii), (iii) and (iv)
(c) (i), (ii) and (iii) (d) (i) and (ii)

Match the Following

17.

List I (Report/Publication)	List II (Published by)
A. Our Common Future	1. Brundtland Commission
B. Limits to Growth	2. P. Ehrlich
C. The Population Bomb	3. D. Meadows

Codes

	A	B	C		A	B	C
(a)	1	2	3	(b)	1	3	2
(c)	3	2	1	(d)	3	1	2

Assertion-Reason

Directions (Q. Nos. 18-19) In the questions given below are two statements labelled as Assertion (A) and other labelled as Reason (R). In the context of two statements which one of the following is correct?
Codes
(a) Both A and R are true, but R is not the correct explanation of A
(b) Both A and R are true and R is the correct explanation of A
(c) Both A and R are incorrect
(d) A is correct, but R is incorrect

18. Assertion (A) Intensive irrigation has led to tremendous rise in agricultural and livestock productivity in the Indira Gandhi Command Area.
Reason (R) Intensive irrigation has led to excessive waterlogging and soil salinity.

19. Assertion (A) Development is dynamic and complex in nature.
Reason (R) The objective of planning is to utilise resources in sustainable manner.

Answers

1. (c) regional planning
2. (c) A positive change in quality
3. (b) Fifth Five-Year Plan
4. (c) Equal distribution of canal water in the command area
5. (b) Deccan Plateau
6. (d) All of the above
7. (c) Pir Panjal, Dhaula Dhar
8. (b) Entire area to the left side of main canal.
9. (c) water logging and soil salinity
10. (b) Increase in agricultural productivity
11. (c) Indira Gandhi Canal Command Area-Ganganagar, Hanumangarh
12. (b) Indira Gandhi Canal Command Area
13. (b) (i) and (ii)
14. (c) (i), (ii), (iii) and (iv)
15. (b) (i), (ii) and (iv)
16. (a) (i), (iii) and (iv)
17. (b)
18. (a) Both A and R are true, but R is not the correct explanation of A
19. (a) Both A and R are true, but R is not the correct explanation of A

Subjective Questions

Short Answer Type Questions

1. Discuss the two types of planning approaches in India.

Or **Define planning. Compare regional of sectoral planning with examples.** CBSE Diksha

Ans. The process of thinking, formulation of schemes or programmes and implementation of a set of actions to achieve goal is referred as planning.

There are two approaches of planning which are as follows

(i) **Sectoral Planning Approach** In this approach, plans are formulated for the development of various sectors of the economy, e.g. agriculture, irrigation, manufacturing, power, construction, transport, communication, social infrastructure, services, etc.

(ii) **Regional Planning Approach** In this approach, the main emphasis is on making such plans which may help to reduce regional disparities and bring uniform economic development across all regions. Thus, this approach aims to reduce regional imbalances.

2. "The target area planning is essential to reduce regional and social disparities in India". Support the statement with suitable example. Competency Based Que

Ans. The target area planning is essential to reduce regional and social disparities in India as in India we can see there is a great regional imbalance. Some resource rich areas are also economically backward because of lack of technology and proper resource utilisation. Planning Commission introduced the target area approach of planning to reduce these disparities.

Some of the examples of programmes and groups directed towards the development of target areas are Command Area Development Programme, Drought Prone Area Development Programme, Desert Development Programme, Hill Area Development Programme, Small Farmers Development Agency (SFDA) and Marginal Farmers Development Agency (MFDA).

3. Point out some salient features of Hill Area Development Programme.

Ans. Features of Hill Area Development Programme are as follows

- It was started in Fifth Five-Year Plan, it covered 15 districts comprising all the hilly districts of Uttarakhand, Mikir hills and North Cachar hills of Assam, Darjeeling district of West Bengal and Nilgiri district of Tamil Nadu.
- Development of horticulture, plantation, agriculture, animal husbandry, poultry, forestry and small-scale and village industry were the main objectives of the programme through which efficient use of local resources may become possible.

- National Committee on the Development of Backward Area recommended in 1981 that all the hill areas having a height above 600 m and not covered under tribal sub-plan be treated as backward hill areas.

4. What were the objectives and strategies of the programme initiated during the Fourth Five Year Plan to address drought-prone areas in India?

Ans. The objectives and strategies of the Drought prone area programme launched during the Fourth five year plan are as follows

- The programme aimed to provide employment and create productive assets in drought-prone areas.
- It initially focused on labour-intensive civil works, it later expanded to irrigation, land development, afforestation, and rural infrastructure.
- Integrated watershed development at the micro-level was a key strategy to restore ecological balance among water, soil, plants, and populations.
- The Planning Commission identified 67 drought-prone districts in semi-arid and arid regions, including Rajasthan, Gujarat, and Maharashtra.

5. What were the shortcomings of Integrated Tribal Development Project in Bharmaur?

Ans. The shortcomings to Integrated Tribal Development Project are as follows

- In terms of infrastructural facilities, the remote villages in Tundah and Kugti areas are still not developed.
- The method of crop cultivation is still traditional in nature.
- Even though pastoralism has declined but still a sizeable portion of the *Gaddis* migrate to Kangra and surrounding areas in order to earn living from wage labour during the cold season.
- It was not implemented equally in whole region.
- All the problem of the region were not addressed by this plan.

6. Write in brief about the physical setting of Bharmaur region.

Ans. The physical setting of Bharmaur region is discussed below

This region lies between 32° 11′ N and 32° 41′ N latitudes and 76° 22′ E and 76° 53′ E longitudes. Spread over an area of about 1,818 sq km, the region mostly lies between an altitude of 1,500 m to 3,700 m above the mean sea level.

This region is popularly known as the homeland of *Gaddis* (a tribal community) and is surrounded by lofty mountains on all sides.

It has Pir Panjal Range in the North and Dhaula Dhar Range in the South. In the East, the extension of Dhaula Dhar Range converges with Pir Panjal near Rohtang pass.

7. Explain the main aims of Bharmaur Tribal Area Development plan.

Ans. The main aims and priorities of this project were as follows

- Improving the quality of life of the *Gaddis*.
- Narrowing the gap in the level of development between Bharmaur and other districts of Himachal Pradesh.
- The highest priority was on development of transport and communication, agriculture and allied activities as well as social and community services.
- To utilise local resources in the efficient manner.
- To create new opportunities for the people.

8. How did the concept of sustainable development evolved. What are the aims of sustainable development?

Ans. The concept of sustainable development emerged in Western world in 1960 because of undesirable effects of industrial development on the environment.

The main aim of sustainable development is to take care of economic, social and ecological spheres of development during the present times as well as conserve all the resources in such a manner that these can be retained for future generations.

It takes into account the development of whole humankind which have a common future.

It is trying to create harmony between development and environment.

9. Discuss the role of World Commission on Environment and Development (WCED) in promotion of the idea of sustainable development.

Ans. The role of World Commission on Environment and Development (WCED) in promotion of the idea of sustainable development is as follows

- This commission was charged with proposing long term solutions for bringing about sustainable development.
- WCED focuses on the overall sustainable development of ecological, social and economic aspects of development.
- This committee believes in the idea of conservation of resources to enable the future generations to use these resources.
- It considers the development of the whole humankind which has a common future.

10. How has the introduction of Indira Gandhi Canal irrigation in the drylands of Rajasthan influenced the environmental conditions of the region positively? Explain in any three points.

Ans. The positive impacts of Indira Gandhi Canal irrigation on the environmental conditions of the dryland area of Rajasthan are as follows

(i) Command Area Development programmes (CAD) i.e. afforestation and pasture development programmes developed the desertic area into a green land.

(ii) Due to availability of moisture for a long time and afforestation, wind erosion has reduced considerably.

(iii) Due to canal development the health of soil is improved as soil erosion is reduced and problem of siltation has also declined.

11. Study the given map carefully and answer the questions that follow.

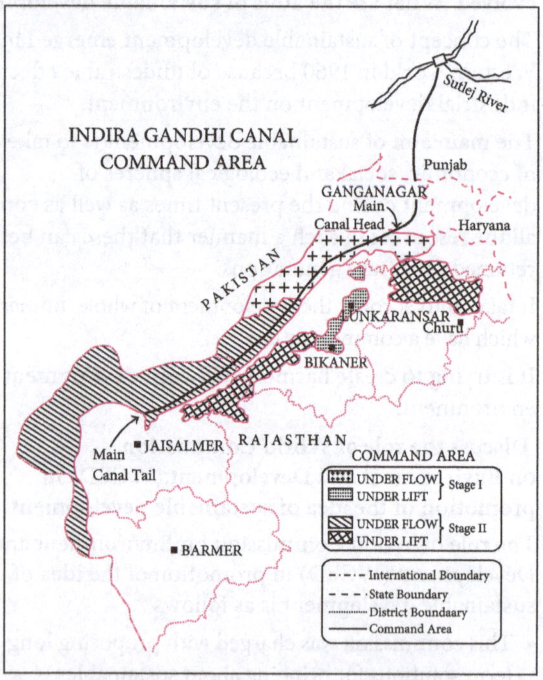

(i) Mention the source of origin of this canal.

(ii) Why is the area to the East of the canal under lift irrigation?

(iii) Explain the economic significance of this canal for the command area.

Ans. (i) The source of origin of Indira Gandhi Canal is the Harike Barrage in Punjab.

(ii) The area of the East of the Indira Gandhi Canal is under lift irrigation as it comprises of desert land dotted with shifting sand dunes. With the help of lift irrigation system, the water is lifted up to make it to flow against the slope of the land.

(iii) The economic significance of this canal is that the irrigation through this canal led to increase in cultivated land and intensity of cropping. Main commercial crops, i.e. wheat, rice, cotton, groundnut replaced the drought resistant crops like gram, bajra and jowar.

Long Answer Type Questions

1. Development is a multi-dimensional concept and signifies the positive, irreversible transformation of the economy, society and environment. Support the statement with suitable arguments from India.

Ans. Development is a multi-dimensional and dynamic concept that is used to describe the state of particular societies and the process of changes experienced by them. Development signifies positive and irreversible transformation of the economy, society and the environment. It refers to qualitative change in the life of an individual, e.g. increasing literacy, longivity, etc. In economic sphere, creating resources, technological developments such as industries, etc are irreversible in nature.

Earlier, development was measured by only the economic growth. Later, the development started including equal access and redistribution along with economic growth. Later, it was realised that development cannot be restricted to only the economic sphere. It must include well-being of the people, improving their living standards, education, health, political and civil rights, etc.

In the case of India, when it was realised that regional imbalances are getting more noticeable, the Planning Commission introduced the 'target area' and target group approaches to planning that aimed at removing regional disparities that have occured due to development. So, area specific plans such as Hill Area Development Programme, Drought-Prone Area Development Programme, etc were launched to make development more balanced.

2. "Hill Area Development Programmes in India were drawn keeping in view their topographical, ecological, social and economic conditions". Support this statement with suitable explanation.

Competency Based Que

Ans. Yes, it is true that Hill Area Development Programmes in India were drawn keeping in view their topographical, ecological, social and economic conditions because the main objectives of these programmes were to develop horticulture, plantation, agriculture, animal husbandry, poultry, forestry, small scale and village industry. By this, efficient use of local resources may become possible.

National Committee on the Development of Backward Area (1981) set a criterion that the hill areas having a height above 600 m and not covered under tribal sub-plan be treated as backward hill areas.

The programme covered all the hilly districts of Uttar Pradesh (present Uttarakhand), Mikir hill and North hills of Assam, Darjeeling district of West Bengal and Nilgiri district of Tamil Nadu.

In drawing up the plans for the region, ecological elements were kept in mind. The aim of plan was to harness local resources without environmental degradation.

Along with economic topographical and ecological sphere, social sphere was also given due attention in implementation of the plan. The objective of plan was to promote marginalised and socially backward classes.

3. State any four achievements in Bharmaur region in Chamba district of Himachal Pradesh after the region was taken under Target area plan in 1970. **CBSE Diksha**

Ans. The four achievements in Bharmaur region in Chamba district of Himachal Pradesh after the region was taken under Target area plan in 1970 are as follows

(i) The most significant contribution of tribal sub-plan in Bharmaur region is the development of infrastructure in terms of schools, healthcare facilities, potable water, roads, communications and electricity.

(ii) It also led to the tremendous increase in literacy rate, improvement in sex ratio and decline in child marriage. The female literacy rate in the region increased from 1.88 per cent in 1971 to 65 per cent in 2011.

(iii) Traditionally, the Gaddis had subsistence agricultural-cum-pastoral economy having emphasis on food grains and livestock production. But presently, the cultivation of pulses and other cash crops has increased in Bharmaur region showing positive signs of growth

(iv) Mostly, people are living settled life and some are also migrating to Kangra during winters to earn their living from wage labour.

4. The Gaddis have experienced geographical and political isolation and socio-economic deprivation since long. State any five reasons because of which this region of Himachal Pradesh has still remained economically and socially backward. **CBSE Diksha**

Ans. The Gaddis have experienced geographical and political isolation and socio-economic deprivation since long. Following are the reasons because of which this region of Himachal Pradesh has still remained economically and socially backward.

(i) This region has Pir Panjal in the North and Dhaula Dhar in the South. In the East, the extension of Dhaula Dhar converges with Pir Panjal near Rohtang Pass making it a difficult terrain.

(ii) The river Ravi and its tributaries "the Budhil and the Tundahen, drain this territory and carve out deep gorges.

(iii) Bharmaur experiences freezing weather conditions and snowfall in winter. Its mean monthly temperature in January remains 4-degree Celsius making it difficult to live comfortable life.

(iv) The region suffers from poor infrastructure i.e. roads, potable water supply, electricity supply, telecommunications, thus disconnecting it from surrounding areas.

(v) Subsistence and pastoral economy has made life of its people very poor due to low resource base.

5. Attaining sustainable development in the command area requires major thrust upon the measures to achieve ecological sustainability. Highlight the measures proposed to promote sustainable development in the command area of Indira Gandhi Rajasthan Canal. **CBSE Sample Paper Term II 2021**

Or **Analyse any five measures for establishing ecological balance in the 'Indira Gandhi Canal Command Area'.** **CBSE 2024**

Ans. The measures proposed to promote sustainable development in the Indira Gandhi Rajasthan Canal Command Area are

- Strict implementation of water management policy is required. The canal project envisages protective irrigation in Stage-I and extensive irrigation of crops and pasture development in Stage-II.
- In general, the cropping pattern shall not include water intensive crops. It shall be adhered to and people shall be encouraged to grow plantation crops such as citrus fruits.
- The Common Area Development (CAD) programmes such as lining of water courses, land development and levelling and warabandi system (equal distribution of canal water in the command area of outlet) shall be effectively implemented to reduce the conveyance loss of water.
- The areas affected by water logging and soil salinity shall be reclaimed.
- The eco-development through afforestation, shelterbelt plantation and pasture development is necessary particularly in the fragile environment of Stage-II.
- The social sustainability in the region can be achieved only if the land allottees having poor economic background are provided adequate financial and institutional support for cultivation of land.

Source Based Questions

1. Read the passage carefully and answer the questions that follow.

There is no uniform economic development over space in any country. Some areas are more developed and some lag behind. This uneven pattern of development over space necessitates that the planners have a spatial perspective and draw the plans to reduce regional imbalance in development. This type of planning is termed as regional planning. The planning process has to take special care of those areas which have remained economically backward. As you know, the economic development of a region depends upon its resource base. But sometimes resource-rich region also remain backward. Economic development requires technology, as well as, investment besides resources. With the planning experience of about one-and-a-half decades, it was realised that regional imbalances in economic development were getting accentuated.

(i) Which of the following is the most important aim of regional planning?

(a) To increase GDP of the country
(b) To reduce inequality between regions
(c) To increase inequality between regions
(d) All of the above

Ans. (b) To reduce inequality between regions

(ii) Economic development of a region requires which of the following components?

(a) Presence of resources (b) Technology
(c) Capital Investment (d) All of these

Ans. (d) All of these

(iii) What are the benefits of planning?

(a) Equal distribution of resources
(b) Reduction in regional imbalances
(c) Spatial development (d) All of these

Ans. (d) All of these

2. Read the passage carefully and answer the questions that follow. CBSE SQP 2022

Bharmaur tribal area comprises Bharmaur and Holi tehsils of Chamba district of Himachal Pradesh. It has been a notified tribal area since 21st November, 1975. Bharmaur is inhabited by '*Gaddi*', a tribal community who have maintained a distinct identity in the Himalayan region as they practiced transhumance and conversed through *Gaddiali* dialect. Bharmaur tribal region has harsh climate conditions, low resource base and fragile environment. These factors have influenced the society and economy of the region. According to the 2011 Census, the total population of Bharmaur sub-division was 39,113 i.e., 21 persons per sq km. It is one of the most (economically and socially) backward areas of Himachal Pradesh. Historically, the *Gaddis* have experienced geographical and political isolation and socio-economic deprivation. The economy is largely based on agriculture and allied activities such as sheep and goat rearing.

The process of development of the tribal area of Bharmaur started in the 1970s, when *Gaddis* were included among 'Scheduled Tribes'. Under the Fifth Five Years Plan, the tribal sub-plan was introduced in 1974 and Bharmaur was designated as one of the five Integrated Tribal Development Project (ITDP) in Himachal Pradesh. This area development plan was aimed at improving the quality of life of the *Gaddis* and narrowing the gap in the level of development between Bharmaur and other areas of Himachal Pradesh. This plan laid the highest priority on development of transport and communications, agriculture and allied activities, and social and community services.

(i) How have the *Gaddi* tribal community maintained a distinct identity in the Himalayan region?

Ans. *Gaddi* tribal communities have maintained a distinct identity in the Himalayan region because of the following reasons

- They practiced transhumance that involves seasonal migration of humans along with their livestock.
- They conserved their culture through their *Gaddiali* dialect.

(ii) State any two achievements of the Bharmaur region in Chamba district of Himachal Pradesh after the region was taken under target area plan in 1970.

Ans. The two achievements of the Bharmaur region after being taken under target area plan in 1970 are as follows

(a) There was a tremendous increase in literacy rate, improvement in sex ratio and decline in child marriage.

(b) The economic activities changed from pastures to pulses and other cash crops.

(iii) Under the Integrated Tribal Development Project, which areas were given the highest priority?

Ans. Under the Integrated Tribal Development Project, the areas which were given the highest priority include development of transport and communications, agriculture and allied activities, and social and community services.

3. Read the passage carefully and answer the questions that follow. CBSE 2024

Integrated Tribal Development Project in Bharmaur Region

This region lies between 32°11′ N and 32°41′ N latitudes and 76°22′ E and 76°53′ E longitudes. Spread over an area of about 1,818 sq km, the region mostly lies between 1,500 m to 3,700 m above the mean sea level.

This region popularly known as the homeland of *Gaddis* is surrounded by lofty mountains on all sides. It has Pir Panjal in the North and Dhaula Dhar in the South. In the East, the extension of Dhula Dhar converges with Pir and the Tundahen, drain this territory, and carve out deep gorges. These rivers divide the region into four physiographic divisions called *Holi*, *Khani*, *Kugti* and *Tundah* areas. Bharmaur experiences freezing weather conditions and snowfall in winter. Its mean monthly temperature in January remains 4°C and in July 26°C.

(i) **Describe the location of Bharmaur region.**

Ans. The Bharmaur region is located between 32°11′ N and 32°41′ N latitudes and 76°22′ E and 76° 53′ E longitudes. It spread over an area of about 1,818 sq km.

(ii) **Why does this region experience harsh climatic conditions? Give one reason.**

Ans. This region mostly lies between 1,500 m to 3,700 m above the mean sea level. Therefore, it experiences a harsh climate.

(iii) **Why is this region economically backward? Explain any one reason.**

Ans. This region is economically backwards due to the lack of job opportunities and high dependence on traditional agriculture and pastoral activities.

4. Read the passage carefully and answer the questions that follow. **CBSE Term II 2022**

The concept of development is dynamic and has evolved during the second half of twentieth century. In the post-World War II era, the concept of development was synonymous to economic growth which is measured in terms of temporal increase in Gross National Product (GNP) and per capita income/per capita consumption. But, even the countries having high economic growth, experienced speedy rise in poverty because of its unequal distribution. So, in 1970s, the phrases such as redistribution with growth and growth and equity were incorporated in the definition of development.

While dealing with the questions related to redistribution and equity, it was realised that the concept of development cannot be restricted to the economic sphere alone. It also includes the issues such as improving the well-being and living standard of people, availing of the health, education and equality of opportunity and ensuring political and civil rights. By 1980s, development emerged as a concept encapsulating widespread improvement in social as well as material well-being of all in a society.

(i) **Explain the meaning of 'multi-dimensional concept of development'.**

Ans. The term 'multi-dimensional development' recognises that human development is not one thing. Rather, human development is a broad term that includes lots of possible factors, such as economic development, social development and environmental management.

(ii) **Development cannot be restricted to the economic sphere only. Comment.**

Ans. The concept of development cannot be restricted to the economic development only as it also includes the issues like improving the well being and living standards of people, availing of the health, education and equality of opportunity.

(iii) **Define the term 'sustainable development'.**

Ans. The term sustainable development was coined by Brundtland Commission with the publication of report 'Our Common Future' in 1987. It defined sustainable development as a development that meets the needs of the present generations without compromising the ability of future generations to meet their own needs.

5. Read the passage carefully and answer the questions that follow.

Indira Gandhi Canal, previously known as the Rajasthan Canal, is one of the largest canal systems in India. Conceived by Kanwar Sain in 1948, the canal project was launched on 31st March, 1958. The canal originates at Harike barrage in Punjab and runs parallel to Pakistan border at an average distance of 40 km in Thar Desert (Marusthali) of Rajasthan. The total planned length of the system is 9,060 km catering to the irrigation needs of a total culturable command area of 19.63 lakh hectares. Out of the total command area, about 70 per cent was envisaged to be irrigated by flow system and the rest by lift system. The construction work of the canal system has been carried out through two stages. The command area of Stage-I lies in Ganganagar, Hanumangarh and Northern part of Bikaner districts. It has a gently undulating topography and its culturable command area is 5.53 lakh hectares.

(i) **The Indira Gandhi Canal originates in which of the following states?**

(a) Rajasthan (b) Punjab
(c) Haryana (d) Uttar Pradesh

Ans. (b) Punjab

(ii) **Which of the following can be a negative effect of Indira Gandhi Canal?**

(a) Decreasing soil moisture (b) Deforestation
(c) Water salinity (d) All of these

Ans. (c) Water salinity

(iii) **Which among the following has been the advantage of introducing irrigation through Indira Gandhi Canal area?**

(a) Increasing agricultural productivity
(b) Increasing crop intensity
(c) Water logging (d) Both (a) and (b)

Ans. (d) Both (a) and (b)

SELF ASSESSMENT TEST

Objective Type Questions

1. Uneven pattern of development over space requires that planners have a spatial perspective. This type of planning approach is referred to as ....

   (a) spatial planning (b) regional planning
   (c) sectoral planning (d) target area planning

2. The Bharmaur Tribal Area is inhabited mainly by which of the following tribes?

   (a) Bakkarwals (b) Gujjars
   (c) *Gaddis* (d) Nagas

3. The Brundtland Commission published its report 'Our Common Future' in the year ....

   (a) 1960 (b) 1991 (c) 1987 (d) 1927

4. The total planned length of the Indira Gandhi Canal System is ....

   (a) 900 km (b) 2,000 km (c) 9,080 km (d) 1,023 km

5. Which of the following measures could be adopted to promote sustainable development in the Indira Gandhi Command Area?

   (a) Avoiding water intensive crops
   (b) Reclaimation of land affected by water logging
   (c) Diversification of economic base
   (d) All of the above

6. **Assertion** (A) The Planning Commission was replaced by NITI Aayog in 2015.

   Reason (R) NITI Aayog was established to involve states in economic policy-making and provide strategic and technical advice to the Central and State governments.

   Codes

   (a) Both A and R are true, and R is the correct explanation of A.
   (b) Both A and R are true, but R is not the correct explanation of A.
   (c) Both A and R are incorrect
   (d) A is correct, but R is incorrect

Short Answer Type Questions

7. India graduated into decentralised multi-level planning. Explain
8. Target area approach and target group of planning differs from each other in certain ways. Elucidate the statement.
9. Mention some salient features of Drought-prone Area Development Programme.
10. There was a target group approach called Integrated Tribal Development Projects (ITDP), explain about its main objectives.

Long Answer Type Questions

11. Development is the positive change in every aspect of life and environment. Elucidate the statement with valid examples.
12. Mention the salient features of concept of sustainable development.

UNIT 4

7 CHAPTER

The use of transport and communication depends upon our need to move things from the place of their availability to the place of their use. Human beings use various methods to move goods, commodities and ideas from one place to another.

YOUR STUDY GOALS

7.1 Transport
7.2 Communication Network

YOUR PRACTICE GOAL

- Objective Type Questions (24 Qs ; MCQs, Statements, Matching, A-R)
- Subjective Questions (12 SAs, 11 LAs)
- Source Based Questions (4 Qs)
- Map Based Questions (3 Qs)

Transport and Communication

7.1 Transport

- Transport is an essential part of country's economy. Transport is important for trade and commerce and it allows people to travel for work, education and emergencies.
- Major means of transport are as follows

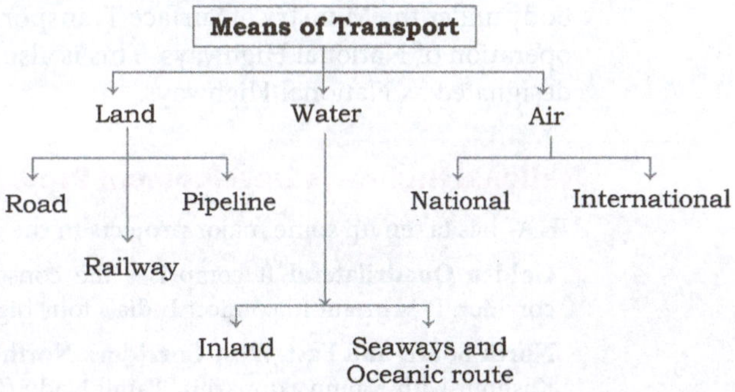

Land Transport

- The pathways and unmetalled roads have been used for transportation in India since ancient times.
- The economic and technological development, metalled roads and railways were developed to move large volumes of goods and people from one place to another.
- Ropeways, cableways and pipelines were developed for the transportation of specific goods under specific conditions.

Road Transport

- India has the **second largest road network** in the world with a total length of about 62.16 lakh km (2020-21). About 85 per cent of passenger and 70 per cent of freight traffic are carried by roads every year.
- Road transport is relatively suitable for shorter distance travel. Road transport in modern sense was very limited in India before World War II.
- In 1943, the **Nagpur Plan** was made for road transport development in India. This plan wasn't implemented due to lack of coordination between the princely states and British India.
- After independence, a **Twenty-Year Road Plan** (1961) was introduced to improve the conditions of roads in India. However, road construction was done around urban areas only. Rural and remote areas had the least connectivity by road.
- Roads are classified as **National Highways** (NH), **State Highways** (SH), **Major District Roads** and **Rural Roads** for construction and maintenance purposes.

Grand Trunk Road

Sher Shah Suri built the *Shahi* (Royal) road to strengthen and unite his empire from the Indus Valley to the Sonar Valley in Bengal. This road was renamed the Grand Trunk (GT) road during the British period. It connects Calcutta and Peshawar. At present, it extends from Amritsar to Kolkata.

National Highways

- The main roads which are constructed and maintained by the central government are known as the National Highways. These connect the state capitals, major cities, important ports, railway junctions, etc.
- These roads are meant for inter-state transport and movement of defence men and materials in strategic areas.
- The length of the National Highways has increased from 19,700 km in 1951 to 1,36,440 km in 2020.
- The National Highways constitute only about 2 per cent of the total road length but carry 40 per cent of the road traffic.
- The **National Highways Authority of India** (NHAI) was operationalised in 1995. It is an autonomous body under the Ministry of Surface Transport. It has the responsibility of development, maintenance and operation of National Highways. This is also the highest (apex) body to improve the quality of the roads designated as National Highways.

National Highways Development Projects

NHAI has taken up some major projects in the country under different phases

- **Golden Quadrilateral** It comprises the construction of a 5,846 km long 4/6 lane, high-density traffic corridor. It is meant to connect India's four big metro cities of Delhi-Mumbai-Chennai-Kolkata.
- **North-South and East-West Corridors** North-South corridor aims at connecting Srinagar in Jammu and Kashmir with Kanniyakumari in Tamil Nadu (including Kochchi-Salem Spur) with a 4,076 km long road.
- The East-West Corridor has been planned to connect Silchar in Assam with the port town of Porbandar in Gujarat with 3,640 km of road length.

State Highways

- These are constructed and maintained by state governments.
- They join the state capitals with district headquarters and other important towns.
- These roads are connected to the National Highways.

District and Rural Roads

- District roads are the connecting link between District Headquarters and the other important nodes in the district.
- Rural roads are vital for providing links in rural areas. About 80 per cent of the total road length in India is categorised as rural roads.
- There is regional variation in the density of rural roads because these are influenced by the nature of the landform.

Bharatmala Project

Bharatmala is a proposed scheme for

- development of state roads along coastal border areas, including connectivity of non-major ports;
- backward areas religious and tourist places connectivity programme;
- **Setubharatam Pariyojana** which focuses on the construction of about 1500 major bridges and 200 rail over bridges/rail under bridges. It also focuses on the development of about 9000 km newly declared National Highways.

Other Roads

- Other roads include Border Roads and International Highways.
- The **Border Road Organisation** (BRO) was established in May 1960 to boost economic development and strengthen defence preparedness through rapid and coordinated improvement of strategically important roads along the Northern and North-Eastern boundary of the country.
- BRO has constructed roads in high-altitude mountainous terrain joining Chandigarh with Manali (Himachal Pradesh) and Leh (Ladakh). This road runs at an average altitude of 4,270 metres above the mean sea level.
- BRO also undertakes snow clearance in high-altitude areas.
- The international highways are meant to promote a friendly relationship with the neighbouring countries by providing effective links with India.

Road Network in India

S. No.	Road Category	Length in Km
1.	National Highways	136440
2.	State Highways	176818
3.	Other Roads	5902539
	Total	6215797

Source *Ministry of Road Transport and Highways Annual Report 2021.*

Atal Tunnel

- It is the **world's longest Highway tunnel** (9.02 km), built by the Border Road Organisation.
- This tunnel connects Manali to Lahaul-Spiti Valley throughout the year. Earlier the valley was cut off for about 6 months each year because 'of' heavy snowfall.
- The tunnel is built with ultra-modern specifications in the Pir Panjal range of the Himalayas at an altitude of 3000 metres from the Mean Sea Level (MSL).

Quick Test 1

1. Name the body which is responsible for maintaining National Highways in India?
2. Which cities does the Golden Quadrilateral connect?
3. Which organisation constructed roads in high-altitude mountainous terrain joining Chandigarh with Manali and Leh?
4. What areas does Bharatmala focus on connecting?

Rail Transport

- Indian railways network is one of the longest in the world. It facilitates the movement of freight and passengers.
- Indian railway was introduced in 1853. The **first line** was constructed from Bombay to Thane covering a distance of 34 km.
- Indian railways is the largest government undertaking in the country.
- The length of the Indian railways network was 67,956 km (2019-20). Its huge size puts pressure on a centralised railway management system. Thus, in India, the railway system has been divided into **17 zones.**
- Replacement of steam engines by diesel and electric engines has increased the speed, as well as the carrying capacity. This replacement also improved the environment at the stations.
- **Metro rail has** revolutionised the urban transport system in India. Using diesel buses by CNG-run vehicles along with the introduction of the metro is a great step towards controlling air pollution in urban centres.
- The railway network is relatively less dense in the hill states, North-Eastern states, central parts of India and Rajasthan.

Rail Guage

- Based on the width of the track of the Indian railways, three categories of rail guage have been made. These are as follows
  (i) **Broad Gauge** The distance between rails in broad gauge is 1.676 metres. The total length of broad gauge lines was 63,950 km (2019-20).
  (ii) **Metre Gauge** The distance between rails is one metre. Its total length was 2,402 km (2019-20).
  (iii) **Narrow Gauge** The distance between the rails in this case is 0.762 metres or 0.610 metres. The total length of the narrow gauge was 1,604 km (2019-20). It is generally confined to hilly areas.
- Indian railways has launched an extensive programme to convert the metre and narrow gauges to broad gauge.

Indian Railways : Railway Zones and Headquarters

Railway Zone	Headquarters	Railway Zone	Headquarters
Central	Mumbai CST	Southern	Chennai
Eastern	Kolkata	South Central	Secunderabad
East Central	Hajipur	South-Eastern	Kolkata
East Coast	Bhubaneswar	South-East Central	Bilaspur
Northern	New Delhi	South-Western	Hubli
North Central	Allahabad	Western	Mumbai (Church Gate)
North-Eastern	Gorakhpur	West Central	Jabalpur
North-East Frontier	Maligaon (Guwahati)	Metro Railway	Kolkata
North-Western	Jaipur		

Konkan Railway

- Konkan railway has been one of the important achievements of the Indian railways since 1998.
- It is a 760 km long rail route connecting Roha in Maharashtra to Mangalore in Karnataka. It is considered an engineering marvel.
- It crosses 146 rivers and streams, nearly 2000 bridges and 91 tunnels. Asia's largest tunnel which is nearly 6.5 km long, also lies on this route. The states of Maharashtra, Goa and Karnataka are partners in this undertaking.

Oil and Gas Pipelines

- Pipelines are the most convenient and efficient mode of transporting liquids and gases over long distances. Even solids can also be transported by pipelines after converting them into slurry.
- **Oil India Limited (OIL)** under the administrative set up of the Ministry of Petroleum and Natural Gas is engaged in the exploration, production and transportation of crude oil and natural gas. It was created as a company in 1959.
- Asia's first cross-country pipeline covering a distance of 1,157 km was constructed by OIL from the Naharkatiya oilfield in Assam to the Barauni refinery in Bihar. It was further extended up to Kanpur in 1966.
- GAIL (India) Ltd. was set up in 1984 as a public sector undertaking to transport, process and market natural gas for its economic use.
- The first 1,700 km long **Hazira-Vijaipur-Jagdishpur** (HVJ) cross-country gas pipeline, was constructed by GAIL (India). It linked Mumbai High and Bassein gas fields with various fertiliser, power and industrial complexes in Western and Northern India.
- India's gas infrastructure has expanded over ten times from 1,700 km to 18,500 km of cross-country pipelines. It is expected to soon reach over 34,000 km as Gas Grid by linking all the gas sources and consuming markets across the country including North-Eastern states.

Quick Test 2

1. When was the first railway line started in India?
2. Mention different rail gauges present in India.
3. What are the two ends of the Konkan railway line?
4. What is the length of first cross country gas pipeline constructed by GAIL (India)?

Water Transport

- Waterways are an important mode of transport for both passenger and cargo traffic in India. It is the cheapest means of transport and is most suitable for carrying heavy and bulky material.
- It is a fuel-efficient and eco-friendly mode of transport.
- Water transport is of two types namely, **inland waterways** and **oceanic waterways**.

Inland Waterways

- Inland waterways was the chief mode of transport before railways was introduced. It faced tough competition from road and railway transport.
- The diversion of river water for irrigation purposes made inland waterways non-navigable in large parts of their courses.
- India has 14,500 km of navigable waterways, contributing about 1% to the country's transportation. It comprises rivers, canals, backwaters[1], creeks[2], etc.

---

1 Backwaters A body of water or a part of a river pushed back by the currents of the sea and separated from it by large areas of sand.
2 Creeks A narrow area of water that flows into the land from the sea, a lake, etc.

- At present, 5,685 km of major rivers are navigable by mechanised flatbottom vessels.
- For the development, maintenance and regulation of national waterways in the country, the **Inland Waterways Authority** was set up in 1986.
- The following waterways have been declared as the National Waterways by the Government

National Waterways of India

Waterways	Stretch	Specification
NW 1	Allahabad- Haldia Stretch (1,620 km)	It is one of the most important waterways in India, which is navigable by mechanical boats up to Patna and by ordinary boats up to Haridwar. It is divided into three parts for developmental purposes (i) Haldia-Farakka (560 km) (ii) Farakka-Patna (460 km) (iii) Patna -Allahabad (600 km)
NW 2	Sadiya- Dhubri Stretch (891 km)	Brahmaputra is navigable by steamers up to Dibrugarh (1,384 km), which is shared by India and Bangladesh.
NW 3	Kottapuram-Kollam Stretch (205 km)	It includes 168 km of West coast canal along with Champakara canal (14 km) and Udyogmandal canal (23 km).
NW 4	—	Specified streches of Godavari and Krishna rivers along with Kakinada Puducherry strech of canals (1,078 km).
NW 5	—	Specified streches of river Brahmani along with Matai river, delta channels of Mahanadi and Brahmani rivers and East coast canals (588 km).

- The Inland Waterways Authority has also identified 10 other inland waterways which could be upgraded.
- The backwaters (Kadal) of Kerala have special significance in the Inland Waterway. They not only provide cheap means of transport, but they are also attracting a large number of tourists to Kerala. The famous **Nehru Trophy Boat Race** (Vallamkali) is also held in the backwaters.

Oceanic Routes

- Approximately 95 per cent of India's foreign trade by volume and 70 per cent by value moves through ocean routes.
- India has a vast coastline of approximately 7,517 km, including islands. 12 major and 200 minor ports provide infrastructural support to these routes.
- Apart from international trade, oceanic routes are also used for the purpose of transportation between the islands and the rest of the country.

Air Transportation

- Air transport is the fastest means of movement from one place to the other. It has reduced distances by minimising the travel time.
- It is essential for a vast country like India for its large distances and the diversity in terrain and climatic conditions.
- Air transport in India was initiated in 1911 when airmail began operation over a small distance of 10 km between Allahabad and Naini. But its real development took place in the post-independent period.
- The **Airport Authority of India** is responsible for providing safe, efficient air traffic and aeronautical communication services in the Indian Air Space.

- **Pawan Hans** is the helicopter service operating in hilly areas and is widely used by tourists in the North-Eastern sector. In addition, Pawan Hans Limited mainly provides helicopter services to the petroleum sector and for tourism.

UDAN (*Ude Desh ka Aam Nagrik*)

- **Regional Connectivity Scheme (RCS)**-UDAN was initiated by the Ministry of Aviation (MoCA) Government of India, to promote regional connectivity by making flying affordable for the common citizen.
- The central idea of the scheme is to encourage airlines to operate flights on regional and remote routes through enabling policies and extending incentives.

Quick Test 3

1 Which scheme is initiated by the government of India to promote regional aviation?
2 Mention the importance of oceanic waterways in India.
3 Who constructed Asia's first cross-country pipeline?
4 Mention one characteristic of National Waterway 1.

7.2 Communication Network

- Human beings have developed different methods of communication over time. In earlier times, horses, camels, dogs, birds and other animals were used to send messages. Initially, the means of communication were also the means of transportation.
- The establishment of the post office, telegraph, printing press, telephone, satellite, etc has made communication much faster and easier.
- Development in the field of science and technology has significantly contributed in bringing about revolution in the field of communication. People use different modes of communication to convey the messages.
- Based on scale and quality, the mode of communication can be divided into personal and mass communication systems.

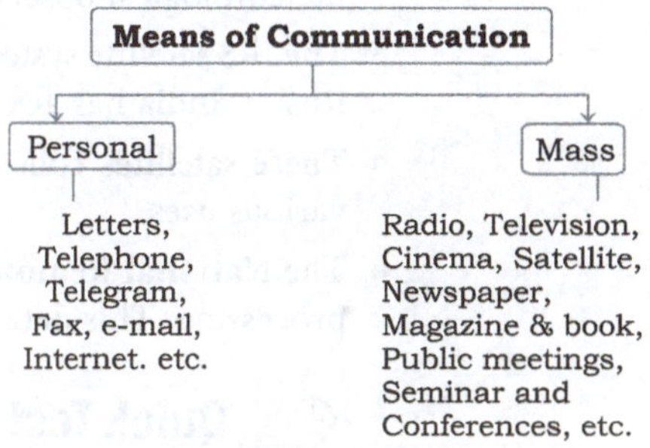

Personal Communication System

- The internet is the most effective and advanced communication system. It is widely used in urban areas.
- It enables the user to establish direct contact through e-mail and access to the world of knowledge and information. It is increasingly used for e-commerce and carrying out money transactions.
- The network through the internet and e-mail provide efficient access to information at a comparatively low cost. It provides us with the basic facilities of direct communication.

Mass Communication System

Radio

- Radio broadcasting started in India in 1923 by the **Radio Club of Bombay**. It became popular from there and changed the socio-cultural life of people.
- The government brought radio under its control in 1930 under the **Indian Broadcasting System**. It was changed to **All India Radio** in 1936 and to **Akashwani** in 1957.
- All India Radio, broadcasts multiple programmes related to information, education and entertainment. Special news bulletins are also broadcast on specific occasions like sessions of parliament and state legislatures.

Television (TV)

- Television broadcasting has emerged as the most effective audio-visual medium for sharing information and educating the masses.
- Initially, the TV services were limited only to the National Capital where it began in 1959. After 1972, several other centres became operational.
- In 1976, TV was separated from All India Radio (AIR) and got a separate identity as **Doordarshan** (DD).
- After INSAT-IA (National Television-DD1) became operational, **Common National Programmes** (CNP) was started for the entire network and its services were extended to the backward and remote rural areas.

Satellite Communication

- Satellites are modes of communication in themselves and regulate the use of other means of communication too. Satellite communication is important for the country for economic and strategic reasons.
- Satellite images can be used for weather forecasting[3], monitoring of natural calamities, surveillance of border areas, etc.
- Based on configuration and purposes, satellite systems in India are grouped as the **Indian National Satellite System** (INSAT) and **Indian Remote Sensing Satellite System** (IRS).
- The INSAT was established in 1983. It is a multi-purpose satellite system for telecommunication, meteorological observation, and various other data and programmes.
- The IRS satellite system became operational with the launch of IRS-IA in March 1988 from Vaikanour in Russia. India has also developed its launching vehicle, PSLV (Polar Satellite Launch Vehicle).
- These satellites collect data in several spectral bands[4] and transmit them to the ground stations for various uses.
- The **National Remote Sensing Centre** (NRSC) at Hyderabad provides facilities for data collection and processing. This data is very useful in the management of natural resources.

Quick Test 4

1. When did radio broadcasting start in India?
2. All India Radio was changed to Akashwani in which year?
3. What are the uses of INSAT I?
4. Name two types of communication networks.

3 Weather Forecasting Weather forecasting is the use of scientific knowledge and technology to predict the weather in a specific location and time.
4 Spectral Bands Spectral bands are regions of a given spectrum, having a specific range of wavelengths of frequencies.

Mind Map

TRANSPORT AND COMMUNICATION

1 Land Transport

Roads

India has one of the second largest road networks

- **National Highways** Main roads maintained by Central Government. These connect the state capitals, major cities, important ports, railway junctions, etc. It constitute only about 2 per cent of the total road length. These are maintained by the central government. Golden Quadrilateral is a 5, 846 km long 4/6 lane highway that connects all the 4 major cities of India. North-South corridor connects Srinagar to Kanyakumari. East-West corridor connects Silchar in Assam to Porbandar in Gujarat.
- **State Highways** Constructed and maintained by State Government. They join the state capitals with district headquarters and other important towns. These roads are connected to the National Highways.
- **District Roads** Connecting links between district headquarters.
- **Rural Roads** Links rural areas.
- **Other Roads** Includes border roads and international roads. Border roads are maintained by BRO.

Railways

- Indian Railways is one of the longest network in the world.
- It was introduced in 1853.
- First line was constructed from Bombay to Thane.

Tracks are divided on the basis of width as

- **Broad Gauge** Distance between rails is 1.676 m.
- **Metre Gauge** Distance between rail is one metre.
- **Narrow Gauge** Distance between rail is 0.762 m. Generally confined to hilly areas.

2 Water Transport

- Cheapest mode of transport.
- Suitable for heavy and bulky material.

Inland Waterways

- India has 14500 km of navigable waterway Example, rivers, canal, creeks, backwater.

Oceanic Routes

- India has a vast coastline of approximately 7,517 km, including islands, 12 major and 200 minor ports.

3 Air Transport

- Fastest means of transportation
- Began in 1911
- Maintained by Airport Authority of India

4 Pipeline

- Convenient and efficient mode of transport
- Can transport liquid, gas, solid (slurry)

Authorities

- **Gas Authority of India Limited** (GAIL) It was set up in 1984. The first 1,700 km long Hazira-Vijaipur-Jagdishpur was constructed by GAIL.
- **Oil India Limited** (OIL) Asia's first cross-country pipeline covering a distance of 1,157 km. It was constructed by OIL from the Naharkatiya oilfield in Assam to the Barauni refinery in Bihar.

5 Personal Communication System

- Communication between two persons.
- **Example** Internet, email, fax

6 Mass Communication System

- Communication to a wide audience at one time

Example

- **Radio** Started in India in 1923 by the Radio Club of Bombay. It was changed to All India Radio in 1936 and to Akashwani in 1957.
- **Tv** Most effective audio-visual medium for sharing information and educating the masses.
- **Satellites** Used for weather forecasting, monitoring of natural calamities, surveillance of border areas, etc.

NCERT Folder

Choose the right answer of the following from the given options

(i) **In how many zones has the Indian railway system been divided?**

(a) 9 (b) 12 (c) 17 (d) 14

Ans. (c) 17

(ii) **On which river and between which two places does the National Waterway No. 1 lie?**

(a) The Brahmaputra, Sadiya- Dhubri

(b) The Ganga, Haldia-Allahabad

(c) West Coast Canal, Kottapuram to Kollam

Ans. (b) The Ganga, Haldia-Allahabad

(iii) **In which of the following year, the first radio programme was broadcast?**

(a) 1911 (b) 1936

(c) 1927 (d) 1923

Ans. (d) 1923

Answer the following questions in about 30 words

(i) **Which activity does transportation convey? Name the three major modes of transportation.**

Ans. Transportation conveys the tertiary activity i.e. transport services for people and goods from one place to another. The three modes of transportation are land, water and air.

(ii) **Discuss advantages and disadvantages of pipeline transportation.**

Ans. Advantages of pipeline transportation are as follows (*Any two*)

- Pipelines are suited to transport liquid and gases.
- It can be laid through difficult terrains as well as under the road.
- It needs very little maintenance and energy consumption.
- It does not require much space.

Disadvantages of pipeline transportation are as follows (*Any two*)

- It cannot be used conveniently to transport solids.
- Initial construction cost is very high.
- Its capacity cannot be increased once it is laid.
- Underground pipeline cannot be easily repaired and detection of leakage is also difficult.

(iii) **What do you mean by communication?**

Ans. Communication means transmission of information from one place, person or group to another. Communication network is used to send information from one place to another.

There are two types of communication

(i) Personal communication

(ii) Mass communication

Answer the following questions in about 150 words

(i) **Which are the chief means of transportation in India? Discuss the factors affecting their development.**

Ans. The chief means of transportation in India include

- **Road Transport** India has a vast road network, with National Highways, State Highways and Rural Roads facilitating connectivity.
- **Rail Transport** It is one of the world's longest networks. Railways are crucial for passenger and freight movement, which connect urban and rural areas.
- **Water Transport** Inland waterways and oceanic routes are vital for heavy cargo transport, with major ports supporting trade.
- **Air Transport** Essential for long-distance and remote area connectivity. Air travel has become more accessible with the UDAN scheme.
- **Pipeline Transport** Pipelines are used to transport oil, gas, and even water, connecting production and demand centres efficiently.

Factors affecting the development of transportation in India are

- **Geographical Terrain** Mountainous, desert and forested regions pose challenges for road and rail networks.
- **Economic Investment** High costs limit infrastructure expansion, especially in less profitable or rural areas.
- **Technological Advancements** Improvements in infrastructure like metro rail, high-speed trains and modern highways accelerate connectivity.
- **Government Policies** Schemes like Bharatmala for roads and UDAN for air travel promote infrastructure growth and accessibility .

(ii) **Give a detailed account of the development of railway transport in India and highlight their importance.**

Ans. Development of Railway Transport in India

Railway transport was developed in India by the Britishers. They developed it with the objective of exploiting resources. In 1853, the first railway line was started from Bombay to Thane covering a distance of 34 km.

Areas around towns, raw material producing areas, hill stations, cantonments towns were well-connected by railways during the British period.

After independence, the railway network has been extended to remote and backward areas of the country. Many initiatives were taken by government to improve the performance and outreach of the railway. With time, meter and narrow gauge are being converted into broad gauge. Steam engines have been replaced by diesel and electronic engines. Metro rail has added new features in railway transport. Currently, country has 17 railway zones. Due to consistent efforts by the government, today Indian railway network is one of the largest rail networks in the world.

Importance of Railways

Importance of Indian railways are as follows

- After independence, Indian railways played a significant role in the development of India. Railways is still the chief means of transport for the masses.
- It has brought people of diverse cultures together for India's freedom struggle.
- Indian railway also contributes to Indian economy in many ways by providing fast and reliable transport medium for various important raw materials and products across the country.

(iii) **Describe the role of roads in the economic development of India.**

Or **"India has one of the largest road networks in the world." Examine the statement.** **CBSE Term II 2022**

Ans. India has the second largest road network in the world. It contributes to the economic development of India as about 80% of passenger traffic and 75% of freight in India is carried by roads every year.

The role of roads in economic development are as follows

- Roads connect the remote villages and backward areas with the cities.
- Road transport establishes easy contacts between farms, fields, factories, and markets.
- It facilitates easy movement of raw materials as well as finished products across the country.
- The National Highways are used to transport men and materials in the strategic areas. They also connect state capitals, important economic and industrial cities, important ports, railway junctions, etc.
- State Highways connect state capitals with district headquarters and commercial towns.
- Border roads accelerate economic development by rapidly improving strategically important roads along North and North-Eastern border of the country.
- International highways also contribute to trade and economic development of India.
- Golden Quadilateral and North-South economic corridor helps in connecting major urban, industrial centres, promoting growth and development.

Exam Pattern Questions

Objective Type Questions

Multiple Choice Questions (MCQs)

1. Nagpur Plan is associated with which of the following?

(a) Railway modernisation (b) Road modernisation
(c) Waterway development (d) Airways development

2. The road between Chandigarh-Manali was constructed by which of the following?

(a) Border Roads Organisation
(b) National Highways Authority of India
(c) Central Public Works Department
(d) State Public Works Department

3. Which of the following metro-cities is not linked with the 'Golden Quadrilateral'? **CBSE 2024**

(a) Mumbai (b) Chennai
(c) Hyderabad (d) Delhi

4. Indian Railway was introduced in 1853 and a railway line was constructed from .... to .... covering a distance of 34 km.

(a) Mumbai (Bombay), Thane
(b) Kolkata (Calcutta), Hugli
(c) Chennai (Madras), Madurai
(d) Bengaluru (Bangalore), Calicut

5. Which one of the following places is the Easternmost station of the 'East-West Corridor'? CBSE 2024

(a) Digboi (b) Silchar
(c) Guwahati (d) Itanagar

6. Which of the following are the correct two terminal places of the North-South Corridor? CBSE 2024

(a) Srinagar and Kanyakumari (b) Delhi and Kanyakumari
(c) Amritsar and Chennai (d) Srinagar and Chennai

7. Which of the following is not true regarding the development of border roads? CBSE 2023

(a) Integration of people of remote areas with major cities.
(b) Strengthening defence preparedness.
(c) Helps in transporting goods to border villages.
(d) Help in developing large scale industries.

8. Name the headquarters of Northern Railway Zone of India.

(a) Lucknow (b) Kanpur
(c) New Delhi (d) Chandigarh

9. Which one of the following is the biggest government undertaking in the country? CBSE 2024

(a) Indian Railways
(b) National Highways Authority of India
(c) Border Roads Organisation
(d) All India Radio

10. Which of the following pairs is not correctly matched?

(a) Central Railway Zone – Mumbai (CST)
(b) Northern Railway Zone – Gorakhpur
(c) North Central Railway Zone – Allahabad
(d) North-East Frontier Railway Zone – Maligaon (Guwahati)

11. The National Waterway 2 lies on which river in India?

(a) Ganga (b) Yamuna
(c) Brahmaputra (d) Chambal

12. Choose the correct option regarding the stretch of National Waterways 2.

(a) Sadiya to Dhubri (b) Sadiya to Haldia
(c) Sadiya to Kollam (d) Sadiya to Allahabad

13. Choose the correct option regarding the stretch of National Waterways 1. CBSE 2024

(a) Allahabad/Prayagraj-Haldia
(b) Sadiya-Dhubri
(c) Kottapuram-Kollam
(d) Kakinada-Puducherry

14. Which of these provide helicopter services in hilly areas in the North-East region in India?

(a) Air India Limited (b) Pawan Hans Limited
(c) Indian Airlines (d) BHEL Limited

15. Which of these are true for road transport in India?

(i) India has the second largest road network in the world.
(ii) About 20 per cent of passenger traffic is carried by roads in India.
(iii) Twenty-year Road Plan was introduced in the year 1961 to improve the conditions of roads.

Codes

(a) (i), (ii) and (iii) (b) (i) and (ii)
(c) (i) and (iii) (d) (ii) and (iii)

16. Which of these states operate the Konkan Railways?

(i) Maharashtra (ii) Goa
(iii) Andhra Pradesh (iv) Karnataka

Codes

(a) (i), (ii) and (iii) (b) (i), (ii), (iii) and (iv)
(c) (i), (ii) and (iv) (d) (i) and (iii)

17. Which of the following is/are the use(s) of satellite communication in India?

(i) Management of natural resources
(ii) Meteorological observation
(iii) Telecommunication

Codes

(a) (i) and (ii) (b) (i), (ii) and (iii)
(c) (ii) and (iii) (d) (i) and (iii)

18. Read the programmes related to the proposed Bharatmala umbrella scheme carefully and choose the correct option. CBSE 2024

(i) Focuses on backward areas, religious and tourist places connectivity programme.
(ii) To interconnect the four metropolitan cities of the country.
(iii) To develop state roads in adjoining coastal areas.
(iv) To connect non-major ports in coastal states

Options

(a) Only (i), (ii) and (iii) are correct.
(b) Only (ii), (iii) and (iv) are correct.
(c) Only (i), (iii) and (iv) are correct.
(d) Only (i), (ii) and (iv) are correct.

Match the Following

19. CBSE 2023

List I (Railway Zone)		List II (Headquarter)	
A.	North Central	1.	Secunderabad
B.	East Central	2.	Allahabad/Prayagraj
C.	West Central	3.	Hajipur
D.	South Central	4.	Jabalpur

Codes

	A	B	C	D		A	B	C	D
(a)	1	2	3	4	(b)	4	3	2	1
(c)	3	4	1	2	(d)	2	3	4	1

CBSE 2024

20.

	List I (National Waterway)		List II (River)
A.	National Waterway 1	1.	Matai
B.	National Waterway 2	2.	Godavari
C.	National Waterway 4	3.	Ganga
D.	National Waterway 5	4.	Brahmaputra

Codes

	A	B	C	D		A	B	C	D
(a)	4	3	2	1	(b)	4	3	1	2
(c)	3	4	1	2	(d)	3	4	2	1

21.

	List I (National Waterway)		List II (Stretch)
A.	NW 1	1.	Sadiya - Dhubri
B.	NW 2	2.	Allahabad - Haldia
C.	NW 3	3.	Kottapuram-Kollam

Codes

	A	B	C		A	B	C
(a)	1	3	2	(b)	2	1	3
(c)	2	3	1	(d)	1	2	3

Assertion-Reason

Directions (Q. Nos. 22-24) In the questions given below are two statements labelled as Assertion (A) and other labelled as Reason (R). In the context of two statements which one of the following is correct?

Codes

(a) Both A and R are true, but R is not the correct explanation of A
(b) Both A and R are true and R is the correct explanation of A
(c) A is incorrect, but R is correct
(d) A is correct, but R is incorrect

22. Assertion (A) Indian railways has been divided into 18 zones.
Reason (R) Large size of railways puts a lot of pressure on a centralised management system.

23. Assertion (A) Water transport is the cheapest of all transport.
Reason (R) India has 17,500 km of navigable waterways.

24. Assertion (A) Waterway is an important mode of transport both for passengers and cargo traffic in India.
Reason (R) It is fuel efficient and eco-friendly mode of transport.

Answers

1. (b) Road modernisation
2. (a) Border Roads Organisation
3. (c) Hyderabad
4. (a) Mumbai (Bombay), Thane
5. (b) Silchar
6. (a) Srinagar and Kanyakumari
7. (d) Help in developing large scale industries.
8. (c) New Delhi
9. (a) Indian Railways
10. (b) Northern Railway Zone-Gorakhpur
11. (c) Brahmaputra
12. (a) Sadiya to Dhubri
13. (a) Allahabad/Prayagraj-Haldia
14. (b) Pawan Hans Limited
15. (c) (i) and (iii)
16. (c) (i), (ii) and (iv)
17. (b) (i), (ii) and (iii)
18. (c) Only (i), (iii) and (iv) are correct.
19. (d)
20. (d)
21. (b)
22. (c) A is incorrect, but R is correct
23. (d) A is correct, but R is incorrect
24. (b) Both A and R are true and R is the correct explanation of A

Subjective Questions

Short Answer Type Questions

1. Evaluate the role and importance of roads in the economic development of India. **CBSE Sample Paper Term II 2021**

Ans. Importance and role of roadways in the economic development in India are

- Roads provides better connectivity between rural and urban areas and hence advancement of rural India occurs.
- Road connectivity is very important in linking intra-state urban areas and inter-states for better transportation of various goods and services and hence for overall development in terms of saving time, money, etc.
- Rural economy would be connected with urban economy through a dense road network.
- A good road network helps to improve import and export in the country.

2. The distribution of roads in India is not uniform. Examine the statement by giving three reasons. **Competency Based Que**

Or **"The density and quality of roads are better in plains as compared to other regions in India". Support the statement with examples.**

Ans. The distribution of roads in India is not uniform. Reasons behind this uneven distribution of roads are

- Roads can be easily constructed at a low cost in plain areas, whereas it is difficult and costly in hilly, mountainous and plateau areas. Therefore, most of the Northern states and Southern states have dense network of roads as compared to Himalayan and North-Eastern states.
- Level of economic development also plays an important role in deciding the network of roads in an area. Therefore, areas having low economic development like, Rajasthan and Madhya Pradesh have less dense network of roads.
- Inaccessible areas also have less density of roads in India, e.g. forested, rainy and high altitude areas have less density of roads.

3. Describe any three characteristics of State Highways of India.

Ans. Three characteristics of State Highways of India are as follows

(i) These are the highways which are constructed and maintained by the state governments. They constitute about 4% of total roads in the country.

(ii) They are meant to connect the state capitals with district headquarters and other important towns.

(iii) These roads are further connected to National Highways, so they can connect these areas to other states.

4. Which are the two types of roads included under the category of 'other roads' in India? Write any two features of each.

Ans. Border Roads and International Highways are included under the category of 'other roads' in India.

These are described below

Border Roads These are strategically important roads along the Northern and North-Eastern boundary of the country.

Characteristics of border roads are as follows

(i) The total length of border roads is 46,870 km. These are constructed by Border Road Organisation (BRO).

(ii) These roads are important to accelerate economic development and strengthening defence preparedness.

International Highway These are the roads which connect India to neighbouring countries.

Characteristics of international highways are as follows

(i) They aim to promote harmonious relationship with neighbouring countries.

(ii) They provide an effective connectivity to neighbouring countries.

5. Explain the functions of Border Road Organisation.

Ans. The Border Road Organisation (BRO) was established in May 1960. Functions of BRO are as follows

- It aims at accelerating economic development and strengthening defence preparedness through rapid and co-ordinated improvement of strategically important roads along the Northern and North-Eastern boundary of the country.
- Apart from the construction and maintenance of roads in strategically sensitive areas, the BRO also undertakes snow clearance in high altitude areas.
- It also contributes to the socio-economic development of border states.

6. Define different gauges of Indian railways.

Or **What are the three categories of the track of Indian railways? Write any one feature of each.**

Or **What are the three categories of Indian railways on the basis of width of track? Write main feature of each category.**

Ans. For answer refer to text page no. 298 under the heading 'Rail Gauge'.

7. What are the steps taken by Indian railways to improve its performance?

Ans. Following are the steps taken by Indian railways after independence to improve its performance

- To convert the metre and narrow gauge into broad gauge.
- Replacement of steam engine and diesel engine into electric engine which may also help in keeping the environment clean and reduce the operational cost.
- Introduction of metro rails in metropolitan towns to provide good means for urban transit system, e.g. Kolkata Metro, operated by Indian railways.

8. Why is the Indian railway system divided into sixteen zones (now eighteen)? Name the headquarters of Eastern, Western, Northern and Southern zones.

Ans. Indian railway system is divided into sixteen zones because it is one of the longest rail networks in the world with the length of 66,030 km. This whole network was controlled by the Centralised Railway System, so to reduce the pressure of this large size network from centralised railway system Indian Railways are divided into zones. Another reason for this division is to provide services throughout the country. Zoning of Railways helps in increasing the efficiency of the Railways.

Each Railway zones have a headquarter among which the headquarter of Eastern Railways is Kolkata, Western Railways zone is Mumbai, Northern Railways zone is New Delhi and Southern Railways zone is Chennai.

9. Examine the role of Inland Waterways Authority of India.

Ans. The role of Inland Waterways Authority of India can be understood through the following points

- The Inland Waterways Authority was set up in 1986.
- It is entrusted with the responsibility of the development, maintenance and regulation of national waterways in the country.
- It does the function of surveying the economic feasibility of new projects and also the administration of waterways.
- It advises the Central government on matters related to Inland Waterways.

10. How are oceanic routes advantageous for India?

Ans. Oceanic routes are advantageous for India because

- These play an important role in the transport sector of India's economy.
- About 95 per cent of India's foreign trade by volume and 70 per cent by value moves through oceanic routes.
- Oceanic routes are advantageous as India has vast coastline of 7,517 km including islands.
- About 185 minor ports and twelve major ports provide infrastructural support to these routes.
- These routes provide international trade service.
- It provides transportation between the Islands and rest of the country.

11. Which is the most effective and advanced personal communication system in India? Explain any four characteristics of it.

Ans. The most effective and advanced personal communication system in India is internet.

It has following characteristics

- With the help of internet, users can directly communicate through e-mail and can get access to the world of knowledge and information.
- Use of internet is increasing for e-commerce and carrying out money transactions.
- The internet is like a huge central warehouse of data, with detailed information on various items.
- It enables us with the basic facilities of direct communication.

This mode of communication is efficient and cost effective.

12. Explain with examples the importance of 'satellite communication' in the world. **CBSE 2024**

Ans. Satellite communication plays a crucial role in global connectivity, enabling telecommunication, broadcasting, and internet services across vast areas. It supports weather forecasting, disaster monitoring, and border surveillance. For example, satellites like INSAT in India provide essential services for telecommunication, meteorological observation, and emergency communication. They also assist in monitoring natural disasters like cyclones and floods. Satellite systems ensure reliable communication, especially in remote or underserved regions, and contribute significantly to economic and strategic development worldwide.

Long Answer Type Questions

1. Write any five characteristics of road transport in India.

Ans. Characteristics of road transport in India are as follows *(Any five)*

(i) With a total length of 54.8 lakh km of roads, India has placed itself among the countries which have a large road network.

(ii) Road transport carries about 85% of passenger and 70% of freight traffic every year. It is preferred for short distance travel as it provides door to door service.

(iii) Roads are mainly concentrated around urban areas, Rural and remote areas are least connected by the roads.

(iv) Distribution of roads is not even throughout the country. Road density is highest in Kerala and lowest in Jammu and Kashmir. Most of the Northern and Southern states have highly dense network of roads as compared to North-East and Himalayan region.

(v) In India, roads are classified on the basis of purpose of construction and maintenance in National Highways (NH), State Highways (SH), major district roads and rural roads.

(vi) Apart from above roads, there are border roads which are constructed for defence purpose and international roads which are constructed to link and connect with neighbouring countries. They are also used for strategic purposes.

2. Which apex body develops the border roads? Explain the importance of border roads with examples.

Ans. The organisation that is responsible for developing border roads is Border Road Organisation (BRO). This organisation was established in 1960 and accelerated the economic development, and strengthened defence preparedness through rapid and coordinated improvement of strategic roads along the Northern and North-Eastern borders.

The importance of border roads for India is

- These are meant to promote harmonious relationship with the neighbouring countries of India by providing effective links and routes.
- These roads are suitable for carrying out international trade with the bordering countries of India which leads to economic development.
- They are most suitable during foreign attacks as troops and defence materials can be easily transported to border posts with the use of these roads.
- These roads are used to provide essential items to the inaccessible areas such as mountain regions in states of Himachal Pradesh, Uttarakhand, Arunachal Pradesh, etc.
- These roads integrate the far off areas of India with the Indian mainland that helps in national integration and unity.

3. Explain with five suitable examples, how the level of economic development and nature of terrain affect the density of roads in India.

Ans. Nature of terrain and level of economic development affect the density of roads in following ways

(i) Construction of roads in plains is easy and cheaper in comparison to hilly and mountainous areas. Therefore, Gangetic plains have high density of roads as compared to hilly North-Eastern states.

(ii) Difficult terrain, thick forest do not provide suitable conditions for the development of roads. That's the reason for having low density of roads in Himalayan and North-Eastern region.

(iii) Sandy soil is also a restriction in the development of roads, that's the reason for less density of roads in Western Rajasthan. Similarly in the sandy region of Gujarat, the density of road is very less.

(iv) Economic development also affects the density of roads. Karnataka Plateau and Maharashtra have high density of roads due to high concentration of industries and urbanisation in these areas.

While in the some states, there is very less density of roads in areas which are economically backward and have less natural resources.

(v) High density of road network is found in Punjab, Haryana and Uttar Pradesh in the Northern India. This is due to advanced agriculture, industry and urbanisation in these areas. Density of roads is also high in West Bengal.

After analysing these example we can say that density of roads is dependent on level of economic development and nature of terrain.

4. What are National Highways? Explain any four uses of National Highways in India.

Ans. The main roads which are constructed and maintained by the central government are known as the National highways.

The main uses of National Highways are given below

(i) These roads are meant for inter-state and strategic defence movements. They are used to move both people and freight across the states of India.

(ii) They carry most of the road traffic in India. They constitute only 2% of the total road length but carries 40% of the road traffic. Thus, they are very important for transportation.

(iii) National Highways are important for industrial development. Most of the industries are located at important modes where National Highways provide good connectivity for the easy movement of raw materials and goods and commodities to the market areas.

(iv) These also connect the state capitals, major cities, important ports, railway junctions, etc and help in carrying out trade and commercial activities across these capitals and cities.

5. Define the term road density. Explain with examples the two main determinants of road density in India.

Or **Explain with examples the two main determinants of road density in India.**

Ans. Density of roads is defined as the length of roads per 100 sq km of surface area. It is a method to compare road network of an area to another area.

The two determinants of road density in India are as follows

Level of Economic Development

- The density of roads is directly proportional to the level of economic development in a region.
- In Northern plains, the density of roads is high mainly due to development of agricultural sector and urbanisation.
- States of Haryana, Punjab and Uttar Pradesh have high density of roads.
- Industrialisation also decides the density of roads. In the industrialised area, there is high density due to development activities.
- In the backward areas the level of economic development is low thus density of roads is also less.

Nature of Terrain

- Nature of terrain directly affects road density. Plains are most suitable for construction of road infrastructure whereas mountains, hills and forested areas are not suitable for construction of roads.
- Gangetic plains have high density of roads whereas Himalayan states like Uttarakhand and North-Eastern states have low density or roads.
- Plateau regions have less dense roads. For example Chhotanagpur plateau region, central highlands region.

6. "Indian railways network is one of the longest networks of the world and has contributed a lot to the growth of the economy." Support the statement. **Competency Based Que**

Or **"Indian railways network is one of the longest in the world." Support the statement.** **CBSE 2023**

Or **Explain the importance of rail transport in India.** **CBSE 2024**

Ans. India has one of the longest railway networks in the world.

It has contributed to the growth of national economy in following ways

- Indian railways form the lifeline of India catering to its needs for large scale movement of traffic, both freight and passenger, thereby contributing to economic growth.
- Railways has also helped in promoting national integration. It connects areas having important mineral resources to regions where there are industries.
- It also helps in transporting raw materials and finished products.
- Apart from the passengers and traffic, the freight also increased tremendously. Development in industrial and agricultural sectors has generated high demand for railway transport.
- Major commodities transported by railways include coal, iron and steel ores, petroleum products and essential commodities such as foodgrains, fertilisers, cement, sugar, salt, edible oils, etc.
- Indian railways also contribute in tourism sector by connecting hill stations, religious places and other important tourist places.
- It is the largest government undertaking which provides employment to millions of people in India.

7. Describe in brief water transport system of India.

Or **Explain why Inland Water Transport is an important mode of transport?** **CBSE 2024**

Ans. There are two types of water transport systems in India

Inland Waterways

- India has 14,500 km of navigable inland waterways which is used for about 1% of country's total transportation.
- It includes rivers, canals, backwaters, creeks, etc. At present, 5,685 km of major rivers are navigable by mechanised vessels.
- The Inland Waterways Authority is responsible for the development, maintenance and regulation of national waterways in the country.
- Currently, there are 111 Inland waterways which are considered as National Waterways.

Oceanic Routes

- India's vast coastline of about 7,517 km including islands easily facilitate this type of transport.
- There are twelve major and 200 minor ports, which provide infrastructural support to these routes.

- About 95% of India's foreign trade by volume and 70% by value moves through oceanic routes.
- Besides trade, its development is also necessary for the transportation between the island and mainland of India.

8. "Waterways is an important mode of transport for both passenger and cargo traffic in India." Support the statement with examples. Competency Based Que

Ans. Waterways are important mode of transport for both passengers and cargo traffic in India in the following ways

- Waterways provide cheapest and most suitable transportation for heavy and bulky material for long distances from one region to another.
- It is a fuel efficient and eco-friendly means of transport as it does not require maintenance and construction of routes, which involves high cost.
- India has 14,500 km of Inland waterways which accounts for 1% of country's transportation.
- At present, over 5,600 km of rivers are navigable by mechanised vessels in India which are used to transport both passenger and freight.
- Backwaters (Kayal) of Kerala have special significance as they provide cheap means of transport as well as tourism activities.
- It reduces congestion and accidents on roads highways as freight can be moved easily with waterways.
- It can be used for transporting both domestic as well as international cargo. India has many major and minor parts, which are facilitating trade within the country as well as internationally.
- Waterways have potential for cruise, tourism and passenger traffic that can contribute to the development of the country.

9. Give an account of air transportation in India.

Or **What is the importance of air transport? Describe any four characteristics of air transport system of India.**

Ans. Air transport facilitates the fastest movement of goods and passengers from one place to another place. It has reduced distances and converted the world into one unit. Air transport has a great importance for a vast country like India where distances are large and the terrain and the climatic conditions are uneven throughout the country. It is also important for our links with other countries. India occupies a central location between Western Europe and Africa on the one hand and South -East and East Asia on the other hand.

Characteristics of air transport system of India are as follows

(i) To provide safe, efficient air traffic and aeronautical communication services in Indian space, there is regulatory body known as Airport Authority of India.

(ii) There are two corporations, Air India and Indian Airlines, which provide air services in India. Air India handles international traffic passengers and cargo whereas Indian Airlines is the major domestic air carrier of the country.

10. "Pipelines are the most convenient and efficient mode of transporting liquids and gases over long distances in India." Examine the statement. CBSE 2024, CBSE Term II 2022

Ans. Pipelines are the most convenient and efficient mode of transporting liquids and gases over long distances in India. The importance of this mode of transport can be seen through the following points

- Without the help of pipelines, liquids and gases cannot be transported over long distances like from refineries to sea ports and petrol pumps, etc.
- If we opt roadways to transport liquids and gases from one place to another, only a limited quantity can be transported.
- There are chances of road accidents or burning of fuel if liquids and gases are transported through other modes of transport like roadways and railways instead of pipelines.
- But in case of pipelines no or few chances of accidents are there and a smooth supply of these commodities take place.
- Pipelines can also transport solids after converting them into slurry (we mixture).
- Its initial set up cost is high, but after that pipelines transport liquids and gases very cheaply.
- It does not require much space.
- Pipelines are energy efficient and environment friendly.

11. How has internet revolutionised the communication services? CBSE Diksha

Ans. Internet is the most effective and advanced source of communication. Introduction of internet has revolutionised the communication system in the following ways

- It enables the user to establish direct contact through e-mail to get access to the world of knowledge and information.

- It is increasingly used for ecommerce and carrying out money transactions.
- The internet is like a huge central warehouse of data which has detailed information on various items. This helps people solving their problems by exploring.
- The network through internet and e-mail provides an efficient access to information at a comparatively low cost. It enables us with the basic facilities of direct communication.

Source Based Questions

1. Read the passage carefully and answer the questions that follow.

The main roads which are constructed and maintained by the central government are known as the National Highways. These roads are meant for inter-state transport and movement of defence men and material in strategic areas. These also connect the state capitals, major cities, important ports, railway junctions, etc. The National Highways constitute only about 2 per cent of the total road length but carry 40 per cent of the road traffic. State Highways are constructed and maintained by state governments. They join the state capitals with district headquarters and other important towns. These roads are connected to the National Highways. These constitute 4 per cent of total road length in the country. District Roads roads are the connecting link between District Headquarters and the other important nodes in the district.

(i) Which of these roads connect state capitals?

(a) District roads (b) National Highways
(c) Rural Roads (d) Border Roads

Ans. (b) National Highways

(ii) Which organisation is responsible for the maintenance of strategic roads in border areas?

(a) Indian Army
(b) Sahastra Seema Bal
(c) Border Road Organisation
(d) National Highways Authority of India

Ans. (c) Border Road Organisation

(iii) Which category of roads constitute the largest proportion of roads in India?

(a) National Highways
(b) Rural Roads
(c) Border Roads
(d) State Highways

Ans. (b) Rural Roads

2. Study the given diagram carefully and answer the questions that follow. **CBSE 2024**

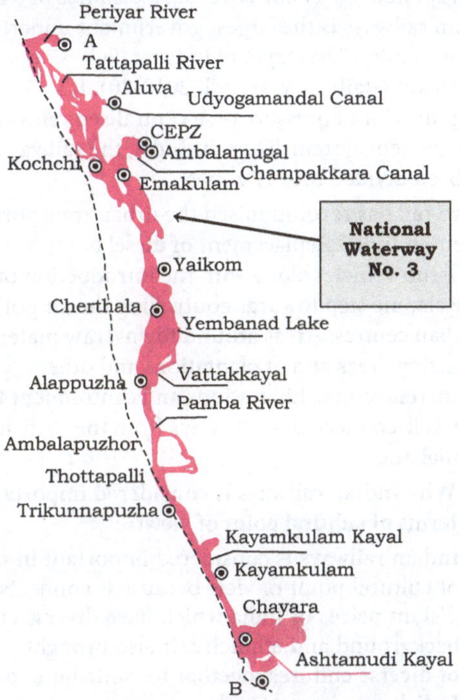

(i) The given diagram is related to which of the following National Waterways of India?

(a) National Waterway 2
(b) National Waterway 3
(c) National Waterway 4
(d) National Waterway 5

Ans. (b) National Waterway 3

(ii) Mark (A) on the diagram is related to which of the following places?

(a) Kakinada (b) Dhubri
(c) Kottapuram (d) Sadiya

Ans. (c) Kottapuram

(iii) Mark (B) on the diagram is related to which of the following places?

(a) Kollam (b) Haldia
(c) Dibrugarh (d) Vallamkali

Ans. (a) Kollam

3. Read the passage carefully and answer the questions that follow.

Indian railways, network is one of the longest in the world. It facilitates the movement of both freight and passengers and contributes to the growth of the economy. Mahatma Gandhi said, the Indian railways "...brought people of diverse cultures together to contribute to India's freedom struggle". Indian railway was introduced in 1853, when a line was constructed from Bombay to Thane covering a distance of 34 km. Indian railways is the largest government undertaking in the country. The length of Indian railways network was 67,956 km (Railway yearbook 2019-20). It's very large size puts a lot of pressure on a centralised railway management system. Thus, in India, the railway system has been divided into 17 zones.

Metro rail has revolutionised the urban transport system in India. Replacement of diesel buses by CNG-run vehicles along with the introduction of metro is a welcome step towards controlling the air pollution in urban centres. Areas around towns, raw material producing areas and of plantations and other commercial crops, hill stations and cantonment towns were well-connected by railways from the British colonial era.

(i) Why Indian railways is considered important in terms of cultural point of view?

Ans. Indian railways is considered important in terms of cultural point of view because it connects distant places of India which have diverse cultural background and ethnicity. It also brought people of diverse cultures together to contribute to India's freedom struggle.

(ii) Mention some points that shows that the urban transport has been revolutionised.

Ans. Introduction of Metro rail, Replacement of diesel buses by CNG-run vehicles are some of the steps that shows the revolutionising nature of the urban transport.

(iii) Why is Konkan railway considered an engineering marvel?

Ans. Konkan railway is considered an engineering marvel because

- This 760 km long rail route connects Roha in Maharashtra to Mangalore in Karnataka which crosses 146 rivers, streams, nearly 2000 bridges and 91 tunnels.
- Asia's largest tunnel which is nearly 6.5 km long also lies on this route.

4. Read the passage carefully and answer the questions that follow.

Human beings have evolved different methods of communication over time. In earlier times, the messages were delivered by beating the drum or hollow tree trunks, giving indications through smoke or fire or with the help of fast runners. Horses, camels, dogs, birds and other animals were also used to send messages. Initially, the means of communication were also the means of transportation. Invention of post office, telegraph, printing press, telephone, satellite, etc has made the communication much faster and easier. Development in the field of science and technology has significantly contributed in bringing about revolution in the field of communication. Among all the personal communication system internet is the most effective and advanced one. It is widely used in urban areas. It enables the user to establish direct contact through e-mail to get access to the world of knowledge and information. It is increasingly used for e-commerce and carrying out money transactions. The internet is like a huge central warehouse of data, with detailed information on various items. The network through internet and e-mail provides an efficient access to information at a comparatively low cost. It enables us with the basic facilities of direct communication.

(i) How has the method of communication evolved?

Ans. Over the years, the methods of communication has evolved from using drums or hollow tree trunks to horses, camels, birds as the method to send messages. Later there were invention of post offices and telegraph methods.

(ii) Development in the field of science has revolutionised the communication system. Comment.

Ans. Introduction of internet in the field of communication is the proof that the communication has been revolutionised. Internet enables the user with basic facilities of direct communication.

(iii) What are the methods of mass communication?

Ans. The methods of mass communication includes television, newspaper and radio.

Map Based Questions

1. Locate and label the following features with appropriate symbols on the outline political map of India.

(i) The international airport located in Assam
(ii) The international airport in Gujarat
(iii) The international airport in Punjab
(iv) The international airport in Karnataka
Or An international Southernmost airport in Kerala
(v) An international airport in Maharashtra

Ans.

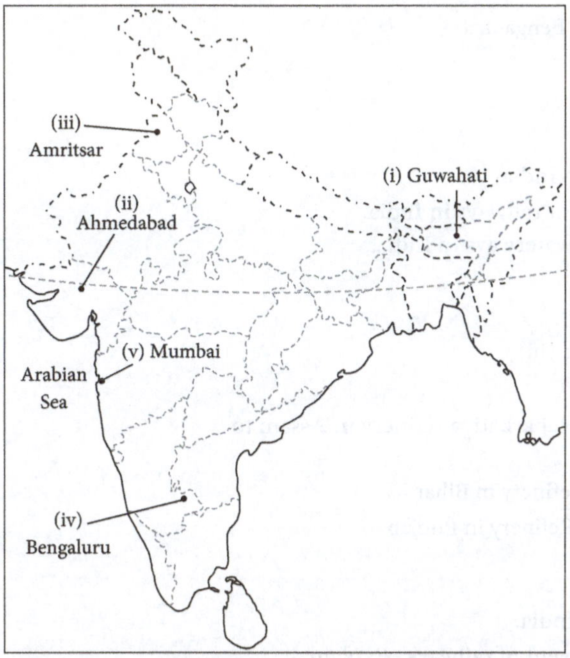

2. On the given political outline map of India, locate and label the following with appropriate symbols.

(i) The international airport in Tamil Nadu
(ii) The international airport in West Bengal
(iii) Delhi international airport
(iv) The Southernmost international airport
(v) The Easternmost international airport
(vi) An international airport in Telangana

Ans.

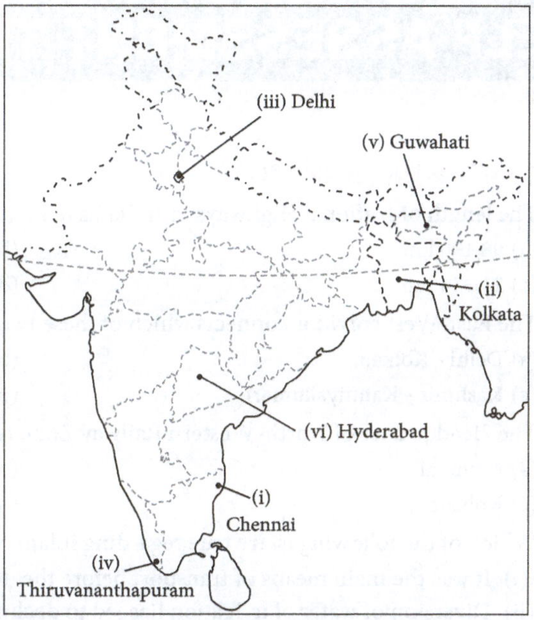

3. On the outline map of India, locate the following

(i) Important towns of Golden Quadrilateral
(ii) Important towns of North-South Corridor
(iii) Important towns of East-West Corridor

Ans.

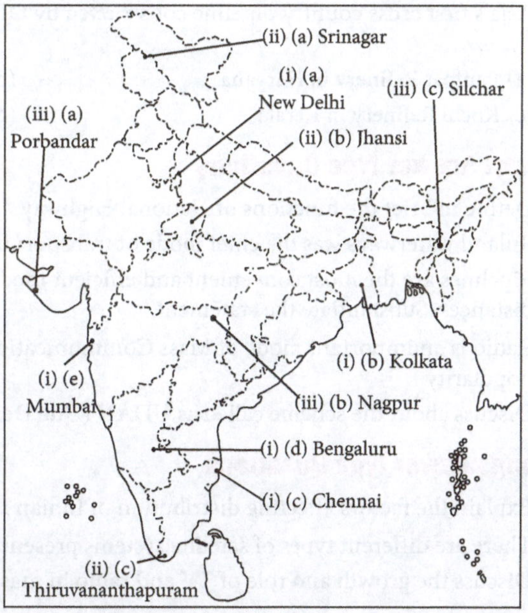

SELF ASSESSMENT TEST

Objective Type Questions

1. The length of National Highways in India have increased from 19,700 km in 1951 to ……….. in 2016.

(a) 98,190 km (b) 1,00,475 km

(c) 21,350 km (d) 12,340 km

2. The East-West corridor connects which of these two cities?

(a) Delhi - Kolkata (b) Porbandar - Silchar

(c) Kashmir - Kanniyakumari (d) Chennai - Bengaluru

3. The Headquarter of North-Western Railway Zone is located at

(a) Mumbai (b) Jaipur

(c) Kolkata (d) Delhi

4. Which of the following is/are true regarding inland waterways in India?

(i) It was the main means of transport before the development of railways in India.

(ii) Diversion of water of irrigation has led to decline of inland waterways in India.

(iii) Inland waterways comprises of rivers, canals, creeks, etc.

Codes

(a) (i) and (ii) (b) (i), (ii) and (iii)

(c) (ii) and (iii) (d) (i) and (iii)

5. Asia's first cross country pipeline constructed by OIL connects Naharkatiya refinery in Assam to ………… .

(a) Panipat Refinery in Haryana (b) Barauni Refinery in Bihar

(c) Kochi Refinery in Kerala (d) Bathinda Refinery in Punjab

Short Answer Type Questions

6. Define in brief the functions of National Highway Authority of India.

7. 'Inland waterways was the chief mode of transport before the advent of railways'. Explain.

8. Pipelines are the most convenient and efficient mode of transporting liquids and gases over long distances. Substantiate the statement.

9. Radio is an important mode of Mass Communication system. Discuss about its journey, how it gained popularity.

10. Discuss about the scheme called as UDAN (Ude Desh Ka Aam Nagrik).

Long Answer Type Questions

11. Explain the factors affecting distribution of Indian railways network.

12. There are different types of satellite systems present in India. Explain with suitable examples.

13. Discuss the growth and role of TV and radio in mass communication.

8 CHAPTER

International Trade

This chapter deals with the concept of international trade and what is the pattern of import and export of goods around the world. International trade is defined as the activity in which there is exchange of goods and services between countries globally.

YOUR STUDY GOALS

8.1 Changing Pattern of India's Exports
8.2 Changing Patterns of India's Import
8.3 Direction of Trade
8.4 Gateways of International trade-Sea Ports
8.5 Airports

YOUR PRACTICE GOAL

- Objective Type Questions (24 Qs ; MCQs, Statements, Matching, A-R)
- Subjective Questions (9 SAs, 6 LAs)
- Source/Graph Based Questions (3 Qs)
- Map Based Questions (3 Qs)

- International Trade is beneficial for all the countries as no country is self-sufficient.
- India's international trade has changed in recent years in terms of volume, composition and direction.
- The nature of India's foreign trade has changed over the years. Though there has been an increase in the total volume of imports and exports, the value of imports is higher than that of exports.

8.1 Changing Pattern of India's Exports

- In exports, the share of agriculture and allied products and manufactured goods has decreased, whereas, the share from crude petroleum and products and other commodities has increased.
- Amongst the agricultural products, there is a decline in the export of traditional items, such as cashews, etc but there is an increase in floricultural products, fresh fruits, marine products and sugar, etc. The decline in traditional items is largely due to the tough international competition.
- China and other East Asian countries are India's major competitors.

- The manufacturing sector alone accounted for 67.8 per cent of India's total value of exports in 2021-22. Gems and jewellery contribute a larger share of India's foreign trade.
- The export of engineering goods has significantly increased.

Composition of India's Exports, 2015-2022 (Percentage share in Exports)

Commodities	2015-16	2016-17	2020-21	2021-22
Agriculture and allied products	12.6	12.3	14.3	11.9
Ore and minerals	1.6	1.9	3.2	2.0
Manufactured goods	72.9	73.6	71.2	67.8
Crude and petroleum products	11.9	11.7	9.2	16.4
Other commodities	1.1	0.5	2.1	1.9

Source : *Economic Survey 2016-17 and 2022-23*

8.2 Changing Patterns of India's Import

- During the 1950s and 1960s, the major imports were foodgrains, capital goods, machinery and equipment. The balance of payment was negative as imports were more than exports.
- After the 1970s, foodgrain import was discontinued due to the success of the Green Revolution.
- During the energy crisis of 1973, the prices of petroleum were increased, and the import budget was also increased.
- Foodgrain import was replaced by fertilisers and petroleum. Machines and equipment, special steel, edible oil and chemicals largely make up the imports.
- There is rise in the import of petroleum products because it is used not only as a fuel but also as an industrial raw material. It is an indicator of rising **industrialisation**[1] and a better standard of living.
- The import of capital goods has declined. The import of food and allied products has also declined.
- India's imports also include pearls, precious and semi-precious stones, gold and silver and non-metal ferrous metals.

India Composition of Import 2015-22 (In percentage)

Commodities	2015-16	2016-17	2020-21	2021-22
Food and allied products	5.1	5.6	4.5	4.4
Fuel (Coal, POL)	25.4	26.7	25.1	31.6
Fertilisers	2.1	1.3	1.9	2.3
Paper board manufacturing and news print	0.8	0.9	0.8	0.7
Capital goods	13.0	13.6	12.7	10.1
Others	38.1	37.0	41.6	38.5

Source : *Economic Survey 2022-23*

1 **Industrialisation** It is the process of shifting a country's economy from agriculture to manufacturing, often using mechanised mass production techniques.

8.3 Direction of Trade

- India has trade relations with most of the countries and major trading blocs of the world.
- India is adopting suitable measures such as import **liberalisation**[2], reduction in import duties, delicensing and change from process to product patents, to double its international trade in five years.
- Most of India's foreign trade is carried through sea and air routes. However, a small portion is also carried through land routes to neighbouring countries like Nepal, Bhutan, Bangladesh and Pakistan.

Direction of India's Import Trade (in crore rupees)

Region	Imports	
	2016-17	**2021-22**
Europe	403972	640577
Africa	193327	368156
North America	195332	378041
Latin America	115762	161995
Asia and ASEAN	1544520	2918577

Source : *Economic Survey 2016-17 and 2022-23*

Quick Test 1

1. State any one reason responsible for a sharp increase in India's international trade since independence.
2. Name any three traditional items that India exports.
3. Why was the import of foodgrains discontinued after 1970?
4. Name four commodities that India imports from other countries.
5. With which countries does India do more trading?

8.4 Gateways of International Trade- Sea Ports

- India is surrounded by sea from three sides and has a long coastline.
- India has a long tradition of sea route trading. It developed many ports with names ending in *pattan*, meaning port.
- India has more ports on its West than its East coast. The ports became important for international trade after the coming of European traders and colonisation of the country by the British. This led to variation in size and quality of ports.
- The extension of railways linked the local markets to regional markets, regional markets to national markets and national markets to the international markets through the ports.
- Due to the partition of the country in 1947, two very important ports, i.e., **Karachi Port** went to Pakistan and **Chittagong Port** to Bangladesh (erstwhile East Pakistan). After this, many new ports, like the Kandla in the West and the Diamond Harbour near Kolkata on river Hugli in the East were developed.
- At present, India has 12 major ports and 200 minor or intermediate ports. The central government manages and controls the major ports and the state governments manage and control the minor ports.
- At present, Indian ports are handling large volumes of domestic, as well as, overseas trade. Most of the ports are equipped with modern infrastructure.
- Earlier, the development and modernisation of ports were the responsibility of the government agencies. Private entrepreneurs and modernisation of ports in India was done to improve their infrastructure, facilities and services to handle cargos.
- The capacity of Indian ports has increased from 20 million tonnes of cargo handling in 1951 to more than 837 million tonnes in 2016.

2 **Liberalisation** Liberalisation is the process or means of removing the control of the state over economic activities.

Important Sea Ports of India

- **Deendayal Port** (Kandla Port)
  - It is situated at the head of the Gulf of Kuchchh. It has been developed as a major port to cater to the needs of Western and North-Western parts of the country and also to reduce the pressure at Mumbai port.
  - The port is specially designed to receive large quantities of petroleum and petroleum products and fertiliser. The offshore terminal at Vadinar has been developed to reduce the pressure at the port.
- **Mumbai**
  - It is a **natural harbour**[3] and the **biggest port** in the country. The port is situated closer to the general routes from the countries of the Middle East, Mediterranean countries, North Africa, North America and Europe.
  - The port is 20 km long and 6-10 km wide with 54 berths and has the **country's largest oil terminal.** Madhya Pradesh, Maharashtra, Gujarat, Uttar Pradesh and parts of Rajasthan constitute the main **hinterlands**[4] of Mumbai ports.
- **Jawaharlal Nehru Port**
  - It was built at Nhava Sheva as a **satellite port**[5] to reduce the pressure at the Mumbai port. It is the **largest container port** in India.
- **Marmagao Port**
  - It is situated at the entrance of the Zuari **estuary**[6]. It is a natural harbour in Goa. It gained significance after its remodelling in 1961 to handle iron-ore exports to Japan.
  - Construction of the Konkan railway has considerably extended the hinterland of this port. Karnataka, Goa and Southern Maharashtra constitute its hinterland.
- **New Mangalore Port**
  - It is located in the state of Karnataka and caters to the needs of the export of iron-ore and iron concentrates.
  - It also handles fertilisers, petroleum products, edible oils, coffee, tea, wood pulp, yarn, granite stone, molasses, etc. Karnataka is the major hinterland for this port.
- **Kochchi Port**
  - It is situated at the head of Vembanad Kayal, popularly known as the **Queen of the Arabian Sea**. It is also a natural harbour. The location of this port is advantageous as it is located close to the Suez-Colombo route.
  - It caters to the needs of Kerala, Southern Karnataka and South-Western Tamil Nadu.
- **Kolkata Port**
  - It is located on the Hugli river, 128 km inland from the Bay of Bengal. It was also developed by the British like the Mumbai port.
  - The port has lost its significance considerably on account of the diversion of exports to other ports such as Visakhapatnam, Paradip and its satellite port, Haldia.
  - Kolkata port is also confronted with the problem of silt accumulation in the Hugli river which provides a link to the sea.

---

3 **Natural Harbour** A harbour is a body of water where ships, boats and barrages seek shelter from stormy weather or are parked for future use.

4 **Hinterland** The hinterland is the inland region lying behind a port and is claimed by the state that owns the coast.

5 **Satellite Port** A satellite port can either already exist or is created near a port that is reaching its capacity. Satellite ports help in reducing pressure over the main port.

6 **Estuary** An estuary is an area where a freshwater river or stream meets the ocean. In estuaries, the salty ocean mixes with a freshwater river, resulting in brackish water.

- Its hinterland covers Uttar Pradesh, Bihar, Jharkhand, West Bengal, Sikkim and the North-Eastern states. Apart from this, it also extends port facilities to India's neighbouring land-locked countries such as Nepal and Bhutan.

- **Haldia Port**
  - It is located 105 km downstream from Kolkata. It has been constructed to reduce the congestion at Kolkata port.
  - It handles bulk cargo like iron ore, coal, petroleum, petroleum products and fertilisers, jute, jute products, cotton and cotton yarn, etc.
- **Paradip Port**
  - It is situated in the Mahanadi delta, about 100 km from Cuttack. The harbours here are deep which are suitable to handle very large vessels.
  - It has been developed mainly to handle large-scale export of iron-ore. Odisha, Chhattisgarh and Jharkhand are the parts of its hinterland.

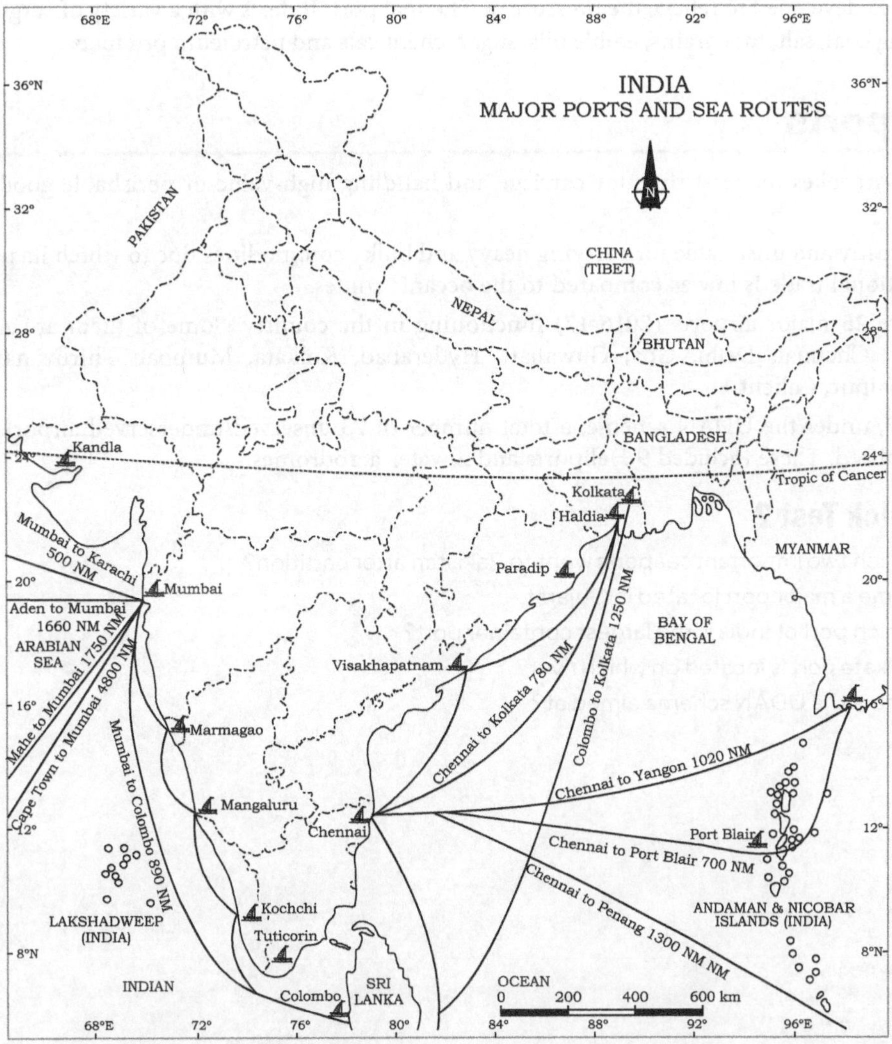

▲ *India-Major Ports and Sea Routes*

- **Visakhapatnam Port**
  - It is located in Andhra Pradesh. It is a land-locked harbour, connected to the sea by a channel, that passes through a solid rock and sand.
  - An outer harbour has been developed for handling iron ore, petroleum and general cargo. Andhra Pradesh and Telangana are the main hinterlands for this port.
- **Chennai Port**
  - It is one of the oldest ports on the Eastern coast. It is an artificial harbour built in 1859.
  - It is not very suitable for large ships because of the shallow waters near the coast. Tamil Nadu and Puducherry are its hinterlands.
- **Ennore**
  - It is a newly developed port in Tamil Nadu. It has been constructed 25 km North of Chennai to relieve the pressure of Chennai port.
- **Tuticorin Port**
  - It was also developed to relieve the pressure of Chennai port. It deals with a variety of cargo, including coal, salt, foodgrains, edible oils, sugar, chemicals and petroleum products.

8.5 Airports

- Air transport takes the least time for carriage and handling high-value or perishable goods over long distances.
- It is very costly and unsuitable for carrying heavy and bulky commodities due to which its participation in international trade is low as compared to the oceanic routes.
- There were 25 major airports (2016-17) functioning in the country. Some of them are Ahmedabad, Bengaluru, Chennai, Delhi, Goa, Guwahati, Hyderabad, Kolkata, Mumbai, Thiruvananthapuram, Srinagar, Jaipur, Calicut.
- Since 2017, under the UDAN scheme, a total number of 73 unserved/underserved airports have been operationalised. These included 9 Heliports and 2 water aerodromes.

Quick Test 2

1. Which two important seaports went to Pakistan after partition?
2. Name a major port located in Gujarat.
3. Which port of India is the largest container port?
4. Kolkata port is located on which river?
5. Wha is the UDAN scheme aimed at?

Mind Map

INTERNATIONAL TRADE

1 Definition and Importance

- International trade involves exchange of goods and services across international borders.
- It plays a significant role in global economy despite contributing only 1% of world trade.

2 Changing Pattern of India's Export

2015-16 to 2021-22

- Decline in Agriculture and traditional items.
- Increase in manufacturing goods, (crude petroleum, marine products).
- Manufacturing sector accounted for 67.8 percent of India's total value of export in 2021-22.

3 Changing Pattern of India's Import

2015-16 to 2021-22

- Major items imported are petroleum, edible oil and fertillisers.
- Shift towards industrial raw materials and luxury items.

4 Direction of Trade

- Different measures like liberalisation, reduction in import duties, delicensing taken by the government.
- Following goals of international trade have been set
  - Modernisation of ports
  - Doubling trade share in next five years

5 Gateways of International Trade-Sea Ports

- **Deendayal Port** (Kandla Port) It is situated at the head of the Gulf of Kuchchh. It is specially designed to receive large quantities of petroleum products and fertilisers.
- **Mumbai** It is a natural harbour and the biggest port in the country. It is 20 km long and 6-10 km wide with 54 berths.
- **Jawaharlal Nehru Port** It was built at Nhava Sheva as a satellite port. It is the largest container port in India.
- **Marmagao Port** It is situated at the entrance of the Zuari Estuary. It is a natural harbour in Goa.
- **New Mangalore Port** It is located in the state of Karnataka. It exports iron-ore and iron concentrates.
- **Kochchi Port** It is situated at the head of Vembanad Kayal(queen of the Arabian sea). It caters to the needs of Kerala, Southern Karnataka and South-Western Tamil Nadu.
- **Kolkata Port** It is located on the Hugli river, 128 km inland from the Bay of Bengal. It was developed by the British.
- **Haldia Port** It is located 105 km downstream from Kolkata. It handles cargo like iron ore, coal, petroleum, jute, etc.
- **Paradip Port** It is situated in the Mahanadi delta. It has been developed mainly to handle large-scale export of iron ore.
- **Visakhapatnam Port** It is located in Andhra Pradesh.
- **Chennai Port** It is oldest port on the Eastern coast. Tamil Nadu and Puducherry are its hinterlands.
- **Ennore** It is constructed 25 km North of Chennai.
- **Tuticorin Port** It deals with a variety of cargo including coal, salt, foodgrains, edible oils, sugar.

6 Airports

- It takes the least time for carriage and handling high-value or perishable goods over long distances.
- It is very costly and unsuitable for carrying heavy and bulky commodities.
- There were 25 major airports (2016-17) functioning in the country.
- Under the UDAN scheme, a total number of 73 unserved/underserved airports have been operationalised. These included 9 Heliports and 2 water aerodromes.

NCERT Folder

Choose the right answer of the following from the given options

(i) **Trade between two countries is termed as**

(a) Internal trade (b) International trade
(c) External trade (d) Local trade

Ans. (b) International trade

(ii) **Which one of the following is a land-locked harbour?**

(a) Visakhapatnam (b) Mumbai
(c) Ennore (d) Haldia

Ans. (a) Visakhapatnam

(iii) **Most of India's foreign trade is carried through**

(a) land and sea (b) land and air
(c) sea and air (d) sea

Ans. (c) sea and air

Answer the following questions in about 30 words

(i) **Mention the characteristics of India's foreign trade.**

Ans. The characteristics of India's foreign trade are as follows

- According to recent study, India's international trade has transformed in terms of volume, composition and direction.
- Although, India's contribution in the world trade is as low as one per cent, of the total volume, yet it plays a significant role in the world economy.
- There has been a sharp rise in India's foreign trade since independence.
- The value of import is higher than that of export which shows an unfavourable balance of trade.

(ii) **Distinguish between port and harbour.**

Ans. Difference between port and harbour are as follows

Port	Harbour
An area situated at the edge of the water body, where boats and ships move and transfer passengers and cargo to/ from land, is called port.	An area next to the shore, where ships and boats are anchored for getting safety from stormy weather, is called harbour.
Ports are a creation of man.	Harbours are both natural and man-made.
Ports provide trading facilities to goods and cargo, from one country to another.	Harbours are used for providing safe anchorage, if the weather is not fit for sailing.

(iii) **Explain the meaning of hinterland.**

Ans. Hinterland is an inland area that lies behind a port and connected to it with roads and railways.
Commodities for export are sent to port from this area and imported commodities are distributed here for sale and consumption. For example, Tamil Nadu and Puducherry are hinterlands of Chennai port.

(iv) **Name important items which India imports from different countries.**

Ans. India imports various items from different countries like petroleum products, capital goods, e.g. non-electrical machinery, transport equipments, manufactures of metals and machine tools, pearls and semi-precious stones , gold and silver, metallic-ferrous ores and metal scrap, non-ferrous metals, electronic goods, etc.

(v) **Name the ports of India located on the East coast.**

Ans. Major ports of India located on the East coast are Kolkata, Haldia, Paradip, Visakhapatnam, Ennore, Chennai, Tuticorin port.

Answer the following questions in about 150 words

(i) **Describe the composition of export and import trade of India.**

Ans. The composition of export and import trade of India is discussed below

Export

- In export, the share of agriculture and allied products and manufactured goods have decreased.
- Share of Crude petroleum and products and other commodities have increased.
- The share of ore and minerals have remained constant over the years from 2015-16 to 2021-22. There is a decline in the export of traditional item, such as cashew, etc.
- Manufacturing sector alone accounted for 67.8 per cent of India's total value of export in 2021-22. Export of engineering goods have increased.

Import

- Foodgrain imports have been replaced by fertilisers and petroleum. The import basket consists of machines, equipments, special steel, edible oil and chemicals.
- Import of food and allied products declined since 2015-2022.

- Other major items of India's import include pearls, precious and semi-precious stones, gold and silver, non-metal ferrous metals.

(ii) Write a note on the changing nature of international trade of India.

Or **"The composition of commodities in India's international trade has been undergoing a change over the years". Examine.** **CBSE 2024**

Ans. The nature of India's international trade has changed with time. Although the total volume of import and export shows a significant increase, the country still shows a negative balance of trade as the value of imports continue to be higher than that of exports. Negative balance of trade is also due to price rise of crude oil and petroleum which is a major component of India's import list.

India has set an aim to increase its share in the international trade within the next few years. To achieve this aim, India has started adopting suitable measures such as import liberalisation, reduction in import duties, delicensing and change from process to product patents.

The composition of commodities have changed in India's international trade. The share of agricultural and allied products have declined whereas, the share of petroleum has increased. Import of capital goods has maintained a steady rise due to rising demands. Non-electrical machinery, transport equipment, manufactures of metal, etc are the main items of capital goods.

Exam Pattern Questions

Objective Type Questions

Multiple Choice Questions (MCQs)

1. What is the reason behind the significant rise in India's international trade.
(a) Rapid growth in manufacturing sector
(b) Liberal policies of the government
(c) Diversification of markets
(d) All of the above

2. Which of the following sector has seen a decline in the composition of exports of India in the last decade?
(a) Manufactured goods (b) Petroleum products
(c) Agriculture and allied products
(d) Both (a) and (c)

3. Which of these is an artificial port/harbour?
(a) Mumbai port (b) Kochchi port
(c) Chennai port (d) Marmagao port

4. Which of these port is situated at the entrance of the Zuari estuary?
(a) Mumbai port (b) Chennai port
(c) Marmagao port (d) Haldia port

5. Which of the following is an inland port?
(a) Kochchi port (b) Ennore port
(c) Haldia port (d) Kolkata port

6. Kolkata port has lost its significance on account of the diversion exports to which port?
(a) Visakhapatnam (b) Paradip port
(c) Haldia port (d) All of these

7. Which one of the following is a natural harbour and the biggest sea port of India? **CBSE 2024**
(a) Kolkata port (b) Chennai port
(c) Mumbai port (d) Kandla port

8. Which of the following is the hinterland of Kolkata port?
(a) Sikkim (b) Uttar Pradesh
(c) West Bengal (d) All of these

9. Paradip port is located in the delta of which of these rivers?
(a) Godavari (b) Ganga (c) Krishna (d) Mahanadi

10. Which of the following is a satellite port of Chennai port?
(a) Kolkata port (b) Haldia port
(c) Tuticorin port (d) Paradip port

11. Under which one of the following categories of commodities, the increase in export is observed from 2010-11 to 2016-17? **CBSE 2025**
(a) Agriculture and allied products
(b) Ore and minerals
(c) Crude and petroleum products
(d) Other commodities

12. Which of the following is a feature of Kandla port? **CBSE SQP 2022**
(a) It is the biggest port of the country.
(b) Its harbour is situated at Zuari estuary.
(c) It is situated at the head of Gulf of Kachchh.
(d) It is the oldest port of India.

13. **Which of the following sea ports in India has been developed specially to import petroleum and fertilisers?** CBSE 2024

(a) Mumbai (b) Marmagao
(c) Kandla (d) Kochchi

14. **Which of the following ports have been arranged correctly from North to South?**

(a) Kolkata, Paradip, Visakhapatnam, Chennai
(b) Chennai, Kolkata, Paradip, Visakhapatnam
(c) Kolkata, Chennai, Paradip, Visakhapatnam
(d) Chennai, Paradip, Visakhapatnam, Kolkata

15. **Which of the following is not an international airport of India?**

(a) Bhopal (b) Bengaluru
(c) Chennai (d) Nagpur

16. **Identify the port based on the characteristic provided below. Mark your answer by choosing the correct option.**

It is a natural harbour and the biggest port of the country. The port is situated closer to the general routes from the countries of Middle East, Mediterranean countries, North Africa, North America and Europe where the major share of country's overseas trade is carried out. The port is 20 km long and 6-10 km wide with 54 berths and has the country's largest oil terminal.

Options

(a) Mangalore port (b) Kandla port
(c) Mumbai port (d) Visakhapatnam port

17. **Arrange the following commodities of Indian export during 2016-17 in descending order of their percentages and choose the correct option.** CBSE 2024

(i) Crude and petroleum products
(ii) Manufactured goods
(iii) Agriculture and allied products
(iv) Ore and minerals

Options

(a) (i), (ii), (iii), (iv) (b) (ii), (i), (iv), (iii)
(c) (iii), (ii), (i), (iv) (d) (ii), (iii), (i), (iv)

18. **Which of the following is true in the context of International trade of India?**

(i) There has been an increase in volume of imports and exports over the years.
(ii) The value of imports are higher than the value of exports.

Codes

(a) Only (i) (b) Only (ii)
(c) Both (i) and (ii) (d) None of these

19. **Which of these products and commodities constitute the export basket of India?**

(i) Manufactured goods
(ii) Crude and petroleum products
(iii) Ores and minerals

Codes

(a) (i) and (ii) (b) (i), (ii) and (iii)
(c) (ii) and (iii) (d) (i) and (iii)

20. **Which of these commodities constitute the imports of India from other countries?**

(i) Machines and equipments
(ii) Edible oil
(iii) Fertilisers
(iv) Iron and steel

Codes

(a) (i), (ii) and (iii) (b) (i), (ii), (iii) and (iv)
(c) (ii), (iii) and (iv) (d) (i), (ii) and (iv)

21. **Which of the following measures have been adopted by India to expand its share in the international trade?**

(i) Trade liberalisation (ii) Increasing export duties
(iii) Delicensing of industries

Codes

(a) (i) and (ii) (b) (i) and (iii)
(c) (i), (ii) and (iii) (d) (ii) and (iii)

22. **Which of the following statements is correct about the ports in India?**

(i) At present, India has 14 major ports and 200 minor or intermediate ports.
(ii) The capacity of Indian ports increased from 20 million tonnes of cargo handling in 1951 to more than 837 million tonnes in 2016.
(iii) The British used the ports as suction points of the resources from their hinterlands.
(iv) New Mangalore Port is located in the state of Karnataka and caters to the needs of the export of iron-ore and iron-concentrates.

Codes

(a) (i), (ii), (iii) (b) (ii), (iii), (iv)
(c) (i), (ii), (iv) (d) (i), (iii), (iv)

Match the Following

23.

	List I (Port)		List II (Satellite port)
A.	Mumbai port	1.	Hugli port
B.	Chennai port	2.	Jawaharlal Nehru port
C.	Kolkata port	3.	Ennore port

Codes

	A	B	C		A	B	C
(a)	3	1	2	(b)	3	2	1
(c)	2	3	1	(d)	2	1	3

Assertion-Reason

24. Assertion (A) India has adopted measures like reducing import duties, delicensing, trade liberalisation.

Reason (R) India aims to expand its share of international trade.

Codes

(a) Both A and R are true, but R is not the correct explanation of A

(b) Both A and R are true and R is the correct explanation of A

(c) Both A and R are incorrect

(d) A is correct, but R is incorrect

Answers

1. (d) All of the above
2. (d) Both (a) and (c)
3. (c) Chennai port
4. (c) Marmagao port
5. (d) Kolkata port
6. (d) All of these
7. (c) Mumbai port
8. (d) All of these
9. (d) Mahanadi
10. (c) Tuticorin port
11. (d) Other commodities
12. (c) It is situated at the head of Gulf of Kachchh.
13. (c) Kandla
14. (a) Kolkata, Paradip, Visakhapatnam, Chennai
15. (a) Bhopal
16. (c) Mumbai port
17. (d) (ii), (iii), (i), (iv)
18. (c) Both (i) and (ii)
19. (b) (i), (ii) and (iii)
20. (b) (i), (ii), (iii) and (iv)
21. (b) (i) and (iii)
22. (b) (ii), (iii), (iv)
23. (c)
24. (b) Both A and R are true and R is the correct explanation of A

Subjective Questions

Short Answer Type Questions

1. What do you understand by international trade? Explain in brief.

Ans. Trade is a tertiary economic activity which means the voluntary exchange of goods and services between two or more parties.

International trade is the exchange of capital, goods and services across international borders or territories.

International trade is mutually beneficial to each country as no country is self-sufficient. In recent years, India's international trade has shown a profound change in terms of volume, composition as well as direction.

In terms of the total volume, India's contribution in the world trade is as low as one per cent however, it still plays an important role in the world economy.

2. Differentiate between exports and imports.

Ans. Differences between exports and imports are as follows

Exports	Imports
When a country produces goods and wants to sell these surplus goods to outside its boundary, then this selling of goods is called as export.	When a country buy some goods or services from other countries because of shortage of that commodity in domestic market, it is known as import.
Foreign exchange is earned by export.	A country invests its earned-foreign exchange for purchasing these commodities and services.
More export is a symbol of positive growth in the economy of a country.	More import may be a symbol of slow growth in economy of a country. But sometimes by importing goods, a country tries to make more profit by converting these goods into valuable ones.

3. How does a country identify whether it is in a position of positive balance of trade or in negative balance of trade?

Ans. A country identifies whether it is in a position of positive balance of trade or in negative balance of trade through the following points

- If a country exports greater value of commodities than its imports, it is in the position of positive balance of trade. The economy may grow in this condition.
- Conversely, if the country imports greater value of commodities than its exports, then it is in the position of negative balance of trade. Its economy then experiences a downward trend.

4. What role international trade plays to connect countries with each other?

Ans. International trade plays the following role to connect countries with each other

- International trade improves relations between two or more countries.
- It mutually benefits both the countries and their economies.
- It promotes friendly relations among trading partners.
- It helps to create international integration and harmony.
- International trade helps in boosting economies of the trading countries.
- International trade helps countries to exchange their raw materials as well as their finished goods with each other, as no country is self-sufficient.

5. "Most of India's foreign trade is carried through sea routes". Explain the statement giving three reasons.

Or **Describe the importance of sea routes in handling India's foreign trade.**

Ans. Most of India's foreign trade is carried through sea routes because

- **Long Coastline** India has a long coastline of 7516.6 km . It enables India to connect with other countries easily by sea route.
- **Open to Sea from Three Sides** India's Peninsular region is open to sea from three sides. This strategic situation in Indian ocean provides a great advantage for India's international trade.
- **Cheapest Means of Transport** Water transport is a cheap means of transport, as it provides a smooth surface and requires no maintenance of sea routes.

6. Explain any four features of Kandla sea port.

Ans. Following are some of the features of Kandla Port

- It is situated at the head of Gulf of Kachchh and it has been developed as a major port.
- This port has been developed to fulfil the needs of Western and North-Western parts of the country and also to reduce the pressure at Mumbai port.
- The port is specially designed to receive large quantities of petroleum and petroleum products and fertiliser.
- The offshore terminal at Vadinar has been developed to reduce the pressure at the port.

7. State the main features of Mumbai port.

Ans. Following are the main features of Mumbai Port

- Mumbai is a natural harbour and the biggest port of the country.
- The port is situated closer to the general routes from the countries of Middle East, Mediterranean countries, North Africa, North America and Europe where the major share of country's overseas trade is carried out.
- The port is 20 km long and 6-10 km wide with 54 berths and it has the country's largest oil terminal. Madhya Pradesh, Maharashtra, Gujarat, Uttar Pradesh and parts of Rajasthan constitute the main hinterlands of Mumbai ports.

8. How many major ports are there in Tamil Nadu? Discuss the important features of these ports.

Ans. In Tamil Nadu, there are three major ports namely Chennai port, Ennore port and Tuticorin port.

Important features of these ports are as follows

For answer refer to page 322 of text under the heading 'Chennai Port', 'Ennore Port' and 'Tuticorin Port'.

9. What are the advantages and disadvantages of air transport?

Ans. Advantages of air transport are

- Air transport has a great advantage in handling high value or perishable goods over long distances.
- It has reduced distances by minimising the travel time.
- It is very much essential for a vast country like India, where distances are large and the terrain and climatic conditions are diverse.

Disadvantages of air transport are

- It is very costly mode of transportation which is not affordable for everyone.
- It is not suitable for carrying heavy and bulky commodities.
- The air transport is not much in use in the international trade due to its high cost.

Long Answer Type Questions

1. "Advancement of international trade of a country is an index of its economic prosperity". Justify the statement with five argument. Competency Based Que

Ans. Advancement of international trade of a country is an index of its economic prosperity. This statement can be justified by the following points

- As every country has limited resources, no country can survive without international trade. Thus, in order to fulfill their demands each country is dependent on international trade worldwide.
- Goods or resources possessed by one country are required by other countries as no country is self sufficient. These differences create conditions for international trade.

- Foreign trade has helped countries to improve their productivity of manufactured goods as it creates conditions of competition among countries in international market.
- Foreign trade helps a country earn foreign exchange, and through investment it strengthens the country's economy. Setting up of MNC's gives opportunities for employment in the country.
- In the recent years, exchange of commodities and goods have been taken over by the exchange of information and knowledge. For example,
  (i) India has emerged as a software giant at the international level and it is earning large foreign exchange through the export of information technology.
  (ii) International trade contributes to India's economic growth, raising income levels of people.

2. India has a long list of its import commodities since many decades. Discuss about the changing pattern of composition of India's import.

Ans. For answer refer to page no. 318 under the heading 'Changing Pattern of Composition of India's Import'.

3. "Despite the set back caused by the partition, Indian ports continued to grow after the independence". Support the statement with examples. Competency Based Que

Ans. India has a long history of international trade *via* seaports. These ports emerged as gateways of international trade after the coming of European traders and colonisation of India by British. These ports linked the local markets to regional markets, regional to national and national to international markets. This process continued till independence.

But India faced a huge loss when Karachi and Chittagong port were lost with the partition of the country. Karachi port went to Pakistan and Chittagong port went to East-Pakistan (now Bangladesh).

To recover from this loss, many new ports were developed. For example, Kandla in the West and Diamond Harbour in East near Kolkata on river Hughli. India recovered successfully from this loss and the growth of Indian ports continued.

Today large volumes of domestic and international trades are handled by these Indian ports. Modern infrastructure facilities are available in most of the Indian ports.

Many private entrepreneurs have been invited for the modernisation of ports in the country. The cargo handling capacity of Indian ports has increased from 20 million tonnes in 1951 to more than 837 million tonnes in 2016-17.

Currently, there are 12 major ports and 200 minor or intermediate ports. A larger part of total traffic is carried through major ports.

4. Compare Mumbai and Kolkata sea ports on the basis of location, hinterland and their significance in world trade.

Ans. Comparison between Mumbai and Kolkata ports can be seen through the following points:

Basis	Mumbai Port	Kolkata Port
Location	Mumbai port is located on the West coast of India. It lies in the state of Maharashtra.	Kolkata port is located on the East coast of India. This port is situated on the Hugli river 128 km inland from the Bay of Bengal in West Bangal state.
Hinterland	The main hinterlands of Mumbai port are Madhya Pradesh, Maharashtra, Gujarat, Uttar Pradesh and ports of Rajasthan.	Kolkata port has a vast hinterland. For example, West Bengal, Bihar, Uttar Pradesh, Jharkhand, Sikkim, Northern parts of Chhattisgarh and some Eastern parts of the country are included in its hinterland.
	The port has overseas trade links with many countries like Middle East, Mediterranean countries, North Africa, North America, Europe and Gulf countries.	Kolkata port has overseas trade links with many countries like South-East Asian countries Australia and New Zealand.
Significance	The major items of export are cotton textiles, leather, tobacco, manganese, machinery, chemical goods, etc while the imports include crude oil, superior quality raw cotton, latest machines, instruments and drugs.	It is the world's most important centre of jute industries. The major items of export are jute products, tea, coal, steel, iron-ore, copper, leather and leather products, textiles, manganese and many other items. The imports consist mainly of machinery crude oil, paper, fertilisers and chemical products.

5. Explain the pattern of the composition of India's import. **CBSE 2025**

Ans. India's import composition has changed significantly over the years in the following ways

- In the 1950s and 1960s, food grains were the major imports due to food shortages. Along with food, capital goods, machinery and equipment were imported to support the industrial development.
- However, after the Green Revolution in the 1970s, food grain imports reduced. Instead, petroleum products and fertilisers became key imports due to the energy crisis of 1973, which pushed up oil prices.
- Over time, as industrialisation grew, the demand for machinery, special steel and chemicals increased. The import of food and allied products decreased, while the import of precious items like pearls, gold and silver remained high.
- Capital goods imports also saw a steady decline. Overall, India's imports shifted towards industrial and energy-related goods.

6. Explain the Indian sea ports as gateways of international trade. **CBSE 2024**

Ans. India's sea ports are crucial gateways for international trade due to their strategic geographic location along major global shipping routes. With a long coastline, India has 12 major and over 200 minor ports that handle most of its trade by volume.

These ports facilitate the import and export of diverse goods like crude oil, electronics and agricultural products, significantly boosting the economy. Ports such as Mumbai, Chennai and Kolkata connect India to markets in Europe, the Middle-East and South-East Asia. Modern infrastructure and trade-friendly policies enhance their efficiency, attracting global shipping traffic. As a bridge between the West and East, India's ports improve trade connectivity and support economic growth, making them vital hubs for international commerce.

Source/Graph Based Questions

1. Read the passage carefully and answer the questions that follow.

India faced serious food shortage during 1950s and 1960s. The major item of import at that time was foodgrain, capital goods, machinery and equipment. The balance of payment was adverse as imports were more than export in spite of all the efforts of import substitution. After 1970s, foodgrain import was discontinued due to the success of Green Revolution but the energy crisis of 1973 pushed the prices of petroleum, and import budget was also pushed up. Foodgrain import was replaced by fertilisers and petroleum. Machine and equipment, special steel, edible oil and chemicals largely make the import basket.

There is a steep rise in the import of petroleum products. It is used not only as a fuel but also as an industrial raw material. It indicates the tempo of rising industrialisation and better standard of living. Sporadic price rise in the international market is another reason for the same. Import of capital goods maintained a steady increase due to rising demand in the export-oriented industrial and domestic sectors. Non-electrical machinery, transport equipment, manufacturers of metals and machine tools were the main items of capital goods. Import of food and allied products declined with a fall in imports of edible oils. Other major items of India's import include pearls and semi-precious stones, gold and silver, metallic-ferrous ores and metal scrap, non-ferrous metals, electronic goods, etc.

(i) What was the reason behind the decline in import of foodgrains in the 1970s?

(a) Construction of Indira Gandhi Canal
(b) Success of Green Revolution
(c) Rise in GDP
(d) All of the above

Ans. (b) Success of Green Revolution

(ii) What is the most important factor behind the rise in import of petroleum products in last few decades?

(a) Increase in industrialisation
(b) Increase in standard of living
(c) Rise in number of personal vehicles
(d) All of the above

Ans. (d) All of the above

(iii) Which of the following capital goods are imported by India?

(a) Transport equipment
(b) Medical equipment
(c) Agricultural equipment
(d) All of the above

Ans. (a) Transport equipment

2. **Study the given graph and answer the questions that follow.** **CBSE 2023**

Changing Pattern of the Composition of India's Exports

Extent of gap between Exports and Imports in India's foreign trade during 2012-13 to 2016-17

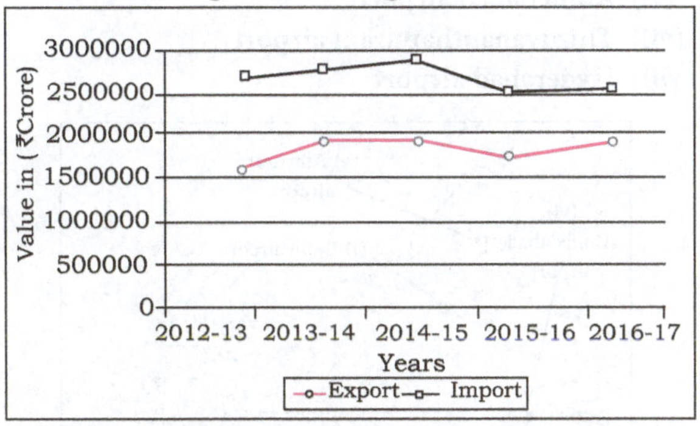

Source : *Economic Survey 2016-17*

(i) **In which year was the gap between imports and exports the maximum?**

Ans. In the year 2012-13, the gap between import and export was maximum.

(ii) **When was the gap between imports and exports minimum?**

Ans. In the year 2016-17, the gap between import and export was minimum.

(iii) **In which year had India's exports shown highest upward trend?**

Ans. In the year 2013-14, India's export had shown highest upward trend.

3. **Study the following data and answer the questions that follow.**

Direction of India's Import trade *(in crore rupees)*

Region	Imports	
	2010-11	2016-17
Europe	3323857	403972
Africa	118612	193327
North America	100602	195332
Latin America	64576	115762
Asia and ASEAN	1029881	1544520

(i) **Which region contributes to largest share in India's imports?**

Ans. Asia region and ASEAN grouping is the largest contributor to India's import.

(ii) **Which mode of transport facilitates the largest proportion of India's exports and imports?**

Ans. The largest proportion of India's exports and imports are managed by sea of air routes.

(iii) **What measures has India adopted to boost trade and industry?**

Ans. India has adopted measures like import liberalisation, reduction in import duties, delicensing and shifting from process to product patents.

Map Based Questions

1. **In the given political outline map of India, locate and label the following with appropriate symbols.**

(i) **The major sea port located in Goa**

(ii) **The Southernmost major sea port of India**

(iii) **The major sea-port in Gujarat**

Or **A major sea port which has been developed after independence to cater the needs of Western and North-Western parts of the country.**

(iv) **The major sea port located in Odisha**

(v) **The major sea port located in Kerala**

Ans.

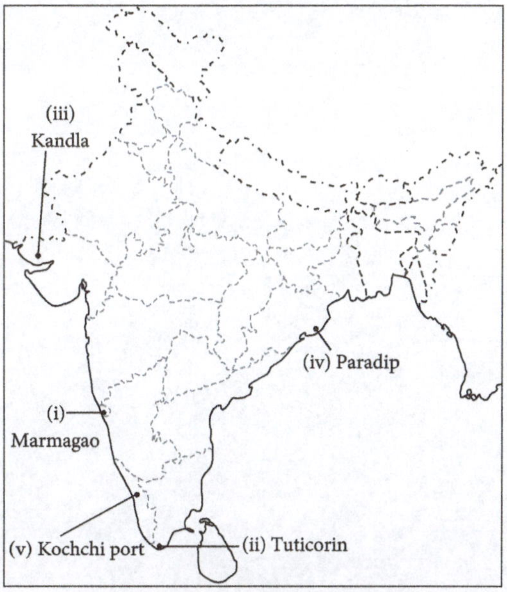

2. On the given political outline map of India, locate and label the following with appropriate symbols.
(i) The major sea port located in Tamil Nadu
(ii) Land-locked harbour in Andhra Pradesh
(iii) A sea port in Karnataka
(iv) The biggest port of India
(v) A sea port in West Bengal

Ans.

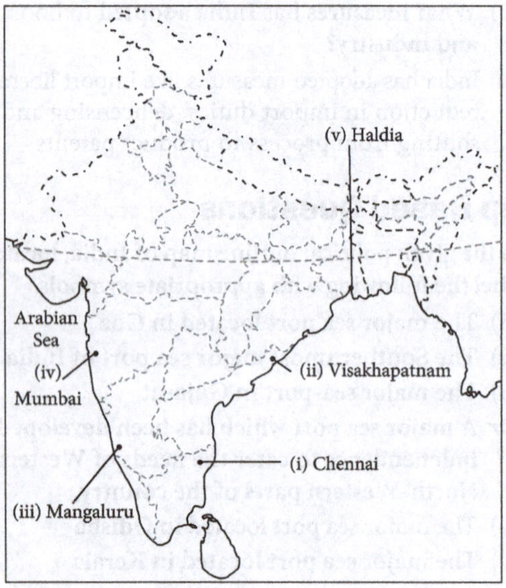

3. On the political outline map of India, locate and label the following international airports of India.
(i) Delhi airport
(ii) Mumbai airport
(iii) Chennai airport
(iv) Kolkata airport
(v) An international airport in Punjab
(vi) Ahmedabad airport
(vii) Thiruvananthapuram airport
(viii) Hyderabad airport

Ans.

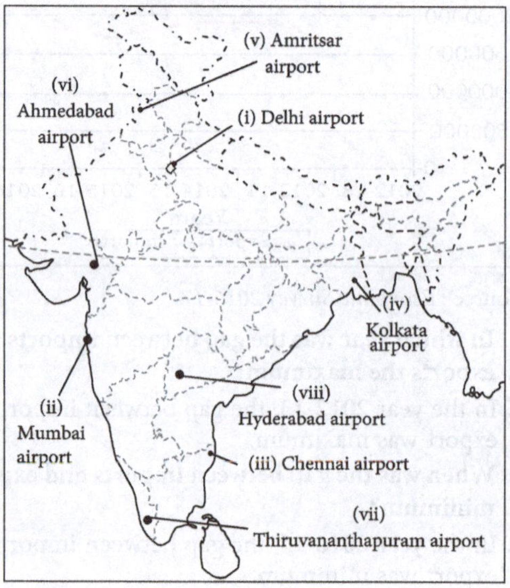

SELF ASSESSMENT TEST

Objective Type Questions

1. If the exports of a country exceed its imports, it results in ...... balance of trade.
   (a) positive
   (b) negative
   (c) unfavourable
   (d) declining
2. The types of goods and services imported and exported by countries is known as
   (a) volume of trade
   (b) composition of trade
   (c) value of trade
   (d) direction of trade
3. The share of which of these products has increased in India's export in the past years?
   (a) Petroleum and crude products
   (b) Agricultural products
   (c) Tea, coffee and cashew
   (d) Minerals and ores
4. Which of the following commodities had the maximum share in the imports of India in 2016-17?
   (a) Iron and steel
   (b) Petroleum products
   (c) Chemical products
   (d) Pearls and precious stones
5. Which of the following ports located at the Vembanad Kayal is also known as 'Queen of the Arabian Sea'?
   (a) Ennore port
   (b) Haldia port
   (c) Marmagao port
   (d) Kochchi port
6. Which of the following statements are true about Deendayal port (Kandla Port)?
   (i) It caters to the needs of the Western and North-Western parts of India.
   (ii) It is a natural harbour located in Goa.
   (iii) It has been developed to reduce pressure at Mumbai port.
   (iv) It primarily handles petroleum and its products.
   Options
   (a) Only (i), (iii) and (iv)
   (b) Only (ii) and (iv)
   (c) Only (i) and (iii)
   (d) All of these

Short Answer Type Questions

7. What do you understand by 'hinterland'? Name hinterlands of any two ports.
8. State any four characteristics of Marmagao port.
9. Explain one of the common property among Ennore, Chennai and Tuticorin port.
10. Air transport plays an important role in the international trade. Explain.

Long Answer Type Questions

11. Discuss in brief about changing patterns of the composition of India's imports.
12. Import of foodgrains decreased in India, after Green Revolution. Justify the statement.

9

CHAPTER

This chapter deals with some of the major geographical issues like environmental pollution, land degradation, problems related to rural and urban areas. Study of the cause of these issues are important to minimise the effects of them on environment and people.

Geographical Perspective on Selected Issues and Problems

YOUR STUDY GOALS

9.1 Environmental Pollution
9.2 Land Degradation
9.3 Urban Waste Disposal
9.4 Rural-Urban Migration
9.5 Problems of Slums

YOUR PRACTICE GOAL

- Objective Type Questions (21 Qs ; MCQs, Statements, Matching, A-R)
- Subjective Questions (7 SAs, 10 LAs)
- Source Based Questions (5 Qs)

9.1 Environmental Pollution

- Environmental pollution is a result of the release of substances and energy from waste products of human activities.
- There are many types of pollution. They are classified based on the medium through which pollutants are transported and spread.
- Pollution can be classified as air pollution, water pollution, land pollution and noise pollution.

Water Pollution

- The increasing population and industries indiscriminately use water that leads to degradation of the quality of water considerably.
- Surface water available from rivers, canals, lakes, etc is never pure. It contains small quantities of suspended particles, organic and inorganic substances. When the concentration of these substances increases, the water becomes polluted, and hence becomes unfit for use.
- Water pollutants are also created from natural sources like erosion, landslides, decay and decomposition of plants and animals, etc.

- Pollutants from human activities like industrial, agricultural and cultural activities are a real cause of concern. Among these activities, industry is the most significant contributor. In such a situation, the **self-purifying**[1] capacity of water is unable to purify the water.
- Water pollution causes various water-borne diseases. Some of them are diarrhoea, intestinal worms, hepatitis, etc. As per the World Health Organisation about one-fourth of the communicable diseases in India are water-borne.

Activities Causing Water Pollution

Industrial Activities

- Industries produce several undesirable products including industrial wastes, polluted waste water, poisonous gases, chemical residuals, numerous heavy metals, dust, smoke, etc.
- Most industrial wastes are disposed off in running water or lakes. Through this, the poisonous elements reach the reservoirs, rivers and other water bodies, which destroy the bio-system of these waters.
- Major water-polluting industries are leather, pulp and paper, textiles and chemicals.

Agricultural and Cultural Activities

- Various types of chemicals are used in modern agriculture like inorganic fertilisers, pesticides and herbicides. They generate water-polluting components.
- These chemicals flow into the rivers, lakes and tanks. These chemicals also infiltrate the soil to reach the groundwater. Fertiliser increases the nitrate content of surface waters.
- Cultural activities such as pilgrimage, religious fairs, tourism, etc also cause water pollution. In India, almost all surface water sources are contaminated and unfit for human consumption.

Namami Gange Programme

- River Ganga is considered a river of national importance. Ganga continuously requires cleaning by effectively controlling the pollution of its water.
- The Union Government has launched the 'Namami Gange Programme' with the following objectives:
  - To develop sewerage treatment systems in towns on the banks of rivers.
  - To monitor the industrial effluents.
  - To develop the river-front.
  - Afforestation along the bank increases biodiversity.
  - Cleaning of the river surface.
  - Development of 'Ganga Grams' in Uttarakhand, Uttar Pradesh, Bihar, Jharkhand and West Bengal.
  - Creating public awareness to avoid adding pollutants into the river even in the form of rituals.

Air Pollution

- Air pollution refers to the addition of contaminants, like dust, fumes, gas, fog, odour, smoke or vapour to the air in substantial proportion and duration that may be harmful to flora and fauna and to property.
- Due to the use of various fuels as energy sources, there is an increase in the emission of toxic gases into the atmosphere that results in the pollution of air.
- Combustion of fossil fuels, mining and industries are the main sources of air pollution. These processes release oxides of sulphur and nitrogen, hydrocarbons, carbon dioxide, carbon monoxide, lead and asbestos.
- Air pollution causes various diseases related to the respiratory, nervous and circulatory systems.

1 **Self-purifying** A natural process of purifying where the water body or any other natural element is capable of removing pollutants itself.

Urban Smog and Acid Rain

- Urban smog is the smoky fog over cities caused by atmospheric pollution. It is very harmful to human health.
- Air pollution can also cause **acid rain**. Rainwater analysis of the urban environment has indicated that the pH value of the first rain after summer is always lower than the subsequent rains.

Noise Pollution

- Noise pollution refers to the presence of any unwanted or disturbing sound in the surroundings that affects the health and well being of humans and other organisms.
- The level of steady noise is measured in terms of decibels[2] (dB).
- The main sources of noise pollution are various factories, mechanised construction and demolition works, automobiles and aircraft, etc. Other sources of noise pollution are sirens and loudspeakers used in various festivals and programmes associated with community activities.
- The biggest source of noise pollution is the noise produced by traffic because its intensity and nature depend upon factors, such as the type of aircraft, vehicle, train and the condition of the road, as well as, that of the vehicle.
- In sea traffic, noise pollution is restricted to the harbour due to loading and unloading activities being carried out. Industries cause noise pollution but with varying intensity depending upon the type of industry.
- Noise pollution is location-specific and its intensity declines with an increase in distance from the source of pollution, i.e. industrial areas, arteries of transportation[3], airports, etc. Noise pollution is hazardous in many metropolitan and big cities in India.

9.2 Land Degradation

- The pressure on agricultural land increases due to the limited availability of land as well as the deterioration of the quality of agricultural land.
- Soil erosion, waterlogging, salinisation and alkalinisation of land lead to land degradation.
- Land degradation is generally a temporary or permanent decline in the productive capacity of the land. (A piece of land becomes a wasteland when it remain unchecked for a long time).
- Two processes that induce land degradation are **natural** and **human activities.**
- The **National Remote Sensing Centre** (NRSC) has classified wastelands by using remote sensing techniques. These wastelands are categorised based on the process of their formation.
- Wastelands can be classified as gullied /ravenous land, desertic or coastal sands, barren rocky areas, steeply sloping land and glacial areas. These wastelands are primarily caused by natural activities.
- Other degraded lands such as waterlogged and marshy areas, land affected by salinity and alkalinity and land with or without scrub, have largely been caused by natural as well as human factors.
- There are some other types of wastelands such as degraded shifting cultivation areas, degraded land under plantation crops, degraded forests, degraded pastures, and mining and industrial wastelands, which are caused by human activities.

2 Decibel It is a unit to measure the intensity of a sound or the power level of an electrical signal by comparing it with a given level on a logarithmic scale.

3 Arteries of transportation The "arteries of transportation" refer to the main routes or pathways that facilitate the movement of people, goods and services across regions.

A Case Study- Jhabua

- Jhabua district is located the Western agro-climatic zone of Madhya Pradesh and is one of the five most underdeveloped districts in India.
- It has a high tribal population, mostly Bhils, who face poverty and problems from degraded land and forests.
- The Government of India's Rural Development and Agriculture Ministries funded watershed management programmes here. These programmes work on improving land, water, and vegetation to support people's livelihoods through resource management and community involvement.
- In the past five years, these programmes have treated 20% of Jhabua's land, improving soil quality and preventing land degradation.
- In Petlawad block, there's a successful partnership between the government, NGOs, and the Bhil community for managing watersheds.
- In Sat Rundi, a hamlet of Karravat village, each household planted and took care of one tree on shared land.
- Villagers also grew fodder grass on pasture land. They protected these areas and also stopped open grazing so that the land could get recovered.
- In village, conflicts on land were solved by sharing the benefits of the improved pasture with a man who had taken their land forcefully.
- This partnership helped to protect common lands, created a sustainable way to feed cattle and brought the community together.

▲ *Community Participation for Land Leveling*

Types and Sources of Pollution

Pollution Types	Pollution Involved	Sources of Pollution
Air Pollution	Oxides of sulphur (SO_2, SO_3), oxides of nitrogen, carbon monoxide, hydro-carbon, ammonia, lead, aldehydes, asbestos and beryllium.	Combustion of coal, petrol and diesel, industrial processes, solid waste disposal, sewage disposal, etc.
Water Pollution	Odour, dissolved and suspended solids, ammonia and urea, nitrate and nitrites, chloride, fluoride, carbonates, oil and grease, insecticide and pesticide residue, tannin, coliform MPM (bacterial count) sulphates and sulphides, heavy metals, e.g. lead, arsenic, mercury, manganese, etc radioactive substances.	Sewage disposal, urban run off, toxic effluents from industries, run-off over cultivated lands and nuclear power plants.
Land Pollution	Human and animal excreta, viruses and bacteria, garbage and vectors therein, pesticides and fertiliser-residue, alkalinity, fluorides, radioactive substances.	Improper human activities, disposal of untreated industrial waste, use of pesticides and fertilisers.
Noise Pollution	High level of noise above tolerance level.	Aircrafts, automobiles, trains, industrial processing and advertising media.

Quick Test 1

1. Name two human activities that lead to pollution of water.
2. Name three air pollutants.
3. What are two types of pollutants that cause land degradation?
4. Which type of diseases are caused by the air pollution?

9.3 Urban Waste Disposal

- Urban waste disposal is a serious problem in India. In metropolitan cities like Mumbai, Kolkata, Chennai, Bengaluru, etc., about 90 per cent of the solid waste is collected and disposed.
- In most other cities and towns in the country, about 30 to 50 per cent of the waste generated are not collected and they accumulate on streets, in open spaces between houses and wastelands, leading to serious health hazards.
- Urban areas are generally overcrowded and congested, with inadequate facilities to support the fast-growing population. All this leads to poor sanitary conditions and bad air.
- Solid waste refers to old and used articles, for example, stained small pieces of metals, broken glassware, plastic containers, polythene bags, ash, floppies, CDs, etc., which is dumped at different places.
- Solid wastes are disposed of from two sources : **household or domestic establishments**, and **industrial or commercial establishments**.
- The household wastes are disposed off either on public lands or on private contractors' sites. On the other hand, solid wastes of industrial units are collected and disposed off through public (municipal) facilities at low-lying public grounds (landfill areas).
- Solid wastes cause health hazards through unpleasant smells, and harbouring of flies and rodents, which act as carriers of diseases like typhoid, diphtheria, diarrhoea, malaria, cholera, etc.
- The dumping of industrial waste into rivers leads to water pollution. River pollution from city-based industries and untreated sewage leads to serious health problems downstream.
- Untreated wastes ferment slowly and release toxic biogas to the atmosphere, including methane. Urban waste should be treated as a resource and utilised for generating energy and compost.

Case Study: A Role Model to Restore the Ecology and Safeguard Human Health in Daurala

- In Daurala near Meerut, a project was started to restore the environment and protect human health, based on the **Polluter Pays** principle.
- This project involved collaboration among Daurala industries, NGOs, government officials, and residents to improve living conditions.
- In 2003, people noticed that Daurala's groundwater was contaminated with heavy metals from untreated industrial wastewater.
- An NGO surveyed the health of residents and found serious health risks from contaminated water.
- The key actions taken included
  - Increasing the capacity of the village's overhead water tank.
  - Laying 900 meters of extra pipeline to provide clean water to residents.
  - Cleaning and desilting[4] a village pond to help recharge the groundwater.
  - Building rainwater harvesting systems to mix groundwater contaminants after rain.
  - Planting 1,000 trees to improve air quality and the overall environment.
  - After three years, these efforts have significantly improved the health and ecology of the village.

9.4 Rural-Urban migration

- Population flow from rural to urban areas is caused by many factors, like high demand for labour in urban areas, low job opportunities in rural areas and unbalanced pattern of development between urban and rural areas.

4 Desilting It is the process of removal of silt from a water body.

- In India, the population in cities is rapidly increasing. At present, 55 per cent of the world's population lives in cities. This proportion might increase to 68 per cent by 2050.
- Urban population grows through natural increase (when birth rate exceeds death rate), net immigration (when people move in rather than out), and sometimes through reclassification of urban areas.

9.5 Problems of Slums

- Slums are areas in cities with poor living conditions and crowded spaces.
- People in slums often move there from villages, looking for work but can't afford proper housing.
- Houses in slums are in bad shape, often old and broken.
- Hygiene is poor, with little access to clean drinking water, toilets and proper ventilation.
- Streets are narrow and often filled with trash, creating health risks.
- Many people have to practice open defecation due to a lack of toilet facilities.
- Drainage systems are unregulated, causing dirty water to collect and spread diseases.
- Most slum residents work in low-paying, risky jobs with no job security.
- They often struggle with undernourishment and lack of proper healthcare.
- Due to poverty, they can't always send their children to school.
- The harsh conditions can lead to problems like drug abuse, crime and social isolation[5].
- The Swachh Bharat Mission is a part of the urban renewable mission launched by the Government of India to improve the quality of life in urban slums. It was launched in 2014 to improve sanitary conditions in the country.

Dharavi-Asia's Largest Slum

- Dharavi is a large slum area in central Bombay (Mumbai).
- Originally, Dharavi was a coastal area. It got filled with waste over time and is now home to many marginalised communities, including Scheduled Castes and poor Muslims.
- It has one main road, called the **ninety-foot road**, which is much narrower than that.
- Most buildings are temporary, two or three storeyed high, with rusty staircases leading to small single rooms that are often shared by large families of up to twelve people.
- The neighbourhood of Dharavi are poor areas which are crowded and have less greenery. It is similar to the Victorian London's East End.
- Despite these conditions, Dharavi produces some of India's most valuable goods, including
  - ceramics and pottery
  - embroidery and zari work
  - leather goods
  - fashionable clothing
  - metalwork, jewellery, wood carvings and furniture

▲ *Slum Area in Dharavi*

Quick Test 2

1. Mention two cities where more than 90% of solid waste is collected and disposed of.
2. What type of disease is caused due to improper solid waste management?
3. Identify two problems of slum dwellers.
4. In which type of activities are slum dwellers engaged?

5 **Social Isolation** It is a condition when a person do not have any contact with others and has little to no social support.

Mind Map

GEOGRAPHICAL PERSPECTIVE ON SELECTED ISSUES AND PROBLEMS

1 Environmental Pollution

Results from the release of substances and energy from waste products of human activities.

Water Pollution

- **Causes** Release of unwanted substances into water body by domestic and industrial activities.
- **Effects** Water-borne diseases like diarrhoea, intestinal worms and hepatitis.

Noise Pollution

Causes Noise coming from factories, mechanised construction, automobiles and aircraft.

Effects

- Causes sleep disruption
- High blood pressure stress

Air Pollution

- **Causes** Addition of contaminants like dust, gas, odour into air by different sources like combustion of fuels, mining industries.
- **Effects** Causes respiratory diseases, nervous and affects circulatory system

Land Degradation

Temporary or permanent decline in productivity of land

Naturally Induced

- Wastelands are caused by natural agents.
  Example, gullied/ravinous wasteland desertic wasteland

Man-Made

- Wastelands are caused by human factors.
  Example, salinity, alkalinity and land with or without scrub.

2 Urban-Waste Disposal

It involves managing waste collected from residential and industrial area.

Household Waste

Wastes generated from domestic activity

Effects Causes health hazards, like cholera, typhoid, malaria.

Industrial Waste

Wastes generated from industrial activity.

Effects

- Water pollution
- Health hazards like diphtheria

3 Rural-Urban Migration

Defined as the flow of population from rural to urban areas.

Causes

- High demand for labour in urban areas
- Low job opportunities in rural areas
- Unbalanced development

Effects

- Change in population density
- Increases pressure on resources
- Environmental impact

4 Problems of Slum

Slum is a densely populated area with poor quality housing and infrastructure.

Causes

Poverty and unemployments, rapid urbanisation, poor planning

Effects

- Drug abuse
- Alcoholism
- Crime
- Social exclusion

NCERT Folder

Choose the right answer of the following from the given options

(i) Which one of the following rivers is highly polluted?

(a) Brahmaputra (b) Sutlej
(c) Yamuna (d) Godavari

Ans. (c) Yamuna

(ii) Which one of the following diseases is caused by water pollution?

(a) Conjunctivitis (b) Diarrhoea
(c) Respiratory infections (d) Bronchitis

Ans. (b) Diarrhoea

(iii) Which one of the following is the cause of acid rain?

(a) Water pollution (b) Land pollution
(c) Noise pollution (d) Air pollution

Ans. (d) Air pollution

(iv) Push and pull factors are responsible for

(a) migration (b) land degradation
(c) slums (d) air pollution

Ans. (a) migration

Answer the following questions in about 30 words

(i) What is the difference between pollution and pollutants?

Ans. Differences between pollution and pollutants are given below

Pollution	Pollutants
Pollution is the addition of undesirable and harmful elements in our environment in large amount over a long period of time.	Pollutants are those elements that deteriorate the quality of land, air or water by getting mixed with them.
Pollution changes the physical, chemical or biological characteristics of air, land and water that is undesirable and affects human life adversely.	Pollutants occur on land, in air or water in the form of gases, solids or liquids.
Types of pollution are air, water, land, etc.	Examples of pollutants are radioactive elements, carbon monoxide, solid waste, etc.

(ii) Describe the major source of air pollution.

Ans. The major source of air pollution are combustion of fossil fuels, mining process and industries. These processes release oxides of sulphur and nitrogen, hydrocarbons, carbon dioxide, carbon monoxide, lead and asbestos. With increasing use of varieties of fuels as sources of energy, there is increase in emission of toxic gases into atmosphere resulting in the pollution of air.

(iii) Mention major problems associated with urban waste disposal in India.

Ans. Major problems associated with urban waste disposal in India are as follows

- When solid waste is not properly disposed off, it becomes problem for humans as well as our environment.
- Due to urban wastes, flies and rodents spread and can cause many diseases like typhoid, diphtheria, diarrhoea, malaria, cholera and other diseases.
- Industrial solid wastes leads to water pollution. These make water unfit for human consumption.
- In India about 30 to 50 per cent of the wastes generated are left uncollected and untreated which accumulate on the streets, in open spaces between houses, in wastelands, etc.

(iv) What are the effects of air pollution on human health?

Ans. Effects of air pollution on human health are as follows

- Various diseases related to respiratory, nervous and circulatory systems are caused by air pollution.
- Air pollution results in the formation of smog in urban areas. This smog has a negative effect on human health.
- Acid rain is also caused by air pollution. According to rainwater analysis of urban environment, pH value of the first rain after summer is always lower than the subsequent rains. That's why the first rain is relatively acidic as compared to subsequent rains.

Answer the following questions in about 150 words

(i) Describe the nature of water pollution in India.

Ans. The nature of water pollution in India can be seen through the following points

- Rise in the pollutants in the water bodies leads to water pollution, which makes it unfit for human use. For example, water bodies like lakes, rivers, oceans, aquifers, groundwater, etc are being increasingly polluted by human activities.

- Quality of water is degraded by indiscriminate use of water by increasing population and industrial expansion.
- No surface water is found in pure form in rivers, canals, lakes, etc as these water sources have small quantities of suspended particles, organic and inorganic substances.
- Water becomes unfit for use when concentration of these substances increases and makes water polluted. It also reduces the self purifying capacity of water.

For source of water pollution refer to page no. 335 under the heading 'Activities Causing Water Pollution'.

(ii) Describe the problem of slums in India.

Or **"Slums are residential areas of serious health and socio-environmental hazards." Support the statement.** **CBSE 2023**

Or **Explain any three problems of slums in India.** **CBSE 2024**

Ans. Slums are those area/colonies which are occupied by those migrants who were forced to migrate from the rural areas to urban areas/centres in search of livelihood but due to high rent and high cost of land, they could not afford proper housing. Thus, they are forced to live in environmentally incompatible and degraded areas.

Problems of slums in India are as follows

- Slums are environmentally incompatible and degraded areas.
- Slums have dilapidated (broken-down) houses where people are forced to live due to poverty or lesser income.
- People of slums face poor hygenic conditions. Thus, they are prone to many diseases and illness.
- The houses in slums have poor ventilation. So, people residing there face suffocation problems.
- Slums have poor quality housing or illegal and inadequate building structures.
- Slums areas are overcrowded and they have narrow street which are under threat of serious hazards e.g. Fire Hazards.
- Slums lack in basic amenities like drinking water, light and toilet facilities.
- They are marked by unregulated drainage system and open defecation.
- Besides this, most of the slum dwellers engage in low-paid, high risk-prone unorganised sectors of the urban economy. Because of such situation they are undernourished, prone to different types of illness.
- Due to poverty, slum dwellers are unable to give proper education to their children.
- Poverty has also made these people vulnerable to drug abuse, alcoholism, crime, vandalism, escapism, apathy and ultimately social exclusion.

(iii) Suggest measures for reduction of land degradation.

Ans. Following are some practices for reduction of land degradation

- **Treatment of Industrial Wastes Water** Industrial waste should be treated properly before discharging into rivers as this river water when used for irrigation may cause land pollution because the toxic elements present in the river water may infiltrate into the soil. After proper treatment, this water can also be used for irrigation.
- **Convert Wastes into Resource** Wastes generated from households and industries should be treated as resource and utilised for generating energy and compost. If this waste is not treated properly and dumped on the land, land gets degraded.
- **Improve Sanitary Conditions** Sanitary conditions can be improved by providing *sulabh swachalayas* (toilet facilities) in slums and other areas where there is absence of these facilities. Thus, we can minimise land degradation in such areas.
- **Watershed Management Programmes** These programmes acknowledge the linkage between land, water and vegetation and attempts to improve livelihoods of people through natural resource management and community participation. These are helpful in preventing land degradation and improving soil quality.
- **Joint Participation of Community and Government** There is an urgent need for joint participation of both government and community for reduction of land degradation.

Exam Pattern Questions

Objective Type Questions

Multiple Choice Questions (MCQs)

1. **Which of these activities are the most significant contributor to water pollution?**

(a) Households (b) Farms
(c) Industries (d) Tourism

2. **Which of the following elements is both a water pollutant and air pollutant?**

(a) Sulphates (b) Carbon monoxide
(c) Ammonia (d) Mercury

3. **Which one of the following diseases is caused by water pollution?** **CBSE 2024**

(a) Hepatitis (b) Asthma
(c) Pneumonia (d) Deafness

4. **Which of the following programmes is launched by the present Union Government for the cleaning of river Ganga?** **CBSE Sample Paper Term I 2021**

(a) Ganga Action Plan
(b) Namami Gange
(c) Ganga Namami Action Plan
(d) Ganga Cleaning Mission

5. **Read the given statement carefully and answer the question that follow.** **CBSE 2024**

"Most of the industrial wastes are disposed off in running water or lakes".

Which among the following groups of industries are the major sources of water pollution?

(a) Leather, pulp and paper
(b) Iron, copper and sugar
(c) Sugar, petrochemicals and fertiliser
(d) Cotton textile, chemical and power plant

6. **Which of the following human body system gets affected the most by water pollution?** **CBSE 2024**

(a) Nervous system
(c) Respiratory system
(b) Circulatory system
(d) Digestive system

7. **Which one of the following is not an objective of Namami Gange Programme?** **CBSE 2024**

(a) Developing sewerage treatment systems in towns
(b) Monitoring of industrial effluents
(c) Afforestation along the banks of the river
(d) To divert the flow of the river from the cities

8. **Identify the practical measure from the following to control air pollution in the metropolitan cities in India. Choose the most appropriate option.** **CBSE 2025**

(a) Public Transport with Ring Railway
(b) Carpooling with Metro Rail
(c) Metro Rail with CNG Buses
(d) Ring Railway with CNG Buses

9. **Respiratory diseases are mainly caused by ...... pollution.**

(a) land (b) water (c) air (d) noise

10. **Which of the following wastelands have been primarily formed by natural agents?**

(a) Barren rocky areas (b) Desertic sands
(c) Steep sloping land (d) All of these

11. **Which of the following tribes is in majority in Jhabua district of Madhya Pradesh?** **CBSE 2024**

(a) Bhil (b) Tharu (c) Bakarwal (d) Gaddi

12. **'Swachh Bharat Mission' has been launched by which one of the following?** **CBSE 2024**

(a) Government of Madhya Pradesh
(b) Government of India
(c) Non-Governmental Organisation
(d) World Health Organisation

13. **Read the following sources of land pollution carefully and choose the correct option.**

(i) Improper human activities
(ii) Untreated industrial waste
(iii) Practice of primitive subsistence agriculture
(iv) Use of pesticides and fertilizers

Options

(a) Only (i), (ii) and (iii) are correct
(b) Only (ii), (iii) and (iv) are correct
(c) Only (i), (ii) and (iv) are correct
(d) Only (i), (iii) and (iv) are correct

14. **Which of the following are the causes of pollution in Yamuna?**

(i) Industrial pollution from Kanpur.
(ii) Domestic waste from Delhi.
(iii) Extraction of water by Haryana and Uttar Pradesh for irrigation.

Codes

(a) (i), (ii) and (iii) (b) (ii) and (iii)
(c) (i) and (iii) (d) (i) and (ii)

15. Choose from the following the prominent feature of an urban area.

(i) Overcrowding
(ii) Good sanitary conditions
(iii) Adequate facilities to support the fast-growing population.
(iv) Congestion

Options
(a) (i), (ii) and (iv)
(b) (i) and (iv)
(c) (i), (ii), (iii), (iv)
(d) (ii), (iii) and (iv)

16. Choose from the following the reason responsible for the acute poverty in Jhabua district.

(i) It is due to degradation of land
(ii) It is due to degradation of forests
(iii) Government policies
(iv) Illiteracy of people

Options
(a) (i) and (ii)
(b) (i) and (iv)
(c) (i) and (iii)
(d) All of these

17. Read the following factors of migration carefully and choose the correct option related to pull factors **CBSE 2024**

(i) Peace and stability
(ii) Unfavourable climate
(iii) Protection from property
(iv) Economic backwardness

Options
(a) Only (i) and (ii) are correct
(b) Only (i) and (iii) are correct
(c) Only (ii) and (iv) are correct
(d) Only (ii) and (iii) are correct

Match the Following

18.

List I (Pollution)	List II (Effects)
A. Water Pollution	1. Smog
B. Air Pollution	2. Alkalinity
C. Land Pollution	3. Diarrhoea

Codes

	A	B	C
(a)	1	2	3
(b)	2	3	1
(c)	3	2	1
(d)	3	1	2

Assertion-Reason

Directions (Q. Nos. 19-21) In the questions given below are two statements labelled as Assertion (A) and other labelled as Reason (R). In the context of two statements which one of the following is correct?

Codes
(a) Both A and R are true, but R is not the correct explanation of A
(b) Both A and R are true and R is the correct explanation of A
(c) Both A and R are incorrect
(d) A is correct, but R is incorrect

19. **Assertion** (A) India is facing a serious problem of urban waste disposal.

Reason (R) About 30 to 50 per cent of the wastes generated are left uncontrolled and untreated.

20. **Assertion** (A) Watershed management is an effective way to prevent land degradation.

Reason (R) Watershed Management programmes acknowledge the linkages between land, water and vegetation and improves the livelihoods of people through natural resource management and community participation.

21. **Assertion** (A) "Slums are residential areas of least choice for living."

Reason (R) "Slums are associated with unregulated drainage, lack of basic amenities like drinking water, toilets, lights, etc." **CBSE 2024**

Answers

1. (c) Industries
2. (c) Ammonia
3. (a) Hepatitis
4. (b) Namami Gange
5. (a) Leather, pulp and paper
6. (d) Ring Railway with CNG Buses
7. (d) To divert the flow of the river from the cities
8. (d) Agricultural runoff
9. (c) air
10. (d) All of these
11. (a) Bhil
12. (b) Government of India
13. (c) Only (i), (ii) and (iv) are correct
14. (b) (ii) and (iii)
15. (b) (i) and (iv) only
16. (a) (i) and (ii)
17. (b) Only (i) and (iii) are correct
18. (d)
19. (b) Both A and R are true and R is the correct explanation of A
20. (b) Both A and R are true and R is the correct explanation of A
21. (b) Both A and R are true and R is the correct explanation of A

Subjective Questions

Short Answer Type Questions

1. How is environmental pollution caused? Mention the four types of pollution responsible for the environmental degradation.

Ans. Pollution of environment is caused by the release of unwanted substances from waste products of human activities.

Pollution of environment is the introduction of pollutants that can cause damage to environment and harm to humans or other living species. It is the addition of an undesirable substance or form of energy to the environment at a rate faster than the environment can accommodate it by dispersion, breakdown, recycling, etc.

The four types of pollution which are responsible for the environmental degradation are

(i) Water pollution (ii) Air pollution

(iii) Land pollution (iv) Noise pollution

2. How do industries pollute India's water bodies? Explain with examples.

Ans. Industries pollute India's water bodies in the following ways

- Waste water, poisonous gases, chemical residuals, numerous heavy metals, nitrate and nitrites, chloride, flourides, insecticides, pesticides, etc from industries contribute to water pollution.
- During the last fifty years, the number of industries in India has grown rapidly. But water pollution is concentrated within a few sections, mainly in the form of toxic wastes and organic pollutants.
- Examples of these industries are leather, pulp and paper, textiles, chemicals, sugar mills, distilleries and thermal power stations.
- Not all industries have treatment facilities for industrial affluents. Small scale industries cannot afford high investments in pollution control equipment.
- Thus, these industries release untreated wastewater into the rivers which pollutes them.
- In India rivers like Ganga, Yamuna are highly polluted by the industrial waste water and untreated effluents

3. State which main pollutants are involved in water pollution?

Ans. Main pollutants which are involved in water pollution are as follows

- Odour, dissolved and suspended solids discharged by industries.
- Ammonia and urea discharged by agricultural activities.
- Nitrate and nitrites caused by industrial activities.
- Chloride, fluoride, carbonates oil and grease discharged by industries.
- Insecticide and pesticide residue discharged by agricultural activities.
- Tannin, coliform MPM (bacterial count) sulphates and sulphides.
- Heavy metals, e.g. lead, arsenic, mercury, manganese discharged by industries which disturbs aquatic life badly.
- Radioactive substances discharged by thermal and atomic power plants..

4. The Ganga and Yamuna rivers are among the most polluted rivers in India. State the sources of pollution of these rivers and also mention their polluted stretches.

Ans. The Ganga and Yamuna are among the most polluted rivers in India.

Following are the source of pollution of these rivers and their polluted stretches.

Ganga river

- Industrial pollution generated from towns like Kanpur.
- Domestic wastes coming from urban centres.
- Dumping of carcasses in the river add pollution to the river water.

Polluted stretches

- Downstream of Kanpur
- Downstream of Varanasi
- Farrakka Barrage

Yamuna

- Extraction of water by Haryana and Uttar Pradesh for irrigation.
- Agricultural runoff resulting in high levels of micro-pollutants in the Yamuna.
- Domestic and industrial waste of Delhi flowing into the river.

Polluted stretches

- Delhi to confluence with Chambal
- Mathura and Agra

5. Define the term air pollution. Explain any two harmful effects of air pollution.

Or **Explain any three consequences of air pollution.**

Or **Explain any three ill effects of air pollution on human health in India.**

Ans. A larger proportion of pollutants like dust fumes, gas, fog, odour, smoke or vapour in air for a long duration is known as air pollution.

The main consequences of air pollution are as follows

- Air pollution is responsible for many diseases that cause harm to our respiratory, nervous and circulatory systems.
- Air pollution is responsible for creating smoky fog over cities which is known as urban smog. It also has negative effects on human health.
- Air pollution is also responsible for acid rains. First rain after summers in urban areas is relatively acidic in nature i.e. it shows lower pH level than the subsequent rains.
- Air pollution may be harmful to flora and fauna and to property.

6. How does migration affect the environment?

Competency Based Que

Ans. Migration often alters the environment in many place whether it is place of destination where a person wants to go to or the place of origin where a person belongs to. Researches from many locations have shown that deforestation and land degradation may occur in destination areas due to the alteration of land use patterns by the migrants.

For example, they build new houses by clearing vegetation or forest cover and use water resources and also discharge households and industrial wastes into water.

Due to conflict displaced people lack the most basic necessities and rely on natural resources for their survival. Unsustainable use of natural resources can lead to environmental degradation. Due to large number of migrants, pollutants are released in the environment at large scale in the form of air, water, land and noise pollutions. Thus, migration affects the environment adversely.

7. How can we improve the condition of slum dwellers?

Competency Based Que

Ans. We can help to improve the condition of slum dwellers with the help of the government by setting aims such as

- To improve the quality of life of poor people by providing access to clean water, improved sanitation and waste management services, and supporting secure land tenure and affordable housing.
- To strengthen the capacity of local people and their institutions to engage with local authorities and other service providers for the sustainable provision of basic services.
- To support income generation activities and community managed savings and credit schemes that enable households, to secure funds for the improvement of basic facilities.

Long Answer Type Questions

1. How are pollutants from human activities responsible for water pollution? Explain with examples.

Ans. Pollutants from human sources are responsible for water pollution. Human beings pollute the water through industrial, agricultural and cultural activities which are discussed below

- **Industrial Sources** Industries are the most significant contributor in pollution. Industries are source of a number of undersirable products including industrial wastes, polluted waste water, posionous gases, chemical residuals, numerous heavy metals, dust and smoke, etc. These industrial wastes are disposed in water bodies like rivers or lakes from where these poisonous elements spread to other water bodies like reservoirs, lakes, rivers, etc. This ultimately destroys the bio-system and pollute water at a larger scale. Industries like leather, pulp and paper, textiles and chemicals, etc are the major water polluting industries.
- **Agricultural Sources** Agriculture has modernised with the use of various types of chemical fertilisers like inorganic fertilisers, pesticides and herbicides, etc. These pollutants are washed down to rivers, lakes, tanks and pollute them.
  These harmful chemicals also infiltrate the soil from where they reach the groundwater. Fertilisers lead to an increase in the nitrate content in surface waters. In India, almost all the surface water sources are contaminated and unfit for human use.
- **Cultural Activities** Activities like pilgrimage, religious fairs, tourism, etc are also contributing factors that cause water pollution.

2. Describe any two sources of air pollution in India and suggest any three measures to overcome the air pollution.

Ans. Two major sources of air pollution are the combustion of fossil fuels and industrial activities. The burning of fossil fuels releases harmful gases like carbon dioxide, carbon monoxide, and oxides of sulfur and nitrogen, while industries emit toxic substances such as lead and asbestos.

Some of the measures to reduce and control air pollution are as follows

- Old automobiles should be replaced by new ones which should be redesigned in such a way that their emission cause minimum pollution.
- As coal produces poisonous gases that are released into the air, so electric engines should be used instead of steam or diesel engines.

- Industrial areas should be located at a safe distance from the residential areas.
- Newly designed smoke free furnaces should be used.
- Forest fires should be checked. Adequate preventive measures should be adopted to protect the forests.
- In industries, there should be the arrangement for pollution control.
- Replace conventional energy sources with the renewable or non-conventional energy sources. It is due to the reason that, non-convetional energy sources produces less smoke during combustion and are eco-friendly as compared to conventional energy sources.
- Cheap devices for controlling air pollution should be developed.
- Air pollution can be checked only through the joint efforts of the government, non- government organisations and the general public.

3. What is noise pollution? Explain any four sources of noise.

Or **Describe three main sources of noise pollution in India.**

Ans. Noise pollution refers to the presence of any unwanted or disturbing sound in the surroundings environment. Presence of these unwanted sounds creates disturbance in the environment which affects the health and well being of humans and other organisms. Noise pollution has become a serious concern now a days because of technological advancements.

Following are the four sources of noise pollution

(i) **Transportation** Cars, trucks, and motorcycles generate significant noise through engines, tires, and horns. Airplanes produce loud sounds during take-off, landing, and while flying at low altitudes.

(ii) **Industrial Activities** Machinery, equipment and processes in factories can create constant noise.

(iii) **Construction Sites** These produces high levels of noise. Use of equipment like hammers, cranes bulldozers create source of noise pollution.

(iv) **Community and Recreational Sources** These include pollutants like loudspeakers, concerts, festivals and events.

4. How can we control noise pollution? Suggest some measures.

Ans. Noise pollution can be effectively controlled by taking the following measures

(i) **Suppression of Noise at Source** This is possible if working methods are improved by

- designing and fabricating quieter machines to replace the noisy ones.
- proper lubrication and better maintenance of machines.
- installing noisy machines in sound proof chambers.
- covering noise producing machine parts with sound absorbing materials to check noise pollution.
- using silencers to control noise from automobiles, ducts, exhausts, etc.

(ii) **Planting of Trees** Planting green trees and shrubs along roads, hospitals, educational institutions, etc help in noise reduction to a considerable extent.

(iii) **Legislative Measures** Strict legislative measures need to be enforced to control the noise pollution such as

- Minimum use of loudspeakers and amplifiers especially near silent zones.
- Banning pressure horns in automobiles.
- Framing a separate Noise Pollution Act.

(iv) **Strict Enforcement**

- The government agencies should strictly enforce the law to curb noise pollution and impose penalties for violation.
- Apart from these meansures, ear pluges, ear muffs, etc can be provided to reduce exposure to noble pollution.

5. Explain how noise pollution has become hazardous in many big cities of India.

Ans. Noise pollution has become hazardous in many big cities of India such as Delhi and Mumbai due to the following factors:

- With the increase in population, the volume of traffic and passengers has increased. This has led to more noise pollution due to vehicular noise.
- More people have become prosperous in the cities. As a result of this, the number of private vehicles such as cars have increased significantly. This has led to traffic jams during peak hours i.e. in the morning and in the evening when people go to and come from their work places. This has increased noise pollution on the roads.
- Rapid industrialisation in and around the residential colonies has also increased noise pollution due to operation of machinery.
- Construction activities have increased to accommodate the ever increasing population in the big cities. These activities generate alot of noise.
- Religious activities, social functions, rallies, etc., create noise pollution particularly in the late hours of the day.

6. How is the degradation of cultivable land one of the serious problems in India? Explain in any three points.

Ans Land degradation refers to the process in which there is deterioration in the quality of land. This results in the decrease of productivity of that land. The degradation of land is one of the serious problems in India as agriculture is the most important activity which requires a good cultivable land. This can be illustrated by the following points

- Pressure on the agricultural land is created because of limited availability of cultivable land and decreasing quality of the land.
- There is decline in the productivity of the cultivable land because of soil erosion, salinisation, water logging and alkalinisation of land.
- Natural and man-made processes also contribute in deteriorating the quality of cultivable land.

7. Land degradation caused by human made processes are more harmful than natural processes in India. Analyse the statement with suitable examples. **Competency Based Que**

Ans. Land degradation is generally understood either as a temporary or a permanent decline in productive capacity of the land.

The causes or factors responsible for land degradation in India are given below

(i) Soil erosion (ii) Waterlogging

(iii) Salinisation (iv) Alkalinisation of land

Land is constantly used without managing its fertility, it is degraded and its productivity declines. Deforestation, overgrazing, mining and quarrying too are responsible for land degradation in India. Thus, land degradation caused by human processes is more harmful than natural processes in India.

Man-made degraded wastelands such as degraded shifting cultivation areas, degraded land under plantation crops, degraded forest, mining and industrial wasteland are 5.8% of the total geographical area of the country.

In states such as Jharkhand, Chhattisgarh, Madhya Pradesh and Odisha, deforestation due to mining has caused severe land degradation.

In states such as Gujarat, Rajasthan, Madhya Pradesh and Maharashtra overgrazing is one of the main reasons for land degradation.

8. How is the use of plastic bags harmful for environmental degradation? Evaluate it by citing suitable reasons. **CBSE Sample Paper Term II 2021**

Ans. Use of plastic bags is harmful for environmental degradation in the following ways

- The major impact of plastic bags on the environment is that it takes many years to for them to decompose.
- Waste from plastic bags poses serious environmental danger to human and animal health. If plastic bags are not properly disposed off, they can impact the environment by causing littering and stormwater drain blockages.
- Animals often confuse the plastic bags for food and consume them, therefore blocking their digestive processes.
- Plastic buried deep in landfills can drain harmful chemicals that spread into groundwater.
- If plastic bags are burned, they release a toxic substance into the air causing ambient air pollution.

9. How is 'urban waste disposal' a serious problem in India? Suggest measures to solve this problem. **CBSE Term II 2022**

Or **Suggest any three measures to solve the problem of 'Urban Waste Disposal' in India and explain them.** **CBSE 2024**

Ans. Urban waste disposal is a serious problem in India which can be seen through the following points

- Solid wastes are threat to human health and can cause various diseases. It creates foul smell and it harbours flies and rodents that can cause typhoid, diphtheria, diarrhoea, malaria, cholera and other diseases.
- Solid waste can create inconvenience rapidly if they are not properly handled. Pollutants can spread through rainwater or wind and can cause further problems.
- Industrial solid waste can cause water pollution if it dumped into water bodies. Rivers in which untreated sewage is dumped also results into various health problems.

We can solve the problem of waste disposal by these methods

- By minimising the use of disposable items and promoting the use of recycled articles.
- Separating biodegradable and non- biodegradable waste before dumping them.
- Recycling the non-biodegradable waste material.
- Stop dumping industrial solid waste into water bodies instead use landfill method of waste disposal. In this method a huge pit is made in an open low lying area, usually away from the places where people reside. The wastes is collected in huge trucks and dumped into the pits. Once the pits are full, they are covered with soil and left for decomposition.

10. Discuss the problems of slums and urban waste disposal in developing countries like India. **CBSE SQP 2022**

Or **Analyse any three problems of slum dwellers in India.** **CBSE 2024**

Ans. Slums are those area/colonies which are occupied by those migrants who were forced to migrate from the rural areas to urban areas/centres in search of livelihood but due to high rent and high cost of land, they could not afford proper housing. Thus, they are forced to live in environmentally incompatible and degraded areas.

Problems of slums in India are as follows

- Slums are environmentally incompatible and degraded areas.
- Slums have dilapidated (broken-down) houses where people are forced to live due to poverty or lesser income.
- People of slums face poor hygenic conditions. Thus, they are prone to many diseases and illness.
- The houses in slums have poor ventilation. So, people residing there face suffocation problems.
- Slums have poor housing or illegal and inadequate building structures.
- Slums are overcrowed having narrow street pattern which is prone to serious hazards, e.g. fire hazards because of congested spaces, which increase the chances of its spread.
- Slums lack in basic amenities like drinking water, light and toilet facilities.
- They are marked by unregulated drainage system and open defecation.
- Besides this, most of the slum dwellers engage in low-paid, high risk-prone unorganised sectors of the urban economy. Because of such situation they are undernourished, prone to different types of illness.
- Due to poverty, slum dwellers are unable to give proper education to their children.
- Poverty has also made these people vulnerable to drug abuse, alcoholism, crime, vandalism, escapism, apathy and ultimately social exclusion.

Source Based Questions

1. Read the passage carefully and answer the questions that follow.

Indiscriminate use of water by increasing population and industrial expansion has led degradation of the quality of water considerably. Surface water available from rivers, canals, lakes, etc is never pure.

It contains small quantities of suspended particles, organic and inorganic substances. When concentration of these substances increases, the water becomes polluted, and hence becomes unfit for use. In such a situation, the self-purifying capacity of water is unable to purify the water. Though water pollutants are also created from natural sources (erosion, landslides, decay and decomposition of plants and animals, etc.) pollutants from human activities are the real causes of concern.

Human beings pollute the water through industrial, agricultural and cultural activities. Among these activities, industry is the most significant contributor. Industries produce several undesirable products including industrial wastes, polluted waste water, poisonous gases, chemical residuals, numerous heavy metals, dust, smoke, etc. Most of the industrial wastes are disposed off in running water or lakes. Consequently, poisonous elements reach the reservoirs, rivers and other water bodies, which destroy the bio-system of these waters.

(i) Which of the following is the largest contributor to water pollution in India?

(a) Agriculture (b) Households
(c) Industry (d) Services

Ans. (c) Industry

(ii) Which among the following is a polluting industry?

(a) Leather industry (b) Pulp and paper industry
(c) Chemicals industry (d) All of these

Ans. (d) All of these

(iii) Indiscriminate use of fertilisers leads to increase in which of the following harmful components in water?

(a) Sulphur (b) Nitrates
(c) Calcite (d) Flouride

Ans. (b) Nitrates

2. Read the passage carefully and answer the questions that follow.

Based on the universal law "Polluter pays", effort to restore the ecology and safeguard the human health with people's participation has taken place in Daurala near Meerut. These efforts are now bearing fruits after a span of three years when Meerut based NGO had developed a model for ecological restoration. The meeting of the Daurala Industries officials, NGOs, Government officials and other stakeholders at Meerut has brought out results. The powerful logics, authentic studies and the pressure of people have brought a new lease of life to the twelve thousand residents of this village. It was in the year 2003 that the pitiable condition of Dauralaites drew the attention of the civil society.

The groundwater of this village was contaminated with heavy metals. The reason was that the untreated wastewater of Daurala industries was leaching to the groundwater table. The NGO conducted a door to door survey of the health status of the residents and came out with a report.

The organisation, the village community and people's representatives sat together to find out sustainable solutions to the health problem. The industrialists showed a keen interest towards checking the deteriorating ecology. The overhead water tank's capacity in the village was enhanced and a 900m extra pipeline was laid to supply potable water to the community.

(i) Daurala was experiencing which of the following type of pollution?

(a) Air pollution (b) Water pollution
(c) Land pollution (d) Noise pollution

Ans. (b) Water pollution

(ii) Which of these measures were taken by the people to dilute the harmful contaminants of groundwater?

(a) Dam construction (b) Rainwater harvesting
(c) Digging of borewells (d) Cleaning rivers

Ans. (b) Rainwater harvesting

(iii) Which of the following played the most important role in resolving the pollution related issues at Daurala?

(a) The Judiciary (b) The Government
(c) The Civil Servants (d) The Civil Society

Ans. (d) The Civil Society

3. Read the passage carefully and answer the questions that follow.

Dharavi–Asia's Largest Slum

"…. Buses merely skirt the periphery. Autorickshaws cannot go there, Dharavi is part of central Bombay where three wheelers are banned. Only one main road traverses the slum, the miscalled 'ninety-foot road', which has been reduced to less than half of that for most of its length.

Some of the side alleys and lanes are so narrow that not even a bicycle can pass. The whole neighbourhood consists of temporary buildings, two or three storeyed high with rusty iron stairways to the upper part, where a single room is rented by a whole family, sometimes accommodating twelve or more people; it is a kind of tropical version of the industrial dwelling of Victorian London's East End.

But Dharavi is a keeper of more sombre secrets than the revulsion it inspires in the rich; a revulsion, moreover, that is, in direct proportion to the role it serves in the creation of the wealth of Bombay.

In this place of shadowless, treeless sunlight, uncollected garbage, stagnant pools of foul water, where the only non-human creatures are the shining black crows and long grey rats, some of the most beautiful, valuable and useful articles in India are made. From Dharavi come delicate ceramics and pottery, exquisite embroidery and zari work, sophisticated leather goods, high-fashion garments, finely-wrought metalwork, delicate jewellery settings, wood carvings and furniture that would find its way into the richest houses, both in India and abroad…

Dharavi was an arm of the sea that was filled by waste, largely produced by the people who have come to live there: Scheduled Castes and poor Muslims. It comprises rambling buildings of corrugated metal, 20 metres high in places, used for the treatment of hides and tanning. There are pleasant parts, but rotting garbage is everywhere…"

(i) What restrictions limit public transportation access to Dharavi?

Ans. Buses only skirt the periphery, and autorickshaws are banned because Dharavi is part of central Bombay.

(ii) What types of items are manufactured in Dharavi that contribute to its economic significance?

Ans. Dharavi produces delicate ceramics, pottery, exquisite embroidery, zari work, leather goods, high-fashion garments, metalwork, jewellery, wood carvings and furniture.

(iii) How has Dharavi's landscape changed from its original state?

Ans. Dharavi was originally an arm of the sea, which was filled in with waste, primarily from the residents who later moved there.

4. Read the passage carefully and answer the questions that follow **CBSE 2024**

Dharavi

There is only one main road that traverses Dharavi, which has been reduced to less than half of that for most of its length. Some of the side alleys and lanes are so narrow that not even a bicycle can pass. The whole neighbourhood consists of temporary buildings, two or three storeyed high with rusty iron stairways to the upper part, where a single room is rented by a whole family, sometimes accommodating 10-12 people; it is a kind of tropical version of the industrial dwelling of Victorian London's East End. But Dharavi is a keeper of more sombre secrets than the revulsion it inspires in the rich; a revulsion, moreover, that is, in direct proportion to the role it serves in the creation of the wealth of Bombay. In this place of shadowless, treeless sunlight, uncollected garbage, stagnant pools of foul water, where the only creatures are the shining black crows and long grey rats, some of the most beautiful, valuable and useful articles in India are made. From Dharavi come delicate ceramics and pottery, exquisite embroidery and zari work, sophisticated leather goods, high-fashion garments, finely-wrought metalwork, delicate jewellery settings, wood carvings and furniture that would find its way into the houses, both in India and abroad.

(i) Describe the physical condition of Dharavi.

Ans. Dharavi has narrow roads, overcrowded temporary buildings, and poor infrastructure. Many areas lack proper sanitation, with stagnant water, uncollected garbage, and limited greenery, creating an unsanitary living environment.

(ii) **Explain one major problem of Dharavi.**

Ans. The major problem in Dharavi is overcrowding, with families living in cramped, poorly ventilated spaces. This, combined with poor sanitation, contributes to health risks and a lack of basic amenities.

(iii) **Explain the main objective of 'Swachh Bharat Mission' in the context of Dharavi.**

Ans. The main objective of the 'Swachh Bharat Mission' in Dharavi is to improve sanitation by eliminating open defecation, enhancing waste management, and promoting cleanliness, ultimately aiming to create a healthier living environment.

5. Read the passage carefully and answer the questions that follow . **CBSE 2024**

Land Degradation

The pressure on agricultural land increases not only due to the limited availability but also by deterioration of quality of agricultural land. Soil erosion, waterlogging, salinisation and alkalinisation of land lead to land degradation. What happens if land is consistently used without managing its fertility ? Land is degraded and productivity declines. Land degradation is generally understood either as a temporary or a permanent decline in productive capacity of the land. Though all degraded land may not be wasteland, but unchecked process of degradation may lead to the conversion to wasteland. There are two processes that induce land degradation. These are natural and created by human beings. National Remote Sensing Centre (NRSC) has classified wastelands by using remote sensing techniques and it is possible to categorise these wastelands according to the processes that have created them. There are a few types of wastelands such as gullied/ravinous land, desertic or coastal sands, barren rocky areas, steep sloping land, and glacial areas, which are primarily caused by natural agents.

There are other types of degraded lands such as waterlogged and marshy areas, land affected by salinity and alkalinity and land with or without scrub, which have largely been caused by natural as well as human factors. There are some other types of wastelands such as degraded shifting cultivation area, degraded land under plantation crops, degraded forests, degraded pastures, and mining and industrial wastelands, that are caused by human action.

(i) **Explain the meaning of land degradation.**

Ans. Land degradation refers to a temporary or permanent decline in the productive capacity of the land.

(ii) **Discuss about the processes other than natural process responsible for land degradation.**

Ans. Mining is one of the man-made processes that is responsible for land degradation.

(iii) **Suggest any two measures to solve the problem of land degradation.**

Ans. Two measures to solve the problem of land degradation are as follows

- Afforestation
- Contour ploughing

SELF ASSESSMENT TEST

Objective Type Questions

1. Which of the following is/are consequence(s) of water pollution?
   (a) Rivers are contaiminated (b) Water-borne diseases
   (c) Degrading quality of groundwater (d) All of these
2. Noise pollution is location specific and its .... declines with distances.
   (a) quality (b) intensity
   (c) pitch (d) frequency
3. Which of the following are the pollutants of water?
   (i) Oil and grease
   (ii) Insecticides and pesticides
   (iii) Heavy metals
   Codes
   (a) (i) and (ii) (b) (i), (ii) and (iii)
   (c) (ii) and (iii) (d) (i) and (iii)
4. Which of the following are push factors of migration?
   (a) Large employment opportunities (b) Better civic amenities
   (c) Civil unrest (d) Better income
5. Slums in India suffer from which of the following problems?
   (a) Lack of basic amenities (b) Over crowded streets
   (c) Unregulated drainage system (d) All of these

Short Answer Type Questions

6. River Ganga and Yamuna have some main polluters which results in the extensive stretches of the polluted water. Discuss
7. Being the citizen of the society you are asked to give some contribution to control the pollution. Give some of your views regarding this.
8. Analyse the main problems caused by urban waste disposal.
9. The living standard of slum dwellers could be uplifted. Give some of your suggestion regarding this problem.
10. Explain some of the characteristics of slum areas.

Long Answer Type Questions

11. Ganga has a national importance but the river requires cleaning by effectively controlling the pollution for its water. Discuss any one initiative taken by the government regarding the same.
12. Noise pollution is an emerging problem today. Suggest some measures to reduce its effects.
13. 'Trends of urbanisation by 2050 is going to pressurise the spatial infrastructure and resources of cities'? Explain in brief.
14. Analyse some of the methods that could be adopted to reduce the problem of land degradation.

PRACTICAL WORK

1. Data– Its Source and Compilation

The data is defined as numbers that represent measurements from the real world. A datum is a single measurement. In other words, logical and numerical information is called data.

Need for Data

Data is essential for various fields, including science, economics, and geography. Some of its key uses include

- **Understanding Trends** Data helps to identify trends in population growth, climate change, and economic development.
- **Decision-Making** Governments and businesses use data to plan policies, allocate resources, and improve efficiency.
- **Statistical Analysis** Researchers analyse data to test hypotheses and derive conclusions.
- **Predictive Analysis** Weather forecasts, stock market trends, and disease outbreaks are predicted using data.

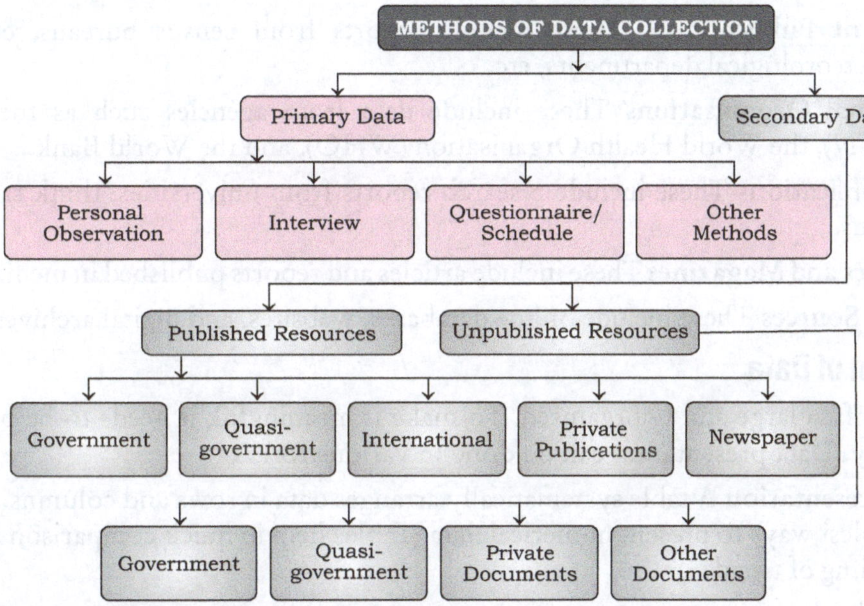

Practical Work

Sources of Data

Data can be collected from two main sources: primary and secondary.

Primary Sources of Data

Primary data is collected firsthand by researchers or organisations for specific purposes. It is original and has not been previously recorded. Some methods of primary data collection include

- **Personal Observation** In this method, researchers observe and record information directly from the field. For example, geographers survey landforms, vegetation, and human settlements.
- **Interviews** In this method, researchers conduct face-to-face or online interviews with individuals or groups to gather insights.
- **Questionnaires** In this method, researchers conduct structured surveys where respondents provide answers to predefined questions.
- **Field Experiments** In this method, scientists collect data on soil quality, air pollution, or water contamination using specialised tools.

Secondary Sources of Data

Secondary data is collected from published or unpublished records. It may include

- **Government Publications** These include reports from census bureaus, economic surveys, meteorological departments, etc.
- **International Organisations** These include data from agencies such as the United Nations (UN), the World Health Organisation (WHO), and the World Bank.
- **Private Publications** These include research reports from universities, think tanks, and corporations.
- **Newspapers and Magazines** These include articles and reports published in media outlets.
- **Electronic Sources** These include online databases, websites, and digital archives.

Presentation of Data

Raw data is often large and unorganised. To make it meaningful, it needs to be presented systematically. Data presentation can be done in various forms

- **Tabular Presentation** A table systematically arranges data in rows and columns. It is one of the simplest ways to present numerical data. Tables help in quick comparison and easy understanding of trends.

  For example

Year	Population (in billions)
2000	1.1
2010	1.2
2020	1.4

- **Graphical Representation** Graphs and charts visually represent data, making it easier to interpret. Some common graphical methods include
- **Bar Graphs** These are used for comparing different categories.
- **Line Graphs** These are used to show trends over time.
- **Pie Charts** These are used to represent the proportions of different components in a dataset.
- **Histograms** These are used to display frequency distributions.
- **Frequency Distribution** Frequency distribution groups data into categories based on numerical intervals. It helps in analysing how data points are spread across a range. For example, exam scores of students can be grouped into different ranges to observe performance trends.
- **Statistical Methods** Statistical techniques such as mean, median, and mode help summarise large datasets effectively. These measures of central tendency give an idea of the overall distribution of data.

Data Processing and Compilation

Once data is collected, it undergoes various processing stages. These stages include

(i) **Editing** In this step, checking for errors, inconsistencies, and missing values is done.

(ii) **Classification** In this step, grouping data based on common characteristics is done.

(iii) **Tabulation** In this step, data is organised into tables.

(iv) **Analysis** In this step, statistical tools are used to derive conclusions.

(v) **Interpretation** In this step, meaningful insights from analysed data are drawn.

Types of Data Representation

Data can be represented in different ways depending on the context and purpose as follows

- **Absolute Data** The actual figures, e.g., total population, production of a crop. This type of data is also known as raw data.
- **Percentage Data** Expressing values as percentages, e.g., literacy rate, unemployment rate.
- **Index Numbers** These measure changes over time, e.g., inflation rate, stock market index.

Grouping of Data

The grouping of the raw data requires determining of the number of classes in which the raw data are to be grouped and what will be the class intervals. The selection of the class interval and the number of classes, however, depends upon the range of raw data.

Making Tally Marks to Obtain Frequency

Group	Numerical of Raw Data	Tally Marks	Number of Individual
0-10	02,02,09,06	||||	4
10-20	10,15,18,12,17	~~||||~~	5
20-30	22,28,26,22,28	~~||||~~	5
30-40	39,32,37,36,35,37,31	~~||||~~ ||	7
40-50	47, 46, 44, 43, 42, 41	~~||||~~ |	6
50-60	53, 57, 50, 51, 58, 59, 56, 58, 56, 59	~~||||~~ ~~||||~~	10
60-70	64, 62, 67, 65, 63, 64, 68, 64	~~||||~~ |||	8
70-80	74, 73, 75, 70, 74, 71	~~||||~~ |	6
80-90	89, 84, 84, 80, 83	~~||||~~	5
90-100	96, 92, 90, 90	||||	4
			$\Sigma f = N = 60$

Process of Classification

Once the number of groups and the class interval of each group are determined, the raw data are classified. It is done by a method popularly known as Four and Cross Method or tally marks

Frequency Distribution

A frequency distribution is a visual representation of how often a value occurs in a set of data. Frequencies are classified as Simple and Cumulative frequencies.

Simple Frequencies are expressed by 'f' and represent the number of individuals falling in each group (as shown in the table below). Cumulative frequencies are expressed by 'Cf' and can be obtained by adding successive simple frequencies in each group with the previous sum. Each simple frequency is associated with its group or class. The exclusive or inclusive methods are used for forming the groups or classes.

Frequency Distribution

Group	f	Cf
00-10	4	4
10-20	5	9
20-30	5	14
30-40	7	21
40-50	6	27
50-60	10	37
60-70	8	45
70-80	6	51
80-90	5	56
90-100	4	60

$\Sigma f = N = 60$

- **Exclusive Method** The upper limit of one group is same as the lower limit of the next group (e.g., 10-20, 20-30).
- **Inclusive Method** In this method, a value equal to the upper limit of a group is included in the same group. Classes are mentioned in different form in this method as shown in the first column of the table below (e.g., 10-19, 20-29).

Frequency Distribution

Group	f	CF
0-9	4	4
10-19	5	9
20-29	5	14
30-39	7	21
40-49	6	27
50-59	10	37
60-69	8	45
70-79	6	51
80-89	5	56
90-99	4	60
	$\sum f = N = 60$	

Graphical Tools in Data Analysis

Frequency Polygon

A frequency polygon is a line graph representing data point distribution. It helps in comparing multiple datasets.

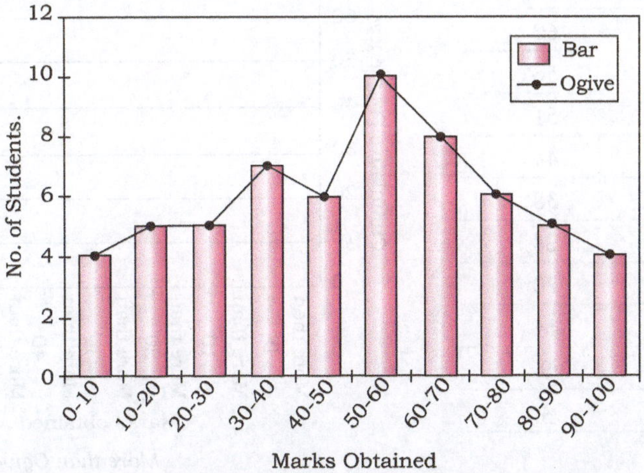

Frequency Distribution Polygon

Practical Work

Ogive (Cumulative Frequency Graph)

When the frequencies are added they are called cumulative frequencies and are listed in a table called cumulative frequency table. The curve obtained by plotting cumulative frequencies is called an Ogive. It is constructed either by the less than method or the more than method.

In the less-than method, we start with the upper limit of the classes and go on adding the frequencies. When these frequencies are plotted, we get a rising curve. For example,

Frequency Distribution : Less than Method

Less than Method	CF
Less than 10	4
Less than 20	9
Less than 30	14
Less than 40	21
Less than 50	27
Less than 60	37
Less than 70	45
Less than 80	51
Less than 90	56
Less than 100	60

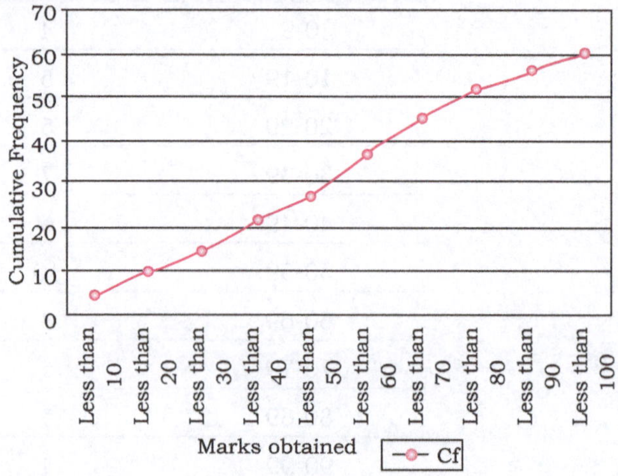

Less than ogive

In the more than method, we start with the lower limits of the classes and from the cumulative frequency, we subtract the frequency of each class. When these frequencies are plotted, we get a declining curve. For example,

Frequency Distribution : More than Method

More than Method	CF
More than 0	60
More than 10	56
More than 20	51
More than 30	44
More than 40	38
More than 50	28
More than 60	20
More than 70	14
More than 80	9
More than 90	4

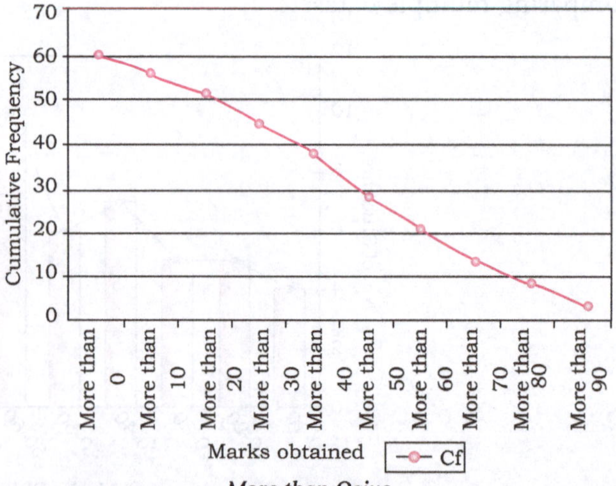

More than Ogive

Practical Work

2. Data Processing

In our daily lives, we come across various numerical data, such as temperatures, population figures, and exam scores. These values help us understand trends and make informed decisions. To simplify this, statistical methods like measures of central tendency help in identifying a single value that best represents an entire dataset.

Measures of Central Tendency

Measures of central tendency are statistical tools used to find a single value that represents the middle or centre of a dataset. This central value helps to summarize data and understand its overall pattern. Each measure provides a different perspective on the data, making them useful in different situations.

The three most commonly used measures of central tendency are

(i) **Mean** The arithmetic average of all values.

(ii) **Median** The middle value when data is arranged in order.

(iii) **Mode** The most frequently occurring value in a dataset.

Mean

Mean is the simple arithmetic average of the different values of a variable. For ungrouped and grouped data, the methods for calculating mean are necessarily different. Mean can be calculated by direct or indirect methods, for both grouped and ungrouped data.

Mean for Grouped Data

Direct Method

While calculating mean from ungrouped data using the direct method, the values for each observation are added and the total number of occurrences are divided by the sum of all observations. The mean is calculated using the following formula

The mean is calculated by summing all the values in a dataset and dividing by the number of values. It provides an overall average, making it useful for comparing datasets.

$$\overline{X} = \frac{\sum x}{N}$$

Where

$\overline{X}$ = Mean

x = A raw score in a series of measures

N = Number of measures

$\sum$ = Sum of a series of measures

$\sum x$ = The sum of all the measures

Example Calculate the mean rainfall for Malwa plateau in Madhya Pradesh from the rainfall of the districts of the region given in the table below.

Districts in Malwa Plateau	Normal Rainfall in mms × Direct Method	Indirect Method $d = x - 800$ *
Indore	979	179
Dewas	1083	283
Dhar	833	33
Ratlam	896	96
Ujjain	891	91
Mandsaur	825	25
Shajapur	977	177
$\sum x$ and $\sum d$	6484	884
$\frac{\sum x}{N}$ and $\frac{\sum d}{N}$	**926.29**	**126.29**

* *Where 800 is assumed mean.*
d is deviation from the assumed mean.

Indirect Method

For a large number of observations, the indirect method is normally used to compute the mean. It helps in reducing the values of the observations to smaller numbers by subtracting a constant value from them.

The following formula is used in computing the mean using indirect method

$$\overline{X} = A + \frac{\sum d}{N}$$

Where,

A = Subtracted constant $\quad \sum d$ = Sum of the coded scores

N = Number of individual observations in a series

Mean for Grouped Data

When data is grouped into class intervals, we use the midpoint of each class and its frequency to calculate the mean.

Direct Method

When scores are grouped into a frequency distribution, the individual values lose their identity. These values are represented by the midpoints of the class intervals in which they are located.

While computing the mean from grouped data using the direct method, the midpoint of each class interval is multiplied with its corresponding frequency (f); all values of fx (the X are the midpoints) are added to obtain $\sum fx$ that is finally divided by the number of observations i. e., N. Hence, the mean is calculated using the following formula

$$\overline{X} = \sum \frac{fx}{N}$$

Where

$\overline{X}$ = Mean $\qquad f$ = Frequencies

x = Midpoints of class intervals

N = Number of observations (it may also be defined as $\sum f$

For example, to compute the mean of the following data, this will be the process

Wage Rate of Factory Workers

Wage Rate (₹/day)	Number of Workers (*f*)
Classes	***f***
50-70	10
70-90	20
90-110	25
110-130	35
130-150	9

Computation of Mean

Classes	Frequency (f)	Mid-points (x)	fx	$d = x - 100$	fd	$u = (x - 100)/20$	fu
50-70	10	60	600	−40	−400	−2	−20
70-90	20	80	1,600	−20	−400	−1	−20
90-110	25	100	2,500	0	0	0	0
110-130	35	120	4, 200	20	700	1	35
130-150	9	140	1,260	40	360	2	18
$\sum fx$ and $\sum fd$	$\sum f = 99$		$\sum fx = 10{,}160$		$\sum fd = 260$		$\sum fu = 13$

Where $N = \sum f = 99$

The mean may be computed as under using the given formula

$$\overline{X} = \sum \frac{fx}{N} = \frac{10{,}160}{99} = 102.6$$

The indirect way of computing the mean for the particular data is as follows

$$\bar{x} = A \pm \frac{\sum fd}{N} = 100 + \frac{260}{99} = 100 + 2.6 = 102.6$$

Indirect Method

The following formula can be used for the indirect method for grouped data. The principles of this formula are similar to that of the indirect method given for ungrouped data. It is expressed as under

$$\bar{x} = A \pm \sum \frac{fd}{N}$$

Where,

A = Midpoint of the assumed mean group

(The assumed mean group in Table 2.3 is 90 - 110 with 100 as midpoint.)

f = Frequency

d = Deviation from the assumed mean group (A)

N = Sum of cases or $\sum f$

i = Interval width (in this case, it is 20)

Median

The median is the value that divides an ordered dataset into two halves. It is useful when the data contains extreme values that might distort the mean.

Steps to Calculate Median

(i) Arrange the data in ascending order.

(ii) Identify the middle value

- If the number of values is odd, the median is the middle value.
- If the number of values is even, the median is the average of the two middle values.

For example, in the dataset [12, 18, 22, 25, 28, 30, 35], the median is 25. If we have an even number of values, say [12, 18, 22, 25, 28, 30], the median is?

Median for Ungrouped Data

When the scores are ungrouped, these are arranged in ascending or descending order. Median can be found by locating the central observation or value in the arranged series. The central value may be located from either end of the series arranged in ascending or descending order. The following equation is used to compute the median

Value of $\left(\frac{N+1}{2}\right)$th item

Median for Grouped Data

When the scores are grouped, we have to find the value of the point where an individual or observation is centrally located in the group. It can be computed using the following formula

$$M = l + \frac{i}{f}\left(\frac{N}{2} - c\right)$$

Practical Work

Where,

M = Median for grouped data
l = Lower limit of the median class
i = Interval
f = Frequency of the median class
N = Total number of frequencies or number of observations
c = Cumulative frequency of the pre-median class.

Examaple Calculate the median for the following distribution

Class	50-60	60-70	70-80	80-90	90-100	100-110
f	3	7	11	16	8	5

Computation of Median

Classes	Frequency (f)	Cumulative Frequency (F)	Calculation of Median Class
50-60	3	3	
60-70	7	10	
70-80	11	21 c	
80-90 (median group)	**16 f**	37	$M = \frac{N}{2}$
90-100	8	45	$\frac{50}{2}$
100-110	5	50	= 25

$\sum f$ or N = 50

The median is computed in the steps given below

(i) Create the frequency table.

(ii) Cumulative frequencies (F) are obtained by adding each normal frequency of the successive interval groups.

(iii) Median number is obtained by $\frac{N}{2}$ i.e. $\frac{50}{2} = 25$ in this case, as shown in column 4 of table above.

(iv) Count into the cumulative frequency distribution (F) from the top towards bottom until the value next greater than $\frac{N}{2}$ is reached. In this example, $\frac{N}{2}$ is 25, which falls in the class interval of 40-44 with cumulative frequency of 37, thus the cumulative frequency of the pre-median class is 21 and actual frequency of the median class is 16.

(v) The median is then computed by substituting all the values determined in the step 4 in the following equation

$$M = l + \frac{i}{f}(m - c) = 80 + \frac{10}{16}(25 - 21)$$

$$= 80 + \frac{5}{8} \times 4 = 80 + 2.5$$

$$M = 82.5$$

Practical Work

Mode

The value that occurs most frequently in a distribution is referred to as mode. It is symbolised as Z or M_0. Mode is a measure that is less widely used compared to mean and median. There can be more than one type of mode in a given data set.

Mode for Ungrouped Data

While computing mode from the given data sets, all measures are first arranged in ascending or descending order. It helps in identifying the most frequently occurring measure easily.

For example, to calculate the mode for the following test scores in geography for ten students: 61, 10, 88, 37, 61, 72, 55, 61, 46, 22, arrange the data in ascending order. Measure 61 occurring three times in the series is the mode in the given dataset.

As no other number is in a similar way in the dataset, it possesses the property of being unimodal.

The data set with multiple modes is bimodal. If three values have equal and highest frequency, the series is trimodal. Similarly, a recurrence of many measures in a series makes it multimodal. However, when there is no measure being repeated in a series it is designated as without mode.

Comparison of Mean, Median, and Mode

Each measure of central tendency serves a different purpose

- **Mean** is best for continuous data without extreme values.
- **Median** is ideal for skewed data or datasets with outliers.
- **Mode** is useful for categorical data and frequency-based analysis.

In a normal distribution, the mean, median, and mode are equal. However, in a biased distribution, they differ

- **Positively Skewed Distribution** Mean > Median > Mode
- **Negatively Skewed Distribution** Mode > Median > Mean

Applications of Central Tendency Measures

- **Education** Analysing student performance using average marks.
- **Economics** Calculating per capita income.
- **Health** Studying average life expectancy.
- **Business** Understanding consumer preferences through mode.
- **Weather Analysis** Determining average rainfall or temperature.

3. Graphical Representation of Data

The data representation plays an important role in decision making. Graphical representation of data provides several benefits

- **Simplifies Complex Data** Large datasets become easier to understand when presented visually.
- **Facilitates Comparison** Helps compare different trends, regions, or time periods effectively.
- **Enhances Decision-Making** Provides a clear view of trends and patterns, aiding in policy-making and business strategies.
- **Saves Time** Visual data is processed faster than textual or numerical data.
- **Improves Communication** Graphs and diagrams make it easier to convey information to a wider audience.

Types of Data Representation

1. Graphical Representation

Graphical methods use visual tools like line graphs, bar diagrams, pie charts, and flow charts to depict data. These methods are categorised into

- **Line Graphs** It is used to show trends over time (e.g., population growth, temperature changes). It is constructed using an X-axis (time) and Y-axis (values).
- **Bar Diagrams** It represents data in rectangular bars. It is of the following types
  - (i) **Simple Bar Diagram** Used for one type of data.
  - (ii) **Multiple Bar Diagram** Compares multiple variables.
  - (iii) **Compound Bar Diagram** Represents different components in a single bar.
- **Pie Charts** It is used to show the proportions of different components in a dataset. It is constructed by dividing a circle into sections based on percentages.
- **Flow Charts** They represent the movement of goods, services, or population from one place to another. They are used in economic geography and transport analysis.

2. Cartographic Representation (Maps)

Maps are used for geographic data representation. Types include

- **Dot Maps** These maps represent the distribution of a particular phenomenon (e.g., population, crops). The dots are placed proportionally based on data values.
- **Choropleth Maps** These maps use different shades or colours to show data variations (e.g., literacy rates, population density). The data is grouped into categories and represented in different intensities.
- **Isopleth Maps** These maps use lines to connect points of equal value (e.g., temperature, rainfall). Common examples include isotherms (temperature) and isohyets (rainfall).

Rules for Effective Data Representation

To ensure clarity and accuracy, the following rules must be followed

- **Selection of Suitable Method** Choose the right graphical or cartographic method based on data type.
- **Selection of Suitable Scale** Ensure that the scale appropriately represents all data points.
- **Proper Design Elements**
  - (i) **Title** Clearly states the purpose of the graph or map.
  - (ii) **Legend** Explains symbols and colours used.
  - (iii) **Labels and Units** Axes and elements must be labeled properly.
  - (iv) **Direction Indicator** (for maps) Shows the North direction for orientation.

Construction of Diagrams and Maps

Steps for Drawing a Line Graph

- Convert data into rounded numbers if needed.
- Draw X-axis (time) and Y-axis (values).
- Choose an appropriate scale.
- Plot data points and join them with a smooth line.

For example, construct a line graph to represent the data given below in the table.

Year	Growth rate in percentage
1901	
1911	0.56
1921	0.30
1931	1.04
1941	1.33
1951	1.25
1961	1.96
1971	2.20
1981	2.22
1991	2.14
2001	1.93
2011	1.79

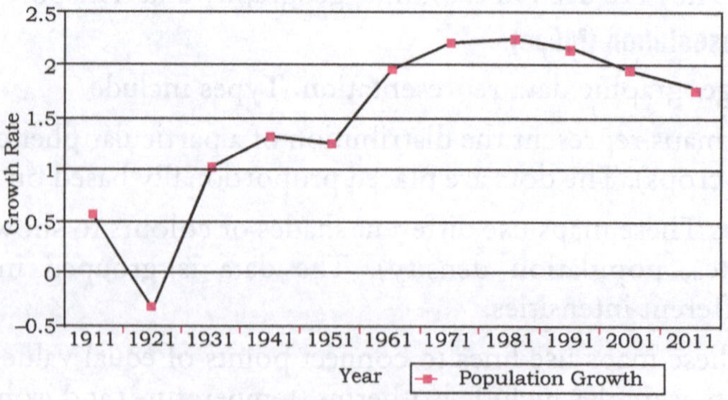

Annual Growth of Population in India 1901-2011

Steps for Constructing a Bar Diagram

- Draw X and Y axes.
- Label categories on the X-axis and values on the Y-axis.
- Draw bars of equal width with appropriate heights.
- Shade bars or use different colours for clarity.

For example, construct a simple bar diagram to represent the rainfall data of Thiruvananthapuram as given in the table below

Month	J	F	M	A	M	J	J	A	S	O	N	D
Rainfall in cm	2.3	2.1	3.7	10.6	20.8	35.6	22.3	14.6	13.8	27.3	20.6	7.5

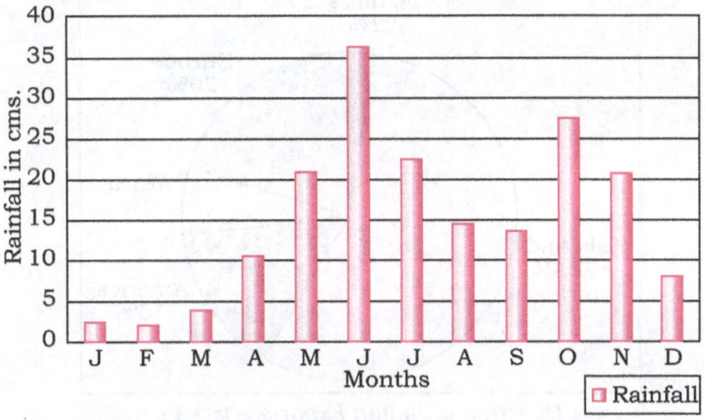

Average Monthly Rainfall of Thiruvananthapuram

Steps for Constructing a Pie Chart

- Calculate the percentage distribution of data.
- Convert percentages into angles using the formula.
- Draw a circle and divide it into sections based on calculated angles.
- Label each section with its respective category.

For example, represent the data given in the table below through a pie chart.

Unit/Region	% of Indian Export
Europe	20.2
Africa	6.5
America	14.8
Asia and ASEAN	56.2
Other	2.3
Total	100

Source : Economic Survey 2011-12

Calculation of degrees will be as follows

Countries	%	Calculation	Degree
Europe	20.2	20.2 × 3.6 = 72.72	73°
Africa	6.5	6.5 × 3.6 = 23.4	23°
America	14.8	14.8 × 3.6 = 53.28	53°
Asia and ASEAN	56.2	56.2 × 3.6 =202.32	203°
Other	2.3	2.3 × 3.6 = 8.28	8°
Total	100		360°

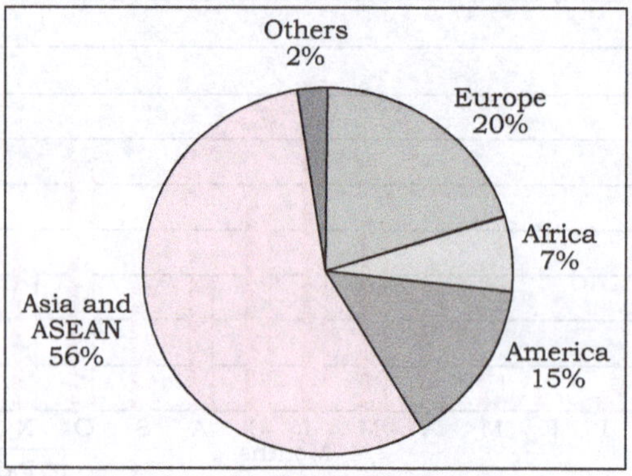

Direction of Indian Exports 2010-11

Steps for Constructing Thematic Maps

The thematic maps are generally classified into quantitative and non-quantitative maps. The quantitative maps are drawn to show the variations within the data. For example, maps depicting areas receiving more than 200 cm, 100 to 200 cm, 50 to 100 cm and less than 50 cm of rainfall. These maps are also called statistical maps.

The non-quantitative maps, on the other hand, depict the non-measurable characteristics in the distribution of given information, such as a map showing high and low rainfall-receiving areas. These maps are also called qualitative maps.

The types of quantitative maps are

(a) Dot maps (b) Choropleth maps (c) Isopleth maps

Dot Maps

The dot maps are drawn to show the distribution of phenomena such as population, cattle, types of crops, etc.

Construction

- Select the size and value of a dot.
- Determine the number of dots in each part using the given scale.
- Place the dots in each part as per the determined number in all parts.

Choropleth Map

The choropleth maps are also drawn to depict the data characteristics as they are related to the administrative units.

Construction

Arrange the data in ascending or descending order.

- Group the data into 5 categories to represent very high, high, medium, low and very low concentrations.
- The interval between the categories may be identified on the following formulae i.e., Range/5 and Range = maximum value - minimum value.
- Patterns, shades or colour to be used to depict the chosen categories should be marked in an increasing or decreasing order.

Isopleth Map

The word Isopleth is derived from Iso meaning equal and pleth means lines. Thus, an imaginary line which joins the places of equal values, is referred as Isopleth.

The more frequently drawn isopleths include Isotherm (equal temperature), Isobar (equal pressure), Isohyets (equal rainfall), Isonephs (equal cloudiness), Isohels (equal sunshine), contours (equal heights), Isobaths (equal depths), Isohaline (equal salinity), etc.

Construction

- An equal interval of values be selected.
- Interval of 5, 10, or 20 is supposed to be ideal.
- The value of Isopleth should be written along the line on either side or in the middle by breaking the line.

Method of Interpolation

For interpolation, follow the following steps

- Firstly, determine the minimum and maximum values given on the map.
- Calculate the range of value i.e. Range = maximum value - minimum value.
- Based on range, determine the interval in a whole number like 5, 10, 15, etc.

The exact point of drawing an Isopleth is determined by using the following formulae.

$$\text{Point of Isopleth} = \frac{\text{Distance between two points in cm}}{\text{Difference between the two values of corresponding points}} \times \text{Interval}$$

The interval is the difference between the actual value on the map and interpolated value.

Practical Work

4. Spatial Information Technology

Spatial Information Technology is an essential field that helps in collecting, storing, retrieving, displaying, managing, and analysing spatial data. The term 'spatial' relates to space and describes features and phenomena distributed across a geographically defined area.

Today, most of the data we use has spatial components, such as municipal addresses, land boundaries, and natural resource locations. Spatial Information Technology integrates various advanced technologies, including Remote Sensing, GPS, GIS, Digital Cartography, and Database Management Systems.

A crucial part of Spatial Information Technology is the Geographic Information System (GIS). A GIS is a system that captures, stores, checks, integrates, manipulates, analyzes, and displays data that are spatially referenced to the Earth. This system combines the strengths of Computer-Assisted Cartography and Database Management Systems and draws knowledge from multiple disciplines, including Geography, Geology, Statistics, Environmental Science, and Public Administration.

Forms of Geographical Information

There are two main types of geographical data: spatial and non-spatial data.

- **Spatial Data** These include positional, linear, and areal forms that define physical locations and features on the Earth's surface.
- **Non-Spatial Data** Also called attribute data, these describe characteristics of spatial features, such as population statistics or land usage.

A GIS database integrates both types of data to create detailed and meaningful geographic analyses. The choice of data sources for GIS applications depends on factors such as application needs, budget constraints, and data structure (vector or raster).

Spatial and Non-spatial Data

Stock Register of a Cycle shop

Part No.	Quantity	Description
101435	54	Wheel Spoke
108943	68	Ball Bearing
105956	25	Wheel Rim
123545	108	Tyre

Literate Population in States 1981

State	%Male	%Female
Kerala	75.3	65.7
Maharashtra	58.8	34.8
Gujarat	54.4	32.3
Punjab	47.2	33.7

GIS data is primarily stored in two formats

(i) **Raster Data** Represents spatial features using a grid of cells. Each cell has an assigned value corresponding to an attribute. Raster data is commonly used for satellite imagery and scanned maps. Raster data is simple and efficient for overlay analysis but requires large storage space and lacks precision.

(ii) **Vector Data** Represents spatial features using points, lines, and polygons. This format is useful for applications that require high precision, such as mapping roads or property boundaries. Vector data is compact and precise but has a complex data structure and limited compatibility with satellite imagery.

Comparison between Raster and Vector Data Models

Raster Model	Vector Model
Advantages • Simple data structure • Easy and efficient overlaying • Compatible with satellite imagery • High spatial variability is efficiently represented • Simple for own programming • Same grid cells for several attributes	**Advantages** • Compact data structure • Efficient for network analysis • Efficient projection transformation • Accurate map output
Disadvantages • Inefficient use of computer storage • Errors in perimeter and shape • Difficult network analysis • Inefficient projection transformation • Loss of information when using large cells, less accurate (although interactive maps)	**Disadvantages** • Complex data structure • Difficult overlay operations • High spatial variability is inefficiently represented • Not compatible with satellite imagery

Advantages of GIS Over Manual Methods

GIS has several advantages over traditional manual methods, such as

- Efficient storage and retrieval of spatial data.
- Ability to overlay multiple maps for comparative analysis.
- Quick and accurate spatial data analysis, such as buffering and proximity analysis.
- Improved decision-making in areas like urban planning, environmental management, and disaster response.

Components of GIS

A GIS consists of five key components

- **Hardware** Includes processing units, storage devices, and input/output systems.
- **Software** Manages data entry, editing, transformation, display, and analysis.
- **Data** The foundation of GIS, including spatial and attribute data.
- **People** Users such as scientists, policymakers, and engineers who interpret GIS data.
- **Procedures** Methods for data retrieval, storage, transformation, and final output presentation.

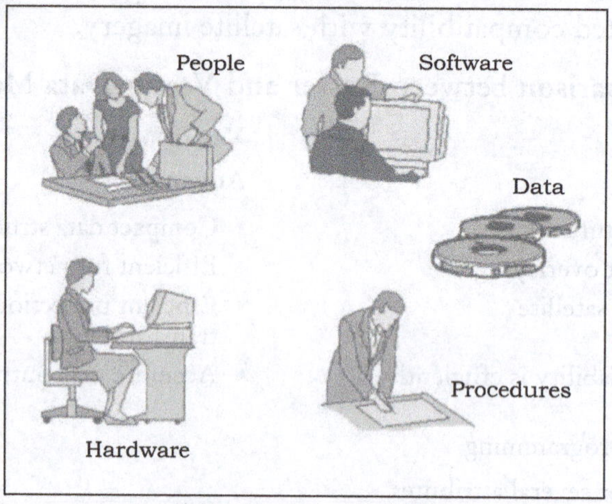

Basic Components of GIS

Sequence of GIS Activities

The main steps in GIS-related activities include

- **Spatial Data Input** To collect data through digitisation, remote sensing, or direct surveys.
- **Entering Attribute Data** To input additional descriptive information.
- **Data Verification and Editing** To ensure data accuracy and correct errors.
- **Data Linkages and Matching** To connect spatial data with attribute data.
- **Spatial Analysis** To apply GIS techniques to analyse patterns and make predictions.

Spatial Analysis Techniques

Spatial analysis in GIS helps in studying real-world processes and solving problems. Some important techniques include

- **Overlay Analysis** Combining multiple layers of maps to identify relationships and changes over time.
- **Buffer Analysis** Creating buffer zones around a feature to study its impact, such as assessing pollution zones or accessibility to healthcare facilities.
- **Network Analysis** Used in transportation and logistics to find the shortest path and optimise travel routes.
- **Digital Terrain Modeling** Creating 3D representations of landscapes for environmental and urban planning.

Viva Voce Questions

1. ***What is data?***

Ans. Data refers to numerical or logical information that represents real-world measurements.

2. ***What are the primary sources of data?***

Ans. Primary sources include personal observation, interviews, questionnaires, and field experiments.

3. ***What are secondary sources of data?***

Ans. Secondary sources include government publications, international organisations, private research reports, newspapers, and electronic sources.

4. ***Why is data important?***

Ans. Data helps in understanding trends, decision-making, statistical analysis, and predictive analysis.

5. ***What are the different ways to present data?***

Ans. Data can be presented using tables, graphs, frequency distributions, and statistical methods.

6. ***What is a tabular representation of data?***

Ans. It is a systematic arrangement of data in rows and columns for better understanding.

7. ***What is a bar graph used for?***

Ans. A bar graph is used to compare different categories of data.

8. ***What is a pie chart?***

Ans. A pie chart is a circular graph divided into sectors representing the proportions of a dataset.

9. ***What is meant by frequency distribution?***

Ans. It is a method of grouping data into intervals to show how often each value occurs.

10. ***What are the three measures of central tendency?***

Ans. Mean, median, and mode are the three measures of central tendency.

11. ***How is the mean calculated?***

Ans. Mean is calculated by dividing the sum of all values by the number of values.

12. ***What is the median?***

Ans. The median is the middle value when data is arranged in ascending order.

13. ***What is the mode in statistics?***

Ans. Mode is the most frequently occurring value in a dataset.

14. ***How does the mean differ from the median?***

Ans. The mean is affected by extreme values, while the median represents the middle value and is less affected by outliers.

15. ***What is a choropleth map?***

Ans. It is a thematic map that uses shades or colours to represent data variations in different regions.

16. ***What is GIS?***

Ans. Geographic Information System (GIS) is a system for capturing, storing, analysing, and displaying spatial data.

17. ***What are the components of GIS?***

Ans. Hardware, software, data, people, and procedures are components of GIS.

18. ***What are raster and vector data?***

Ans. Raster data represents spatial features using a grid of cells, while vector data uses points, lines, and polygons.

19. ***What is overlay analysis in GIS?***

Ans. It is a technique that combines multiple layers of maps to study relationships and changes.

20. ***What do you mean by buffer analysis?***

Ans. Buffer analysis creates zones around a feature to study its impact, such as pollution zones or accessibility to services.

SAMPLE QUESTION PAPER 1

A Highly Simulated Sample Question Paper for CBSE Class XII

(SOLVED)

GEOGRAPHY

- This question paper contains 30 questions. All questions are compulsory.
- This question paper is divided into five sections – Sections A, B, C, D and E.
- Section A – Questions no. 1 to 17 are Multiple Choice (MCQ) Type Questions carrying 1 mark each.
- Section B – Questions no. 18 and 19 are Source Based Questions carrying 3 marks each.
- Section C – Questions no. 20 to 23 are Short Answer (SA) Type Questions carrying 3 marks each. Answer to these questions shall be written in 80 to 100 words.
- Section D – Questions no. 24 to 28 are Long Answer (LA) Type Questions carrying 5 marks each. Answer to these questions shall be written in 120 to 150 words.
- Section E – Questions no. 29 and 30 are Map Based Questions.

Time : 3 hours **Max. Marks : 70**

SECTION A

1. Consider the following statements about primitive subsistence agriculture. **(1)**

I. Shifting cultivation involves clearing a forest area, burning the vegetation and using the ash to fertilize the soil.

II. After a few years of cultivation, the soil loses fertility and the farmers move to a new area.

III. This method is widely practiced in densely populated regions of India.

IV. Shifting cultivation is known by different names in different regions, such as Jhum in North-East India.

Which of the above statements are correct?

(a) II and IV (b) I, III and IV (c) I, II and IV (d) I, II and III

2. Arrange the following Indian ports from South to North in the Indian Ocean. **(1)**

I. Tuticorin **II. Chennai**

III. Vishakhapatnam **IV. Haldia**

Codes

(a) I, II, III, IV (b) II, I, IV, III (c) III, IV, II, I (d) IV, III, II, I

3. Identify the scholar who gave the following concept. **(1)**

According to him, man is able to accelerate, slow or stop the progress of a country's development. He is like the traffic controller in a large city, who alters the rate, not the direction of progress; and perhaps the phrase 'Stop-and-Go Determinism'.

Options

(a) Ellen C semple (b) Griffth Taylor (c) Paul Vidal de la Blache (d) Ratzel

4. Where is headquarter of North Railway Zone is located? **(1)**

(a) Chandigarh (b) New Delhi (c) Kanpur (d) Lucknow

5. Which of the following statements are correct about air transportation in India? **(1)**

I. It is essential for a vast country like India, where distances are large and the terrain and climatic conditions are diverse.

II. Air transport in India made a beginning in 1911 when airmail operation commenced over a little distance of 10 km between Allahabad and Naini.

III. The Airport Authority of India is responsible for providing safe, efficient air traffic and aeronautical communication services in the Indian Air Space.

IV. Pawan Hans is the helicopter service operating in hilly areas and is widely used by tourists in North-Western sector.

Codes

(a) I, II, III (b) II, III, IV (c) I, III, IV (d) I, II, IV

6. Choose from the following the objectives of Namami Gange Programme. **(1)**

(i) Developing sewerage treatment systems in towns,

(ii) Monitoring of domestic effluents.

(iii) Development of river front.

Codes

(a) (i), (ii) and (iii) (b) (i) and (iii) (c) only (ii) (d) only (iii)

7. Assertion (A) Water pollutants are also created from human activities. **(1)**

Reason (R) Various types of chemicals used in industries are ejected to the river water.

Codes

(a) Only Assertion is correct

(b) Only Reason is correct

(c) Both Statements are correct. Statement II correctly explains statement I.

(d) Both are correct but not related to each other

8. Consider the following statements and choose the correct option from the given options. **(1)**

I. There has been increase in area under forest in India.

II. It is due to the increase in demarcated area under forest rather than an actual increase in forest cover.

Options

(a) Only statement I is correct

(b) Both the statements are true and statement II correctly present the reason for statement I

(c) Only Statement II is correct

(d) Both the statements I and II are incorrect

9. Which of the following defines the concept of balance of trade? **(1)**

(a) The volume of goods and services a country imports compared to what it exports.

(b) The difference between a country's total exports and total imports.

(c) The value of a country's exports being greater than its imports.

(d) The value of a country's imports being greater than its exports.

10. Which of the following statements are correct about World Trade Organisations? **(1)**

I. GATT was transformed into the World Trade Organisation from 1st January, 1948.

II. WTO is the only international organisation dealing with the global rules of trade between nations.

III. WTO also covers trade in services, such as telecommunication and banking and other issues such as intellectual rights.

IV. The influential nations in the WTO focus on their own commercial interests.

Codes

(a) I, II and III (b) II, III and IV

(c) I, III and IV (d) I, II and IV

FULLY SOLVED

11. **Which of the following statements about regional trade blocs is not accurate based on the given information?** (1)

(a) Regional trade blocs aim to promote trade between geographically proximate countries with similar and complementary trading items.
(b) The primary goal of regional trade blocs is to encourage global free trade by removing all trade tariffs worldwide.
(c) Regional trade blocs have emerged partly due to the failure of global organisations to enhance intra-regional trade.
(d) None of the above

12 **Which of the following is incorrectly matched?** (1)

(a) Gurumahisani iron ore mines – Odisha
(b) Noamundi iron ore mines – Jharkhand
(c) Rajhara iron ore mines – Bihar
(d) Kudremukh iron ore mines – Karnataka

13. **Match the following** (1)

	List-I (Waterways)		List-II (Stretch)
A.	NW1	1.	Allahabad-Haldia stretch (1,620 km)
B.	NW2	2.	Sadiya-Dhubri stretch (891 km)
C.	NW3	3.	Specified stretches of Godavari and Krishna rivers along with Kakinada Puducherry
D.	NW4	4.	Specified stretches of river Brahmani along with Matai river, delta channels of Mahanadi and Brahmani rivers and East Coast canals.

Codes

	A	B	C	D		A	B	C	D
(a)	1	2	4	3	(b)	3	1	2	4
(c)	4	1	3	2	(d)	2	1	3	4

14. **Arrange the following railway zones from West to East.** (1)

I. Central **II. Eastern** **III. East Central** **IV. East Coast**

Codes

(a) I, III, IV, II (b) I, II, III, IV (c) IV, III, II, I (d) II, III, IV, I

Study the following map and answer the following questions no. 15-17.

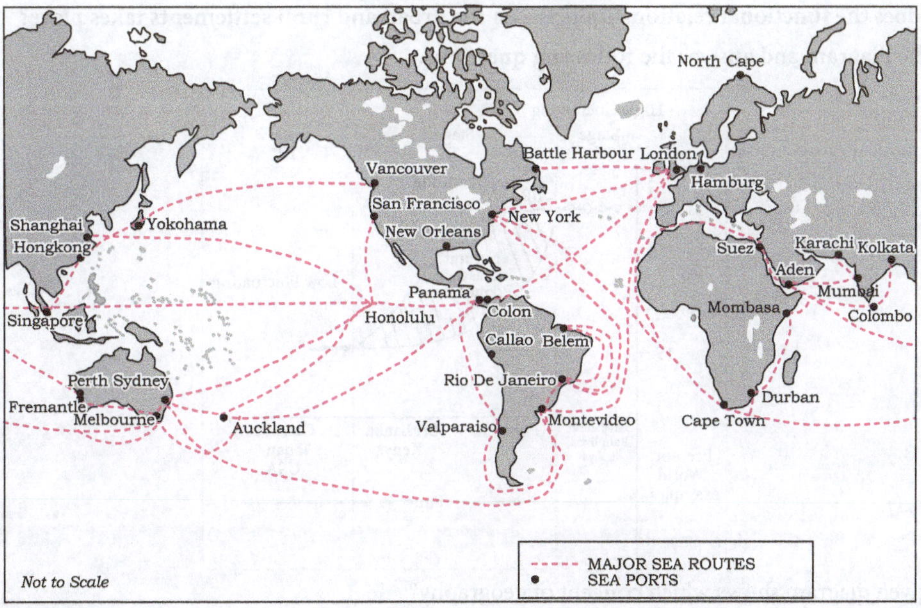

15. **Which of the following is not a port shown on the major sea routes in this map?** **(1)**
(a) Shanghai (b) Auckland (c) Buenos Aires (d) Montevideo

16. **Which of the following ports is located in Australia?** **(1)**
(a) Auckland (b) Fremantle (c) Singapore (d) Colombo

17. **Which port lies on the Eastern coast of South America?** **(1)**
(a) Belem (b) Valparaiso (c) Honolulu (d) Yokohama

SECTION B

18. **Read the given source and answer the questions that follow.**

Human Settlement means cluster of dwellings of any type or size where human beings live. For this purpose, people may erect houses and other structures and command some area or territory as their economic support-base. Thus, the process of settlement inherently involves grouping of people and apportioning of territory as their resource base.

Settlements vary in size and type. They range from a hamlet to metropolitan cities. With size, the economic character and social structure of settlements changes and so do its ecology and technology. Settlements could be small and sparsely spaced; they may also be large and closely spaced. The sparsely located small settlements are called villages, specializing in agriculture or other primary activities. On the other hand, there are fewer but larger settlements which are termed as urban settlements specializing in secondary and tertiary activities.

The rural settlements derive their life support or basic economic needs from land based primary economic activities, whereas, urban settlements, depend on processing of raw materials and manufacturing of finished goods on the one hand and a variety of services on the other.

Cities act as nodes of economic growth; provide goods and services not only to urban dwellers but also to the people of the rural settlements in their hinterlands in return for food and raw materials. This functional relationship between the urban and rural settlements takes place through transport and communication network.

Rural and urban settlements differ in terms of social relationship, attitude and outlook. Rural people are less mobile and therefore, social relations among them are intimate. In urban areas, on the other hand, way of life is complex and fast, and social relations are formal.

(i) **Why do people need human settlements?** **(1)**
(ii) **What is the basic difference between rural and urban settlements?** **(1)**
(iii) **How does the functional relationship between the urban and rural settlements takes place?** **(1)**

19. **Observe the diagram and answer the following questions.**

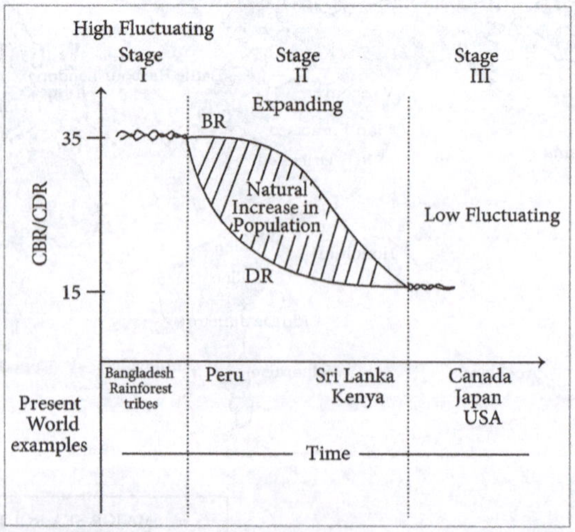

(i) The given diagram shows which concept of geography? **(1)**
(ii) What is the purpose of this diagram? **(1)**
(iii) What does the transition from high fluctuating stage to low fluctuating stage indicate? **(1)**

FULLY SOLVED

SECTION C

20. What are the various sources of noise pollution in urban areas? **(3)**

Or "Urban solid waste is a nuisance for metropolitan cities." Explain briefly.

21. Study the map and answer the following questions. **(3)**

(i) Which inland waterway is shown in the map?

(ii) Which industrial regions of Europe are connected through this waterway?

(iii) State any two characteristics of this waterway.

22. What is telecommunication? What is it important? **(3)**

23. Give an account of production and use of coal in India. **(3)**

SECTION D

24. The assessment, efficient use and conservation of water become necessary to water development. Discuss it in Indian perspective. **(5)**

25. Give a detailed account of the changes in the demographic profile of India over the last century. **(5)**

Or "The adolescent population of India has high potentials but they are also vulnerable if not properly guided". Explain.

26. What do you mean by Quinary activities? Discuss the new trends in Quinary services. **(5)**

Or What is medical tourism? Explain the scope of medical services in India for overseas patients. How does outsourcing of medical tests and data interpretation help in this?

27. State any three economic and two social and cultural factors influencing the distribution of population in the world.

Or What would be the consequences of the condition of positive population growth and negative population growth/decline? Explain. **(5)**

28. Where is intensive subsistence agriculture practiced in the world? What are its two types? Describe any two characteristics of each type. **(5)**

Or Discuss about the factors that influences the Industrial locations in the world. **(5)**

SECTION E

29. On the political map of India mark and indicate any five of the following features. (Any five) **(1 × 5 = 5)**

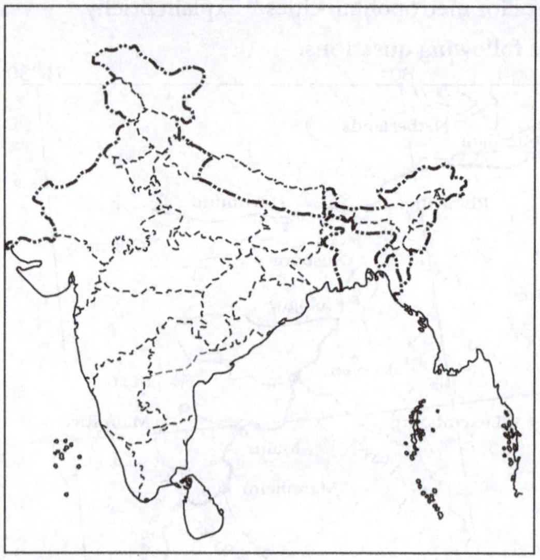

(i) The state with the highest level of urbanisation.
(ii) The state with highest density in India.
(iii) The leading producer state of rice in Eastern India.
(iv) Shimoga Manganese mine.
(v) Barauni oil refinery.
(vi) A city in Karnataka having 10 million plus population.
(vii) A coal mine in West Bengal.

30. In the given political map of the world seven features are shown by (i), (ii), (iii), (iv), (v), (vi) and (vii) Identify any five features with the help of the information given below and write their correct names on the lines as marked in the map. **(1 × 5 = 5)**

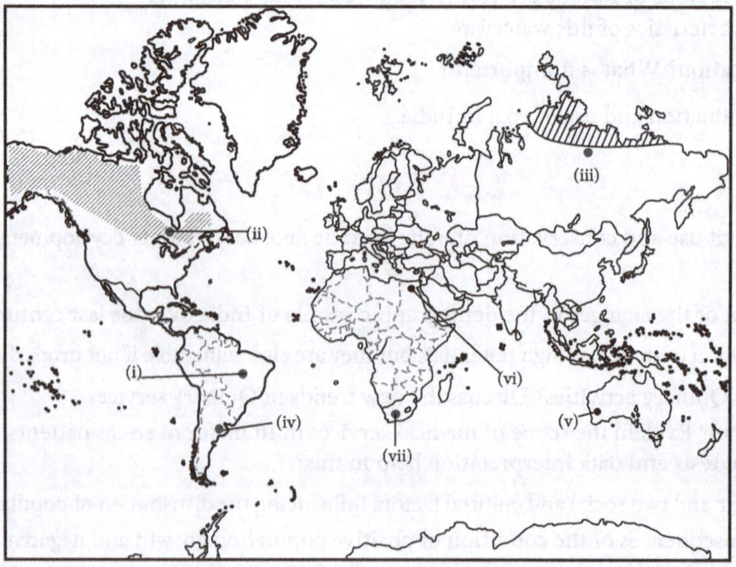

(i) The largest country in South America.
(ii) An area of subsistence gathering.
(iii) An area of nomadic herding.
(iv) An area of extensive commercial grain farming.
(v) A terminal station of Australian Trans-Continental Railway.
(vi) A major sea port.
(vii) A major airport.

ANSWERS

1. (c) I, II and IV
2. (c) III, IV, II, I
3. (b) Griffith Taylor
4. (b) New Delhi
5. (a) I, II, III
6. (b) (i) and (iii)
7. (c) Both Statements are correct. Statement II correctly explains statement I.
8. (b) Both the statements are true and statement II correctly present the reason for statement I
9. (c) The value of a country's exports being greater than its imports.
10. (b) II, III and IV
11. (d) None of the above
12. (c) Rajhara iron ore mines – Bihar
13. (a)
14. (b) I, II, III, IV
15. (c) Buenos Aires
16. (b) Fremantle
17. (a) Belem
18. (i) People need human settlements for the following purposes
    - For human habitation.
    - For doing economic activities such as commerce, agricultural practices etc.
    - For administration purpose.
    - For defense purpose etc.

    (ii) The basic difference between rural and urban settlements is that the rural settlements derive their life support or basic economic needs from land based primary economic activities.

    On the other hand, urban settlements depend on processing of raw materials and manufacturing of finished goods on the one hand and a variety of services on the other.

    (iii) This functional relationship between the urban and rural settlements takes place through transport and communication network.
19. (i) The given diagram shows the theory of Demographic transition which is a popular theory in population geography.

    (ii) The purpose of this diagram is to highlight the different stages of demographic transition which take place differently in different courtiers.

    (iii) The transition from high fluctuating stage to low fluctuating stage indicates the shift from Rural Agrarian economy to Urban Industrial economy.
20. Noise pollution is the state of unbearable and uncomfortable noise levels to human beings caused by different sources.

    Sources of Noise Pollution

    The main sources of noise pollution are

    (i) **Traffic** Traffic of vehicles on the roads is the biggest source of noise pollution. Vehicles such as trucks, buses, motorcycles cause varying levels of pollution of noise.

    (ii) **Construction** Construction and demolition activities require heavy machinery, which creates large amount of noise in the residential areas.

    (iii) **Industries** Industries use large number of moving parts, which leads to more noise pollution. These noises have a significant impact on the workers.

    (iv) **Community Activities** Noise from the community activities such as festival celebrations, programmes, loudspeakers create noise.

    (v) **Transport** Noise from the transport services such as Railways, Airways, trucks etc. cause noise pollution.

Or Urban areas generate a large amount of solid waste, both from the households as well as the industries. In the metropolitan areas where people live in congested places, the problem of solid waste is more serious. It has created multiple problems in the metropolitan regions.

These are:

(i) Solid waste such as metal pieces, glassware, plastic containers, polythene bags, ashes, floppies are dumped at many places that pollute the land in these areas.

FULLY SOLVED

(*ii*) The waste from households and industries is disposed off on private lands or collected and disposed by the municipal facilities in landfill areas. It creates foul smell in these regions.

(*iii*) Ashes and debris from industries, thermal power houses and construction of buildings poses serious consequences for the public health.

(*iv*) Solid waste acts as carriers of diseases because flies, rodents etc harbour upon the solid waste which spreads diseases such as typhoid, diptheria, malaria and cholera etc.

21. (i) The Rhine Inland waterway is shown in the map.

(ii) It connects the industrial areas of Switzerland, Germany, France, Belgium and the Netherlands.

(iii) The two characteristics of this waterway are as follows

(a) Rhine river flows through a rich coalfield, making the whole basin a prosperous manufacturing area.

(b) More than 20,000 ocean-going vessels and 2,00,000 inland vessels exchange their cargoes each year through this route.

22. Telecommunication is the exchange of information over significant distances by electronic means. Importance of telecommunication are:

(*i*) Modern technology has changed the old pattern of communication. It has made communication independent of transport.

(*ii*) The use of mobile phones and internet has brought a revolution in modern communication.

(*iii*) It has reduced the speed with which messages are sent to destination. It has reduced the communication time from weeks to minutes.

(*iv*) It has made the communication direct and instantaneous at any time and from anywhere irrespective of location.

(*v*) It is now easier to cater to a wide range of audience across the world through radio, television or internet.

Or The climatic conditions of any region decide the demand for tourism. The climate of a region attracts tourists in the following ways :

(*i*) People from colder places seek to visit warm places. That's why the Mediterranean lands and Southern Europe, due to their considerable higher temperature, sunny days and less rainfall attract tourists from Europe.

(*ii*) People from warmer regions like to visit colder places. That's why tourists from Northern plains of India prefer to go to tourist places located in the Himalayan region or other hill stations.

(*iii*) Climatic conditions of a region also provide some adventurous activities to do and attract tourists. For example, ice skating and skiing in snowy regions, sea surfing on beaches, etc.

23. About 80% of coal found in India is bituminous coal of non-coking grade. In India, coal is found in two rock sequences:

(*i*) Gondwana Fields It is mainly found in river valleys of Damodar, Godavari, Mahanadi, Sone, etc. The important coal mines are Jharia, Raniganj, Bokaro, Korba, Singareni, etc.

(*ii*) Tertiary Coal Fields It is found in Western and Eastern region of Himalayas. Meghalaya, Assam, Jammu and Kashmir and Arunachal Pradesh are important states where tertiary coal is produced.

Uses of coal are as follows:

- It is mainly used for generation of thermal power.
- It is also used in smelting of iron ore.

24. India accounts 4 per cent of the world's water resources. The total water available from precipitation in the country in a year is about 4000 cubic km. The availability from surface water and replenishable groundwater is 1869 cubic km. Out of this, only 60 per cent can be put to beneficial uses. Thus, the total utilisable water resource in the country is only 1122 cubic km. India has traditionally been an agrarian economy and about two-third of its population has been dependent on agriculture.

The share of agricultural sector in total water utilisation is much higher than other sectors. The per-capita availability of water is dwindling day-by-day due to increase in population. The available water resources are also getting polluted with industrial, agricultural and domestic effluents and this in turn, is further limiting the availability of usable water resources.

India has to take quick steps and make effective policies and laws and adopt effective measures for its conservation. Besides developing water saving technologies and methods, attempts are also to be made to prevent pollution. There is need to encourage watershed development, rainwater harvesting, water recycling and reuse, and conjunctive use of water for sustaining water supply in long run.

25. Over the last century, there have been different trends in the demography of India. It can be explained with the help of four distinct phases of demographic changes. These are:

(*i*) **Phase 1–1901 to 1921** This period was the period of stagnant or stationary population growth. The growth of population was very slow and even negative. During this phase, both birth rates and death rates were high. It was due to poor health and medical facilities, illiterate population, inefficient food distribution and other basic necessities.

(*ii*) **Phase 2–1921 to 1951** During this period, there was a steady increase in the population of India. The birth rate was higher whereas the death rate remained low. This was because of higher levels of health and sanitation, improvements in food distribution, and availability of health services to the population.

(*iii*) **Phase 3–1951 to 1981** During this phase, there was large scale growth of India's population, known as population explosion. The birth rates were very high but the death rates declined. This was because of development activities that were introduced after independence which improved the standard of living of the people. There was international migration from Tibet, Bangladesh, Nepal, Pakistan, which also contributed to a very large rate of growth of population.

(*iv*) **Phase 4–1981 to Present** In the current phase, the population growth rate has started to decline. The birth rate is now showing a downward trend. This is the result of an increase in mean age of marriage, improved quality of life because of higher education levels of females in the country.

Or The adolescent population of India are an important component of India's population. In India's total population, the share of adolescents is almost 21% (2011). The male adolescents constitute 52% whereas, females are 48%. The adolescent population has huge amount of potential as they form a major economic and demographic force in the country. But they are vulnerable and face many challenges. These are:

(*i*) **Illiteracy** Many of the adolescents are still illiterate because they have no access to proper education. The females are particularly more vulnerable as they drop out of the schools at an early age. Various social norms such as early marriage, household work affect their access to education.

(*ii*) **Child Marraige** There are widespread child marriages which leads to discrimination against the adolescents. It leads to high mental stress and they are not able to utilise their potentials. Early pregnancy and child births are harmful for the adolescent girls.

(*iii*) **Poor Health** Adolescent population in India face high rates of infections diseases such as HIV, mental retardness, low intake of nutrition as well as high rates of adolescent maternal mortality that results in very poor health of these adolescents.

(*iv*) **Low Skills** The adolescents have very low levels of skills due to which they are not able to utilise their talents properly.

(*v*) **Vulnerable to Abuse** The adolescent population is highly vulnerable to social evils such as drug abuse, alcoholism, commitence of crimes and juvenille delinquency etc. They should be provided proper guidance so that their vulnerabilities can be reduced and their energy can be utilised for development of the country.

26. **Quinary Activities** Quinary activities are services that focus on the creation, re-arrangement and interpretation of new and existing ideas, data interpretation and the use and evaluation of new technologies.

Often referred to as gold collar professional, they represent a sub-division of the tertiary sector representing special and highly paid skills of senior business executives, government officials, research scientists, financial and legal consultants, etc. Their importance in the structure of advanced economies far outweighs their numbers.

New Trends in Quinary Services New trends in Quinary services include Knowledge Processing Outsourcing (KPO) and home shoring, which an alternative to outsourcing.

Knowledge Process Outsouring Knowledge Process Outsouring refers to the service industry where there are highly skilled workers. It can also be termed as information driven knowledge outsouring. It enables the companies to create additional business opportunities. The examples of KPO industry are research and development services, intellectual property research, banking sector and legal profession.

Homeshoring Homeshoring is an operational model in various organisations in which the employees work and perform all official tasks from a home or external office. The companies hire employees, who work from their domestic location but are connected to the company via internet. Homeshoring enables a company to reduce infrastructure and maintenance cost of a physical office.

Or **Medical Tourism** When medical treatment is combined with international tourism activity, it is known as medical tourism.

Scope of Medical Tourism in India The growing medical facilities have made India a favourable destination for the overseas medical tourists. The medical infrastructure in India has developed because of emergence of large number of hospitals, tertiary care clinics which provide highly specialised services at cheaper costs as compared to the developed countries.

Development of advanced transport and communication facilities have also facilitated the flow of tourists for medical purposes. They can now easily visit places which were earlier inaccessible to them due to social, cultural and transport infrastructural issues. Affordable international fares have contributed to the development of this industry in India.

Specialist doctors, nurses and paramedical staff have also emerged in India. They provide quality healthcare to the overseas medical tourists combining the traditional techniques and the modern methods. Thus, medical tourism can emerge as a huge industry in India.

Role of Outsouring of Medical Tests and Data Interpretation Outsouring of medical tests and data interpretation can help in improving the quality of healthcare for the overseas medical tourists. It results in higher levels of specialised healthcare because the reading of medical tests such as radiology images, ultrasound tests and MRIs becomes more accurate. It leads to better diognosis and gives utmost quality healthcare to the people of overseas country.

27. The three economic factors influencing the distribution of population in the world are as follows:

(i) **Minerals** Areas with mineral deposits attract industries, which generate huge employment and skilled and semi skilled workers that settle in these areas.

(ii) **Urbanisation** Urban centres offer better employment opportunities, education and medical facilities and better means of communication which attract population.

(iii) **Industrialisation**Industrial belts provide job opportunities. These attract not only factory workers, but also transport operators, shopkeepers, bank employees, doctors, teachers and other service providers.

Two social and cultural factors influencing the distribution of population in the world are as follows:

(i) **Religious and Cultural Significance** Places having religious importance and cultural significance tend to attract number of people due to which they are densely populated.

(ii) **Social and Political Unrest** Places where there is political turmoil and social unrest are not fit for living. Thus, people tend to move away from those areas. This makes them sparsely populated.

Or **Positive Population Growth** Growth of population at high rate, beyond a certain level creates problem in the way of development. Some consequences of positive population growth are given below

- The growth of population leads to pressure on land and its natural resources.
- The drinking water will not be available and it will become scarce. The water reserves are depleting in many regions of the world.
- Forests are being cleared for demand of more land and soil for agriculture which leads to soil erosion.
- The growth of population leads to adverse effects on the quality of workforce. Therefore, per capita income of work may go down.
- The important consequences are poverty, unemployment, disparity and malnutrition which also rise rapidly.

Negative Population Growth/Decline in Population The decline in population is also a major problem. It can be understood from following points

- The population declines when the available resources are insufficient to support the population.
- The basic structure of the society itself becomes unstable. Due to it, there occurs a great chaos.

- Lesser number of people are available for working as most of population comprises of old and aged people.

Thus, the growth and decline of population both leads to adverse impact on the economic and social framework of a country.

28. Intensive subsistence agriculture is largely practiced in densely populated regions of monsoon Asia. There are two types of intensive subsistence agriculture which are as follows

(i) **Intensive subsistence agriculture dominated by wet paddy cultivation** This type of agriculture is characterised by dominance of the rice crop. Landholdings are very small due to the high density of population. Farmers work with the help of family labour leading to intensive use of land. Use of machinery is limited and most of the agricultural operations are done by manual labour. In this type of agriculture, the yield per unit area is high but labour productivity is low.

(ii) **Intensive subsistence agriculture dominated by crops other than paddy** Due to the difference in relief, climate, soil and some of the other geographical factors, it is not practical to grow paddy in many parts of monsoon Asia. Wheat, soya bean, barley and sorghum are grown in Northern China, Manchuria, North Korea and North Japan. Most of the characteristics of this type of agriculture are similar to those dominated by wet paddy except that irrigation is often used.

Or The factors influencing the industrial location in the world are as follows

(i) **Access to Market** Market affects the location of an industry. A manufacturing unit is established near the market area. Areas having more population are big markets for manufactured goods, as compared to areas having less population. Apart from it, areas having population with more purchasing power form big markets.

(ii) **Access to Raw Material** Industries that use heavy, bulky and weight-losing raw material are established near the source of raw material.
For example, in sugar industries, sugarcane is a perishable and weight-losing raw material. To reduce the transport cost, industries are located near the source of raw material.

(iii) **Access to Sources of Energy** Industries using more power and energy are established near the source of energy. For example, aluminium industry.

(iv) **Access to Transportation and Communication** Industries are located in areas that have efficient transport network to get raw material from various regions and supply manufactured goods to market.

(v) **Government Policies** Favourable government policies that promote industrial location is also important in deciding the location of an industry.

29.

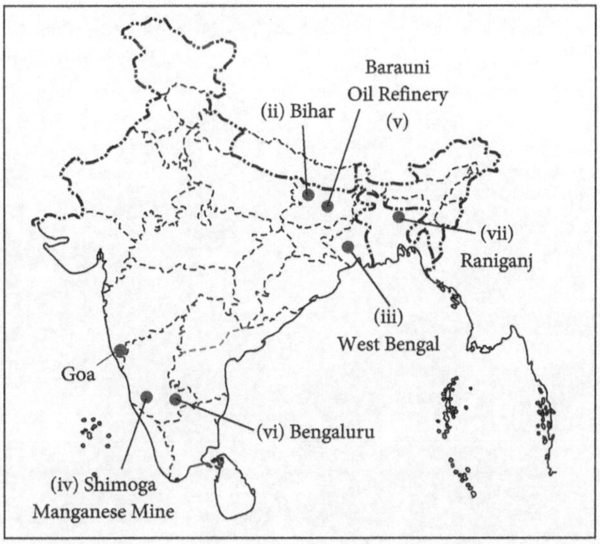

30.

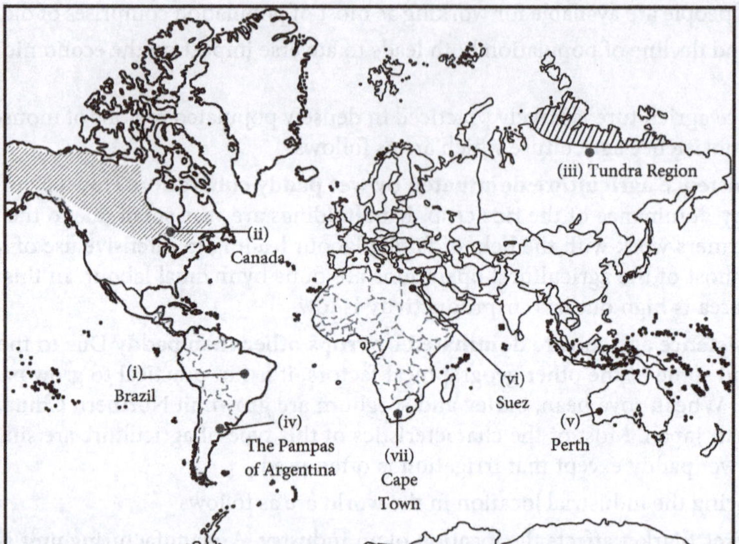
(iii) Tundra Region
(ii)
Canada
(i)
Brazil
(iv)
The Pampas
of Argentina
(vi)
Suez
(vii)
Cape
Town
(v)
Perth

SAMPLE QUESTION PAPER 2

A Highly Simulated Sample Question Paper for CBSE Class XII

(SOLVED)

GEOGRAPHY

- This question paper contains 30 questions. All questions are compulsory.
- This question paper is divided into five sections – Sections A, B, C, D and E.
- Section A – Questions no. 1 to 17 are Multiple Choice (MCQ) Type Questions carrying 1 mark each.
- Section B – Questions no. 18 and 19 are Source Based Questions carrying 3 marks each.
- Section C – Questions no. 20 to 23 are Short Answer (SA) Type Questions carrying 3 marks each. Answer to these questions shall be written in 80 to 100 words.
- Section D – Questions no. 24 to 28 are Long Answer (LA) Type Questions carrying 5 marks each. Answer to these questions shall be written in 120 to 150 words.
- Section E – Questions no. 29 and 30 are Map Based Questions.

Time : 3 hours ***Max. Marks : 70***

SECTION A

1. Which of the following is not a sub-field of Social Geography? **(1)**

(a) Military Geography (b) Behavioural Geography
(c) Gender Geography (d) Geography of Leisure

2. Which of the following is not a 'pull factor' of migration? **(1)**

(a) More job opportunities (b) Security of life and property
(c) Poor living conditions (d) Better living conditions

3. Which of the following pair is incorrectly matched? **(1)**

List I		List II	
A.	Phase I	1.	stagnant or stationary phase of growth
B.	Phase II	2.	steady population growth
C.	Phase III	3.	population explosion in India
D.	Phase IV	4.	decline in the population

Codes

	A	B	C	D
(a)	1	2	3	4
(b)	4	3	2	1
(c)	1	3	2	4
(d)	3	4	2	1

4. Assertion (A) Intensive subsistence agriculture dominated by crops other than paddy is not suitable to grow paddy in many parts of monsoon Asia.

Reason (R) It is due to a number of geographical factors like climate, relief, soil, etc. **(1)**

Codes

(a) Only assertion is correct (b) Only reason is correct
(c) Both statements are correct. Statement II correctly explains statement I
(d) Both are correct but not related to each other

5. Consider the following statements and choose the correct option from the given options.
I. Personal and professional services are not well developed in Rural Marketing Centres.
II. Rural Marketing Centres are of rudimentary type or very basic centres. (1)

Codes

(a) Only statement I is correct
(b) Both the statements are true and statement II correctly present the reason for statement I
(c) Only statement II is correct
(d) Both the statements I and II are incorrect

6. Assertion (A) Railways are most suited for large volume bulky materials over longer distances.
Reason (R) As compared to railways, road transport is economical for short distances. (1)

(a) Only assertion is correct
(b) Only reason is correct
(c) Both assertion and reason are correct and reason is the correct explanation for assertion
(d) Both assertion and reason are correct but reason is not the correct explanation for assertion

7. Which of the following schools of thought attributed the current social problems to development of capitalism? (1)

(a) Radical School (b) Behavioural School (c) Welfare School (d) Humanistic School

8. Read the following information carefully and identify the correct option for the type of agriculture. (1)

- **The farms are not extensive but moderate in size.**
- **Important crops are wheat, barley, oats, rye, and maize.**
- **Soil fertility maintained through crop rotation and inter cropping.**

Options

(a) Commercial grain farming (b) Mixed farming
(c) Dairy farming (d) Truck farming

9. Accordin to Demographic Transition theory there are three stages of population growth. Identify the stage from given description.

Both fertility and mortality decline considerably. The population is either stable or grows slowly. The population becomes urbanised, literate and has high technical know- how and deliberately controls the family size.

(a) Stage 1 (b) Stage 2 (c) Stage 3 (d) None

10. Which of the following parts of a river have the best quality water? (1)

(a) The delta part (b) The part in the mountains
(c) The plains part (d) The part in the valleys

11. Which of the following refineries is field based? (1)

(a) Barauni (b) Bina (c) Visakhapatnam (d) Numaligarh

12. Arrange the following Ports from North to South (1)

I. Kolkata Port **II. Haldia Port** **III. Chennai Port** **IV. Kochchi Port**

Codes

(a) I, II, III, IV (b) IV, III, II, I (c) I, III, IV, II (d) II, III, IV, I

13. Which of the following pair is correctly matched? (1)

List I (Approach to Human Development)	List II (Feature)
A. Income	1. Newest approach
B. Welfare	2. People are active recipients
C. Basic needs	3. Given by ILO
D. Capability	4. Friedrich Ratzel

14. **Arrange the following Railway Zones from East to West.**

I. Eastern **II. East Central** **III. East Coast** **IV. Western**

Codes

(a) I, II, III, IV (b) II, III, IV, I (c) IV, III, II, I (d) I, IV, III, II

Study the graph and answer the following questions no. 15-17.

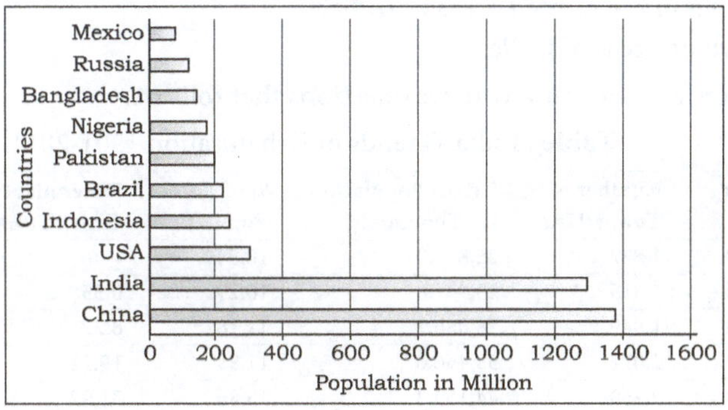

Most Populous Countries

15. **The highest population of the country ranges between.**

(a) 0-200 million (b) 1000-1200 million (c) 400-800 million (d) 1200-1400 million

16. **Identify the African Country that has very low population.**

(a) Mexico (b) Pakistan (c) Nigeria (d) Brazil

17. **Which country has population more than 250 million but less than 400 million.**

(a) Mexico (b) China (c) USA (d) Indonesia

SECTION B

18. **Read the following paragraph and answer the questions that follow.**

The nature of problems faced by Indian agriculture varies according to agro-ecological and historical experiences of its different regions. Hence, most of the agricultural problems in the country are region specific. Yet, there are some problems which are common and range from physical constraints to institutional hindrances.

Irrigation covers only about 33 per cent of the cultivated area in India. The crop production in rest of the cultivated land directly depends on rain. Poor performance of South-West monsoon also adversely affects the supply of canal water for irrigation. On the other hand, the rainfall in Rajasthan and other drought-prone areas is too meagre and highly unreliable. Even the areas receiving high annual rainfall experience considerable fluctuations. This makes them vulnerable to both droughts and floods. Drought is a common phenomenon in the low rainfall areas, which may also experience occasional floods. The flash floods in drylands of Maharashtra, Gujarat and Rajasthan in 2006 and 2017 are examples of this phenomenon. Droughts and floods continue to be the twin menace in Indian agriculture.

The yield of the crops in the country is low in comparison to the international level. Per hectare output of most of the crops such as rice, wheat, cotton and oilseeds in India is much lower than that of the U.S.A, Russia and Japan. Because of the very high pressure on the land resources, the labour productivity in Indian agriculture is also very low in comparison to international level. The vast rainfed areas of the country, particularly drylands which mostly grow coarse cereals, pulses and oilseeds have low yields. The inputs of modern agriculture are very expensive. This resource intensive approach has become unmanageable for marginal and small farmers as they have very meagre or no saving to invest in agriculture. To tide over these difficulties, most of such farmers have resorted to availing credit from various institutions and moneylenders. Crop failures and low returns from agriculture have forced them to fall in the trap of indebtedness.

Indian peasantry had been exploited for a long time as there had been unequal distribution of land. Among the three revenue systems operational during British period, i.e., Mahalwari, Ryotwari and Zamindari, the last one was most exploitative for the peasants. After Independence, land reforms were accorded priority, but these reforms were not implemented effectively due to lack of strong political will. Most of the state governments avoided taking politically tough decisions which went against strong political lobbies of landlords. Lack of implementation of land reforms has resulted in continuation of inequitous distribution of cultivable land which is detrimental to agricultural development.

(i) State any two major problems of Indian agriculture? (1)

(ii) Which crops are grown in the rainfed areas of India? (1)

(iii) Give examples of dryland areas of India. (1)

19. Study the table given below and answer any three questions that follows.

Table : India -Trends of Urbanisation 1901-2011

Year	Number of Towns/UAs	Urban Population (In Thousands)	% of Total Population	Decennial Growth (%)
1901	1,827	25,851.9	10.84	–
1911	1,815	25,941.6	10.29	0.35
1921	1,949	28,086.2	11.18	8.27
1931	2,072	33,456.0	11.99	19.12
1941	2,250	44,153.3	13.86	31.97
1951	2,843	62,443.7	17.29	41.42
1961	2,365	78,936.6	17.97	26.41
1971	2,590	1,09,114	19.91	38.23
1981	3,378	1,59,463	23.34	46.14
1991	4,689	2,17,611	25.71	36.47
2001	5,161	2,85,355	27.78	31.13
2011	6,171	3,77,000	31.16	31.08

(i) In which years the urban population of India experienced stagnant condition? (1)

(ii) What do you understand by the term 'Urban Agglomeration'? (1)

(iii) Increasing urbanisation has lead to which type of problems in our country? (1)

SECTION C

20. 'Migration affects the society in a number of ways, both positively and negatively'. Discuss the consequences of the migration in its social context.

Or 'Population Growth beyond a certain level leads to problems'. Describe.

21. Study the map and answer the following questions.

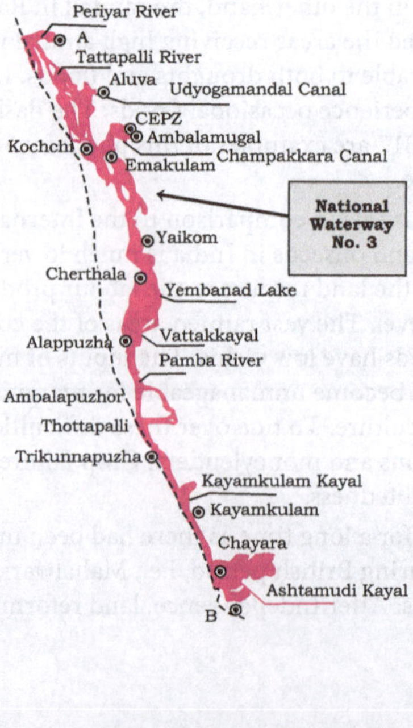

(i) Discuss about the stretch of National Waterways 3.
(ii) Write one specification of National Waterways 3.
(iii) Mention one feature of water transportation.

22. For human development sustainability, productivity and empowerment are essential ingredients. Explain. **(3)**

23. State the physical factors which determine the pattern of population distribution. **(3)**

SECTION D

24. "Medical tourism brings abundant benefits to developing countries." Explain. **(5)**

Or Discuss the significance and growth of the service sector in modern economic development.

25. Discuss the main features of different types of rural settlements.

Or Name any three factors that determine the clustered or compact rural settlement in India.

26. What is mixed farming? Where is it practised in the world? Give four characteristics of mixed farming. **(5)**

Or 'Today international trade has become the basis of world's economy'. Define the statement with example.

27. Trade is essentially buying and selling of items produce elsewhere. Elucidate.

Or Transport is an essential tertiary activity. Validate.

28. Classify minerals into two groups on the basis of chemical and physical properties and give one example of minerals of each group. Mention any two features of the three mineral belts of India. **(5)**

SECTION E

29. Locate and label the following on the given map of India. (Any five) **(5)**

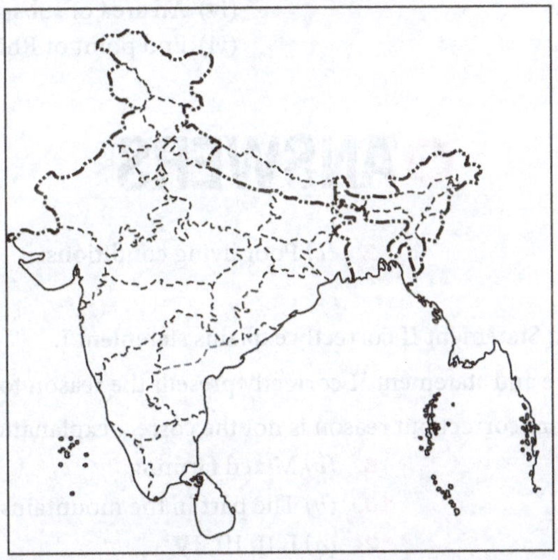

(i) The state with the lowest level of urbanisation.
(ii) Important node of North-South corridor.
(iii) A sea port in Odisha.
(iv) The leading state for wheat production.
(v) Khetri copper mine.
(vi) An oil refinery in Gujarat.
(vii) A coal mine in Tamil Nadu.

30. **In the given political map of the world seven features are shown by (i), (ii), (iii), (iv), (v), (vi) and (vii) Identify any five features with the help of the information given below and write their correct names on the lines marked in the map.** **(5)**

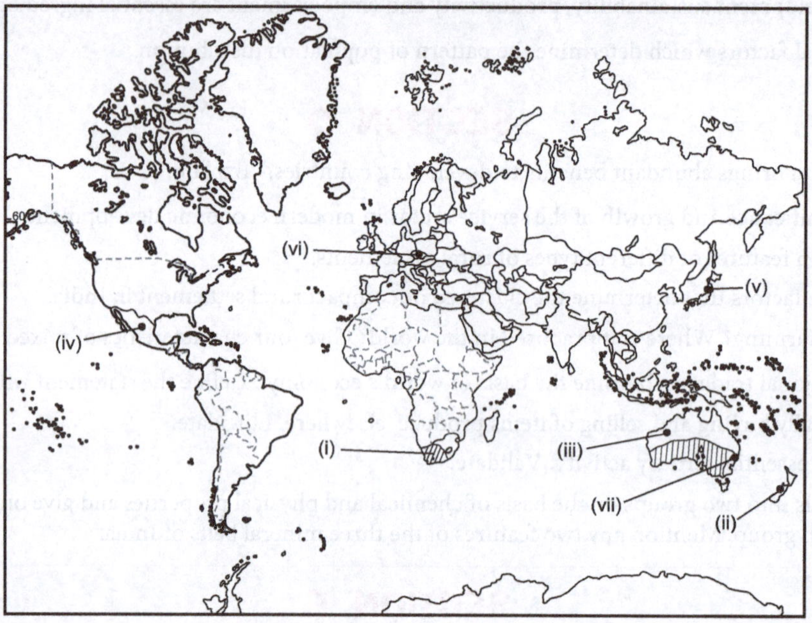

(i) Areas of commercial extensive grain farming
(ii) An area of commercial livestock rearing
(iii) Largest country in oceania
(iv) An area of subsistence agriculture
(v) A major Airport
(vi) End point of Rhine river waterway
(vii) A sea port

ANSWERS

1. (a) Military Geography
2. (c) Poor living conditions
3. (a)
4. (c) Both statements are correct. Statement II correctly explains statement I.
5. (b) Both the statements are true and statement II correctly present the reason for statement I
6. (d) Both assertion and reason are correct but reason is not the correct explanation for assertion
7. (a) Radical School
8. (b) Mixed farming
9. (c) Stage 3
10. (b) The part in the mountains
11. (d) Numaligarh
12. (a) I, II, III, IV
13. (c) Basic needs - Given by ILO
14. (a) I, II, III, IV
15. (d) 1200-1400 million
16. (a) Mexico
17. (c) USA
18. (i) Two major problems of Indian agriculture are
    - Floods
    - Drought

    (ii) Oilseeds, cereal and pulses are the crops which are grown in the rainfed areas of India. These are particularly grown in dryland parts of these areas.

(iii) Examples of dryland areas of India are the North Western desert regions of Rajasthan, the plateau region of Central India, the Alluvial plains of Ganga Yamuna river basin, the Central highlands of Gujarat, Maharashtra and Madhya Pradesh.

19 (i) The urban population of India experienced stagnant condition in the years 1921-31 and 1951-61.

(ii) An urban area together with its urban outgrowth is known as urban agglomeration. Urban agglomeration is a highly developed spatial form of integrated cities.

(iii) Increasing urbanisation has lead to different types of problems in our country such as

- Slum development
- Water pollution
- Problem of Solid waste

20. Migration creates both benefits and problems. Its consequences can be observed in economic, social, cultural, political and demographic terms. In its social milieu, its positive contribution and negative consequences are given under the following headings

Positive Contribution of Migration

Migrants act as agents of social change. The new ideas related to new technologies, family planning, girls' education etc, get diffused from urban to rural areas through them. Migration leads to intermixing of people from diverse cultures. It has positive contribution such as evolution of composite culture and breaking through the narrow considerations and broadening the mental horizon of the people.

Negative Effects of Migration

Its serious negative consequences are anonymity, which leads to social vacuum and sense of dejection among individuals. Gradually, this feeling can also motivate people to fall in the trap of anti-social activities like crime and drug abuse.

Or A small increase in population is essential for any country. But population growth beyond a certain level can create problem for a country. These problems are mentioned below

- Rising population leads to depletion of resource at a very fast rate. The Earth has a limited capacity to generate raw materials such as minerals, fuels etc. Overpopulation leads to depletion of these resources.
- Due to overpopulation, there is increasing pollution of air, water which harms the natural environment and causes faster degradation of the environment.
- Increasing growth of population also leads to an increase in young population. It increases the number of dependent people on the working population. It also increases the pressure on economic resources of the country.

21. (i) National Waterways 3 stretches from Kottapuram- Kollam in Arabian Sea. This Waterway has a length of 205km.

(ii) It includes 168 km of West coast canal along with Champakara canal (14 km) and Udyogmandal canal (23 km).

(iii) It is the cheapest means of transportation and is most suitable for carrying heavy and bulky material.

22. Human Development refers to development that results in building a better life for the people by enlarging their choices. Sustainability, productivity and empowerment are the pillars of Human Development. *The importance of these in Human Development are as follows*

(*i*) Sustainability ensures continuity in the availability of opportunities. It means that all the environmental, financial and human resources should be used keeping in mind the future generations. For example: If a community will not stress upon sending the girl child to school then many opportunities will be lost to these young girls when they grow up. It will reduce the quality of their lives.

(*ii*) Productivity ensures that humans are able to work in an efficient manner. Productivity of the people is increased by building people's capabilities. The capability of people can be raised by providing them better education and health facilities.

FULLY SOLVED

(*iii*) Empowerment results in more number of choices to the people. The power to make choices comes due to increasing freedom and capabilities. People are empowered by Good Governance and people-oriented policies of the government. Socially and economically disadvantaged groups should be empowered particularly.

23. In India, there is uneven distribution of population due to various factors. Important physical factors which determine the pattern of population distribution are given below

(*i*) There is a close relationship between climate and population distribution. The climate, terrain and availability of water largely determine the pattern of the population distribution.

(*ii*) Since, there is availability of sufficient water and fertile plain land in Northern plains, the population density in Northern part of India is high in comparison to Southern states. Whereas, there is rough terrain in Himalayas, therefore population density is also low in Himalayan states like Himachal Pradesh, Sikkim and Arunachal Pradesh.

(*iii*) However, due to availability of transport, communication, resources and other developmen–tal facilities, the concentration of population has become moderate to high in areas which were earlier sparsely populated e.g. Rajasthan, Jharkhand.

24. When medical treatment is combined with international tourism activity, it is known as medical tourism. It has brought enormous benefits for the developing countries. These benefits are

(*i*) **Economic Development** The tourists that visit developing countries from the developed countries gives economic boost to the visiting country as these tourists visit various large as well as smaller cities for the purpose of medical healthcare. It also generates more employment in these cities.

(*ii*) **Local Employment Opportunities** As medical tourists visit a country, they help in providing business opportunities and employment to the local population. There is generation of direct employment such as hotels, transport services, eateries as well as direct employment for providing goods and services.

(*iii*) **Generation of Foreign Reserves** When foreign tourists visit the developing countries, they bring in foreign currency, which helps in generation of foreign income and resources for the country. It helps in reducing the trade deficit.

(*iv*) **Creation of Medical Infrastructure** As the demand for specialised services increases, it leads to increasing medical infrastructure in the country. The quality of healthcare for the domestic population also increases and also becomes cheaper. This leads to decline in diseases and improving health conditions for the people in the country.

(*v*) **Improvements in Transport and Communication** Medical tourism also leads to developments in transport and communication facilities as medical tourists require air travel, roads and railways etc to travel from their home country to the foreign country as well as move within the foreign country. Increasing communication services help in outsourcing medical tests and data interpretation services.

Or Service sector is significant for modern economic development for the following reasons

- **Facilitates Flow of Money** Service sector facilitates the flow of money in an economy. For example, buying and selling of items. Trading helps in the exchange of money and commodities among different regions. International trade also helps in flow of foreign currency.
- **Contributes in GDP** In developed countries, a large proportion of GDP is contributed by service sector, as it is a major sector of economy in these countries.
- **Provides Employment** Apart from generating revenue, service sector also provides employment to people. About 45 to 75 per cent of population in developed countries is engaged in service sector.
- **Growth of Towns** Growth of services contributes in growth of existing centres and emergence of new centres. For example, new forms of trade which include money exchange at international level has produced many centres and institutions such as trading centres or collection and distribution points.
- **Supports Economic Development** In the initial stages of economic development, larger proportion of people work in the primary sector. As economy develops proportion of population in tertiary activity increases. Making and maintaining highways and bridges, maintaining fire fighting departments and supplying or supervising education and customer care are among the services most often supervised or performed by governments or companies.

FULLY SOLVED

25. Rural settlements are sparsely located small settlements. These are divided into four types i.e. clustered settlement, semi-clustered settlement, hamleted settlement, dispersed settlement.

Following are the features of different types of rural settlements

(i) **Clustered Settlements** It is an area of closely built block of houses. The general living area is distinct and separated from the surrounding farms and pastures. These settlements are found in fertile alluvial plains and the North-Eastern states. People also live in compact villages for security reasons such as in Bundelkhand region of central India.

(ii) **Semi-clustered Settlements** It is formed due to clustering in a restricted area of dispersed settlement. It may also result from segregation or fragmentation of a large compact area. Such settlement are widespread in the Gujarat plains and some parts of Rajasthan.

(iii) **Hamleted Settlement** These settlements are formed due to social or ethnic factors. They have different names in different parts of the country like Panna, Para, Nagla, Dhani, etc. Each hamlet is a unit and has a number of houses. Such settlements are found in the middle and lower Ganga plain, Chhattisgarh and lower valleys of the Himalayas.

(iv) **Dispersed Settlement** This settlement appears in the form of isolated huts or hamlets of few huts in remote jungles. The houses may be of temporary use. It is found in Meghalaya, Uttarakhand, Himachal Pradesh, Kerala, etc.

Or The three factors that determine the clustered or compact rural settlement in India are as follows

- **Fertile Alluvial Plain** It provides a plain surface where houses can be easily build. Fertile plains provide more agricultural land which attracts people to engage in agriculture. More concentration of population results in a compact or clustered rural settlement pattern.
- **Water** It is another reason that can cause people to live in compact conditions. Scarcity of water forces the people to live together for maximum utilisation of the available water, e.g. compact settlements of Rajasthan.
- **Security or Defence** - It is another reason that cause people to live in compact settlements e.g. people of Bundelkhand region and Nagaland live in compact settlements for security reasons.
- **Nature of Terrain** It plays an important role in determining the shape and size of rural settlements. For example, plain areas have compact and larger settlements with dense population, whereas mountainous areas have scattered and hamleted rural settlements. E.g.: Meghalaya, Uttarakhand and Himachal Pradesh have scattered types of rural settlement.

26. Mixed farming refers to the practise of raising crops along with animal husbandry. Thus, it involves both growing crops and keeping livestock.

Areas of Practise

Mixed farming is practised in the developed parts of the world and the temperate parts of the Southern continents. It includes countries of North-Western Europe, Eastern-North America, and certain parts of Eurasia.

Four characteristics of Mixed farming in the world are

(i) Mixed farms are smaller in size where crops like wheat, barley, oats, maize, rye, etc are grown. Fodder crops are also grown in these farms to feed the livestock.

(ii) The fertility of the soil is maintained by practising crop rotation and intercropping. Crop rotation means growing different crops at different times whereas intercropping refers to growing different rows of different crops in the same agricultural fields.

(iii) It involves high capital expenditure because agriculture is practised with the help of farm machinery and buildings are constructed to keep the livestock. It also requires large use of chemical fertilisers and green manures, which involves large costs.

(iv) It provides an alternative source of income to the farmer because the products obtained from animals such as cattle, sheep, pig, and poultry are also sold in the markets along with the crops.

Or International trade is the basis of world economy in modern times because of the following

- Different countries of the world have differences in their resource base. International trade helps in reducing uneven economic development.

FULLY SOLVED

- With international trade, developing and the underdeveloped countries earn foreign exchange. With the help of foreign exchange, these countries can invest in their economic development.
- As the international trade flourishes, the domestic industry gets a boost as it produces more to fulfil the demands of international markets.
- New technologies and new ideas are also transferred between countries. With the help of this, countries innovate and make better products and provides better services.
- Employment Increase in international trade results in increasing employment generation as new industries are setup to fulfil the demands of exports.
- International trade also results in improved standard of living because of the increasing levels of eco nomic and social developments in the country.

27. Trading is essentially buying and selling of the items produced elsewhere and specifically intended for profit. The towns and cities where all these works take place are known as trading centres. The rise of trading from barter at the local level to money-exchange of international scale has produced many centres and institutions such as trading centres or collection and distribution points. The types of trading are as follows

- **Retail Trading** This is the business activity concerned with the sale of goods directly to the consumers. Most of the retail trading takes place in fixed establishments or stores solely devoted to selling. Street peddling, handcarts, trucks, door-to-door, mail-order, telephone, automatic vending machines and internet are examples of non-store retail trading.
- **Wholesale Trading** It constitutes bulk business through numerous intermediary merchants and supply houses and not through retail stores. Some large stores including chain stores are able to buy directly from the manufacturers. However, most retail stores procure supplies from an intermediary source. Wholesalers often extend credit to retail stores to such an extent that the retailer operates very largely on the wholesaler's capital.

Or Transport is a tertiary activity which is essential for a nation's economy. It is a service by which people, materials and manufactured goods are physically carried from one location to another. It is an organised industry created to satisfy the basic need of mobility.

Speedy and efficient transport systems assist in the production, distribution and consumption of goods in the modern developing societies. Transport distance can be measured as kilometre distance or actual distance of route length; time distance or the time taken to travel on a particular route; and cost distance or the expense of travelling on a route.

Factors affecting demand for transport is influenced by the size of population. The larger the population size, the greater is the demand for transport. Some of the commonly used form of transport are roadways, railways and airways. They can vary in distance covered, cost and goods or manpower transported. Railways are the cheapest option to carry large amount of cargo over large distances, whereas airways are the fastest but usually expensive compared to road and railways transport.

28. Minerals are classified on the basis of their physical properties and chemical properties such as

- **Metallic Minerals** Metallic minerals are those that are rich in metals. They are used to obtain a variety of metals like copper, gold, iron, etc. Bauxite, iron ore are some examples of metallic minerals. There are two types of metallic minerals i.e. ferrous and non-ferrous. Ferrous minerals include iron, manganese etc. Non-ferrous minerals include copper, bauxite, etc.
- **Non-metallic Minerals** Non-metallic minerals are those that do not have metal components. Non-metallic minerals are mica, limestone, graphite, etc.

Features of the three mineral belts are

(i) **North-Eastern Plateau Region**

- It covers Chotanagpur in Jharkhand, Odisha Plateau, West Bengal and parts of Chhattisgarh.
- It contains minerals such as Iron-ore, coal, manganese, bauxite and mica.

(ii) **South-Western Plateau Region**

- It extends over Karnataka, Goa, Tamil Nadu uplands and Kerala.
- It is rich in ferrous minerals and iron-ore, manganese and limestone. It also contains Neyveli lignite coal.

(iii) **North-Western Region**
- It extends along Aravalli in Rajasthan and parts of Gujarat.
- Minerals are associated with Dharwar system of rocks. Minerals found here include copper, zinc, sandstone, granite and marble.

29.

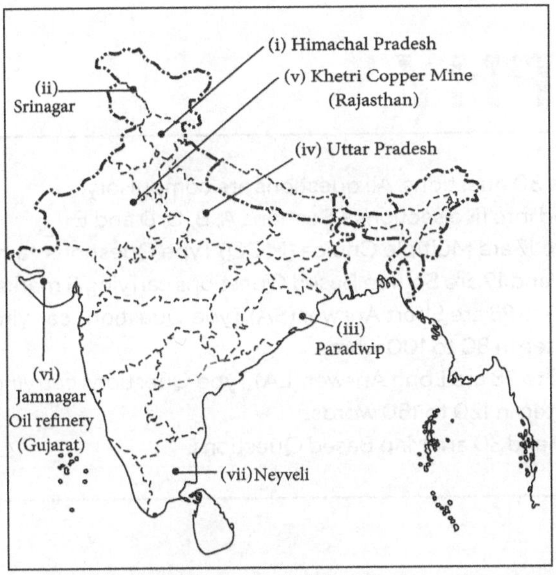

30.

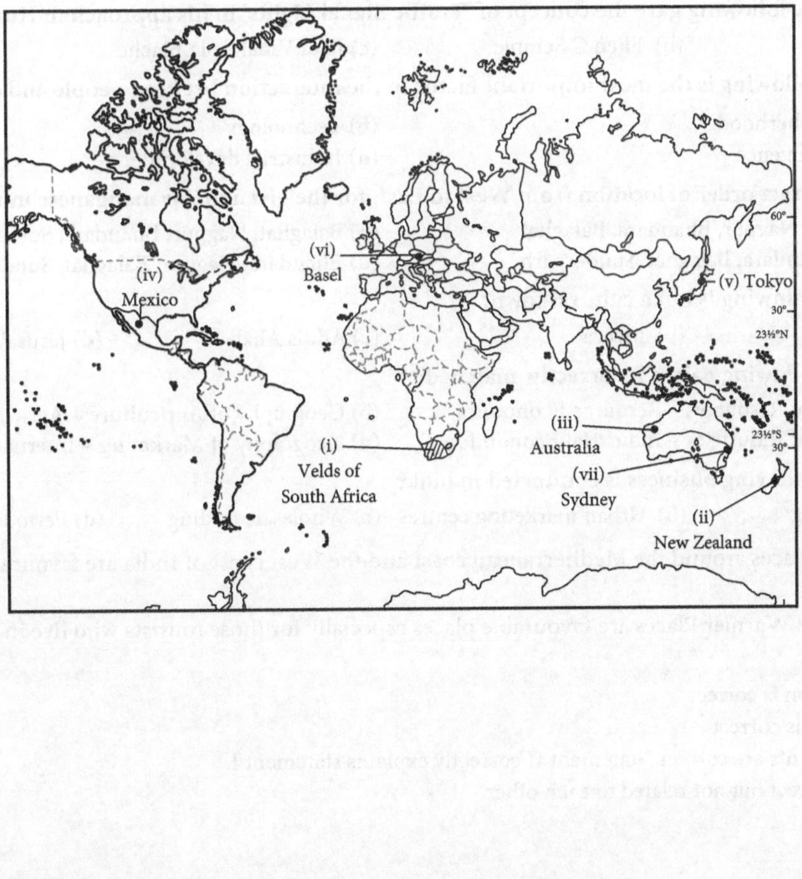

SAMPLE QUESTION PAPER 3

A Highly Simulated Sample Question Paper for CBSE Class XII

(UNSOLVED)

GEOGRAPHY

- This question paper contains 30 questions. All questions are compulsory.
- This question paper is divided into five sections – Sections A, B, C, D and E.
- Section A – Questions no. 1 to 17 are Multiple Choice (MCQ) Type Questions carrying 1 mark each.
- Section B – Questions no. 18 and 19 are Source Based Questions carrying 3 marks each.
- Section C – Questions no. 20 to 23 are Short Answer (SA) Type Questions carrying 3 marks each. Answer to these questions shall be written in 80 to 100 words.
- Section D – Questions no. 24 to 28 are Long Answer (LA) Type Questions carrying 5 marks each. Answer to these questions shall be written in 120 to 150 words.
- Section E – Questions no. 29 and 30 are Map Based Questions.

Time : 3 hours **Max. Marks : 70**

SECTION A

1. Who among the following gave the concept of 'Traffic Signal Lights' in his approach in Human Geography? **(1)**

(a) Ratzel (b) Ellen C Semple (c) Paul Vidal de la Blache (d) Griffith Taylor

2. Which of the following is the most important factor in the interaction between people and environment? **(1)**

(a) Human brotherhood (b) Technology
(c) Human intelligence (d) Industrial development

3. Identify the correct order of location from West to East, for the given major manganese mines of India. **(1)**

(a) Sundergarh, Nagpur, Bhandara, Balaghat (b) Balaghat, Nagpur, Bhandara, Sundergarh
(c) Nagpur, Bhandara, Balaghat, Sundergarh (d) Bhandara, Nagpur, Balaghat, Sundergarh

4. Which of the following is not a cultural town? **(1)**

(a) Varanasi (b) Mecca (c) Addis Ababa (d) Jerusalem

5. Which of the following pair is incorrectly matched? **(1)**

(a) Geography of Resources – Resource Economics (b) Geography of Agriculture – Agricultural Sciences
(c) Geography of Industries – Industrial Economics (d) Geography of Marketing – International Trade

6. Which of the following business is conducted in bulk? **(1)**

(a) Retail trading (b) Urban marketing centres (c) Wholesale trading (d) Periodic markets

7. Assertion (A) Places around the Mediterranean coast and the West coast of India are favourable for tourists' attraction.

Reason (R) The Warmer Places are favourable places especially for those tourists who live in colder regions. **(1)**

Codes

(a) Only assertion is correct
(b) Only reason is correct
(c) Both statements are correct. Statement II correctly explains statement I.
(d) Both are correct but not related to each other

8. **Consider the following statements and choose the correct option from the given options.** **(1)**

I. Products of gathering activity cannot compete at the global market.

II. Synthetic products of better quality and cheap prices are available in global markets.

Codes

(a) Only statement I is correct
(b) Both the statements are correct and statement II correctly present the reason for statement I
(c) Only statement II is correct
(d) Both the statements I and II are incorrect

9. **Arrange the following water management programme in the correct order as per their formation year.** **(1)**

I. Pradhan Mantri Krishi Sinchayee Yojana **II. Atal Bhujal Yojana**

III. Neeru- Meeru **IV. Haryali**

Codes

(a) III, IV, I, II (b) I, II, III, IV (c) II, I, III, IV (d) III, I, IV, II

10. **Read the following information carefully and identify the correct option for measure of human development.**

It is a holistic and sustainable approach to development. Bhutan is the only official country to proclaim it. It encourages us to think of the spiritual, non-material and qualitative aspects of development. This simply means material progress cannot come at the cost of happiness.

Options

(a) HDI (b) Gross National Happiness
(c) GDP (d) Human Poverty Index

11. **Identify the medieval town of India.** **(1)**

(a) Varanasi (b) Mumbai (c) Agra (d) Chennai

12. **Assertion** (A) The high-tech industries which are regionally concentrated, self-sustained and highly specialised are called technopolis. **(1)**

Reason (R) The Silicon Valley near San Francisco and Silicon Forest near Seattle are examples of technopolis.

Codes

(a) Only assertion is correct
(b) Only reason is correct
(c) Both assertion and reason are correct and reason is the correct explanation for assertion
(d) Both assertion and reason are correct but reason is not the correct explanation for assertion

13. **Which of the following is a feature of water transport?** **(1)**

(a) It does not require any construction and thus reduces costs.
(b) The energy cost is low in water transport.
(c) The oceans are linked and can be navigated in all directions.
(d) All of the above

14. **Match the following List I with List II.** **(1)**

	List I (Types of Pollution)		List II (Sources)
A.	Air pollution	1.	Industrial processing
B.	Water pollution	2.	Combustion of coal
C.	Land pollution	3.	Industrial waste
D.	Noise pollution	4.	Agricultural runoff

Codes

	A	B	C	D		A	B	C	D
(a)	1	2	3	4	(b)	2	4	3	1
(c)	4	3	2	1	(d)	3	4	2	1

UNSOLVED

Study the given map and answer the following questions no. 15-17.

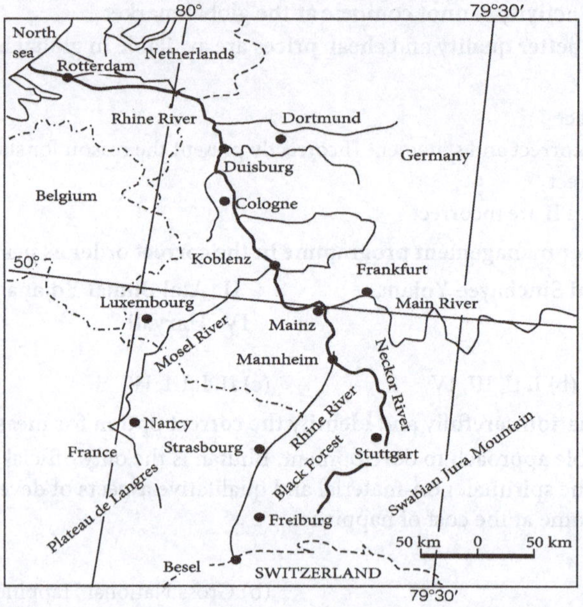

15. Which of the following cities marks the Southernmost point of the Rhine river shown on this map?

(a) Frankfurt (b) Freiburg (c) Basel (d) Stuttgart

16. How many countries does the Rhine river pass through according to this map?

(a) 3 (b) 4 (c) 5 (d) 6

17. Which geographical feature is located to the East of the Rhine river in Germany?

(a) Plateau de Langres (b) Jura Mountains (c) Black Forest (d) Netherlands Lowlands

SECTION B

18. Read the following paragraph and answer the questions that follow.

The main roads which are constructed and maintained by the Central Government are known as the National Highways. These roads are meant for inter-state transport and movement of defence men and material in strategic areas. These also connect the state capitals, major cities, important ports, railway junctions, etc. The length of the National Highways has increased from 19,700 km in 1951 to 1, 36,440 km in 2020. The National Highways constitute only about 2 per cent of the total road length but carry 40 per cent of the road traffic. The National Highways Authority of India (NHAI) was operationalised in 1995. It is an autonomous body under the Ministry of Surface Transport. It is entrusted with the responsibility of development, maintenance and operation of National Highways. This is also the apex body to improve the quality of the roads designated as National Highways.

NHAI has taken up some major projects in the country under different phases: Golden Quadrilateral comprises construction of 5,846-km long 4/6 lane, high density traffic corridor, to connect India's four big metro cities of Delhi-Mumbai-Chennai-Kolkata. With the construction of Golden Quadrilateral, the time, distance and cost of movement among the mega cities of India will be considerably minimized. North-South and East-West Corridors: North-South corridor aims at connecting Srinagar in Jammu and Kashmir with Kanniyakumari in Tamil Nadu (including Kochchi-Salem Spur) with 4,076-km long road. The East-West Corridor has been planned to connect Silchar in Assam with the port town of Porbandar in Gujarat with 3,640- km of road length.

State Highways are constructed and maintained by state governments. They join the state capitals with district headquarters and other important towns. These roads are connected to the National Highways. These constitute 4 per cent of total road length in the country. District Roads These roads are the connecting link between District Headquarters and the other important nodes in the district. They account for 14 per cent of the total road length of the country.

(i) Why National Highways are important for a country? **(1)**

(ii) What is the main function of NHAI? **(1)**

(iiii) Name the cities which are connected by North-South-East-West Corridor Project of India. **(1)**

19. Study the figure given below and answer the questions that follows.

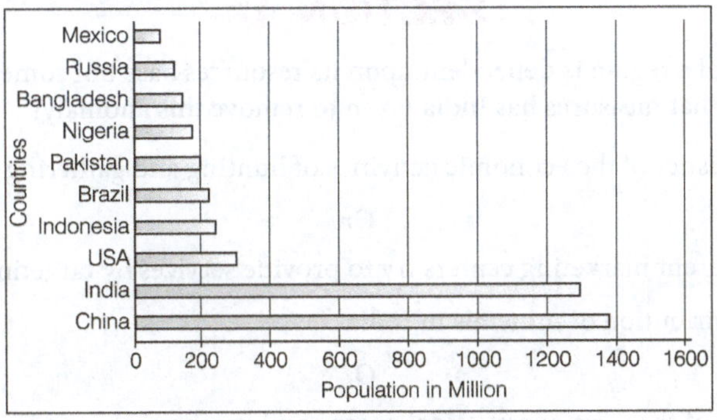

(i) Out of the 10 most populous countries of the world, how many are located in Asia? **(1)**

(ii) State the factors which affect population distribution of a region. **(1)**

(iii) The fifth most populous country is a part of which continent of the world? **(1)**

SECTION C

20. Write in brief about the mineral belts of India with the examples of minerals extracted. **(3)**

Or Write a detailed note on the petroleum resources of India.

21. Study the map given below and answer the following questions.

India-Distribution of Cotton and Jute

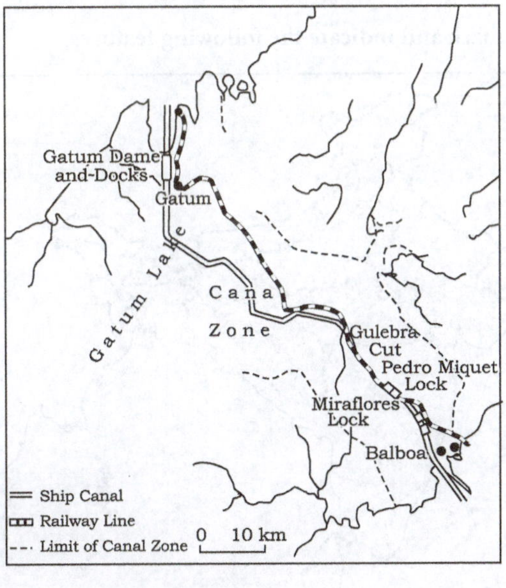

(i) Identify and name the canal shown in the map. **(1)**

(ii) Mention any one characteristic of this canal. **(1)**

(iii) Which oceans are connected through this canal? **(1)**

22. "Equity is one of the most important pillars of Human Development." Explain any three human values that are required to give equal access to opportunities for everybody. **(3)**

23. Why is the quality of water resource declining in India? Explain any four reasons.

SECTION D

24. "Economic development of a region is dependent upon its resources base but sometimes resource rich regions also remain backward". What measures has India taken to remove this anomaly? **(5)**

25. Explain any five characteristics of the economic activities of hunting and gathering practiced in the world. **(5)**

Or

How can you say that different marketing centers try to provide services by targeting different markets?

26. Give a brief account of distribution of minerals in India. **(5)**

Or

Explain any three features of the solar energy, tidal energy and geothermal energy.

27. Examine any five factors that influence the location of industries in the world. **(5)**

Or

Discuss about the primary differences between household industries, small scale manufacturing and large-scale manufacturing industries.

28. How far the trend of birth and death rate in India has determined the growth of population? **(5)**

Or

Discuss the religious composition in population of India which shows the secular fabric of Indian society.

SECTION E

29. On the political map of India mark and indicate the following features. **(1 × 5 = 5)**

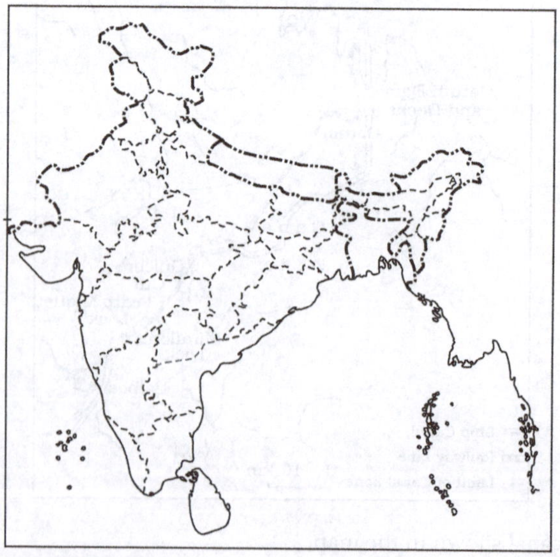

(i) A state with low level of urbanisation
(ii) A seaport in Gujarat
(iii) The leading producer of Rice
(iv) Leading producer oilseeds
(v) An oil refinery in Assam
(vi) A Manganese region in Odisha
(vii) Jharia coal mine

30 In the given political map of the world seven features are shown by (i), (ii), (iii), (iv) and (v) and (vii). Identify any five features with the help of the information given below and write their correct names on the lines as marked in the map. **(1 × 5 = 5)**

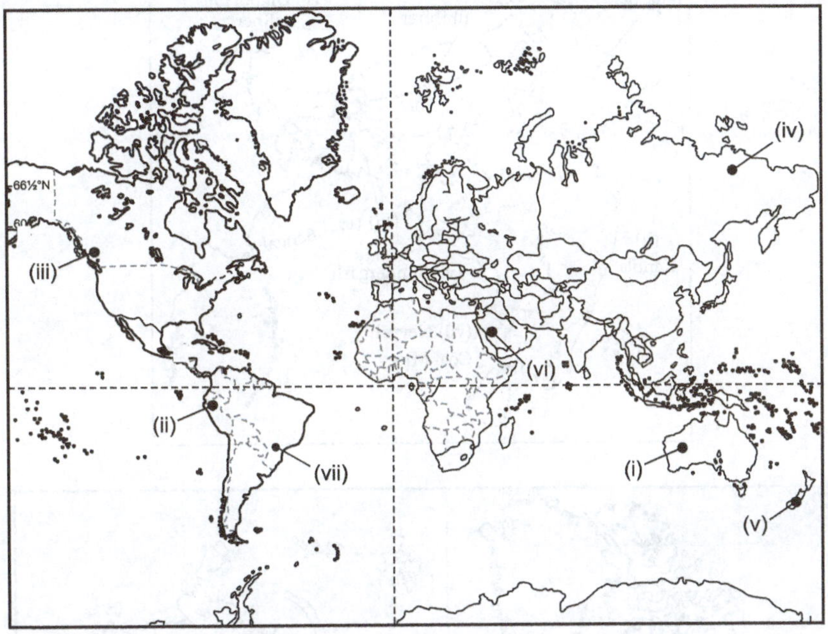

(i) A country that practises commercial livestock rearing.
(ii) An area of subsistence gathering.
(iii) A terminal station of Trans-Candian Railway.
(iv) Largest European country.
(v) An Area of Extensive commercial grain farming.
(vi) A major Air port
(vii) A major Sea port

UNSOLVED

ANSWERS

1. (*d*) Griffith Taylor
2. (*b*) Technology
3. (*c*) Nagpur, Bhandara, Balaghat, Sundergarh
4. (*c*) Addis Ababa
5. (*d*) Geography of Marketing – International Trade
6. (*c*) Wholesale trading
7. (*c*) Both statements are correct. Statement II correctly explains statement I.
8. (*b*) Both the statements are true and statement II correctly present the reason for statement I
9. (*a*) III, IV, I, II
10. (*b*) Gross National Happiness
11. (*c*) Agra
12. (*d*) Both assertion and reason are correct but reason is not the correct explanation for assertion
13. (*d*) All of the above
14. (*b*)
15. (*c*) Basel
16. (*b*) 4
17. (*c*) Black Forest

29.

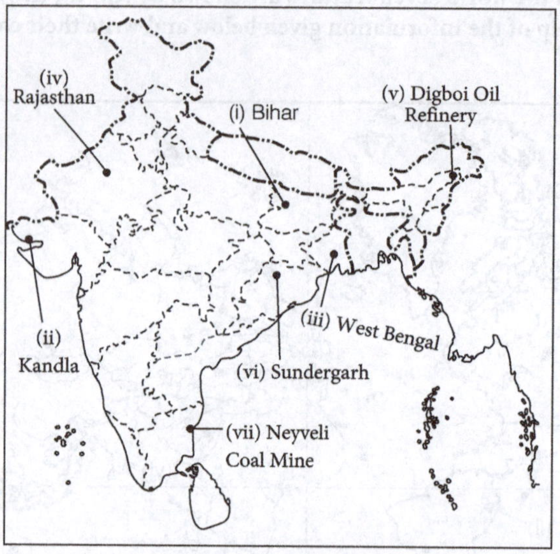

30.

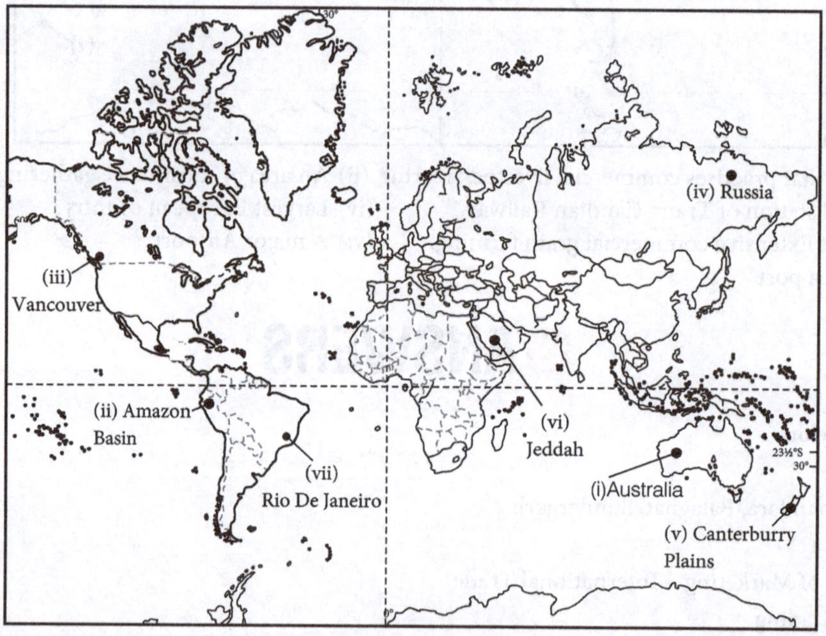

UNSOLVED

SAMPLE QUESTION PAPER 4

A Highly Simulated Sample Question Paper for CBSE Class XII

(UNSOLVED)

GEOGRAPHY

- This question paper contains 30 questions. All questions are compulsory.
- This question paper is divided into five sections – Sections A, B, C, D and E.
- Section A – Questions no. 1 to 17 are Multiple Choice (MCQ) Type Questions carrying 1 mark each.
- Section B – Questions no. 18 and 19 are Source Based Questions carrying 3 marks each.
- Section C – Questions no. 20 to 23 are Short Answer (SA) Type Questions carrying 3 marks each. Answer to these questions shall be written in 80 to 100 words.
- Section D – Questions no. 24 to 28 are Long Answer (LA) Type Questions carrying 5 marks each. Answer to these questions shall be written in 120 to 150 words.
- Section E – Questions no. 29 and 30 are Map Based Questions.

Time : 3 hours **Max. Marks : 70**

SECTION A

1. Arrange the following factors affecting land degradation by their impact. **(1)**

I. Overuse of chemical fertilisers　　II. Soil erosion

III. Waterlogging　　IV. Salinisation

Codes

(a) II, IV, III, I　　(b) I, II, III, IV

(c) IV, III, II, I　　(d) 1, 3, 2, 4

2. Arrange the sources of pollution in the order of their contribution to water pollution. **(1)**

I. Urban runoff　　II. Industrial effluents

III. Sewage disposal　　IV. Agricultural runoff

Codes

(a) II, IV, III, I　　(b) I, II, III, IV

(c) IV, III, I, II　　(d) II, III, IV, I

3. Assertion (A) Nomadic herding is practiced over vast horizontal as well as vertical distances.

Reason (R) Nomads migrate from plains to high altitude pastures during winter season and from high altitude pastures to plains during summer season. **(1)**

Codes

(a) Only Assertion is correct

(b) Only Reason is correct

(c) Both statements are correct. Statement II correctly explains statement I

(d) Both are correct but not related to each other

4. Which of the following pair is correctly matched? (1)

	List I (States)		List II (Copper Producing Region)
(a)	Jharkhand	–	Balaghat
(b)	Madhya Pradesh	–	Agnigundala
(c)	Rajasthan	–	Jhunjhunu
(d)	Andhra Pradesh	–	Singhbhum

5. Assertion (A) Sustainable development aims to meet the needs of the present without compromising the ability of future generations to meet their own needs.

Reason (R) It was realised that the concept of development is restricted to the economic sphere. (1)

Codes

(a) Both A and R are true and R is the correct explanation of A
(b) Both A and R are true, but R is not the correct explanation of A
(c) Both A and R are false
(d) A is true, but R is false

6. Grape cultivation is mainly practised in which of the following regions? (1)

(a) Tropical Region
(b) Mediterranean Region
(c) Tundra Region
(d) Steppes Region

7. Consider the following statements and choose the correct option from the given options. (1)

I. Population density is important as it provides a deep analysis of population over a piece of land.
II. It is important to know this because land has a limited capacity to sustain life.

Codes

(a) Only statement I is correct
(b) Both the statements are true and statement II correctly present the reason for statement I
(c) Only statement II is correct
(d) Both the statements I and II are incorrect

8. Read the following information carefully and identify the correct option for inland national water ways. (1)

It is one of the most important waterways in India. It stretches from Allahabad to Haldia covering around 1620 km. It is divided into three parts for developmental purposes. It is navigable by mechanical boats up to Patna and ordinary boats upto Haridwar.

Options

(a) NW3
(b) NW2
(c) NW1
(d) NW5

9. Which of the following is a feature of State highways? (1)

(a) Central Governments are responsible to construct and maintain these highways.
(b) These roads connect the state capitals with district headquarters and other important towns.
(c) These roads are also connected to the National Highways.
(d) Both (b) and (c)

10. Which of the following measures have been adopted by India to expand its share in the International Trade? (1)

(a) Trade liberalisation
(b) Delicencing of industries
(c) Increasing export duties
(d) Both (a) and (b)

11. 'India' was merged with Air India to form a single airline in which of the following years? (1)

(a) 2009
(b) 2011
(c) 1981
(d) 2010

12. Match the following. **(1)**

List I (Crops)		List II (Major States of Production)	
A.	Wheat	1.	Maharashtra
B.	Bajra	2.	Gujarat
C.	Groundnut	3.	West Bengal
D.	Jute	4.	Uttar Pradesh

Codes

	A	B	C	D		A	B	C	D
(a)	1	2	3	4	(b)	2	1	4	3
(c)	4	1	2	3	(d)	2	4	3	1

13. Which of the following pair is incorrectly matched? **(1)**

List I (Activity)		List II (Region)
(a) Nomadic Herding	–	Madagascar
(b) Commercial Livestock Rearing	–	Australia
(c) Plantation Agriculture	–	USA
(d) Market Gardening	–	Western Europe

14. The oil and Natural Gas Commission was set up in .... **(1)**

(a) 1981 (b) 1947 (c) 1956 (d) 1921

15. Study the graph and answer the following questions no. 15-17. **(1)**

Table 2.1 : India – Trends of Urbanisation 1901-2011

Year	Number of Towns /UAs	Urban Population (in Thousands)	% of Total Population	Decennial Growth (%)
1901	1,827	25,851.9	10.84	—
1911	1,815	25,941.6	10.29	0.35
1921	1,949	28,086.2	11.18	8.27
1931	2,072	33,456.0	11.99	19.12
1941	2,250	44,153.3	13.86	31.97
1951	2,843	62,443.7	17.29	41.42
1961	2,365	78,936.6	17.97	26.41
1971	2,590	1,09,114	19.91	38.23
1981	3,378	1,59,463	23.34	46.14
1991	4,689	2,17,611	25.71	36.47
2001	5,161	2,85,355	27.78	31.13
2011*	6,171	3,77,000	31.16	31.08

Source: Census of India, 2011 http.//www.censusindia.gov.in (Provisional)

15. Which decade witnessed the highest decennial growth rate in urban population?

(a) 1941-1951 (b) 1971-1981 (c) 1961-1971 (d) 1981-1991

16. The number of towns/UAs in India crossed 5,000 for the first time in **(1)**

(a) 1991 (b) 2001 (c) 2011 (d) 1981

17. Between 1901 and 2011, the percentage of urban population to total population increased from approximately

(a) 11% to 31% (b) 10% to 25% (c) 15% to 35% (d) 13% to 28% **(1)**

UNSOLVED

SECTION B

18. Read the following paragraph and answer the questions that follow.

Many towns and cities perform specialised services. Some towns and cities specialise in certain functions and they are known for some specific activities, products or services. However, each town performs a number of functions. Towns supporting administrative headquarters of higher order are administrative towns, such as Chandigarh, New Delhi, Bhopal, Shillong, Guwahati, Imphal, Srinagar, Gandhinagar, Jaipur, Chennai, etc. Industrial towns Industries constitute prime motive force of these cities, such as Mumbai, Salem, Coimbatore, Modinagar, Jamshedpur, Hugli, Bhilai, etc. Transport Cities may be ports primarily engaged in export and import activities such as Kandla, Kochchi, Kozhikode, Vishakhapatnam, etc., or hubs of inland transport, such as Agra, Dhulia, Mughalsarai, Itarsi, Katni, etc. Commercial towns and cities specializing in trade and commerce are kept in this class. Kolkata, Saharanpur, Satna, etc, are some examples.

Mining towns have developed in mineral rich areas such as Raniganj, Jharia, Digboi, Ankaleshwar, Singrauli, etc. Garrison Cantonment towns emerged as garrison towns such as Ambala, Jalandhar, Mhow, Babina, Udhampur, etc. Starting as centres of education, some of the towns have grown into major campus towns, such as Roorkee, Varanasi, Aligarh, Pilani, Allahabad, etc. Religious and cultural towns Varanasi, Mathura, Amritsar, Madurai, Puri, Ajmer, Pushkar, Tirupati, Kurukshetra, Haridwar, and Ujjain came to prominence due to their religious/cultural significance.

(i) **Shillong, Guwahati, Imphal and Srinagar are examples of which category of towns?** **(1)**

(ii) **State any three examples of transport cities of India.** **(1)**

(iii) **Roorkee, Varanasi, Aligarh, Pilani, Allahabad come under which types of towns of India?** **(1)**

19. Observe the diagram and answer the following questions.

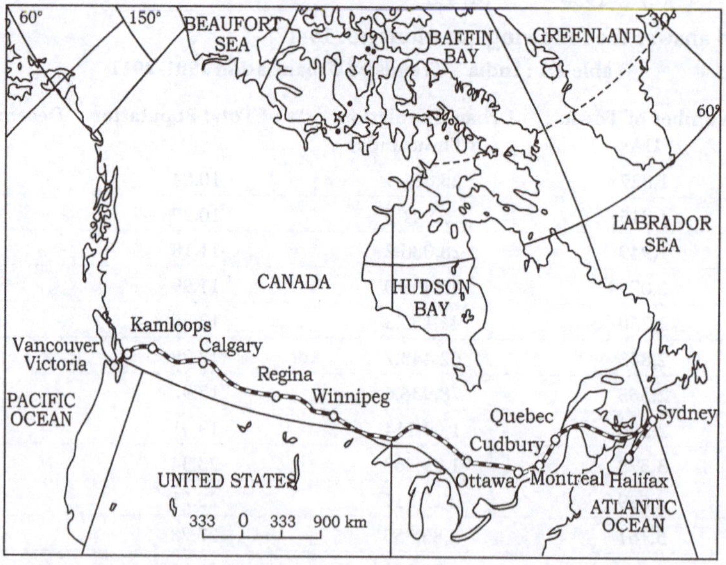

(i) The given map indicates which Trans-Continental Railway line of the world? **(1)**

(ii) Why this Trans-Continental Railway line is considered important in terms of economic point of view? **(1)**

(iii) Name the important export commodities which are supplied through this railway line. **(1)**

UNSOLVED

SECTION C

20. "People prefer to live in certain regions of the world and not in others." Support the statement with suitable arguments. **(3)**

Or What do you understand by migration? Describe two different patterns of migration.

21. **Study the map and answer the following questions.** **(3)**

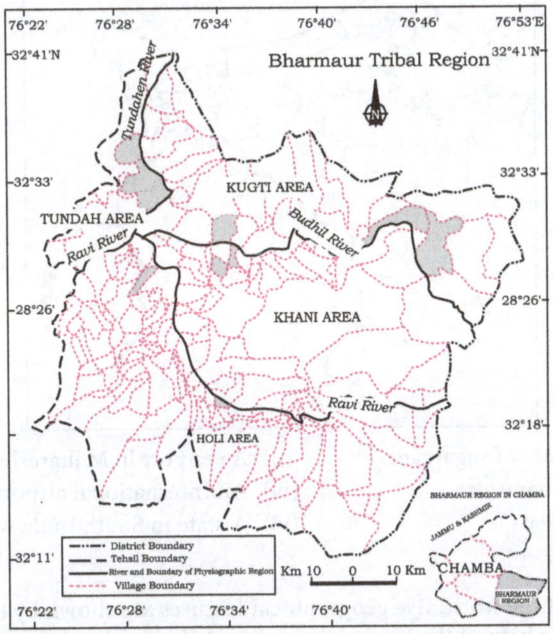

(i) Which is the primary community inhabiting Bharmaur, Himachal Pradesh?

(ii) What was the aim of introducing the tribal sub-plan in Bharmaur under the Fifth Five-Year Plan?

(iii) What is the primary occupation of the Gaddi tribal community in the Bharmaur tribal area?

22. 'Implementating comprehensive measures for reducing air pollution requires collaborative efforts between government agencies and non-government agencies and the general public.' Justify in brief. **(3)**

23. Humanisation of nature is different from Naturalisation of humans. Explain how. **(3)**

SECTION D

24. Describe the watershed development and management programmes initiated by the Central and State Governments in India. Explain them with five points. **(5)**

25. Explain the three aspects of international Trade. **(5)**

Or Discuss the role of any three regional blocs in the promotion of trade.

26. What do equity and sustainability refer to within the concept of human development? **(5)**

Or How are countries classified under different categories under the HDI?

27. Compare and contrast between primary and secondary activities. **(5)**

Or 'Industries should be located at points where the production costs are minimum'. Evaluate several factors affecting the location of Industries.

28. Discuss the benefits of Satellite communication in India. **(5)**

Or 'Communication is an integral part of exchanging information'. Explain.

UNSOLVED

SECTION E

29. On the political map of India mark and indicate the following features. (Any five) **(1 × 5 = 5)**

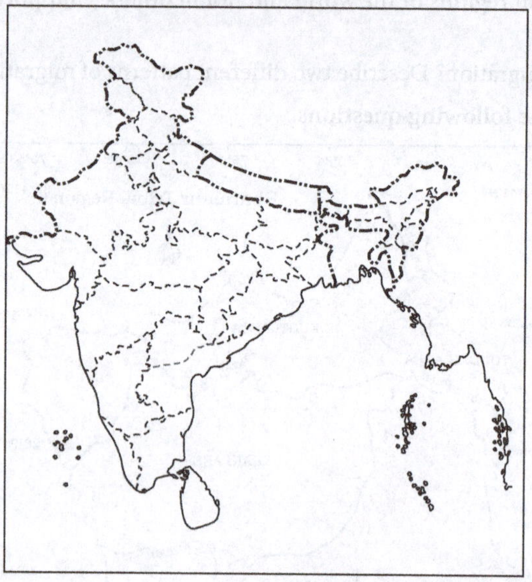

(i) The leading producer state of sugarcane.
(ii) A sea port in Maharashtra
(iii) An iron ore mine in Maharashtra
(iv) An International airport in Tamil Nadu
(v) Leading producer of wheat
(vi) A state in South India with high level of urbanisation
(vii) Koraput bauxite mine

30. In the given political map of the world five geographical features are shown by (i), (ii), (iii), (iv) and (v). Identify the features with the help of the information given below and write their correct names on the lines marked in the map. **(1 × 5 = 5)**

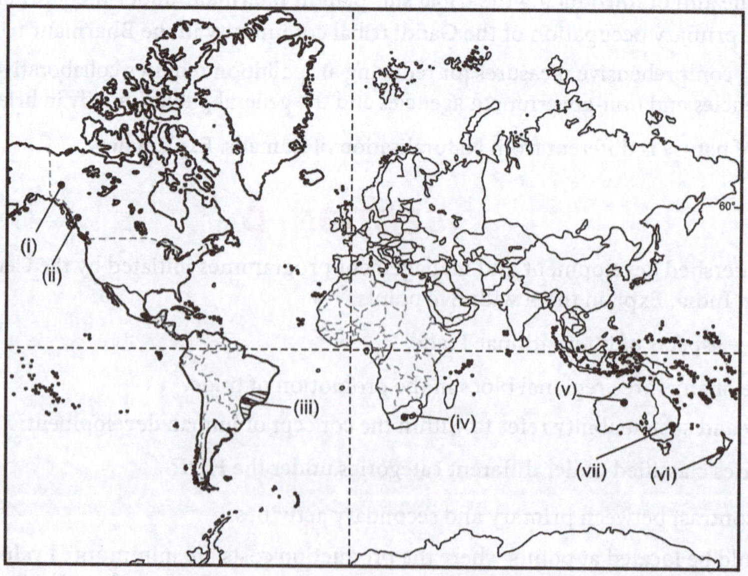

(i) Largest country in North America
(ii) A major sea port
(iii) An area of mixed farming
(iv) An area of extensive commercial grain farming
(v) An area of commercial livestock rearing
(vi) A major Airport
(vii) A terminal station of Australian Trans-Continental Railway

ANSWERS

1. (a) II, IV, III, I
2. (a) II, IV, III, I
3. (a) Only assertion is correct
4. (c) Rajasthan - Jhunjhunu
5. (d) A is true, but R is false
6. (b) Mediterranean Region
7. (b) Both the statements are true and statement II correctly present the reason for statement I
8. (c) NW1
9. (d) Both (b) and (c)
10. (d) Both (a) and (b)
11. (b) 2011
12. (c)
13. (c) Plantation Agriculture - USA
14. (c) 1956
15. (b) 1971-1981
16. (b) 2001
17. (a) 11% to 31%

29.

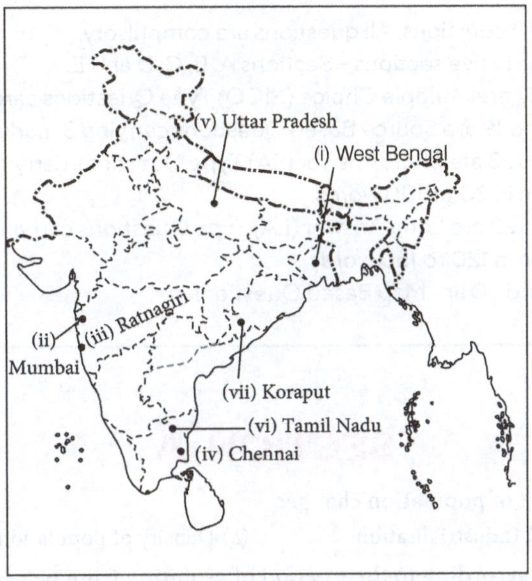

30.

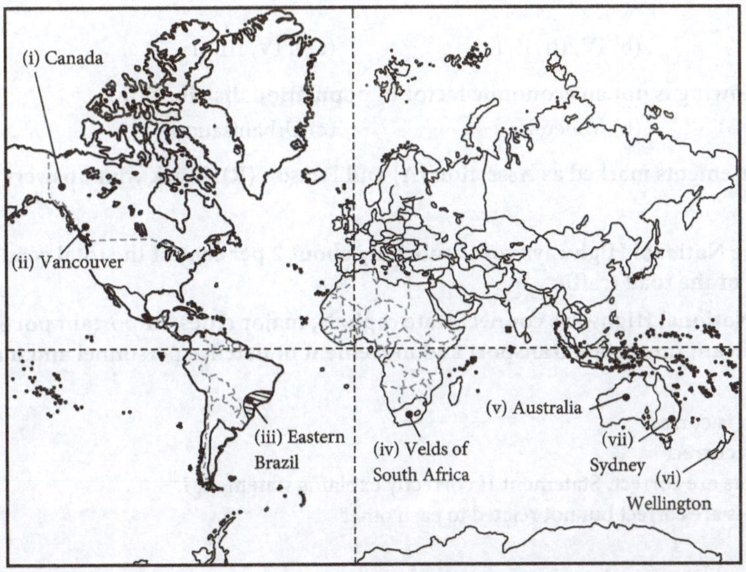

SAMPLE QUESTION PAPER 5

A Highly Simulated Sample Question Paper for CBSE Class XII

(UNSOLVED)

GEOGRAPHY

- This question paper contains 30 questions. All questions are compulsory.
- This question paper is divided into five sections – Sections A, B, C, D and E.
- Section A – Questions no. 1 to 17 are Multiple Choice (MCQ) Type Questions carrying 1 mark each.
- Section B – Questions no. 18 and 19 are Source Based Questions carrying 3 marks each.
- Section C – Questions no. 20 to 23 are Short Answer (SA) Type Questions carrying 3 marks each. Answer to these questions shall be written in 80 to 100 words.
- Section D – Questions no. 24 to 28 are Long Answer (LA) Type Questions carrying 5 marks each. Answer to these questions shall be written in 120 to 150 words.
- Section E – Questions no. 29 and 30 are Map Based Questions.

Time : 3 hours **Max. Marks : 70**

SECTION A

1. What is the major component of population change? **(1)**

(a) Migration (b) Industrialisation (c) Density of population (d) Urbanisation

2. Arrange the following towns according to their period of evolution from newest to oldest.

I. Chandigarh II. Goa III. Hyderabad IV. Prayagraj

Codes

(a) I, II, II, IV (b) IV, III, II, I (c) I, IV, III, II (d) III, II, IV, I **(1)**

3. Which of the following is not an economic factor of population distribution? **(1)**

(a) Climate (b) Mineral (c) Urbanisation (d) Industrialisation

4. There are two statements marked as Assertion (A) and Reason (R). Mark your answers as per the codes given below. **(1)**

Assertion (A) The National Highways constitute only about 2 per cent of the total road length in India but carry 40 per cent of the road traffic.

Reason (R) The National Highways connect state capitals, major cities, important ports, and railway junctions, facilitating significant inter-state transport and movement of defence personnel and materials.

Codes

(a) Only assertion is correct
(b) Only reason is correct
(c) Both statements are correct. Statement II correctly explains statement I.
(d) Both statements are correct but not related to each other

5. Assertion (A) Many Industries benefit from nearness to a leader industry.
Reason (R) Linkages between industries increases savings and profits for all the industries. (1)

Codes
(a) Only assertion is correct
(b) Only reason is correct
(c) Both statements are correct. Statement II correctly explains statement I.
(d) Both statements are correct but not related to each other

6. Which of the following best describes the features of gathering? (1)
(a) Low capital/Skill investment
(b) Low yield per person
(c) Non-surplus in production
(d) All of these

7. Assertion (A) Mediterranean regions have been inhabited from early periods in history.
Reason (R) Plain areas are favourable for the production of crops and to build roads and industries. (1)

Codes
(a) Only assertion is correct
(b) Only reason is correct
(c) Both assertion and reason are correct and reason is the correct explanation for assertion
(d) Both assertion and reason are correct but reason is not the correct explanation for assertion

8. Which of these type of stores employ highly skilled specialists? (1)
(a) Consumer cooperatives
(b) Departmental stores
(c) Chain stores
(d) Permanent shops

9. Given below are the export of some Principal Commodities (in crore rupees). Arrange them in decreasing order. (1)

I. Agriculture and allied products
II. Ores and Minerals
III. Manufactured goods
IV. Mineral fuels and Lubricants

Codes
(a) III, IV, I, II
(b) I, II, III, IV
(c) IV, III, II, I
(d) I, III, II, IV

10. Read both the statements I and II and choose the correct option. (1)

I. An uneducated child cannot make the choice to be a doctor.
II. His/her choice has got limited by her lack of education.

Options
(a) Only statement I is correct
(b) Both the statements are true and statement II correctly present the reason for statement I
(c) Only statement II is correct
(d) Both the statements I and II are incorrect

11. Match the following. (1)

List I (Level of Human Development)	List II (Score in Development Index)
A. Very high	1. Below 0.549
B. High	2. Between 0.550 to 0.699
C. Medium	3. Above 0.800
D. Low	4. Between 0.700 to 0.799

Codes

	A	B	C	D
(a)	3	4	2	1
(b)	1	3	4	2
(c)	1	4	3	2
(d)	4	1	2	3

12. Identify the administrative town. (1)
(a) Bhilai
(b) Surat
(c) Chandigarh
(d) Bhubaneshwar

UNSOLVED

13. Singreni coal field is located in (1)

(a) Telangana (b) Tamil Nadu (c) Maharashtra (d) Punjab

14. Which of the following pair is correctly matched? (1)

	Managanese mines		States
A.	Kendujhar	–	Bihar
B.	Bhandara	–	Kerala
C.	Jhabua	–	Madhya Pradesh
D.	Belgaum	–	Odisha

Study the given graph carefully and answer the following questions no. 15-17.

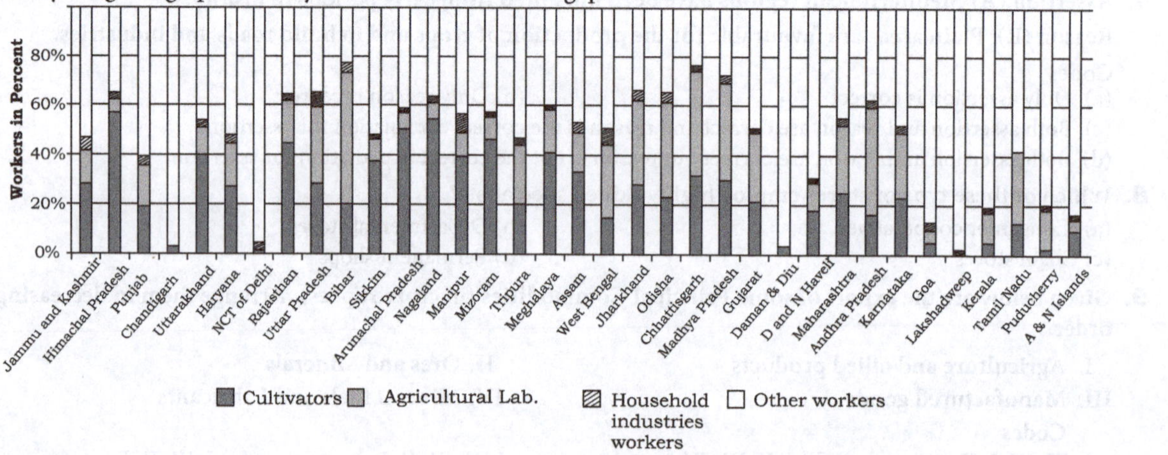

India-Occupational Structure, 2011

15 Which state has the higher proportion of cultivators as compared to others? (1)

(a) himachal Pradesh (b) goa
(c) tamil nadu (d) Rajasthan

16. In which of the following Union territory, there is very high percentage of agricultural labourers? (1)

(a) NCT of Delhi (b) Chandigarh
(c) Puducherry (d) Lakshadweep

17. Which state has higher proportion of other workers? (1)

(a) Bihar (b) Goa
(c) Madhya Pradesh (d) Chhatiisgarh

SECTION B

18. Read the following paragraph and answer the questions that follow.

One of the great advantages of water transportation is that it does not require route construction. The oceans are linked with each other and are negotiable with ships of various sizes. All that is needed is to provide port facilities at the two ends. It is much cheaper because the friction of water is far less than that of land. The energy cost of water transportation is lower. Water transport is divided into sea routes and inland waterways.

Rivers, canals, lakes and coastal areas have been important waterways since time immemorial. Boats and steamers are used as means of transport for cargo and passengers. The development of inland waterways is dependent on the navigability width and depth of the channel, continuity in the water flow, and transport technology in use. Rivers are the only means of transport in dense forests. Very heavy cargo like coal, cement, timber and metallic ores can be transported through inland waterways. In ancient times, riverways were the main highways of transportation as in the case of India. But they lost importance because of competition from railways, lack of water due to diversion for irrigation, and their poor maintenance.

The significance of rivers as inland waterways for domestic and international transport and trade has been recognised throughout the developed world. Despite inherent limitations, many rivers have been modified to enhance their navigability by dredging, stabilising river banks, and building dams and barrages for regulating the flow of water. The following river waterways are some of the world's important highways of commerce.

(i) Why water transport is advantageous for people? **(1)**

(ii) Despite having many advantages, water transport is declining. State any two reasons. **(1)**

(iii) The development of inland waterways is dependent on many factors. State any two important factors. **(1)**

19. Observe the diagram and answer the following questions.

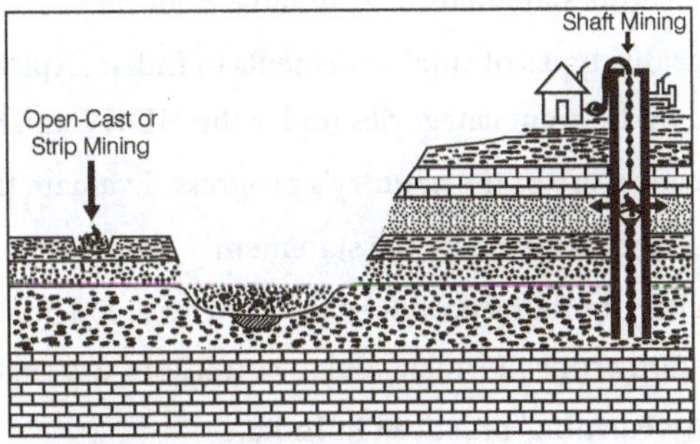

(i) The given diagram shows which type of economic activity? **(1)**

(ii) In which type of mining the output is large and rapid? **(1)**

(iii) In which mining process accidents like underground fires, leakage of poisonous gases and flooding may occur? **(1)**

SECTION C

20. There is an increasing popularity of Air Transport in India. Justify the statement. **(3)**

Or What are the types of roads found in India? Describe briefly the role of Pradhan Mantri Gran Sadak Yojana increasing rural connectivity.

21. Study the map and answer the following questions. **(3)**

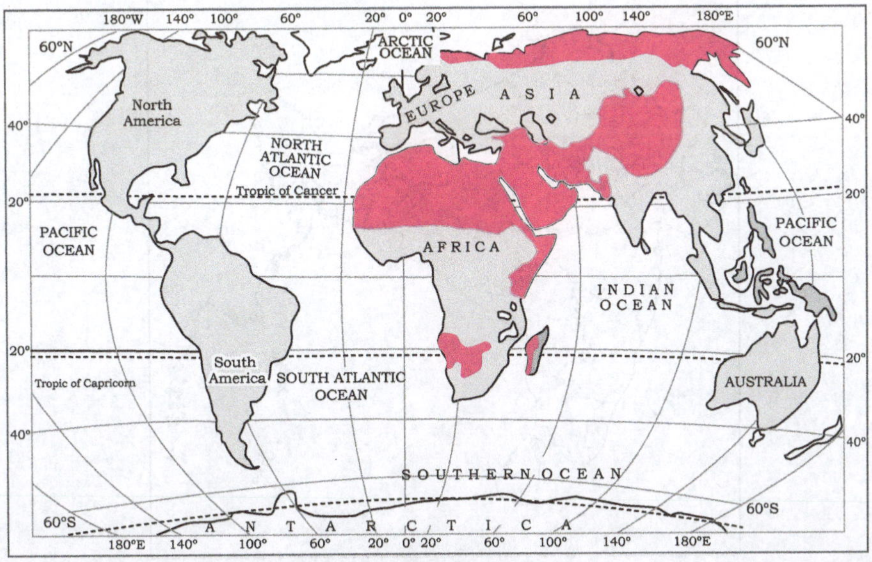

(i) Which was the earliest economic activity performed in the world?

(ii) Which type of activities are performed in these regions?

(iii) Why does gathering have a low chance of becoming a global economic activity?

22. Discuss some of the measures that can be adopted to minimise the effects of air pollution. **(3)**

23. Urban waste disposal has led to various environmental problems in large cities of the world. **(3)**

SECTION D

24. Why did the population of India rise at a faster rate during 1951-1981? After which period the growth rate has declined and why? **(5)**

25. "Hill Area Development Programmes in India were drawn keeping in view their topographical, ecological, social and economic conditions." Support this statement with suitable examples. **(5)**

Or What are the characteristics of various types of rural settlements in India? Explain with examples.

26. How does countries are classified in different categories under the HDI? Explain in brief. **(5)**

Or 'Gross National Happiness' is the measure of the country's progress. Evaluate the statement.

27. Transport is an essential tertiary activity. Elucidate the statement **(5)**

Or Trade is essentially buying and selling of items produced de elsewhere. Elucidate.

28. Give a brief account of the plantation crops in India. Which conditions are required for these crops to grow? **(5)**

Or Describe any five features of 'Dairy Farming' practised in India.

SECTION E

29. On the political map of India mark and locate the following features. (Any five) **(1 × 5 = 5)**

(i) The state having the highest population density

(ii) An iron-ore mine in Jharkhand

(iii) An oil refinery in Bihar

(iv) The leading cotton producing state

(v) The leading wheat producing state

(vi) An International Airport in West Bengal

(vii) A bauxite mine in Madhya Pradesh

UNSOLVED

30. **In the given political map of the world five geographical features are shown by (i), (ii), (iii), (iv), (v), (vi) and (vii). Identify any five features with the help of the information given below and write their correct names on the lines marked in the map.** **(1 × 5 = 5)**

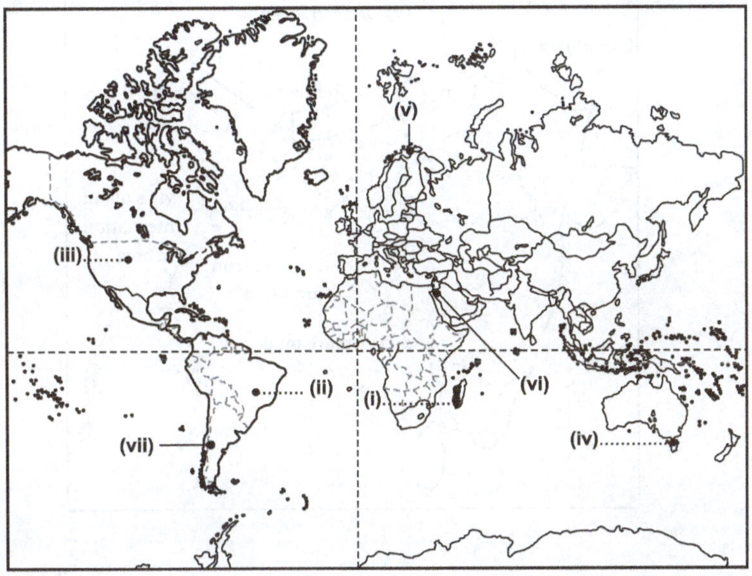

(i) An area of Nomadic herding
(ii) Largest country in South America
(iii) An area of extensive commerical grain cultivation
(iv) An Island where dairy farming is practised
(v) A sea port in Europe
(vi) An Inland Water way
(vii) An International Airport

ANSWERS

1. *(a)* Migration
2. *(a)* I, II, III, IV
3. *(a)* Climate
4. *(c)* Both statements are correct. Statement II correctly explains statement I.
5. *(c)* Both statements are correct. Statement II correctly explains statement I.
6. *(d)* All of the above
7. *(c)* Both assertion and reason are correct and reason is the correct explanation for assertion
8. *(c)* Chain stores
9. *(a)* III, IV, I, II
10. *(b)* Both the statements are true and statement II correctly present the reason for statement I
11. *(c)*
12. *(c)* Chandigarh
13. *(a)* Telangana
14. *(c)* Jhabua - Madhya Pradesh
15. *(b)* Possibilism
16. *(a)* To Keep the campus warm in winters
17. *(b)* Due to harsh climate

29.

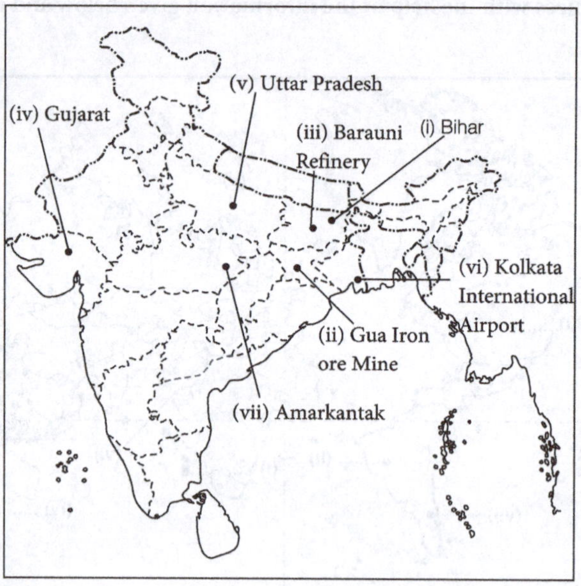

30.

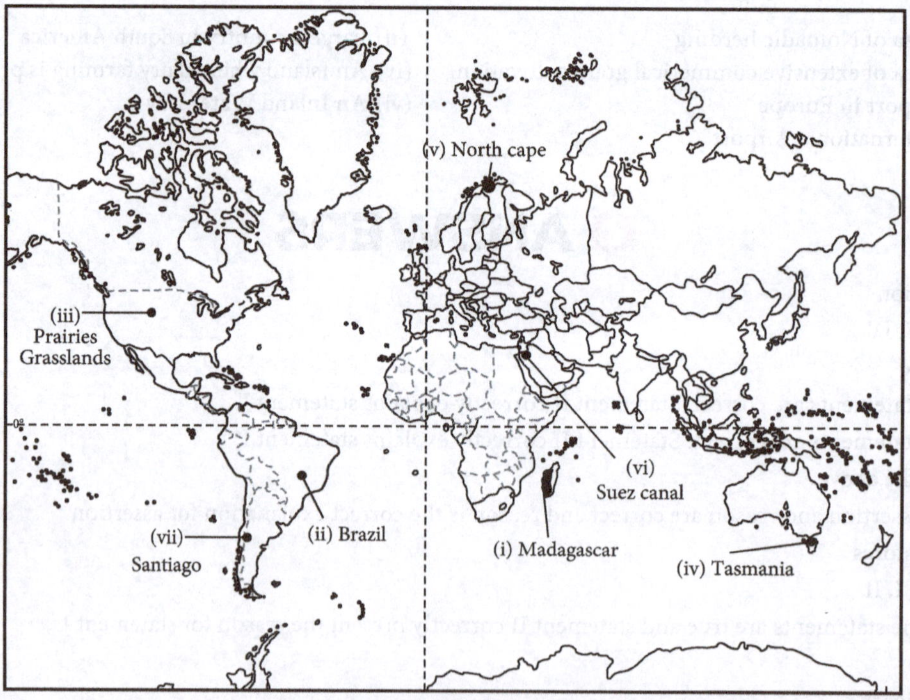

UNSOLVED

CBSE SOLVED PAPER 2025

GEOGRAPHY

- This question paper contains 30 questions. All questions are compulsory.
- This question paper is divided into five sections – Sections A, B, C, D and E.
- **Section A** – Question no. 1 to 17 are Multiple Choice (MCQ) Type Questions. Each question carries 1 mark.
- **Section B** – Question no. 18 and 19 are Source Based Questions. Each question carries 3 marks.
- **Section C** – Question no. 20 to 23 are Short Answer (SA) Type Questions. Answer to these questions shall be written in 80 to 100 words.
- **Section D** – Question no. 24 to 28 are Long Answer (LA) Type Questions. Answer to these questions shall be written in 120 to 150 words.
- **Section E** – Question no. 29 and 30 are Map Based Questions. Each question carries 5 marks.
- There is no overall choice given in the question paper. However an internal choice has been provided in a few questions in all sections other than Section A.

Time : 3 hours **Max. Marks : 70**

SET - 1 (64/2/1)

SECTION A

1. 'Human geography is the synthetic study of relationship between human societies and Earth's surface.' This definition of human geography is given by .... (1)

(a) Vidal-de-la-Blache
(b) Richard Hartshorne
(c) Ritter
(d) Ratzel

2. Which one of the following is the core concern of geography discipline ? (1)

(a) To understand population distribution and the factors affecting the same.
(b) To understand the relationship between resource distribution and its utilisation.
(c) To understand the Earth as the home of human beings and its sustainability.
(d) To understand the Earth as the home of natural resources and their estimation.

3. The concept of 'Neodeterminism' was introduced by (1)

(a) Ehrlich (b) C. Semple
(c) Griffith Taylor (d) Humboldt

4. Read the following statements about ports carefully and choose the correct option. (1)

(i) The ports provide the facilities of loading, unloading and storage of cargo.
(ii) The importance of ports is judged by the size of its hinterland.
(iii) The quantity of cargo handled by a port indicates the level of development of its hinterland.
(iv) Ports are the chief gateways of the world trade.

Options

(a) Only (i), (ii) and (iii) are correct.
(b) Only (i), (iii) and (iv) are correct.
(c) Only (i), (ii) and (iv) are correct.
(d) Only (ii), (iii) and (iv) are correct.

5. Two statements are given below. They are Assertion (A) and Reason (R). Read both the statements carefully and choose the correct option. (1)

Assertion (A) 'World Trade Organisation (WTO) is widening the gulf between rich and poor by making rich countries richer'.

Reason (R) 'The influential nations in the WTO focus on their own commercial interests.'

Options

(a) Both (A) and (R) are correct and (R) is the correct explanation of (A).
(b) Both (A) and (R) are correct, but (R) is not the correct explanation of (A).
(c) (A) is correct, but (R) is incorrect.
(d) (A) is incorrect but (R) is correct.

6. **Choose the correct option to fill the blank. The act of opening up economies for trading is known as** (1)

(a) Balanced trade (b) Unilateral trade
(c) Free trade (d) Bilateral trade

7. **Arrange the following towns of India from the oldest to the newest order based on their historical evolution and choose the correct option.** (1)

(i) Jaipur (ii) Chandigarh
(iii) Madurai (iv) Jamshedpur

Options
(a) (iii), (i), (ii), (iv) (b) (iii), (i), (iv), (ii)
(c) (i), (iii), (iv), (ii) (d) (i), (iii), (ii), (iv)

8. **Read the following statement related to the objectives of smart city mission carefully and choose the correct option.** (1)

(i) To promote the city with clean and sustainable environment.
(ii) To provide decent quality of life to its citizens.
(iii) To provide employment to the job seekers.
(iv) To make the city less vulnerable to disasters.

Options
(a) Only (ii), (iii) and (iv) are correct.
(b) Only (i), (iii) and (iv) are correct.
(c) Only (i), (ii) and (iii) are correct.
(d) Only (i), (ii) and (iv) are correct.

9. **Local names like Panna, Para, Palli, Nagla, Dhani etc. are examples of which of the following types of rural settlements in India?** (1)

(a) Clustered settlement (b) Semi-clustered settlement
(c) Hamleted settlement (d) Dispersed settlement

10. **Two statements are given below. They are Assertion (A) and Reason (R). Read both the statements carefully and choose the correct option.** (1)

Assertion (A) 'The agriculturally rich states of Punjab, Haryana and Western Uttar Pradesh are facing the crisis of groundwater depletion.'

Reason (R) More groundwater is utilised for irrigation than water-table recharge.'

Options
(a) Both (A) and (R) are correct and (R) is correct reason of (A).
(b) Both (A) and (R) are correct, but (R) is not the correct reason of (A).
(c) (A) is not correct, but (R) is correct.
(d) (A) is correct, but (R) is not correct.

11. **Read the following statements related to Indira Gandhi Canal Project carefully and choose the correct option.** (1)

(i) Indira Gandhi Canal project was conceived by Kanwar Sain in 1950 and it was launched in 1981.
(ii) Introduction of canal irrigation has brought perceptible changes in the agricultural economy of the command area.
(iii) Spread of canal irrigation has led to increase in cultivated area and crop intensity.
(iv) Traditional crops of jowar, bajra has been replaced by rice and wheat etc.

Options
(a) Only (i), (ii) and (iv) are correct.
(b) Only (i), (ii) and (iii) are correct.
(c) Only (i), (ii) and (iv) are correct.
(d) Only (ii), (iii) and (iv) are correct.

12. **Read the following statements related to international trade of India carefully and choose the correct option.** (1)

(i) India has a long coastline surrounded by ocean from three sides.
(ii) Indian coasts have large number of well-developed sea ports.
(iii) Kandla port exports huge amount of iron-ore.
(iv) The transportation cost by water is very cheap for voluminous items.

Options
(a) Only (i), (ii) and (iv) are correct.
(b) Only (i), (ii) and (iii) are correct.
(c) Only (i), (iii) and (iv) are correct.
(d) Only (ii), (iii) and (iv) are correct.

13. **Why is it that slums are the areas of residence with least choice ? Choose the correct options.** (1)

(i) They have dilapidated houses with poor ventilation.
(ii) The basic facilities like lights and toilets are difficult to get.
(iii) Hygienic conditions and drinking water are improper.
(iv) Better drainage facilities are available.

Options
(a) Only (i), (ii) and (iii) are correct.
(b) Only (ii), (iii) and (iv) are correct.
(c) Only (i), (iii) and (iv) are correct.
(d) Only (i), (ii) and (iv) are correct.

14. **The watershed management programme in Jhabua district of Madhya Pradesh is funded by which one of the following ministries?** (1)
(a) Rural Development (b) Environment
(c) Transport (d) Irrigation

Study the following table carefully and answer the Question No. 15 to 17.

Composition of India's export: 2009-2017
(Percentage share in exports)

Commodities	2000-10	2010-11	2015-16	2016-17
Agriculture and allied products	10.0	9.9	12.6	12.3
Ore and minerals	4.9	4.0	1.6	1.9
Manufactured goods	67.4	68.0	72.9	73.6
Crude and petroleum products	16.2	16.8	11.9	11.7
Other commodities	1.5	1.2	1.1	0.5

15. **Under which one of the following category of commodities, increase in export is continuously observed?** (1)
(a) Agriculture and allied products (b) Ore and minerals
(c) Manufactured goods (d) Other commodities

16. **Under which one of the following category of commodities, maximum decline in export is recorded from 2015-16 to 2016-17?** (1)
(a) Agriculture and allied products
(b) Ore and minerals
(c) Crude and petroleum products
(d) Other commodities

17. **Under which one of the following categories of commodities, the increase in export is observed from 2010-11 to 2016-17?** (1)
(a) Agriculture and allied products
(b) Ore and minerals
(c) Crude and petroleum products
(d) Other commodities

SECTION-B

18. **Read the passage carefully and answer the questions that follow.** (3)

Hunting and Food Gathering

The earliest human beings depended on their immediate environment for their sustenance. They subsisted on: (a) animals which they hunted; and (b) the edible plants which they gathered from forests in the vicinity.

Primitive societies depended on wild animals. People located in very cold and extremely hot climates survived on hunting. The people in the coastal areas still catch fish though fishing has experienced modernisation due to technological development. Many species, now have become extinct or endangered due to illegal hunting (poaching). The early hunters used primitive tools made of stones, twigs or arrows so the number of animals killed was limited.

Gathering and hunting are the oldest economic activity known. These are carried out at different orientation.

Gathering is practised in regions with harsh climatic conditions. It often involves primitive societies, who extract both plants and animals to satisfy their needs for food, shelter and clothing. This type of activity often requires a small amount of capital investment and operates at very low level of technology. The yield per person is very low and little or no surplus is produced.

(i) Examine the impact of poaching on wild animals. (1)
(ii) Why was hunting of animals limited in early times? Explain. (1)
(iii) Why did early man depend upon his immediate natural environment? Explain. (1)

19. **Study the following table carefully and answer the questions that follow.** (3)

Composition of Total Cultivable Land

Agricultural Land use Categories	As a percentage of Reporting Area		As a percentage of Total Cultivable Land	
	1950-51	2014-15	1950-51	2014-15
Culturable waste land	8.0	4.0	13.4	6.8
Fallow other than current fallow	6.1	3.6	10.2	6.2
Current fallow	3.7	4.9	6.2	8.4
Net area sown	41.7	45.5	70.0	78.4
Total Cultivable Land	59.5	58.0	100.00	100.00

(i) Mention the reason for the decrease in cultivable waste land in 2014-15 as compared to 1950-51. (1)
(ii) Mention the reason for the increase in current fallow during 2014-15 as compared to 1950-51. (1)
(iii) Explain the reason of continuous increase in net area sown. (1)

SECTION-C

20. Examine the role of climate, water availability and soil fertility on the distribution of world population. **(3)**

Or Examine three stages of demographic transition theory.

21. Study the map of Rhine waterways and answer the questions that follow. **(3)**

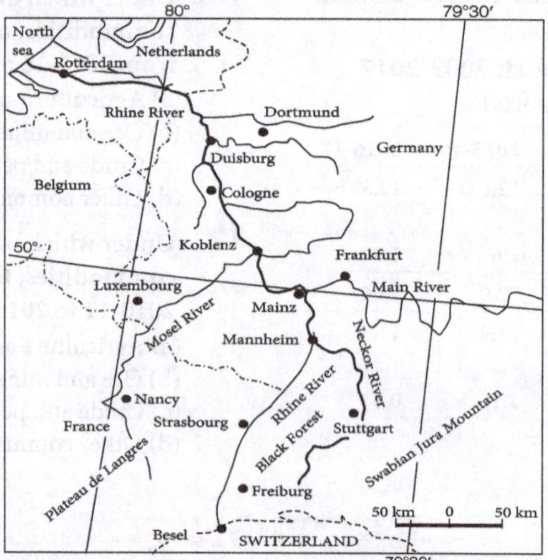

(i) Name the country in which most of Rhine river lies.

(ii) Name two countries whose industrial areas are connected by river Rhine.

(iii) Why is river Rhine world's most heavily used waterway?

22. Explain the main characteristics of rural roads in India. **(3)**

23. Suggest the measures to achieve the objectives of 'Namami Gange Programme'. **(3)**

SECTION-D

24. Explain the concept of human development. Examine four approaches to human development. **(5)**

25. Explain the main features of large scale manufacturing industries in the world. **(5)**

Or

Explain the main features of 'High-tech' industries in the world. **(5)**

26. Assess the growth and significance of service sector in the development of the world economy. **(5)**

Or

Assess the growth and significance of transport and communication services in the world economy. **(5)**

27. Analyse the rural-urban characteristics of Indian population. **(5)**

Or

Analyse the main features of the composition of working population in India.

28. "Petroleum is an essential source of energy and many byproducts are associated with its refining". Explain this statement with examples. **(5)**

Or

"The generation of energy through non-conventional sources is the need of the hour for sustainable development". Explain the statement with examples.

SECTION - E

29. On the outline political map of the world, seven geographical features have been marked as A, B, C, D E, F, and G. Identify any five of them and write their names on the lines drawn near them. (5)

A. Major sea port in Germany.
B. Terminal station of Trans-Siberian Railway.
C. An international airport.
D. An area of subsistence gathering.
E. An important waterway.
F. An area of 'Nomadic Herding'.
G. An area of extensive commercial grain farming.

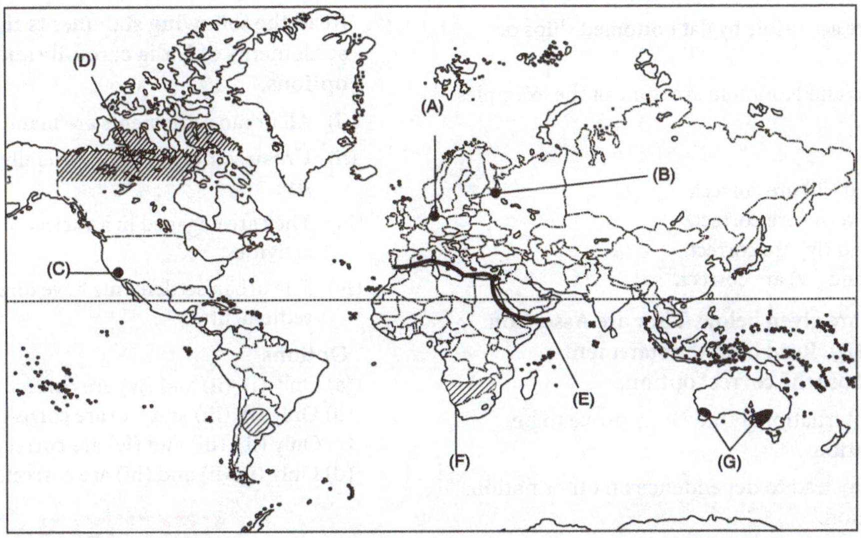

30. On the given political outline map of India, locate and label any five the following geographical features with appropriate symbols. (5)

(i) Important iron ore mines in Odisha.
(ii) An important seaport in Kerala.
(iii) A copper mine in Rajasthan.
(iv) An oil refinery in Bihar.
(v) An international airport in Punjab.
(vi) A state with highest density of population.
(vii) A state leading in the production of jute.

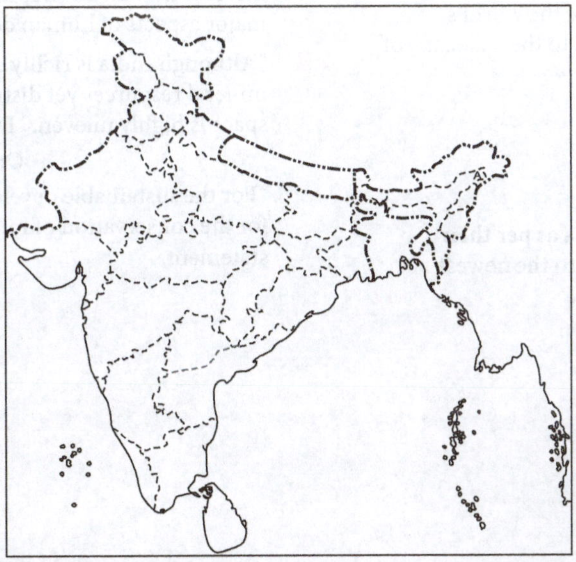

SET- 2 (64/2/2)

(Uncommon Questions from Set 1)

SECTION-A

4. **Read the following statements regarding inland ports carefully and choose the correct option.** (1)

(i) These ports are located away from the sea coast.

(ii) These ports are linked to sea by inland water bodies.

(iii) These ports are accessible by flat bottomed ships or barges.

(iv) Kochchi, Aden and Honolulu are some of the examples of inland port.

Options

(a) Only (i), (ii) and (iii) are correct.
(b) Only (i), (ii) and (iv) are correct.
(c) Only (i), (iii) and (iv) are correct.
(d) Only (ii), (iii) and (iv) are correct.

5. **Two statements are given below. They are Assertion (A) and Reason (R). Read both the statements carefully and choose the correct option.** (1)

Assertion (A) 'International trade may prove to be detrimental to nations.'

Reason (R) 'It may lead to dependence on other nations causing exploitation.'

Options

(a) Both (A) and (R) are correct and (R) is correct explanation of (A).
(b) Both (A) and (R) are correct, but (R) is not the correct explanation of (A).
(c) (A) is correct, but (R) is not correct.
(d) (A) is incorrect but (R) is correct.

6. **Choose the correct option to fill the blank.** (1)

"in modern times, trade is the basis of the world's economic organisation and is related to the .... of nations".

(a) bilateral trade policy
(b) multi-lateral trade policy
(c) foreign trade policy
(d) internal need policy.

7. **Arrange the following towns of India as per their historical evolution from the oldest to the newest order and choose the correct option.** (1)

(i) Chennai (ii) Gandhinagar
(iii) Patna (iv) Lucknow

Options

(a) (iii), (iv), (ii), (i) (b) (iii), (iv), (i), (ii)
(c) (iv), (iii), (i), (ii) (d) (iv), (iii), (ii), (i)

8. **Read the following statements regarding urban settlements of India carefully and choose the correct options.** (1)

(i) All urban settlements are manufacturing centres.

(ii) Urban settlements are generally compact and larger in size.

(iii) They are engaged in a variety of non-agricultural activities.

(iv) The urban settlements have direct relation with rural settlements.

Options

(a) Only (i), (ii) and (iv) are correct.
(b) Only (i), (iii) and (iv) are correct.
(c) Only (ii), (iii) and (iv) are correct.
(d) Only (i), (ii) and (iii) are correct.

SECTION - C

22. Explain the main features of State Highways in India. (3)

23. Suggest the measures to solve the problems of urban waste disposal in India. (3)

SECTION - D

24. Explain the approach suggested by Amartya Sen to increase human development and examine the four major aspects of human development. (5)

28. "Although India is richly endowed with a variety of mineral resources yet distribution of minerals over space is highly uneven." Evaluate the statement. (5)

Or

"For the sustainable development there is urgent need for the conservation of mineral resources." Evaluate the statement. (5)

SET- 3 (64/2/3)

(Uncommon Questions from Set 1 & 2)

SECTION-A

4. Read the following statements regarding outports carefully and choose the correct option. (1)

(i) These are deep water ports.
(ii) They are built away from the actual ports.
(iii) These ports are also known as ferry ports.
(iv) Piraeus is an example of outport for Athens in Greece.

Options

(a) Only (i), (ii) and (iii) are correct.
(b) Only (i), (ii) and (iv) are correct.
(c) Only (i), (iii) and (iv) are correct.
(d) Only (ii), (iii) and (iv) are correct.

5. Two statements are given below. They are Assertion (A) and Reason (R). Read both the statements carefully and choose the correct option.

Assertion (A) 'The chief gateways of the world are harbours and ports'.

Reason (R) 'Cargoes and travellers are transported through them'.

Options

(a) (A) is correct, but (R) is incorrect.
(b) (A) is incorrect but (R) is correct.
(c) Both (A) and (R) are correct and (R) is the correct explanation of (A).
(d) Both (A) and (R) are correct, but (R) is not the correct explanation of (A).

6. Choose the correct option to fill the blank. (1)

.... were originally developed for refuelling, watering and collecting food items.

(a) Entreports (b) Ports of Call
(c) Packet Stations (d) Comprehensive Ports

7. Arrange the following towns of India as per their location from North to South direction and choose the correct option. (1)

(i) Nagpur (ii) Hyderabad
(iii) Madurai (iv) Lucknow

Options

(a) (i), (iv), (ii), (iii) (b) (i), (iv), (iii), (ii)
(c) (iv), (i), (iii), (ii) (d) (iv), (i), (ii), (iii)

8. Read the following statements regarding medieval towns in India carefully and choose the correct option. (1)

(i) About 100 of the existing towns have their roots in medieval period.
(ii) Varanasi, Madurai and Prayag are some of its examples.
(iii) Most of the towns were developed as headquarters of the kingdoms.
(iv) These are mostly fort towns built on ruins of ancient towns.

Options

(a) Only (i), (ii) and (iii) are correct.
(b) Only (i), (ii) and (iv) are correct.
(c) Only (i), (iii) and (iv) are correct.
(d) Only (ii), (iii) and (iv) are correct.

SECTION-C

22. Explain the main features of National Highways in India. (3)

23. Suggest the measures to solve the problems of slums in India. (3)

SECTION-D

27. Analyse the growth of population in India since 1921. (5)

Or

With respect to adolescent population, analyse the challenges of Indian society.

28. "In the Indian context, the non-conventional sources of energy are more equitably distributed and are environment friendly". In the context of this statement, analyse the future prospect of India in meeting its clean energy demand. (5)

Or

"Nuclear energy has emerged as a viable source in recent times". Analyse the statement in context of India.

ANSWERS

Set-1

1. (d) Ratzel
2. (c) To understand the Earth as the home of human beings and its sustainability.
3. (c) Griffith Taylor
4. (a) Only (i), (ii) and (iii) are correct.
5. (d) A is incorrect but R is correct.
6. (c) Free Trade
7. (b) (iii), (i), (iv), (ii)
8. (d) Only (i), (ii) and (iv) are correct.
9. (c) Hamleted Settlement
10. (a) Both (A) and (R) are correct and (R) is the correct reason of (A).
11. (d) (ii), (iii) and (iv) only are correct.
12. (a) Only (i), (ii) and (iii) are correct.
13. (a) Only (i), (ii) and (iii) are correct.
14. (a) Rural Development
15. (c) Manufactured goods
16. (a) Agriculture and allied products
17. (d) Other commodities
18. (i) Poaching has led to many species becoming endangered or extinct. Illegal hunting disrupts the natural balance and reduces the population of wild animals, threatening biodiversity. The loss of these animals also affects ecosystems, as each species plays a crucial role in maintaining environmental stability.
    (ii) In early times, hunting was limited because people used primitive tools like stones, twigs and arrows. These tools were not very efficient, so they could only hunt a small number of animals. Additionally, the need to preserve animals for future survival and the small-scale nature of early societies also limited hunting.
    (iii) Early man depended on his immediate natural environment for survival because it provided everything needed for sustenance. They hunted animals for food and gathered plants for nourishment, shelter and clothing. Since there were no advanced tools or technology, they relied on the resources around them to meet their basic needs.
19. (i) Over the years, there has been increased government focus on land reclamation, irrigation projects and improving agricultural practices. The development of infrastructure, such as irrigation systems and the use of modern farming techniques have made previously unusable land suitable for cultivation. Additionally, afforestation programs, better land management practices and the rise in agricultural productivity have contributed to reducing wasteland areas.
    (ii) The increase in current fallow land is primarily due to inadequate irrigation, poor soil fertility and inefficient agricultural practices. Additionally, climatic factors like droughts and irregular rainfall contribute to land being left uncultivated for a season. Farmers often face economic difficulties, leading to reduced agricultural activity and fallow land.
    (iii) The continuous increase in the net area sown in India is mainly due to the expansion of irrigation facilities, the use of high-yielding variety seeds and the adoption of modern farming techniques. Apart from this, government policies like subsidies for fertilisers and improved infrastructure have encouraged farmers to cultivate more land.
20. Climate, water availability and soil fertility play significant roles in determining the distribution of the world's population. People tend to live in areas where freshwater is easily accessible, as it is crucial for drinking, agriculture, industries and daily activities. This is why river valleys are densely populated.

    Areas with a comfortable climate, minimal seasonal variation and pleasant weather attract more people, whereas extreme climates like deserts or regions with heavy rainfall tend to have low populations. Additionally, regions with fertile loamy soils support intensive agriculture, leading to higher population densities as they can sustain farming and related activities.

    Or The demographic transition theory describes population changes in three stages
    (i) In the first stage, both fertility and mortality rates are high due to epidemics, poor food supply and low life expectancy leading to slow population growth.
    (ii) In the second stage, fertility remains high, but mortality decreases due to improvements in sanitation and health causing rapid population growth.
    (iii) In the third stage, both fertility and mortality decline significantly, leading to stable or slow population growth. Societies become urbanised, literate and technologically advanced with deliberate family size control.
21. (i) Major part of the Rhine river lies in Germany.
    (ii) Germany and the Netherlands are the two countries whose industrial areas are connected by the river Rhine.
    (iii) The Rhine river is the world's most heavily used waterway because it connects major industrial regions across Switzerland, Germany, France, Belgium and the Netherlands, facilitating the transport of vast amounts of cargo.
22. Rural roads in India are primarily built to connect villages with towns and cities, facilitating the movement of people and goods.

    These roads are often in poor condition with many being unpaved or poorly maintained, especially in remote areas. The quality of rural roads varies across regions, with some being narrow and prone to damage during monsoons.

Despite these challenges, rural roads play a crucial role in transporting agricultural products, providing access to healthcare, education and markets and connecting rural areas to urban centers. The government has initiated schemes like the Pradhan Mantri Gram Sadak Yojana (PMGSY) to improve rural road infrastructure.

23. To achieve the objectives of the 'Namami Gange Programme', the following measures can be taken

- **Pollution Control** Install sewage treatment plants to prevent untreated wastewater from flowing into the Ganga.
- **Afforestation** Plant trees along the riverbanks to prevent soil erosion and improve water quality.
- **Waste Management** Promote solid waste management systems in nearby towns and villages to avoid waste dumping in the river.
- **Public Awareness** Educate people about the importance of river conservation and the impact of pollution.
- **Ganga Rejuvenation Projects** Undertake cleaning, dredging and restoring natural habitats along the river.
- **Promote Sustainable Practices** Encourage eco-friendly practices in industries along the river.

24. The concept of human development, introduced by Dr. Mahbub-ul-Haq, focuses on enlarging people's choices and improving their lives. It emphasises health, education and access to resources, enabling individuals to lead meaningful, purposeful lives.

The four approaches to human development are

(i) **Income Approach** This approach links human development to income levels. Higher income is seen as reflecting greater freedom and better quality of life, which results in higher human development.

(ii) **Welfare Approach** In this approach, people are viewed as passive recipients of development. The focus is on increasing government spending on education, health and social services to improve human development.

(iii) **Basic Needs Approach** Proposed by the International Labour Organisation (ILO), this approach focuses on providing six basic needs - health, education, food, water, sanitation and housing. It emphasises fulfilling the essential requirements of life but does not focus on expanding choices.

(iv) **Capability Approach** Developed by Prof. Amartya Sen, this approach highlights the importance of building human capabilities in health, education and access to resources, enabling people to lead meaningful lives and expand their choices.

25. Large scale manufacturing involves a large market, various raw materials, enormous energy, specialised workers, advanced technology, assembly-line mass production and large capital. This kind of manufacturing developed in the last 200 years, in the United Kingdom, North-Eastern USA and Europe. Now it has spread to almost all over the world.

Some features of large-scale manufacturing industries are as follows

- These industries typically require significant capital investment and are located in areas with access to essential resources, such as raw materials, water and energy. They often employ a large workforce and are highly mechanised to increase efficiency and production.
- The distribution of large-scale industries is influenced by factors like raw material availability, transportation, market proximity and government policies. Industries like steel, petrochemicals and automobiles are concentrated in regions with favourable conditions such as cheap labour and abundant resources.
- Large-scale industries are also important for economic development, as they generate employment, boost technological innovation and contribute significantly to the economy.

Or High-tech industries are the most advanced form of manufacturing, driven by intensive research and development (R&D). These industries focus on producing products that require advanced scientific and engineering knowledge. In high-tech industries, a significant portion of the workforce consists of highly skilled, professional (white-collar) workers, like engineers and researchers, while the number of production (blue-collar) workers is comparatively low.

One of the defining characteristics of high-tech industries is the use of advanced technologies such as robotics, Computer-Aided Design (CAD) and electronic controls in manufacturing processes. These industries also focus on the constant development of new chemical and pharmaceutical products. The industrial landscape of high-tech industries is marked by low, modern buildings, office-plant-lab spaces and business parks for startups.

High-tech industries are often regionally concentrated in areas known as technopolies, which are self-sustained, specialised regions. Examples of technopolies include Silicon Valley in California and Silicon Forest near Seattle which are hubs for technology and innovation.

26. The service sector has experienced significant growth in the world economy in the following ways

- This sector includes a wide range of activities such as finance, healthcare, education, information technology, tourism and entertainment. As economies become more industrialised, the demand for services increases, leading to the expansion of this sector.
- The rise of information technology and globalisation has particularly boosted the service industry, enabling services to be provided internationally.
- The service sector contributes significantly to GDP and employment, especially in developed countries. It fosters innovation, enhances productivity and drives economic modernisation. Additionally, it supports other sectors, such as manufacturing, by providing essential services like logistics, marketing and research.

Thus, the service sector plays a crucial role in enhancing overall economic growth and improving the quality of life globally.

Or

Transport and communication services are crucial to the growth and integration of the global economy in the following ways

- These services enable the movement of goods, people and information across vast distances, facilitating trade, investment and cultural exchange. The expansion of transportation infrastructure, such as roads, railways, airways and shipping routes, has reduced the costs of moving goods, connecting markets and enhancing international trade.
- Advancements in communication services, particularly through the internet, tele-communications, and satellite technology have revolutionised global connectivity. They have made it possible to exchange information instantly, thus enabling businesses to operate more efficiently, enhance productivity and access new markets.
- Transport and communication services have also led to the development of global supply chains, enabling the efficient production and distribution of goods. Additionally, they have played a vital role in the rise of the service sector, particularly in tourism, finance and e-commerce. Therefore, these services are integral to the continued growth of the world economy.

27. The rural-urban characteristics of Indian population can be analysed by the following points

- The Indian population exhibits distinct rural-urban characteristics. Rural areas are predominantly engaged in agriculture, with a lower literacy rate, limited access to healthcare and lower standards of living.
- These regions often lack basic infrastructure like roads, sanitation and electricity. In contrast, urban areas have higher literacy rates, better healthcare and more access to modern amenities.
- The economy in urban areas is diversified, with industries, services and trade playing a significant role. The migration of people from rural to urban areas in search of better employment opportunities and improved living conditions is a notable trend, leading to urbanisation.

This shift has resulted in a growing demand for housing, infrastructure and resources in urban areas, contributing to challenges such as overcrowding and pollution.

Or The main features of the composition of the working population in India can be defined by the following points

- A large proportion of the workforce, especially in rural areas, relies on farming and related activities for livelihood. However, there has been a gradual shift towards the secondary and tertiary sectors, particularly in urban areas with growth in industries, services and technology.
- The working population in India also faces challenges such as underemployment and low wages, especially in informal sectors. There is a high dependence on family-based work in rural areas, while urban areas show a greater involvement in formal sector jobs.
- Additionally, the workforce in India is predominantly young, with a growing number of women participating in economic activities, although gender disparity remains.

The composition highlights a need for skill development and diversification of employment opportunities.

28. Petroleum is a crucial source of energy that powers various industries, transportation, and households. It is refined to produce a wide range of byproducts, each serving different purposes in the economy. The main products derived from petroleum include petrol, diesel and kerosene, which are widely used as fuels for vehicles, machinery and heating. In addition to these fuels, petroleum refining also produces other valuable byproducts like lubricants, bitumen and wax. Lubricants are essential for machinery and engine maintenance, while bitumen is used in road construction. Petrochemicals, such as plastic, synthetic rubber and fertilisers are also derived from petroleum, playing a key role in various industries.

Thus, petroleum not only provides energy but also contributes to the production of essential products used in daily life, making it a vital resource for modern economies. The refining process, therefore, has far-reaching effects beyond just providing fuel.

Or

The generation of energy through non-conventional sources is essential for sustainable development, as conventional sources like coal, oil and natural gas are depleting and causing environmental harm. For example,

- Non-conventional sources, such as solar, wind, hydropower and biomass, offer renewable and eco-friendly alternatives.
- Solar energy harnesses the power of the sun, providing an abundant and clean source of energy. It is increasingly used for electricity generation in rural and remote areas. Wind energy, through wind turbines also offers a renewable and efficient method of power generation, especially in coastal and hilly regions.
- Hydropower, generated through the flow of water, is another widely used non-conventional energy source. It not only produces electricity but also helps in irrigation and flood control. Biomass energy, derived from plant and animal waste, contributes to reducing dependency on fossil fuels.

These non-conventional energy sources are sustainable, reduce carbon emissions and help in achieving long-term environmental goals, making them vital for future development.

29.

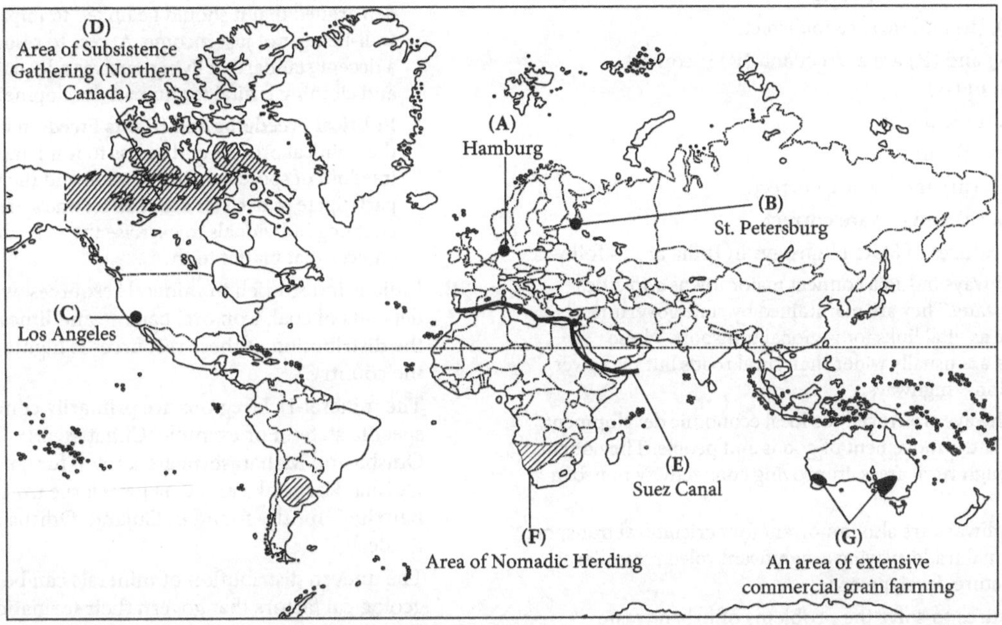
(D)
Area of Subsistence
Gathering (Northern
Canada)
(A)
Hamburg
(B)
St. Petersburg
(C)
Los Angeles
(E)
Suez Canal
(F)
Area of Nomadic Herding
(G)
An area of extensive
commercial grain farming

30.

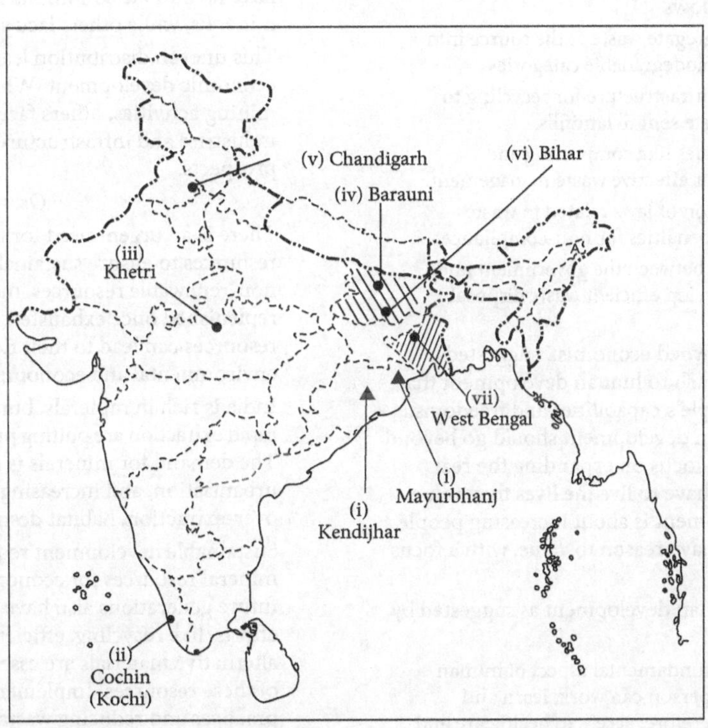
(v) Chandigarh
(vi) Bihar
(iv) Barauni
(iii)
Khetri
(vii)
West Bengal
(i)
Mayurbhanj
(i)
Kendijhar
(ii)
Cochin
(Kochi)

Set-2

4. (a) Only (i), (ii) and (iii) are incorrect.
5. (a) Both (A) and (R) are correct and (R) is correct explanation of (A).
6. (c) Foreign trade policy
7. (b) (iii), (iv), (i), (ii)
8. (c) Only (ii), (iii) and (iv) are correct.
11. (a) Only (i), (ii) and (iv) are correct.
22. The main features of State Highways in India are as follows
    - State highways in India connect major towns and cities within a state. They are maintained by state governments and serve as vital links for regional transport. These highways are usually wider than rural roads but narrower than national highways.
    - State highways are crucial for local economic development, facilitating the movement of goods and people. They often pass through rural areas, improving connectivity to urban centers.
    - These highways are also important for agricultural transport and regional trade, playing a significant role in state-level infrastructure development.
23. Some measures to solve the problems of urban waste disposal in India are as follows
    - Encourage citizens to segregate waste at the source into biodegradable and non-biodegradable categories.
    - Increase awareness and infrastructure for recycling to reduce the volume of waste sent to landfills.
    - Adopt modern technologies like composting and waste-to-energy plants for effective waste management.
    - Ensure the implementation of laws related to waste management, including penalties for non-compliance.
    - Encourage collaboration between the government and private companies to develop efficient waste disposal systems.
24. Prof. Amartya Sen, a renowned economist, suggested a broad and inclusive approach to human development that focuses on improving people's capabilities and freedoms. He emphasised that human development should go beyond just economic growth and focus on expanding the real opportunities that people have to live the lives they value. According to Sen, development is about increasing people's abilities to lead lives they have reason to value, with a focus on freedom and choice.

    Four major aspects of human development as suggested by Amartya Sen are
    - **Health** Good health is a fundamental aspect of human development. A healthy person can work, learn and contribute to society. Therefore, access to healthcare and improvements in public health systems are crucial for enhancing human development.
    - **Education** Education expands people's knowledge and skills which enables them to make better life choices and participate fully in society. It helps in developing individual capabilities which is essential for increasing freedoms and opportunities.
    - **Economic Resources** While economic growth is important, Sen argued that it should be linked to improving people's well-being, not just income. Access to resources that ensure a decent standard of living, such as adequate food, shelter and clothing is vital for human development.
    - **Political Freedoms and Rights** Freedom to participate in the political process and access to fundamental rights like freedom of speech and expression and the right to participate in decisions that affect one's life are the key for enabling individuals to exercise their capabilities and make choices that matter to them.
28. India is indeed rich in mineral resources, with significant deposits of coal, iron ore, bauxite and limestone. However, the distribution of these resources is highly uneven across the country.

    The mineral-rich regions are primarily concentrated in specific states. For example, Chhattisgarh, Jharkhand, Odisha and Maharashtra are known for coal deposits, while Odisha, Karnataka and Goa have large iron ore reserves. Bauxite is mostly found in Gujarat, Odisha and Madhya Pradesh.

    The uneven distribution of minerals can be attributed to the geological factors that govern their formation. Some regions have favourable conditions for the accumulation of specific minerals, while others lack such resources.

    This uneven distribution leads to regional disparities in economic development. While certain areas benefit from mining activities, others face a lack of mineral-based industries and infrastructure, affecting their growth prospects.

    Or

    There is an urgent need for the conservation of mineral resources to ensure sustainable development. Minerals are non-renewable resources, meaning they cannot be replenished once exhausted. Over-exploitation of these resources can lead to their depletion, causing severe environmental and economic problems.

    India is rich in minerals, but the uneven distribution and rapid extraction are putting pressure on these finite resources. The demand for minerals is rising due to industrialisation, urbanisation, and increasing population which leads to over-extraction, habitat destruction and pollution.

    Sustainable development requires a balance between using mineral resources for economic growth and ensuring that future generations also have access to them. Conservation efforts, like recycling, efficient use and exploration of alternative materials are essential to prolong the availability of these resources. Implementing eco-friendly mining practices and reducing wastage can help in achieving long-term sustainability.

Set-3

4. (d) Only (ii), (iii) and (iv) are correct.
5. (c) Both (A) and (R) are correct and (R) is the correct explanation of (A).
6. (b) Ports of call

7. (d) (iv), (i), (ii), (iii)
8. (b) Only (i), (ii) and (iv) are correct.

22. The main features of National Highways (NHs) in India are
- National Highways connect major cities, states and important ports which ensures smooth interstate travel and transport of goods.
- NHs are designed to handle heavy traffic and are usually wider, well-maintained and built to high-quality standards.
- They play a crucial role in national defense, linking border areas and facilitating the movement of security forces.
- National Highways are managed and maintained by the central government.
- NHs facilitate both domestic and international trade by linking key routes to neighboring countries.

23. To solve the problems of slums in India, the following measures can be taken
- The government should promote the construction of affordable and low-cost housing to accommodate slum dwellers and reduce overcrowding.
- Implement slum redevelopment programs to improve living conditions without displacing residents.
- Offer vocational training and skill-building programs to empower slum dwellers with better job opportunities.
- Ensure better urban planning to prevent the growth of unplanned slums and promote organised, sustainable development.

27. The population of India has witnessed significant growth since 1921. In 1921, India's population was approximately 250 million. However, the growth was slow and fluctuating due to factors like high mortality rates, epidemics, and famines. Between 1921 and 1951, the population growth was modest, with a decadal growth rate of about 1.25%.

After 1951, India's population growth accelerated, especially post-independence. This was due to improved healthcare, better sanitation, and advances in medical technology, which significantly reduced mortality rates. The population increased by about 21% between 1951 and 1961.

From 1981 to 2011, India's population grew rapidly, with the 2011 Census showing a population of 1.21 billion, marking an increase of over 17% from the previous decade. The growth rate, however, showed signs of slowing down due to government policies promoting family planning and education.

Despite this, India's population continues to grow, presenting both challenges and opportunities for the nation.

Or

The adolescent population in India faces several challenges that impact their overall well-being and development. One major issue is lack of access to quality education in rural areas, limiting their opportunities for skill development and future employment.

Another challenge is health-related concerns, such as malnutrition and poor healthcare facilities, especially in underdeveloped regions. Many adolescents struggle with inadequate nutrition, leading to stunted growth and developmental issues.

Social pressures also play a significant role, especially in terms of early marriages for girls, leading to restricted personal growth and education. Moreover, the rise of mental health issues among adolescents, such as stress, anxiety and depression, is a growing concern due to academic pressure and societal expectations.

Gender inequality and lack of awareness about rights further complicate the situation, especially for girls. Therefore, addressing these challenges requires effective policies and programmes focused on education, healthcare and gender equality.

28. In India, non-conventional sources of energy such as solar, wind, biomass and hydropower are more equitably distributed across regions compared to conventional fossil fuels. This presents a significant advantage in addressing the country's clean energy demand. Solar energy, for instance, is abundant in states like Rajasthan and Gujarat, while coastal regions have strong potential for wind energy. Biomass is widely available in rural areas and small-scale hydropower can be harnessed in hilly regions.

The future prospects of India meeting its clean energy demand look promising, especially with the government's push towards renewable energy. India has set ambitious targets, aiming for 500 GW of non-fossil fuel-based energy capacity by 2030. Furthermore, India is also focusing on energy storage technologies and smart grids to ensure a reliable supply of renewable energy.

With the continued growth of renewable infrastructure, technological advancements and global collaboration, India can significantly reduce its reliance on fossil fuels and work towards a sustainable, clean energy future.

Or

In recent times, nuclear energy has emerged as a viable source of power for India due to its potential to meet the growing energy demand while reducing dependence on fossil fuels. India has limited reserves of coal and oil, making it essential to explore alternative energy sources. Nuclear energy offers a sustainable solution, as it can produce large amounts of electricity with minimal environmental impact compared to traditional sources like coal and natural gas.

India has made significant progress in developing its nuclear energy sector, with several nuclear power plants operational and others in development, such as the Kudankulam nuclear power plant. The government has also signed nuclear cooperation agreements with countries like the USA, Russia and France to enhance its nuclear technology capabilities.

While concerns about safety and waste disposal remain, advancements in technology, improved safety measures and global cooperation make nuclear energy an increasingly important component of India's energy mix for the future.

